CW00688586

Women in Culture

Women in Culture

An Intersectional Anthology for Gender and Women's Studies

Second Edition

Edited by

Bonnie Kime Scott, Susan E. Cayleff, Anne Donadey, and Irene Lara

WILEY Blackwell

This edition first published 2017
Editorial material and organization © 2017 John Wiley & Sons, Ltd
Edition history: Blackwell Publishing Ltd (1e, 1998, edited by Lucinda Joy Peach)

Registered Office
John Wiley & Sons, Ltd, The Atrium, Southern Gate, Chichester, West Sussex, PO19 8SQ, UK

Editorial Offices
350 Main Street, Malden, MA 02148-5020, USA
9600 Garsington Road, Oxford, OX4 2DQ, UK
The Atrium, Southern Gate, Chichester, West Sussex, PO19 8SQ, UK

For details of our global editorial offices, for customer services, and for information about how to apply for permission to reuse the copyright material in this book please see our website at www.wiley.com/wiley-blackwell.

The right of Bonnie Kime Scott, Susan E. Cayleff, Anne Donadey, and Irene Lara to be identified as the authors of the editorial material in this work has been asserted in accordance with the UK Copyright, Designs and Patents Act 1988.

All rights reserved. No part of this publication may be reproduced, stored in a retrieval system, or transmitted, in any form or by any means, electronic, mechanical, photocopying, recording or otherwise, except as permitted by the UK Copyright, Designs and Patents Act 1988, without the prior permission of the publisher.

Wiley also publishes its books in a variety of electronic formats. Some content that appears in print may not be available in electronic books.

Designations used by companies to distinguish their products are often claimed as trademarks. All brand names and product names used in this book are trade names, service marks, trademarks or registered trademarks of their respective owners. The publisher is not associated with any product or vendor mentioned in this book.

Limit of Liability/Disclaimer of Warranty: While the publisher and authors have used their best efforts in preparing this book, they make no representations or warranties with respect to the accuracy or completeness of the contents of this book and specifically disclaim any implied warranties of merchantability or fitness for a particular purpose. It is sold on the understanding that the publisher is not engaged in rendering professional services and neither the publisher nor the author shall be liable for damages arising herefrom. If professional advice or other expert assistance is required, the services of a competent professional should be sought.

Library of Congress Cataloging-in-Publication Data

Names: Scott, Bonnie Kime, 1944– editor.
Title: Women in culture : an intersectional anthology for gender and women's studies / edited by
    Bonnie Kime Scott, Susan E. Cayleff, Anne Donadey, and Irene Lara.
Description: Chichester, West Sussex, UK : John Wiley & Sons, 2017. | Earlier edition: 1998. |
    Includes bibliographical references and index.
Identifiers: LCCN 2016004209 | ISBN 9781118541128 (pbk.) | ISBN 9781119120193 (epub)
Subjects: LCSH: Women. | Women in popular culture. | Sex role. | Social values. | Feminist criticism.
Classification: LCC HQ1233 .W596 2017 | DDC 305.4–dc23
LC record available at http://lccn.loc.gov/2016004209

A catalogue record for this book is available from the British Library.

Cover image: From the collection of Olivia Robles © Linda Vallejo 2015

Set in 10.5/13pt Minion by SPi Global, Pondicherry, India

1   2017

Contents

Acknowledgments

Every effort has been made to trace the copyright holders but if any have been inadvertently overlooked the publishers will be pleased to make the necessary arrangement at the first opportunity.

The editors also want to thank their graduate student assistants, Alyssa Brooke-Gay and Lorena Gonzalez for assembling materials, Helen Lockett for constructing the index, and Teddi Brock, Administrative Coordinator of the Women's Studies Department at San Diego State University, for budgetary assistance. Their Women's Studies colleagues, Anh Hua, Sara Giordano, Huma Ahmed-Ghosh, and Esther Rothblum provided valuable resources, advice and support. For our pedagogy resources we are indebted to Jerrica Escoto, Cristina Dominguez, Melissann Herron, Katie White, Alyssa Brooke-Gay, Jessica Heredia, and Ashley Green, graduate students experienced in teaching WMSNT 102, the humanities-based introduction to our coursework.

List of Sources

1.1 Sandra Cisneros, "My Name" from *The House on Mango Street*, pp. 10–11. New York: Vintage, 1991. © 1984 by Sandra Cisneros. Reproduced with permission of Susan Bergholz Literary Services and Bloomsbury Publishing plc. 1.2 Jacinta Bunnell and Nat Kusinitz, "The new pronoun they invented suited everyone just fine" from *Sometimes the Spoon Runs Away with Another Spoon Coloring Book*, words by Jacinta Bunnell, pictures by Nat Kusinitz. Oakland, CA: PM Press, 2010. Reproduced with permission of PM Press. 1.3 Marilyn Frye, "Oppression" from *The Politics of Reality: Essays in Feminist Theory*, pp. 1–7. Berkeley, CA: The Crossing Press, 1983. Reproduced with permission of Marilyn Frye. 1.4 Audre Lorde, "Age, Race, Class, and Sex: Women Redefining Difference" from *Sister Outsider: Essays and Speeches*, pp. 114–23. Freedom, CA: The Crossing Press, 1984. Reproduced with permission of Abner Stein Agency. 1.5 Alice Walker, "Womanist" from *In Search of Our Mothers' Gardens: Womanist Prose*, pp. xi–xii. San Diego: Harcourt Brace Jovanovich, 1983. 1.6 Michael S. Kimmel, "Masculinity as Homophobia: Fear, Shame, and Silence in the Construction of Gender Identity" from *Theorizing Masculinities*, ed. Harry Brod and Michael Kaufman; pp. 124–26; 131–41. Thousand Oaks, CA: Sage, 1994. Reproduced with permission of Sage Publications, Inc. 1.7 Kate Bornstein, "Abandon Your Tedious Search: The Rulebook Has Been Found!" from *Gender Outlaw: On Men, Women and the Rest of Us*, pp. 45–52. New York: Routledge, 1994. Reproduced with permission of Taylor & Francis Group LLC. 1.8 Rosemary Marangoly George, "Feminists Theorize Colonial/Postcolonial" from *Cambridge Companion to Feminist Literary Theory*, ed. Ellen Rooney, pp. 211–16; 220–23, 227–31. Cambridge, UK: Cambridge University Press, 2006. Reproduced with permission of Cambridge University Press.

2.1 Gloria Anzaldúa, "To Live in the Borderlands Means You" from *Borderlands/La Frontera: The New Mestiza*, 2nd ed., pp. 216–17. San Francisco: Aunt Lute, 1999. Reproduced with permission of Aunt Lute Books. 2.2 Evelyn Alsultany, "Los Intersticios: Recasting Moving Selves" from *This Bridge We Call Home: Radical*

Visions for Transformation, ed. Gloria E. Anzaldúa and AnaLouise Keating, pp. 106–10. New York: Routledge, 2002. Reproduced with permission of Taylor & Francis Group LLC. 2.3 Paula Gunn Allen, "Where I Come From Is Like This" from *The Sacred Hoop: Recovering the Feminine in American Indian Traditions*, pp. 43–50. Boston: Beacon Press, 1992. Reproduced with permission of Beacon Press. 2.4 Barbara Ehrenreich and Arlie Russell Hochschild, "Introduction" from *Global Woman: Nannies, Maids, and Sex Workers in the New Economy*, ed. Barbara Ehrenreich and Arlie Russell Hochschild, pp. 1–13, 285–86. New York: Metropolitan, 2002. Reproduced with permission of Granta Publications and Henry Holt & Co. 2.5 Melanie Kaye/Kantrowitz and Irena Klepfisz with Bernice Mennis, "*In Gerangl*/In Struggle: A Handbook for Recognizing and Resisting Anti-Semitism" from *The Tribe of Dina: A Jewish Women's Anthology*, ed. Melanie Kaye/Kantrowitz and Irena Klepfisz, pp. 304–05. Montpelier, VT: Sinister Wisdom, 1986. 2.6 Eli Clare, "losing home" from *Exile & Pride: Disability, Queerness and Liberation*, pp. 31–37, 46–49. South End Press, 1999, 2009. Reproduced with permission of Duke University Press and Eli Clare.

3.1 Evelyn Sharp, "The Women at the Gate" from *Rebel Women*, pp. 7–19. London: John Lane Company, 1910. Public domain. 3.2 Sojourner Truth, "A'n't I A Woman?" Delivered at 1851 Women's Convention, Akron, Ohio. Public domain. 3.3 Adrienne Rich, "When We Dead Awaken: Writing as Re-Vision" from *On Lies, Secrets, and Silence: Selected Prose 1966–1978*, excerpts from pp. 34–49. New York: Norton, 1979. "Aunt Jennifer's Tigers" (© 1993, 1951 by Adrienne Rich) and the lines from "Snapshots of a Daughter-in-Law" (© 1993, 1997, 1963 by Adrienne Rich) from Adrienne Rich, *Collected Early Poems: 1950–1970*. All material reproduced with permission of W.W. Norton & Company, Inc. 3.4 Benita Roth, excerpts from *Separate Roads to Feminism: Black, Chicana, and White Feminist Movements in America's Second Wave*, pp. 11–14. Cambridge, UK: Cambridge University Press, 2004. Reproduced with permission of Cambridge University Press and Benita Roth. 3.5 Carol Boyce Davies, "Feminist Consciousness and African Literary Criticism" from *Ngambika: Studies of Women in African Literature*, ed. Carole Boyce Davies and Anne Adams Graves, pp. 1–3, 12–17. Trenton, NJ: Africa World Press, 1986. Reproduced with permission of Africa World Press. 3.6 Blanche Wiesen Cook, "The Historical Denial of Lesbianism," in *Radical History Review* Volume 20 (1979), pp. 60–65. Reproduced with permission of Duke University Press and MARHO: The Radical Historians Organization, Inc. 3.7 Aurora Levins Morales, "The Historian as Curandera," from *Medicine Stories: History, Culture, and the Politics of Integrity*, pp. 23–38. Boston: South End Press, 1998. Reproduced with permission of The Permissions Company, Inc., on behalf of the author, www.auroralevinsmorales.com.

4.1 Joy Kogawa, "Obasan" from *Obasan*, pp. 231–36. New York: Anchor, 1994. Reproduced with permission of the Sandra Dijkstra Literary Agency and Random House LLC. 4.2 Wendy Maruyama, "The Tag Project: Executive Order 9066." 4.3 Guerrilla Girls, "Do Women Have to be Naked to Get Into the Met. Museum?" 4.4 Esther Newton, "The Mythic Mannish Lesbian: Radclyffe Hall and the New Woman," excerpts from *Signs: Journal of Women in Culture and Society* 9.4 (Summer 1984), pp. 557–75. Reproduced with permission of University of Chicago Press and Esther Newton. 4.5 Virginia Woolf, "Shakespeare's Sister" from *A Room of One's Own*, pp. 41–43, 44–50, 111–12. Orlando: Harcourt, 2005. Reproduced with permission of Harcourt Brace and of The Society of Authors on behalf of the estate of Virginia Woolf. 4.6 Maythee Rojas, "Creative Expressions" excerpts from *Women of Color and Feminism*, pp. 107–31. Berkeley, CA: Seal Press, 2009. Reproduced with permission of Perseus Books Group. 4.7 Jean Kilbourne, "Beauty and the Beast of Advertising" from *Media and Values: Redesigning Women*. Center for Media Literacy (Winter 1990). Reproduced with permission of Center for Media Literacy. 4.8 Andi Zeisler, "Pop and Circumstance: Why Pop Culture Matters" excerpts from *Feminism and Pop Culture*. Berkeley, CA: Seal Press, 2008, pp. 1–21). Reproduced with permission of Perseus Books Group.

5.1 Maiana Minahal, "poem on trying to love without fear" from *Color of Violence: The Incite! Anthology*, ed. Incite! Women of Color against Violence, pp. 267–69. Cambridge, MA: South End Press, 2006. Reproduced with permission of Maiana Minahal. 5.2 Audre Lorde, "Uses of the Erotic: The Erotic as Power" from *Sister Outsider: Essays and Speeches*, pp. 53–59. Freedom, CA: Crossing Press, 1984. Reproduced with permission of Abner Stein Agency. 5.3 "The Happiest Day of My Life" from *Dear Sisters: Dispatches from the Women's Liberation Movement*, ed. Rosalyn Baxandall and Linda Gordon New York: Basic Books, 2000, p. 163. Reproduced with permission of Perseus Books Group. 5.4 Heather Corinna, "An Immodest Proposal" from *Yes Means Yes: Visions of Female Sexual Power and a World without Rape*, ed. Jaclyn Friedman and Jessica Valenti, pp. 179–86. Berkeley, CA: Seal Press, 2008. Reproduced with permission of Perseus Books Group, Jaclyn Friedman, and Jessica Valenti. 5.5 Kathy Peiss, "'Charity Girls' and City Pleasures: Historical Notes on Working-Class Sexuality, 1880–1920" from *Powers of Desire: the Politics of Sexuality*, ed. Ann Snitow, Christine Stansell, and Sharon Thompson, pp. 74–87. New York: Monthly Review, 1983. Reproduced with permission of Monthly Review Press. 5.6 Indiana University Empowerment Workshop, "When you Meet a Lesbian: Hints for the Heterosexual Woman" Public domain. 5.7 Gay and Lesbian Speakers' Bureau, "Heterosexuality Questionnaire." The Heterosexuality Questionnaire has been used in SpeakOUT's speaker training curriculum since it was called the Gay and Lesbian Speakers' Bureau. Established in 1972, SpeakOUT is now the oldest LGBTQIA speakers' bureau in the United States. 5.8 Judith Lorber and Lisa Jean Moore, "Aligning Bodies, Identities, and Expressions: Transgender Bodies" from *Gendered Bodies: Feminist Perspectives*, pp. 118–21. New York: Oxford University Press, 2011. Reproduced with permission of Oxford University Press. 5.9 R.W. Connell, "Masculinity Politics on a World Scale" from *Masculinities*, 2nd ed., pp. 260–65. Berkeley, CA: University of California Press, 2005. Reproduced with permission of University of California Press. 5.10 Prentis Hemphill, "Brown Boi Health Manifesto" from *Freeing Ourselves: A Guide to Health and Self Love for Brown Bois*, pp. 118–19. Brown Boi Project, 2011. Reproduced with permission of Brown Boi Project.

6.1 Janice Mirikitani, "Recipe" from *Shedding Silence*, p. 20. Berkeley: Celestial Arts, 1987. Reproduced with permission of Janice Mirikitani. 6.2 Rose Weitz, "A History of Women's Bodies" from *The Politics of Women's Bodies: Sexuality, Appearance, Behavior*, ed. Rose Weitz, pp. 3–11. New York: Oxford University Press, 2003. Reproduced with permission of Oxford University Press. 6.3 Gloria Steinem, "If Men Could Menstruate" from *Ms Magazine*, October 1978, p. 110. Reproduced with permission of Gloria Steinem. 6.4 Laura Hershey, "Women and Disability and Poetry (Not Necessarily in That Order)," Jan 26, 2010, from www.laurahershey.com. Reproduced with permission of R. Stephens. 6.5 Morrie Turner, "Do we call you handicapped?" *Wee Pals*, 8–3, 1981. Reproduced with permission from Creators Syndicate International for the artist. 6.6 Eric Anderson, "Maintaining Masculinity: Homophobia at Work" from *In the Game: Gay Athletes and the Cult of Masculinity*, pp. 25–30. Albany: SUNY Press, 2005. Reproduced with permission of State University of New York Press. 6.7 Judith Ortiz Cofer, "The Story of My Body" from *The Latin Deli: Prose and Poetry*, pp. 135–46. Athens: University of Georgia Press, 1993. Reproduced with permission of University of Georgia Press. 6.8 Maysan Haydar, "Veiled Intentions: Don't Judge a Muslim Girl by her Covering" from *Body Outlaws: Rewriting the Rules of Beauty and Body Image*, ed. Ophira Edut, pp. 258–65. Emeryville, CA: Seal Press, 2003. Reproduced with permission of Perseus Books Group.

7.1 Meridel le Sueur, "Sequel to Love" from *Writing Red: An Anthology of American Women Writers*, ed. Charlotte Nekola and Paula Rabinowitz, pp. 36–38. New York: Feminist Press, 1987. 7.2 Loretta J. Ross, Sarah L. Brownlee, Dazon Dixon Diallo, Luz Rodriquez, and SisterSong Women of Color Reproductive Health Project, "Just Choices: Women of Color, Reproductive Health and Human Rights" from *Policing the National Body: Sex, Race, and Criminalization. A Project of the Committee on Women, Population, and the Environment*, ed. Jael Silliman and Anannya Bhattacharjee, pp. 154–60, 168–74. Cambridge, MA: South End Press, 2002. Reproduced with permission of Loretta J. Ross. 7.3 Etobssie Wako and Cara Page. "Depo Diaries and the Power of Stories" from *Telling Stories to Change the World: Global Voices on the Power of Narrative to Build Community and Make Social Justice Claims*, ed. Rickie Solinger, Madeline Fox, and Kayhan Irani, pp. 101–07. New York: Routledge, 2008. Reproduced with permission of Taylor & Francis Group LLC. 7.4 Karen J. Warren, "Women, People of Color, Children, and Health" and "Women and Environmental Justice" from *Ecofeminist Philosophy: A Western Perspective on What It Is and Why It Matters*, pp. 10–16, 18–19. Lanham, MD: Rowman & Littlefield, 2000. Reproduced with permission of Rowman & Littlefield Publishing Group LLC. 7.5 Ynestra King, "Healing the Wounds: Feminism, Ecology, and the Nature/Culture Dualism from *Reweaving the World: The Emergence of Ecofeminism*, ed. Irene Diamond and Gloria Feman Orenstein, pp. 106–21. San Francisco: Sierra Club Books, 1990. Reproduced with permission of Ynestra King. 7.6 Vandana Shiva, "Mad Cows and Sacred Cows," excerpts from *Stolen Harvest: The Hijacking of the Global Food Supply*, pp. 57–78. Cambridge, MA: South End Press, 2000. 7.7. Favianna

Rodriguez, "Green our Communities! Plant Urban Gardens." Reproduced with permission of Favianna Rodriguez. 7.8 Greta Gaard, "Toward a Queer Ecofeminism", "Sexualizing Nature, Naturalizing Sexuality" from *New Perspectives on Environmental Justice: Gender, Sexuality, and Activism*, ed. Rachel Stein, pp. 21–29. New Brunswick, NJ: Rutgers University Press, 2004.

8.1 Charlotte Perkins Gilman, "The Yellow Wallpaper," 1892. Public domain. 8.2 Carol Bohmer and Andrea Parrot, "Scope of the Problem" from *Sexual Assault on Campus: The Problem and the Solution*, pp. 18–40. New York: Lexington Books, 1993. Reproduced with permission of Rowman & Littlefield. 8.3 Colleen Jamison, "Sexual Assault Prevention Tips Guaranteed to Work!" from http://feminally.tumblr. com/post/168208983/sexual-assault-prevention-tips-guaranteed-to-work (posted Aug. 21, 2009). 8.4 Martha R. Mahoney, "Legal Images of Battered Women: Redefining the Issue of Separation," from *Michigan Law Review*, 90.1 (Oct. 1991), pp.1–19. Reproduced with permission of Martha R. Mahoney and Michigan Law Review. 8.5 Alicia Gaspar de Alba and Georgina Guzmán, "Feminicidio: The 'Black Legend' of the Border" from *Making a Killing: Femicide, Free Trade, and La Frontera*, ed. Alicia Gaspar de Alba with Georgina Guzmán, pp. 1–11.Austin: University of Texas Press, 2010. Reproduced with permission of University of Texas Press. 8.6 Cheryl Chase, "Hermaphrodites with Attitude: Mapping the Emergence of Intersex Political Activism" from *GLQ: A Journal of Lesbian and Gay Studies*, 4.2 (1998), pp. 189–203, 208–11. Reproduced with permission of Duke University Press. 8.7 Andrea Smith, "Heteropatriarchy and the Three Pillars of White Supremacy: Rethinking Women of Color Organizing" from *Color of Violence: The Incite! Anthology*, ed. Incite! Women of Color against Violence, pp. 66–73. Cambridge, MA: South End Press, 2006. Reproduced with permission of A. Smith.

9.1 Helena María Viramontes, "The Moths" from *The Moths and Other Stories*, 2nd ed., pp. 27–34. Houston: Arte Público Press, 1995. Reproduced with permission of Arte Público Press. 9.2 Ama R. Saran, "My Guardian Spirits" from *Wings of Gauze: Women of Color and the Experience of Health and Illness*, ed. Barbara Bair and Susan E. Cayleff, pp. 23–25. Detroit: Wayne State University Press, 1993. Reproduced with permission of Wayne State University Press. 9.3 E. M. Broner, "Honor and Ceremony in Women's Rituals" from *The Politics of Women's Spirituality: Essays by Founding Mothers of the Movement*, ed. Charlene Spretnak, pp. 234–44. Reproduced with permission of Random House LLC and Frances Goldin Literary Agency. 9.4 Alifa Rifaat, "My World of the Unknown" from *Distant View of a Minaret and Other Stories*, trans. Denys Johnson-Davies, pp. 61–76. London: Quartet Books, 1983. 9.5 Inés Maria Talamantez, "Seeing Red: American Indian Women Speaking about Their Religious and Political Perspectives" from *In Our Own Voices: Four Centuries of American Women's Religious Writing*, ed. Rosemary Skinner Keller and Rosemary Radford Ruether, pp. 398–401, 406–409. San Francisco: Harper San Francisco, 1995. Reproduced with permission of Rosemary Radford Ruether. 9.6 Terry Tempest Williams, "The Clan of One-Breasted Women" from *Refuge: An Unnatural History of Family and Place*, pp. 281–90. New York: Vintage, 1992. © 1991 by Terry Tempest Williams. Reproduced with permission of Pantheon Books, an imprint of the Knopf Doubleday Publishing Group, a division of Random House LLC. 9.7 Lori Arviso Alvord and Elizabeth Cohen Van Pelt, "Life out of Balance" from *The Scalpel and the Silver Bear*. pp. 59–61, 65–76. New York: Bantam, 1999. Reproduced with permission of William Morris Endeavour Entertainment and Bantam Books, an imprint of Random House, a division of Random House LLC.

10.1 bell hooks, "Feminism: A Transformational Politic" from *Talking Back: Thinking Feminist, Thinking Black*, pp. 19–26. Boston: South End Press, 1989. 10.2 Rebekah Putnam and Carri Bennett, "If I had a hammer ... I'd SMASH Patriarchy" from *Habitual Freak* zine, issue 2 (Sept 1994). 10.3 Judy Freespirit and Aldebaran, "Fat Liberation Manifesto" (1973), from *The Fat Studies Reader,* ed. Esther Rothblum and Sondra Solovay, pp. 341–42. New York: NYU Press, 2009. Reproduced with permission of NYU Press. 10.4 Jenny Morris, "Fighting Back" from *Pride against Prejudice: A Personal Politics of Disability*, pp. 169–80. London: Women's Press, 1991. Reproduced with permission of Jenny Morris. 10.5 Julie Sze, "Expanding Environmental Justice: Asian American Feminists' Contribution" from *Dragon Ladies: Asian American Feminists Breathe Fire*, ed. Sonia Shah, pp. 90–99. Boston: South End Press, 1997. Reproduced with permission of Julie Sze. 10.6 M. Jacqui Alexander, "El Mundo Zurdo and the Ample Space of the Erotic" subsection in "Remembering This Bridge, Remembering Ourselves: Yearning, Memory, and Desire" from *This Bridge We Call Home: Radical Visions for Transformation*, ed. Gloria E. Anzaldúa and AnaLouise Keating, pp. 97–103. New York: Routledge, 2002. Reproduced with permission of Taylor & Francis. 10.7 AnaLouise Keating, "From Intersections to Interconnections: Lessons for Transformation *from This Bridge Called My Back: Radical Writings by Women of Color*" from *The Intersectional Approach: Transforming the Academy through Race, Class, and Gender*, ed. Michele Tracy Berger and Kathleen Guidroz, pp. 84–95. Chapel Hill: University of North Carolina Press, 2009. Reproduced with permission of University of North Carolina Press. 10.8 Sabrina Margarita Sandata, 1998, "All Sleeping Women Now Awake and Move" from *Bamboo Girl* zine, issue 7. Reproduced with permission from M. Alcantara. 10.9 Maya Angelou, "Still I Rise" from *And Still I Rise*. New York: Random House, Virago, 1978. Reproduced with permission of Penguin Random House LLC and Little Brown.

General Introduction

What distinguishes this introductory text to Gender and Women's Studies from others currently available is its rich inclusion of the sort of humanities content that was vital to the emergence of the women's movement. Each chapter leads off with an outstanding piece of creative writing. Readings connect with and give voice to the lives of a diverse set of women and expressions of gender worldwide. The texts offer vibrant images, evocative language, and well-articulated ideas. Using these as models, students will find themselves better prepared to express their experience and frame their own arguments in service of the activism that is so central to Gender and Women's Studies. Social issues are addressed throughout, but without stressing quantitative, social science–based approaches. The reintegration of humanities content works to support interdisciplinary studies, which Women's Studies has fostered throughout its history.

The current anthology emerges from a thorough revision of the 1998 textbook, *Women in Culture: A Women's Studies Anthology*, edited by the late Lucinda Joy Peach. There was much to admire in this work, including its attention to feminist terminology and use of thematic sections, each with an introduction, exercises, and bibliography. These features are retained in the updated work. Discussion questions provided for each chapter encourage creative thought and activism in students, both in and beyond the classroom. Additional resources in the text are a historical timeline inclusive of major feminist writings and a glossary of key terms used in the readings, reflecting both past and present concerns of Women's Studies. In order to make standpoints clear, the names of many feminist thinkers included in our chapter introductions are preceded with identity labels, which are mostly drawn from identities the individuals have embraced themselves. Related to this, good topics for discussion are, first, that certain identities that have been dominant, such as heterosexual, white, or Euro-, are often not embraced in self-identifications; and second, that terms for identities are fluid and subject to change. Instructors will find supplemental materials focused on pedagogical approaches, as well as media resources, and suggested assignments, by chapter, at the companion website www.wiley.com\go\scott\womeninculture.

Many of the foundational readings contained in the 1998 text were well worth retaining, but much of the feminist conversation has moved on from debates about various waves and theoretical schools of feminism, and Women's Studies has grown to support greater dialogue and diversity. The former edition placed an emphasis upon representations of women in "American culture." Though its US-based content remains strong and is representative of numerous communities, the new text works for greater intersections among women's cultures worldwide. Finally, for the updated version we found it essential to explore work related to racially diverse, LGBT (lesbian, gay, bisexual, and transgender)/queer/trans feminisms and masculinities that have continued to emerge in the last two decades.

The thematic chapters that comprise the body of this new text are designed as follows:

Our intention with the initial chapter, titled "Introduction to Feminist Concepts and Issues," is to define key terms that lay a foundation for all future work in Women's Studies. These include feminism(s); sex and gender; standpoint; social location, privilege, oppression, and resistance; intersectionality; transnational feminisms; interdisciplinarity; and representation.

The second chapter, "Stories of Identity and Community," includes personal narratives and scholarly essays about identities across differences and commonalities. These readings address the complexity of self-definition for individuals within families and communities, and the negotiation of group identities for shared activisms.

Chapter 3, "Histories of Feminism," introduces feminist efforts to bring a diverse set of women back into history and historiography. We explore multiple versions of the history of feminism, ranging through time, as told from decentered, postcolonial, and transnational perspectives.

Chapter 4, "Representations of Women and Gender in Arts and Media," concerns cultural representations of women, both in traditional arts and in popular culture. It historicizes women's struggle for inclusion in artistic canons and display spaces and allows us to see women as creators of alternate self-defined images and genres.

Chapter 5, "Sexualities and Genders," promotes an understanding of the culturally constructed nature of LGBT and queer sexualities, gender identities, heterosexual privilege, transphobia, and homophobia. It redefines desire and the erotic across sexualities.

We move next to "Body Politics" in Chapter 6. This identifies ideas and expressions that alienate women from our bodies. Furthermore, the readings offer strategies for reclaiming the body and healing the mind/body/spirit split typical of Western thought. Concerns include racialized and gendered bodies, bodies with disabilities, and masculinities.

The seventh chapter, titled "Reproductive and Environmental Justice," presents women-led and conceptualized movements to sustain the wellbeing of women and the earth, both in the United States and internationally, with particular attention to ways women of color have assumed leadership in these movements.

Chapter 8, "Violence and Resistance," documents women's responses to culturally sanctioned, gendered violence and rape, which may range in location from intimate partners' relationships to widespread contexts of war and colonial occupation.

Chapter 9, concerning "Healing and Spirituality," draws on various cultural knowledges to present woman-centered perspectives on spirituality by healers, activists, ritualists, scholars, and creative writers. The readings present feminist critiques of racism, heteropatriarchal religions, and Eurocentric medical and other corporate-driven institutions. It also examines the meaning of life and death, wellness and illness, the relationships between people, land bases, and all living things, and the role of spirituality and healing in relation to social justice.

The final chapter, "Activism for the Future," shows ways that Women's Studies encourages activisms both locally and globally, responding to continuing and new issues and challenges, and serving to further social justice.

1

Introduction to Feminist Concepts and Issues

By Anne Donadey

Contents

Original publication details: 1.1 Sandra Cisneros, "My Name" from *The House on Mango Street*, pp. 10–11. New York: Vintage, 1991. © 1984 by Sandra Cisneros. Reproduced with permission of Susan Bergholz Literary Services and Bloomsbury Publishing plc. 1.2 Jacinta Bunnell and Nat Kusinitz, "The new pronoun they invented suited everyone just fine" from *Sometimes the Spoon Runs Away with Another Spoon Coloring Book*, words by Jacinta Bunnell, pictures by Nat Kusinitz. Oakland, CA: PM Press, 2010. Reproduced with permission of PM Press. 1.3 Marilyn Frye, "Oppression" from *The Politics of Reality: Essays in Feminist Theory*, pp. 1–7. Berkeley, CA: The Crossing Press, 1983. Reproduced with permission of Marilyn Frye. 1.4 Audre Lorde, "Age, Race, Class, and Sex: Women Redefining Difference" from *Sister Outsider: Essays and Speeches*, pp. 114–23. Freedom, CA: The Crossing Press, 1984. Reproduced with permission of Abner Stein Agency. 1.5 Alice Walker, "Womanist" from *In Search of Our Mothers' Gardens: Womanist Prose*, pp. xi–xii. San Diego: Harcourt Brace Jovanovich, 1983. 1.6 Michael S. Kimmel, "Masculinity as Homophobia: Fear, Shame, and Silence in the Construction of Gender Identity" from *Theorizing Masculinities*, ed. Harry Brod and Michael Kaufman; pp. 124–26; 131–41. Thousand Oaks, CA: Sage, 1994. Reproduced with permission of Sage Publications, Inc. *(continued on page 2)*

Women in Culture: An Intersectional Anthology for Gender and Women's Studies, Second Edition. Edited by Bonnie Kime Scott, Susan E. Cayleff, Anne Donadey, and Irene Lara. © 2017 John Wiley & Sons, Ltd. Published 2017 by John Wiley & Sons, Ltd.

Feminism has many different definitions and facets. A popular definition of feminism is "the radical notion that women are people." The *Merriam-Webster's Collegiate Dictionary* defines it as "1: the theory of the political, economic, and social equality of the sexes; 2: organized activity on behalf of women's rights and interests." Feminism thus includes both scholarship and activism. African American public intellectual bell hooks takes issue with a narrow definition of feminism that focuses only on seeking equality with men. She importantly asks, to *which* men do *which* women seek to be equal, given that not all men are equal? She highlights the extent to which this narrow definition of feminism only focuses on gender issues and therefore applies best to the situation of white, middle-class women. She goes on to redefine feminism more broadly and radically: "Feminism as a movement to end sexist oppression directs our attention to systems of domination and the inter-relatedness of sex, race, and class oppression" ("Feminism" 31). The most complete definition of feminism is probably that of Black lesbian writer-activist Barbara Smith: "Feminism is the political theory and practice that struggles to free *all* women: women of color, working-class women, poor women, disabled women, lesbians, old women – as well as white, economically privileged, heterosexual women. Anything less than this vision of total freedom is not feminism, but merely female self-aggrandizement" (25).

Intersectional Feminism

Smith's and hooks's definitions are intersectional, a term that means that they do not only focus on one issue such as gender but broaden the analysis to encompass other vectors of identity and of human domination such as race and racism, social class and classism, sexual orientation, colonialism and imperialism, disability, national origin, religion, and age. This wide-ranging approach, which has created a paradigm shift in Women's Studies, Ethnic Studies, and other fields, has come to be known as intersectionality (Crenshaw) but is also variously termed "Black feminist thought" (Collins), "multiracial feminism" (Zinn and Dill), "multicultural feminism" (Shohat), "US Third-World feminism"

Original publication details: 1.7 Kate Bornstein, "Abandon Your Tedious Search: The Rulebook Has Been Found!" from *Gender Outlaw: On Men, Women and the Rest of Us*, pp. 45–52. New York: Routledge, 1994. Reproduced with permission of Taylor & Francis Group LLC. 1.8 Rosemary Marangoly George, "Feminists Theorize Colonial/Postcolonial" from *Cambridge Companion to Feminist Literary Theory*, ed. Ellen Rooney, pp. 211–16; 220–23, 227–31. Cambridge, UK: Cambridge University Press, 2006. Reproduced with permission of Cambridge University Press.

(Sandoval), "multiple consciousness" (King), and multi-axial approach (Brah 189). Intersectionality can be traced back to African American activist-intellectuals Sojourner Truth and Anna Julia Cooper in the nineteenth century. While others had also made connections between some issues such as gender and class, gender and sexual orientation, race and class, or race and colonialism, the focus on race, class, gender, and sexual orientation as profoundly interwoven and interlocking vectors is an original contribution to scholarship by 1970s and 1980s US feminists of color.[1] They theorized the interrelatedness of race, gender, and imperialism (e.g., Elizabeth "Betita" Martinez in 1972; Mitsuye Yamada in 1981); race, gender, and class (e.g., Angela Davis in 1981); race, gender, class, and sexual orientation (e.g., the Combahee River Collective in 1977; Cherríe Moraga and Gloria Anzaldúa in 1981; Audre Lorde; and Adrienne Rich); colonialism, race, class, and gender (e.g., Gayatri Chakravorty Spivak in 1985). Starting around the 1990s, scholars from various countries addressing the intersections among gender, race, and nationalism (e.g., Ella Shohat; Deniz Kandiyoti; Floya Anthias; and Nira Yuval-Davis) and among disability and other vectors such as gender (e.g., Susan Wendell) and gender, race, and class (e.g., Rosemarie Garland Thomson and Jenny Morris) have made important additions to this scholarship. By the year 2000, gender identity had been added as a key factor that LGBTQQI (lesbian, gay, bisexual, transgender, queer, questioning, and intersex) activists urged must be considered in discussions of oppression and identity. This is explored in this chapter and in Chapter 5. A central lesson feminists have learned through debates between single-focus and intersectional approaches is that our standpoint (our worldview, the ways in which we make sense of our life experiences and of the world around us) is influenced by our social location (the time and place in which we live and the information to which we have access, as well as the social categories or groups to which we are perceived as belonging).

The readings in this introductory section illustrate some of the main issues discussed above. Chicana creative writer Sandra Cisneros's chapter, "My Name," from her acclaimed novel *The House on Mango Street*, first published in 1984, opens the anthology. The character of young Esperanza shares her standpoint with readers with respect to the difficulties of having multiple identities in a world that fragments you because it expects you to be only one thing. Bilingual and bicultural, Esperanza struggles to find her place. Her first name, Spanish for hope, is also related to the verb *esperar*, to wait. This double meaning reflects her sense of double belonging – being between Anglo and Latino cultures – and her hope for a better future for women. Her sense of connection to the strong woman in her lineage after whom she was named makes her reflect on the dual meaning of her name – both hope and waiting, a metaphor for the need to be able to fit in your lineage and cultures without letting them completely determine your identity or your place in society. Her attentiveness to various levels of linguistic meaning reflects her awareness of the different value associated with Anglo and Latino cultures in the United States – her "silver"-sounding name in Spanish sounds like "tin," a much less valued metal, in English.

In her book *The Politics of Reality* (1983), from which a portion of the chapter on "Oppression" is excerpted here, white lesbian feminist philosopher Marilyn Frye provides a critical definition of oppression as "a system of interrelated barriers and forces which reduce, immobilize and mold people who belong to a certain group, and effect their subordination to another group" (33). Oppression is a system that unfairly targets certain people based on their perceived group membership (for example their perceived race, gender, social class, or sexual orientation), rather than judging them on their individual characteristics (7–8). It includes specific unpaid or poorly paid functions that members of the oppressed group are expected to provide to members of the dominant group. Frye gives the example of women being expected to provide service work of a personal, sexual, and emotional nature for men (9). She highlights the fact that oppression is made to appear natural so oppressed people internalize it through socialization (33–34). Internalized oppression leads people who are the target of one form of oppression to believe the negative messages against their groups and sometimes to end up acting against their own self-interests. Conversely, internalized domination leads members of a dominant group to believe that they are naturally entitled to a superior status and to the advantages derived from that status. It thus serves to hide the existence of dominant group privilege (see Adams, Bell, and Griffin).

Afro-Caribbean lesbian writer Audre Lorde's essay "Age, Race, Class, and Sex: Women Redefining Difference" (1984) develops central concepts for wide-ranging feminist social justice projects: the dangers of a world view that arranges perceived group differences into hierarchical binary oppositions such as male/female, white/black, mind/body, self/other, or culture/nature[2]; the ways in which various forms of oppression are structured similarly to create a norm that is seen as superior (the "mythical norm"); the need to recognize each other's oppression and resistance ("the edge of each other's battles"); the need to learn from histories of oppression and resistance so we do not have to reinvent the wheel generation after generation; and the need for intersectional activist approaches so that an inclusive feminist agenda does not solely focus on gender issues but includes a commitment to fighting for racial and economic justice and against heterosexism (the primacy of heterosexuality) and ageism (privileging adults versus older people and children). In beautifully evocative language, Lorde invites us to imagine "patterns for relating across our human differences as equals," a project that is as central to a socially just future today as it was in the early 1980s when she first articulated it. For instance, pretending to be color-blind and to not "see" differences (especially racial ones) only leads us to conceptualize equality in terms of sameness and to feel guilty over noticing differences, thus resulting in avoidance of the topic and immobilization rather than social justice activism. The ideology of color-blindness implies that difference is bad and that it is therefore impolite to notice or dialogue about differences. More problematically, it encourages the denial of racism (Frankenberg) and of the existence of power differences between groups, makes racism a taboo topic, and signals that people of color are expected to act white and assimilate (Sue). Instead, Lorde invites us to explore differences and create new ways of working together as *equals through differences*.

Because feminists active in the movement have tended to be the ones with more access to financial resources, time, and education, the leadership of the movement has historically tended to be primarily white, middle/upper-class, and heterosexual. Debates over whether feminism should focus on gender issues narrowly defined or should adopt a broader, intersectional focus have to do in great part with who sets the agenda and what issues are primary in their lives. As a result, issues of importance to women of color, working-class women, women with disabilities, indigenous women, and lesbians or queer people have historically not been fully included in feminist agendas. While many feminists of color focused on redefining feminism more broadly, as explained above, some selected a different term altogether to reflect their intersectional approaches in reaction against mainstream feminism's inability to fully include race issues in the 1970s and early 1980s. In her book *In Search of Our Mothers' Gardens: Womanist Prose* (1983), African American novelist Alice Walker famously coined the adjective "womanist" and created a definition of the term that mimics the standard format of a dictionary definition. Her definition is purposefully grounded in African American vernacular language, history, and culture and progressively broadens to include lesbian existence, female solidarity, and men, culminating in a holistic and spiritual view of feminism based on love. It is to be noted that while many critics refer to Walker's concept as womanism, Walker herself only coined the adjective womanist – presumably seeking to create an intersectional approach that many could identify with rather than trying to impose a new doctrine or movement.

Feminists of color have disagreed with some white radical feminists and lesbian separatist feminists who called for women to separate from men as a solution to sexist oppression and male domination. While feminists such as hooks, Lorde, Walker, Martinez, and others have taken men from their own cultural backgrounds to task for engaging in sexist oppression, they also insist that these men are their allies in the fight against racism and white supremacy. As early as 1972, Martinez insisted that Latinas "have the right to expect that our most enlightened men will join in the fight against sexism; it should not be our battle alone" (33). Lorde also powerfully reminds white feminists that female cross-racial solidarity is not a given but something that must be achieved through recognition of the different issues with which various women struggle: "Some problems we share as women, some we do not. You fear your children will grow up to join the patriarchy and testify against you, we fear our children will be dragged from a car and shot down in the street, and you will turn your backs upon the reasons they are dying."

In "Masculinity as Homophobia: Fear, Shame, and Silence in the Construction of Gender Identity" (1994), white sociologist Michael S. Kimmel picks up on Lorde's concept of the mythical norm. The gender-based mythical norm is often referred to as "hegemonic masculinity" (a term coined by R. W. Connell and various collaborators), which Kimmel defines as the masculinity of those who have power in society. As Lorde described hierarchical binary oppositions, Kimmel shows that hegemonic masculinity defines itself in opposition to anything feminine and teaches men that the only emotion appropriate for them to display is aggression (Frye similarly refers to anger, *Politics* 14), which leads to violence (see Chapter 8). Since men are not supposed to be feminine, they are encouraged to look down upon women, distance themselves from men who are perceived as being gay, and attack the masculinity of men who have less power in the culture, such as men of color. Kimmel shows how homophobia, sexism, and racism can be wielded by men to defend their own sense of masculinity. Lorde's insight that the "mythical norm" is set up in such a way that very few people can feel that they are a part of it and Frye's distinction between oppression and suffering can help explain what

Kimmel describes as a major "paradox in men's lives, a paradox in which men [as a group] have virtually all the power and yet do not feel [individually] powerful," thus leading yet again to frustration and anger.

In an essay that is widely available online, white anti-racist feminist activist Peggy McIntosh makes a similar point with respect to white people and race, claiming that "whites are carefully taught not to recognize white privilege, as males are taught not to recognize male privilege." Internalized domination serves to hide the existence of dominant group privilege. McIntosh points out that it is easier for people in general to see the ways in which we are oppressed than it is to recognize ways in which we are privileged. Privilege is the flip side of oppression, and she challenges white readers to become more aware of the ways in which whiteness functions as a mythical norm granting whites "unearned privileges." A dominant upbringing systematically trains white people to become blind to white privilege or to see it as a natural entitlement, and McIntosh provides many daily examples of how white privilege functions for individuals in society. By focusing on men and white people, Kimmel and McIntosh demonstrate that analyses of oppression can yield important insights into the role that privilege and internalized domination play in the maintenance of structures of oppression, as well as open up avenues for self-awareness and social change through alliance politics.

Redefinitions of Gender

As scholars have widened the purview of feminism from a single-minded focus on gender to intersectional approaches, they have also refined and redefined what we mean by gender and women in significant ways. Whereas the generic definitions of sex and gender are that sex refers to the biological sexual characteristics with which one is born and gender to social constructions of sex, feminists such as anthropologist of sexuality Gayle Rubin have complicated our understandings of the relationship between the two terms. For Rubin, the "sex/gender system" is "the set of arrangements by which a society transforms biological sexuality into products of human activity" (159). This definition acknowledges that sex and gender cannot be easily pulled apart along the lines of nature versus culture but that they constantly interface with one another. This redefinition is important because women's oppression is often justified with reference to female biology (the ideas that women bear children and are supposedly more emotional and naturally inclined to raise children and to work out of love – that is, for free). White postmodernist feminist and queer studies scholar Judith Butler reverses the biological justifications for women's secondary status by claiming that since we can only conceive of sexual difference through our cultural understandings of it as male and female, "perhaps this construct called 'sex' is as culturally constructed as gender" and sex turns out "to have been gender all along" (7, 8). In "Abandon Your Tedious Search: The Rulebook Has Been Found!" (1994), white transgender intellectual, activist, and performance artist Kate Bornstein participates in this debate by deconstructing the "rules of gender," our society's expectation of rigid distinctions between males and females. Through the use of analysis, personal examples, and humor, she demonstrates that these supposedly natural rules are in fact constructions that contribute to marginalizing gender-nonconforming people. The binary opposition between male and female obscures the existence of people who do not fit into either category: intersex people (who are born with some male and female physical sexual characteristics) and transgender people (people whose gender identity – that is, their personal and psychological sense of being male or female or on a continuum – is at odds with their sex assigned at birth, or people whose gender identity does not fit easily into the male/female, heterosexual/homosexual binary). Sometimes the terms trans*, transgender, and queer are used interchangeably. For transgender persons, being referred to as one's gender of choice – signified by correct and preferred name and pronouns – is a major issue in the struggle for respectful recognition. Feminists have long fought for gender-inclusive language (e.g., firefighter instead of fireman, mail carrier for mailman, or staffing the desk instead of manning the desk). Transgender activists have coined gender-neutral pronouns such as "ze" and "hir" (Bornstein, *My Gender Workbook* 36); others use they/them/theirs to refer to one person. Children's coloring book authors Jacinta Bunnell and Nat Kusinitz's thoughtful cartoon "The New Pronoun They Invented Suited Everyone Just Fine" (2010) illustrates this issue and encourages us to be creative in modifying language to reflect more inclusive ways of perceiving identities for future generations. Chapter 5, on sexualities and genders, develops these issues at greater length.

Postcolonial and Transnational Feminisms

As feminists from various locations have developed intersectional definitions of oppression and feminism, they have also focused on strategies of resistance to oppression and on the importance of women's agency (the awareness that women are not just oppressed and victimized but that they also find ways, both large and small, of setting their own course and making their own decisions even in contexts in which they have very limited options). Even in situations of oppression that are marked by what Frye calls the double bind – the absence of viable choices – it is important to recognize that people still manage to exert some amount of agency and should not only be seen as disempowered victims. For instance, Cisneros ends her chapter with her protagonist selecting a new, mysterious name full of promise for herself. Walker highlights a history of African American women's organized resistance to slavery, referencing Harriet Tubman's participation in the Underground Railroad.

Feminists focusing on the lives of women in colonized parts of the world have similarly insisted on the importance of acknowledging the agency and resistance of women to three specific forms of oppression. The first form of oppression is created by colonialism and imperialism, which rely on a discourse of Third World women as victims of their own cultures and religions to justify military intervention, conquest, and the exploitation of natural resources and human labor in the colonies. The second one comes from masculinist (male-dominated) nationalist resistance to colonialism that equates liberation from colonial domination with regaining manhood (which entails keeping women in secondary positions – see hooks, "Reflections"). The third difficulty originates with Western feminists who, when they only focus on gender issues, ignore the detrimental impact that their own colonizing governments have had on women from colonized countries and may end up reinforcing colonial oppression under the guise of so-called feminist sisterhood. In "Feminists Theorize Colonial/Postcolonial" (2006), Indian postcolonial feminist scholar Rosemary Marangoly George clarifies the central contribution of postcolonial feminist Gayatri Chakravorty Spivak to the field. Spivak explained that between the colonialist discourse of "white men saving brown women from brown men" and the male "nativist" (nationalist) argument that local women who conform to oppressive cultural or religious practices are doing so entirely of their own free will, there is almost no space for local women to express their concerns in ways that will actually be heard on their own merits as opposed to being coopted, reframed, and manipulated by either side. The problems are compounded when Western feminists exhibit colonialist attitudes and start acting as "white women saving brown women from brown men." In that difficult context, postcolonial/Third World/transnational feminists are often attacked and dismissed in their own countries as being Westernized and inauthentic representatives of their cultures by a masculinist leadership that does not want to question male privilege (see also Narayan). In the West, their critiques of Western colonial practices and discourses often go unheard, and their complex feminist positions are simplified and used to justify a colonialist critique of their cultures or religions as being backwards and in need of Western salvation. With the renewed Islamophobia in the West after the destruction of the World Trade Center towers in New York City on September 11, 2001, and the state of permanent warfare in which the West has been engaged ever since, creating new waves of refugee populations from the Middle East, these patterns have gained renewed centrality and call for careful analysis on the part of scholars and citizens alike.

Finally, Spivak distinguishes between two meanings of the term "representation": it can refer to political representation (gaining the right to vote, having politicians who speak for their various constituent groups) and visual or textual representation (the ways that various groups are portrayed in society through stereotypes, as well as counternarratives and resistance to stereotypes). Women's Studies is an interdisciplinary field (it includes scholars trained in various fields, from English and Comparative Literary Studies to the Social Sciences and History, and increasingly includes researchers in the Natural Sciences). It focuses on analyzing, critiquing, and bettering women's status in society and promoting activism for social justice. In general, humanities scholars will tend to focus on issues of cultural/visual/textual representations and social science scholars on political representation and access. Both aspects of representation are important for all social justice projects and will be addressed in various chapters in the volume.

Discussion Questions

1. In what ways do Cisneros's and Walker's essays demonstrate an intersectional approach? What vectors of identity are most salient for each? How are these vectors presented as interrelated?

2. Why does Frye argue against too broad a definition of oppression? What problems does she envision if oppressors can also be viewed as oppressed?
3. Explain Frye's theory of the double bind oppressed people experience. Can you think of some examples? Explain her analogy of oppression as a bird cage. What makes this analogy rhetorically effective?
4. In what ways are the poetic style used by Cisneros and Lorde and the humorous style used by Cisneros and Bornstein particularly effective to convey their message? Why and how does style give their message a more powerful punch?
5. Can you think of concrete examples of Kimmel's notion of "hegemonic masculinity" and of his idea (also evident in Bornstein's piece) that "our peers are a kind of gender police"? How can we counter these practices?
6. George explains that nineteenth-century "European texts repeatedly justified and explained colonial domination by reinforcing a series of hierarchized oppositions such as civilized/savage, modern/traditional, mature/childlike, and, most signifi-cantly, rational/irrational." Can you think of some examples that show that these patterns of colonial thinking continue today? For example, which cultures are still described in popular media as uncivilized, which religions as traditional, and which gender as irrational?
7. How do *you* define feminism? Has your definition been somewhat modified after doing the readings in this chapter? Why, or why not?

Notes

1. The terms "women of color" and "people of color" began to be used widely in the United States in the 1970s and 1980s to indicate coalitional and intersectional identities among groups facing oppressions based on race and other factors. These terms were created by people belonging to these groups and should not be confused with the earlier terms "colored women" and "colored people," which were derogatory terms used during the Jim Crow segregation era in the United States to refer to African American people. The two sets of terms are not interchangeable.
2. White feminist anthropologist Sherry Ortner argued that women are devalued in most cultures because they are seen as being closer to nature and the body and men are identified with culture and the mind, which are seen as superior values.

References

Adams, Maurianne, Lee Anne Bell, and Pat Griffin, eds. *Teaching for Diversity and Social Justice*. 2nd ed. New York: Routledge, 2007.

Anthias, Floya, and Nira Yuval-Davis. Introduction. Ed. Nira Yuval-Davis and Floya Anthias. *Woman-Nation-State*. Houndmills, UK: Macmillan, 1989. 1–15.

Bornstein, Kate. *My Gender Workbook: How to Become a Real Man, a Real Woman, the Real You, or Something Else Entirely*. New York: Routledge, 1998.

Brah, Avtar. *Cartographies of Diaspora: Contesting Identities*. London: Routledge, 1996.

Butler, Judith. *Gender Trouble: Feminism and the Subversion of Identity*. New York: Routledge, 1990.

Collins, Patricia Hill. 1990. *Black Feminist Thought: Knowledge, Consciousness, and the Politics of Empowerment*. New York: Routledge, 2000.

Combahee River Collective. 1977. "A Black Feminist Statement." *This Bridge Called My Back: Writings by Radical Women of Color*. Ed. Cherríe Moraga and Gloria Anzaldúa. New York: Kitchen Table Press, 1983. 210–18.

Connell, R. W., and James W. Messerschmidt. "Hegemonic Masculinity: Rethinking the Concept." *Gender and Society* 19.6 (2005): 829–59.

Cooper, Anna Julia. 1892. *A Voice from the South*. Intro. Mary Helen Washington. New York: Oxford University Press, 1988.

Crenshaw, Kimberlé Williams. "Demarginalizing the Intersection of Race and Sex: A Black Feminist Critique of Antidiscrimination Doctrine, Feminist Theory, and Antiracist Politics." *University of Chicago Legal Forum* 140 (1989): 139–67.

Crenshaw, Kimberlé Williams. "Mapping the Margins: Intersectionality, Identity Politics, and Violence against Women of Color." *Stanford Law Review* 43 (1991): 1241–99.

Davis, Angela Y. *Women, Race and Class*. New York: Random House, 1981.

Frankenberg, Ruth. *White Women, Race Matters: The Social Construction of Whiteness*. Minneapolis: University of Minnesota Press, 1993.

Frye, Marilyn. *The Politics of Reality: Essays in Feminist Theory*. Freedom, CA: Crossing Press, 1983.

hooks, bell. "Feminism: A Movement to End Sexist Oppression." *Feminist Theory: From Margin to Center*. Boston, MA: South End Press, 1984. 17–31.

hooks, bell. "Reflections on Race and Sex." *Yearning: Race, Gender, and Cultural Politics*. Boston: South End Press, 1990. 57–64.

Kandiyoti, Deniz. "Identity and Its Discontents: Women and the Nation." *Millenium: Journal of International Studies* 20.3 (1991): 429–43.

King, Deborah K. "Multiple Jeopardy, Multiple Consciousness: The Context of a Black Feminist Ideology." *Signs* 14.1 (Autumn 1988): 46–73.

Martinez, Elizabeth. 1972. "La Chicana." *Chicana Feminist Thought: The Basic Historical Writings*. Ed. Alma M. García. New York: Routledge, 1997. 32–34.

McIntosh, Peggy. 1988. "White Privilege and Male Privilege: A Personal Account of Coming to See Correspondences through Work in Women's Studies" (Wellesley College, Center for Research on Women. Wellesley, MA. 1–19). http://www.collegeart.org/pdf/diversity/white-privilege-and-male-privilege.pdf (last accessed December 20. 2015).

Merriam-Webster's Collegiate Dictionary Electronic Edition. Springfield, MA: Merriam-Webster, Inc., 2003 (Boston, MA: Credo Reference, 2012). http://www.credoreference.com.libproxy.sdsu.edu/entry.do?id=12730173 (last accessed September 6. 2013).

Moraga, Cherríe, and Gloria Anzaldúa, eds. 1981. *This Bridge Called My Back: Writings by Radical Women of Color*. New York: Kitchen Table Press, 1983.

Narayan, Uma. "Contesting Cultures: 'Westernization,' Respect for Cultures, and Third-World Feminists." *Dislocating Cultures: Identities, Traditions, and Third World Feminism*. New York: Routledge, 1997. 1–39.

Ortner, Sherry B. "Is Female to Male as Nature Is to Culture?" *Feminist Studies* 1.2 (Autumn 1972): 5–31.

Rich, Adrienne. *Blood, Bread and Poetry: Selected Prose 1979–1985*. New York: Norton, 1986.

Rich, Adrienne. "Disloyal to Civilization: Feminism, Racism, Gynephobia (1978)." *On Lies, Secrets, and Silence: Selected Prose 1966–1978*. New York: Norton, 1979. 275–310.

Rubin, Gayle. "The Traffic in Women: Notes on the 'Political Economy' of Sex." *Toward an Anthropology of Women*. Ed. Rayna Reiter. New York: Monthly Review Press, 1975. 157–210.

Sandoval, Chela. "U.S. Third World Feminism: The Theory and Method of Oppositional Consciousness in the Postmodern World." *Genders* 10 (1991): 1–24.

Shohat, Ella, ed. *Talking Visions: Multicultural Feminism in a Transnational Age*. New York: New Museum of Contemporary Art and Cambridge, MA: MIT Press, 1998.

Smith, Barbara. 1982. "Racism and Women's Studies." *Making Face, Making Soul. Haciendo Caras: Creative and Critical Perspectives by Feminists of Color*. Ed. Gloria Anzaldúa. San Francisco: Aunt Lute Books, 1990. 25–28.

Spivak, Gayatri Chakravorty. 1985. "Can the Subaltern Speak?" *Colonial Discourse and Post-Colonial Theory: A Reader*. Ed. Patrick Williams and Laura Chrisman. New York: Columbia UP, 1994. 66–111.

Sue, Derald Wing. *Microaggressions in Everyday Life: Race, Gender, and Sexual Orientation*. Hoboken, NJ: John Wiley & Sons, Inc., 2010.

Thomson, Rosemarie Garland. *Extraordinary Bodies: Figuring Physical Disability in American Culture and Literature*. New York: Columbia UP, 1997.

Wendell, Susan. "Toward a Feminist Theory of Disability." *Hypatia* 4.2 (Summer 1989): 104–24.

Yamada, Mitsuye. 1981. "Invisibility is an Unnatural Disaster: Reflections of an Asian American Woman." *This Bridge Called My Back: Writings by Radical Women of Color*. Ed. Cherríe Moraga and Gloria Anzaldúa. New York: Kitchen Table Press, 1983. 35–40.

Zinn, Maxine Baca, and Bonnie Thornton Dill. "Theorizing Difference from Multiracial Feminism." *Feminist Studies* 22.2 (Summer 1996): 321–31.

1.1

My Name

Sandra Cisneros

In English my name means hope. In Spanish it means too many letters. It means sadness, it means waiting. It is like the number nine. A muddy color. It is the Mexican records my father plays on Sunday mornings when he is shaving, songs like sobbing.

It was my great-grandmother's name and now it is mine. She was a horse woman too, born like me in the Chinese year of the horse – which is supposed to be bad luck if you're born female – but I think this is a Chinese lie because the Chinese, like the Mexicans, don't like their women strong.

My great-grandmother. I would've liked to have known her, a wild horse of a woman, so wild she wouldn't marry. Until my great-grandfather threw a sack over her head and carried her off. Just like that, as if she were a fancy chandelier. That's the way he did it.

And the story goes she never forgave him. She looked out the window her whole life, the way so many women sit their sadness on an elbow. I wonder if she made the best with what she got or was she sorry because she couldn't be all the things she wanted to be. Esperanza. I have inherited her name, but I don't want to inherit her place by the window.

At school they say my name funny as if the syllables were made out of tin and hurt the roof of your mouth. But in Spanish my name is made out of a softer something, like silver, not quite as thick as sister's name – Magdalena – which is uglier than mine. Magdalena who at least can come home and become Nenny. But I am always Esperanza.

I would like to baptize myself under a new name, a name more like the real me, the one nobody sees. Esperanza as Lisandra or Maritza or Zeze the X. Yes. Something like Zeze the X will do.

1.2

The New Pronoun They Invented Suited Everyone Just Fine

Jacinta Bunnell and Nat Kusinitz

**The new pronoun they invented
suited everyone just fine.**

1.3

Oppression

Marilyn Frye

It is a fundamental claim of feminism that women are oppressed. The word "oppression" is a strong word. It repels and attracts. It is dangerous and dangerously fashionable and endangered. It is much misused, and sometimes not innocently.

The statement that women are oppressed is frequently met with the claim that men are oppressed too. We hear that oppressing is oppressive to those who oppress as well as to those they oppress. Some men cite as evidence of their oppression their much-advertised inability to cry. It is tough, we are told, to be masculine. When the stresses and frustrations of being a man are cited as evidence that oppressors are oppressed by their oppressing, the word "oppression" is being stretched to meaninglessness: it is treated as though its scope includes any and all human experience of limitation or suffering, no matter the cause, degree or consequence. Once such usage has been put over on us, then if ever we deny that any person or group is oppressed, we seem to imply that we think they never suffer and have no feelings. We are accused of insensitivity; even of bigotry. For women, such accusation is particularly intimidating, since sensitivity is one of the few virtues that has been assigned to us. If we are found insensitive, we may fear we have no redeeming traits at all and perhaps are not real women. Thus are we silenced before we begin: the name of our situation drained of meaning and our guilt mechanisms tripped.

But this is nonsense. Human beings can be miserable without being oppressed, and it is perfectly consistent to deny that a person or group is oppressed without denying that they have feelings or that they suffer …

The root of the word "oppression" is the element "press." *The press of the crowd; pressed into military service; to press a pair of pants; printing press; press the button.* Presses are used to mold things or flatten them or reduce them in bulk, sometimes to reduce them by squeezing out the gasses or liquids in them. Something pressed is something caught between or among forces and barriers which are so related to each other that jointly they restrain, restrict or prevent the thing's motion or mobility. Mold. Immobilize. Reduce.

The mundane experience of the oppressed provides another clue. One of the most characteristic and ubiquitous features of the world as experienced by oppressed people is the double bind – situations in which options are reduced to a very few and all of them expose one to penalty, censure or deprivation. For example, it is often a requirement upon oppressed people that we smile and be cheerful. If we comply, we signal our docility and our acquiescence in our situation. We need not, then, be taken note of. We acquiesce in being made invisible, in our occupying no space. We participate in our own erasure. On the other hand, anything but the sunniest countenance exposes us to being perceived as mean, bitter, angry or dangerous. This means, at the least, that we may be found "difficult" or unpleasant to work with, which is enough to cost one one's livelihood; at worst, being seen as mean, bitter, angry or dangerous has been known to result in rape, arrest, beating and murder. One can only choose to risk one's preferred form and rate of annihilation.

Another example: it is common in the United States that women, especially younger women, are in a bind where neither sexual activity nor sexual inactivity is all right. If she is heterosexually active, a woman is open to censure and punishment for being loose, unprincipled or a whore. The "punishment" comes in the form of criticism, snide and embarrassing remarks, being treated as an easy lay by men, scorn from her more restrained female friends. She may have to lie and hide her behavior from her parents. She must juggle the risks of unwanted pregnancy and dangerous contraceptives. On the other hand, if she refrains from heterosexual activity, she is fairly constantly harassed by men who try to persuade her into it and pressure her to "relax" and "let her hair down"; she is threatened with labels like "frigid," "uptight," "man-hater," "bitch" and "cocktease." The same parents who would be disapproving of her sexual activity may be worried by her inactivity because it suggests she is not or will not be popular, or is not sexually normal. She may be charged with lesbianism. If a woman is raped, then if she has been heterosexually active she is subject to the presumption that she liked it (since her activity is presumed to show that she likes sex), and if she has not been heterosexually active, she is subject to the presumption that she liked it (since she is supposedly "repressed and frustrated"). Both heterosexual activity and heterosexual non-activity are likely to be taken as proof that you wanted to be raped, and hence, of course, weren't *really* raped at all. You can't win. You are caught in a bind, caught between systematically related pressures.

Women are caught like this, too, by networks of forces and barriers that expose one to penalty, loss or contempt whether one works outside the home or not, is on welfare or not, bears children or not, raises children or not, marries or not, stays married or not, is heterosexual, lesbian, both or neither. Economic necessity; confinement to racial and/or sexual job ghettos; sexual harassment; sex discrimination; pressures of competing expectations and judgments about *women, wives* and *mothers* (in the society at large, in racial and ethnic subcultures and in one's own mind); dependence (full or partial) on husbands, parents or the state; commitment to political ideas; loyalties to racial or ethnic or other "minority" groups; the demands of self-respect and responsibilities to others. Each of these factors exists in complex tension with every other, penalizing or prohibiting all of the apparently available options. And nipping at one's heels, always, is the endless pack of little things. If one dresses one way, one is subject to the assumption that one is advertising one's sexual availability; if one dresses another way, one appears to "not care about oneself" or to be "unfeminine." If one uses "strong language," one invites categorization as a whore or slut; if one does not, one invites categorization as a "lady" – one too delicately constituted to cope with robust speech or the realities to which it presumably refers.

The experience of oppressed people is that the living of one's life is confined and shaped by forces and barriers which are not accidental or occasional and hence avoidable, but are systematically related to each other in such a way as to catch one between and among them and restrict or penalize motion in any direction. It is the experience of being caged in: all avenues, in every direction, are blocked or booby trapped.

Cages. Consider a birdcage. If you look very closely at just one wire in the cage, you cannot see the other wires. If your conception of what is before you is determined by this myopic focus, you could look at that one wire, up and down the length of it, and be unable to see why a bird would not just fly around the wire any time it wanted to go somewhere. Furthermore, even if, one day at a time, you myopically inspected each wire, you still could not see why a bird would have trouble going past the wires to get anywhere. There is no physical property of any one wire, *nothing* that the closest scrutiny could discover, that will reveal how a bird could be inhibited or harmed by it except in the most accidental way. It is only when you step back, stop looking at the wires one by one, microscopically, and take a macroscopic view of the whole cage, that you can see why the bird does not go anywhere; and then you will see it in a moment. It will require no great subtlety of mental powers. It is perfectly *obvious* that the bird is surrounded by a network of systematically related barriers, no one of which would be the least hindrance to its flight, but which, by their relations to each other, are as confining as the solid walls of a dungeon.

It is now possible to grasp one of the reasons why oppression can be hard to see and recognize: one can study the elements of an oppressive structure with great care and some good will without seeing the structure as a whole, and hence without seeing or being able to understand that one is looking at a cage and that there are people there who are caged, whose motion and mobility are restricted, whose lives are shaped and reduced.

The arresting of vision at a microscopic level yields such common confusion as that about the male door-opening ritual. This ritual, which is remarkably widespread across classes and races, puzzles many people, some of whom do and some of whom do not find it offensive. Look at the scene of the two people approaching a door. The male steps slightly ahead and opens the door. The male holds the door open while the female glides through. Then the male goes through. The door closes after them. "Now how," one innocently asks, "can those crazy womenslibbers say that is oppressive? The guy *removed* a barrier to the lady's smooth and unruffled progress." But each repetition of this ritual has a place in a pattern, in fact in several patterns. One has to shift the level of one's perception in order to see the whole picture.

The door-opening pretends to be a helpful service, but the helpfulness is false. This can be seen by noting that it will be done whether or not it makes any practical sense. Infirm men and men burdened with packages will open doors for able-bodied women who are free of physical burdens. Men will impose themselves awkwardly and jostle everyone in order to get to the door first. The act is not determined by convenience or grace. Furthermore, these very numerous acts of unneeded or even noisome "help" occur in counterpoint to a pattern of men not being helpful in many practical ways in which women might welcome help. What *women* experience is a world in which gallant princes charming commonly make a fuss about being helpful and providing small services when help and services are of little or no use, but in which there are rarely ingenious and adroit princes at hand when substantial assistance is really wanted either in mundane affairs or in situations of threat, assault or terror. There is no help with the (his) laundry; no help typing a report at 4 a.m.; no help in mediating disputes among relatives or children. There is nothing but advice that women should stay indoors after dark, be chaperoned by a man, or when it comes down to it, "lie back and enjoy it."

The gallant gestures have no practical meaning. Their meaning is symbolic. The door-opening and similar services provided are services which really are needed by people who are for one reason or another incapacitated – unwell, burdened with parcels, etc. So the message is that women are incapable. The detachment of the acts from the concrete realities of what women need and do not need is a vehicle for the message that women's actual needs and interests are unimportant or irrelevant. Finally, these gestures imitate the behavior of servants toward masters and thus mock women, who are in most respects the servants and caretakers of men. The message of the false helpfulness of male gallantry is female dependence, the invisibility or insignificance of women, and contempt for women.

One cannot see the meanings of these rituals if one's focus is riveted upon the individual event in all its particularity, including the particularity of the individual man's present conscious intentions and motives and the individual woman's conscious perception of the event in the moment. It seems sometimes that people take a deliberately myopic view and fill their eyes with things seen microscopically in order not to see macroscopically. At any rate, whether it is deliberate or not, people can and do fail to see the oppression of women because they fail to see macroscopically and hence fail to see the various elements of the situation as systematically related in larger schemes.

As the cageness of the birdcage is a macroscopic phenomenon, the oppressiveness of the situations in which women live our various and different lives is a macroscopic phenomenon. Neither can be *seen* from a microscopic perspective. But when you look macroscopically you can see it – a network of forces and barriers which are systematically related and which conspire to the immobilization, reduction and molding of women and the lives we live.

1.4

Age, Race, Class, and Sex: Women Redefining Difference

Audre Lorde

Much of Western European history conditions us to see human differences in simplistic opposition to each other: dominant/subordinate, good/bad, up/down, superior/inferior. In a society where the good is defined in terms of profit rather than in terms of human need, there must always be some group of people who, through systematized oppression, can be made to feel surplus, to occupy the place of the dehumanized inferior. Within this society, that group is made up of Black and Third World people, working-class people, older people, and women.

As a forty-nine-year-old Black lesbian feminist socialist mother of two, including one boy, and a member of an inter-racial couple, I usually find myself a part of some group defined as other, deviant, inferior, or just plain wrong. Traditionally, in american society, it is the members of oppressed, objectified groups who are expected to stretch out and bridge the gap between the actualities of our lives and the consciousness of our oppressor. For in order to survive, those of us for whom oppression is as american as apple pie have always had to be watchers, to become familiar with the language and manners of the oppressor, even sometimes adopting them for some illusion of protection. Whenever the need for some pretense of communication arises, those who profit from our oppression call upon us to share our knowledge with them. In other words, it is the responsibility of the oppressed to teach the oppressors their mistakes. I am responsible for educating teachers who dismiss my children's culture in school. Black and Third World people are expected to educate white people as to our humanity. Women are expected to educate men. Lesbians and gay men are expected to educate the heterosexual world. The oppressors maintain their position and evade responsibility for their own actions. There is a constant drain of energy which might be better used in redefining ourselves and devising realistic scenarios for altering the present and constructing the future.

Institutionalized rejection of difference is an absolute necessity in a profit economy which needs outsiders as surplus people. As members of such an economy, we have *all* been programmed to respond to the human differences between us with fear and loathing and to handle that difference in one of three ways: ignore it, and if that is not possible, copy it if we think it is dominant, or destroy it if we think it is subordinate. But we have no patterns for relating across our human differences as equals. As a result, those differences have been misnamed and misused in the service of separation and confusion.

Certainly there are very real differences between us of race, age, and sex. But it is not those differences between us that are separating us. It is rather our refusal to recognize those differences, and to examine the distortions which result from our misnaming them and their effects upon human behavior and expectation.

Racism, the belief in the inherent superiority of one race over all others and thereby the right to dominance. Sexism, the belief in the inherent superiority of one sex over the other and thereby the right to dominance. Ageism. Heterosexism. Elitism. Classism.

It is a lifetime pursuit for each one of us to extract these distortions from our living at the same time as we recognize, reclaim, and define those differences upon which they are imposed. For we have all been raised in a society where those distortions were endemic within our living. Too often, we pour the energy needed for recognizing and exploring difference into pretending those differences are insurmountable barriers, or that they do not exist at all. This results in a voluntary isolation, or false and treacherous connections. Either way, we do not develop tools for using human difference as a springboard for creative change within our lives. We speak not of human difference, but of human deviance.

Somewhere, on the edge of consciousness, there is what I call a *mythical norm*, which each one of us within our hearts knows "that is not me." In america, this norm is usually defined as white, thin, male, young, heterosexual, christian, and financially secure. It is with this mythical norm that the trappings of power reside within this society. Those of us who stand outside that power often identify one way in which we are different, and we assume that to be the primary cause of all oppression, forgetting other distortions around difference, some of which we ourselves may be practicing. By and large, within the women's movement today, white women focus upon their oppression as women and ignore differences of race, sexual preference, class, and age. There is a pretense to a homogeneity of experience covered by the word *sisterhood* that does not, in fact, exist.

Unacknowledged class differences rob women of each other's energy and creative insight. Recently, a women's magazine collective made the decision for one issue to print only prose, saying poetry was a less "rigorous" or "serious" art form. Yet even the form our creativity takes is often a class issue. Of all the art forms, poetry is the most economical. It is the one which is the most secret, which requires the least physical labor, the least material, and the one which can be done between shifts, in the hospital pantry, on the subway, and on scraps of surplus paper. Over the last few years, writing a novel on tight finances, I came to appreciate the enormous differences in the material demands between poetry and prose. As we reclaim our literature, poetry has been the major voice of poor, working-class, and Colored women. A room of one's own may be a necessity for writing prose, but so are reams of paper, a typewriter, and plenty of time. The actual requirements to produce the visual arts also help determine, along class lines, whose art is whose. In this day of inflated prices for material, who are our sculptors, our painters, our photographers? Where we speak of a broadly based women's culture, we need to be aware of the effect of class and economic differences on the supplies available for producing art.

As we move toward creating a society within which we can each flourish, ageism is another distortion of relationship which interferes with our vision. By ignoring the past, we are encouraged to repeat its mistakes. The "generation gap" is an important social tool for any repressive society. If the younger members of a community view the older members as contemptible or suspect or excess, they will never be able to join hands and examine the living memories of the community, nor ask the all-important question, "Why?" This gives rise to a historical amnesia that keeps us working to invent the wheel every time we have to go to the store for bread.

We find ourselves having to repeat and relearn the same old lessons over and over that our mothers did because we do not pass on what we have learned, or because we are unable to listen. For instance, how many times has this all been said before? For another, who would have believed that once again our daughters are allowing their bodies to be hampered and purgatoried by girdles and high heels and hobble skirts?

Ignoring the differences of race between women and the implications of those differences presents the most serious threat to the mobilization of women's joint power.

As white women ignore their built-in privilege of whiteness and define *woman* in terms of their own experience alone, then women of Color become "other," the outsider whose experience and tradition is too "alien" to comprehend. An example of this is the signal absence of the experience of women of Color as a resource for women's studies courses. The literature of women of Color is seldom included in women's literature courses and almost never in other literature courses, nor in women's studies as a whole. All too often, the excuse given is that the literatures of women of Color can only be taught by Colored women, or that they are too difficult to understand, or that classes cannot "get into" them because they come out of experiences that are "too different." I have heard this argument presented by white women of otherwise quite clear intelligence, women who seem to have no trouble at all teaching and reviewing work that comes out of the vastly different experiences of Shakespeare, Molière, Dostoyevsky, and Aristophanes. Surely there must be some other explanation.

This is a very complex question, but I believe one of the reasons white women have such difficulty reading Black women's work is because of their reluctance to see Black women as women and different from themselves. To examine Black women's literature effectively requires that we be seen as whole people in our actual complexities – as individuals, as women, as human – rather than as one of those problematic but familiar stereotypes provided in this society in place of genuine images of Black women. And I believe this holds true for the literature of other women of Color who are not Black.

The literatures of all women of Color recreate the textures of our lives, and many white women are heavily invested in ignoring the real differences. For as long as any difference between us means one of us must be inferior, then the recognition of any difference must be fraught with guilt. To allow women of Color to step out of stereotypes is too guilt provoking, for it threatens the complacency of those women who view oppression only in terms of sex.

Refusing to recognize difference makes it impossible to see the different problems and pitfalls facing us as women.

Thus, in a patriarchal power system where whiteskin privilege is a major prop, the entrapments used to neutralize Black women and white women are not the same. For example, it is easy for Black women to be used by the power structure against Black men, not because they are men, but because they are Black. Therefore, for Black women, it is necessary at all times to separate the needs of the oppressor from our own legitimate conflicts within our communities. This same problem does not exist for white women. Black women and men have shared racist oppression and still share it, although in different ways. Out of that shared oppression we have developed joint defenses and joint vulnerabilities to each other that are not duplicated in the white community, with the exception of the relationship between Jewish women and Jewish men.

On the other hand, white women face the pitfall of being seduced into joining the oppressor under the pretense of sharing power. This possibility does not exist in the same way for women of Color. The tokenism that is sometimes extended to us is not an invitation to join power; our racial "otherness" is a visible reality that makes that quite clear. For white women there is a wider range of pretended choices and rewards for identifying with patriarchal power and its tools.

Today, with the defeat of the ERA, the tightening economy, and increased conservatism, it is easier once again for white women to believe the dangerous fantasy that if you are good enough, pretty enough, sweet enough, quiet enough, teach the children to behave, hate the right people, and marry the right men, then you will be allowed to coexist with patriarchy in relative peace, at least until a man needs your job or the neighborhood rapist happens along. And true, unless one lives and loves in the trenches it is difficult to remember that the war against dehumanization is ceaseless.

But Black women and our children know the fabric of our lives is stitched with violence and with hatred, that there is no rest. We do not deal with it only on the picket lines, or in dark midnight alleys, or in the places where we dare to verbalize our resistance. For us, increasingly, violence weaves through the daily tissues of our living – in the supermarket, in the classroom, in the elevator, in the clinic and the schoolyard, from the plumber, the baker, the saleswoman, the bus driver, the bank teller, the waitress who does not serve us.

Some problems we share as women, some we do not. You fear your children will grow up to join the patriarchy and testify against you, we fear our children will be dragged from a car and shot down in the street, and you will turn your backs upon the reasons they are dying.

The threat of difference has been no less blinding to people of Color. Those of us who are Black must see that the reality of our lives and our struggle does not make us immune to the errors of ignoring and misnaming difference. Within Black communities where racism is a living reality, differences among us often seem dangerous and suspect. The need for unity is often misnamed as a need for homogeneity, and a Black feminist vision mistaken for betrayal of our common interests as a people. Because of the continuous battle against racial erasure that Black women and Black men share, some Black women still refuse to recognize that we are also oppressed as women, and that sexual hostility against Black women is practiced not only by the white racist society, but implemented within our Black communities as well. It is a disease striking the heart of Black nationhood, and silence will not make it disappear. Exacerbated by racism and the pressures of powerlessness, violence against Black women and children often becomes a standard within our communities, one by which manliness can be measured. But these woman-hating acts are rarely discussed as crimes against Black women.

As a group, women of Color are the lowest paid wage earners in america. We are the primary targets of abortion and sterilization abuse, here and abroad. In certain parts of Africa, small girls are still being sewed shut between their legs to keep them docile and for men's pleasure. This is known as female circumcision, and it is not a cultural affair as the late Jomo Kenyatta insisted, it is a crime against Black women.

Black women's literature is full of the pain of frequent assault, not only by a racist patriarchy, but also by Black men. Yet the necessity for and history of shared battle have made us, Black women, particularly vulnerable to the false accusation that anti-sexist is anti-Black. Meanwhile, womanhating as a recourse of the power-less is sapping strength from Black communities, and our very lives. Rape is on the increase, reported and unreported, and rape is not aggressive sexuality, it is sexu-alized aggression. As Kalamu ya Salaam, a Black male writer points out, "As long as male domination exists, rape will exist. Only women revolting and men made conscious of their responsibility to fight sexism can collectively stop rape."[1]

Differences between ourselves as Black women are also being misnamed and used to separate us from one another. As a Black lesbian feminist comfortable with the many different ingredients of my identity, and a woman committed to racial and sexual freedom from oppression, I find I am constantly being encouraged to pluck out some one aspect of myself and present this as the meaningful whole, eclipsing or denying the other parts of self. But this is a destructive and fragmenting way to live. My fullest concentration of energy is available to me only when I integrate all the parts of who I am, openly, allowing power from particular sources of my living to flow back and forth freely through all my different selves, without the restrictions of externally imposed definition. Only then can I bring myself and my energies as a whole to the service of those struggles which I embrace as part of my living.

A fear of lesbians, or of being accused of being a lesbian, has led many Black women into testifying against themselves. It has led some of us into destructive alliances, and others into despair and isolation. In the white women's commu-nities, heterosexism is sometimes a result of identifying with the white patriarchy, a rejection of that interdependence between women-identified women which allows the self to be, rather than to be used in the service of men. Sometimes it reflects a die-hard belief in the protective coloration of heterosexual relationships, sometimes a self-hate which all women have to fight against, taught us from birth.

Although elements of these attitudes exist for all women, there are particular resonances of heterosexism and homophobia among Black women. Despite the fact that woman-bonding has a long and honorable history in the African and African-american communities, and despite the knowledge and accomplishments of many strong and creative women-identified Black women in the political, social and cultural fields, heterosexual Black women often tend to ignore or discount the existence and work of Black lesbians. Part of this attitude has come from an under-standable terror of Black male attack within the close confines of Black society, where the punishment for any female self-assertion is still to be accused of being a lesbian and therefore unworthy of the attention or support of the scarce Black male. But part of this need to misname and ignore Black lesbians comes from a very real fear that openly women-identified Black women who are no longer dependent upon men for their self-definition may well reorder our whole concept of social relationships.

Black women who once insisted that lesbianism was a white woman's problem now insist that Black lesbians are a threat to Black nationhood, are consorting with the enemy, are basically un-Black. These accusations, coming from the very women to whom we look for deep and real understanding, have served to keep many Black lesbians in hiding, caught between the racism of white women and the homophobia of their sisters. Often, their work has been ignored, trivialized, or misnamed, as with the work of Angelina Grimke, Alice Dunbar-Nelson, Lorraine Hansberry. Yet women-bonded women have always been some part of the power of Black communities, from our unmarried aunts to the amazons of Dahomey.

And it is certainly not Black lesbians who are assaulting women and raping children and grandmothers on the streets of our communities.

Across this country, as in Boston during the spring of 1979 following the unsolved murders of twelve Black women, Black lesbians are spearheading movements against violence against Black women.

What are the particular details within each of our lives that can be scrutinized and altered to help bring about change? How do we redefine difference for all women? It is not our differences which separate women, but our reluctance to recognize those differences and to deal effectively with the distortions which have resulted from the ignoring and misnaming of those differences.

As a tool of social control, women have been encouraged to recognize only one area of human difference as legitimate, those differences which exist between women and men. And we have learned to deal across those differences with the urgency of all oppressed subordinates. All of us have had to learn to live or work or coexist with men, from our fathers on. We have recognized and negotiated these differences, even when this recognition only continued the old dominant/subordinate mode of human relationship, where the oppressed must recognize the master's difference in order to survive.

But our future survival is predicated upon our ability to relate within equality. As women, we must root out internalized patterns of oppression within ourselves if we are to move beyond the most superficial aspects of social change. Now we must recognize differences among women who are our equals, neither inferior nor superior, and devise ways to use each other's difference to enrich our visions and our joint struggles.

The future of our earth may depend upon the ability of all women to identify and develop new definitions of power and new patterns of relating across difference. The old definitions have not served us, nor the earth that supports us. The old patterns, no matter how cleverly rearranged to imitate progress, still condemn us to cosmetically altered repetitions of the same old exchanges, the same old guilt, hatred, recrimination, lamentation, and suspicion.

For we have, built into all of us, old blueprints of expectation and response, old structures of oppression, and these must be altered at the same time as we alter the living conditions which are a result of those structures. For the master's tools will never dismantle the master's house.

As Paulo Freire shows so well in *The Pedagogy of the Oppressed*,[2] the true focus of revolutionary change is never merely the oppressive situations which we seek to escape, but that piece of the oppressor which is planted deep within each of us, and which knows only the oppressors' tactics, the oppressors' relationships.

Change means growth, and growth can be painful. But we sharpen self-definition by exposing the self in work and struggle together with those whom we define as different from ourselves, although sharing the same goals. For Black and white, old and young, lesbian and heterosexual women alike, this can mean new paths to our survival.

> *We have chosen each other*
> *and the edge of each other's battles*
> *the war is the same*
> *if we lose*
> *someday women's blood will congeal*
> *upon a dead planet*
> *if we win*
> *there is no telling*
> *we seek beyond history*
> *for a new and more possible meeting.*[3]

Notes

1. From Kalamu ya Salaam, "Rape: A Radical Analysis, an African-American Perspective," *Black Books Bulletin*, 6(4) (1980).
2. Paulo Freire, *The Pedagogy of the Oppressed* (New York: Seabury Press, 1970).
3. From "Outlines," unpublished poem.

1.5

Womanist

Alice Walker

Womanist

1. From *womanish*. (Opp. of "girlish," i.e., frivolous, irresponsible, not serious.) A black feminist or feminist of color. From the black folk expression of mothers to female children, "You acting womanish," i.e., like a woman. Usually referring to outrageous, audacious, courageous or *willful* behavior. Wanting to know more and in greater depth than is considered "good" for one. Interested in grown-up doings. Acting grown up. Being grown up. Interchangeable with another black folk expression: "You trying to be grown." Responsible. In charge. *Serious.*

    .   .   .

2. *Also*: A woman who loves other women, sexually and/or nonsexually. Appreciates and prefers women's culture, women's emotional flexibility (values tears as natural counter-balance of laughter), and women's strength. Sometimes loves individual men, sexually and/or nonsexually. Committed to survival and whole-ness of entire people, male *and* female. Not a separatist, except periodically, for health. Traditionally universalist, as in: "Mama, why are we brown, pink, and

yellow, and our cousins are white, beige, and black?" Ans.: "Well, you know the colored race is just like a flower garden, with every color flower represented." Traditionally capable, as in: "Mama, I'm walking to Canada and I'm taking you and a bunch of other slaves with me." Reply: "It wouldn't be the first time."

.   .   .

3.   Loves music. Loves dance. Loves the moon. *Loves* the Spirit. Loves love and food and roundness. Loves struggle. *Loves* the Folk. Loves herself. *Regardless.*

.   .   .

4.   Womanist is to feminist as purple to lavender.

1.6

Masculinity as Homophobia: Fear, Shame, and Silence in the Construction of Gender Identity

Michael S. Kimmel

All masculinities are not created equal; or rather, we are all *created* equal, but any hypothetical equality evaporates quickly because our definitions of masculinity are not equally valued in our society. One definition of manhood continues to remain the standard against which other forms of manhood are measured and evaluated. Within the dominant culture, the masculinity that defines white, middle class, early middle-aged, heterosexual men is the masculinity that sets the standards for other men, against which other men are measured and, more often than not, found wanting. Sociologist Erving Goffman (1963) wrote that in America, there is only "one complete, unblushing male":

> a young, married, white, urban, northern heterosexual, Protestant father of college education, fully employed, of good complexion, weight and height, and a recent record in sports. Every American male tends to look out upon the world from this perspective. ... Any male who fails to qualify in any one of these ways is likely to view himself ... as unworthy, incomplete, and inferior. (p. 128)

This is the definition that we will call "hegemonic" masculinity, the image of masculinity of those men who hold power, which has become the standard in psychological evaluations, sociological research, and self-help and advice literature for teaching young men to become "real men" (Connell, 1987). The hegemonic definition of manhood is a man *in* power, a man *with* power, and a man *of* power. We equate manhood with being strong, successful, capable, reliable, in control. The very definitions of manhood we have developed in our culture maintain the power that some men have over other men and that men have over women.

Our culture's definition of masculinity is thus several stories at once. It is about the individual man's quest to accumulate those cultural symbols that denote manhood, signs that he has in fact achieved it. It is about those standards being used against women to prevent their inclusion in public life and their consignment to a devalued private sphere. It is about the differential access that different types of men have to those cultural resources that confer manhood and about how each of these groups then develop their own modifications to preserve and claim their manhood. It is about the power of these definitions themselves to serve to maintain the real-life power that men have over women and that some men have over other men.

This definition of manhood has been summarized cleverly by psychologist Robert Brannon (1976) into four succinct phrases:

1. "No Sissy Stuff!" One may never do anything that even remotely suggests femininity. Masculinity is the relentless repudiation of the feminine.
2. "Be a Big Wheel." Masculinity is measured by power, success, wealth, and status. As the current saying goes, "He who has the most toys when he dies wins."
3. "Be a Sturdy Oak." Masculinity depends on remaining calm and reliable in a crisis, holding emotions in check. In fact, proving you're a man depends on never showing your emotions at all. Boys don't cry.
4. "Give 'em Hell." Exude an aura of manly daring and aggression. Go for it. Take risks.

These rules contain the elements of the definition against which virtually all American men are measured. Failure to embody these rules, to affirm the power of the rules and one's achievement of them is a source of men's confusion and pain. Such a model is, of course, unrealizable for any man. But we keep trying, valiantly and vainly, to measure up. American masculinity is a relentless test.[1] The chief test is contained in the first rule. Whatever the variations by race, class, age, ethnicity, or sexual orientation, being a man means "not being like women." This notion of anti-femininity lies at the heart of contemporary and historical conceptions of manhood, so that masculinity is defined more by what one is not rather than who one is.

This, then, is the great secret of American manhood: *We are afraid of other men.* Homophobia is a central organizing principle of our cultural definition of manhood. Homophobia is more than the irrational fear of gay men, more than the fear that we might be perceived as gay. "The word 'faggot' has nothing to do with homosexual experience or even with fears of homosexuals," writes David Leverenz (1986). "It comes out of the depths of manhood: a label of ultimate contempt for anyone who seems sissy, untough, uncool" (p. 455). Homophobia is the fear that other men will unmask us, emasculate us, reveal to us and the world that we do not measure up, that we are not real men. We are afraid to let other men see that fear. Fear makes us ashamed, because the recognition of fear in ourselves is proof to ourselves that we are not as manly as we pretend, that we are, like the young man in a poem by Yeats, "one that ruffles in a manly pose for all his timid heart." Our fear is the fear of humiliation. We are ashamed to be afraid.

Shame leads to silence – the silences that keep other people believing that we actually approve of the things that are done to women, to minorities, to gays and lesbians in our culture. The frightened silence as we scurry past a woman being hassled by men on the street. That furtive silence when men make sexist or racist jokes in a bar. That clammy-handed silence when guys in the office make gay-bashing jokes. Our fears are the sources of our silences, and men's silence is what keeps the system running. This might help to explain why women often complain that their male friends or partners are often so understanding when they are alone and yet laugh at sexist jokes or even make those jokes themselves when they are out with a group.

The fear of being seen as a sissy dominates the cultural definitions of manhood. It starts so early. "Boys among boys are ashamed to be unmanly," wrote one educator in 1871 (cited in Rotundo, 1993, p. 264). I have a standing bet with a friend that I can walk onto any playground in America where 6-year-old boys are happily playing and by asking one question, I can provoke a fight. That question is simple: "Who's a sissy around here?" Once posed, the challenge is made. One of two things is likely to happen. One boy will accuse another of being a sissy, to which that boy will respond that he is not a sissy, that the first boy is. They may have to fight it out to see who's lying. Or a whole group of boys will surround one boy and all shout "He is! He is!" That boy will either burst into tears and run home crying, disgraced, or he will have to take on several boys at once, to prove that he's not a sissy. (And what will his father or older brothers tell him if he chooses to run home crying?) It will be some time before he regains any sense of self-respect.

Violence is often the single most evident marker of manhood. Rather it is the willingness to fight, the desire to fight. The origin of our expression that one has a chip on one's shoulder lies in the practice of an adolescent boy in the country or small town at the turn of the century, who would literally walk around with a chip of wood balanced on his shoulder – a signal of his readiness to fight with anyone who would take the initiative of knocking the chip off (see Gorer, 1964, p. 38; Mead, 1965).

As adolescents, we learn that our peers are a kind of gender police, constantly threatening to unmask us as feminine, as sissies. One of the favorite tricks when I was an adolescent was to ask a boy to look at his fingernails. If he held his palm toward his face and curled his fingers back to see them, he passed the test. He'd looked at his nails "like a man." But if he held the back of his hand away from his face, and looked at his fingernails with arm outstretched, he was immediately ridiculed as a sissy.

As young men we are constantly riding those gender boundaries, checking the fences we have constructed on the perimeter, making sure that nothing even remotely feminine might show through. The possibilities of being unmasked are everywhere. Even the most seemingly insignificant thing can pose a threat or activate that haunting terror. On the day the students in my course "Sociology of Men and Masculinities" were scheduled to discuss homophobia and male-male friendships, one student provided a touching illustration. Noting that it was a beautiful day, the first day of spring after a brutal northeast winter, he decided to wear shorts to class. "I had this really nice pair of new Madras shorts," he commented. "But then

I thought to myself, these shorts have lavender and pink in them. Today's class topic is homophobia. Maybe today is not the best day to wear these shorts."

Our efforts to maintain a manly front cover everything we do. What we wear. How we talk. How we walk. What we eat. Every mannerism, every movement contains a coded gender language. Think, for example, of how you would answer the question: How do you "know" if a man is homosexual? When I ask this question in classes or workshops, respondents invariably provide a pretty standard list of stereotypically effeminate behaviors. He walks a certain way, talks a certain way, acts a certain way. He's very emotional; he shows his feelings. One woman commented that she "knows" a man is gay if he really cares about her; another said she knows he's gay if he shows no interest in her, if he leaves her alone.

Now alter the question and imagine what heterosexual men do to make sure no one could possibly get the "wrong idea" about them. Responses typically refer to the original stereotypes, this time as a set of negative rules about behavior. Never dress that way. Never talk or walk that way. Never show your feelings or get emotional. Always be prepared to demonstrate sexual interest in women that you meet, so it is impossible for any woman to get the wrong idea about you. In this sense, homophobia, the fear of being perceived as gay, as not a real man, keeps men exaggerating all the traditional rules of masculinity, including sexual predation with women. Homophobia and sexism go hand in hand.

The stakes of perceived sissydom are enormous – sometimes matters of life and death. We take enormous risks to prove our manhood, exposing ourselves disproportionately to health risks, workplace hazards, and stress-related illnesses. Men commit suicide three times as often as women. Psychiatrist Willard Gaylin (1992) explains that it is "invariably because of perceived social humiliation," most often tied to failure in business:

> Men become depressed because of loss of status and power in the world of men. It is not the loss of money, or the material advantages that money could buy, which produces the despair that leads to self-destruction. It is the "shame," the "humiliation," the sense of personal "failure." … A man despairs when he has ceased being a man among men. (p. 32)

In one survey, women and men were asked what they were most afraid of. Women responded that they were most afraid of being raped and murdered. Men responded that they were most afraid of being laughed at (Noble, 1992, pp. 105–106).

Homophobia as a Cause of Sexism, Heterosexism, and Racism

Homophobia is intimately interwoven with both sexism and racism. The fear – sometimes conscious, sometimes not – that others might perceive us as homosexual propels men to enact all manner of exaggerated masculine behaviors and attitudes to make sure that no one could possibly get the wrong idea about us. One of the centerpieces of that exaggerated masculinity is putting women down, both by excluding them from the public sphere and by the quotidian put-downs in speech and behaviors that organize the daily life of the American man. Women and gay men become the "other" against which heterosexual men project their identities, against whom they stack the decks so as to compete in a situation in which they will always win, so that by suppressing them, men can stake a claim for their own manhood. Women threaten emasculation by representing the home, workplace, and familial responsibility, the negation of fun. Gay men have historically played the role of the consummate sissy in the American popular mind because homosexuality is seen as an inversion of normal gender development. There have been other "others." Through American history, various groups have represented the sissy, the non-men against whom American men played out their definitions of manhood, often with vicious results. In fact, these changing groups provide an interesting lesson in American historical development.

At the turn of the 19th century, it was Europeans and children who provided the contrast for American men. The "true American was vigorous, manly, and direct, not effete and corrupt like the supposed Europeans," writes Rupert Wilkinson (1986). "He was plain rather than ornamented, rugged rather than luxury seeking, a liberty loving common man or natural gentleman rather than an aristocratic oppressor or servile minion" (p. 96). The "real man" of the early 19th century was neither noble nor serf. By the middle of the century, black slaves had replaced the effete nobleman. Slaves were seen as dependent, helpless men, incapable of defending their women and children, and therefore less than manly. Native Americans were cast as foolish and naive children, so they could be infantilized as the "Red Children of the Great White Father" and therefore excluded from full manhood.

By the end of the century, new European immigrants were also added to the list of the unreal men, especially the Irish and Italians, who were seen as too passionate and emotionally volatile to remain controlled sturdy oaks, and Jews, who were seen as too bookishly effete and too physically puny to truly measure up. In the mid-20th century, it was also Asians – first the Japanese during the Second World War, and more recently, the Vietnamese during the Vietnam War – who have served as unmanly templates against which American men have hurled their gendered rage. Asian men were seen as small, soft, and effeminate – hardly men at all.

Such a list of "hyphenated" Americans – Italian-, Jewish-, Irish-, African-, Native-, Asian-, gay – composes the majority of American men. So manhood is only possible for a distinct minority, and the definition has been constructed to prevent the others from achieving it. Interestingly, this emasculation of one's enemies has a flip side – and one that is equally gendered. These very groups that have historically been cast as less than manly were also, often simultaneously, cast as hypermasculine, as sexually aggressive, violent rapacious beasts, against whom "civilized" men must take a decisive stand and thereby rescue civilization. Thus black men were depicted as rampaging sexual beasts, women as carnivorously carnal, gay men as sexually insatiable, southern European men as sexually predatory and voracious, and Asian men as vicious and cruel torturers who were immorally disinterested in life itself, willing to sacrifice their entire people for their whims. But whether one saw these groups as effeminate sissies or as brutal uncivilized savages, the terms with which they were perceived were gendered. These groups become the "others," the screens against which traditional conceptions of manhood were developed.

Being seen as unmanly is a fear that propels American men to deny manhood to others, as a way of proving the unprovable – that one is fully manly. Masculinity becomes a defense against the perceived threat of humiliation in the eyes of other men, enacted through a "sequence of postures" – things we might say, or do, or even think, that, if we thought carefully about them, would make us ashamed of ourselves (Savran, 1992, p. 16). After all, how many of us have made homophobic or sexist remarks, or told racist jokes, or made lewd comments to women on the street? How many of us have translated those ideas and those words into actions, by physically attacking gay men, or forcing or cajoling a woman to have sex even though she didn't really want to because it was important to score?

Power and Powerlessness in the Lives of Men

I have argued that homophobia, men's fear of other men, is the animating condition of the dominant definition of masculinity in America, that the reigning definition of masculinity is a defensive effort to prevent being emasculated. In our efforts to suppress or overcome those fears, the dominant culture exacts a tremendous price from those deemed less than fully manly: women, gay men, nonnative-born men, men of color. This perspective may help clarify a paradox in men's lives, a paradox in which men have virtually all the power and yet do not feel powerful (see Kaufman, 1993).

Manhood is equated with power – over women, over other men. Everywhere we look, we see the institutional expression of that power – in state and national legislatures, on the boards of directors of every major U.S. corporation or law firm, and in every school and hospital administration. Women have long understood this, and feminist women have spent the past three decades challenging both the public and the private expressions of men's power and acknowledging their fear of men. Feminism as a set of theories both explains women's fear of men and empowers women to confront it both publicly and privately. Feminist women have theorized that masculinity is about the drive for domination, the drive for power, for conquest.

This feminist definition of masculinity as the drive for power is theorized from women's point of view. It is how women experience masculinity. But it assumes a symmetry between the public and the private that does not conform to men's experiences. Feminists observe that women, as a group, do not hold power in our society. They also observe that individually, they, as women, do not feel powerful. They feel afraid, vulnerable. Their observation of the social reality and their individual experiences are therefore symmetrical. Feminism also observes that men, as a group, *are* in power. Thus, with the same symmetry, feminism has tended to assume that individually men must feel powerful.

This is why the feminist critique of masculinity often falls on deaf ears with men. When confronted with the analysis that men have all the power, many men react incredulously. "What do you mean, men have all the power?" they ask. "What are you talking about? My wife bosses me around. My kids boss me around. My boss bosses me around. I have no power at all! I'm completely powerless!"

Men's feelings are not the feelings of the powerful, but of those who see themselves as powerless. These are the feelings that come inevitably from the discontinuity between the social and the psychological, between the aggregate analysis that reveals how men are in power as a group and the psychological fact that they do not feel powerful as individuals. They are the feelings of men who were raised to believe themselves entitled to feel that power, but do not feel it. No wonder many men are frustrated and angry.

This may explain the recent popularity of those workshops and retreats designed to help men to claim their "inner" power, their "deep manhood," or their "warrior within." Authors such as Bly (1990), Moore and Gillette (1991, 1992, 1993a, 1993b), Farrell (1986, 1993), and Keen (1991) honor and respect men's feelings of powerlessness and acknowledge those feelings to be both true and real. "They gave white men the semblance of power," notes John Lee, one of the leaders of these retreats (quoted in *Newsweek*, p. 41). "We'll let you run the country, but in the meantime, stop feeling, stop talking, and continue swallowing your pain and your hurt." (We are not told who "they" are.)

Often the purveyors of the mythopoetic men's movement, that broad umbrella that encompasses all the groups helping men to retrieve this mythic deep manhood, use the image of the chauffeur to describe modern man's position. The chauffeur appears to have the power – he's wearing the uniform, he's in the driver's seat, and he knows where he's going. So, to the observer, the chauffeur looks as though he is in command. But to the chauffeur himself, they note, he is merely taking orders. He is not at all in charge.[2]

Despite the reality that everyone knows chauffeurs do not have the power, this image remains appealing to the men who hear it at these weekend workshops. But there is a missing piece to the image, a piece concealed by the framing of the image in terms of the individual man's experience. That missing piece is that the person who is giving the orders is also a man. Now we have a relationship *between* men – between men giving orders and other men taking those orders. The man who identifies with the chauffeur is entitled to be the man giving the orders, but he is not. ("They," it turns out, are other men.)

The dimension of power is now reinserted into men's experience not only as the product of individual experience but also as the product of relations with other men. In this sense, men's experience of powerlessness is *real* – the men actually feel it and certainly act on it – but it is not *true*, that is, it does not accurately describe their condition. In contrast to women's lives, men's lives are structured around relationships of power and men's differential access to power, as well as the differential access to that power of men as a group. Our imperfect analysis of our own situation leads us to believe that we men need *more* power, rather than leading us to support feminists' efforts to rearrange power relationships along more equitable lines.

Philosopher Hannah Arendt (1970) fully understood this contradictory experience of social and individual power:

> Power corresponds to the human ability not just to act but to act in concert. Power is never the property of an individual; it belongs to a group and remains in existence only so long as the group keeps together. When we say of somebody that he is "in power" we actually refer to his being empowered by a certain number of people to act in their name. The moment the group, from which the power originated to begin with ... disappears, "his power" also vanishes. (p. 44)

Why, then, do American men feel so powerless? Part of the answer is because we've constructed the rules of manhood so that only the tiniest fraction of men come to believe that they are the biggest of wheels, the sturdiest of oaks, the most virulent repudiators of femininity, the most daring and aggressive. We've managed to disempower the overwhelming majority of American men by other means – such as discriminating on the basis of race, class, ethnicity, age, or sexual preference.

Masculinist retreats to retrieve deep, wounded, masculinity are but one of the ways in which American men currently struggle with their fears and their shame. Unfortunately, at the very moment that they work to break down the isolation that governs men's lives, as they enable men to express those fears and that shame, they ignore the social power that men continue to exert over women and the privileges from which they (as the middle-aged, middle-class white men who largely make up these retreats) continue to benefit – regardless of their experiences as wounded victims of oppressive male socialization.[3]

Others still rehearse the politics of exclusion, as if by clearing away the playing field of secure gender identity of any that we deem less than manly – women, gay men, nonnative-born men, men of color – middle-class, straight, white men can reground their sense of themselves without those haunting fears and that deep shame that they are unmanly and will be exposed by other men. This is the manhood of racism, of sexism, of homophobia. It is the manhood that is so chronically insecure that it trembles at the idea of lifting the ban on gays in the military, that is so threatened by women in the workplace that women become the targets of sexual harassment, that is so deeply frightened of equality that it must ensure that the playing field of male competition remains stacked against all newcomers to the game.

Exclusion and escape have been the dominant methods American men have used to keep their fears of humiliation at bay. The fear of emasculation by other men, of being humiliated, of being seen as a sissy, is the leitmotif in my reading of the history of American manhood. Masculinity has become a relentless test by which we prove to other men, to women, and ultimately to ourselves, that we have successfully mastered the part. The restlessness that men feel today is nothing new in American history; we have been anxious and restless for almost two centuries. Neither exclusion nor escape has ever brought us the relief we've sought, and there is no reason to think that either will solve our problems now. Peace of mind, relief from gender struggle, will come only from a politics of inclusion, not exclusion, from standing up for equality and justice, and not by running away.

Notes

1. Although I am here discussing only American masculinity, I am aware that others have located this chronic instability and efforts to prove manhood in the particular cultural and economic arrangements of Western society. Calvin, after all, inveighed against the disgrace "for men to become effeminate," and countless other theorists have described the mechanics of manly proof. (See, for example, Seidler, 1994.)
2. The image is from Warren Farrell, who spoke at a workshop I attended at the First International Men's Conference, Austin, Texas, October 1991.
3. For a critique of these mythopoetic retreats, see Kimmel and Kaufman, 1994.

References

Arendt, H. (1970). *On revolution*. New York: Viking.

Bly, R. (1990). *Iron John: A book about men*. Reading, MA: Addison-Wesley.

Brannon, R. (1976). The male sex role–and what it's done for us lately. In R. Brannon & D. David (Eds.), *The forty-nine percent majority* (pp. 1–40). Reading, MA: Addison-Wesley.

Connell, R. W. (1987). *Gender and power*. Stanford, CA: Stanford University Press.

Farrell, W. (1986). *Why men are the way they are*. New York: McGraw-Hill.

Farrell, W. (1993). *The myth of male power: Why men are the disposable sex*. New York: Simon & Schuster.

Gaylin, W. (1992). *The male ego*. New York: Viking.

Goffman, E. (1963). *Stigma*. Englewood Cliffs, NJ: Prentice Hall.

Gorer, G. (1964). *The American people: A study in national character*. New York: Norton.

Kaufman, M. (1993). *Cracking the armour: Power and pain in the lives of men*. Toronto: Viking Canada.

Keen, S. (1991). *Fire in the belly*. New York: Bantam.

Kimmel, M., & Kaufman, M. (1994). Weekend warriors: The new men's movement. In H. Brod & M. Kaufman (Eds.), *Theorizing Masculinities* (pp. 259–288). Thousand Oaks, CA: Sage.

Leverenz, D. (1986). Manhood, humiliation and public life: Some stories. *Southwest Review*, 71, Fall.

Mead, M. (1965). *And keep your powder dry*. New York: William Morrow.

Moore, R., & Gillette, D. (1991). *King, warrior. magician lover*. New York: HarperCollins.

Moore, R., & Gillette, D. (1992). *The king within: Accessing the king in the male psyche*. New York: William Morrow.

Moore, R., & Gillette, D. (1993a). *The warrior within: Accessing the warrior in the male psyche*. New York: William Morrow.

Moore, R., & Gillette, D. (1993b). *The magician within: Accessing the magician in the male psyche*. New York: William Morrow.

Noble, V. (1992). A helping hand from the guys. In K. L. Hagan (Ed.), *Women respond to the men's movement*. San Francisco: HarperCollins.

Rotundo, E. A. (1993). *American manhood: Transformations in masculinity from the revolution to the modern era*. New York: Basic Books.

Savran, D. (1992). *Communists, cowboys and queers: The politics of masculinity in the work of Arthur Miller and Tennessee Williams*. Minneapolis: University of Minnesota Press.

Seidler, V. J. (1994). *Unreasonable men: Masculinity and social theory*. New York: Routledge.

Wilkinson, R. (1986). *American tough: The tough-guy tradition and American character*. New York: Harper & Row.

1.7

Abandon Your Tedious Search: The Rulebook Has Been Found!

Kate Bornstein

The rules of gender are termed the "natural attitude" of our culture (the real, objective facts) per Harold Garfinkel's 1967 *Studies in Ethnomethodology*. I like to read these rules every now and then to see how each rule has continued to play a part in my life – it's frighteningly accurate. I keep in touch with these rules – it helps me figure out new ways of breaking them. Here are Mr. Garfinkel's rules, and a few ideas about each:

1. There are two, and only two, genders (female and male).

The first question we usually ask new parents is: Is it a boy or a girl? There's a great answer to that one going around: "We don't know; it hasn't told us yet." Personally, I think no question containing *either/or* deserves a serious answer, and that includes the question of gender.

> I'm a member of a commercial electronic bulletin board service called **America Online**. My screen name is **OutlawGal**. I inevitably get two queries: "What makes you an outlaw?" to which I always reply that I break the laws of nature. The second question is almost always, "M or F?" to which I answer, "Yes." Anyone who has a sense of humor about that is someone I want to keep talking with.

2.   One's gender is invariant. (If you are female/male, you always were female/male and you always will be female/male.)

*The latest transsexual notable has been
Renee Richards who has succeeded in hit-
ting the benefits of sex discrimination back
into the male half of the court. The public
recognition and success that it took Billie
Jean King and women's tennis years to get,
Renee Richards has achieved in one set. The
new bumper stickers might well read: "It
takes castrated balls to play women's tennis."*
— Janice G. Raymond,
The Transsexual Empire, 1979

Despite her vicious attack on transsexuals, Raymond's book is a worthwhile read, chiefly for its intelligent highlighting of the male-dominated medical profession, and that profession's control of transsexual surgery. Raymond and her followers believe in some essential thing called "woman," and some other essential thing called "man," and she sees transgendered people as encroaching in her space. Raymond obeys the rules: in her world view, there can be no mutable gender.

There have been both cultural feminists
and hard-line fundamentalists who have
agreed that I was not only born male, but
that no matter what happened to me, and
no matter my choices, I will remain male
'til the day I die. I no longer dispute people
like that: that's how they're going to experience me no matter what I say or do. As
long as they neither threaten me nor keep
me from entering any public space, I feel
more sorry for them than anything else.

3.   Genitals are the essential sign of gender. (A female is a person with a vagina; a male is a person with a penis.)

I never hated my penis; I hated that it made
me a man – in my own eyes, and in the
eyes of others. For my comfort, I needed a
vagina – I was convinced that the only way
I could live out what I thought to be my
true gender was to have genital surgery

to construct a vagina from my penis. Fortunately, I don't regret having done this.

It's real interesting all the papers you have to sign before actually getting male-to-female gender reassignment surgery. I had to acknowledge the possibility of every surgical mishap: from never having any sensation in my genitals, to never having another orgasm in my life, to the threat of my newly-constructed labia falling off. As it turned out, I have some slight loss of feeling on the surface of the skin around my vagina, but I can achieve orgasms, and the last time I looked my labia were still in place. Like I said, I'm lucky; some folks aren't.

4. Any exceptions to two genders are not to be taken seriously. (They must be jokes, pathology, etc.)

I remember one time walking into a Woolworth's in Philadelphia. I'd been living as a woman for about a month. I came through the revolving doors, and stood face to face with a security guard – a young man, maybe nineteen or twenty years old. He did a double take when he saw me and he began to laugh – very loud. He just laughed and laughed. I continued round through the revolving doors and left the store. I agreed with him that I was a joke; that I was the sick one.

I went back in there almost a year later. He came on to me.

5. There are no transfers from one gender to another except ceremonial ones (masquerades).

The Mummers' Parade is held annually on New Year's Day in Philadelphia. Hundreds of men – mostly blue-collar family men – dress up in sequins, feathers, and gowns, and parade up and down the main streets of the City of Brotherly Love.

In most shamanic cultures, there exists a ceremonial rite whereby spiritual leaders, like the Siberian "soft man," need to live part of their lives as another gender before attaining the rank of spiritual leader.

> *The transformation [from man to "soft man"] takes place gradually when the boy is between ages eight and fifteen, the critical years when shamanistic inspiration usually manifests itself. The Chukshi feel that this transformation is due to powerful spirits.*
> – Walter L. Williams,
> *The Spirit and the Flesh*, 1986

6.   Everyone must be classified as a member of one gender or another. (There are no cases where gender is not attributed.)

Do you know anyone to whom you've not assigned the gender male or the gender female? Isn't that a hoot? That alone makes it important for each of us to question gender's grip on our society.

7.   The male/female dichotomy is a "natural" one. (Males and females exist independently of scientists' [or anyone else's] criteria for being male or female.)

There is black on one side of a spectrum, and

white
on the other

with a middle ground of grey, or
some would say there's a rainbow between the two.
There is
left, and

right

and a middle ground of center
There is birth on one side,

and death on the other side
and a middle ground of life.

Yet we insist that there are two,   And we insist that this
only two genders: male and female.   is the way of nature.

Blue   yellow

                              green.

                                                             Nature?

Nature?   Nature.

8.   Membership in one gender or another is "natural." (Being female or male is not dependent on anyone's deciding what you are.)

In the mid-80s, when I first got involved with women's politics, and gay and lesbian politics, I saw these buttons that read:

or

I thought they were particularly relevant to my situation as a transsexual. But I found out otherwise. If I attempt to decide my own gender, I am apparently transgressing against nature – never mind what the buttons said.

When I entered the women's community in the mid-80s, I was told that I still had male energy. (I never knew what "male energy" was, but I later figured out that it was the last of my male privilege showing.) They said that I'd been socialized as a male, and could never truly be a female; that what I was, in fact, was a castrated male. And that hurt me for a long time – over a year, in fact.

I kept hearing people define me in terms *they* were comfortable with. It's easy to play victim, and to say that these people were being malicious, but assuming the worst about others is simply not truth, and it's not a loving or empowering way to look at other people. So, I began to look at their investment in defining me. What I found was that each person who was anxious to define me had a stake in maintaining his or her own membership in a given gender. I began to respect the needs of those who had a stake in their genders.

So I began to say things like, "Yep, I'm a castrated man all right, if that's what you see." And my joy at the look on their faces was the beginning of my sense of humor about all of this – I was no longer humiliated by their definitions of me.
I still have my

button – it's more nostalgic than anything else.

Somewhere, Beyond the Rules

So there are rules to gender, but rules can be broken. On to the next secret of gender – gender can have ambiguity. There are many ways to transgress a prescribed gender code, depending upon the world view of the person who's doing the transgressing: they range from preferring to be somewhat less than rigidly-gendered, to preferring an entirely non-definable image. Achievement of these goals ranges from doing nothing, to maintaining several wardrobes, to full surgical transformation.

> It doesn't really matter what a person decides to do, or how radically a person plays with gender. What matters, I think, is how aware a person is of the options. How sad for a person to be missing out on some expression of identity, just for not knowing there are options.

And then I found out that gender can have fluidity, which is quite different from ambiguity. If ambiguity is a refusal to fall within a prescribed gender code, then fluidity is the refusal to remain one gender or another. Gender fluidity is the ability to freely and knowingly become one or many of a limitless number of genders, for any length of time, at any rate of change. Gender fluidity recognizes no borders or rules of gender.

> A fluid identity, incidentally, is one way to solve problems with boundaries. As a person's identity keeps shifting, so do individual borders and boundaries. It's hard to cross a boundary that keeps moving!

It was the discovery of my own ambiguity and fluidity of gender that led me to my gender change. It was figuring out these two concepts that allowed me to observe these factors – inhibited or in full bloom – in the culture, and in individuals.

References

Garfinkel, Harold. *Studies in Ethnomethodology*. Englewood Cliffs, N.J.: Prentice-Hall, 1967.
Raymond, Janice G. *The Transsexual Empire*. Boston: Beacon Press, 1979.
Williams, Walter L. *The Spirit and the Flesh*. Boston: Beacon Press, 1986.

1.8

Feminists Theorize Colonial/Postcolonial
Rosemary Marangoly George

Postcolonial feminist theory's project can be described as one of interrupting the discourses of postcolonial theory and of liberal Western feminism, while simultaneously refusing the singular "Third World Woman" as the object of study. From the early 1980s onward, postcolonial feminism in the West has been centrally concerned with the terms in which knowledge about non-Western women was produced, circulated, and utilized. In postcolonial literary analyses, issues of location, of representation, of "voicing" female subjecthood, and of the expansion of the literary canon emerged as important foci. As a critical approach, the postcolonial literary feminism that would radically alter the study of literature in the Western academy can be traced to a few key critical essays written in the early 1980s. In this essay I discuss a range of the most significant contributions to postcolonial literary feminism and situate them in relation to the work of numerous scholars in the fields of colonial and postcolonial studies and feminist literary scholarship. I will present Gayatri Chakravorty Spivak, a feminist and cultural theorist, born and educated in India and based in the United States as an exemplary critical figure; a discussion of the trajectory of her work will allow us to consider some of the major ideas in the field. Postcolonial feminist literary critics negotiate with a wide range of related discourses in order to revise the terms in which the location of the critic and of the literary subject are understood. Indeed, postcolonial feminist criticism contests the very location of literature itself.

Much of the theoretical energy of early postcolonial feminist scholarship focused on challenging Western feminist literary theory's investment in first world women's texts, in uninterrogated national literary traditions, and in a benevolent, ultimately patronizing, reception of third world women, in and out of literary texts. At the same time, postcolonial feminists scrutinized the gendered blind spots of the mostly masculinist postcolonial critique of relations of power in colonial contexts and newly independent states. Thus postcolonial feminist scholarship has as its characteristic markings: the fashioning of cautionary signposts, the disclosure of absences, an insistence on what cannot be represented in elite texts, an emphasis on the more than "purely literary," and the persistent embedding of gendered difference in a larger understanding of race, nationality, class, and caste. Despite the disciplining tone of many of the occasions for such scholarship, in the late 1990s and early 2000s, a postcolonial feminist approach harnesses the wisdom of many different critical strands; a coalitional scholarship, it is indebted even as it contributes to scholarship in a range of fields that extend feminist discourse beyond any simple notion of the literary or of gender.

I use the term "postcolonial" in this essay to refer to a critical framework in which literary and other texts can be read against the grain of the hegemonic discourse in a colonial or neocolonial context: this framework insists on recognizing, resisting, and overturning the strictures and structures of colonial relations of power. It takes its inspiration from and constantly refers to the intellectual work that contributed to the end of Europe's colonial occupation of the globe, from the mid-twentieth century to the present. But the postcolonial critical framework is more than a condensed theory of decolonization. Rather, it is a methodology especially invested in examining culture as an important site of conflicts, collaborations, and struggles between those in power and those subjected to power. While colonial control over far-flung empires was largely accomplished through use of force, the "superiority" of the colonizer was crucially reinforced through cultural "persuasion." British colonizers spread the secular scripture of English literature through the colonial education system as a means of establishing the "innate" superiority of British culture (and therefore of British rule) in the minds of the native elites. As Cheikh Hamidou Kane, the Senegalese writer, noted in his 1963 novel, *Ambiguous Adventure*: "The cannon compels the body, the school bewitches the soul."[1]

Anticolonial national struggles and postcolonial literary discourse developed an implicit conviction that cultural sites have the potential to change social and political reality. Indeed, the urgency to end colonial rule was often first publicly expressed in cultural texts. In the present, the term "postcolonial" is differently invoked by different practitioners. For the most part, however, this critical stance counters the usual relations of power between First and Third World locations in the linked arenas of economics, politics, and cultural production.

Like other scholars and cultural practitioners arguing from the margins in the 1980s and 1990s, postcolonial theorists in the West and elsewhere were engaged in the task of widening the range of literary texts and practices understood as worthy of scholarly attention, that is, as canonical. In order to achieve this goal, the role of literary texts in society had to be retheorized: thus, for instance, Ngugi Wa Thiongo argued for two literary categories: the literature of oppression and the literature of struggle; he thus challenged the conventional practice of distinguishing among literary texts solely on the bases of form (*Writers in Politics*, 1981). Other scholars, for example, those working on testimonials or on transcribed oral texts, argued for a reevaluation of the *type* of texts considered worthy of analysis. Concurrently, postcolonial literary criticism finally put to rest the humanist notion that the best literary texts transcended politics by carrying within them the pearls of what would be *universally* acknowledged as wisdom. By disclosing, as Edward Said did in *Orientalism* (1978) and *Culture and Imperialism* (1992), that literary texts were shaped by and in turn shaped the ruling ideologies of their day, they demonstrated the logic of tracing both colonial and anticolonial ideologies through literature.[2] Postcolonial feminists intervened to insist that men and women experience aspects of colonialism and postcolonialism differently. Yet they also vigorously maintained that gender was not *invariably* a fundamental marker of difference. Postcolonial feminists have noted, for example, that European women in the colonial period wrote frequently about their "Eastern Sisters," but that there were very few instances in which alliances between women *as women* overcame the difference of race under a colonial system. As a result, gender must be understood as operating in tandem with the pressures of race, class, sexuality, and location.

In the late 1980s and 1990s, postcolonial theorists were very invested in reexamining colonial and "native" discourses from the nineteenth and early twentieth century, produced and circulated in Europe and in the colonies, especially those that constructed "modernity" in opposition to "traditional" or "native" customs. European texts repeatedly justified and explained colonial domination by reinforcing a series of hierarchized oppositions such as civilized/savage, modern/traditional, mature/ childlike, and, most significantly, rational/irrational. Dipesh Chakrabarty's *Provincializing Europe* (2000) is an example of a postcolonial critical text that attempts to undo the central position that Europe has held as "the Universal" in non-European locations thanks to the legacy of these colonialist oppositions. While Europe in the late twentieth and early twenty-first century is clearly no longer the embodiment of the universal human, a certain Europe still occupies a central position in the scholarly imagination. Postcolonial criticism aims to "provincialize Europe" and to counter the hegemonic weight of an Enlightenment universalist world view by insisting on the humanity of colonized peoples and on the value of non-European thought and culture. Postcolonial feminists bring to this revisionary reading of center and periphery a keen sense of the gendered dynamics of knowledge production in colonial discourse and in the postcolonial critique of the same.

Arguably, one of the inaugural moments of postcolonial feminist literary criticism in the West was the publication of Spivak's "Three Women's Texts and a Critique of Imperialism" in the Fall 1985 issue of *Critical Inquiry*. In this short essay, Spivak forced a rethinking of the ways in which literary texts, especially those written by women, had been deployed in feminist arguments. Spivak brilliantly focuses on Charlotte Brontë's *Jane Eyre*, one of the "cult texts" of Western academic feminism; she argues that in the novel, as in twentieth-century feminist criticism, Jane Eyre and Bertha Mason Rochester become who they are – heroine and less than human, respectively – because of the politics of imperialism. Prior to Spivak's essay, the authoritative feminist critical analysis of *Jane Eyre* was the lynchpin chapter in Sandra Gilbert's and Susan Gubar's hugely successful *The Madwoman in the Attic* (1979). Despite titling their book after the experiences of *Jane Eyre*'s Creole Bertha, who is declared insane and locked in the attic of her husband Mr. Rochester's English country house, Gilbert and Gubar were quite oblivious to Bertha's significance, except insofar as she served as Jane's "dark double": Bertha would do for Jane what Jane could not herself do. Gilbert's and Gubar's reading of the novel brought to a crescendo the feminist celebration of Jane as the solitary heroine who begins life "without connections, beauty or fortune" and ends having acquired all three *and* the power to narrate her version of the story of her life. In these readings Jane's triumph is her transformation, seemingly through the power of her first-person narrative, from a timid, impoverished governess into a desirable woman the hero cannot live without. When the first-person narrator begins the last chapter of the novel with "Dear Reader, I married him," the immolation of Bertha and her leap to her death (the plot event that allows Jane finally to accept Mr. Rochester's marriage proposal) is quite easily forgotten in the celebratory conclusion to the romance plot.

"Three Women's Texts and a Critique of Imperialism" made the feminist argument exemplified by Gilbert's and Gubar's work completely untenable, by demonstrating how "the feminist individualist heroine of British fiction," the fully individual feminine subject that is the apotheosis of liberal feminism, comes into being through violence done to the Other. Spivak argues that this becoming of the subject/the individual is brought about not just by marriage and childbearing, but by "soul making" – a task that requires the violence done to the soulless, less than human Other. With much assistance from the Caribbean novelist Jean Rhys's *Wide Sargasso Sea* (1965), Spivak demonstrates that "so intimate a thing as personal and human identity might be determined by the politics of imperialism."[3] Using Rhys's narrative, which tells Bertha's version of the story of her marriage to Mr. Rochester, Spivak deftly demonstrates that "the active ideology of imperialism … provides the discursive field" for the Brontë novel. Following Spivak, we might ask: Where do Mr. Rochester's wealth and Jane's fortune come from? Why is Bertha initially considered an attractive match? And how is it that her legal rights as Mr. Rochester's wife are so easily disregarded by the narrative and the reader? The resulting discussion of the novel's imbrication in the global relations of domination established under British imperialism significantly alters our understanding of the gendered politics of fiction. If the study of eighteenth-century English novels and conduct books demonstrates, as Nancy Armstrong argues, that "the modern individual was first and foremost a female," in the wake of Spivak's essay postcolonial feminists argued that the nineteenth- and twentieth-century English woman of liberal feminism was first and foremost authorized by the economic, political, social, and cultural axioms of British imperialism.[4]

The 1990s saw the publication of many essays, special editions of journals, and books that reexamined the much-trammeled terrain of eighteenth- to twentieth-century British literary, legal, and other texts with a view to explicating the investment in Empire that had gone unnoticed in earlier scholarship. Of these projects, Lata Mani's analysis of the British colonial discussion of the custom of *sati* (spelt "suttee" in the colonial period) in nineteenth-century India illustrates colonial discourse's construction of "native custom and practice" as barbaric, thus rationalizing the imposition of a "civilizing" European colonial rule. But Mani also interrogates the patriarchal "native" representation of this custom in which newly widowed wives immolated themselves on their husbands' funeral pyres. As she shows, *sati* was not a practice followed all over the Indian subcontinent, nor was it the necessary fate of all widows in a particular caste or class. Rather, it was practiced sporadically in scattered incidents that were, however, scrupulously recorded by British observers. Mani's study discloses the use to which the burning widow (referred to as the *sati*) was put in simultaneously furthering the colonial project and protecting indigenous patriarchal power. Mani argues that the *satis* "become sites on which various versions of scripture/tradition/law are elaborated and contested" (p. 115).[5] She demonstrates that the elaborate narratives compiled by eyewitnesses contain no record of the widows' motivations, utterances, reasoning, or subjectivity, or even of their pain. In Mani's words: "… even reading against the grain of a discourse ostensibly about women, one learns so little about them … neither subject, nor object, but ground – such is the status of women in the discourse on *sati*" (p. 118). Despite the colonizers' stated concern for the wellbeing of native women, the real purpose of this debate around the practice of *sati* was to reinforce the "necessity" of the regulatory presence of British colonial rule.

In her 1988 essay "Can the Subaltern Speak?" Spivak succinctly notes that the same nineteenth-century descriptions of *sati* (even after the abolition of this rite by William Bentinck in 1829) allow us to understand the way in which colonial rule presented itself: as "white men saving brown women from brown men." Against this colonialist reading of the anti-*sati* campaign, Spivak places the Indian nativist argument, which she condenses into the phrase, "the women actually wanted to die." She argues that "the two sentences go a long way to legitimize each other. One never encounters the testimony of the women's voice-consciousness. Such a testimony would not be ideology-transcendent or 'fully' subjective, of course, but it would have constituted the ingredients for producing a countersentence."[6] Spivak points to what will become a major preoccupation of postcolonial feminist writing: namely, if and how disenfranchised women can represent, speak, and act *for themselves*, despite oppressive conditions. Postcolonial feminism unflinchingly acknowledges that there are many obstacles in the path of securing such "voice-consciousness." Yet, despite the odds, postcolonial feminist discourse strives to create the space for this "countersentence" to be spoken by the "gendered subaltern."

Postcolonial feminist criticism developed in this period in relation to other critical feminist projects as well. From the early 1960s onward, there was a powerful and multifaceted movement by US-based "women of color" (as they began to call themselves) for equal rights in all spheres of life. This struggle emerged from and alongside the feminist and civil rights movements of the 1960s–1970s, with women of color insisting on the double oppression they faced on account of their race and gender. As part of their resistance to racial and gendered prejudices, women of color in the United States also developed powerful critiques of mainstream white feminism for its race-related blind spots, and against the masculinist bias of nationalist struggles for racial uplift within their own communities. Like postcolonial theorists, these women were inspired by nationalist struggles in the third world. Thus women of color in the United States argued that they were also "third world women," despite the irony of their geographic location.

Two texts from the early 1980s consolidated theorizing from this position: the poetic and incisive *This Bridge Called My Back*, edited by Cherríe Moraga and Gloria Anzaldúa, with a foreword by Toni Cade Bambara (1981), and Chandra Mohanty's "Under Western Eyes: Feminist Scholarship and Colonial Discourses" (1984). These early texts, emblematic of this critical tradition, connected the US-based women of color critique (conventionally linked with US feminist and civil rights movements) with the then-burgeoning postcolonial feminist critique (whose arena was usually defined in the United States as "foreign," given its preoccupation with the contours of the erstwhile colonial spaces of Britain and her former colonies and the general amnesia about US imperialism).

Mohanty's "Under Western Eyes" was first published in 1984 in the academic journal *Boundary 2*, then republished in Teresa de Lauretis's influential anthology *Feminist Studies/Critical Studies* in 1986, then reprinted in *Feminist Review* in 1988 and again in 1991 in the immensely important *Third World Women and the Politics of Feminism*, edited by Mohanty, Russo, and Torres.[7] Very widely read, this essay engaged both women of color and postcolonial feminist concerns and soon became constitutive of both fields. In the essay Mohanty formulates a theoretically nuanced critique of the "discursive colonialism" toward "third world women" practiced by elite women, both in the geographic West and outside it. She maps the contours of privilege in feminist writing and the effects of such West-oriented feminism on the non-West. She pinpoints the effect of feminist analysis that constructs a singular and generic "third world woman" as the object of study. Third world women always function in such work as "a homogenous, powerless group ... often located as the implicit victim of particular socioeconomic systems" (*Third World Women*, p. 57).

Mohanty's concern is that even as elite feminism intervenes in traditional disciplinary analysis, an "ethnocentric universalism is produced in western feminist analysis" and "a homogenous notion of the oppression of women is assumed, which, in turn, produces the image of an 'average third world woman'" – one who is studied most often in terms of her fertility (p. 56). Mohanty thus both names and challenges the objectification of women in the third world as perennial victims within scholarship on topics as seemingly disparate as economic development, male violence, familial systems, genital mutilation, and "the Islamic code." Marking the gap between the heterogeneous conditions in which women live their lives in the third world and the monolithic "third world woman" of elite feminist discourse, "Under Western Eyes" is a foundational text for all contemporary feminist endeavors, even those that are not readily identified as postcolonial. The cautions that Mohanty offers are now part of the "common sense" of the field. Yet, even as recently as 2001–2, the discussion of Afghan women in the mainstream US media provided many examples of the imperialist first world reading of third world women that Mohanty vociferously and painstakingly critiqued in an essay written more than twenty years ago!

Mohanty's essay, along with some of the writing produced in parallel discussions such as Denise Riley's *"Am I That Name?" Feminism and the Category of "Women" in History* (1988), Judith Butler's *Gender Trouble* (1990), and other work on this topic, began to disassemble one of feminist literary criticism's most revered and "natural" categories – that of "the woman" and, subsequently, of "the woman writer." A long-presumed, *automatic* unity based in gender was repeatedly challenged by these feminists, who were quick to point to the ways in which women were *multiply* constituted subjects. As Mohanty states: "by women as a category of analysis, I am referring to the crucial assumption that all of us of the same gender, across classes and cultures, are somehow socially constituted as a homogeneous group identified *prior to the process of analysis*" (p. 56, my emphasis). Yet "women" as a category of analysis has long been considered central to feminist theory and practice. What does it mean for feminist discourse and practice to give up the category of women as foundational? Postcolonial feminism had only to turn to anticolonial discourse to see the very special place it granted to women and to understand that this special status was to be firmly resisted.

Postcolonial feminists were especially astute in noting *and refusing* the exalted yet largely symbolic status allotted to women in many nationalist struggles. Indeed, gender symbolism in colonial and postindependence periods remains essentially unchanged: women were paradoxically both central (as symbolic figures) and marginal (in terms of actual changes in their material circumstances) to nationalist projects, just as they had been to colonial projects. Partha Chatterjee's influential essay on "The Nationalist Resolution of the Women's Question" in the Indian context best surveys the terrain in which such discussions of women as subjects and objects of discourse played out.[8] Chatterjee argues that nationalism resolved the women's question through the separation of the domain of culture into two spheres: the material and the spiritual. Colonialism, it was believed, had left the spiritual or private realm of culture untouched; this realm was embodied by the Indian woman. The spiritual sphere was thus a space in which the nation imagined itself as already free; cultural arenas were seen as not always in the same subordinate relation to the colonizers as economic or political arenas. What resulted from this nationalist reasoning was a firm association of women with the spiritual, cultural, and private realms. Indian nationalists deftly invoked prevalent patriarchal gender inequalities to resist colonial interference in the intimate reaches of "native" lives. As a consequence, reforming women's lives became a contentious arena of struggle between colonists and nationalists. Mrinalini Sinha's discussion of the age of consent (for marriage) debates in late nineteenth- and early twentieth-century British India provides a good illustration of the gendered dynamics of social reform.[9]

During independence struggles and immediately after, most nations were figured as female, and women were the ground on which national identity was erected. In Loomba's succinct reformulation of Benedict Anderson's argument: "If the nation is an imagined community, that imagining is profoundly gendered" (*Colonialism-Postcolonialism*, p. 215). Postcolonial feminist scholars have argued that while women may make minimal gains when mobilized as symbols of the new nation, they are easily returned to the domestic or to a depoliticized private sphere when independence is achieved. As Deniz Kandiyoti notes: "the vagaries of nationalist discourse are reflected in changing portrayals of women as victims of social back-wardness, icons of modernity, as boundary markers or privileged bearers of cultural authenticity."[10] In these symbolic sites, Kandiyoti argues, women's claims to "enfranchised citizenry" ("Identity and its Discontents," p. 378) are ultimately limited because they are "held hostage" to the needs of the nation and tenaciously subjected to patriarchal control in the familial sphere. That is, they are caught in the role of mother/daughter/wife in both familial *and* national discourse. This disposition does not go unchallenged, however. As Lila Abu-Lughod makes clear in her discussion of the Middle East, "women themselves actively participate in these debates and social struggles, with feminism, defined in sometimes quite different ways, having become by now an inescapable term of reference."[11] Thus women in these locations are simultaneously participants in and hostages to nationalist projects – both empowered and undercut by the weight of their symbolic place.

As in the colonial era, in the postindependence period women are also the primary objects of reform and manipulation, especially under state-sanctioned modernization projects. Reforming/modernizing the lives of women in the Middle East, as Abu-Lughod demonstrates, is regulatory and emancipatory: modernity in the Middle East, she argues, introduces an era of the consolidation of the domestic as the proper arena for women within a new, heterosexual nuclear family model, with the man as head of household and the concomitant devaluation of women's homosocial networks. "The forms of feminism in the Middle East tied to modernity," she writes, "ushered in new forms of gendered subjection (in the double sense of subject positions for women and forms of domination) as well as new experiences and possibilities" (*Remaking Women*, p. 13).

Elite women's writing in these locations reflects the pride, ambivalence, and tension of embodying the locally defined ideal of womanhood. Popular literature by women in the newly independent nations expresses a desire to evolve into a female subject who is "free" from the many representations of proper womanhood that are abundantly produced in various nationalist texts, yet the contours of this desired self are defined by these representations. Thus in a range of texts, including *Changes: A Love Story* by the Ghanaian writer Ama Ata Aidoo, *Nervous Conditions* by the Zimbabwean writer Tsitsi Dangarembga, *Women of Sand and Myrrh* by the Lebanese writer Hanan al-Shaykh, and *That Long Silence* by the Indian writer Shashi Deshpande, frustration at the appropriation of the body, labor and intellect of the female subject by state, communal, or familial projects forms a central theme of the realist plot.[12] For the women in these fictional texts, belonging to, indeed, being the showpiece of a newly independent nation holds no guarantees.

Increasingly, postcolonial scholars within the Western academy have begun to theorize a "new" Diaspora Studies that considers the effects of mass migrations beyond the groups (Jews, Greeks, Armenian) to which the term "diaspora" was exclusively applied before the 1960s. As Western academia slowly opened up to scholarly articulations of diasporic experiences of travel and resettlement, of cultural production "on the road," as it were, of cross-continental links that endure over generations and of the differentiated, diasporic sense of belonging and citizenship in all locations, new issues relating to gender and sexuality in a cross-continental framework are elaborated upon by feminists. Diaspora Studies serves as an interesting site for feminist and other scholars, straddling as it does several geographic locations that are held in one framework. Thus an immigrant's view of the West is both linked to and distinguished from one or more parts of the non-Western world.

Forty years after women of color in the United States associated themselves with "women in the third world," the changes in immigration law, the movement of capital and jobs, globalization, and other economic and political forces all call for reformulations of the relations between people who live in and move among different corners of the planet. For example, under the rubric of Diaspora Studies, one can study the long history of the transportation of "indentured labor" from China and South Asia to meet the demands of a plantation economy after the abolition of slavery in the nineteenth century. We might ponder how gendered, labor, sexual, and familial relations were reorganized in these circumstances. Moving to the current phase of globalization, we may ask who are the subalterns and elites in the new global economies. What was the impact of the changes in immigration law in 1965 on racial and class dynamics in the United States? Consider the full implications of the slogan "We Are Here Because You Were There" that is frequently used by black and Asian British subjects protesting about various aspects of race relations in the United Kingdom. How are citizenship, gender, sexuality, and familial dynamics reformulated in a diasporic context? How does the conventional understanding of nationality signify in the age of what Aihwa Ong has called "flexible citizenship" in her study of transnational Asians? Newly emerging feminist scholarship on these issues goes well beyond the "literary" and beyond a pristine understanding of gender as an isolated factor.

Also, other well-established areas of study – such as Asian Studies and Asian American or Latin American Studies – come into conversation with postcolonial studies under the aegis of diaspora. Asian American Studies over the past decade has moved well beyond a purely national understanding of its scope to study the effects of US imperialism in Asia, new immigration, and transnational labor arrangements that stretch from Asia to the United Kingdom and out into other geographies. Thus a novel such as Jessica Hagedorn's *Dogeaters* (1991), set in the Philippines in the Marcos era, can be classified both as postcolonial fiction (given its clear elaboration of the impact of US imperialism on the Philippines) and as a classic Asian American novel framed by the protagonist Rio's immigration to the United States. As the novel makes clear, the United States shapes Rio's everyday life well before she steps onto US shores. Increasingly, the foods, music, television channels, languages, and peoples of the Philippines are now visible and established in thriving Filipino American communities in the United States. There are many such local contact zones where third world meets first world and irreversibly mix the categories of "West" and "non-West." The so-called "mainstream" cultures of the West are now irreversibly colored by the contributions from their immigrant populations and thus by past and present imperial policies.

Returning our attention to postcolonial literary feminist criticism: literary critical feminist territorial boundaries are not as clear-cut in the twenty-first century as they were imagined to be even a decade ago. We are at the threshold of a new location, one that *approaches* what we might call "global literary studies" – a situation that calls for a radical rethinking of the claims we have become accustomed to making when we produce feminist and/or literary scholarship. We can no longer make claims about how literary texts function as cultural artifacts and as political tools without having to think hard about how such texts might play out in other locations. This is not to suggest glibly that today information and influence circulate easily among scholars working in different parts of the world, but rather to argue that we cannot proceed with our scholarly projects oblivious to how our work speaks to scholarship or readership in different locations. Writing to this enlarged audience alerts one to the kinds of theoretical and practical negotiations that will soon be required *as a matter of course* in the era of global literary studies. Many cultural practices (literary and nonliterary) are produced every day across the globe, and many theorists and intellectuals (whose names do not appear here) continue to reflect on and articulate the significance of such work. The challenge for postcolonial feminist scholarship within the Western academy is to look beyond this location and engage with literary texts and literary criticism produced elsewhere, but always with a clear understanding of the pitfalls of apprehending the world with the aid of the old imperial analytical tools supplied by our common history of colonialism.

Notes

I would like to thank Ellen Rooney for her generosity with insights and countless conversations about this essay.

1. Quoted by Ngugi Wa Thiongo in *Homecoming: Essays on African and Caribbean Literature, Culture and Politics* (London: Heinemann, 1972), p. 45.

2. See also Moira Ferguson's *Colonialism and Gender Relations from Mary Wollstonecraft to Jamaica Kincaid: East Caribbean Connections* (New York: Columbia University Press, 1993), Firdous Azim's *The Colonial Rise of the Novel* (London: Routledge, 1993), among a host of other scholarly books on this topic.

3. Catherine Belsey and Jane Moore, eds., *The Feminist Reader: Essays in Gender and the Politics of Literary Criticism* (New York: Oxford University Press, 1987), p. 183.

4. See Nancy Armstrong, *Desire and Domestic Fiction: A Political History of the Novel* (New York: Oxford University Press, 1987), p. 66. See also the chapter "The Authoritative Englishwoman: Setting up Home and Self in the Colonies," in my *The Politics of Home: Postcolonial Relocations and Twentieth-Century Fiction* (Cambridge: Cambridge University Press, 1996), pp. 35–64.

5. See Lata Mani, "Contentious Traditions: the Debate on Sati in Colonial India," in Kumkum Sangari and Sudesh Vaid, eds., *Recasting Women: Essays in Colonial History* (New Delhi: Kali for Women Press, 1989), pp. 88–126.

6. Gayatri Chakravorty Spivak, "Can the Subaltern Speak?," in Patrick Williams and Laura Chrisman, eds., *Colonial Discourse and Postcolonial Theory: A Reader* (New York: Columbia University Press, 1994), p. 93.

7. Chandra Talpade Mohanty, Ann Russo, and Lourdes Torres, eds., *Third World Women and the Politics of Feminism* (Bloomington: Indiana University Press, 1991).

8. See Partha Chatterjee, "The Nationalist Resolution of the Women's Question," Sangari and Vaid, eds., in *Recasting Women*, pp. 233–53.

9. See Mrinalini Sinha, "Potent Protests: the Age of Consent Controversy, 1891" in Sinha, *Colonial Masculinity* (1995; reprinted New Delhi: Kali for Women Press, 1997), pp. 138–80.

10. Deniz Kandiyoti, "Identity and its Discontents: Women and the Nation," in Williams and Chrisman, eds., *Colonial Discourse*, pp. 376–91. See also N. Yuval-Davis and F. Anthias, eds., *Women-Nation-State* (London: Macmillan, 1989); and Kumari Jayawardena, *Feminism and Nationalism in the Third World* (London: Zed, 1988).

11. Lila Abu-Lughod, "Introduction: Feminist Longings and Postcolonial Conditions," in Abu-Lughod, ed., *Remaking Women: Feminism and Modernity in the Middle East* (Princeton: Princeton University Press, 1998), pp. 3–31.

12. See Ama Ata Aidoo, *Changes: A Love Story* (London: The Women's Press, 1991); Tsitsi Dangarembga, *Nervous Conditions* (London: The Women's Press, 1988); Hanan al-Shaykh, *Women of Sand and Myrrh* (London: Quartet Press, 1989); and Shashi Deshpande, *That Long Silence* (London: Virago, 1988).

Further Reading

Leela Gandhi, *Postcolonial Theory: A Critical Introduction* (New York: Columbia University Press, 1998).

Ania Loomba, *Colonialism-Postcolonialism* (New York: Routledge, 1998).

Chandra Talpade Mohanty, Ann Russo, and Lourdes Torres, eds., *Third World Women and the Politics of Feminism* (Bloomington: Indiana University Press, 1991).

Edward Said, *Culture and Imperialism* (New York: Vintage, 1994).

Edward Said, *Orientalism* (New York: Random House, 1993).

Gayatri Chakravorty Spivak, *The Spivak Reader*, eds. Donna Landry and Gerald MacLean (New York: Routledge, 1996).

Patrick Williams and Laura Chrisman, eds., *Colonial Discourse and Postcolonial Theory* (New York: Columbia University Press, 1994).

2

Stories of Identity and Community

By Irene Lara

Contents

Original publication details: 2.1 Gloria Anzaldúa, "To Live in the Borderlands Means You" from *Borderlands/La Frontera: The New Mestiza*, 2nd ed., pp. 216–17. San Francisco: Aunt Lute, 1999. Reproduced with permission of Aunt Lute Books. 2.2 Evelyn Alsultany, "Los Intersticios: Recasting Moving Selves" from *This Bridge We Call Home: Radical Visions for Transformation*, ed. Gloria E. Anzaldúa and AnaLouise Keating, pp. 106–10. New York: Routledge, 2002. Reproduced with permission of Taylor & Francis Group LLC. 2.3 Paula Gunn Allen, "Where I Come From Is Like This" from *The Sacred Hoop: Recovering the Feminine in American Indian Traditions*, pp. 43–50. Boston: Beacon Press, 1992. Reproduced with permission of Beacon Press. 2.4 Barbara Ehrenreich and Arlie Russell Hochschild, "Introduction" from *Global Woman: Nannies, Maids, and Sex Workers in the New Economy*, ed. Barbara Ehrenreich and Arlie Russell Hochschild, pp. 1–13, 285–86. New York: Metropolitan, 2002. Reproduced with permission of Granta Publications and Henry Holt & Co. 2.5 Melanie Kaye/Kantrowitz and Irena Klepfisz with Bernice Mennis, "*In Gerangl*/In Struggle: A Handbook for Recognizing and Resisting Anti-Semitism" from *The Tribe of Dina: A Jewish Women's Anthology*, ed. Melanie Kaye/Kantrowitz and Irena Klepfisz, pp. 304–05. Montpelier, VT: Sinister Wisdom, 1986. 2.6 Eli Clare, "losing home" from *Exile & Pride: Disability, Queerness and Liberation*, pp. 31–37, 46–49. South End Press, 1999, 2009. Reproduced with permission of Duke University Press and Eli Clare.

Women in Culture: An Intersectional Anthology for Gender and Women's Studies, Second Edition.
Edited by Bonnie Kime Scott, Susan E. Cayleff, Anne Donadey, and Irene Lara.
© 2017 John Wiley & Sons, Ltd. Published 2017 by John Wiley & Sons, Ltd.

Women's Studies argues for the power of storytelling as a feminist praxis – the constant interface between theory and practice in which theory influences practice and activist experiences refine thought – for knowledge production, consciousness raising, teaching critical and compassionate thinking, revising dominant histories, and inspiring activism (hooks; Levins Morales; Solinger, Fox, and Irani). In Women's Studies we recognize that whoever tells, documents, and interprets people's stories has the power to create and perpetuate reality, including people's sense of identity and community. Thus we study the ways telling one's individual and collective stories is central to liberation struggles against oppressive laws, policies, institutions, beliefs, and versions of history, as well as those against colonizing, imperialist, and heteropatriarchal governments. For example, women of color health advocates Cara Page and Etobssie Wako helped found Depo Diaries: A National Storytelling Project for women to document their experiences using the controversial Depo-Provera contraceptive that is disproportionately promoted in poor communities. They established this project because, as Wako describes it, she believes "in the power of the personal narrative as a means to transcend oppressive practices and systems and promote just communities" (see Chapter 7).

Working to understand how an individual's story has larger political implications is captured in the feminist dictum "the personal is political." A common praxis during the US civil rights and women's movements of the 1960s and 1970s was to create spaces for women to give voice to their stories and listen to the stories of others across differences and commonalities, providing opportunities for consciousness raising (Adams, Bell, and Griffin). The related praxis of women's "testimonio," from the Latin American social movements' tradition of oral autobiography bearing witness and challenging official dominant stories, including those that erase, distort, or demean women's diverse voices, is also considered an effective tool for social justice, creativity, and/or healing (e.g., Menchú, Latina Feminist Group).

Further grounding the textbook's introduction to feminist concepts in the life experiences of a diverse set of women and gender identities, this second chapter presents several personal narratives and scholarly articles that explore identity and community. As seen throughout the readings, one's identity – who a person is, perceives oneself to be, or is perceived to be – is complex. It changes according to geographical, cultural, historical, economic, and life cycle contexts, is affected by power relations, and can be a source of empowerment and healing, as well as privilege and oppression. A Women's Studies intersectional approach to understanding identity and community also entails analyzing the ways that one's race, ethnicity, nationality, region, language, religion, sex,

gender, sexuality, class, age, ability, size, history, and additional differences all simultaneously operate to give shape to a person's life. As also discussed in Chapter 1, although
we are focusing our studies on girls and women, one's sex is not the primary or only
vector of identity. The self is a dynamic amalgamation of all social categories and related
systems of dominance and oppression; therefore analyzing how they all interact and
constitute one another provides a more complete picture of reality, and helps us to more
effectively challenge and dismantle unjust systems.

The concept of intersectionality first emerged to explain the experiences of women of
color who were marginalized by mainstream white feminism *and* male-centered, nationalist, anti-racism movements as well as race- and gender-blind labor organizations. Citing
Black critical race and feminist theorist Kimberlé Crenshaw, credited with being the first
to theorize the term, Latina feminist scholar Maythee Rojas also explains that the
intersection of race and gender makes women of color's "challenges to confronting racism and misogyny more difficult" (27) since engaging in one single strategy is not fully
effective. Intersectionality has since developed to more directly account also for class,
sexuality, nationality, religion, ability, and additional social differences. It recognizes that
most people experience some privileges and some oppressions, that our status can
change across time and place, and that being privileged in some ways may mitigate
being oppressed in others and vice versa depending on the context. In our readings in
this chapter for example, Eli Clare experiences the privilege of being white and educated
and the oppression of being queer, working class, and a person with a disability, and
Evelyn Alsultany experiences the privilege of being an able-bodied, middle-class, US
citizen able to travel abroad and the oppression of being a multiethnic, Muslim woman
of color. All of these factors shape people's sense of identity and the stories they tell to
make sense of their experiences.

One's identity is related to one's "social location," discussed in Chapter 1 as "the time
and place in which we live and the information to which we have access, as well as the
social categories or groups to which we are perceived as belonging," and that inform
what we believe and how we treat each other. Although some may assume that classi-
fying humans into such groups is a neutral act of description, on the contrary, feminist
and other scholars committed to social justice have shown that such categorization is
"used to establish and maintain a particular kind of social order" (Kirk and Okazawa-Rey
54). Accordingly, as elaborated in Chapter 5, within sexual orientation groups, being
heterosexual is deemed superior, dominant, and normal, while being lesbian, pansexual,
queer, or asexual is deemed inferior, subordinate, and deviant. As Audre Lorde theorizes,
as discussed in Chapter 1, labeling people based on real or presumed differences is a way
to prescribe privileges – unearned advantages often seen as natural entitlements – to
some, and oppressions – unearned disadvantages – to others, thus perpetuating structural inequalities. People from privileged groups experience more power and status
compared to those from oppressed groups, and are also called "dominant" because they
establish the social norms that people from "subordinate" groups are expected to follow
(Adams, Bell, and Griffin). Moreover, beyond categorizing people into binary social
groups that are deemed either privileged or oppressed, social justice theorists recognize
the existence of "border social groups" (Adams, Bell, and Griffin) that may or may not be

dominant or subordinate, depending on the personal, political, cultural, and historical context. So, for example, being transgender or gender-nonconforming in some indigenous cultures, particularly before Christian colonization, is not demeaned (as also suggested in Chapter 5), or being mixed race but able to "pass" as white may decrease discrimination and violence. Both are experiences that complicate a rigid binary understanding of privilege and oppression.

Although these identity categories are socially constructed and many postmodern writers have argued for the need to deconstruct them in order to destabilize the social structures that create their limiting and controlling meanings (e.g., Butler, particularly in reference to sex and gender), this does not make the effects of sexism, classism, racism, ageism, and other oppressive systems on actual people and groups any less real (Keating). Indeed, many argue that addressing social inequities and healing historical injustices entails "reclaiming identity" (Moya) and "restor[ing] to the dehistoricized a sense of identity," as Jewish Puerto Rican feminist Aurora Levins Morales elaborates in "The Historian as Curandera" (1998) in Chapter 3. Queer and straight women of color writers, such as those anthologized in the landmark *This Bridge Called My Back: Writings by Radical Women of Color* (Moraga and Anzaldúa) for example, have worked to reclaim and restore identities on their own terms, while resisting and transforming the stories told from dominant perspectives that have historically rendered them invisible or hypervisible, and stereotyped, victimized, demonized, and/or "otherized" them. To "other" or "otherize" is to deem someone from a specific group inferior, different, and marginal in relation to a presumed superior "self" who is deemed normal and at the center (akin to Lorde's "mythical norm" concept). To establish oppositional relationships of "them" (the others) versus "us" can be a dehumanizing process used to justify injustices (Kirk and Okazawa-Rey 55–56).

By creating what Cherríe Moraga described as experiential "theory in the flesh" (Moraga and Anzaldúa 23) and sharing their stories, feminist writers help us to see the connection between individual identity and social group identity by showing us that our "personal" issues are often actually "about who we are assumed to be based on our race or class or our gender or sexuality" (Rojas 5) or a mix of these and additional identity markers. That is, we are often treated a certain way based on what society assumes about the particular group of which we are, or are perceived to be, a part. Likewise, we too treat others based on our conscious or unconscious suppositions. Moreover, we internalize dominant beliefs about ourselves and the groups of which we are a part, and act accordingly, sometimes to our own self-detriment (Adams, Bell, and Griffith). Identity labels can thus be both empowering and limiting.

As womanist scholar AnaLouise Keating elaborates in her 2002 essay in Chapter 10, many *This Bridge* writers bravely "risk[ed] self-exposure" as they "dr[ew] on their personal experiences to explore the stereotypes and the limitations in identity labels," "challenge[d] assumptions of sameness," and yet insisted on their commonalities while maintaining the importance of recognizing differences. In dialogue with Chicana lesbian creative writer and theorist Gloria Anzaldúa (2002), Keating critiques the way identity categories are fixed, set up in opposition to one another, and can keep people from truly seeing and deeply listening to one another, and thus ultimately from creating the widespread social change that is needed in local and global communities. Anzaldúa theorizes the creation of a new sense of community where: "Nothing is fixed. The pulse of existence, the heart of the universe is fluid. Identity, like a river, is always changing, always in transition, always in nepantla [an in between space]" (2002, 556) and "[y]ou share a category wider than any social position or racial label" (558). In Chapter 10, Keating elaborates on this spiritual identity category that emphasizes our "radical interrelatedness" with all existence, akin to many indigenous, Buddhist, and other philosophies of interconnection.

Identity is connected to community in various ways. Community is generally defined as "a body of persons… having a common history or common social, economic, and political interests" and "a unified body of individuals" (*Merriam-Webster's Collegiate Dictionary*) that share one or more vectors of identity. For example, the stories in this chapter include intersectional reflections on being a bicultural Laguna Pueblo woman with multiethnic white ancestry (Gunn Allen) and being a white "dyke" with a mixed class rural background and a disability (who now identifies as a transgender man) (Clare). One's identification with a given community can thus be based on feeling affinity because you share one or more social group categories. Writers have addressed the value and joy of creating community – joining under the banner of "African ascendant women" (Dillard) or "the lesbian community" (Rothblum) for example – to collectively raise consciousness, politically organize, create art, produce knowledge, and/or provide emotional support based on such social group identities. Interestingly, Jewish white lesbian psychologist Esther Rothblum's research on lesbian communities in the United States shows a desire for connectedness built on personal and organizational relationships, support, and similarities "based on shared hobbies and politics, not necessarily shared sexuality" (469). This is different from the situation in the 1970s when more silences and discrimination against people who identify as LGBTQ (lesbian, gay, bisexual, trans, and queer) arguably necessitated more sexuality-based communities. Nevertheless, queer and trans people of color collectives on and off university campuses continue to emerge as a way to conscientiously center the intersectional experiences of being LGBTQ and a person of color and thus build community around addressing related political-personal concerns (e.g., Quesada, Gomez, and Vidal-Ortiz; King, Mikalson, and Glennon-Zukoff).

Writers have also engaged the limits of a "politics of identity," which includes essentialism, the belief that people have a stable, unchanging, and true core identity (as opposed to a relational identity that evolves through time, experience, and our sociopolitical context). Indeed, in the name of a "unified community," many experience the pressure to silence certain parts of themselves. In nationalist movements, for example, issues of colonialism, class, and race have historically subsumed concerns related to gender and sexual oppression (Rojas). In mainstream LGBTQ movements, white, middle-class, able-bodied, and urban values are often not recognized as being the dominant lens, denying the diverse realities of, for example, queers of color, undocumented queer immigrants, and – as discussed by Clare in this chapter – rural and working-class lesbians, gays, bisexuals, and transgender people.

Rather than completely dismissing communities that can be oppressive (including one's cultural family), many engage the strategy called "disidentification" by Latino queer theorist José Muñoz. For many LGBTQ people of color whose identities may be both nurtured and rejected by their heteropatriarchal families, to "disidentify" signals the simultaneous working "on, with, and against" (Muñoz 12) family structures as they negotiate the racism, classism, and sexism of dominant cultures and the sexual and gender oppression within their own homes, neighborhoods, and regional communities. Indeed, as the editors of *Colonize This! Young Women of Color on Today's Feminism* describe it, "family is only a safe zone until you kiss another woman, question the faith or go to the movies with a white boy" among other ways of expressing one's individuality (Rehman and Hernández xxv). Such differences and "dissent" are supposed to be suppressed "in order to look strong in the face of racism" and additional oppressions (xxv). These dilemmas contextualize queer Filipina-American Maiana Minahal's "poem on trying to love without fear" (2006), included in Chapter 5.

"Community" can be a paradoxical place where people feel safe and supported in some ways, some of the time, but also vulnerable, betrayed, and policed. Nevertheless, many forward a "commitment to the spirit of community" (Dillard 84) whereby one's personhood entails recognizing our interdependence as part of a human community and caring for one another across differences and commonalities, as manifested in the sub-Saharan African concept of "Ubuntu" (I am because we are) (Dillard), the Mayan concept "In Lak'ech" (you are my other me), and the Zen Buddhist concept of "interbeing" (Pérez), and also touched on in Chapter 9. The readings in this chapter help us to critically think about how one's identities and communities materially and spiritually affect people's lives, in what contexts they form and change, and who has the power to define oneself and others. Moreover, they ask us to consider the process and effects of belonging and participation: who is included and who is excluded in certain communities and why?

Borderland Identities and Communities

Beginning with Anzaldúa's poem "To Live in the Borderlands Means You" (1987/1999), we are introduced to a view of identity informed by the racialized body, place, and the transculturation process (that entails cultural loss, the creation of new cultural forms, and the persistence of non-dominant worldviews and practices all mediated through power relations). She speaks from the complex standpoint of a "new mestiza" that acknowledges you "are neither *hispana india negra española/ni gabacha* ... [hispanic indian black spanish/nor a white woman]" yet "caught in the crossfire between camps." In her influential *Borderlands/La Frontera: The New Mestiza*, where this poem was published, Anzaldúa challenges dichotomous views that force her to choose or emphasize certain aspects of her identity over others in the name of assimilating to dominant cultures. Anzaldúa explores identity and community beyond the rigid divisions imposed by inter-related national, racial, ethnic, language, sexual, and gender borders. Grounded in the geopolitical realities of the United States-Mexico region and its specific histories of settler colonialism, imperialism, and global capitalism and her experiences as a Chicana whose ancestors have lived in what is now the state of Texas for six generations, Anzaldúa also questions the western modern philosophical borders between the material and spiritual worlds, and the divisions between one's body, mind, and spirit.

Instead, Anzaldúa claims a third space, what she refers to as "the Borderlands," a material and symbolic world where oppositional binaries (like man versus woman, Anglo versus Indian, and us versus them) are interrogated, multiple identities and communities are negotiated, and the expectation that you choose allegiance to one part of your self at the cost of disavowing another part of your self is challenged. In the Borderlands, the effects of oppressive histories and systems of inequality are recognized and resisted. In the Borderlands, multiplicity, difference, and ambiguity *also* become cultural assets rather than deficits (e.g., you are a "forerunner of a new race, half and half – both woman and man, neither – a new gender"). Without romanticizing its stories, Anzaldúa offers us the concept of the Borderlands as a place of possibility, where one can envision one's whole, multiple self as a spiritual, sexual, creative, and intellectual embodied being.

Multiethnic Identities and Communities

Building on Anzalduan theories of identity and community as politically, culturally, and historically situated, Evelyn Alsultany describes the challenges of living in the Borderland-like concept of "*los intersticios*," defined as "the spaces between the different worlds" inhabited (Anzaldúa, 20). As she argues in her essay "Los Intersticios: Racasting Moving Selves" (2002), society lacks a framework that accounts for simultaneously being two or more ethnicities (or races, nationalities, religions, and other social categories for that matter). Alsultany makes a case for reconceptualizing multiethnic identities so they can be perceived and experienced "as unitary and whole rather than fragmented and dislocated." Indeed, not being recognized as "complex unitary subjects" can lead to feelings of alienation, not belonging, and dislocation, from one's self as well as one's supposed communities. Discussing the political function of a framework that creates rigid racial and ethnic categories that separate people from one another, Alsultany asserts that "[a]n inability to conceptualize multiethnic persons reflects a colonial ideology of categorization and separation based on 'pure blood' criteria – a system constructed for the white colonists to maintain power." Experiencing "differing dislocations in multiple contexts" – she is called a "gringa" (a word often used disparagingly to describe a US American woman) when traveling in Latin America, claimed as "Latina" when speaking Spanish in the United States, and perceived as "Arab" in other contexts – has led to the fracturing of her identity. Alsultany ultimately advocates for the personal and social value of claiming "in between spaces" that blur oppositional dichotomies and question essentialist assumptions based on either/or binaries. Most recently, Alsultany is among a wave of scholars writing about Arab and Arab American identities and communities – especially contesting their problematic representations after 9/11 – that further address these and additional related issues of violence and belonging from intersectional feminist perspectives (Abdulhadi, Alsultany, and Naber).

Tribal American Indian Women's Identity

Native American feminist Paula Gunn Allen's essay "Where I Come from Is Like This" (1986/1992) reflects on modern American Indian women's struggle to "reconcile traditional tribal definitions of women with industrial and postindustrial [Western] non-Indian definitions," which are often assumed to be superior by dominant society. Recognizing that there are many tribes and they approach women's identities and roles differently (ranging from women wielding power and autonomy to being devalued and viewed as a secondary adjunct to the family), she nevertheless asserts that an Indian woman's self-definition centers on her tribal identity whereby "her destiny is necessarily that of her people." That is, she cares about issues of sovereignty and self-determination that affect the whole tribal community. Moreover, a tribal definition of womanhood is quite distinct from Western cultural beliefs about womanhood largely based on sexuality, such as the madonna versus whore dichotomy and other dominant ideas about women's bodies further discussed in Chapters 4, 5, and 6. She draws on her memory of growing up as a "half-breed" with her Laguna Pueblo mother and grandmothers to offer her readers a diversity of non-romanticized images of American Indian women, claiming that although "the tribes see women variously … they do not question the power of femininity." Although one might interpret Allen's assertion as folding gender into sex and essentializing women, from a Laguna Pueblo worldview, femininity is a quality associated with human women *and* revered supernatural female figures and natural energies, and also extends beyond the female sex.

Allen also acknowledges the significant role of oral storytelling in maintaining "the fragile web of identity" for American Indian women, especially given the modern-colonial legacy of being subjected to a white, Christian education that largely represents Indians in derogatory or simplified ways (for example, as savages or "exotic curios"). It is through stories that "her tribal sense of relationship to all that is continues to flourish." Indeed, in all of the stories Allen's mother told her, "she told me who I was, who I was supposed to be, whom I came from, and who would follow me." This oral tribal education continues to counter the dehumanization and pressure to assimilate by dominant cultural institutions and works to maintain a sense of American Indian – and Laguna Pueblo, more specifically – identity and community.

Mothers and Motherwork

Akin to Allen's discussion of the significance of Native women's tribal identity accounting for the whole community in the face of cultural destruction and the imperative to survive, writers theorize the ways that "motherwork" acknowledges "that *individual* survival, empowerment, and identity require *group* survival, empowerment, and identity" (Hill Collins 59, our emphasis). Indeed, as elaborated by Black feminist sociologist Patricia Hill Collins, motherwork is the physical and emotional labor by biological *and* cultural maternal figures that aims to ensure the survival of families and communities of color in the context of the social inequalities that undermine their survival (including

reproductive and environmental justice issues discussed in Chapter 7). A similar imperative to survive in homophobic and transphobic cultural contexts and *thrive* in spite of
socially hostile environments drives LGBTQ families of all races, classes, and gender identities to create new forms of family and familial community networks. In Women's Studies
we critically study the ways that culture teaches us what it means to be a "good" or "bad"
woman in relationship to becoming or being a mother. We also take an intersectional
approach to understanding motherhood by analyzing how gender inequality, racism,
economic exploitation, and heteronormativity work together to affect the lives of
biological mothers *and* people with maternal roles across social locations. Such work
destabilizes the notions that "true" women must become mothers and maternal identity
is necessarily connected to biology or a "feminine" body, as well as the mainstream
presumption that mothering takes place within a heteronormative, nuclear family dominated by a patriarch. Such scholarship helps us to critically discern the social pressures
associated with motherhood, as well as consider the multiple ways that being a mother,
participating in motherwork, and building families is mediated by one's identity and
systems of privilege and oppression (Hill Collins; O'Reilly; Epstein; Weston; Lewin).

The "Introduction" to *Global Woman* (2002), by white feminist scholars Barbara
Ehrenreich and Arlie Russell Hochschild, also shifts the center of analysis to make visible
the stories of working mothers from underdeveloped poor countries who are largely
forced by economic necessity to leave their own children and migrate to wealthier
countries to work as nannies for the children of other women, who themselves are
choosing or are financially compelled to work outside the home in greater numbers.
Within the context of global economic inequality, this "feminization of migration" is motivated by motherwork. Many women bear the costs of being without their own families
in order to ensure their survival.

Global Identities and Transnational Communities

In addition to situating the stories of women who work as nannies within the context of
post-1970s globalization (an interactive ongoing process "between the people, companies, and governments of different nations ... driven by international trade and
investment and aided by information technology" that has accelerated with late capitalism's opening of free markets (Globalization 101), Ehrenreich and Hochschild discuss the
experiences of other domestic workers and sex workers in the contemporary global
economy. These are the three primary low-paying, largely private (and thus more
susceptible to being oppressive) jobs that "pull" migrant women from their local communities in the "systematic transfer of caring work from poor countries to rich." Engaging
with a racially, ethnically, and nationally diverse demographic of women workers, the
scholars discuss how their identities and lives are affected by global capitalism. Bringing
to bear a feminist transnational approach to the lives of migrant women includes
acknowledging the globalization of women's work, the ways migrating women maintain
social relations across national and cultural borders, and "bring[ing] the world's most
invisible women into the light ... as full human beings." As suggested by the authors,

building a sense of community and solidarity between women workers in the developed and the underdeveloped world is challenging given the vast power differences. However, doing so could potentially transform the oppressive aspects of globalization that affect everyone's lives.

Jewish Identity – Religious Minority Identity – Resisting Oppression through Community

In their essay "*In Gerangl*/In Struggle" (1986), Jewish feminist writers and activists Melanie Kaye/Kantrowitz and Irena Klepfisz with Bernice Mennis tackle oppression based on ethnic and religious identity. Since the specific social groups within the social structures of identity categories are organized into hierarchies, examining the vectors of identity also entails analyzing the systems of privilege and oppression with which they are associated. For example, in the United States within the category of religion, Christian Protestants are the dominant privileged social group and Jews, Muslims, Hindus, Buddhists, other minoritized religious groups, and Atheists are the targeted groups. The authors specifically discuss how anti-Semitism, hatred toward and/or discrimination against Jews, operates in individuals and institutions through three strategies: fostering silence (the focus of the selection excerpted in this chapter), preventing Jewish solidarity, and isolating Jews from other groups. In line with Women's Studies social justice approaches that address oppression alongside resistance, their Handbook as a whole elaborates strategies for resistance: breaking silence, building Jewish identity, pride and solidarity, and creating coalitions. Informed by consciousness-raising praxis, this guide is designed to be engaged by Jews in groups with the aim of creating a space to collectively tackle systems of anti-Semitic oppression and contradict the ways dominant society often keeps people split from their marginalized identities and each other. This contribution serves as an example of identity groups coming together in community to work toward liberation.

Queer and Exile Identities

In his contribution "losing home" (1997/2009), Eli Clare addresses the yearning to belong and feel whole in whatever community in which you find yourself. As a white, dyke and queer identified, mixed-class, disabled person who grew up in rural Oregon, left, and returned (and now identifies as a transgender man), Clare reflects on the continual process of "losing home." Feeling exiled from "home" is a common feeling that can be read in other stories documented in this chapter. Such "exile identities" bridge the experiences of those who are literally exiled as refugees from their home countries and those who are de facto exiles. As a Chicana lesbian, for example, Anzaldúa brings the experiences of these communities together in her discussion of homophobia as the "fear of going home" (1987, 19) to her cultural community as well as the fear and intolerance toward people who identify as LGBTQ.

Clare's contribution also reminds us that even social justice–oriented communities that espouse visions of inclusivity and acceptance of the "other" have blind spots and can perpetuate inequalities. He specifically critiques queer movements as largely grounded in urban, white, and somewhat affluent LGBTQ culture and with limited success at building political alliances across classes and races. Clare poignantly relates losing a connection to his rural, working-class culture and "a daily sustaining connection to a landscape" (the backwoods of Oregon) when he states, "My loss of home is about being queer," and later elaborates from an intersectional perspective, "My loss of home, my exile, is [also] about class." Clare laments the loss, or more accurately, the social conditions that occasion his loss of home (including homophobia, the lack of economic justice, cultural educational and artistic opportunities, and a queer social justice community, and the culture of violence in which he experienced severe sexual and physical abuse). His sense of identity is a "maze created by dyke identity, class location, and white rural roots" and while he has "lived among dykes and created chosen families and homes, not rooted in geography, but in shared passion, imagination, and values," he still grieves what he has lost. Clare ultimately sees leaving as necessary for his healing and queer and economic survival, and while he hates feeling exiled – "the sense of being pushed out, compelled to leave" – he cannot envision returning and somewhat accepts that "displacement, marked by my sense of never quite belonging, has become an ordinary condition in my life." Like other authors in this chapter, Clare's sense of his own intersectional identity informs his wide-ranging worldview.

Discussion Questions

1. With Gloria Anzaldúa's poem in mind, how have literal and metaphorical borders split or affected your sense of identity and community?
2. Why is living without borders and being a "crossroads" important for Anzaldúa? How might these ideas apply to analyzing any other reading in the chapter?
3. What does Evelyn Alsultany mean by "my body becomes marked with meaning as I enter public space"? Discuss this idea in relation to Eli Clare or other authors in the chapter.
4. Explain why Alsultany is wary of being otherized as well as being identified with.
5. How does Paula Gunn Allen integrate and/or negotiate her tribal identity with her understanding of American Indian womanhood? Why do you think her mother tells her to "never forget you are Indian"?
6. As suggested by "Global Woman," how are the identities and lives of mothers, nannies, maids, and sex workers produced by global capitalism?
7. What do you think is Eli Clare's main goal in telling his identity and community story? What are the various meanings of "losing home" for Clare?
8. How does anti-Semitism foster silences according to Melanie Kaye/Kantrowitz and Irena Klepfisz? How might being part of any oppressed religion affect one's sense of identity and community?

References

Abdulhadi, Rabab, Evelyn Alsultany, and Nadine Naber, eds. *Arab and Arab American Feminisms: Gender, Violence, and Belonging.* New York: Syracuse University Press, 2011.

Adams, Maurianne, Lee Anne Bell, and Pat Griffin, eds. *Teaching for Diversity and Social Justice,* 2nd ed New York: Routledge, 2007.

Anzaldúa, Gloria. 1987. *Borderlands/La Frontera: The New Mestiza,* 2nd ed. San Francisco, CA: Aunt Lute Press. 1999.

Anzaldúa, Gloria. "now let us shift … the path of conocimiento … inner work, public acts." *this bridge we call home: radical visions for transformation* Ed. Gloria E. Anzaldúa and AnaLouise Keating. New York: Routledge, 2002. 540–78.

Butler, Judith. *Gender Trouble: Feminism and the Subversion of Identity.* New York: Routledge, 1989.

Dillard, Cynthia B. "Pedagogies of Community are Pedagogies of the Spirit: Living Ubuntu." *Learning to (Re)member the Things We've Learned to Forget: Endarkened Feminisms, Spirituality, and the Sacred Nature of Research and Teaching.* New York: Peter Lang, 2012. 83–105.

Epstein, Rachel, ed. *Who's Your Daddy? And Other Writings on Queer Parenting.* Toronto: Sumach Press, 2009.

Globalization 101. A Project of SUNY Levin Institute. 25 September, 2014. http://www.globalization101.org/what-is-globalization/(last accessed December 20, 2015).

Hill Collins, Patricia. "Shifting the Center: Race, Class, and Feminist Theorizing about Motherhood." *Representations of Motherhood.* Ed. Donna Bassin, Margaret Honey, and Meryle Mahrer Kaplan. New Haven, CT: Yale University Press, 1994. 56–74.

hooks, bell. "Telling the Story." *Teaching Critical Thinking: Practical Wisdom.* New York: Routledge, 2010. 49–53.

Keating, AnaLouise. "Forging El Mundo Zurdo: Changing Ourselves, Changing the World." *this bridge we call home: radical visions for transformation.* Ed. Gloria E. Anzaldúa and AnaLouise Keating. New York: Routledge, 2002. 519–30.

King, Nia, Terra Mikalson, and Jessica Glennon-Zukoff. *Queer and Trans Artists of Color: Stories of Some of Our Lives.* CreateSpace Independent Publishing Platform, 2014.

Kirk, Gwyn, and Margo Okazawa-Rey. "Identities and Social Locations: Who am I? Who are my People?" *Women's Lives, Multicultural Perspectives.* Ed. Kirk and Okazawa-Rey. Mountain View, CA: Mayfield Publishing, 1998. 51–60.

Latina Feminist Group. *Telling to Live: Latina Feminist Testimonios.* Durham, NC: Duke University Press, 2001.

Levins Morales, Aurora. *Medicine Stories: History, Culture, and the Politics of Integrity.* Cambridge, MA: South End Press, 1998.

Lewin, Ellen. *Lesbian Mothers: Accounts of Gender in American Culture.* Ithaca, NY: Cornell University Press, 1993.

Menchú, Rigoberta. *I, Rigoberta Menchú: An Indian Woman in Guatemala.* Ed. Elisabeth Burgos-Debray. Trans. Ann Wright. London: Verso, 1984.

Merriam-Webster's Collegiate Dictionary Electronic Edition. Springfield, MA: Merriam-Webster, Inc., 2003 (Boston, MA: Credo Reference, 2012). http://search.credoreference.com.libproxy.sdsu.edu/content/entry/mwcollegiate/community/0?searchId=bdaa82ef-cc4b-11e5-8eec-1207b0fa605f&result=0 (last accessed February 2, 2016).

Moya, Paula M. L. "Introduction: Reclaiming Identity." *Reclaiming Identity: Realist Theory and the Predicament of Postmodernism.* Ed. Paula M. L. Moya and Michael Hames-Garcia. Berkeley: University of California Press, 2000. 1–28.

Moraga, Cherríe, and Gloria Anzaldúa, eds. 1981. *This Bridge Called My Back: Writings by Radical Women of Color*, 2nd ed. New York: Kitchen Table, Women of Color Press, 1983.

Muñoz, José Esteban. *Disidentifications: Queers of Color and the Performance of Politics*. Minneapolis: University of Minnesota Press, 1999.

O'Reilly, Andrea, ed. *Twenty-first Century Motherhood: Experience, Identity, Policy, Agency*. New York: Colombia, 2010.

Pérez, Laura. "Writing with Crooked Lines." *Fleshing the Spirit: Spirituality and Activism in Chicana, Latina, and Indigenous Women's Lives*. Ed. Elisa Facio and Irene Lara. Tucson: University of Arizona Press, 2014. 23–33.

Quesada, Uriel, Letitia Gomez, and Salvador Vidal-Ortiz, eds. *Queer Brown Voices: Personal Narratives of Latina/o LGBT Activism*. Austin: University of Texas Press, 2015.

Rehman, Bushra, and Daisy Hernández, eds. "Introduction." *Colonize This! Young Women of Color on Today's Feminism*. Berkeley, CA: Seal Press, 2002. xvii–xxviii.

Rojas, Maythee. "Defining Identities." *Women of Color and Feminism*. Berkeley, CA: Seal Press, 2009. 1–31.

Rothblum, Esther. "Where is the 'Women's Community?' Voices of Lesbian, Bisexual, and Queer Women, and Heterosexual Sisters." *Feminism and Psychology* 20:4 (2010): 454–72.

Solinger, Rickie, Madeline Fox, and Kayhan Irani, eds. *Telling Stories to Change the World: Global Voices on the Power of Narrative to Build Community and Make Social Justice Claims*. New York: Routledge, 2008.

Weston, Kath. *Families We Choose: Lesbians, Gays, Kinship*. New York: Columbia University Press, 1997.

2.1

To Live in the Borderlands Means You

Gloria Anzaldúa

To live in the Borderlands means you
    are neither *hispana india negra española*
    ni gabacha, eres mestiza, mulata, half-breed
    caught in the crossfire between camps
    while carrying all five races on your back
    not knowing which side to turn to, run from;

To live in the Borderlands means knowing
    that the *india* in you, betrayed for 500 years,
    is no longer speaking to you,
    that *mexicanas* call you *rajetas*,
    that denying the Anglo inside you
    is as bad as having denied the Indian or Black;

Cuando vives en la frontera
    people walk through you, the wind steals your voice,
    you're a *burra, buey*, scapegoat,
    forerunner of a new race,
    half and half – both woman and man, neither –
    a new gender;

To live in the Borderlands means to
    put *chile* in the borscht,
    eat whole wheat *tortillas,*
    speak Tex-Mex with a Brooklyn accent;
    be stopped by *la migra* at the border checkpoints;

Living in the Borderlands means you fight hard to
    resist the gold elixir beckoning from the bottle,
    the pull of the gun barrel,
    the rope crushing the hollow of your throat;

In the Borderlands
    you are the battleground
    where enemies are kin to each other;
    you are at home, a stranger,
    the border disputes have been settled
    the volley of shots have shattered the truce
    you are wounded, lost in action
    dead, fighting back;

To live in the Borderlands means
    the mill with the razor white teeth wants to shred off
    your olive-red skin, crush out the kernel, your heart
    pound you pinch you roll you out
    smelling like white bread but dead;

To survive the Borderlands
    you must live *sin fronteras*
    be a crossroads.

gabacha – a Chicano term for a white woman
rajetas – literally, "split," that is, having betrayed your word
burra – donkey
buey – oxen
sin fronteras – without borders

2.2
Los Intersticios: Recasting Moving Selves
Evelyn Alsultany

Ethnicity in such a world needs to be recast so that our moving selves can be acknowledged. … Who am I? When am I? The questions that are asked in the street, of my identity, mold me. Appearing in the flesh, I am cast afresh, a female of color – skin color, hair texture, clothing, speech, all marking me in ways that I could scarcely have conceived of.

          – Meena Alexander (66)

I'm in a graduate class at the New School in New York City. A white female sits next to me and we begin "friendly" conversation. She asks me where I'm from. I reply that I was born and raised in New York City and return the question. She tells me she is from Ohio and has lived in New York for several years. She continues her inquiry: "Oh … well, how about your parents?" (I feel her trying to map me onto her narrow cartography; New York is not a sufficient answer. She analyzes me according to binary axes of sameness and difference. She detects only difference at first glance, and seeks to pigeonhole me. In her framework, my body is marked, excluded, not from this country. A seemingly "friendly" question turns into a claim to land and belonging.) "My father is Iraqi and my mother Cuban," I answer. "How interesting. Are you a U.S. citizen?"

I am waiting for the NYC subway. A man also waiting asks me if I too am Pakistani. I reply that I'm part Iraqi and part Cuban. He asks if I am Muslim, and I reply that I am Muslim. He asks me if I am married, and I tell him I'm not. In cultural camaraderie he leans over and says that he has cousins in Pakistan available for an arranged marriage if my family so desires. (My Cubanness, as well as my own relationship to my cultural identity, evaporates as he assumes that Arab plus Muslim equals arranged marriage. I can identify: he reminds me of my Iraqi relatives and I know he means well.) I tell him that I'm not interested in marriage but thank him for his kindness. (I accept his framework and respond accordingly, avoiding an awkward situation in which he realizes that I am not who he assumes I am, offering him recognition and validation for his [mis]identification.)

I am in a New York City deli waiting for my bagel to toast. The man behind the counter asks if I'm an Arab Muslim (he too is Arab and Muslim). I reply that yes, I am by part of my father. He asks my name, and I say, "Evelyn." In utter disdain, he tells me that I could not possibly be Muslim; if I were truly Muslim I would have a Muslim name. What was I doing with such a name? I reply (after taking a deep breath and telling myself that it's not worth getting upset over) that my Cuban mother named me and that I honor my mother. He points to the fact that I'm wearing lipstick and have not changed my name, which he finds to be completely inappropriate and despicable, and says that I am a reflection of the decay of the Arab Muslim in America.

I'm on an airplane flying from Miami to New York. I'm sitting next to an Ecuadorian man. He asks me where I'm from. I tell him. He asks me if I'm more Arab, Latina, or American, and I state that I'm all of the above. He says that's impossible. I must be more of one ethnicity than another. He determines that I am not really Arab, that I'm more Latina because of the camaraderie he feels in our speaking Spanish.

I am in Costa Rica. I walk the streets and my brown skin and dark hair blend in with the multiple shades of brown around me. I love this first-time experience of blending in! I walk into a coffee shop for some café con leche, and my fantasy of belonging is shattered when the woman preparing the coffee asks me where I'm from. I tell her that I was born and raised in New York City by a Cuban mother and an Arab father. She replies, "Que eres una gringa."

I am shocked by the contextuality of identity: that my body is marked as gringa in Costa Rica, as Latina in some U.S. contexts, Arab in others, in some times and spaces not adequately Arab, or Latina, or "American," and in other contexts simply as *other*.

My body becomes marked with meaning as I enter public space.[1] My identity fractures as I experience differing dislocations in multiple contexts. Sometimes people otherize me, sometimes they identify with me. Both situations can be equally problematic. Those who otherize me fail to see a shared humanity and those who identify with me fail to see difference; my Arab or Muslim identity negates my Cuban heritage. Identification signifies belonging or home, and I pretend to be that home for the mistaken person. It's my good deed for the day (I know how precious it can be to find a moment of familiarity with a stranger). The bridge becomes my back as I feign belonging, and I become that vehicle for others, which I desire for myself. Although it is illusory, I do identify with the humanity of the situation – the desire to belong in this world, to be understood. But the frameworks used to (mis)read my body, to disconnect me, wear on me. I try to develop a new identity. What should I try to pass for next time? Perhaps I'll just say I'm Cuban to those who appear to be Arab or South Asian. A friend suggests I say I'm an Italian from Brooklyn. I wonder if I could successfully pass for that. Ethnicity needs to be recast so that our moving selves can be acknowledged.

> *They would chop me up into little fragments and tag each piece with a label. ...*
> *Who, me confused? Ambivalent? Not so. Only your labels split me.*
> *– Gloria Anzaldúa, "La Prieta" (205)*

This Bridge Called My Back revolutionized how we saw ourselves as women of color. Our experiences – unacknowledged by the dominant culture and by feminist, ethnic, and/or queer movements – were finally named. *This Bridge* insisted on a theory of the flesh through which to bridge the contradictions in our lives: "We do this bridging by naming our selves and by telling our stories in our own words" (Moraga, 23). *Bridge* authors powerfully addressed the multiple displacements women of color often experience, or what Gloria Anzaldúa calls "los intersticios:" "Alienated from her mother culture, 'alien' in the dominant culture, the woman of color does not feel safe within the inner life of her Self. Petrified, she can't respond, her face caught between *los intersticios*, the spaces between the different worlds she inhabits" (*Borderlands*, 20). Many multiethnic women identify strongly with this experience of being alienated in different ways from our various communities, trapped in a space of dislocation. Our complex selves can't be acknowledged as unified and whole.

When we're not acknowledged as complex unitary subjects, we become caught in los intersticios, haciendo caras to get by. Lisa Suhair Majaj, born to a Palestinian father and a white American mother, growing up in Lebanon and Jordan, has spent much of her life in los intersticios: "I learned to live as if in a transitional state, waiting always for the time that we would go to Palestine, to the United States, to a place where I would belong. But trips to Iowa and to Jerusalem taught me that once I got there, 'home' slipped away inexplicably materializing again just beyond reach.

If a sense of rootedness was what gave life meaning, as my parents' individual efforts to ward off alienation implied, this meaning seemed able to assume full import only in the imagination" (71). Majaj's lived experiences are not mapped out; there are no ready frameworks to understand her identity as complex and simultaneously Arab and American. She never felt like she fully belonged anywhere and found herself searching for "home," a space of belonging. Yet she recurringly experienced belonging as deferment: "In my experience cultural marginality has been among the most painful of alienations. My childhood desire, often desperate, was not so much to be a particular nationality, to be American or Arab, but to be wholly one thing or another: to be *something* that I and the rest of the world could understand, categorize, label, predict" (79, author's emphasis).

We carry this pain with us as we live in los intersticios. To "belong," we must fragment and exclude particular parts of our identity. Dislocation results from the narrow ways in which the body is read, the rigid frameworks imposed on the body in public space. At the end of the day, I'm tired of wearing masks, being misunderstood, projected upon, otherized, erased. "I am tired of being afraid to speak who I am: American and Palestinian, not merely half one thing and half of another, but both at once – and in that inexplicable melding that occurs when two cultures come together, not quite either, so that neither American nor Arab find themselves fully reflected in me, nor I in them" (Majaj, 68). Identity must be reconceptualized so that we can speak our own identities as we live and interpret them in multiple contexts. But how can we create a space for the articulation of multiethnic identities as unitary and whole rather than fragmented and dislocated?

If we change the reading/framework/lens, we can transform dislocation into location. We must reconstruct "belonging" to embrace the experiences of all human beings. As Adrian Piper (a light-skinned African-American woman who grew up in los intersticios, alienated from the black community for her light skin complexion and alienated from the white community for her blackness) has stated, "the racial categories that purport to designate any of us are too rigid and oversimplified to fit anyone accurately. But then, accuracy was never their purpose" (110).

Racial categories' purpose has usually been geopolitical. In "Dislocated Identities: Reflections of an Arab Jew," Ella Shohat discusses how today's dominant frameworks do not account for her identity as an Arab Jew and illustrates the ways in which these categories have been recently constructed as antithetical. Such frameworks have a political function. For her grandmother's generation and for hundreds of prior generations, Jewishness was inextricably linked to Arabness; they were not binary categories but logically linked: an Arab could be Muslim, Jewish, Christian, or any other faith. It was when she arrived in Israel from Iraq (as a refugee) that her grandmother had to learn such imposed constructed distinctions. New cartographies were created within which her identity became dislocated: "For Middle Easterners, the operating distinction had always been 'Muslim,' 'Jew,' and 'Christian,' not Arab versus Jew. The assumption was that 'Arabness' referred to a common shared culture and language, albeit with religious differences" (8). In the U.S. context this binarism between Arab and Jew operates, allowing for the narration of "a singular Jewish memory, i.e., a European one" (8).

Shohat's experience points to the political nature of categorization. Meanings attached to identities shift not only over time and space but also according to political circumstance. That such meanings change indicates that we can alter them. We can create a new cartography. An inability to conceptualize multiethnic persons reflects a colonial ideology of categorization and separation based on a "pure blood" criteria – a system constructed for the white colonists to maintain power. Rigid racial categories keep us separate. Multiethnic identity comes as a surprise and a danger within this framework as people attempt to place us, to make sense within the schemas available for understanding people and the world. Our identities transgress the constructed categories and become threatening. As Piper explains, "These incidents and others like them had a peculiar cognitive feel to them, as though the individuals involved felt driven to make special efforts to situate me in their conceptual mapping of the world, not only by naming or indicating the niche in which they felt I belonged, but by seeking my verbal confirmation of it … [an attempt to] locate me within the rigid confines of [their] stereotype of black people" (83).

I seek to decolonize these essentialized frameworks, so that I can move through public space without strategizing a performance, selecting a mask for each scenario. I want to expand los intersticios, creating a space for us all in our multiplicities to exist as unified subjects. It is a nonessentialist way of relating that creates a space to articulate multiple identifications and unlimited interpretations of those dimensions. This new space begins with a question: Ask me who I am. Don't project your essentialisms onto my body and then project hatred because I do not conform to your notions of who I'm supposed to be. There is no essentialized blueprint. Opening up the possibility of articulating the variety of ways we experience and negotiate our identities benefits everyone, not just the multiethnic. Recasting our moving selves begins with an openness and a willingness to listen, which leads to dialogue.

Note

I would like to thank Marisol Negrón, Alexandra Lang, María Helena Rueda, Ericka Beckman, Karina Hodoyan, Sara Rondinel, Jessi Aaron, and Cynthia María Paccacerqua for their feedback in our writing seminar at Stanford University with Mary Pratt. I would especially like to thank Mary Pratt for her invaluable feedback, and AnaLouise Keating and Gloria Anzaldúa for their thoughtful editing.

1. Although such episodes are not exclusive to "public space," I will not be dealing with the complex dynamics of "private space" in this piece.

References

Alexander, Meena. *The Shock of Arrival: Reflections on Postcolonial Experience*. Boston: South End Press, 1996.

Anzaldúa, Gloria. "La Prieta." *This Bridge Called My Back: Writings by Radical Women of Color*. Eds. Cherríe Moraga and Gloria Anzaldúa. 1981. New York: Kitchen Table/Women of Color Press, 1983. 198–209.

Anzaldúa, Gloria. *Borderlands/La frontera: The New Mestiza*. San Francisco: Aunt Lute Press, 1987.

Moraga, Cherríe. "Entering the Lives of Others: Theory in the Flesh." *This Bridge Called My Back: Writings by Radical Women of Color*. Eds. Cherríe Moraga and Gloria Anzaldúa. 1981. New York: Kitchen Table/Women of Color Press, 1983. 23.

Majaj, Lisa Suhair. "Boundaries: Arab/American." *Food for Our Grandmothers: Writings by Arab-American and Arab-Canadian Feminists*. Ed. Joanna Kadi. Boston: South End Press, 1994. 65–86.

Shohat, Ella. "Dislocated Identities: Reflections of an Arab Jew." *Movement Research: Performance Journal* #5 (Fall–Winter 1992): 8.

Piper, Adrian. "Passing for White, Passing for Black." *Talking Visions: Multicultural Feminism in a Transnational Age*. Ed. Ella Shohat. Cambridge, MA: MIT Press, 1999. 75–112.

2.3

Where I Come from is Like This

Paula Gunn Allen

I

Modern American Indian women, like their non-Indian sisters, are deeply engaged in the struggle to redefine themselves. In their struggle they must reconcile traditional tribal definitions of women with industrial and postindustrial non-Indian definitions. Yet while these definitions seem to be more or less mutually exclusive, Indian women must somehow harmonize and integrate both in their own lives.

An American Indian woman is primarily defined by her tribal identity. In her eyes, her destiny is necessarily that of her people, and her sense of herself as a woman is first and foremost prescribed by her tribe. The definitions of woman's roles are as diverse as tribal cultures in the Americas. In some she is devalued, in others she wields considerable power. In some she is a familial/clan adjunct, in some she is as close to autonomous as her economic circumstances and psychological traits permit. But in no tribal definitions is she perceived in the same way as are women in western industrial and postindustrial cultures.

In the west, few images of women form part of the cultural mythos, and these are largely sexually charged. Among Christians, the madonna is the female prototype, and she is portrayed as essentially passive: her contribution is simply that of birthing. Little else is attributed to her and she certainly possesses few of the characteristics that are attributed to mythic figures among Indian tribes. This image is countered (rather than balanced) by the witch-goddess/whore characteristics designed to reinforce cultural beliefs about women, as well as western adversarial and dualistic perceptions of reality.

The tribes see women variously, but they do not question the power of femininity. Sometimes they see women as fearful, sometimes peaceful, sometimes omnipotent and omniscient, but they never portray women as mindless, helpless, simple, or oppressed. And while the women in a given tribe, clan, or band may be all these things, the individual woman is provided with a variety of images of women from the interconnected supernatural, natural, and social worlds she lives in.

As a half-breed American Indian woman, I cast about in my mind for negative images of Indian women, and I find none that are directed to Indian women alone. The negative images I do have are of Indians in general and in fact are more often of males than of females. All these images come to me from non-Indian sources, and they are always balanced by a positive image. My ideas of womanhood, passed on largely by my mother and grandmothers, Laguna Pueblo women, are about practicality, strength, reasonableness, intelligence, wit, and competence. I also remember vividly the women who came to my father's store, the women who held me and sang to me, the women at Feast Day, at Grab Days, the women in the kitchen of my Cubero home, the women I grew up with; none of them appeared weak or helpless, none of them presented herself tentatively. I remember a certain reserve on those lovely brown faces; I remember the direct gaze of eyes framed by bright-colored shawls draped over their heads and cascading down their backs. I remember the clean cotton dresses and carefully pressed hand-embroidered aprons they always wore; I remember laughter and good food, especially the sweet bread and the oven bread they gave us. Nowhere in my mind is there a foolish woman, a dumb woman, a vain woman, or a plastic woman, though the Indian women I have known have shown a wide range of personal style and demeanor.

My memory includes the Navajo woman who was badly beaten by her Sioux husband; but I also remember that my grandmother abandoned her Sioux husband long ago. I recall the stories about the Laguna woman beaten regularly by her husband in the presence of her children so that the children would not believe in the strength and power of femininity. And I remember the women who drank, who got into fights with other women and with the men, and who often won those battles. I have memories of tired women, partying women, stubborn women, sullen women, amicable women, selfish women, shy women, and aggressive women. Most of all I remember the women who laugh and scold and sit uncomplaining in the long sun on feast days and who cook wonderful food on wood stoves, in beehive mud ovens, and over open fires outdoors.

Among the images of women that come to me from various tribes as well as my own are White Buffalo Woman, who came to the Lakota long ago and brought them the religion of the Sacred Pipe which they still practice; Tinotzin [Tonantzin] the goddess who came to Juan Diego to remind him that she still walked the hills of her people and sent him with her message, her demand and her proof to the Catholic bishop in the city nearby. And from Laguna I take the images of Yellow Woman, Coyote Woman, Grandmother Spider (Spider Old Woman), who brought the light, who gave us weaving and medicine, who gave us life. Among the Keres she is known as Thought Woman who created us all and who keeps us in creation even now. I remember Iyatiku, Earth Woman, Corn Woman, who guides and counsels the people to peace and who welcomes us home when we cast off this coil of flesh as huskers cast off the leaves that wrap the corn. I remember Iyatiku's sister, Sun Woman, who held metals and cattle, pigs and sheep, highways and engines and so many things in her bundle, who went away to the east saying that one day she would return.

II

Since the coming of the Anglo-Europeans beginning in the fifteenth century, the fragile web of identity that long held tribal people secure has gradually been weakened and torn. But the oral tradition has prevented the complete destruction of the web, the ultimate disruption of tribal ways. The oral tradition is vital; it heals itself and the tribal web by adapting to the flow of the present while never relinquishing its connection to the past. Its adaptability has always been required, as many generations have experienced. Certainly the modern American Indian woman bears slight resemblance to her forebears – at least on superficial examination – but she is still a tribal woman in her deepest being. Her tribal sense of relationship to all that is continues to flourish. And though she is at times beset by her knowledge of the enormous gap between the life she lives and the life she was raised to live, and while she adapts her mind and being to the circumstances of her present life, she does so in tribal ways, mending the tears in the web of being from which she takes her existence as she goes.

My mother told me stories all the time, though I often did not recognize them as that. My mother told me stories about cooking and childbearing; she told me stories about menstruation and pregnancy; she told me stories about gods and heroes, about fairies and elves, about goddesses and spirits; she told me stories about the land and the sky, about cats and dogs, about snakes and spiders; she told me stories about climbing trees and exploring the mesas; she told me stories about going to dances and getting married; she told me stories about dressing and undressing, about sleeping and waking; she told me stories about herself, about her mother, about her grandmother. She told me stories about grieving and laughing, about thinking and doing; she told me stories about school and about people; about darning and mending; she told me stories about turquoise and about gold; she told me European stories and Laguna stories; she told me Catholic stories and Presbyterian stories; she told me city stories and country stories; she told me political stories and religious stories. She told me stories about living and stories about dying. And in all of those stories she told me who I was, who I was supposed to be, whom I came from, and who would follow me. In this way she taught me the meaning of the words she said, that all life is a circle and everything has a place within it. That's what she said and what she showed me in the things she did and the way she lives.

Of course, through my formal, white, Christian education, I discovered that other people had stories of their own – about women, about Indians, about fact, about reality – and I was amazed by a number of startling suppositions that others made about tribal customs and beliefs. According to the un-Indian, non-Indian view, for instance, Indians barred menstruating women from ceremonies and indeed segregated them from the rest of the people, consigning them to some space specially designed for them. This showed that Indians considered menstruating women unclean and not fit to enjoy the company of decent (nonmenstruating) people, that is, men. I was surprised and confused to hear this because my mother had taught me that white people had strange attitudes toward menstruation: they thought something was bad about it, that it meant you were sick, cursed, sinful, and weak and that you had to be very careful during that time. She taught me that menstruation was a normal occurrence, that I could go swimming or hiking or whatever else I wanted to do during my period. She actively scorned women who took to their beds, who were incapacitated by cramps, who "got the blues."

As I struggled to reconcile these very contradictory interpretations of American Indians' traditional beliefs concerning menstruation, I realized that the menstrual taboos were about power, not about sin or filth. My conclusion was later borne out by some tribes' own explanations, which, as you may well imagine, came as quite a relief to me.

The truth of the matter as many Indians see it is that women who are at the peak of their fecundity are believed to possess power that throws male power totally out of kilter. They emit such force that, in their presence, any male-owned or -dominated ritual or sacred object cannot do its usual task. For instance, the Lakota say that a menstruating woman anywhere near a yuwipi man, who is a special sort of psychic, spirit-empowered healer, for a day or so before he is to do his ceremony will effectively disempower him. Conversely, among many if not most tribes, important ceremonies cannot be held without the presence of women. Sometimes the ritual woman who empowers the ceremony must be unmarried and virginal so that the power she channels is unalloyed, unweakened by sexual arousal and penetration by a male. Other ceremonies require tumescent women, others the presence of mature women who have borne children, and still others depend for empowerment on postmenopausal women. Women may be segregated from the company of the whole band or village on certain occasions, but on certain occasions men are also segregated. In short, each ritual depends on a certain balance of power, and the positions of women within the phases of womanhood are used by tribal people to empower certain rites. This does not derive from a male-dominant view; it is not a ritual observance imposed on women by men. It derives from a tribal view of reality that distinguishes tribal people from feudal and industrial people.

Among the tribes, the occult power of women, inextricably bound to our hormonal life, is thought to be very great; many hold that we possess innately the blood-given power to kill – with a glance, with a step, or with a judicious mixing of menstrual blood into somebody's soup. Medicine women among the Pomo of California cannot practice until they are sufficiently mature; when they are immature, their power is diffuse and is likely to interfere with their practice until time and experience have it under control. So women of the tribes are not especially inclined to see themselves as poor helpless victims of male domination. Even in those tribes where something akin to male domination was present, women are perceived as powerful, socially, physically, and metaphysically. In times past, as in times present, women carried enormous burdens with aplomb. We were far indeed from the "weaker sex," the designation that white aristocratic sisters unhappily earned for us all.

I remember my mother moving furniture all over the house when she wanted it changed. She didn't wait for my father to come home and help – she just went ahead and moved the piano, a huge upright from the old days, the couch, the refrigerator. Nobody had told her she was too weak to do such things. In imitation of her, I would delight in loading trucks at my father's store with cases of pop or fifty-pound sacks of flour. Even when I was quite small I could do it, and it gave me a belief in my own physical strength that advancing middle age can't quite erase. My mother used to tell me about the Acoma Pueblo women she had seen as a child carrying huge ollas (water pots) on their heads as they wound their way up the tortuous stairwell carved into the face of the "Sky City" mesa, a feat I tried to imitate with books and tin buckets. ("Sky City" is the term used by the Chamber of Commerce for the mother village of Acoma, which is situated atop a high sandstone table mountain.) I was never very successful, but even the attempt reminded me that I was supposed to be strong and balanced to be a proper girl.

Of course, my mother's Laguna people are Keres Indian, reputed to be the last extreme mother-right people on earth. So it is no wonder that I got notably non-white notions about the natural strength and prowess of women. Indeed, it is only when I am trying to get non-Indian approval, recognition, or acknowledgment that my "weak sister" emotional and intellectual ploys get the better of my tribal woman's good sense. At such times I forget that I just moved the piano or just wrote a competent paper or just completed a financial transaction satisfactorily or have supported myself and my children for most of my adult life.

Nor is my contradictory behavior atypical. Most Indian women I know are in the same bicultural bind: we vacillate between being dependent and strong, self-reliant and powerless, strongly motivated and hopelessly insecure. We resolve the dilemma in various ways: some of us party all the time; some of us drink to excess; some of us travel and move around a lot; some of us land good jobs and then quit them; some of us engage in violent exchanges; some of us blow our brains out. We act in these destructive ways because we suffer from the societal conflicts caused by having to identify with two hopelessly opposed cultural definitions of women. Through this destructive dissonance we are unhappy prey to the self-disparagement common to, indeed demanded of, Indians living in the United States today. Our situation is caused by the exigencies of a history of invasion, conquest, and colonization whose searing marks are probably ineradicable. A popular bumper sticker on many Indian cars proclaims: "If You're Indian You're In," to which I always find myself adding under my breath, "Trouble."

III

No Indian can grow to any age without being informed that her people were "savages" who interfered with the march of progress pursued by respectable, loving, civilized white people. We are the villains of the scenario when we are mentioned at all.

We are absent from much of white history except when we are calmly, rationally, succinctly, and systematically dehumanized. On the few occasions we are noticed in any way other than as howling, bloodthirsty beings, we are acclaimed for our noble quaintness. In this definition, we are exotic curios. Our ancient arts and customs are used to draw tourist money to state coffers, into the pocketbooks and bank accounts of scholars, and into support of the American-in-Disneyland promoters' dream.

As a Roman Catholic child I was treated to bloody tales of how the savage Indians martyred the hapless priests and missionaries who went among them in an attempt to lead them to the one true path. By the time I was through high school I had the idea that Indians were people who had benefited mightily from the advanced knowledge and superior morality of the Anglo-Europeans. At least I had, perforce, that idea to lay beside the other one that derived from my daily experience of Indian life, an idea less dehumanizing and more accurate because it came from my mother and the other Indian people who raised me. That idea was that Indians are a people who don't tell lies, who care for their children and their old people. You never see an Indian orphan, they said. You always know when you're old that someone will take care of you – one of your children will. Then they'd list the old folks who were being taken care of by this child or that. No child is ever considered illegitimate among the Indians, they said. If a girl gets pregnant, the baby is still part of the family, and the mother is too. That's what they said, and they showed me real people who lived according to those principles.

Of course the ravages of colonization have taken their toll; there are orphans in Indian country now, and abandoned, brutalized old folks; there are even illegitimate children, though the very concept still strikes me as absurd. There are battered children and neglected children, and there are battered wives and women who have been raped by Indian men. Proximity to the "civilizing" effects of white Christians has not improved the moral quality of life in Indian country, though each group, Indian and white, explains the situation differently. Nor is there much yet in the oral tradition that can enable us to adapt to these inhuman changes. But a force is growing in that direction, and it is helping Indian women reclaim their lives. Their power, their sense of direction and of self will soon be visible. It is the force of the women who speak and work and write, and it is formidable.

Through all the centuries of war and death and cultural and psychic destruction have endured the women who raise the children and tend the fires, who pass along the tales and the traditions, who weep and bury the dead, who are the dead, and who never forget. There are always the women, who make pots and weave baskets, who fashion clothes and cheer their children on at powwow, who make fry bread and piki bread, and corn soup and chili stew, who dance and sing and remember and hold within their hearts the dream of their ancient peoples – that one day the woman who thinks will speak to us again, and everywhere there will be peace. Meanwhile we tell the stories and write the books and trade tales of anger and woe and stories of fun and scandal and laugh over all manner of things that happen every day. We watch and we wait.

My great-grandmother told my mother: Never forget you are Indian. And my mother told me the same thing. This, then, is how I have gone about remembering, so that my children will remember too.

2.4

Introduction to *Global Woman: Nannies, Maids, and Sex Workers in the New Economy*

Barbara Ehrenreich and Arlie Russell Hochschild

"Whose baby are you?" Josephine Perera, a nanny from Sri Lanka, asks Isadora, her pudgy two-year-old charge in Athens, Greece.

Thoughtful for a moment, the child glances toward the closed door of the next room, in which her mother is working, as if to say, "That's my mother in there."

"No, you're *my* baby," Josephine teases, tickling Isadora lightly. Then, to settle the issue, Isadora answers, "Together!" She has two mommies – her mother and Josephine. And surely a child loved by many adults is richly blessed.

In some ways, Josephine's story – which unfolds in an extraordinary documentary film, *When Mother Comes Home for Christmas*, directed by Nilita Vachani – describes an unparalleled success. Josephine has ventured around the world, achieving a degree of independence her mother could not have imagined, and amply support-ing her three children with no help from her ex-husband, their father. Each month she mails a remittance check from Athens to Hatton, Sri Lanka, to pay the children's living expenses and school fees. On her Christmas visit home, she bears gifts of pots, pans, and dishes. While she makes payments on a new bus that Suresh, her oldest son, now drives for a living, she is also saving for a modest dowry for her daughter, Norma. She dreams of buying a new house in which the whole family can live. In the meantime, her work as a nanny enables Isadora's parents to devote themselves to their careers and avocations.

But Josephine's story is also one of wrenching global inequality. While Isadora enjoys the attention of three adults, Josephine's three children in Sri Lanka have been far less lucky. According to Vachani, Josephine's youngest child, Suminda, was two – Isadora's age – when his mother first left home to work in Saudi Arabia. Her middle child, Norma, was nine; her oldest son, Suresh, thirteen. From Saudi Arabia, Josephine found her way first to Kuwait, then to Greece. Except for one two-month trip home, she has lived apart from her children for ten years. She writes them weekly letters, seeking news of relatives, asking about school, and complaining that Norma doesn't write back.

Although Josephine left the children under her sister's supervision, the two youn-gest have shown signs of real distress. Norma has attempted suicide three times.

Suminda, who was twelve when the film was made, boards in a grim, Dickensian orphanage that forbids talk during meals and showers. He visits his aunt on holidays. Although the oldest, Suresh, seems to be on good terms with his mother, Norma is tearful and sullen, and Suminda does poorly in school, picks quarrels, and otherwise seems withdrawn from the world. Still, at the end of the film, we see Josephine once again leave her three children in Sri Lanka to return to Isadora in Athens. For Josephine can either live with her children in desperate poverty or make money by living apart from them. Unlike her affluent First World employers, she cannot both live with her family and support it.

Thanks to the process we loosely call "globalization," women are on the move as never before in history. In images familiar to the West from television commercials for credit cards, cell phones, and airlines, female executives jet about the world, phoning home from luxury hotels and reuniting with eager children in airports. But we hear much less about a far more prodigious flow of female labor and energy: the increasing migration of millions of women from poor countries to rich ones, where they serve as nannies, maids, and sometimes sex workers. In the absence of help from male partners, many women have succeeded in tough "male world" careers only by turning over the care of their children, elderly parents, and homes to women from the Third World. This is the female underside of globalization, whereby millions Josephines from poor countries in the south migrate to do the "women's work" of the north – work that affluent women are no longer able or willing to do. These migrant workers often leave their own children in the care of grandmothers, sisters, and sisters-in-law. Sometimes a young daughter is drawn out of school to care for her younger siblings.

This pattern of female migration reflects what could be called a worldwide gender revolution. In both rich and poor countries, fewer families can rely solely on a male breadwinner. In the United States, the earning power of most men has declined since 1970, and many women have gone out to "make up the difference." By one recent estimate, women were the sole, primary, or coequal earners in more than half of American families.[1] So the question arises: Who will take care of the children, the sick, the elderly? Who will make dinner and clean house?

While the European or American woman commutes to work an average twenty-eight minutes a day, many nannies from the Philippines, Sri Lanka, and India cross the globe to get to their jobs. Some female migrants from the Third World do find something like "liberation," or at least the chance to become independent breadwinners and to improve their children's material lives. Other, less fortunate migrant women end up in the control of criminal employers – their passports stolen, their mobility blocked, forced to work without pay in brothels or to provide sex along with cleaning and child-care services in affluent homes. But even in more typical cases, where benign employers pay wages on time, Third World migrant women achieve their success only by assuming the cast-off domestic roles of middle- and high-income women in the First World – roles that have been previously rejected, of course, by men. And their "commute" entails a cost we have yet to fully comprehend.

The migration of women from the Third World to do "women's work" in affluent countries has so far received little scholarly or media attention – for reasons that are easy enough to guess. First, many, though by no means all, of the new female migrant workers are women of color, and therefore subject to the racial "discounting" routinely experienced by, say, Algerians in France, Mexicans in the United States, and Asians in the United Kingdom. Add to racism the private "indoor" nature of so much of the new migrants' work. Unlike factory workers, who congregate in large numbers, or taxi drivers, who are visible on the street, nannies and maids are often hidden away, one or two at a time, behind closed doors in private homes. Because of the illegal nature of their work, most sex workers are even further concealed from public view.

At least in the case of nannies and maids, another factor contributes to the invisibility of migrant women and their work – one that, for their affluent employers, touches closer to home. The Western culture of individualism, which finds extreme expression in the United States, militates against acknowledging help or human interdependency of nearly any kind. Thus, in the time-pressed upper middle class, servants are no longer displayed as status symbols, decked out in white caps and aprons, but often remain in the background, or disappear when company comes. Furthermore, affluent careerwomen increasingly earn their status not through leisure, as they might have a century ago, but by apparently "doing it all" – producing a full-time career, thriving children, a contented spouse, and a well-managed home. In order to preserve this illusion, domestic workers and nannies make the house hotel-room perfect, feed and bathe the children, cook and clean up – and then magically fade from sight.

The lifestyles of the First World are made possible by a global transfer of the services associated with a wife's traditional role – child care, homemaking, and sex – from poor countries to rich ones. To generalize and perhaps oversimplify: in an earlier phase of imperialism, northern countries extracted natural resources and agricultural products – rubber, metals, and sugar, for example – from lands they conquered and colonized. Today, while still relying on Third World countries for agricultural and industrial labor, the wealthy countries also seek to extract something harder to measure and quantify, something that can look very much like love. Nannies like Josephine bring the distant families that employ them real maternal affection, no doubt enhanced by the heartbreaking absence of their own children in the poor countries they leave behind. Similarly, women who migrate from country to country to work as maids bring not only their muscle power but an attentiveness to detail and to the human relationships in the household that might otherwise have been invested in their own families. Sex workers offer the simulation of sexual and romantic love, or at least transient sexual companionship. It is as if the wealthy parts of the world are running short on emotional and sexual resources and have had to turn to poorer regions for fresh supplies.

There are plenty of historical precedents for this globalization of traditional female services. In the ancient Middle East, the women of populations defeated in war were routinely enslaved and hauled off to serve as household workers and concubines for the victors. Among the Africans brought to North America as slaves in the sixteenth through nineteenth centuries, about a third were women and children, and many of those women were pressed to concubines, domestic servants, or both. Nineteenth-century Irishwomen – along with many rural Englishwomen – migrated to English towns and cities to work as domestics in the homes of the growing upper middle class. Services thought to be innately feminine – child care, housework, and sex – often win little recognition or pay. But they have always been sufficiently in demand to transport over long distances if necessary. What is new today is the sheer number of female migrants and the very long distances they travel. Immigration statistics show huge numbers of women in motion, typically from poor countries to rich. Although the gross statistics give little clue· as to the jobs women eventually take, there are reasons to infer that much of their work is "caring work," performed either in private homes or in institutional settings such as hospitals, hospices, child-care centers, and nursing homes.

The statistics are, in many ways, frustrating. We have information on legal migrants but not on illegal migrants,[2] who, experts tell us, travel in equal if not greater numbers. Furthermore, many Third World countries lack data for past years, which makes it hard to trace trends over time; or they use varying methods of gathering information, which makes it hard to compare one country with another. Nevertheless, the trend is clear enough for some scholars, including Stephen Castles, Mark Miller, and Janet Momsen, to speak of a "feminization of migration."[3] From 1950 to 1970, for example, men predominated in labor migration to northern Europe from Turkey, Greece, and North Africa. Since then, women have been replacing men. In 1946, women were fewer than 3 percent of the Algerians and Moroccans living France; by 1990, they were more than 40 percent.[4] Overall, half of the world's 120 million legal and illegal migrants are now believed to be women.

Patterns of international migration vary from region to region, but women migrants from a surprising number of sending countries actually outnumber men, sometimes by a wide margin. For example, in the 1990s, women make up over half of Filipino migrants to all countries and 84 percent of Sri Lankan migrants to the Middle East.[5] Indeed, by 1993 statistics, Sri Lankan women such as Josephine vastly outnumbered Sri Lankan men as migrant workers who'd left for Saudi Arabia, Kuwait, Lebanon, Oman, Bahrain, Jordan, and Qatar, as well as to all countries of the Far East, Africa, and Asia.[6] About half of the migrants leaving Mexico, India, Korea, Malaysia, Cyprus, and Swaziland to work elsewhere are also women. Throughout the 1990s women outnumbered men among migrants to the United States, Canada, Sweden, the United Kingdom, Argentina, and Israel.[7]

Most women, like men, migrate from the south to the north and from poor countries to rich ones. Typically, migrants go to the nearest comparatively rich country, preferably one whose language they speak or whose religion and culture they share. There are also local migratory flows: from northern to southern Thailand, for instance, or from East Germany to West. But of the regional or cross-regional flows, four stand out. One goes from Southeast Asia to the oil-rich Middle and Far East – from Bangladesh, Indonesia, the Philippines, and Sri Lanka to Bahrain,

Oman, Kuwait, Saudi Arabia, Hong Kong, Malaysia, and Singapore. Another stream of migration goes from the former Soviet bloc to western Europe – from Russia, Romania, Bulgaria, and Albania to Scandinavia, Germany, France, Spain, Portugal, and England. A third goes from south to north in the Americas, including the stream from Mexico to the United States, which scholars say is the longest-running labor migration in the world. A fourth stream moves from Africa to various parts of Europe. France receives many female migrants from Morocco, Tunisia, and Algeria. Italy receives female workers from Ethiopia, Eritrea, and Cape Verde.

Female migrants overwhelmingly take up work as maids or domestics. As women have become an ever greater proportion of migrant workers, receiving countries reflect a dramatic influx of foreign-born domestics. In the United States, African-American women, who accounted for 60 percent of domestics in the 1940s, have been largely replaced by Latinas, many of them recent migrants from Mexico and Central America. In England, Asian migrant women have displaced the Irish and Portuguese domestics of the past. In French cities, North African women have replaced rural French girls. In West Germany, Turks and women from the former East Germany have replaced rural native-born women. Foreign females from countries outside the European Union made up only 6 percent of all domestic workers in 1984. By 1987, the percentage had jumped to 52, with most coming from the Sri Lanka, Thailand, Argentina, Colombia, Brazil, El Salvador, and Peru.[8]

The governments of some sending countries actively encourage women to migrate in search of domestic jobs, reasoning that migrant women are more likely than their male counterparts to send their hard-earned wages to their families rather than spending the money on themselves. In general, women send home anywhere from half to nearly all of what they earn. These remittances have a significant impact on the lives of children, parents, siblings, and wider networks of kin – as well as on cash-strapped Third World governments. Thus, before Josephine left for Athens, a program sponsored by the Sri Lankan government taught her how to use a microwave oven, a vacuum cleaner, and an electric mixer. As she awaited her flight, a song piped into the airport departure lounge extolled the opportunity to earn money abroad. The songwriter was in the pay of the Sri Lanka Bureau of Foreign Employment, an office devised to encourage women to migrate. They lyrics say:

> *After much hardship, such difficult times,*
> *How lucky I am to work in a foreign land.*
> *As the gold gathers so do many greedy flies.*
> *But our good government protects us from them.*
> *After much hardship, such difficult times,*
> *How lucky I am to work in a foreign land.*
> *I promise to return home with treasures for everyone.*

Why this transfer of women's traditional services from poor to rich parts of the world? The reasons are, in a crude way, easy to guess. Women in Western countries have increasingly taken on paid work, and hence need other – paid domestics and caretakers for children and elderly people – to replace them.[9] For their part, women in poor countries have an obvious incentive to migrate: relative and absolute poverty. The "care deficit" that has emerged in the wealthier countries as women enter the workforce *pulls* migrants from the Third World and postcommunist nations; poverty *pushes* them.

In broad outline, this explanation holds true. Throughout western Europe, Taiwan, and Japan, but above all in the United States, England, and Sweden, women's employment has increased dramatically since the 1970s. In the United States, for example, the proportion of women in paid work rose from 15 percent of mothers of children six and under in 1950 to 65 percent today. Women now make up 46 percent of the U.S. labor force. Three-quarters of mothers of children eighteen and under and nearly two-thirds of mothers of children age one and younger now work for pay. Furthermore, according to a recent International Labor Organization study, working Americans averaged longer hours at work in the late 1990s than they did in the 1970s. By some measures, the number of hours spent at work have increased more for women than for men, and especially for women in managerial and professional jobs.

Meanwhile, over the last thirty years, as the rich countries have grown much richer, the poor countries have become – in both absolute and relative terms – poorer. Global inequalities in wages are particularly striking. In Hong Kong, for instance, the wages of a Filipina domestic are about fifteen times the amount she could make as a schoolteacher back in the Philippines. In addition, poor countries turning to the IMF or World Bank for loans are often forced to undertake measures of so-called structural adjustment, with disastrous results for the poor and especially for poor women and children. To qualify for loans, governments are usually required to devalue their currencies, which turns the hard currencies of rich countries into gold and the soft currencies of poor countries into straw. Structural adjustment programs also call for cuts in support for "noncompetitive industries," and for the reduction of public services such as health care and food subsidies for the poor. Citizens of poor countries, women as well as men, thus have a strong incentive to seek work in more fortunate parts of the world.

But it would be a mistake to attribute the globalization of women's work to a simple synergy of needs among women – one group, in the affluent countries, needing help and the other, in poor countries, needing jobs. For one thing, this formulation fails to account for the marked failure of First World governments to meet the needs created by its women's entry into the workforce. The downsized American – and to a lesser degree, western European – welfare state has become a "deadbeat dad." Unlike the rest of the industrialized world, the United States does not offer public child care for working mothers, nor does it ensure paid family and medical leave. Moreover, a series of state tax revolts in the 1980s reduced the number of hours public libraries were open and slashed school-enrichment and after-school programs. Europe did not experience anything comparable. Still, tens of millions of western European women are in the workforce who were not before – and there has been no proportionate expansion in public services.

Secondly, any view of the globalization of domestic work as simply an arrangement among women completely omits the role of men. Numerous studies, including some of our own, have shown that as American women took on paid employment, the men in their families did little to increase their contribution to the work of the home. For example, only one out of every five men among the working couples whom Hochschild interviewed for *The Second Shift* in the 1980s shared the work at home, and later studies suggest that while working mothers are doing somewhat less housework than their counterparts twenty years ago, most men are doing only a little more.[10] With divorce, men frequently abdicate their child-care responsibilities to their ex-wives. In most cultures of the First World outside the United States, powerful traditions even more firmly discourage husbands from doing "women's work." So, strictly speaking, the presence of immigrant nannies does not enable affluent women to enter the workforce; it enables affluent *men* to continue avoiding the second shift.

The men in wealthier countries are also, of course, directly responsible for the demand for immigrant sex workers – as well as for the sexual abuse of many migrant women who work as domestics. Why, we wondered, is there a particular demand for "imported" sexual partners? Part of the answer may lie in the fact that new immigrants often take up the least desirable work, and, thanks to the AIDS epidemic, prostitution has become a job that ever fewer women deliberately choose. But perhaps some of this demand, grows out of the erotic lure of the "exotic." Immigrant women may seem desirable sexual partners for the same reason that First World employers believe them to be especially gifted as caregivers: they are thought to embody the traditional feminine qualities of nurturance, docility, and eagerness to please. Some men feel nostalgic for these qualities, which they associate with a bygone way of life. Even as many wage-earning Western women assimilate to the competitive culture of "male" work and ask respect for making it in a man's world, some men seek in the "exotic Orient" or "hot-blooded tropics" a woman from the imagined past.

Of course, not all sex workers migrate voluntarily. An alarming number of women and girls are trafficked by smugglers and sold into bondage. Because trafficking is illegal and secret, the numbers are hard to know with any certainty. Kevin Bales estimates that in Thailand alone, a country of 60 million, half a million to a million women are prostitutes, and one out of every twenty of these is enslaved.[11] Many of these women are daughters whom northern hill-tribe families have sold to brothels in the cities of the south. Believing the promises of jobs and money, some begin the voyage willingly, only to discover days later that the "arrangers" are traffickers who steal their passports, define them as debtors, and enslave them as prostitutes. Other women and girls are kidnapped, or sold by their impoverished families, and then trafficked to brothels. Even worse fates befall women from neighboring Laos and Burma, who flee crushing poverty and repression at home only to fall into the hands of Thai slave traders.

If the factors that pull migrant women workers to affluent countries are not as simple as they at first appear, neither are the factors that push them. Certainly relative poverty plays a major role, but, interestingly, migrant women often do not come from the poorest classes of their societies.[12] In fact, they are typically more affluent and better educated than male migrants. Many female migrants from the Philippines and Mexico, for example, have high school or college diplomas and have held middle-class – albeit low paid – jobs back home. One study of Mexican migrants suggests that the trend is toward increasingly better-educated female migrants. Thirty years ago, most Mexican-born maids in the United States had been poorly educated maids in Mexico. Now a majority have high school degrees and have held clerical, retail, or professional jobs before leaving for the United States.[13] Such women are likely to be enterprising and adventurous enough to resist the social pressures to stay home and accept their lot in life.

Noneconomic factors – or at least factors that are not immediately and directly economic – also influence a woman's decision to emigrate. By migrating, a woman may escape the expectation that she care for elderly family members, relinquish her paycheck to a husband or father, or defer to an abusive husband. Migration may also be a practical response to a failed marriage and the need to provide for children without male help. In the Philippines, contributor Rhacel Salazar Parreñas tells us, migration is sometimes called a "Philippine divorce." And there are forces at work that may be making the men of poor countries less desirable as husbands. Male unemployment runs high in the countries that supply female domestics to the First World. Unable to make a living, these men often grow demoralized and cease contributing to their families in other ways. Many female migrants tell of unemployed husbands who drink or gamble their remittances away. Notes one study of Sri Lankan women working as maids in the Persian Gulf: "It is not unusual … for the women to find upon their return that their Gulf wages by and large have been squandered on alcohol, gambling and other dubious undertakings while they were away."[14]

To an extent then, the globalization of child care and housework brings the ambitious and independent women of the world together: the career-oriented upper-middle-class woman of an affluent nation and the striving woman from a crumbling Third World or postcommunist economy. Only it does not bring them together in the way that second-wave feminists in affluent countries once liked to imagine – as sisters and allies struggling to achieve common goals. Instead, they come together as mistress and maid, employer and employee, across a great divide of privilege and opportunity.

This trend toward global redivision of women's traditional work throws a new light on the entire process of globalization. Conventionally, it is the poorer countries that are thought to be dependent on the richer ones – a dependency symbolized by the huge debt they owe to global financial institutions. What we explore in this book, however, is a dependency that works in the other direction, and it is a dependency of a particularly intimate kind. Increasingly often, as affluent and middle-class families in the First World come to depend on migrants from poorer regions to provide child care, homemaking, and sexual services, a global relationship arises that in some ways mirrors the traditional relationship between the sexes. The First World takes on a role like that of the old-fashioned male in the family – pampered, entitled, unable to cook, clean, or find his socks. Poor countries take on a role like that of the traditional woman within the family – patient, nurturing, and self-denying. A division of labor feminists critiqued when it was "local" has now, metaphorically speaking, gone global.

To press this metaphor a bit further, the resulting relationship is by no means a "marriage," in the sense of being openly acknowledged. In fact, it is striking how invisible the globalization of women's work remains, how little it is noted or discussed in the First World. Trend spotters have had almost nothing to say about the fact that increasing numbers of affluent First World children and elderly persons are tended by immigrant care workers or live in homes cleaned by immigrant maids. Even the political groups we might expect to be concerned about this trend – antiglobalization and feminist activists – often seem to have noticed only the most extravagant abuses, such as trafficking and female enslavement. So if a metaphorically gendered relationship has developed between rich and poor countries, it is less like a marriage and more like a secret affair.

But it is a "secret affair" conducted in plain view of the children. Little Isadora and the other children of the First World raised by "two mommies" may be learning more than their ABC's from a loving surrogate parent. In their own living rooms, they are learning a vast and tragic global politics.[15] Children see. But they also learn how to disregard what they see. They learn how adults make the visible invisible. That is their "early childhood education."

The globalization of women's traditional role poses important challenges to anyone concerned about gender and economic inequity. How can we improve the lives and opportunities of migrant women engaged in legal occupations such as nannies and maids? How can we prevent trafficking and enslavement? More basically, can we find a way to counterbalance the systematic transfer of caring work from poor countries to rich, and the inevitable trauma of the children left behind? Before we can hope to find activist solutions, we need to see these women as full human beings. They are strivers as well as victims, wives and mothers as well as workers – sisters, in other words, with whom we in the First World may someday define a common agenda.

Notes

1. See Ellen Galinsky and Dana Friedman, *Women: The New Providers*, Whirlpool Foundation Study, Part 1 (New York: Families and Work Institute, 1995), p. 37.
2. Editors' note: It is important to note the discursive shift toward using "documented" and "undocumented" to describe migrants instead of "legal" and "illegal" because these terms problematically link human beings to criminality. In 2013, the Associated Press and several newspapers changed their stylebook accordingly.
3. In addition to material directly cited, this introduction draws from the following works: Kathleen M. Adams and Sara Dickey, eds., *Home and Hegemony: Domestic Service and Identity Politics* in *South and Southeast Asia* (Ann Arbor: University of Michigan Press, 2000); Floya Anthias and Gabriella Lazaridis, eds., *Gender and Migration* in *Southern*

Europe: Women on the Move (Oxford and New York: Berg, 2000); Stephen Castles and Mark J. Miller, *The Age of Migration: International Population Movements in the Modern World* (New York and London: The Guilford Press, 1998); Noeleen Heyzer, Geertje Lycklama à Nijehold, and Nedra Weerakoon, eds., *The Trade in Domestic Workers: Causes, Mechanisms, and Consequences of International Migration* (London: Zed Books, 1994); Eleanore Kofman, Annie Phizacklea, Parvati Raghuram, and Rosemary Sales, *Gender and International Migration* in *Europe: Employment, Welfare, and Politics* (New York and London: Routledge, 2000); Douglas S. Massey, Joaquin Arango, Graeme Hugo, Ali Kouaouci, Adela Pellegrino, and J. Edward Taylor, *Worlds in Motion: Understanding International Migration at the End of the Millennium* (Oxford: Clarendon Press, 1999); Janet Henshall Momsen, ed., *Gender, Migration, and Domestic Service* (London: Routledge, 1999); Katie Willis and Brenda Yeoh, eds., *Gender and Immigration* (London: Edward Elgar Publishers, 2000).

4. Illegal migrants are said to make up anywhere from 60 percent (as in Sri Lanka) to 87 percent (as in Indonesia) of all migrants. In Singapore in 1994, 95 percent of Filipino overseas contract workers lacked work permits from the Philippine government. The official figures based on legal migration therefore severely underestimate the number of migrants. See Momsen, 1999, p. 7.

5. Momsen, 1999, p. 9.

6. Sri Lanka Bureau of Foreign Employment, 1994, as cited in G. Gunatilleke, *The Economic, Demographic, Sociocultural and Political Setting for Emigration from Sri Lanka International Migration*, vol. 23 (3/4), 1995, pp. 667–98.

7. Anthias and Lazaridis, 2000; Heyzer, Nijehold, and Weerakoon, 1994, pp. 4–27; Momsen, 1999, p. 21; "Wistat: Women's Indicators and Statistics Database," version 3, CD-ROM (United Nations, Department for Economic and Social Information and Policy Analysis, Statistical Division, 1994).

8. Geovanna Campani, "Labor Markets and Family Networks: Filipino Women in Italy," in Hedwig Rudolph and Mirjana Morokvasic, eds., *Bridging States and Markets: International Migration in the Early 1990s* (Berlin: Edition Sigma, 1993), p. 206.

9. This "new" source of the Western demand for nannies, maids, child-care, and elder-care workers does not, of course, account for the more status-oriented demand in the Persian Gulf states, where most affluent women don't work outside the home.

10. For information on male work at home during the 1990s, see Arlie Russell Hochschild and Anne Machung, *The Second Shift: Working Parents and the Revolution at Home* (New York: Avon, 1997), p. 277.

11. Kevin Bales, *Disposable People: New Slavery in the Global Economy* (Berkeley: University of California Press, 1999), p. 43.

12. Andrea Tyree and Katharine M. Donato, "A Demographic Overview of the International Migration of Women," in *International Migration: The Female Experience*, ed. Rita Simon and Caroline Bretell (Totowa, N.J: Rowman & Allanheld, 1986), p. 29. Indeed, many immigrant maids and nannies are more educated than the people they work for. See Pei-Chia Lan's paper in this volume.

13. Momsen, 1999, pp. 10, 73.

14. Grete Brochmann, *Middle East Avenue: Female Migration from Sri Lanka to the Gulf* (Boulder, Colo.: Westview Press, 1993), pp. 179, 215.

15. On this point, thanks to Raka Ray, Sociology Department at the University of California, Berkeley.

2.5

From In Gerangl/*In Struggle: A Handbook for Recognizing and Resisting Anti-Semitism and for Rebuilding Jewish Identity and Pride*

Melanie Kaye/Kantrowitz and Irena Klepfisz
with Bernice Mennis

The following outline was begun in 1982 and developed over the past three years as we led workshops and continued our own consciousness-raising. It is incomplete, is meant not to be read and absorbed, but used and discussed, ideally by Jews in groups or in correspondence with other Jews. A good procedure might be to take one or several paragraphs to talk about at a given gathering. Each section also has suggested exercises for discussion. Some of the topics naturally overlap. We expect this outline to require revision and hope to hear from those who use and change it.

Strategies of Anti-Semitism

Anti-Semitism operates through ordinary avenues of prejudice and hatred, in individuals and in institutions. In addition there are gambits particular to anti-Semitism, widely used in situations like mainstream US culture – or the women's movement – which are not overtly rabidly Jewhating (vs. Hitler's Germany or the Ku Klux Klan). Recognizing these strategies, we are ourselves less vulnerable to their manipulation; we can expose them to others, and develop strategies of resistance.

In this handbook, we have organized strategies of anti-Semitism into three major categories according to how they affect Jews: Fostering Silence; Preventing Jewish Solidarity; and Isolating Jews from Other Groups. (Strategies for resistance have also been organized into parallel categories: Breaking Silence; Building Jewish Identity, Pride and Solidarity; Creating Coalitions.)

I.   Fostering Silence

A.   *The Christian Assumption*

Because the US (and most other western societies) are ostensibly secular, yet Christianity is the assumed underpinning, Jews and Jewishness are often invisible. Jewishness just "doesn't come up." To bring it up seems impolite or disruptive. Thus Jews remain invisible even to each other, unable to bond.

B.   The Myth of the Powerful Jew

Because Jews are assumed to be rich, privileged and running the world, prejudice against us is made to seem trivial, not potentially dangerous. What's the point of mentioning it? How can we be so selfish as to expect others to pay attention to something so insignificant (like an elephant complaining about a flea)?

C.   The Complexity Argument

Often when we point to an instance of anti-Semitism we're told that the issue is very complex, subtle, unclear. This is a strategy to make us apologetic, unsure (and to excuse gentile inaction). In fact, the *majority* of instances of anti-Semitism are pretty clear. The sense that an oppressive behavior is "subtle" often reflects an early stage of consciousness, as in the early phases of feminism we found instances of sexism "subtle." Similar instances we now consider blatant and outrageous, a result of growing confidence in our perception.

D.   Jewish Disagreement

Defining anti-Semitism is a task for Jews. But Jews don't always agree – due to assimilation, denial, fear, ignorance of each other's Jewish experience and just plain diversity. Often these differences are used to silence and invalidate us when we speak about anti-Semitism: "But so-and-so doesn't think it's anti-Semitic and she's a Jew..."

E.   The Demand for Perfection

Jewish women articulating issues and problems of Jewish identity, seeking strategies against anti-Semitism, will make mistakes – because we are beginning. Some people will criticize not just the mistakes but the fact that we speak before we have every detail worked out. As women, as lesbians, as political thinkers, we have all at one time or another been told to keep quiet until we could formulate a fool-proof theory, until we had resolved or named every complexity. Such a demand for perfection is stifling, nothing more than a convoluted, covert strategy to shut us up.

F.   The Myth of Jewish Paranoia

The charge of anti-Semitism is frequently countered by the accusation that Jews are paranoid and overly sensitive. Jews are not paranoid. Rather, we are fearful. And rightly so, given our long history of expulsions, pogroms and massacres, given that 6,000,000 – one-third – of our people were exterminated just over forty years ago.

G.   *Resistance Makes It Worse*

We are told it is better not to make a fuss, not to draw attention to ourselves. We are told that if we point out anti-Semitism, it will get worse, and, in the end, we will be responsible for it. (Often, it's Jews who say this, out of fear.) We are told that unless anti-Semitism is outrageous – killing us – we should let it go, not focus on it. This strategy allows anti-Semitic forces to gain strength and momentum without any Jewish opposition or resistance.

2.6

losing home

eli clare

I must find the words to speak of losing home. Then I never want to utter them again. They throb like an abscessed tooth, simply hurt too much. *Homesick* is a platitude. I need to grab at seemingly unrelated words. *Queer. Exile. Class.* I reach for my red and gold *American Heritage Dictionary* but restrain myself. I know the definitions. I need to enter the maze created by dyke identity, class location, and white rural roots.

Let me start with *queer*, the easiest point of entry. In its largest sense, queer has always been where I belong. A girl child not convinced of her girlness. A backwoods hick in the city. A dyke in a straight world. A gimp in an ableist world. The eldest child of a poor father and a working-class mother, both teachers who tried to pull themselves up by their own bootstraps, using luck and white privilege.

In its narrower sense, queer has been home since I became conscious of being a dyke. At age 17, I left the backwoods of Oregon with a high school diploma and a scholarship to college, grateful not to have a baby or a husband. A year later, after months of soul-searching, I finally realized that I was a dyke and had been for years. Since then, I have lived among dykes and created chosen families and homes, not rooted in geography, but in shared passion, imagination, and values. Our collective dyke household in Oakland with its vegetable garden in the front yard and chicken coop in the back. The women's circle on the Great Peace March from Los Angeles to Washington, DC. The Women's Encampment for a Future of Peace and Justice in upstate New York. Queer potlucks in Ann Arbor, where I now live. Whether I've been walking across the country for peace or just hanging out listening to lesbian gossip, learning to cook tofu, or using red-handled bolt cutters to cut fence at the Army Depot, being a dyke in dyke community is as close as I've ever felt to belonging. And still I feel queer.

Exile. If *queer* is the easiest, then *exile* is the hardest. I lie when I write that home is being a dyke in dyke community. Rather, home is particular wild and ragged beaches, specific kinds of trees and berry brambles, the exact meander of the river I grew up near, the familiar sounds and sights of a dying logging and fishing town. Exile is the hardest because I have irrevocably lost that place as actual home. Let me return to *queer*.

Queer people – using the narrow definition – don't live in Port Orford, or at least I have never found them. And if we did, we would have to tolerate a lack of community, unspoken disdain, a wicked rumor mill, and the very real possibility of homophobic violence. Now if I moved back and lived quietly, never saying the word *dyke* but living a woman-centered life, no one would shoot at my house, throw stones through my windshield, or run me out of town. Muscles Smith at the cannery, Bonnie Wagner at the one-room library, and Dick Tucker at the lumber mill would just shake their heads and talk about Bob Craig's oldest back from the city. As long as I maintained the balance – my unspoken queerness weighed against their tacit acceptance – I would be fine.

Urban, middle-class queer activists may mock this balance as simply another "don't ask, don't tell" situation contributing to queer invisibility. While I agree that it isn't the ideal relationship between queer people and straight people, it is far better than the polite and disdainful invisibility bestowed on us by many middle-class, liberal heterosexuals.

If you don't believe me, let me take you to my maternal grandfather's funeral. At the service I sat with family, my sister to the right, my great aunt Esther to the left, my aunt Margaret in front of us, her lover of many years to her right. Barb is an African American lesbian, an unmistakable butch whether or not she's in heels and a skirt. I am quite sure my aunt has never introduced Barb to Uncle John or Aunt Esther, Uncle Henry or Aunt Lillian as her partner, lover, or girlfriend. Yet Barb is unquestionably family, sitting with my grandfather's immediate relatives near the coffin, openly comforting my aunt. My grandfather was a mechanic in Detroit; his surviving brothers and sisters are Lutheran corn farmers from southern Illinois. Most of them never graduated from high school, still speak German at home, and have voted Republican all their lives. From the perspective of many middle and upper-class urban folks, they are simple rednecks, clods, hillbillies. Working-class writer and activist Elliott maps out three definitions of the word *redneck:*

Its denotation:
  "A member of the white rural laboring class...."[1]

Its connotation:
  "A person who advocates a provincial, conservative, often bigoted sociopolitical attitude characteristic of a redneck...."[2]

And lastly its usage by progressives, including many who are queer:
  "1. Any person who is racist, violent, uneducated and stupid (as if they are the same thing), woman-hating, gay-bashing, Christian fundamentalist, etc. 2. Used as a synonym for every type of oppressive belief except classism."[3]

Many urban queer folks would take one look at my great aunts and uncles and cast them as over-the-top rednecks and homophobes.

Yet in this extended working-class family, unspoken lesbianism balanced against tacit acceptance means that Barb is family, that Aunt Margaret and she are treated as a couple, and that the overt racism Barb would otherwise experience from these people is muffled. Not ideal, but better than frigid denial, better than polite manners and backhanded snubs, better than middle-class "don't ask, don't tell," which would carefully place Barb into the category marked "friend" and have her sit many pews away from immediate family at her lover's father's funeral.*

At the same time, it is a balance easily broken. In Port Orford I would never walk down Main Street holding hands with a woman lover. That simple act would be too much. It is also a balance most readily achieved among family or folks who have known each other for decades. If I moved back and lived down the road from a dyke – closeted or not – who hadn't grown up in Port Orford, whose family of origin didn't live in town, who was an "outsider," I would worry about her safety.

It isn't that outside the bounds of this fragile balance these rural white people are any more homophobic than the average urban person. Rather the difference lies in urban anonymity. In Ann Arbor if a group of frat boys yells, "Hey, lezzie!" at me or the man sitting next to me on the bus whispers "queer" and spits at me, I'll defend myself in whatever ways necessary, knowing chances are good that I'll never see these men again, or if I do, they won't remember me. On the other hand, in Port Orford if someone harassed me – the balance somehow broken, some invisible line over-stepped, drunken bravado overcoming tacit acceptance – I would know him, maybe work with his wife at the cannery, see his kids playing up the river at Butler Bar, encounter him often enough in the grocery store and post office. He would likewise know where I lived, with whom I lived, what car I drove, and where I worked. This lack of anonymity is a simple fact of rural life, one that I often miss in the city, but in the face of bigotry and violence, anonymity provides a certain level of protection.

If I moved back to Port Orford, the daily realities of isolation would compete with my concerns about safety. Living across the street from the chainsaw shop, I would have to drive an hour to spend an evening at a dyke potluck, three hours to hang out at a women's bookstore or see the latest queer movie, seven hours to go to a LGBT pride march. I don't believe I could live easily and happily that isolated from queer community, nor could I live comfortably while always monitoring the balance, measuring the invisible lines that define safety. My loss of home is about being queer.

Let me return now to *exile*. It is a big word, a hard word. It implies not only loss, but a sense of allegiance and connection – however ambivalent – to the place left behind, an attitude of mourning rather than of good riddance. It also carries with it the sense of being pushed out, compelled to leave. Yes, my loss of home is about being queer, but is it *exile*? To answer that, I need to say another thing about anonymity, isolation, and safety, a messier thing.

---

* Reading this story now in 2009, I'm struck by the ways I've downplayed racism and my own white privilege. Even though Barb and Margaret did experience tacit acceptance, which possibly muffled direct expressions of overt racism, I know that in my extended white rural family Barb navigated a strong undercurrent of covert racism, including suspicion, curiosity, stereotyping, and disrespectful humor. It is all too easy for me to manifest white privilege by disregarding this undercurrent. – E.C., 2009

Throughout my childhood and young adulthood, my father, along with a number of other adults, severely sexually and physically abused me, tying me up, using fire and knives and brute force on my body. My father, who taught for 30 years at the local high school. My father, whom everyone in town knew and respected, even if they thought he was quirky, odd, prone to forgetfulness and unpredictable anger. He no longer lives there, although some of the other adults who abused me still do. In the years since leaving Port Orford, I have been able to shake my perpetrators' power away from me, spending long periods of time uncovering the memories and working through persistent body-deep terror, grief, and confusion. I've done this work in community, supported by many friends, a few good professionals, and a political framework that places the violence I experienced into a larger context. For much of that time, I could not have returned to Port Orford and been physically safe. I lived a kind of exile, knowing I needed the anonymity of a small city halfway across the country to protect me, a city where no one knew my father, where not a single person had participated either tangentially or centrally in my abuse. Today my safety depends less on anonymity and more on an internal set of resources. Even so, I don't know how I would deal, if I moved back, with seeing a small handful of my perpetrators on a regular basis, being known as Bob's kid everywhere I went. Simply put, my desire for community, for physical safety, for emotional well-being and psychological comfort compelled me to leave. Being a queer is one piece of this loss, this exile; abuse is another.

And class is a third. If *queer* is the easiest and *exile* the hardest, then *class* is the most confusing. The economics in Port Orford are simple: jobs are scarce. The life of a Pacific Northwest fishing and logging town depends on the existence of salmon and trees. When the summer salmon runs dwindle and all the old growth trees are cut, jobs vanish into thin air. It is rumored that fishermen now pay their boat mortgages by running drugs – ferrying marijuana, crack, and cocaine from the freighters many miles out at sea back to the cannery where they are then picked up and driven in-land. Loggers pay their bills by brush cutting – gathering various kinds of ferns to sell by the pound to florists – and collecting welfare. What remains is the meager four-month-a-year tourist season and a handful of minimum-wage jobs – pumping gas, cashiering, flipping burgers. The lucky few work for the public school district or own land on which they run milk cows and sheep. In short, if I moved back, I probably wouldn't find work. Not only are jobs scarce, but my CP makes job-hunting even harder. Some jobs, like cashiering or flipping burgers, I simply can't do; I don't have enough manual dexterity. Other jobs, like clerical work that requires a lot of typing, I can do but more slowly than many people. Still other jobs I can do well, but potential employers are reluctant to hire me, confusing disability with inability. And if, miraculously, I did find work, the paycheck probably wouldn't stretch around food, gas, and rent.

To leap from economic realities to class issues in Port Orford holds no challenge. The people who live in dying rural towns and work minimum- or sub-minimum-wage jobs – not temporarily but day after day for their whole working lives – are working-class and poor people. There are some middle-class people who live in Port

Orford: the back-to-the-land artists who grow marijuana for money (or did until the federal crackdown more than a decade ago), the young teachers whose first jobs out of college bring them to Pacific High School, the retirees who have settled near Port Orford, lured to Oregon by cheap land. But these people don't stay long. The artists burn out. The young teachers find better jobs in other, more prosperous towns. The retirees grow older and find they need more services than are available in Curry County. The people who stay are poor and working-class. I left because I didn't want to marry and couldn't cashier at Sentry's Market. I left because I hoped to have money above and beyond the dollars spent on rent and food to buy books and music. I left because I didn't want to be poor and feared I would be if I stayed. I will never move back for the same reasons. My loss of home, my exile, is about class.

***

My leaving gave me a dyke community but didn't change my class location. Before I left, I was a rural, mixed-class, queer child in a straight, rural, working-class town. Afterwards, I was an urban-transplanted, mixed-class, dyke activist in an urban, mostly middle-class, queer community. Occasionally I simply feel as if I've traded one displacement for another and lost home to boot. Most of the time, however, I know that it is life-blood for me to live openly in relative safety as a dyke among dykes; to live thousands of miles away from the people who raped and tortured me as a child; to live in a place where finding work is possible; to live with easy access to books and music, movies and concerts, when I can afford them. But I hate the cost, hate the kind of exile I feel.

This displacement, marked by my sense of never quite belonging, has become an ordinary condition in my life, only noticed when I meet new people or travel to new places. Some years ago, a friend and I took a trip to lesbian land in Oregon, visiting WomanShare, Oregon Women's Land (OWL), and the Healing Ground, hanging out with dykes, hiking in the mountains, splitting firewood, planting trees. When we left WomanShare heading north, Janice told us about a dyke-owned natural food store in Myrtle Creek and asked us to say hello to Judith if we stopped. Two hours later we pulled off Interstate 5 into a rickety little logging town. My friend, a Jewish dyke who grew up in suburban Cleveland and suburban Detroit, noticed the John Birch sign tacked under the "Welcome to Myrtle Creek" sign, while I noticed the familiar ramshackle of Main Street, the hills checkered with overgrown clearcuts, the one-ton pickups with guns resting in their rear windows. We parked and started to make a shopping list: fruit, bread, cheese, munchies for the road. I could feel Marjorie grow uncomfortable and wary, the transition from lesbian land to town, particularly one that advertised its John Birch Society, never easy. On the other hand, I felt alert but comfortable in this place that looked and smelled like home. In white, rural, Christian Oregon, Marjorie's history as an urban, middle-class Jew and mine as a rural, mixed-class gentile measured a chasm between us.

As we walked into the grocery store, the woman at the cash register smiled and said, "Welcome, sisters," and all I could do was smile back. Judith wanted news from WomanShare, asked about Janice and Billie, answered our questions about Eugene, already knew about the woman from Fishpond who had committed suicide a week earlier. News of her death moved quickly through this rural dyke community; as we traveled north, we heard women from southern Oregon to Seattle talking about and grieving for this woman. As I stood in Judith's store, I began to understand that OWL, WomanShare, Rainbow's End, Fly Away Home, Fishpond, and the Healing Ground weren't simply individual, isolated pieces of lesbian land, created and sustained by transient, urban dykes. They are links in a thriving rural, queer network. When Judith asked where I was from, I tried to explain what it meant to discover this network a mere hundred miles east of my unarticulated dyke childhood. I smiled some more as Judith told stories about being a dyke in Myrtle Creek, stories interrupted as she greeted customers by name and exchanged local gossip and news. Marjorie and I left 45 minutes later with a bag of groceries and a pile of stories. As we drove north, I reached out to my ever-present sense of displacement and found it gone for the moment.

I certainly don't believe that I can cure my displacement with a simple move back to the Oregon mountains where I could live at OWL or WomanShare. The questions of safety and paying the rent would still be too big and eventually compel me to leave again. My displacement, my exile, is twined with problems highlighted in the intersection of queer identity, working-class and poor identity, and rural identity, problems that demand not a personal retreat, but long-lasting, systemic changes. The exclusivity of queer community shaped by urban, middle-class assumptions. Economic injustice in the backwoods. The abandonment of rural working-class culture. The pairing of rural people with conservative, oppressive values. The forced choice between rural roots and urban queer life. These problems are the connective tissue that brings the words *queer, class*, and *exile* together. Rather than a relocation back to the Oregon mountains, I want a redistribution of economic resources so that wherever we live – in the backwoods, the suburbs, or the city – there is enough to eat; warm, dry houses for everyone; true universal access to health care and education. I want queer activists to struggle against homophobic violence in rural areas with the same kind of tenacity and creativity we bring to the struggle in urban areas. I want rural, working-class, and poor queer people to be leaders in our communities, to shape the ways we will celebrate the 50th anniversary of Stonewall. I want each of us to be able to bring our queerness home.

Notes

Editor's note: This essay first appeared in *Queerly Classed: Gay Men and Lesbians Write About Class*. Ed. Susan Raffo. Boston, MA: South End Press, 1997.

1. Elliot, "Whenever I Tell You the Language We Use Is a Class Issue, You Nod Your Head in Agreement – And Then You Open Your Mouth" in *Out of the Closet: Lesbians Speak*, ed. Julia Penelope (Freedom, CA: Crossing Press, 1994), 277.
2. Ibid., 278.
3. Ibid., 280.

3

Histories of Feminism

By Bonnie Kime Scott

Contents

Original publication details: 3.1 Evelyn Sharp, "The Women at the Gate" from *Rebel Women*, pp. 7–19.
London: John Lane Company, 1910. Public domain. 3.2 Sojourner Truth, "A'n't I A Woman?" Delivered
at 1851 Women's Convention, Akron, Ohio. Public domain. 3.3 Adrienne Rich, "When We Dead
Awaken: Writing as Re-Vision" from *On Lies, Secrets, and Silence: Selected Prose 1966–1978*, excerpts
from pp. 34–49. New York: Norton, 1979. "Aunt Jennifer's Tigers" (© 1993, 1951 by Adrienne Rich)
and the lines from "Snapshots of a Daughter-in-Law" (© 1993, 1997, 1963 by Adrienne Rich) from
Adrienne Rich, *Collected Early Poems: 1950–1970*. All material reproduced with permission of W.W.
Norton & Company, Inc. 3.4 Benita Roth, excerpts from *Separate Roads to Feminism: Black, Chicana,
and White Feminist Movements in America's Second Wave*, pp. 11–14. Cambridge, UK: Cambridge
University Press, 2004. Reproduced with permission of Cambridge University Press and Benita Roth.
3.5 Carol Boyce Davies, "Feminist Consciousness and African Literary Criticism" from *Ngambika:
Studies of Women in African Literature*, ed. Carole Boyce Davies and Anne Adams Graves, pp. 1–3,
12–17. Trenton, NJ: Africa World Press, 1986. Reproduced with permission of Africa World Press. 3.6
Blanche Wiesen Cook, "The Historical Denial of Lesbianism," in *Radical History Review* Volume 20
(1979), pp. 60–65. Reproduced with permission of Duke University Press and MARHO: The Radical
Historians Organization, Inc. 3.7 Aurora Levins Morales, "The Historian as Curandera," from
Medicine Stories: History, Culture, and the Politics of Integrity, pp. 23–38. Boston: South End Press,
1998. Reproduced with permission of The Permissions Company, Inc., on behalf of the author,
www.auroralevinsmorales.com.

Women in Culture: An Intersectional Anthology for Gender and Women's Studies, Second Edition.
Edited by Bonnie Kime Scott, Susan E. Cayleff, Anne Donadey, and Irene Lara.
© 2017 John Wiley & Sons, Ltd. Published 2017 by John Wiley & Sons, Ltd.

The nature of women's presence – or lack of it – in history and historical writing has long been a feminist concern. Moreover, feminist movements have taken up different issues and approaches over time, and as expressed by variously identified groups, worldwide. It is important to recognize that women's experiences differ tremendously, depending upon their historical moment, location, sexuality, race, nationality, religion, education, ableness, and economic wellbeing, as well as their gender (see Basu). Thanks to the assertions of women of color within women's movements, feminist theory has come to acknowledge that the experience of oppression comes from many more sources than gender, and that the experience of multiple oppressions is "intersectional," meaning complex and synergetic, not simply additive (see Bell, Parker and Guy-Sheftall, eds; Moraga and Anzaldúa, eds; and Ruiz and DuBois, eds). The readings in this chapter offer diverse versions of the history of feminism, including its intersections with other activist movements for change, the recovery of lost and denied histories (a notable example being that of lesbian history), feminist approaches to women's writing and oral histories, and lessons applied to future collaboration. Many of the methods for sharing histories offered in this chapter apply well to feminist pedagogy (the art of teaching). The historical timeline offered in this text can be seen as an extension of this chapter. It lists many of the key events and publications that contribute to the women's movement and other related movements for change, transnationally.

Diverse Experiences of the Suffrage Movement

Women's campaign to gain voting rights was an important item, alongside other socially oriented issues, on the agenda of late nineteenth and early twentieth-century advocates for women's rights, in an era sometimes identified as "First-wave" feminism. As its history grows longer, the problem of dividing the women's movement into "waves" of comparable dimensions has been the subject of debate (see Berger, ed; Dicker; and Hewitt, ed.). Our earliest selection comes from a women's rights convention held in Akron, Ohio, in 1851, three years after the Seneca Falls convention, the event that is generally recognized for inaugurating the women's suffrage movement in the United States. It serves as a useful reminder that feminist and anti-racist struggles have repeatedly arisen side by side – in this case with the abolitionist movement against slavery. A participant in both movements, Sojourner Truth was already articulating the experience of multiple oppressions in her famous speech, "A'n't I a Woman?" (1851). Born a slave on a New York estate in 1797, Truth gained her freedom in 1826 and through court action was able to recover one of her sons, sold illegally into slavery in Alabama. After moving to Massachusetts, she took the name Sojourner Truth, emphasizing her sense of earthly mission, in 1843. Membership in the Northampton Association brought her into contact with abolitionists William Lloyd Garrison and Frederick Douglass, as well as Olive Gilbert, an abolitionist-feminist who later wrote the narrative of her life. Some of the white suffragists present in Akron were reluctant to mix abolition with women's rights and tried to prevent Truth from making her speech. Others did not wish to hear women's voices concerning their rights at all, as several of the male clergy present at the church in Akron made clear. The false assumptions of these men about women's lives are alluded to in Truth's extemporaneous speech. Her remarks first appeared in print in 1881 in a volume whose editors included Elizabeth Cady Stanton and Susan B. Anthony. The speech is presented as Frances D. Gage, the president of the meeting, recalled it, complete with descriptions of Truth's appearance, her confident style, the difficult reception she was given, and Gage's own handling of the situation.

Women's suffrage had its own proponents in the British Isles, their origins dating from about 1865, when a reform act was proposed to grant women the vote. British and Irish suffragettes used a variety of strategies, including pageantry, mass marches, and (especially for the Women's Social and Political Union) militancy that included attacks on public buildings and hunger strikes. The latter resulted in forced feedings of imprisoned women, and in some cases, death. Evelyn Sharp's short story, "The Women at the Gate" (1910), provides a sense of crowd dynamics and police brutality at a suffrage rally. It focuses upon the experience of a woman who is about to join the demonstration outside the gate of the British House of Commons, where hundreds of male legislators sat sheltered in disbelief. The would-be demonstrator is surrounded by others who comment on the proceedings from a variety of perspectives: a male worker cries out support for a woman who is being carted off after her arrest, expressing his wish that the labor movement had the suffragists' "pluck"; an elite woman retreating from the melee finds the disheveled demonstrators an embarrassment to her sex; a veteran compares the scene with his own experience of war, and endorses the importance of struggling for an idea. As she works up her courage to play her own part in the demonstration, the central woman in the story begins to sense a new order, transcending class divisions. Presumably white and well educated, she realizes that she and the worker beside her have a better understanding between them than suffragettes have with the Prime Minister. She moves forward to become the thirteenth woman subjected to police battering and arrest, having a better idea what it is that she seeks. *Shoulder to Shoulder* is the title of both a 1974 BBC TV miniseries and a book (Mackenzie) that document the British suffrage movement. The 2004 film, *Iron Jawed Angels*, represents the parallel suffrage struggle in the United States during the 1910s.

Re-visioned and Recovered Histories

Scholars identified with the "Second wave" of feminism (1960s to early 1980s) looked "back with new eyes" (as Adrienne Rich put it), challenging old academic canons and practices in history, literature, and psychology, some seeking a discipline of their own. Marilyn Jacoby Boxer chronicles the development of Women's Studies programs, having participated in the first in the United States at San Diego State University. Laurel Thatcher Ulrich's re-vision of history includes the insight, used for her book title, that *Well Behaved Women Seldom Make History*. Rich's essay "When We Dead Awaken: Writing as Re-Vision" (1979) was first delivered at the Modern Language Association Conference in 1971. The title alludes to a 1900 play by the Norwegian Henrik Ibsen that displayed emerging feminist consciousness. She also revisits critically Virginia Woolf's creative recovery of women's history in *A Room of One's Own* (excerpted in Chapter 4 of this text). Rich applies the act of re-vision, further, to her own poetry, written in successive stages of her life. Some of this was modeled on male poets, or retreated into a male point of view; some conformed with styles of the day, or accepted false, gendered dichotomies. In later work, she has moved on from this essay as well, aware that in the next decade Black and lesbian feminists would intensify and deepen the call for re-vision.

One such example is Blanche Wiesen Cook's "The Historical Denial of Lesbianism" (1979), a book review written to address the homophobia displayed in a recent biography, *Miss Marks and Miss Wooley*, which serves as a case study of flawed history. In her re-vision of the 47-year relationship of Mary Woolley, a long-term president of Mount Holyoke College, and Jeanette Marks, her former student and a much-published English professor, Cook refers to the same archived letters as the biographer, overcoming her distortion and concealment of the relationship. Cook finds that the women demonstrated high regard for each other's careers throughout their lives, which had socialist, feminist, and international dimensions. Dismissing such euphemisms as the "Boston marriage" and the requirement of "genital proofs" of attachment, she offers instead a more open, humanizing definition of lesbianism based on their example: "they chose each other, and they loved each other" creating "a living environment in which to work creatively and independently," adapting over time to each other's needs. Additional groundbreaking studies of women's shared lives are Carroll Smith-Rosenberg's 1975 article "The Female World of Love and Ritual" and Lillian Faderman's 1981 book *Surpassing the Love of Men: Romantic Friendship and Love between Women from the Sixteenth Century to the Present*.

With her decolonial feminist approach of "The Historian as Curandera [Healer]" (1998), Aurora Levins Morales seeks to restore an oppressed and traumatized people's sense of connection to a history that has been taken away from them by colonizing powers, reestablishing their enduring capacity for creativity and resistance. While she deals most directly with Puerto Rican history as told through the stories of rural, poor, indigenous, mestizo, Black, and mulatto women, she notes analogous forms of historical dispossession in numerous global locations. Like other feminist historians, she asks different questions, disrupts formerly standard answers, construes events differently, and questions standards of objectivity and disciplinary boundaries. Where names and plausible accounts of indigenous women are missing, she imagines their lives, noting that Virginia Woolf used a similar technique in recovering Shakespeare's sister. She also weights evidence differently: skeptical of the authority of written accounts over oral histories, discounting ideas of passive victims and flawless heroes, finding traces of the lives of real women in the production of food and the earning of wages, and recovering global networks of power and exchange. Levins Morales also emphasizes the importance of making curandera histories available to those who need them most, and particularly the next generation, whose history has been hidden from them.

Though women have long been co-creators of African oral literature, the emergence of African women writers and critics has gradually changed male domination of both fields and called for a re-vision of previous emphases and approaches. In "Feminist Consciousness and African Literary Criticism" (1986), Carol Boyce Davies offers both a historical review of traditional and European influences, and an articulation of the agendas of African feminist critics. She notes that traditional societies saw girls' education as a barrier to women's roles as wives and mothers, and that colonial administrators were equally prone toward educating only boys. Similarly, early African male critics reflected European and American "phallic" criticism that devalued women's writing and experience, or they mythologized "Mother Africa." African feminists seek their own, not Western, agendas and interpretations of culture. They detect, for example, utility in extended families, particularly for childcare and household responsibilities. They attend to women's traditions for social networking, cooperative endeavors, and income-generating work. But they also acknowledge "difficult" traditions such as genital mutilation, excesses of polygamy, obligatory motherhood, and preference of sons. Boyce Davies suggests that through its African American and Caribbean diaspora, African feminism is connected to Alice Walker's "womanist" definition. In defining an African feminist critical approach, Boyce Davies links with the work of African American critics such as Deborah McDowell, Barbara Christian, Mary Helen Washington, Alice Walker, and Barbara Smith. Some of the African feminists' projects correspond to early feminist critical efforts elsewhere. Activities begin with building a canon of women writers and critics capable of revising their earlier dismissal. Consciousness of images of women in African literature involves encouragement of accurate portrayals and available choices, rather than stereotypes of "long-suffering," voiceless, or earth-mother identities. Finally, a revised African aesthetic can emerge, based on experiential themes that reflect distinct political and cultural realities and that link oral with written literature. The effort to represent women's historical experiences with respect to global location has been furthered by works such as Estelle Freedman's *No Turning Back: The History of Feminism and the Future of Women*, Bonnie G. Smith's edited collection, *Women's History in Global Perspective,* and Filomina Chioma Steady's edited collection, *The Black Woman Cross-Culturally.*

Intersections and Connections

The development of the key feminist concept of intersectionality came from the activist experience and re-vision of African American and Chicana feminists in the 1980s, as described by Benita Roth in "Feminist Movements and Intersectionality" from *Separate Roads to Feminism* (2004). Awareness of the intersectional nature of oppressions began by relating the feminist concern with gender to race/ethnicity. Next came sensitivity to class, and finally, sexual orientation, with various groups contributing to the complexity of this vision; areas of awareness continue to be added. Roth notes that feminism was not an identification encouraged among activists (and particularly the men) in Black communities. In early work, Frances Beal suggested the term "double jeopardy" for the race/gender experience of Black women; sensitive to class dynamics, the Third World Women's Alliance suggested the term "triple jeopardy." Audre Lorde and the Combahee River Collective, founded in the 1970s by several Black feminists, furthered awareness of heterosexism.

As Roth illustrates, from the inception of the Chicano movement, feminists asserted the importance of Chicana liberation, while distinguishing themselves from Anglo feminists by urging racial/ethnic, national, linguistic, and class dynamics alongside gender. As with African American groups, insights about lesbian experience gained recognition later. Turning jeopardy to advantage, Paula Moya argues that being at the intersectional point of oppressions is advantageous to knowing how power functions and applying this awareness to activisms. Working from lived experiences and embodied knowledge, women of color could engage in a continual process of revision and application to activism. Through long and sometimes difficult discussions, intersectionality is now part of mainstream feminism.

AnaLouise Keating advances the discussion further in her essay "From Intersections to Interconnections: Lessons for Transformation from *This Bridge Called My Back: Radical Writings by Women of Color*" (2009), included in Chapter 10. In charting the progress of feminism after *This Bridge*, which was first published by Cherríe Moraga and Gloria Anzaldúa in 1981, she acknowledges difficult debates that followed. She reminds us of ideas not fully realized and assumptions about racial identity, labeling, and stereotyping not adequately challenged, seeking improved forms of alliance. The first of her three lessons is to make productive use of differences to discover commonalities and thereby work for revolutionary change. In support, she cites Anzaldúa's concept of El Mundo Zurdo, which departs from dualistic or oppositional approaches and moves toward relational ones, despite the risk of personal exposure. The second lesson is the recognition of the interrelatedness of being, a holistic approach that requires rethinking the oppositional strategies that have been vital to survival. Indeed, painful clashes continued to surface among contributors to a second volume she co-edited with Anzaldúa, *this bridge we call home: radical visions for transformation* (2002). Finally, she develops ways to listen humbly, deeply, with "raw openness," recognizing the complexity of other persons and having the willingness to be changed. Another concept from Anzaldúa, "nepantla" or "in-between space," allows the loosening of boundaries and opens "transgressive opportunities for change."

That feminist history learns from the approaches and omissions of its own past is evident throughout these selections. It is also clear that history can be applied to activism, and that many more projects lie ahead.

Discussion Questions

1. Give two examples of feminists asserting the value of oral tradition in the recording of women's history.
2. Give two historic examples of the failure to acknowledge the importance of lesbian experience. Explain at least one reason behind these omissions.
3. Discuss one repeated stereotype of women's role in history that is resisted by feminist historians in multiple readings.
4. Give examples of colonial attitudes and policies that have inhibited women's and/or indigenous people's roles and their representation in history.
5. List several cultural practices dependent upon women that feminist historians have brought to our attention.
6. How can women's historians serve a healing and uniting function?
7. Give examples of the ways that the writing of women's history demands asking different questions and reading the evidence anew.

References

Anzaldúa, Gloria E., and AnaLouise Keating, eds. *this bridge we call home: radical visions for transformation*. New York: Routledge, 2002.

Basu, Amrita. *Women's Movements in the Global Era: The Power of Local Feminisms*. Boulder, CO: Westview, 2010.

Bell, Roseann, Bettye J. Parker, and Beverly Guy-Sheftall, eds. *Sturdy Black Bridges*. Garden City, NY: Anchor/Doubleday, 1979.

Berger, Melody, ed. *We Don't Need Another Wave: Dispatches from the Next Generation of Feminists*. Emeryville, CA: Seal Press, 2006.

Boxer, Marilyn Jacoby. *When Women Ask the Questions: Creating Women's Studies in America*. Baltimore: Johns Hopkins University Press, 1998.

Dicker, Rory Cooke. *A History of U. S. Feminisms*. Berkeley: Seal Press, 2008.

Faderman, Lillian. *Surpassing the Love of Men. Romantic Friendship and Love between Women from the Sixteenth Century to the Present*. New York: Morrow, 1981.

Freedman, Estelle. *No Turning Back: The History of Feminism and the Future of Women*. New York: Ballantine, 2002.

Hewitt, Nancy A., ed. *No Permanent Waves: Recasting Histories of U.S. Feminism*. New Brunswick: Rutgers University Press, 2010.

Iron Jawed Angels. Dir. Katja von Garnier. HBO Films, 2004. Film.

Mackenzie, Midge, ed. *Shoulder to Shoulder: A Documentary*. New York: Vintage, 1975.

Moraga, Cherríe, and Gloria Anzaldúa, eds. *This Bridge Called My Back: Radical Writings by Women of Color*, expanded and revised 3rd ed. Berkeley: Third Woman Press, 2002.

Ruiz, Vicki L., and Ellen Carol DuBois, eds. *Unequal Sisters: An Inclusive Reader in U.S. Women's History*, 4th ed. New York: Routledge, 2008.

Smith, Bonnie G., ed. *Women's History in Global Perspective*. Urbana: University of Illinois Press, 2004.

Smith-Rosenberg, Carroll. "The Female World of Love and Ritual." *Signs: Journal of Women in Culture and Society* 1.1 (1975): 1–29.

Steady, Filomina Chioma. *The Black Woman Cross-Culturally*. Cambridge, MA: Schenkman, 1981.

Ulrich, Laurel Thatcher. *Well Behaved Women Seldom Make History*. New York: Knopf, 2007.

3.1

The Women at the Gate

Evelyn Sharp

"Funny, isn't it?" said the young man on the top of the omnibus.

"No," said the young woman from whom he appeared to expect an answer, "I don't think it is funny."

"Take care," said the young man's friend, nudging him, "perhaps she's one of them!"

Everybody within hearing laughed, except the woman, who did not seem to be aware that they were talking about her. She was on her feet, steadying herself by grasping the back of the seat in front of her, and her eyes, non-committal in their lack of expression, were bent on the roaring, restless crowd that surged backwards and forwards in the Square below, where progress was gradually becoming an impossibility to the stream of traffic struggling towards Whitehall. The thing she wanted to find was not down there, among the slipping horses, the swaying men and women, the moving lines of policemen; nor did it lurk in those denser blocks of humanity that marked a spot, here and there, where some resolute, battered woman was setting her face towards the gate of St. Stephen's; nor was the thing she sought to be found behind that locked gate of liberty where those in possession, stronger far in the convention of centuries than locks or bars could make them, stood in their well-bred security, immeasurably shocked at the scene before them and most regrettably shaken, as some of them were heard to murmur, in a lifelong devotion to the women's cause.

The searching gaze of the woman on the omnibus wandered for an instant from all this, away to Westminster Bridge and the blue distance of Lambeth, where darting lamps, like will-o'-the-wisps come to town, added a touch of magic relief to the dinginess of night. Then she came back again to the sharp realism of the foreground and found no will-o'-the-wisps there, only the lights of London shining on a picture she should remember to the end of her life. It did not matter, for the thing beyond it all that she wanted to be sure of, shone through rain and mud alike.

"Lookin' for a friend of yours, p'raps?" said a not unfriendly woman with a baby, who was also standing up to obtain a more comprehensive view of what was going on below.

"No," was the answer again, "I am looking at something that isn't exactly there; at least –

"If I was you, miss," interrupted the facetious youth, with a wink at his companion, "I should chuck looking for what ain't there, and –"

She turned and smiled at him unexpectedly.

"Perhaps you are right," she said. "And yet, if I didn't hope to find what isn't there, I couldn't go through with what I have to do to-night."

The amazed stare of the young man covered her, as she went swiftly down the steps of the omnibus and disappeared in the crowd.

"Balmy, the whole lot of 'em!" commented the conductor briefly.

The woman with the passionless eyes was threading her way through the straggling clusters of people that fringed the great crowd where it thinned out towards Broad Sanctuary. A girl wearing the militant tricolour in her hat, brushed against her, whispered, "Ten been taken, they say; they're knocking them about terribly to-night!" and passed noiselessly away. The first woman went on, as though she had not heard.

A roar of voices and a sudden sway of the throng that pinned her against some railings at the bottom of Victoria Street, announced the eleventh arrest. A friendly artisan in working clothes swung her up till she stood beside him on the stone coping, and told her to "ketch on." She caught on, and recovered her breath laboriously.

The woman, who had been arrested after being turned back from the doors of the House repeatedly for two successive hours, was swept past in the custody of an inspector, who had at last put a period to the mental and physical torment that a pickpocket would have been spared. A swirling mass of people, at once interested and puzzled, sympathetic and uncomprehending, was swept along with her and round her. In her eyes was the same unemotional, detached look that filled the gaze of the woman clinging to the railings. It was the only remarkable thing about her; otherwise, she was just an ordinary workaday woman, rather drab-looking, undistinguished by charm or attraction, as these things are generally understood.

"Now then, please, every one who wants a vote must keep clear of the traffic. Pass along the foot-way, ladies, if you please; there's no votes to be had in the middle of the roadway," said the jocular voice of the mounted constable, who was backing his horse gently and insistently into the pushing, struggling throng.

The jesting tone was an added humiliation; and women in the crowd, trying to see the last of their comrade and to let her know that they were near her then, were beaten back, hot with helpless anger. The mounted officer came relentlessly on, successfully sweeping the pavement clear of the people whom he was exhorting with so much official reasonableness not to invade the roadway. He paused once to salute and to avoid two men, who, having piloted a lady through the backwash of the torrent set in motion by the plunging horse, were now hoisting her into a place of safety just beyond the spot where the artisan and the other woman held on to the railings.

"Isn't it terrible to see women going on like this?" lamented the lady breathlessly. "And they say some of them are quite nice – like us, I mean."

The artisan, who, with his neighbour, had managed to evade the devastating advance of the mounted policeman, suddenly put his hand to his mouth and emitted a hoarse cheer.

"Bravo, little 'un!" he roared. "Stick to it!" "Votes for women, I say! Votes for women!"

The crowd, friendly to the point of admiring a struggle against fearful odds which they yet allowed to proceed without their help, took up the words with enthusiasm; and the mud-bespattered woman went away to the haven of the police station with her war-cry ringing in her ears.

The man who had led the cheer turned to the woman beside him, as though to justify his impulse.

"It's their pluck," he said. "If the unemployed had half as much, they'd have knocked sense into this Government long ago!"

A couple of yards away, the lady was still lamenting what she saw in a plaintive and disturbed tone. Unconsciously, she was putting herself on the defensive.

"I shouldn't blame them," she maintained, "if they did something really violent, like – like throwing bombs and things. I could understand that. But all this – all this silly business of trying to get into the House of Commons, when they know before-hand that they can't possibly do it – oh, it's so sordid and loathsome! Did you see that woman's hair, and the way her hat was bashed in, and the mud on her nose? Ugh!"

"You can't have all the honour and glory of war, and expect to keep your hair tidy too," observed one of the men, slightly amused.

"War!" scoffed his wife. "There's none of the glory of war in this."

Her glance ranged, as the other woman's had done, over the dull black stream of humanity rolling by at her feet, over the wet and shining pavements, casting back their myriad distorted reflections in which street lamps looked like grinning figures of mockery – over the whole drear picture of London at its worst. She saw only what she saw, and she shuddered with distaste as another mounted officer came sidling through the crowd, pursuing another hunted rebel woman, who gave way only inch by inch, watching her opportunity to face once more towards the locked gate of liberty. Evidently, she had not yet given sufficient proof of her un-alterable purpose to have earned the mercy of arrest; and a ring of compassionate men formed round her as a body-guard, to allow her a chance of collecting her forces. A reinforcement of mounted police at once bore down upon the danger spot, and by the time these had worked slowly through the throng, the woman and her supporters had gone, and a new crowd had taken the place of the former one.

"Oh, there's none of the glory of war in that!" cried the woman again, a tremble in her voice.

"There is never any glory in war – at least, not where the war is," said her second companion, speaking for the first time. His voice travelled to the ear of the other woman, still clinging to the railings with the artisan. She glanced round at him swiftly, and as swiftly let him see that she did not mean to be recognized; and he went on talking as if he had not seen her turn round.

"This is the kind of thing you get on a bigger scale in war," he said, in a half-jesting tone, as if ashamed of seeming serious. "Same mud and slush, same grit, same cow-ardice, same stupidity and beastliness all round. The women here are fighting for something big; that's the only difference. Oh, there's another, of course; they're taking all the kicks themselves and giving none of 'em back. I suppose it has to be that way round when you're fighting for your souls and not for your bodies."

"I didn't know you felt like that about it," said the woman, staring at him curiously. "Oh, but of course you can't mean that real war is anything like this wreched scuffle of women and police!"

"Oh, yes," returned the other, in the same tone of gentle raillery. "Don't you remember Monsieur Bergeret? He was perfectly right. There is no separate art of war, because in war you merely practise the arts of peace rather badly, such as baking and washing, and cooking and digging, and travelling about. On the spot it is a wretched scuffle; and the side that wins is the side that succeeds in making the other side believe it to be invincible. When the women can do that, they've won."

"They don't look like doing it to-night, do they?" said the woman's husband breezily. "Thirteen women and six thousand police, you know!"

"Exactly. That proves it," retorted the man, who had fought in real wars. "They wouldn't bring out six thousand police to arrest thirteen men even if they all threw bombs, as your wife here would like to see."

"The police are not there only to arrest the women –"

"That's the whole point," was the prompt reply. "You've got to smash an idea as well as an army in every war, still more in every revolution, which is always fought exclusively round an idea. If thirteen women batter at the gates of the House of Commons, you don't smash the idea by arresting the thirteen women, which could be done in five minutes. So you bring out six thousand police to see if that will do it. That is what lies behind the mud and the slush – the idea you can't smash."

A man reeled along the pavement and lurched up against them.

"Women in trousers! What's the country coming to?" he babbled; and bystanders laughed hysterically.

"Come along; let's get out of this," said the woman's husband hurriedly; and the trio went off in the direction of the hotel.

The woman with the passionless eyes looked after them. "He sees what we see," she murmured.

"Seems he's been in the army, active service, too," remarked the artisan in a sociable manner. "I like the way he conversed, myself."

"He understands, that is all," explained his companion. "He sees what it all means – all this, I mean, that the ordinary person calls a failure because we don't succeed in getting into the House. Do you remember, in 'Agamemnon' – have you read 'Agamemnon'?"

It did not strike her as strange that she should be clasping iron railings in Westminster, late on a wet evening, talking to a working man about Greek tragedy. The new world she was treading to-night, in which things that mattered were given their true proportions, and important scruples of a lifetime dwindled to nothingness, gave her a fresh and a whimsical insight into everything that happened; and the odd companion that chance had flung her, half an hour ago, became quite easily the friend she wanted at the most friendless moment she had ever known.

The man, without sharing her reasons for a display of unusual perception, seemed equally unaware of any strangeness in the situation.

"No, miss, I haven't read it," he answered. "That's Greek mythology, isn't it? I never learnt to speak Greek."

"Nor I," she told him; "but you can get it translated into English prose. It reminds me always of our demonstrations in Parliament Square, because there is a chorus in it of stupid old men, councillors, they are, I think, who never understand what is going on, however plainly it is put to them. When Cassandra prophesies that Agamemnon is going to be murdered – as we warn the Prime Minister when we are coming to see him – they pretend not to see what she is driving at, because if they did, they would have to do something. And then, when her prophecy comes true and he is murdered – of course, the analogy ends here, because we are not out to murder anybody, only to make the Prime Minister hear our demands – they run about wringing their hands and complaining; but nobody does anything to stop it. It really is rather like the evasions of the Home Office when people ask questions in Parliament about the prison treatment of the Suffragettes, isn't it?"

"Seems so," agreed her new friend, affably.

"And then," continued the woman, scorn rising in her voice, "when Clytaemnestra comes out of the house and explains why she has murdered her husband, they find plenty to say because there is a woman to be blamed, though they never blamed Agamemnon for doing far worse things to her. That is the way the magistrate and the daily papers will talk to-morrow, when our women are brought up in the police court."

"That's it! Always put all the blame on the women," said the artisan, grasping what he could of her strange discourse.

Big Ben tolled out ten strokes, and his companion, catching her breath, looked with sudden apprehension at the moving, throbbing block of people, now grown so immense that the police, giving up the attempt to keep the road clear, were merely concerned in driving back the throng on four sides and preserving an open space round the cluster of buildings known to a liberty-loving nation as the People's House. The gentlemen, who still stood in interested groups behind the barred gates of it, found the prospect less entertaining now that the action had been removed beyond the range of easy vision; and some of the bolder ones ventured out into the hollow square, formed by an unbroken line of constables, who were standing shoulder to shoulder, backed by mounted men who made little raids from time to time on the crowd behind, now fast becoming a very ugly one. Every possible precaution was being taken to avoid the chance of annoyance to any one who might still wish to preserve a decorous faith in the principle of women's liberty.

Meanwhile, somewhere in that shouting, hustling, surging mass of humanity, as the woman onlooker knew full well, was the twelfth member of the women's deputation that had been broken up by the police, two hours ago, before it could reach the doors of the House; and knowing that her turn had come now, she pictured that twelfth woman beating against a barrier that had been set up against them both ever since the world grew civilized. There was not a friend near, when she nodded to the artisan and slipped down from her temporary resting-place. The respectable and sympathetic portion of the crowd was cut off from her, away up towards Whitehall, whither it had followed the twelfth woman. On this side of Parliament Square all the idlers, all the coarse-tongued reprobates of the slums of Westminster, never far distant from any London crowd, were herded together in a stupid, pitiless, ignorant mob. The slough of mud underfoot added the last sickening touch to a scene that for the flash of an instant made her heart fail.

"St. James's Park is the nearest station, miss," said the man, giving her a helping hand. "Don't advise you to try the Bridge; might find it a bit rough getting across."

She smiled back at him from the kerbstone, where she stood hovering a second or two on the fringe of the tumult and confusion. Her moment's hesitation was gone, and the sure look had come back to her eyes.

"I am not going home," she told him. "I am the thirteenth woman, you see."

She left the artisan staring at the spot near the edge of the pavement where the crowd had opened and swallowed her up.

"And she so well-informed too!" he murmured. "I don't like to think of it – I don't like to think of it!"

Shortly after midnight two men paused, talking, under the shadow of Westminster Abbey, and watched a patrol of mounted police that ambled at a leisurely pace across the deserted Square. The light in the Clock Tower was out. Thirteen women, granted a few hours' freedom in return for a word of honour, had gone to their homes, proudly conscious of having once more vindicated the invincibility of their cause; and some five or six hundred gentlemen had been able to issue in safety from the stronghold of liberty, which they had once more proved to themselves to be impregnable. And on the morrow the prisoners of war would again pay the price of the victory that both sides thought they had won.

"If that is like real war too," said one of the men to the other, who had just made these observations aloud, "how does anybody ever know which side has won?"

"By looking to see which side pays the price of victory," answered the man who had fought in real wars.

3.2

And A'n't I a Woman?

Sojourner Truth

[Frances D. Gage describes Sojourner Truth's delivery of her speech as follows.]

There were very few women in those days who dared to "speak in meeting"; and the august teachers of the people were seemingly getting the better of us, while the boys in the galleries, and the sneerers among the pews, were hugely enjoying the discomfiture as they supposed, of the "strong-minded." Some of the tender-skinned friends were on the point of losing dignity, and the atmosphere betokened a storm. When, slowly from her seat in the corner rose Sojourner Truth, who, till now, had scarcely lifted her head. "Don't let her speak!" gasped half a dozen in my ear. She moved slowly and solemnly to the front, laid her old bonnet at her feet, and turned her great speaking eyes to me. There was a hissing sound of disapprobation above and below. I rose and announced, "Sojourner Truth," and begged the audience to keep silence for a few moments.

The tumult subsided at once, and every eye was fixed on this almost Amazon form, which stood nearly six feet high, head erect, and eyes piercing the upper air like one in a dream. At her first word there was a profound hush. She spoke in deep tones, which, though not loud, reached every ear in the house, and away through the throng at the doors and windows.

[What follows is Truth's speech as recorded by Gage in *History of Woman Suffrage*.]

"Wall, chilern, whar dar is so much racket dar must be somethin' out o' kilter. I tink dat 'twixt de niggers of de Souf and de womin at de Norf, all talkin' 'bout rights, de white men will be in a fix pretty soon. But what's all dis here talkin' 'bout?

"Dat man ober dar say dat womin needs to be helped into carriages, and lifted ober ditches, and to hab de best place everywhar. Nobody eber helps me into carriages, or ober mud-puddles, or gibs me any best place!" And raising herself to her full height, and her voice to a pitch like rolling thunder, she asked. "And a'n't I a woman? Look at me! Look at my arm! (and she bared her right arm to the shoulder, showing her tremendous muscular power). I have ploughed, and planted, and gathered into barns, and no man could head me! And a'n't I a woman? I could work as much and eat as much as a man – when I could get it – and bear de lash as well! And a'n't I a woman? I have borne thirteen chilern, and seen 'em mos' all sold off to slavery, and when I cried out with my mother's grief, none but Jesus heard me! And a'n't I a woman?

"Den dey talks 'bout dis ting in de head; what dis dey call it?" ("Intellect," whispered some one near.) "Dat's it, honey. What's dat got to do wid womin's rights or nigger's rights? If my cup won't hold but a pint, and yourn holds a quart, wouldn't ye be mean not to let me have my little half-measure full?" And she pointed her significant finger, and sent a keen glance at the minister who had made the argument. The cheering was long and loud.

"Den dat little man in black dar, he say women can't have as much rights as men, 'cause Christ wan't a woman! Whar did your Christ come from?" Rolling thunder couldn't have stilled that crowd, as did those deep, wonderful tones, as she stood there with outstretched arms and eyes of fire. Raising her voice still louder, she repeated, "Whar did your Christ come from? From God and a woman! Man had nothin' to do wid Him." Oh, what a rebuke that was to that little man.

Turning again to another objector, she took up the defense of Mother Eve. I cannot follow her through it all. It was pointed, and witty, and solemn; eliciting at almost every sentence deafening applause; and she ended by asserting: "If de fust woman God ever made was strong enough to turn de world upside down all alone, dese women togedder (and she glanced her eye over the platform) ought to be able to turn it back, and get it right side up again! And now dey is asking to do it, de men better let 'em." Long-continued cheering greeted this. "'Bleeged to ye for hearin' on me, and now ole Sojourner han't got nothin' more to say."

Amid roars of applause, she returned to her corner, leaving more than one of us with streaming eyes, and hearts beating with gratitude. She had taken us up in her strong arms and carried us safely over the slough of difficulty turning the whole tide in our favor. I have never in my life seen anything like the magical influence that subdued the mobbish spirit of the day, and turned the sneers and jeers of an excited crowd into notes of respect and admiration. Hundreds rushed up to shake hands with her, and congratulate the glorious old mother, and bid her God-speed on her mission of "testifyin' agin concerning the wickedness of this 'ere people."

Reference

Stanton, Elizabeth Cady, Anthony, Susan B. and Gage, Matilda Joslyn (eds) (1889) *History of Woman Suffrage*, 2nd edn, vol. 1 (Rochester, NY: Charles Mann).

3.3
When We Dead Awaken: Writing as Re-Vision
Adrienne Rich

Ibsen's *When We Dead Awaken* is a play about the use that the male artist and thinker – in the process of creating culture as we know it – has made of women, in his life and in his work; and about a woman's slow struggling awakening to the use to which her life has been put.

It's exhilarating to be alive in a time of awakening consciousness; it can also be confusing, disorienting, and plainful. This awakening of dead or sleeping consciousness has already affected the lives of millions of women, even those who don't know it yet. It is also affecting the lives of men, even those who deny its claims upon them. The argument will go on whether an oppressive economic class system is responsible for the oppressive nature of male/female relations, or whether, in fact, patriarchy – the domination of males – is the original model of oppression on which all others are based. But in the last few years the women's movement has drawn inescapable and illuminating connections between our sexual lives and our political institutions. The sleepwalkers are coming awake, and for the first time this awakening has a collective reality; it is no longer such a lonely thing to open one's eyes.

Re-vision – the act of looking back, of seeing with fresh eyes, of entering an old text from a new critical direction – is for women more than a chapter in cultural history: it is an act of survival. Until we can understand the assumptions in which we are drenched we cannot know ourselves. And this drive to self-knowledge, for women, is more than a search for identity: it is part of our refusal of the self-destructiveness of male-dominated society. A radical critique of literature, feminist in its impulse, would take the work first of all as a clue to how we live, how we have been living, how we have been led to imagine ourselves, how our language has trapped as well as liberated us, how the very act of naming has been till now a male prerogative, and how we can begin to see and name – and therefore live – afresh. A change in the concept of sexual identity is essential if we are not going to see the old political order reassert itself in every new revolution. We need to know the writing of the past, and know it differently than we have ever known it; not to pass on a tradition but to break its hold over us.

For writers, and at this moment for women writers in particular, there is the challenge and promise of a whole new psychic geography to be explored. But there is also a difficult and dangerous walking on the ice, as we try to find language and images for a consciousness we are just coming into, and with little in the past to support us. I want to talk about some aspects of this difficulty and this danger.

Jane Harrison, the great classical anthropologist, wrote in 1914 in a letter to her friend Gilbert Murray:

> By the by, about "Women," it has bothered me often – why do women never want to write poetry about Man as a sex – why is Woman a dream and a terror to man and not the other way around?... Is it mere convention and propriety, or something deeper?[1]

I think Jane Harrison's question cuts deep into the myth-making tradition, the romantic tradition; deep into what women and men have been to each other; and deep into the psyche of the woman writer. Thinking about that question, I began thinking of the work of two twentieth-century women poets, Sylvia Plath and Diane Wakoski. It strikes me that in the work of both Man appears as, if not a dream, a fascination and a terror; and that the source of the fascination and the terror is, simply, Man's power – to dominate, tyrannize, choose, or reject the woman. The charisma of Man seems to come purely from his power over her and his control of the world by force, not from anything fertile or life-giving in him. And, in the work of both these poets, it is finally the woman's sense of *herself* – embattled, possessed – that gives the poetry its dynamic charge, its rhythms of struggle, need, will, and female energy. Until recently this female anger and this furious awareness of the Man's power over her were not available materials to the female poet, who tended to write of Love as the source of her suffering, and to view that victimization by Love as an almost inevitable fate. Or, like Marianne Moore and Elizabeth Bishop, she kept sexuality at a measured and chiseled distance in her poems.

One answer to Jane Harrison's question has to be that historically men and women have played very different parts in each other's lives. Where woman has been a luxury for man, and has served as the painter's model and the poet's muse, but also as comforter, nurse, cook, bearer of his seed, secretarial assistant, and copyist of manuscripts, man has played a quite different role for the female artist. Henry James repeats an incident which the writer Prosper Merimee described, of how, while he was living with George Sand,

> he once opened his eyes, in the raw winter dawn, to see his companion, in a dressing-gown, on her knees before the domestic hearth, a candlestick beside her and a red *madras* round her head, making bravely, with her own hands the fire that was to enable her to sit down betimes to urgent pen and paper. The story represents him as having felt that the spectacle chilled his ardor and tried his taste; her appearance was unfortunate, her occupation an inconsequence, and her industry a reproof – the result of all which was a lively irritation and an early rupture.[2]

[1]   J. G. Stewart, *Jane Ellen Harrison: A Portrait from Letters* (London: Merlin, 1959), p. 140.
[2]   Henry James, "Notes on Novelists," in *Selected Literary Criticism of Henry James*, Morris Shapira, ed. (London: Heinemann, 1963), pp. 157–58.

The specter of this kind of male judgment, along with the misnaming and thwarting of her needs by a culture controlled by males, has created problems for the woman writer: problems of contact with herself, problems of language and style, problems of energy and survival.

In rereading Virginia Woolf's *A Room of One's Own* (1929) for the first time in some years, I was astonished at the sense of effort, of pains taken, of dogged tentativeness, in the tone of that essay. And I recognized that tone. I had heard it often enough, in myself and in other women. It is the tone of a woman almost in touch with her anger, who is determined not to appear angry, who is *willing* herself to be calm, detached, and even charming in a roomful of men where things have been said which are attacks on her very integrity. Virginia Woolf is addressing an audience of women, but she is acutely conscious – as she always was – of being overheard by men: by Morgan and Lytton and Maynard Keynes and for that matter by her father, Leslie Stephen.[3] She drew the language out into an exacerbated thread in her determination to have her own sensibility yet protect it from those masculine presences. Only at rare moments in that essay do you hear the passion in her voice; she was trying to sound as cool as Jane Austen, as Olympian as Shakespeare, because that is the way the men of the culture thought a writer should sound.

No male writer has written primarily or even largely for women, or with the sense of women's criticism as a consideration when he chooses his materials, his theme, his language. But to a lesser or greater extent, every woman writer has written for men even when, like Virginia Woolf, she was supposed to be addressing women. If we have come to the point when this balance might begin to change, when women can stop being haunted, not only by "convention and propriety" but by internalized fears of being and saying themselves, then it is an extraordinary moment for the woman writer – and reader.

I have hesitated to do what I am going to do now, which is to use myself as an illustration. For one thing, it's a lot easier and less dangerous to talk about other women writers. But there is something else. Like Virginia Woolf, I am aware of the women who are not with us here because they are washing the dishes and looking after the children. Nearly fifty years after she spoke, that fact remains largely unchanged. And I am thinking also of women whom she left out of the picture altogether – women who are washing other people's dishes and caring for other people's children, not to mention women who went on the streets last night in order to feed their children. We seem to be special women here, we have liked to think of ourselves as special, and we have known that men would tolerate, even romanticize us

<hr>

[3] A. R., 1978: This intuition of mine was corroborated when, early in 1978, I read the correspondence between Woolf and Dame Ethel Smyth (Henry W. and Albert A. Berg Collection, The New York Public Library, Astor, Lenox and Tilden Foundations); in a letter dated June 8, 1933, Woolf speaks of having kept her own personality out of *A Room of One's Own* lest she not be taken seriously: "… how personal, so will they say, rubbing their hands with glee, women always are; *I even hear them as I write.*" (Italics mine.)

as special, as long as our words and actions didn't threaten their privilege of tolerating or rejecting us and our work according to *their* ideas of what a special woman ought to be. An important insight of the radical women's movement has been how divisive and how ultimately destructive is this myth of the special woman, who is also the token woman. Every one of us here in this room has had great luck – we are teachers, writers, academicians; our own gifts could not have been enough, for we all know women whose gifts are buried or aborted. Our struggles can have meaning and our privileges – however precarious under patriarchy – can be justified only if they can help to change the lives of women whose gifts – and whose very being – continue to be thwarted and silenced.

My own luck was being born white and middle-class into a house full of books, with a father who encouraged me to read and write. So for about twenty years I wrote for a particular man, who criticized and praised me and made me feel I was indeed "special." The obverse side of this, of course, was that I tried for a long time to please him, or rather, not to displease him. And then of course there were other men – writers, teachers – the Man, who was not a terror or a dream but a literary master and a master in other ways less easy to acknowledge. And there were all those poems about women, written by men: it seemed to be a given that men wrote poems and women frequently inhabited them. These women were almost always beautiful, but threatened with the loss of beauty, the loss of youth – the fate worse than death. Or, they were beautiful and died young, like Lucy and Lenore. Or, the woman was like Maud Gonne, cruel and disastrously mistaken, and the poem reproached her because she had refused to become a luxury for the poet.

A lot is being said today about the influence that the myths and images of women have on all of us who are products of culture. I think it has been a peculiar confusion to the girl or woman who tries to write because she is peculiarly susceptible to language. She goes to poetry or fiction looking for *her* way of being in the world, since she too has been putting words and images together; she is looking eagerly for guides, maps, possibilities; and over and over in the "words' masculine persuasive force" of literature she comes up against something that negates everything she is about: she meets the image of Woman in books written by men. She finds a terror and a dream, she finds a beautiful pale face, she finds La Belle Dame Sans Merci, she finds Juliet or Tess or Salome, but precisely what she does not find is that absorbed, drudging, puzzled, sometimes inspired creature, herself, who sits at a desk trying to put words together.

So what does she do? What did I do? I read the older women poets with their peculiar keenness and ambivalence: Sappho, Christina Rossetti, Emily Dickinson, Elinor Wylie, Edna Millay, H. D. I discovered that the woman poet most admired at the time (by men) was Marianne Moore, who was maidenly, elegant, intellectual, discreet. But even in reading these women I was looking in them for the same things I had found in the poetry of men, because I wanted women poets to be the equals of men, and to be equal was still confused with sounding the same.

I know that my style was formed first by male poets: by the men I was reading as an undergraduate – Frost, Dylan Thomas, Donne, Auden, MacNiece, Stevens, Yeats. What I chiefly learned from them was craft.[4] But poems are like dreams: in them you put what you don't know you know. Looking back at poems I wrote before I was twenty-one, I'm startled because beneath the conscious craft are glimpses of the split I even then experienced between the girl who wrote poems, who defined herself in writing poems, and the girl who was to define herself by her relationships with men. "Aunt Jennifer's Tigers" (1951), written while I was a student, looks with deliberate detachment at this split.[5]

> Aunt Jennifer's tigers stride across a screen,
> Bright topaz denizens of a world of green.
> They do not fear the men beneath the tree;
> They pace in sleek chivalric certainty.
>
> Aunt Jennifer's fingers fluttering through her wool
> Find even the ivory needle hard to pull.
> The massive weight of Uncle's wedding band
> Sits heavily upon Aunt Jennifer's hand.
>
> When Aunt is dead, her terrified hands will lie
> Still ringed with ordeals she was mastered by.
> The tigers in the panel that she made
> Will go on striding, proud and unafraid.

In writing this poem, composed and apparently cool as it is, I thought I was creating a portrait of an imaginary woman. But this woman suffers from the opposition of her imagination, worked out in tapestry, and her life-style, "ringed with ordeals she was mastered by." It was important to me that Aunt Jennifer was a person as distinct from myself as possible – distanced by the formalism of the poem, by its objective, observant tone – even by putting the woman in a different generation.

I finished college, published my first book by a fluke, as it seemed to me, and broke off a love affair. I took a job, lived alone, went on writing, fell in love. I was young, full of energy, and the book seemed to mean that others agreed I was a poet. Because I was also determined to prove that as a woman poet I could also have what was then defined as a "full" woman's life, I plunged in my early twenties into marriage and had three children before I was thirty. There was nothing overt in the environment to warn me: these were the fifties, and in reaction to the earlier wave of feminism, middle-class women were making careers of domestic perfection, working to send their

---

[4]   A. R., 1978: Yet I spent months, at sixteen, memorizing and writing imitations of Millay's sonnets; and in notebooks of that period I find what are obviously attempts to imitate Dickinson's metrics and verbal compression. I knew H. D. only through anthologized lyrics; her epic poetry was not then available to me.

[5]   A. R., 1978: Texts of poetry quoted herein can be found in A. R., *Poems Selected and New: 1950–1974* (New York: Norton, 1975).

husbands through professional schools, then retiring to raise large families. People were moving out to the suburbs, technology was going to be the answer to everything, even sex; the family was in its glory. Life was extremely private; women were isolated from each other by the loyalties of marriage. I have a sense that women didn't talk to each other much in the fifties – not about their secret emptinesses, their frustrations. I went on trying to write; my second book and first child appeared in the same month. But by the time that book came out I was already dissatisfied with those poems, which seemed to me mere exercises for poems I hadn't written. The book was praised, however, for its "gracefulness"; I had a marriage and a child. If there were doubts, if there were periods of null depression or active despairing, these could only mean that I was ungrateful, insatiable, perhaps a monster.

About the time my third child was born, I felt that I had either to consider myself a failed woman and a failed poet, or to try to find some synthesis by which to understand what was happening to me. What frightened me most was the sense of drift, of being pulled along on a current which called itself my destiny, but in which I seemed to be losing touch with whoever I had been, with the girl who had experienced her own will and energy almost ecstatically at times, walking around a city or riding a train at night or typing in a student room. In a poem about my grandmother I wrote (of myself): "A young girl, thought sleeping, is certified dead" ("Halfway"). I was writing very little, partly from fatigue, that female fatigue of suppressed anger and loss of contact with my own being; partly from the discontinuity of female life with its attention to small chores, errands, work that others constantly undo, small children's constant needs. What I did write was unconvincing to me; my anger and frustration were hard to acknowledge in or out of poems because in fact I cared a great deal about my husband and my children. Trying to look back and understand that time I have tried to analyze the real nature of the conflict Most, if not all, human lives are full of fantasy – passive day-dreaming which need not be acted on. But to write poetry or fiction, or even to think well, is not to fantasize, or to put fantasies on paper. For a poem to coalesce, for a character or an action to take shape, there has to be an imaginative transformation of reality which is in no way passive. And a certain freedom of the mind is needed – freedom to press on, to enter the currents of your thought like a glider pilot, knowing that your motion can be sustained, that the buoyancy of your attention will not be suddenly snatched away. Moreover, if the imagination is to transcend and transform experience it has to question, to challenge, to conceive of alternatives, perhaps to the very life you are living at that moment. You have to be free to play around with the notion that day might be night, love might be hate; nothing can be too sacred for the imagination to turn into its opposite or to call experimentally by another name. For writing is re-naming. Now, to be maternally with small children all day in the old way, to be with a man in the old way of marriage, requires a holding- back, a putting-aside of that imaginative activity, and demands instead a kind of conservatism. I want to make it clear that I am *not* saying that in order to write well, or think well, it is necessary to become unavailable to others, or to become a devouring ego. This has been the myth of the masculine artist and thinker; and I do not accept it. But to be a female human being trying to fulfill traditional female functions in a traditional way is in direct conflict with the subversive function of the imagination. The word traditional is important here. There must be ways, and we will be finding out more and more about them, in which the energy of creation and the energy of relation can be united. But in those years I always felt the conflict as a failure of love in myself. I had thought I was choosing a full life: the life available to most men, in which sexuality, work, and parenthood could coexist. But I felt, at twenty-nine, guilt toward the people closest to me, and guilty toward my own being.

I wanted, then, more than anything, the one thing of which there was never enough: time to think, time to write. The fifties and early sixties were years of rapid revelations: the sit-ins and marches in the South, the Bay of Pigs, the early antiwar movement, raised large questions – questions for which the masculine world of the academy around me seemed to have expert and fluent answers. But I needed to think for myself – about pacifism and dissent and violence, about poetry and society, and about my own relationship to all these things. For about ten years I was reading in fierce snatches, scribbling in notebooks, writing poetry in fragments; I was looking desperately for clues, because if there were no clues then I thought I might be insane. I wrote in a notebook about this time:

> Paralyzed by the sense that there exists a mesh of relationships – e.g., between my anger at the children, my sensual life, pacifism, sex (I mean sex in its broadest significance, not merely sexual desire) – an interconnectedness which, if I could see it, make it valid, would give me back myself, make it possible to function lucidly and passionately. Yet I grope in and out among these dark webs.

I think I began at this point to feel that politics was not something "out there" but something "in here" and of the essence of my condition.

In the late fifties I was able to write, for the first time, directly about experiencing myself as a woman. The poem was jotted in fragments during children's naps, brief hours in a library, or at 3:00 A.M. after rising with a wakeful child. I despaired of doing any continuous work at this time. Yet I began to feel that my fragments and scraps had a common consciousness and a common theme, one which I would have been very unwilling to put on paper at an earlier time because I had been taught that poetry should be "universal," which meant, of course, nonfemale. Until then I had tried very much *not* to identify myself as a female poet. Over two years I wrote a ten-part poem called "Snapshots of a Daughter-in-Law" (1958–1960), in a longer looser mode than I'd ever trusted myself with before. It was an extraordinary relief to write that poem. It strikes me now as too literary, too dependent on allusion; I hadn't found the courage yet to do without authorities, or even to use the pronoun "I" – the woman in the poem is always "she." One section of it, No. 2, concerns a woman who thinks she is going mad; she is haunted by voices telling her to resist and rebel, voices which she can hear but not obey.

2.

Banging the coffee-pot into the sink
she hears the angels chiding, and looks out
past the raked gardens to the sloppy sky.
Only a week since They said: *Have no patience.*

The next time it was: *Be insatiable.*
Then: *Save yourself; others you cannot save.*
Sometimes she's let the tapstream scald her arm,
a match burn to her thumbnail,

or held her hand above the kettle's snout
right in the woolly steam. They are probably angels,
since nothing hurts her anymore, except
each morning's grit blowing into her eyes.

The poem "Orion," written five years later, is a poem of reconnection with a part of myself I had felt I was losing – the active principle, the energetic imagination, the "half-brother" whom I projected, as I had for many years, into the constellation Orion. It's no accident that the words "cold and egotistical" appear in this poem, and are applied to myself.

There is a companion poem to "Orion," written three years later, in which at last the woman in the poem and the woman writing the poem become the same person. It is called "Planetarium," and it was written after a visit to a real planetarium, where I read an account of the work of Caroline Herschel, the astronomer, who worked with her brother William, but whose name remained obscure, as his did not.

In closing I want to tell you about a dream I had last summer. I dreamed I was asked to read my poetry at a mass women's meeting, but when I began to read, what came out were the lyrics of a blues song. I share this dream with you because it seemed to me to say something about the problems and the future of the woman writer, and probably of women in general. The awakening of consciousness is not like the crossing of a frontier – one step and you are in another country. Much of woman's poetry has been of the nature of the blues song: a cry of pain, of victimization, or a lyric of seduction.[6] And today, much poetry by women – and prose for that matter – is charged with anger. I think we need to go through that anger, and we will betray our own reality if we try, as Virginia Woolf was trying, for an objectivity, a detachment, that would make us sound more like Jane Austen or Shakespeare. We know more than Jane Austen or Shakespeare knew: more than Jane Austen because our lives are more complex, more than Shakespeare because we know more about the lives of women – Jane Austen and Virginia Woolf included.

Both the victimization and the anger experienced by women are real, and have real sources, everywhere in the environment, built into society, language, the

---

[6] A. R., 1978: When I dreamed that dream, was I wholly ignorant of the tradition of Bessie Smith and other women's blues lyrics which transcended victimization to sing of resistance and independence?

structures of thought. They will go on being tapped and explored by poets, among others. We can neither deny them, nor will we rest there. A new generation of women poets is already working out of the psychic energy released when women begin to move out towards what the feminist philosopher Mary Daly has described as the "new space" on the boundaries of patriarchy.[7] Women are speaking to and of women in these poems, out of a newly released courage to name, to love each other, to share risk and grief and celebration.

To the eye of a feminist, the work of Western male poets now writing reveals a deep, fatalistic pessimism as to the possibilities of change, whether societal or personal, along with a familiar and threadbare use of women (and nature) as redemptive on the one hand, threatening on the other; and a new tide of phallocentric sadism and overt woman-hating which matches the sexual brutality of recent films. "Political" poetry by men remains stranded amid the struggles for power among male groups; in condemning U.S. imperialism or the Chilean junta the poet can claim to speak for the oppressed while remaining, as male, part of a system of sexual oppression. The enemy is always outside the self, the struggle somewhere else. The mood of isolation, self-pity, and self-imitation that pervades "nonpolitical" poetry suggests that a profound change in masculine consciousness will have to precede any new male poetic – or other – inspiration. The creative energy of patriarchy is fast running out; what remains is its self-generating energy for destruction. As women, we have our work cut out for us.

3.4

From *Separate Roads to Feminism*
Benita Roth

Feminist Movements and Intersectionality: Recasting the Second Wave
Many African American women activists and many Chicana activists became *feminists*, choosing a political label and a political path that was not encouraged by male (and many female) activists in their communities (Blackwell 2000; Cortera 1977; García 1990, 1997; Gray White 1999; Harris 1999; hooks 1981, 1984; Moraga and Anzaldúa 1979; Saldívar-Hull 1991; B. Smith 1983; Springer 2001). In the groups and organizations they formed, they espoused a feminism that incorporated analyses of the consequences of mutually reinforcing oppressions of gender, race/ethnicity, and class (and, less frequently, sexual orientation), analyses which in turn influenced white feminists, such that feminists today acknowledge as axiomatic the necessity of recognizing multiple sources of domination in women's (and men's) lives. In short, in Black and Chicana feminisms of the second wave we find the roots of feminist insights about the *intersectionality* of inequalities in people's lives. I wish to take

---

[7]   Mary Daly, *Beyond God the Father: Towards a Philosophy of Women's Liberation* (Boston: Beacon, 1973).

seriously what this feminist scholarship has to say about exploring the social world in the very examination of the movements that gave rise to that scholarship.

Theory on the intersectionality of oppressions was part of Black and Chicana feminist thinking from the start of their organizing. In her 1970 piece "Double Jeopardy," Frances Beal argued that Black women occupied a social space constituted by their gender, race, and class (and subsequently, the Third World Women's Alliance named its newspaper *Triple Jeopardy* in order to incorporate the insight that class oppression intersected with race and gender). Later in the 1970s, the Combahee River Collective explicitly took an intersectional stance; they added heterosexism as a key component of Black women's oppression, ending the relative silence in Black feminist theory over lesbianism. The need to do their "politics in the cracks," what Springer (2001:155) has characterized as "interstitial politics," with Black feminists caught between the blind spots of most of white feminism and most of Black liberationism – all this meant that Black feminists early on saw the shortcomings of a "monist" (D. H. King 1988) politics that focused on only one axis of oppression. Although Black feminism varied in its organizational form and ideology, in its theory it was nonetheless characterized by a consistent examination of interlocking oppressions and oriented toward action agendas that linked solutions for gender oppression with solutions to other forms of oppression.

Although differently situated in the racial/ethnic hierarchy and left political milieu, Chicana feminists initially organized an interstitial politics as well, in and around the Chicano movement. Feminists in the Chicano movement challenged that movement's shortcomings regarding the liberation of the Chicana in her community, arguing from the inception of their movement that it was only with Chicanas' liberation as women that the entire community could move forward (Cortera 1976a, 1976b; Flores 1971a, 1971b; *La Raza* 1972; Longauex y Vasquez 1970; Nieto-Gomez 1976; Rincon 1971; Sosa Riddell 1974). Chicana feminist organizing was therefore interstitial in its formation, but not in its aims; feminists strove to stay linked to streams in the Chicano liberation movement, and sought to distinguish themselves from what was seen as a very different "Anglo" form of feminist praxis. In an intersectional way, Chicana feminists analyzed their situation as women as the result not just of gender but of racial/ethnic, national, linguistic, and class dynamics. Later critiques by Chicana lesbian feminists deepened this analytical intersectionality by filling in earlier lacunae around issues of heteronormativity.[8]

---

[8] On a more general note, the later "addition" of heterosexism to intersectional analyses in feminisms of color does not reflect total silence about sexuality, as will become clear in the narrative of this work. Rather, early in the emergence of second-wave feminisms, and particularly in communities of color, questions of lesbianism and homosexuality were broached in an inconsistent way. Clearly, criticisms of lesbian feminists of color as to their movements' failure to incorporate a struggle against heterosexism as an element of their political agenda were accepted and influential (see Alarcón, Castillo, and Moraga 1993; Alarcón 1999 [1987]; Castillo 1994; Clarke 1983; Combahee River Collective 1981; Lorde 1982, 1984; Moraga 1983; Moraga and Alarcón 1979; Pérez 1991; B. Smith 1979, 1983; Trujillo 1991).

Thus, theories of intersecting oppressions as mutually constitutive were rooted in feminist politics, born of experience and created to guide activism (see Anzaldúa 1999 [1987]; Beal 1970; Cortera 1977; Crenshaw 1989, 1995; Hill Collins 1990; D. H. King 1988; Naples 1998a, 1998b; Sacks 1989; Sandoval 1990, 1991; Spelman 1982; Thorton Dill 1983). As Kimberlé Crenshaw (1995:358) wrote, for women of color, there was (and is) a "need to account for multiple grounds of identity when considering how the social world is constructed." The need to account for one's disadvantaged position as part of a disadvantaged community was based on experience, but it promoted a particular kind of knowledge; as Paula Moya has written, a kind of "epistemic privilege" comes from being at the intersecting point of oppressions, such that women of color actually have "a special advantage with respect to possessing or acquiring knowledge about how fundamental aspects of our society (such as race, class, gender, and sexuality) operate to sustain matrices of power" (2001:479). And knowledge of the intersectionality of oppressions at the core of women's lives then further facilitated a particular kind of awareness when it came to political activism, one that relied on "new subjectivity," constant political revision, and the "capacity to recenter [one's politics] depending on the kinds of oppression to be confronted" (Sandoval 1991:14).

Thus, feminists of color constructed intersectional theory on the basis of their lived experiences and embodied knowledge. Their theories were oriented toward guiding their activism; in a continuing process, theory and activism constructed further definitions of what constituted a feminist agenda. There were, however, some silences in the earlier constructions of intersectional feminist theory around questions of heteronormativity and sexuality. Early feminists on the left broke silences about the effects of gender domination, racial/ethnic domination, and class domination in their lives; they did so in order to argue for a politics of liberation that would address these dominations simultaneously. But while the archival record of political discussion reflects feminists' displeasure with sexual double standards, there was initially little *written* discussion of homophobia and little *written* theorizing about the oppressiveness of heterosexism. These lacunae in intersectional feminist theory were, of course, filled by feminists who reacted to initial silences with very loud shouts. For example, Black feminists in the Third World Women's Alliance would stress the jeopardy that Black women faced as a result of gender, race, and class oppression; later Black feminists in the Combahee River Collective would include critiques of heterosexism and homophobia in their analyses of what needed to change in order to liberate women. By the 1990s, the intersectional political agenda of feminists of color – the need to simultaneously analyze and battle dominations of gender, class, race/ethnicity, *and* sexuality – migrated to the "mainstream" of feminist scholarship and activism, moving beyond the starting point of their own feminist movements. If the reader wonders where there were feminists discussing the constraints of heterosexuality and whether I am leaving them out, rest assured of my certainty that the discussions were taking place; the reader can draw her own conclusions as to why it took many feminists a little while to circulate their discussions about heteronormativity in written form.

Conclusion

Feminists on Their Own and for Their Own

Revisiting and "Re-Visioning" Second-Wave Feminisms

Second-Wave Feminisms, Plural

The social divisions – the social inequities – of race/ethnicity, class, and gender that structured feminisms into organizationally distinct movements – Black, Chicana, and white – operated at several levels. The macrostructure of postwar American society created unequal sets of resources, privilege, and opportunity for feminists situated in different racial/ethnic communities, and these inequalities created obstacles to cross-racial/ethnic organizing. Feminists in oppositional movement communities organized in specific intramovement contexts that shaped their visions of what they could *and* should do. As they organized, they kept a sense of themselves as leftists who wished to do their politics the right way.

In previous chapters, I have shown that organizing within oppositional political milieus was never simply a question of feminists co-opting resources and splitting off from parent movements. Instead, the historical record gives us discussion, debate, and ambivalence about how to organize as feminists. White women's liberationists worked to separate themselves from a largely hostile, dismissive, and fragmenting white Left, but nonetheless saw themselves as leftists; Black feminists organized in a neotraditionalized, increasingly militant Black movement that battled white donor fatigue (see McAdam 1982) and U.S. government interference, but did not want to further enervate their movement; and Chicana feminists worked for changes to the Chicano movement as a whole even as they organized new Chicana-led groups. In a crowded and competitive social movement sector/field, feminists were faced with choices about liberation, as parent movements demanded that they not withdraw their energies from mixed-gender groups, and as the consensus regarding the ethos of organizing one's own became hegemonic. All of these factors combined structured second-wave feminisms on the left along racial/ethnic lines.

Why is it important to have a different vision of the second wave as composed of feminisms? For one thing – and I hope it is clear from this book and from other work done on second-wave feminisms – we need to understand just how broadly appealing the feminist project (writ large) was. Second-wave feminisms' appeal in the 1960s and 1970s was not limited to "bourgeois" white women, was *never* in fact practiced *only* by those women. When the second wave of feminism is seen as feminisms, the audacity of all feminists who challenged the status quo from wherever they were situated is recaptured and highlighted, and we are forced to recognize the power of feminist visions. Black women formed feminist groups despite a political climate that asked them to choose between fighting racism or sexism; Chicanas organized around their issues, with their efforts all but ignored by "mainstream" feminists and opposed by many in their own communities; white women's

liberationists grew strong despite the ridicule of their activist brothers. This plural-
istic reality of feminist organizing has been underexplored from the start; by ignoring
it, we minimize the significance of feminisms as part of the cycle of postwar
popular protest.

References

Alarcón, Norma, Ana Castillo, and Cherríe Moraga. 1993. "Introduction." In *The Sexuality of
    Latinas*, edited by Norma Alarcón, Ana Castillo, and Cherríe Moraga. Berkeley: Third
    Woman Press.
Anzaldúa, Gloria. 1999 [1987]. *Borderlands/La Frontera: The New Mestiza*. San Francisco:
    Aunt Lute Books.
Beal, Frances. 1970. "Double Jeopardy: To Be Black and Female." In *The Black Woman: An
    Anthology*, edited by Toni Cade (Bambara). New York: New American Library.
Blackwell, Maylei. 2000. "Geographies of Difference: Mapping Multiple Feminist Insurgencies
    and Transnational Public Cultures in the Americas (Mexico)." Ph.D. diss., University of
    California, Santa Cruz.
Castillo, Ana. 1994. *Massacre of the Dreamers: Essays on Xicanisma*. New York: Plume/
    Penguin.
Clarke, Cheryl. 1983. "The Failure to Transform: Homophobia and the Black Community." In
    Home Girls: A Black Feminist Anthology, edited by Barbara Smith. New York: Kitchen
    Table/Women of Color Press.
Combahee River Collective. 1981. "A Black Statement." In *This Bridge Called My Back:
    Writings by Radical Women of Color*, edited by Cherríe Moraga and Gloria Anzaldúa.
    Watertown, MA: Persephone Press.
Cortera, Marta. 1976a. *Diosa y Hembra: The History and Heritage of Chicanas in the U.S.*
    Austin, TX: Information Systems Development.
Cortera, Marta. 1976b. "Chicana Identity (platica de Marta Cortera)." *Caracol* 2:6
    (February): 14–15, 17.
Cortera, Marta. 1977. *The Chicana Feminist*. Austin, TX: Information Systems Development.
Crenshaw, Kimberlé. 1989. "Demarginalizing the Intersection of Race and Sex: A Black
    Feminist Critique of Antidiscrimination Doctrine, Feminist Theory and Antiracist
    Politics." *The University of Chicago Legal* Forum:139–167.
Crenshaw, Kimberlé. 1995. "Mapping the Margins: Intersectionality, Identity Politics and
    Violence Against Women." In *Critical Race Theory: The Key Writings That Formed the
    Movement*, edited by Kimberlé Crenshaw, Neil Gotanda, Gary Peller, and Kendall
    Thomas. New York: The New Press (357–383).
Flores, Francisca. 1971a. "Conference of Mexican Women: Un Remolino." *Regeneración* 1:10.
Flores, Francisca. 1971b. "Editorial." *Regeneración* 1:10.
García, Alma. 1990. "The Development of Chicana Feminist Discourse, 1970–1980." In
    Unequal Sisters: A Multicultural Reader in U.S. Women's History, edited by Ellen Carol
    DuBois and Vicki L. Ruiz. New York and London: Routledge.
García, Alma. 1997. *Chicana Feminist Thought: The Basic Historical Writings*. New York and
    London: Routledge.
Gray White, Deborah. 1999. *Too Heavy a Load: Black Women in Defense of Themselves,
    1894–1994*. New York and London: W. W. Norton.

Harris, Duchess. 1999. "'All of Who I Am in the Same Place': The Combahee River Collective." *Womanist Theory and Research* 2:1 (Fall).

Hill Collins, Patricia. 1990. *Black Feminist Thought: Knowledge, Consciousness, and the Politics of Empowerment*. Boston: Unwin Hyman.

hooks, bell. 1981. *Ain't I a Woman: Black Women and Feminism*. Boston: South End Press.

hooks, bell. 1984. *Feminist Theory: From Margin to Center*. Boston: South End Press.

King, Deborah H. 1988. "Multiple Jeopardy, Multiple Consciousness: The Context of a Black Feminist Ideology." *Signs* 14:1 (Autumn).

La Raza Unida Party. 1972. "Mujeres Find Excellent Expression in La Raza Unida Party." Unpublished convention report (El Paso, Texas, September 1–5). Women's Liberation Ephemera Files, Special Collections, Northwestern University.

Longauex y Vasquez, Enriqueta. 1970. "The Mexican-American Woman." In *Sisterhood is Powerful*, edited by Robin Morgan. New York: Vintage Books.

Lorde, Audre. 1982. *Zami: A New Spelling of My Name*. Freedom, CA: Crossing Press.

Lorde, Audre. 1984. *Sister Outsider: Essays and Speeches*. Freedom, CA: Crossing Press.

McAdam, Doug. 1982. *Political Process and the Development of Black Insurgency 1930–1970*. Chicago: University of Chicago Press.

Moraga Cherríe. 1983. *Loving in the War Years: Lo que nunca pasó par sus labias*. Boston: South End Press.

Moraga, Cherríe, and Gloria Anzaldúa. 1979. "Introduction." In *This Bridge Called My Back: Writings by Radical Women of Color*, edited by Cherríe Moraga and Gloria Anzaldúa. Watertown, MA: Persephone Press.

Moya, Paula M. L. 2001. "Chicana Feminism and Postmodernist Theory." *Signs: Journal of Women in Culture and Society* 26:2:441–483.

Naples, Nancy. 1998a. *Grassroots Warriors: Activist Mothering, Community Work, and the War on Poverty*. New York and London: Routledge.

Naples, Nancy. 1998b. Editor, *Community Activism and Feminist Politics: Organizing Across Race, Class, and Gender*. Philadelphia: Temple University Press.

Nieto-Gomez, Ana. 1976. "Chicana Feminism." *Caracol* 2:5 (January):3–5.

Pérez, Emma. 1991. "Sexuality and Discourse: Notes from a Chicana Survivor." In *Chicana Lesbians: The Girls Our Mothers Warned Us About*, edited by Carla Trujillo. Berkeley: Third Woman Press (159–184).

Rincon, Bernice. 1971. "La Chicana: 'Her Role in the Past and Her Search for a New Role in the Future.'" *Regeneración* 1:10:15–18.

Sacks, Karen. 1989. "Toward a Unified Theory of Class, Race and Gender." *American Ethnologist* 16:3.

Saldívar-Hull, Sonia. 1991. "Feminism on the Border: From Gender Politics to Geopolitics." In *Criticism in the Borderlands*, edited by Hector Calderón and José David Saldívar. Durham, NC: Duke University Press.

Sandoval, Chela. 1990. "Feminism and Racism: A Report on the 1981 National Women's Studies Association Conference." In *Making Face, Making Soul/Hacienda Caras: Creative and Critical Perspectives by Women of Color*, edited by Gloria Anzaldúa. San Francisco: An Aunt Lute Foundation Book.

Sandoval, Chela. 1991. "U.S. Third World Feminism: The Theory and Method of Oppositional Consciousness in the Postmodern World." *Genders* 10 (Spring):1–24.

Smith, Barbara. 1979. "Notes for Yet another Paper on Black Feminism, or Will the Real Enemy Please Stand Up?" *Conditions 5: The Black Woman's Issue*:123–127.

Smith, Barbara. 1983. "Introduction." In *Home Girls: A Black Feminist Anthology*, edited by
    Barbara Smith. New York: Kitchen Table/Women of Color Press.
Sosa Riddell, Adaljiza. 1974. "Chicanas and El Movimiento." *Aztlán* 5:1:155–165.
Spelman, Elizabeth V. 1982. "Theories of Race & Gender/The Erasure of Black Women."
    Quest: A Feminist Quarterly 5:4:36–62.
Springer, Kimberly. 2001. "The Interstitial Politics of Black Feminist Organizations."
    Meridians: feminism, race, transnationalism 1:2:155–191.
Thorton Dill, Bonnie. 1983. "Race, Class and Gender: Prospects for an All-Inclusive
    Sisterhood." *Feminist Studies* 9:1 (Spring).

3.5

Feminist Consciousness and African Literary Criticism

Carole Boyce Davies

African written literature has traditionally been the preserve of male writers and critics. Today, however, accompanying an ever-growing corpus of literature by African women writers, a new generation of critics, most of them women, is impacting on this male-dominated area. The perspectives of these critics exhibit a double influence, and consequently a tension of sorts. On the one hand there is a grounding in the need to liberate African peoples from neo-colonialism and other forms of race and class oppression, coupled with a respect for certain features of traditional African cultures. On the other, there is the influence of the international woman's movement and the recognition that a feminist consciousness is necessary in examining the position of women in African societies. The tension involved in this double allegiance provides a nexus from which this criticism grows.

In examining the relative scarcity of women in African written literary tradition a few points reveal themselves. First of all, there is ample evidence of women's creativity in the production of oral literature, as there is nothing inherently male about literary creativity. According to Finnegan,

> The limitations on this general mastery of the art of storytelling arise from local conventions about the age and sex of the narrators. In some societies, it appears, these are quite free; in others there is a definite emphasis on one or another category as being the most suitable one for a storyteller. In some areas it is the women, often the old women, who tend to be the most gifted ... Elsewhere it is the men who tend to be the more expert ... [1]

The available research makes it clear that there was equal billing for male and female in the oral literary tradition and that while there was specialization in certain genres according to gender, there was no large scale exclusion of one group from the creative process.

As opposed to that, the first African writers to achieve prominence were male. Reasons for this are obvious. The selection of males for formal education was fostered by the colonial institutions which made specific choices in educating male and female. Then too, the sex role distinctions common to many African societies supported the notion that western education was a barrier to a woman's role as wife and mother and an impediment to her success in these traditional modes of acquiring status. With few exceptions, girls were kept away from formal and especially higher education.[2] The colonial administrations were therefore willing accomplices because they imported a view of the world in which women were of secondary importance. Clearly then, European colonialism, as well as traditional attitudes of and to women, combined to exclude African women from the educational processes which prepare one for the craft of writing.

The criticism of African literature was subject to similar historical realities. The earliest critics of African literature were European academicians who communicated the Western male-oriented mode of creating and evaluating literature. The first critical works were authored by European and American critics in the 1950's and '60's (Janheinz Jahn, Ulli Beier, Gerald Moore and others)[3] who, while they performed an invaluable service in the development of a written literary tradition, maintained the Western critical manner of approaching literary texts solely from the point of view of male experience. This Ellman appropriately defines as "phallic criticism"[4] as it excludes a host of woman-oriented configurations. The second school of critics of African literature, continental Africans like writers Ezekiel Mphalele, Eldred Jones, and Eustace Palmer[5] and Caribbean critics, like Oscar Dathorne and John Ramsaran,[6] to a large extent maintained this reductionism as it relates to women in the literature.

Most of the women who appear as contributors in the early anthologies and journals are bibliographers like Margaret amosu.[7] The few women critics, Lilyan Kesteloot, Molly Mahood[8] and later Omolara Ogundipe-Leslie,[9] for example, had to utilize the same critical apparata as their male contemporaries. This meant turning a blind eye to women in African literature. Even when the first major African women writers appeared – Ama Ata Aidoo (1965), Flora Nwapa and Grace Ogot (1966) – the same type of alliance which was created by male critics and writers was not formed between the women critics and writers. Instead, without the benefit of a feminist focus, there was a reluctance to bring the works of African women writers under serious but sensitive critical evaluation.

Defining an African Feminist Critical Approach

African feminist criticism is definitely engaged criticism in much the same way as progressive African literary criticism grapples with decolonization and feminist criticism with the politics of male literary dominance. This criticism therefore is both textual and contextual criticism: textual in that close reading of texts using the literary establishment's critical tools is indicated; contextual as it realizes that analyzing a text without some consideration of the world with which it has a material relationship is of little social value. So the dichotomy between textual and contextual criticism, the perennial argument about form and content, common in literary circles finds some resolution here.

Our task here is to identify critical approaches and standards and criteria which have been applied so far to the study of African literature from a feminist perspective and which can be utilized and built upon for further examination of women in/and African literature. In a larger sense, African literary criticism, in general, if it be unbiased in the future will have to come to grips with issues such as the treatment of women characters and the growing presence of African women writers.

The African feminist theoretical framework previously outlined, along with the work of feminist theorists, combine in a unique fashion in this approach.... African feminist critics must take what is of value from both mainstream feminist criticism and African literary criticism, keeping in mind that both are offshoots from traditional European literary criticism and in some cases its adversaries. The result then is not reduction but refinement geared specifically to deal with the concrete and literary realities of African women's lives.

It is important to underscore the fact that a substantial amount of literature exists on the development of a feminist aesthetic,[10] on one hand, and a Black/African aesthetic[11] on the other. The work of Black feminist critics[12] in the United States also provides an important focus especially when examining African women writers and the question of their exclusion from the literary canon(s).

For this reason, Katherine Frank's "Feminist Criticism and the African Novel,"[13] the only published work known to this writer to deal directly with this subject, loses by not understanding the critical connection between feminist criticism and African literature by not taking into consideration how African-American feminists apply feminist theory to Black literature. There, the geo-cultural differences notwithstanding, lies the link – in the explorations of Deborah McDowell, Barbara Christian, Mary Helen Washington, Alice Walker, Barbara Smith and others. For example, her questions about whether "gender or race is the most significant defining characteristic of a writer" is already answered. For Black/African feminists never make that distinction. It is not a question of either/or, but one of an acceptance of BOTH and the balances and conflicts that go with that twin acceptance. Frank, moreover is guilty of some gross distortions in the way in which she interprets feminism, for example her conclusion: "Feminism, by definition, is a profoundly individualistic philosophy: it values personal growth and individual fulfilment over any larger communal needs or good" (p. 45) is just the kind of conclusion that some retrograde males have made. Quite to the contrary, feminism is not individualistic but openly speaks of "sisterhood" and the need for "women" to advance in society to be on at least an equal level with men for the society's overall good. Frank also, much like Ojo-Ade in his "Female Writers, Male Critics"[14] reads feminism solely as a Western import forgetting the African-American women, like Sojourner Truth's contribution to feminism and the many African women in history whose lives and deeds can be clearly read as "feminist." Frank, nonetheless has made an important contribution to the discussion and importantly delineates the various types of feminist literary theory which can be applied. For example, she sees the need for a literary history of African women writers which would account for the "lost lives" in African literary history. Our position is that women writers are not simply seeing themselves in conflict with traditionalism but are pointing out to society where some of the inequities lie and thereby are directly involved in a struggle to reshape society.

African feminist criticism so far has engaged in a number of critical activities which can be conveniently categorized as follows: 1) Developing the canon of African women writers; 2) Examining stereotypical images of women in African literature; 3) Studying African women writers and the development of an African female aesthetic; and 4) Examining women in oral traditional literature.

1.   Developing the Canon of African Women Writers

In a sense this task is two-fold – the development of a canon of African women writers and a parallel canon of critical works with the final aim of expanding the African literary canon. To this end, it encourages women writers, yet challenges their work by providing criticism which is not punitive but challenging and which seeks to elucidate the woman writer's view of the world.[15] In this instance it is one with feminist critics in the discovering of writers considered by establishment to be minor or unimportant. It re-evaluates dismissed women writers by providing critical studies which reveal specific woman-oriented configurations. An excellent example is the case of Flora Nwapa, clearly a victim of literary politics. Cavalierly dismissed by many critics[16] as unimportant, after re-vision she is credited with recreating that oral culture that African society is noted for and making important contributions to her genre. Ernest Emenyonu's rebuttal, "Who Does Flora Nwapa Write For," which explores Nwapa's aesthetic connections with Igbo oral culture,[17] Lloyd Brown's work on Nwapa in his *Women Writers of Black Africa*, and Naana Banyiwa-Horne's essay in this collection are examples of the reassessment of this writer. Published in the same year (1966), Nwapa's *Efuru*, which has a similar plot as Elechi Amadi's *The Concubine*, has not received the same critical acceptance as Amadi's book. Yet while the former provides a resolution which is favorable to women or at least shows the protagonist grappling with the conflicts, Amadi, without any more significant creative ability than Nwapa, shows woman simply as object, unable to exert any control over her life.

2.   The Examination of Female Stereotypes and Images in the Works of African Writers

The approach here is the identification of negative and positive images. African women writers have been attacked for dwelling on the "woman as victim" image and African male writers for locking women into postures of dependence and for defining women only in terms of their association with men. Clearly the study of images of women is not a "dead-ended" enterprise nor one exhausted by Little, as Frank puts it, for Little himself has done questionable work. The study of images is an important developmental step in feminist criticism. It represents the first realization that something is wrong and is usually the first rung of consciousness for the critic. Beyond that it becomes a challenge to established male writers to recognize distortions just as it is for racist writers to recognize and correct racial caricatures. For women writers the "woman as victim" character performs a political function, directly stimulating empathetic identification in the readers and in a sense challenging them to change. Nnu Ego in Emecheta's *The Joys of Motherhood* is the best example. It is such an excellent example of the undesirable "long-suffering" character presented by a woman writer to make a statement on the depths to which women's lives can descend. A positive image, then, is one that is in tune with African historical realities and does not stereotype or limit women into postures of dependence or submergence. Instead it searches for more accurate portrayals and ones which suggest the possibility of transcendence. Writers like Ngugi wa Thiong'o and Ousmane Sembène have demonstrated this possibility in their creation of characters like Waaringa and N'Deye Touti. Flora Nwapa, Ama Ata Aidoo, Mariama Bâ, Buchi Emecheta and other women writers have worked to provide truthful assessments of women's lives, the positive and negative and to demonstrate the specific choices that women must often make. Thus African feminist critics seek to make writers conscious of unrelenting, uniformly undesirable stereotypes and other shortcomings in female portraiture. Included here also is making visible the "invisible woman," or audible, the mute, voiceless woman, the woman who exists only as tangential to man and his problems. Additionally it explores the idealization of women and motherhood in the Négritude vein – woman as supermother, symbol of Africa, earth as muse, how this supports or distorts the creation of a female mythos and how it conforms to the realities of women's lives.

3. African Women Writers and the Development of an African Female Aesthetic

An important cornerstone of this criticism is the examination of the works of African women writers. It looks at the themes and topics which engage women writers, their language, characterization, the forms they use, images and the like. It demands new examinations into the principles of composition, thought and expression of African women writers. New studies of oral literature from this perspective are necessary, and this is discussed separately below. In the case of written literature, previous work of African-American feminist critics who are still working in this area, provide valuable examples. Mary Helen Washington, for example, in her introduction to *Black Eyed Susans*[18] provides an excellent summation of the themes which are common to African-American women's writing: Growing up Black and Female; The Intimidation of Color; The Black Woman and the Myth of the White Woman; The Black

Mother-Daughter Relationship; The Disappointment of Romantic Love; Reconciliation between Black men and women. How similar are these to themes in African women's writing?

My examination of African woman's literature reveals some concerns are similar and others that are unique to African women: 1) motherhood (the presence or absence of it/its joys and pains); 2) the vagaries of living in a polygamous marriage; 3) the oppression of colonialism and white rule; 4) the struggle for economic independence; 5) the achievement of a balance between relationships with men and friendships with other women; 6) the fickleness of husbands; 7) the importance of having a support system, particularly in the urban environment; 8) the mother-daughter conflict or relationship; 9) the mother-son relationship; 10) above all, the definition of self or the development of a separate self over and beyond, but not separate from, tradition or other "man-made" restrictions. While there are similarities arising out of women's lives internationally, and while some of these themes also appear in the works of male writers, like Nuruddin Farah, the literature reveals that there are differences which point to the specific types of oppression African women face in the various cultures. For example, although we are dealing with the literature of two groups of Black women, each group has both distinct and common political and cultural realities which inform its literary concerns.

Comparative assessments of the two bodies of literature and with women's writing in other parts of the world may throw light on the uniqueness of the African woman's literary experience or its participation in an overall female aesthetic. For example, one finds the recurrence of certain forms like the epistolary form, the journal, the letter and other modes of story narration which appear here as in other women's works. Also, the inclusion within the narrative of "small talk" is often considered a weakness in women writers who have not "mastered form." But Pauline Nalova Lyonga in her recent dissertation "Uhamiri. A Feminist Approach to African Literature"[19] demonstrates a thematic and formal continuity between African women's oral and written literature. Importantly, if we are to apply the critical criteria of the literary establishment which is European and male dominated, many of these African female forms are dismissed as weaknesses. The same battle that African literary theorists had to wage to make the European/American critics realize that other African-based aesthetic criteria have to be applied to African literature, in effect has to be waged for African women writers.

4. Women in/and African Oral Literature and Comparative Studies

The examination of women in oral literature and/or of the aesthetics of oral literature created by women as compared to that created by men is another task which so far has not been sufficiently attacked. This critical inquiry is in some ways subsumed in the previous category but important enough to stand on its own. Finnegan's work raises some concerns but obviously was not geared to that endeavor, so it contains relatively little material of relevance to us. There is, however, some available material with which critics can work.[20] A few interesting studies have been done on women in the mythology and how that carries over into the written literature.[21] Several studies of the oral literature of specific groups include some discussion of women as creator/performer and as subject.[22] Several researchers (sociologists, anthropologists) have found it important to look at women's oral literature in addition to their main interests and some work is being done exclusively on African women's oral literature.[23] But there remains much more to be done. There is an overall male bias in approaching oral literary studies (as is the case in written literary studies) which assumes that the artist is always male and which consequently overlooks a large body of material or does not look for specific aesthetic features common to women when women's work is included.

All of the above cut across a number of time periods (pre-colonial, colonial and neo-colonial contexts), political systems (socialist and capitalist states) and settings (rural and urban locales). A number of areas remain uncovered: Language, symbolic structure and how these are revealed in the works of male and female African writers is a relatively unexplored area. Additionally, in defining an African female aesthetic, it may be worthwhile to make comparisons with the art of African women and its images of women and the female characterizations of African male artists.

Any exposition of a critical approach such as this one must lay claims to incompleteness. It is a step towards a larger end rather than the end itself. This introduction represents a summary of the currents in African feminist criticism and the directions it can take. Inevitably it is derivative and its tasks in many ways are identical to the tasks of mainstream feminist theorists and African literary theorists. Obviously, it must utilize the philosophical developments of both and arrive at a necessary synthesis. The contributors in this volume are all engaged in this task, though they are not alone as several important papers emerge each year. Another collection entitled *Critical Perspectives on Women Writers from Africa*[24] edited by Brenda Berrian and Mildred Mortimer is in press. Many of the papers in this collection were presented at forums like the African Literature Association annual conferences and women's conferences which give time and space to the presentation of women's issues in literary criticism. Each of the areas outlined above must, of necessity be expanded upon and developed. A host of research possibilities reveal themselves. This is only a beginning.

Notes

1. Ruth Finnegan, *Oral Literature in Africa*, (London, Oxford University Press, 1970), pp. 375–376. The written African literature is correctly defined as "Modem Written Literature" in recognition that Africa has a long and distinguished oral literary tradition referred to as oral literature and, more recently, "orature."
2. Ama Ata Aidoo, for example, describes her somewhat unique position coming from one of those families which saw Western formal education as important for all and especially for women, in "To Be A Woman," *Sisterhood is Global*, ed. by Robin Morgan (New York, Anchor/Doubleday, 1984), p. 259.

3. See for example works like Ulli Beier ed. *Introduction to African Literature* (London, Longman, 1967); Janheinz Jahn, *Approaches to African Literature* (Ibadan University Press, 1959); and several other books and journals which were published in the 1950's and 1960's.

4. Mary Ellman, *Thinking About Women* (New York, Harcourt Brace Jovanovich, 1968), pp. 28–54.

5. Novelist Ezekiel Mphalele has published several articles on African literature along with his book *The African Image* (London, Faber, 1962); Eldred Jones has edited a number of volumes of *African Writing Today* but is only now (Vol. 15 forthcoming) devoting space to women in African literature; Eustace Palmer, *An Introduction to the African Novel* (London, Heinemann, 1972) follows the Western critical mold exclusively. A range of perspectives exist among African critics of the late 70's and 80's however.

6. O.R. Dathorne, *African Literature in the Twentieth Century* (Heinemann, 1976) had published several other essays and monographs on African literature before this work which does contain some limited discussion of African women writers; John Ansuman Ramsaran, *New Approaches to African Literature* (Ibadan University Press, 1965).

7. Margaret amosu is the only woman to appear in Ulli Beier's *Introduction to African Literature* cited above. Her contribution is a "Selected Bibliography of Critical Writing," pp. 265–270. She had earlier published "A Preliminary Checklist of creative African Writing in the European Languages" (University of Ibadan, 1964).

8. Lilyan Lagneau-Kesteloot who is one of the few European women critics of the 60's wrote an article "Problems of the Literary Critic in Africa," *Abbia*, 8, (1965), pp. 29–44 but does not discuss the woman as critic. Molly Mahood for some years taught at Ibadan and was a mentor of teacher/critics like Oyin Ogunba. Among her works are "Drama in Newborn States," *Presence Africaine* 60 (1966), pp. 16–33.

9. Omolara Ogundipe-Leslie's work, like other African women critics writing in the late sixties and early 1970's had been geared completely to mainstream criticism. In the late 70's, however, her critical orientation became first Marxist and then Marxist/feminist. Recently, however, she published an essay, "Not Spinning on the Axis of Maleness" in *Sisterhood is Global*, pp. 498–504. This is an important step for it is the first feminist statement that has come from this critic. It is directed at an international audience and should have some bearing on future critical works by her and contribute to African feminist literary theory. A short piece "The Female Writer and Her Commitment" appeared in *The Guardian* (Lagos), December 21, 1983, p. 11. Ms. Ogundipe-Leslie has for years had to struggle almost singly in a male-dominated academic climate which Ama Ata Aidoo also describes.

10. Among them are essays in Cheryl L. Brown and Karen Olson, *Feminist Criticism* Essays on Theory, Poetry and Prose (New Jersey, The Scarecrow Press, Inc., 1978). Cheri Register's Review essay, "Literary Criticism" in *Signs* (Winter, 1980) is a fairly comprehensive sampling of the issues and theorists of feminist criticism. Essays in Elizabeth Abel, ed., *Writing and Sexual Difference* (University of Chicago Press, 1982) and Elaine Showalter, *Feminist Criticism* (New York, Random House, 1985) are additional examples.

11. See Addison Gayle, *The Black Aesthetic* (New York, Doubleday, 1971); Carolyn Fowler's introduction to her *Black Arts and Black Aesthetics: A Bibliography* (Atlanta, First World Foundation, 1984); Zirimu and Gurr, *Black Aesthetics* (Nairobi, East African Publishing House, 1973); Wole Soyinka, *Myth, Literature and the African World* (London, Cambridge University Press, 1976); Chinweizu et al, *Towards the Decolonization of*

African Literature (Washington, D.C., Howard University Press, 1983); Johnson, Cailler, Hamilton and Hill-Lubin, *Defining the African Aesthetic* (Washington, D.C., Three Continents Press, 1982).

12. Section Five of *But Some of Us Are Brave*, edited by Gloria T. Hull, Patricia Bell Scott and Barbara Smith (New York, The Feminist Press, 1982) is devoted to literature and con-tains Barbara Smith's "Toward a Black Feminist Criticism," pp. 157–175 which is also published separately in booklet form and distributed by The Crossing Press, 1982. Deborah McDowell, "New Directions in Black Feminist Criticism," *Black American Literature Forum* 14:4 (Winter, 1980), 153–159; Claudia Tate's *Black Women Writers at Work* (New York, Continuum, 1983), Alice Walker's essays in *In Search of Our Mothers' Gardens*, Mary Helen Washington's many essays and a number of other works address this issue. Toni Cade Bambara's *The Black Woman: An Anthology* (New York, New American Library, 1970) includes essays like Francis Beale's "Double Jeopardy: To Be Black and Female" which discuss the particular situation of Black American women. Deborah McDowell is preparing an extensive manuscript on feminist criticism as applied to African-American literature. Barbara Christian, *Black Feminist Criticism: Perspectives on Black Women Writers* (New York, Pergamon Press, 1985) includes Buchi Emecheta in her study.

13. Katherine Frank, "Feminist Criticism and the African Novel," *African Literature Today* 14 (London: Heinemann, 1984), 34–48.

14. Although it has a catchy introduction and conclusion, Femi Ojo-Ade's "Female Writers, Male Critics" does not deal with criticism but is a study of Flora Nwapa and Ama Ata Aidoo. Ojo-Ade is well recognized for an overtly belligerent, condescending-to-female-writers-and-critics language and oral style of presentation which contradicts some of the points he makes in his conclusion "Criticism, Chauvinism, Cynicism … Commitment." While he seems to be arguing for fairness to women here, his tone may betray his true attitude to this subject. Most Black women welcome men as fellow explorers in this field and rarely descend to the gross abuses he suggests, in his final paragraph, that are lev-elled against male critics. It seems instead a rehashing of some of the early stereotypical language of "women's liberation."

15. Carole Boyce Davies and Elaine Savory Fido, "African Women Writers" in *African Literature in the Twentieth Century* ed. by Oyekan Owomoyela (University of Nebraska Press, forthcoming). This chapter attempts a literary history of African women writers which approaches the works from a womanist critical perspective. Roseann P. Bell had earlier called for a "mutual supportive and critical system sympathetic to our needs" in "The Absence of the African Woman Writer," op. cit., p. 498.

16. See Eustace Palmer's review "Elechi Amadi and Flora Nwapa" in African Literature Today 1–4 (1968–70), 56–58.

17. Ernest N. Emenyonu, "Who Does Flora Nwapa Write For?" *African Literature Today* 7 (London: Heinemann, 1975): 28–33.

18. (New York, Anchor/Doubleday, 1975).

19. Unpublished Ph.D. Dissertation, University of Michigan, 1985.

20. Elizabeth Gunner, "Songs of Innocence and Experience: Women as Composers and Performers of *Izibongo*, Zulu Praise Poetry," in *Research in African Literatures* 10:2 (1979), 239–267. Harold Scheub, *African Oral Narratives, Proverbs, Riddles, Poetry and Song* (Boston, G. K. Hall, 1977) is a comprehensive bibliography of African oral litera-ture. A number of dissertations and theses and other collections contain material which is rarely used and which needs to be reviewed for women's contributions.

21. Chidi Ikonne, "Women in Igbo Folktales" presented at the 1982 (Howard) ALA conference is an example. So is Nama's paper on women in Gikuyu mythology in this work.

22. Examples are Marion Kilson, *Royal Antelope and Spider: West African Mende Tales* (Cambridge, Mass: The Press of Langdon Associates, 1976). See also Donald Cosentino's review in *Research in African Literatures* 10 (1979): 296–307 which discusses the question of woman as performer and makes reference to his own collection and to Mama Ngembe, a highly reputed oral artist. Thirty-nine of the forty stories included in Harold Scheub's *The Xhosa "Ntsomi"* (Oxford, Clarendon Press, 1975) were told by women. See Jeff Opland's review of A. C. Jordan, *Tales From Southern Africa* (Berkeley, University of California Press, 1978) in the same issue of *RAL* pp. 307–314.

23. For example Beverly B. Mack "'*Waka Daya Ba Ta Kare Nika*': One Song Will Not Finish the Grinding: Hausa Women's Oral Literature" in *Contemporary African Literature* ed. by Wylie et al (Three Continents Press, 1983), 15–46; Enoch T. Mvula, "Tumbuka Pounding Songs in the Management of Familial Conflicts" *Cross Rhythms* 2 ed. by Daniel Avorgbedor and Kwesi Yankah (Indiana University, Department of Folklore, The Trickster Press, 1985), 93–113. Mvula is doing some further research on African women's oral literature in East Africa.

24. (Washington, D.C., Three Continents Press, forthcoming). Brenda Berrian's *Bibliography of American Women Writers and Journalists* (Three Continents, 1985) will contribute significantly to the study of African women writers and definitely establishes that there is a substantial body of literature by African women.

3.6

The Historical Denial of Lesbianism

Blanche Wiesen Cook

Miss Marks and Miss Woolley by Anna Mary Wells, New York: Houghton Mifflin, 1978.

The historical denial of lesbianism accompanies the persistent refusal to acknowledge the variety and intensity of women's emotional and erotic experiences. That denial involves the notion so prevalent in 19th century medical textbooks that physical love between women was experimental masturbation, studious preparation for marriage. It involves the notion that women without men are lonely asexual spinsters and that erotic and sexual pleasure without male penetration is not erotic or sexual pleasure.

Old fantasies die hard; and heterosexist definitions denying the reality, the diversity, the vast range of perfectly pleasurable relations between women continue to prevail. Elsewhere I have written about the cost to women of this mandated societal ignorance.[1] Crude and dehumanizing stereotypes about lesbians not only persist, they are now being exploited by reactionaries as a key weapon in their organizing campaigns. These stereotypes result from the fact that women's friendships have been obscured and trivialized, "not merely unsung," as Vera Brittain once wrote, "but mocked, belittled and falsely interpreted."[2]

Thus companionate women who have lived together all their adult lives have been branded, on no evidence whatsoever, 'lonely spinsters.' Jane Addams, for example, lived with Mary Rozet Smith for 40 years. They loved each other, slept in the same room and in the same bed. Yet Jane Addams' biographers insist that "Life ... forever eluded her." She was, after all, a lonely asexual spinster. Our prejudices are such that it has been considered "gentlemanly" to label a woman lonely and lifeless, rather than lesbian. Denied information about the many lesbians whose lives were not only moral and ordinary but admired and exemplary, bigots have been able to perpetuate the myth of lesbianism as deviance, sickness and criminality.

In literature as well as politics the lesbianism of distinguished women has been denied, and when not deniable utterly trivialized. Only recently Leon Edel in the *New York Times* attempted to squirm away from Virginia Woolf's lesbian friendships so clearly presented in her own words. In a review of the fourth volume of Virginia Woolf's letters Edel quoted Virginia's sister Vanessa Bell: "But do you really like going to bed with women? – and how do you do it?" Then Edel quoted Virginia Woolf's answer: "Women alone stir my imagination." But Edel could hardly bear it: "This can only be a thought of the moment," he insisted. Any reader less circumscribed by the limitations of male need and heterosexist imaginings will lose count of the many moments throughout Virginia Woolf's letters devoted to the women she loved – notably Violet Dickinson, Vita Sackville-West, and Dame Ethel Smyth.[3]

Miss Marks and Miss Woolley is one of the more interesting examples of the historical denial of lesbianism. Despite all its flaws it reintroduces two fascinating and formidable women, far too long ignored. Jeannette Marks and Mary Woolley were independent and virgorous women. Learned and caring, they were politically engaged and professionally successful. Among the first generation of academic women, they were associated with Wellesley and Mt. Holyoke, with literature, and with movements for international peace, women's suffrage, and the Equal Rights Amendment. Surrounded by friends, the women with whom they studied and worked, Marks and Woolley offered each other deep affection, keen and helpful criticism, and the kind of nurturing love that freed them from stifling and petty obstacles.

During their 47-year-long relationship, Mary Woolley – president of Mt. Holyoke – seemed to outsiders to dominate the environment. She was the public figure, older, more professionally secure. Jeannette Marks was 12 years younger; and when they vowed "lifelong fidelity" to each other in 1900 Woolley had just been appointed to the presidency, while Marks had still not finished her graduate work at Wellesley. As concerned for her own work as President Woolley was for hers, Jeannette Marks not only feared that she might be eclipsed by the public demands of Woolley's position, but that the public attitude toward her role in Mary Woolley's life might be harmful to Woolley, and their relationship. There were crises. There were storms. There was time apart; time to grow, alone and separated as well as together in public and quiet.

In 1905, during a particularly strained period, that included the death of Mary Woolley's beloved mother, Jeannette Marks wrote: 'If I say I will come next summer, will you take care of me and help give me a chance to do the work I long to do?… If I give all to you and give up the idea that I must protect myself from you, will you really care for my work as well as loving me?" (93)

Above all, Jeannette Marks sought confirmation that neither woman would ever be reduced to dependency or servility. She wrote Woolley about her need to believe in Woolley's regard for her work. "I would not take a kingdom for the proof at the dinner table as well as in the quiet of our bedroom that you depend on me; there is no gift equal to the dignity that you can confer on me in that way."

This is one of innumerable letters and notes Marks and Woolley wrote to each other daily. Theirs is a very well documented life. Yet anna Mary Wells' tone throughout this book denies and diminishes their life together. The above letter, for example, is clearly an expression of Marks' need not to be consumed by the public demands of her lover's position, and not to have her own work belittled. But the letter is oddly edited, and Wells concludes that Marks was "on the verge of an emotional breakdown" because it is so "full of self-pity and making violently ambivalent demands." (92–93) The sentence Wells omits would have told us so much: "I cannot be happy away from you, yet supposing I should be worthless because I have given in to you…." (quoted later, and in an entirely different context, p. 252).

Much of the relationship Marks and Woolley created together was devoted to nurturing and protecting each other's autonomy and individuality. It was the kind of relationship strong, creative women who love each other require. Despite Wells' reference to Marks as an "appendage," it is clear from the passionate intensity of their letters that until Mary Woolley's death in 1947, both women specifically avoided the perils of an arrangement wherein one partner might fall into the shadowy abyss of the role of "wife" or factor. Jeannette Marks and Mary Woolley led full and inspiring lives. And they deserve a full and inspiring book. *Miss Marks and Miss Woolley* is not that book. It is more an academic history of women's colleges, Mt. Holyoke in particular. Wells gives us a full account of their academic careers; an interesting survey of the barriers first Woolley and then Marks, who was Woolley's student at Wellesley, overcame with such gusto; and a running river of the kind of gossip that seems of more concern to Wells than to Marks and Woolley and their friends. It is an on-campus account, with several forays abroad on behalf of international peace. About Jeannette Marks' socialist and feminist contributions to Woolley's vision we learn little, except that Wells thought Marks impolitic, if not cheeky. Actually Wells seems not to understand the full significance, either emotional or political, of these women's lives.

Ultimately the author is incapable of telling us very much about her subjects because she is appalled by them. Yet Wells was the first to use the Woolley-Marks papers and this book serves to give us some sense of the vast work women's biographers have now to do. For the fact that Anna Mary Wells saved this valuable correspondence from total obscurity, we will always be grateful. Committed to reclaiming the pioneering president of Mt. Holyoke from oblivion, Wells acknowledged that Woolley's friendship with Marks was important to her life, to her career.

However Wells defined that friendship, she recognized its significance, despite her initial reaction recorded in the preface:

> The first few that I read were ardent love letters expressed in terms that shocked and embarrassed me. My immediate impulse was to abandon my plans for the book.... I had supposed myself to be open-minded and tolerant about sexual deviation, but it now appeared that I was not so at all when it occurred in women I admired and respected. (ix)

"Admired and respected." They were after all beloved lady professors who wore pearls and occasionally long dresses with plunging necklines. Yet, a victim of out dominant cultural perversity, Wells can only conclude that they were asexual spinsters. On the other hand, since Marks and Woolley were clearly not asexual spinsters, and all their letters proved that, Mt. Holyoke's former president David Truman decided to close the collection until 1999 and to hide the fact that Mt. Holyoke possessed the letters. Regardless of Wells' initial upset, and to her everlasting credit, she appealed for continued access to the material, and to the right to use her notes – temporarily denied – and contacted archivists and historians for support. I was then part of an American Historical Association committee that protested this attempt at pre-publication censorship. Following appeals from many archivists and historians the decision was reversed. Except for a "packet" of letters of unknown content and size, still closed until 1999, the correspondence is now available to scholars.

There is much to do in that collection. The entire political dimension of their lives, the nature of their socialism, feminism, and internationalism remains unexplored. Then, since Wells denies the possibility of sexuality in women, she inevitably diminishes the quality of their life together. "I was," Wells explains, "careful to avoid the use of the words 'lesbian' or 'homosexual', since both seem to me imprecise as well as pejorative." Wells even asserts that "there is substantial doubt that Sappho herself was Lesbian." She concludes: "My own opinion, for what it is worth, is that ... they voluntarily renounced all physical contact...." (x–xi) Wells, alas, seriously expects us to believe that two women who lived together for almost 50 years never hugged, never kissed, never warmed each other's bodies on a cold South Hadley night.

Even if they did renounce all physical contact we can still argue that they were lesbians: they chose each other, and they loved each other. Women who love women, who choose women to nurture and support and to form a living environment in which to work creatively and independently are lesbians. Genital "proofs" to confirm lesbianism are never required to confirm the heterosexuality of men and women who live together for 20, or 50, years. Such proofs are not demanded even when discussing ephemeral love relations between adult women and men.

We know, for example, that General Eisenhower and his friend Kay Summersby were passionately involved with each other. They looked ardently into each other's eyes. They held hands. They cantered swiftly across England's countryside. They played golf and bridge and laughed. They were inseparable. But they never "consummated" their love in the acceptable, traditional, sexual manner. Now does that fact render Kay Summersby and Dwight David Eisenhower somehow less in love? Were they not heterosexual?[4]

What are we talking about then? Bigotry and foolishness. But a dangerous bigotry and a cruel foolishness – capable of wrecking joy, depriving people of job security, severing mother from child, and creating havoc amidst the gossip impinging on the relationship. Jeannette Marks knew that; and dealt with it directly. But Anna Mary Wells completely distorts that fact.

Wells' most grievous analytic fault is her distortion of Jeannette Marks' life. Her contempt based on Mt. Holyoke gossip, Wells concludes that Marks' entire life was miserable. She criticizes Marks' conduct as professor and chair of Mr. Holyoke's English Department as "erratic and self-defeating." She dismisses her professional achievements as unsubstantial, despite Marks' *nineteen* published and largely well received books. And she insists that emotionally Jeannette Marks was unsatisfied, underdeveloped, and unhappy. The truth is Jeannette Marks was a vital person with many enthusiasms. She travelled widely. She wanted to be alone and with other people. She wanted to remove herself from the towering and stifling shadows of Mt. Holyoke. She had affairs. She wrote books. She lived with others. And when she returned to Mary Woolley she did so refreshed and eagerly; fortified and prepared once again for the slander and incessant gossip of small town South Hadley. Woolley was always relieved and happy to have her return; and always offered to resign when the unending gossip or other challenges directly threatened their home.

The changing needs of their lives, and their ability to fulfill those needs ensured their life together. Mary Woolley and Jeannette Marks were not oppressed women. And they did not oppress each other. Their relationship required courage, boldness. It involved the fear of being replaced or left. They believed in the harmony and essential rhythms of their own unique natures. Their ability to remain independent and to protect each other's different needs seems entirely beyond Wells' comprehension. She has written, in fine, a mean-spirited little book. It certainly will not be the last book about these two great ladies who have so much to tell us about the ongoing struggle to create deeply caring and entirely fulfilled lives.

Notes

1. See, "Female Support Networks and Political Activism: Lillian Wald, Crystal Eastman and Emma Goldman," in *Chrysalis*, III, Autumn 1977; reprinted by Out and Out Books, 1979, pamphlet.

2. Vera Brittain, *Testament of Friendship: The Life of Winifred Holtby* (London: Macmillan, 1947), 2.

3. Leon Edel, "Triumphs and Symptoms," a review of *The Letters of Virginia Woolf*, vol. 4, in *The New York Times Book Review*, 25 March 1979; see Blanche Wiesen Cook, "'Women Alone Stir My Imagination': Lesbianism and the Cultural Tradition," *Signs*, vol. 4, no. 4, Summer 1979.

4. Kay Summersby Morgan, *Past Forgetting: My Love Affair with Dwight David Eisenhower* (NY: Simon & Schuster, 1976), published posthumously.

3.7

The Historian as Curandera

Aurora Levins Morales

"Until lions write books, history will always glorify the hunter."

South African proverb

One of the first things a colonizing power or repressive regime does is attack the sense of history of those they wish to dominate by attempting to take over and control their relationships to their own past. When the invading English rounded up the harpists of Ireland and burned their harps, it was partly for their function in carrying news and expressing public opinion, for their role as opposition media; but it was also because they were repositories of collective memory. When the Mayan codices were burned, it was the Mayan sense of identity, rooted in a culture with a past, that was assaulted. The prohibitions against slaves speaking their own languages, reading and writing, playing drums, all had obvious uses in attempting to prevent organized resistance, but they were also ways of trying to control the story of who slaves thought they were.

One important way that colonial powers seek to disrupt the sense of historical identity of the colonized is by taking over the transmission of culture to the young. Native American and Australian aboriginal children were taken from their families by force and required to abandon the language, dress, customs and spirituality of their own people. Irish and Welsh children in English-controlled schools, and Puerto Rican, Mexican, Native American and Chinese children in U.S. public schools, were punished and ridiculed for speaking their home languages.

Invading the historical identities of the subjugated is one part of the task, accomplished through the destruction of records, oral traditions and cultural forms and through interfering with the education of the young. The other part is the creation of an imperial version of our lives. When a controlling elite of any kind comes to power, it requires some kind of a replacement origin myth, a story that explains the new imbalances of power as natural, inevitable and permanent, as somehow inherent to the natures of master and slave, invader and invaded, and therefore unchangeable. A substitute for the memories of the colonized. Official history is designed to make sense of oppression, to say that the oppressed are oppressed because it is their nature to be oppressed. A strong sense of their own history among the oppressed undermines the project of domination. It provides an alternative story, one in which oppression is the result of events and choices, not natural law.

Imperial histories also fulfill a vital role for those who rule. Those who dominate must justify themselves and find ways to see their own dominance as not only legitimate but the only acceptable option. So the founding fathers spoke of the need to control democracy so that only those with the experience of managing wealth would be deemed fit to hold public office; some slave holders framed the kidnapping and enslavement of West Africans as beneficial to the enslaved, as offering them the bless-ings of a higher state of civilization; misogynist patriarchs speak of protecting woman from her own weak nature; and the colonized everywhere are defined as in need of improvement, which only a better management of their labor and resources can offer.

In his 1976 essay "Defensa de la palabra," Uruguayan writer Eduardo Galeano wrote: "What process of change can move a people that does not know who it is, nor where it came from? If it doesn't know who it is, how can it know what it deserves to be?" The role of a socially committed historian is to use history, not so much to document the past as to restore to the dehistoricized a sense of identity and possi-bility. Such "medicinal" histories seek to re-establish the connections between peoples and their histories, to reveal the mechanisms of power, the steps by which their current condition of oppression was achieved through a series of decisions made by real people to dispossess them; but also to reveal the multiplicity, creativity and persistence of resistance among the oppressed.

*****

History is the story we tell ourselves about how the past explains our present, and how the ways in which we tell it are shaped by contemporary needs. When debates raged in 1992 about the quincentennial of Columbus' arrival in the Americas, what was most significant about all the voices in the controversy, the official pomp and ceremony, the outraged protests of indigenous and other colonized peoples of the Americas, and the counter-attacking official responses, is that each of these posi-tions had something vital to say about the nature of our contemporary lives and relationships, which our conflicting interpretations of the events of 1492 simply highlighted.

All historians have points of view. All of us use some process of election through which we choose which stories we consider important and interesting. We do his-tory from some perspective, within some particular worldview. Storytelling is not neutral. Curandera historians make this explicit, openly naming our partisanship, our intent to influence how people think.

Between 1991 and 1996 I researched and wrote *Remedios,* a medicinal version of Puerto Rican history, told through the lives of women not so much because the pasts of Puerto Rican women were inherently important to talk about, but because I wanted to change the way Puerto Rican women think of ourselves historically. As a result, I did not attempt to write a comprehensive general history, but rather to frame historic events in ways that would contribute to decolonizing the historical identities and imaginations of Puerto Rican women and to the creation of a culture of resistance.

Remedios is testimonio, both in the sense of a life story, an autobiography of my relationship to my past, and, like the testimonios of Latin American torture survivors, in bearing witness to a much larger history of abuse and resistance in which many women and men participated. One of the most significant ways in which *Remedios* differs from conventional historical writing is in how explicitly I proclaim that my interest in history lies in its medicinal uses, in the power of history to provide those healing stories that can restore the humanity of the traumatized, and not for any inherent interest in the past for its own sake. *Remedios* does not *tell* history so much as it *interrogates* it. It seeks to be provocative rather than comprehensive, looking for potency, more than the accumulation of information.

In the writing, I chose to make myself visible not only as a historian with an agenda, but also as a subject of this history and one of the traumatized seeking to recover herself. My own work became less and less about creating a reconstructed historical record and more and more a use of my own relationship to history, my questions and challenges, my mapping of ignorance and contradiction, my anger and sorrow and exhilaration, to testify, through my personal responses to them, to how the official and renegade stories of the past impact Puerto Rican women. To explore, by sharing how I had done so in my own life, the ways that recaptured history could be used as a tool of recovery from a multitude of blows. In writing *Remedios*, I made myself the site of experimentation and engaged in a process of decolonizing my own relationship to history as one model of what was possible.

As I did so, I evolved a set of understandings or instructions to myself about how to do this kind of work, a kind of curandera's handbook of historical practice. The rest of this essay is that handbook.

1.   Tell Untold or Undertold Histories

The first and most obvious choice is to seek out and tell those histories that have not been told or have not been told enough. If history books looked like the population of the world, they would be full of women, poor people, workers, children, people of color, slaves, the colonized. In the case of *Remedios*, where I had already chosen to tell Puerto Rican history through the lives of women, this meant continually seeking out and emphasizing the stories of women who were poor, African, indigenous, mestiza and mulatta, women enslaved and indentured, rural women, emigrant women in the United States.

2.   Centering Women Changes the Landscape

Making truly medicinal history requires that we do more than just add women (or any other "disappeared" group of people) to the existing frameworks. We need to ask, "If women are assumed to be the most important people in this story, how will that change the questions we ask? How will it change our view of what events and processes are most important? How will it change the answers to questions that have already been asked?

For example, if you ask, "Until what point did the indigenous Arawak people of Puerto Rico have a significant impact on the society?" most Puerto Rican historians will say that the Arawaks stopped playing a major part by around 1550 because they no longer existed as a people. But what no longer existed in 1550 were organized lowland villages, caciques, war bands – in other words, those aspects of social organization that European men would consider most important and be most likely to recognize. If we ask the same question centered on women, we would need to look at those areas of life in which women had the most influence. Evidence from other parts of the Americas shows that traditional cultures survived longest in those arenas controlled by non-elite women. If we put women at the center, it may be that Arawak culture continued to have a strong influence on rural Puerto Ricans until much later, particularly in the practices of agriculture and medicine, certain kinds of spirituality, childrearing, food preparation, and in the production of cloth and pottery.

Similarly, in exploring when Puerto Ricans first began to have a distinct sense of nationality other than as Spanish colonial settlers, the usual evidence considered is the publication of newspapers or the formation of patriotic societies, activities dominated by men. How did women experience nationality? If, as José Luís Gonzalez asserts, the first people to see themselves as Puerto Rican were Black because they lacked mobility and were, perforce, committed to Puerto Rico, what about the impact of women's mobility or lack of it? Did women experience a commitment to Puerto Rican identity as a result of childbearing and extended family ties? Did they feel Puerto Rican earlier or later than men?

If women are at the center, what is the significance, what were the gains and losses of the strongly feminist Puerto Rican labor movement of the early 20th Century? Medicinal history does not just look for ways to "fit in" more biographies of people from underrepresented groups. It shifts the landscape of the questions asked.

3. Identify Strategic Pieces of Misinformation and Contradict Them

In challenging imperial histories, some kinds of misinformation have more of an impact than others. Part of the task of a curandera historian is diagnosis. We need to ask ourselves what aspects of imperial history do the most harm, which lies are at the foundations of our colonized sense of ourselves. Some of these strategic pieces of misinformation will be the same for all projects, and I name several below. Some will be of central importance only to specific histories. In the case of Puerto Rican history, a few of the specific lies I decided were important to debunk were the absence or downplaying of Africa and African people from official histories, the idea that there was such a thing as "pure" Spanish culture in 1492 or at any time since and the invisibility of Puerto Ricans' relations with people from the other islands, especially the French, English and Dutch colonies. The first is about erasure, the other two deal with ideas of national or cultural purity.

4. Make Absences Visible

The next three points deal with the nature and availability of historical evidence. When you are investigating and telling the history of disenfranchised people, you can't always find the kind and amount of written material you want. But in

medicinal history the goal is as much to generate questions and show inconsistencies as it is to document people's lives.

For example, tracing absences can balance a picture, even when you are unable to
fill in the blanks. Lack of evidence doesn't mean you can't name and describe what is
missing. Tracing the outlines of a woman-shaped hole in the record, talking about
the existence of women about whom we know only general information, can be a
powerful way of correcting imperial history. I wrote one piece about the indigenous
women known to have been brought to Puerto Rico from other parts of Central,
South and North America who left little trace of their real names, and even less of
what nations they carne from.

> We are your Indian grandmothers from Eastern America, stolen from our homes and
> shipped to wherever they needed our work. From Tierra Firme to the islands. From
> one island to another. From this side to that, each colony raiding for its own supply ...
> They have passenger lists with the names of those who came west over the ocean to
> take our lands, but our names are not recorded ... Some of us died so far from home
> we couldn't even imagine the way back: Cherokee in Italy, Tupi in Portugal, Inuit in
> Denmark. Many of us were fed into the insatiable gold mines of el imperio alongside
> the people of your island, and they called us simply indias. But we were as different
> from one another as Kongo from Wolof, Italian from Dane ... We are the ancestors of
> whom no record has been kept. We are trace elements in your bodies, minerals coloring
> your eyes, residue in your fingernails. You were not named for us. You don't know the
> places where our bones are, but we are in your bones. Because of us, you have relatives
> among the many tribes. You have cousins on the reservations ...

It is also possible to use fictitious characters to highlight an absence, as Virginia
Woolf does in *A Room of One's Own* when she speaks of Shakespeare's talented and
fictitious sister, for whom no opportunities were open. I wrote a similar piece about
the invented sister of a Spanish chronicler who visited Puerto Rico in the 18th
century to make visible the absence of women chroniclers.

5.   Asking Questions Can Be as Good as Answering Them

Another way of dealing with lost history is to ask speculative questions. "What
if?" is a legitimate tool of investigation, and the question can be as valuable as an
answer. Proposing a radically different interpretation is a way of opening up how
we think about events, even when there is no way to prove anything. It is useful
to ask, "What would have to be different for us to understand this story in this
other way?"

The chronicles of the Spanish conquest of Puerto Rico have relatively little to say
about the cacica Guanina and her liaison with the Spaniard Cristóbal Sotomayor.
The popularized version I grew up on goes something like this. Innocent Indian
maiden sees the most handsome man she's ever laid eyes on, far surpassing anyone
in her whole culture. She falls in love with him, even though he has enslaved her

community, who are dying like flies. She becomes his lover, and when her people plot an uprising, she runs to warn him. He doesn't take her seriously, not because he's arrogant, but because he's brave, and promptly rides into an ambush and dies. Guanina is beside herself with grief. Her brother the chief finds her dead body lying across her slain lover, the two are buried side by side and the lilies of Spain entwine with the wildflowers of Puerto Rico upon their graves.

On the face of it, this is an extremely unlikely tale. Guanina was the niece of the high cacique of Puerto Rico, in a matrilineal society in which sisters' children inherited. At eighteen she would have been considered a full adult, and a woman of influence and prestige. Puerto Rico, called Boriken by the Arawaks, was not settled by European colonists until 1508. By the time Guanina and Sotomayor are known to have been lovers, the Arawaks of Boriken on the eve of the 1511 uprising had had eighteen years of news from Hispaniola and had a pretty good idea of what was likely to happen to them. Beth Brant, writing on Pocahontas, argues that indigenous women sometimes sought out liaisons with European men as a way of creating ties of kinship, in the hope that such a bond would help them fend off the worst consequences of invasion. If all we do is assume, for a moment, that Guanina was not naive, but was an intelligent woman, used to seeing herself as important, and that she was thinking about what she was doing, the colonialist story becomes completely implausible. My reinterpretation of Guanina's story is based on that implausibility and simply proposes another possible set of motives and understandings that could explain the known facts of her life and death and leave us with a sense of her dignity and purpose. It is speculative, and without hard evidence, but it opens up important questions about how to understand the actions of smart people in intolerable conditions.

6.   What Constitutes Evidence?

Another issue to keep in mind is the bias built into historical standards of evidence. Although there is an increasing acceptance of other forms of documentation, the reliance is still heavily on the written. Which means that we accept an immense body of experience as unavailable for historical discussion. The fact that something was written down does not make it true, as any critical consumer of the media knows. It simply means that someone with sufficient authority to write things down recorded their version of events or transactions while someone else did not. It is evidence of some of what they did, some of what they wanted others to think they did and some of what they thought about it. No more. Of course even something as partial as this is a treasure trove, but when we rely on written records we need to continually ask ourselves what might be missing, what might have been recorded in order to manipulate events and in what direction, and in what ways we are allowing ourselves to assume that objectivity is in any way connected with literacy. We need to remind ourselves that much of what we want to know wasn't written about, and also think about ways to expand what we will consider as contributing to evidence.

Is the oral tradition of a small town, handed down over fourteen generations, about the mass exodus of local men to the gold mines of Brazil, really less reliable than what women tobacco workers charged with civil offenses deposed before a judge whose relatives owned tobacco fields? As historians of the under-represented, we need to question the invalidation of non-literate mechanisms of memory.

7.   Show Agency

One of the big lies of imperial history is that only members of the elite act, and everyone else is acted upon. In our attempts to expose the cruelty of oppression, we sometimes portray oppressed communities as nothing more than victims and are unable to see the full range of responses that people always make to their circumstances. People who are being mistreated are always trying to figure out a strategy. Those strategies may be shortsighted, opportunistic, ineffective or involve the betrayal of others, but they nevertheless represent a form of resistance. Politically, it's essential that we learn to develop strategies that hold out for real transformation whenever possible and that take everyone's well-being into account. But in telling the history of our struggles with each other over time, it's important to recognize that resistance takes many forms. We need to dismantle the idea of passive victimization, which leaves us feeling ashamed and undeserving of freedom. Even under the most brutal conditions, people find ways to assert their humanity. Medicinal history must find ways to show the continual exercise of choice by people who appear powerless.

8.   Show Complexity and Embrace Ambiguity and Contradiction

In order to do this, we must also give up the idea that people are 100 percent heroic or villainous. In searching out a history of resistance, the temptation is to find heroic figures and either overlook their failings or feel betrayed when we find that they have some. Human beings are not all resistance or collaboration and complicity. Popular imperial history tends to be ahistorical and simplistic, focused on exceptional personalities instead of complex social processes. If we ignore what is contradictory about our own impulses toward solidarity or betrayal in an attempt to simplify history into good and evil, we will sacrifice some of the most important lessons to be gained.

We need more than just the heroic stories of militant resistance. Stories of accommodation, collaboration and outright defeat are just as important because they give us ways to understand our position as caused rather than just existing. If we want to give people a sense of agency, of having always been actors as well as acted upon, we must be willing to tell stories full of contradiction that show the real complexity of the causes of their current conditions.

For example, Nzinga, born in 1585, was a queen among the Mbundu of what is now Angola. She was a fierce anti-colonial warrior, a militant fighter, a woman holding power in a male-dominated society, and she laid the basis for successful Angolan resistance to Portuguese colonialism all the way into the 20th century. She was also an elite woman living from the labor of others, murdered her brother and his children, fought other African people on behalf of the Portuguese and collaborated in the slave trade.

I tell her story in two different ways, once at the end of her life, celebrating her anti-colonial militancy and the power of her memory for Black women, and once from the point of view of the woman on whose back she literally sat as she negotiated with the Portuguese governor. It is in many ways more empowering when we show our heroic figures as contradictory characters full of weaknesses and failures of insight. Looking at those contradictions enables us to see our own choices more clearly and to understand that imperfect people can have a powerful, liberating impact on the world.

9.   Reveal Hidden Power Relationships

Imperial history obscures the power relations that underlie our daily lives. This is one of the ways that immense imbalances of power and resources are made to seem natural. In telling the history of an oppressed community, we need to expose those relationships of unequal power whether they come from outside our group or lie within it. Puerto Rican liberal feminists of the late 19th century, all those "firsts" in the arts and education, came primarily from an hacendado class made affluent by the slave-produced profits of the sugar industry Many of the leaders of the 1868 Lares uprising against Spain were coffee planters angered by their growing dependence on newly arrived merchants and the credit they offered.

Another way to expose unequal power is to reveal hidden economic relationships. I did this in part by following the products of Puerto Rican Women's labor to their destinations and tracing the objects of their daily use to their sources. This both shows the degree of control exerted on our lives by the profit-seeking of the wealthy and uncovers relationships we have with working people in other parts of the world. In the 1600s ginger grown by Puerto Rican women and men was sold to English smugglers from Jamaica and ended up spicing the daily gingerbread of London's working poor. One of the main items imported in exchange was used clothing made in the mills of England and the Low Countries. This reveals a different relationship between Puerto Ricans and English people than the "great civilization/insignificant primitive colony" story told in the 1923 *Encyclopaedia Britannica* we had in my home, which described Puerto Rico as a small island with no natural resources. Telling Puerto Rican community college students that the stagehands for Shakespeare's productions probably ate Puerto Rican food on their lunch breaks changes their relationship to that body of "high culture."

Similarly, Puerto Rican women and children picked and processed coffee that was considered the best in the world at the turn of the century. Yauco coffee was served in the wealthiest homes of New York, Paris and Vienna. Mrs. J.P. Morgan bought her personal supply from Yauco, and all those philosophers, poets and painters drank it at their salons. Juxtaposing photographs of coffee workers who earned pennies for their labor with the silver coffeepots and reclining gentry who consumed the coffee restores Puerto Rican women's labor to its place in an international web of trade and profit.

I wrote one piece in which I described the lunch preparations of a rural Puerto Rican neighbor and showed how the food she set on the table was a map of the world, showing her connections to people in Malaysia, Ethiopia, Portugal and many other places. I described the vegetables grown and canned in the Imperial and Salinas Valleys of California by Mexican and Filipina women and promoted as the "modern" replacement for fresh produce to Puerto Rican housewives of the late '40s and '50s. I read this piece as part of a talk I gave at a small college in Michigan, including a section about bacalao, the dry salt cod that is a staple protein of Puerto Rican cuisine.

> The bacalao is the fin-tip of a vast movement in which the shadows of small fishing boats skim across the Grand Banks of Nova Scotia hauling cod from immense schools of feeding fish, salt it down in their holds and return with rumors of great lands to fourteenth-century Basque fishing villages and Portuguese port towns. Return to Iceland, to New Brunswick and Nova Scotia, to build up the great shipping fortunes of Massachusetts. The flaking yellow flesh makes her part of a wide Atlantic net of people who live from the cod: catch the cod, salt the cod, pack and ship the cod, sell the cod, import and export the cod, stretch a piece of it into food for a family for a week."

After the talk, a man came up to me, deeply moved, to tell me that he had grown up in a Nova Scotia fishing village and his family had packed cod. I thanked him and told him we had eaten it for breakfast. "So did we!" he exclaimed. "We ate it with green bananas," I told him. "We ate it with potatoes," he replied, and we embraced. The last place he had expected to hear about his own life was in a talk on Puerto Rican women's history. Revealing this kind of connection increases a sense of our common interests and uncovers the importance of our labor in the international scheme of things.

10. Personalize

The majority of historical figures who are known by name are members of elite groups, while everyone else tends to be known en masse. However, there are quite a few places where the names of individual people who are poor, female, dark, etc., can be found in written records. Using the names of individual real people, and any details we know about their lives, to dramatize and personalize the social condition of a group makes those conditions far more real. When the disenfranchised appear only in crowd scenes, it reinforces a sense of relative unimportance.

In writing about the lives of recently freed slave women in Puerto Rico, I used names of real women found in a footnote in a book on slavery in San Juan that contained the details of what family members they sought out after emancipation and what work they did. This has an entirely different impact than writing, "many freed women sought out their relatives and contracted to work for them."

The best-documented Arawak women are cacicas, members of the indigenous ruling class known as nitainos. Most of the stories about Arawak women focus on cacicas like Guanina, Loiza or Anacaona. But we know that the majority of Arawak women belonged to the naboría laborer class. I found a list of indigenous women both from Boriken and from the smaller islands of the Eastern Caribbean who were being branded as slaves on one particular day in 1515. Many were given two names in the record, one Spanish and one Arawak or Carib and many others simply renamed Maria or Catalina. By using names that were at least imposed on real women, and the few facts recorded about them, their anonymity in the imperial records is at least made visible and the realities of their lives during the conquest become more tangible. Here is an example from my poem "1515: Naborías:"

> They were not cacicas.
> They were not heirs to yuca fields.
> There were no concessions made to their status.
> They were not "queens."
>
> Their names are recorded in the lists of work gangs
> sent to the mines, the conucos, the kitchens, the laundries
> of the Spanish invaders.
> > Mancaney, field hand.
> > Francisquilla, cook.
> > Ana, baker.
> > Catalina, pig woman.
>
> They were the working women of Boriken.
> They were called out of their names.
> Casually recorded under the names of Catholic saints,
> or the queens of the myriad kingdoms of Spain, renamed
> after little sisters or mothers left behind in Estremadura,
> Navarra, Castilla, Sevilla, León
> or a favorite prostitute from a port town,
> or a beauty out of some ballad of the old land.
> They were not born Catalina, Ana, Francisquilla …
>
> The account books of the governor say *herrose* –
> branded on this day – was Elvira Arumaita
> from the island of Guadalupe
> with a son they called Juaníco.
> *herrose*, a Carib called Beatríz, and her son, Juaníco.
> *herrose*, a Carib, Juana Cabarotaxa, from the island of Santa Cruz,

> and
> *herrose*, a little girl called Anita, Carib,
> from the aforementioned island
> which we now call Guadalupe, and *herrose*,
> also from Guadalupe, Magdalena Guavrama
> Carib, and her child.
>
> They were already here, enslaved, escaped,
> and to their great misfortune, recaptured
> and branded this day by Captain Juan Ponce de León,
>   Ana Taguas, Violante Ateyba
>   Leonor Yayguana written down as belonging
>   to the rebel cacique Abey,
>   and Isabel Guayuca with her son, once again Juaníco,
>   once owing loyalty to the collaborator Cayey.
> They were women under two masters,
> the crumbling authority of the caciques
> and the new and violent usage of the señores ...

In cases where we really don't have names, documented elements in the lives of a social group can still be personalized by writing a personal narrative that conveys the reality of such a life. I used figures on average wages of women working in coffee, sugar and garment work in the early 20th century along with a list of the prices of housing and essential foods to write an internal monologue about the kinds of choices a single mother of several children has to make during the dead season of the sugar cane industry when there is little work and a lot of illness. Details like the difference between feeding your children unbroken rice, broken rice or cornmeal make the actual struggles of such women visible and felt in a way that lists of numbers alone cannot.

11.   Show Connection and Context

One element of imperial history is that events tend to be seen as caused by extraordinary personalities acting on one another without showing us the social context. For example, many of the great discoveries and inventions we are taught about in elementary and high school were being pursued by many people at once, but the individual who received the patent is described as a lone explorer rather than part of a group effort. Rosa Parks didn't "get tired" one day and start the Montgomery bus boycott. She was a trained organizer, and her role, as well as the time and place of the boycott, was the result of careful planning by a group of civil rights activists. Just as medicinal history must restore individuality to anonymous masses of people, it must also restore social context to individuals singled out as the actors of history.

12.   Restore Global Context

One element of imperial history that is particularly strong in the United States is a sense that the rest of the world is irrelevant. Few U.S. residents are knowledgeable about the geography, politics, culture and history of other countries. In 1968, when I was fourteen, I spent a summer in Cuba. One of the most striking things for me was opening the paper each day to find regular ongoing coverage of dozens of countries I had only heard of before as occasional "hot spots" or tourist destinations. Imperial history tends to talk about the world outside of imperial headquarters episodically, as if it existed only when the attention of the empire was upon it.

The way I was taught ancient history left me with an impression of a darkened world in which nothing happened until the lights of civilization were turned on, first in Mesopotamia, then in Ancient Greece, then Rome, then spreading northwestward into Europe. Only then, as European expansion took off, did the Americas, Asia and Africa appear. It was at home, from my father, that I learned of Chinese merchants trading with East Africa in the 12th century, or the vast expanse and intellectual achievements of the Islamic empire.

One of the tasks, therefore, of medicinal history is to show that all parts of the world coexist and always have. (Contrary to popular expressions like "Stone Age people" or "just entering the 20th century," all people now alive are living at the same time, whatever our technologies or forms of social organization.) We also need to show that complexity and change exist and always have existed in all parts of the world.

One of my current projects is a curriculum that starts from Shakespeare's England and connects his life and writings to events and people in the rest of the world. How many of us are ever asked to think about what was happening in China, Peru, and Mali while *Hamlet* was being written? In my Puerto Rican history project, I included an ancient and a medieval section in which I showed the diversity and vitality of people's lives in the three regions from which Puerto Ricans originate: West Africa, the Mediterranean and the Caribbean. I wanted7 to create a sense of balance among the regions long before 1492.

As a discipline, history is taught by regions and time periods, in ways that often make it difficult to focus on linkages. Medicinal history can restore a sense of the global to fragmented colonial histories. The arrival of the Spanish in the Caribbean is closely connected with the expulsions of Jews and Moslems from Spain, linking the history of San Juan with that of Constantinople and Marrakech. The upheavals that the slave trade brought to West Africa, and the conflicts among and within African nations have a direct bearing on who showed up in the slave markets of the island. The fact that General Nelson Miles, who led the U.S. invasion of Puerto Rico in 1898, was also the most prominent military commander of the wars against the Plains Indians is not just biographical information about Miles' career. It connects the stories of peoples affected by U.S. expansion from Puerto Rico to the Dakotas, from Idaho and Arizona to Hawaii and the Philippines. Re-establishing a sense of the connectedness of world events is a critical piece of the work of the activist historian.

13. Access and Digestibility

If the purpose of medicinal history is to transform the way we see ourselves histori-cally, to change our sense of what's possible, then making history available to those who need it most is not a separate process from the researching and interpreting. The task of the curandera historian includes delivery.

To do exciting, empowering research and leave it in academic journals and uni-versity libraries is like manufacturing unaffordable medicines for deadly diseases. We need to share our work in ways that people can assimilate, not in the private languages and forms of scholars. This is the difference between curanderas and pharmaceutical companies. Pharmaceuticals are going into indigenous and other people-of-color communities worldwide to steal and patent traditional science, technology and even the plants themselves and produce medicines that are com-pletely out of reach of the people who invented them. We need to be careful, in doing historical research about oppressed communities, to see that the active ingredients get back to the people whose ancestors generated our work.

A good medicine also includes a delivery system, something that gets it to the parts of your body that need it. Those who are hungriest for what we dig up don't read scholarly journals and shouldn't have to. As historians we need to either be art-ists and community educators or find people who are and figure out how to collab-orate with them. We can work with community groups to create original public history projects that really involve people. We can see to it that our work gets into at least the local popular culture through theater, murals, historical novels, posters, films, children's books or a hundred other art forms. We can work with elementary and high-school teachers to create curricula. Medicinal history is a form of healing and its purposes are conscious and overt.

14. Show Yourself in Your Work

One of the pretenses of history is that being rigorous about research is the same as being objective. Since history is a collection of stories about people in conflict, and all our families were involved, it seems a ridiculous claim. Objectivity isn't all it's cracked up to be anyway. Being objective is often understood to mean not taking sides; but failing to take sides when someone is being hurt is immoral. In writing about the past, we are choosing to bear witness to the impact of that past on the people around us. We don't stand apart from history. We are in the midst of it right this minute and the stances we take matter. A committed moral stance does not mean that we cannot be rigorous. While the agenda of the activist historian is to rescue a sense of worth for the oppressed, our ability to see worth in the contradic-tory and ambiguous means we welcome the full picture. We don't, in the narrow sense, have an axe to grind.

Part of what oppression tries to teach us is that as intellectuals we need not involve ourselves and that it is undignified to do so. Certainly to talk and write openly about our personal, emotional and intellectual stakes in our work is frowned on, and lets us in for ridicule and disrespect. Nevertheless, it's important for people's historians not to hide ourselves. Part of what keeps our work honest is acknowledging why we care about it and who we are in relationship to it. We often write the books we most need to read, and do research that in some way touches on core issues in our lives. Revealing this is a way of shedding the cloak of apartness and revealing our humanity.

15.   Cross Borders

At a lecture I gave on my historical research, someone asked how I found all these myriad connections between seemingly unrelated topics. I realized, as I answered her, that the key thing had been allowing myself to be widely curious, across all boundaries of discipline, geography and time. Academic training and the workings of the higher education marketplace exert powerful pressures on us to narrow our interests and not cross into unfamiliar territory. A commitment to the study of connections requires us to continually do so. The categories of discipline, geography and historical period are themselves constructed in obedience to certain priorities that don't necessarily serve the projects of medicinal history. Borders are generally established in order to exercise control, and when we center our attention of the historical empowerment of the oppressed, we inevitably swim rivers, lift barbed wire and violate "no trespassing" signs.

4

Women and Gender in Arts and Media

By Bonnie Kime Scott

Contents

Original publication details: 4.1 Joy Kogawa, "Obasan" from *Obasan*, pp. 231–36. New York: Anchor, 1994. Reproduced with permission of the Sandra Dijkstra Literary Agency and Random House LLC. 4.2 Wendy Maruyama, "The Tag Project: Executive Order 9066." 4.3 Guerrilla Girls, "Do Women Have to be Naked to Get Into the Met. Museum?" 4.4 Esther Newton, "The Mythic Mannish Lesbian: Radclyffe Hall and the New Woman," excerpts from *Signs: Journal of Women in Culture and Society* 9.4 (Summer 1984), pp. 557–75. Reproduced with permission of University of Chicago Press and Esther Newton. 4.5 Virginia Woolf, "Shakespeare's Sister" from *A Room of One's Own*, pp. 41–43, 44–50, 111–12. Orlando: Harcourt, 2005. Reproduced with permission of Harcourt Brace and of The Society of Authors on behalf of the estate of Virginia Woolf. 4.6 Maythee Rojas, "Creative Expressions" excerpts from *Women of Color and Feminism*, pp. 107–31. Berkeley, CA: Seal Press, 2009. Reproduced with permission of Perseus Books Group. 4.7 Jean Kilbourne, "Beauty and the Beast of Advertising" from *Media and Values: Redesigning Women*. Center for Media Literacy (Winter 1990). Reproduced with permission of Center for Media Literacy. 4.8 Andi Zeisler, "Pop and Circumstance: Why Pop Culture Matters" excerpts from *Feminism and Pop Culture*. Berkeley, CA: Seal Press, 2008, pp. 1–21). Reproduced with permission of Perseus Books Group.

Women in Culture: An Intersectional Anthology for Gender and Women's Studies, Second Edition.
Edited by Bonnie Kime Scott, Susan E. Cayleff, Anne Donadey, and Irene Lara.
© 2017 John Wiley & Sons, Ltd. Published 2017 by John Wiley & Sons, Ltd.

Representations of women abound in arts and media of various periods, types, and global locations. In many cases they are coercive, telling women how they should look and behave to be feminine and heterosexual, as well as offering degrading racial stereotypes or postcolonial biases. Women engaged in the creation of arts and media have their own history, which shows their striving to develop voices, discourses, and genres (creative forms) to express experiences marked by gender, cultural, racial, and sexual differences, as well as historical and personal traumas (See Carpenter; Ticknor; Scott, ed.). The women's images referred to in this chapter range from classic paintings to recent websites. Studying women in arts and media promotes the development of feminist terminology and critical practices for analytical thinking and writing. Indeed, each chapter of this text has included creative writing to demonstrate how instrumental arts and media are to the articulation of feminist concerns.

Reading an image for gendered dynamics of power is an important feminist tool. It applies equally well to the study of classical Western art and current advertising. In an essay titled "Ways of Seeing," based on a TV series, John Berger focused upon the female nude in famous paintings as an object for male viewing and ownership. He observed that traditionally, "Men look at women. Women watch themselves being looked at" (Berger 1973, 47). The tradition of female nudes "being looked at" has been parodied by the performance art group Guerrilla Girls, who have also moved to have women artists better represented in cultural institutions (see Pollock). Feminist critical viewing applies equally well to ads that fragment the female body, or represent men in powerful, upright positions and women in submissive, reclining postures. Latina lesbian photographer Laura Aguilar and Cuban-American performance artist, sculptor, and video artist Ana Mendieta offer their own ways of seeing the female body, be it large or petite, with Mendieta exploring its merger with the earth. bell hooks offers the "oppositional gaze" as a critical stance for the Black observer.

Women Writing Their Experience

Challenges to women as writers are present in several readings – Japanese-Canadian poet and novelist Joy Kogawa's *Obasan* (1994), the fiction that leads off the chapter, English feminist novelist Virginia Woolf's imaginary portrait of "Shakespeare's Sister" (1929/2005), and lesbian English novelist Radclyffe Hall's forerunning lesbian novel *The Well of Loneliness* (1928). Kogawa's *Obasan* describes the experience of a Canadian family of Japanese descent in the World War II era. Anxious about possible collaboration with Japan by these citizens, Canada pursued a repressive policy of repatriation and displacement comparable to the development of detention camps for Japanese-Americans in the United States. The dehumanizing effect of internment in the United States is represented in this chapter by a photo of a portion of furniture-maker, artist, and educator Wendy Maruyama's installation "The Tag Project: Executive Order 9066" (2012) which traveled through several US cities. As part of an exhibit, 120,000 replicas of identification tags that internees had to wear during their relocation hang like columns, each representing one of the camps they were assigned to. A fuller explanation of the entire installation, including the luggage and wall cabinets incorporating documentary photography, can be accessed at http://thetagproject.wordpress.com.

The cultured family of the Kogawa's protagonist in *Obasan*, Megumi Naomi Nakane, was fragmented in the relocation process, and their desirable property in Vancouver sold. The title honors the aunt who cared for Naomi and her brother through her childhood years of exile, their struggles culminating on the Baker beet farm in Alberta. The adult Naomi finds the voice to resist a newspaper account sent to her by another aunt, whose more fortunate exile took her to Toronto. The clipping quotes Phil Baker, president of Alberta Sugar Beet Growers, as he boasts of the productivity of Japanese workers. A representative family poses, grinning over a pile of harvested beets. Naomi's reaction rewrites this nationalist Canadian media account, even as it responds to Aunt Emily's need to document history. With harsh, surreal imagery, Naomi evokes the ways dirt, insects, and temperatures literally and metaphorically invaded her body, as well as the psychological impact of her absent aunt's archive, its effect resembling an invasive surgical operation. Kogawa thus offers a model for writing the history as well as the personal experience of trauma and provides her readers with an emotionally effective way of countering dominant representations of oppressed people.

In the fictionalized essay *A Room of One's Own* (1929), Woolf finds it "queer" that in imaginative writing by men, women like Cleopatra are of the highest importance, but in real life during the era of Shakespeare, women were uneducated, married off at a young age, and subjected to a husband's will and violence. Goaded by a bishop's proclamation that no woman could have the genius of Shakespeare, Woolf imagines what might have happened to his sister. While she is as adventurous and imaginative as her brother, Judith Shakespeare gets no schooling, remains at home to do domestic chores, and is beaten when she resists the family's marriage plans. She cannot survive in London where she goes to enter the theater, and loses what Woolf considers the overly prized quality of "chastity."

Elsewhere in *A Room of One's Own*, Woolf celebrates the advent of the middle-class woman writer and the success of English novelists such as Jane Austen and Charlotte Brontë. She feels that genius could not yet emerge from the working class, but she suspects its manifestation in unanticipated places, such as histories of witchcraft. Woolf's concern that anger had negative effects on the woman writer is disputed by Chicana feminist professor and author Maythee Rojas in this chapter. Woolf's hope that women will feel freer to discuss the body and sexuality set an important agenda.

Lesbian cultural anthropologist Esther Newton's "The Mythic Mannish Lesbian: Radclyffe Hall and the New Woman" (1984) historicizes the developing discourse (theory and vocabulary) of lesbian identity, focusing upon feminist ambivalence toward Hall's novel, *The Well of Loneliness*. Middle-class Victorian women had sought an education and they celebrated the female friendships cultivated in women's cultural institutions, forming long-term female couples that supported a passive, passionless view of women's sexuality. By 1928, the expression of ardent same-sex love, often with one member of the couple displaying "mannish" qualities, was emerging. This was accompanied by the supposed science of "sexology," which supplied pathological terms such as "invert" to what it assumed was a regrettable pattern – a male trapped in a female body, aspiring to masculine power and prerogatives. Hall subscribed to this doctrine, particularly as articulated by the English physician and sexologist Havelock Ellis. Stephen Gordon, her lead character, demonstrates "mannish" symptoms and the psychological effects of hating her body and thinking her soul is entrapped. As lesbian discourses have diversified, feminists have expressed ambivalence over Hall's limited formulations. Others of her generation, including Virginia Woolf (in *Orlando*) and American novelist, poet and playwright, Djuna Barnes (in *Ladies Almanack* and *Nightwood*), were simultaneously investigating more varied and affirmative lesbian expression, with Woolf's *Orlando* ranging through time and global location. Their obscure publications and use of lesbian coding evaded the censors that plagued *The Well of Loneliness*.

Race, Gender, and Sexuality in Pop Culture

Designed to appeal to a mass audience and often working hand in hand with capitalist economics, popular culture has the power to limit and degrade our perceptions of ourselves, or to resist sexist, homophobic, racist, and xenophobic (foreign-hating) stereotypes. Analysis of popular culture permits us to question the old hierarchical division between "high" and "low" culture that dismisses mass culture. Feminist critiques and cultural innovators continue to strive for images that break through such stereotypes and offer more diverse possibilities. Author and film-maker Jean Kilbourne's "Beauty and the Beast of Advertising," written in 1990 (see http://www.jeankilbourne.com/lectures/for updated statistics), focuses on damaging ads pervasive in TV and media. Many of these teach dangerous stereotypes – that power belongs to white Anglo men, that children as well as women are sex objects, that addictive substances are desirable, that women are responsible for childrearing and housekeeping, that one must strive to be tall, thin, light-skinned, heterosexual, and young, and that sexuality is a dirty joke. Kilbourne's film series, *Killing us Softly: Advertising's Image of Women* (now in its fourth version), sustains her critique, using a wide variety of advertisements. Though it is important to acknowledge and collect resistant images now appearing in ads, many of the patterns pointed out by Kilbourne persist.

In demonstrating "why pop culture matters," American feminist author and magazine editor Andi Zeisler's article "Pop and Circumstance: Why Pop Culture Matters" (2008) offers a long list of the forms it takes: TV, movies, radio, websites, fashion magazines, tabloids, board games, toys, and online pursuits. She finds that popular musical themes enfold events such as Hurricane Katrina and the Vietnam War. Pop culture circulates worldwide, exporting disorders and desires to cultures distant from Western sources. Her history of feminist cultural studies includes Berger's "Ways of Seeing" and the work of British feminist film theorist Laura Mulvey, which resists and flips the controlling male gaze in film. She attests to progress made through feminist resistance: women now go to work, have access to legal abortions, appear on talk shows, occasionally take lead roles in rock groups, and produce Hollywood films. Still the percentages are disappointing. In 2013, only 1.9% of the directors of the top-grossing films were female, according to Stacie L. Smith, Media Studies professor (Keegan; see also Haskell). Counter messages have also emerged in pop culture, demanding study and response. Women characters also remain badly unrepresented, according to Martha M. Lausen, executive director of the Center for the Study of Women in Television and Film at San Diego State University. In the top-grossing films of 2013, "females comprised 15% of protagonists, 29% of major characters, and 30% of all speaking characters" (Lausen). The media arts organization Women Make Movies counters this with its support for independent films by and about women.

With "Creative Expressions" (2009), Maythee Rojas demonstrates ways women of color have made remarkable departures from the norm through pop culture. Affirmative terminology is one way to defy patterns of subordination, one example being Chicana/o "Alter-native" culture. Strategies include indulging in irreverent, "inappropriate" behavior, laying claim to anger as its own force, rather than a negative stereotype, and addressing important issues of gender, race, and sexuality. Still, popular culture functions in the context of the capitalist system, requiring publishing from the margins, or turning poverty on its head by opting for inexpensive materials. Rojas draws her examples from a range of popular genres, including cartoons, movies, websites, essays, poetry, standup comedy, and photography, showing ways that both stereotypes and enabling terms have evolved with changing historical contexts. Her essay's own historical moment is at the start of President Barak Obama's administration in 2008. At that time a *New Yorker* cover played the first couple against stereotypes and fears of Black power and Muslim force; Hillary Clinton was becoming a pop culture icon as Secretary of State, alongside Brittany Spears.

Among Rojas's diverse examples is Korean-American cartoonist Lela Lee's "little Asian girl," Kim, who defies the submissive Asian stereotype, also addressed by Kogawa. Kim gives a foul-mouthed response to the racial stereotyping experienced on her "First Day at School." Lee's bold cartoon met problems with marketing, criticism from an ambivalent Asian American community, and accusations of self-serving racial representation, to which she responded with a more diverse set of characters. Rojas credits Black lesbian feminist author and activist Audre Lorde's essay "The Uses of Anger" with opening this discussion into ways that the stereotype of the angry Black woman, still seen in films, has a history of more complexly registered emotions, dating back to films featuring African American jazz singer Billie Holiday. Those reclaiming anger include Native American poet and educator Joy Harjo, confronting ways that the anger stereotype has been used to repress Native American resistance, and Japanese-American feminist author Mitsuye Yamada, combatting "harmless" renditions of Asian women. An online confrontation of

Asian pornography is manifested in Chinese-American performer Kristina Wong's website (www.kristinawong.com). A final example in yet another genre is *Persepolis*, a graphic novel and later a film by Iranian-French graphic artist and film director Marjane Satrapi, which represents reactions of a young woman subjected to fundamentalist doctrines of Islam following the ouster of its Shah.

National politics, coupled with xenophobia, have also elicited notable responses in pop culture, as Rojas notes. The dragon lady, performed by Chinese-American silent film star Anna May Wong, played to xenophobia. Western governments could use such stereotypes (e.g., the victimized Asian sex worker or the veiled Muslim woman) as pretexts for their own selective cultural interventions, as in the Bush administration's use of the burqa to justify the military intervention in Afghanistan. As a counter-narrative, Rojas cites Satrapi's autobiographical *Persepolis*. This work and a subsequent film adaptation both critique fundamentalism and assert an affirmative relationship for women of the Islamic faith.

Transnational exchange and collaboration in feminist arts and media present a promising direction for continuing work. There is an ongoing history of feminists organizing to produce independent work and critique establishment practices. Notable examples include the non-profit media arts organization Women Make Movies, established in 1972. It remains a fine source of an international selection of films. In the arts, Guerrilla Girls began in 1985, when an anonymous group of seven feminist women artists donned gorilla costumes to campaign against gender and racial inequality in the art establishment. They sustain their work through richly illustrated publications, posters, and performance art, bringing humor as well as compelling data to their work. Their poster, included in the chapter, "Do Women Have to be Naked to Get into the Met. Museum?" reimagines the female nude, posed for the controlling male gaze, transforming her into a guerrilla girl, her protest backed by statistics.

Discussion Questions

1. What are some of the sources of feminist anger mentioned in our readings and how do these relate to both gender and race?
2. Give two examples of feminist counter-narrative. What sorts of strategies apply?
3. List and discuss six forms of pop culture involving representations of women.
4. Name a stereotypical attitude attributed to Asian women and ways two authors have resisted this.
5. What sorts of cultural conditions would have prevented Shakespeare's sister from achieving literary success, according to Woolf?
6. How did Stephen Gordon view her sexuality in Radclyffe Hall's *The Well of Loneliness*?
7. Give two examples of women finding a voice for expression of their experience.
8. How has the male gaze functioned in two artistic genres? Name a leading theorist on this subject.
9. How have representations of same-sex love changed in stages between the Victorian age and the late twentieth century?

References

Barnes, Djuna. *Ladies Almanack*. 1928. New York: Dalkey Archive, 1992.

Barnes, Djuna. *Nightwood*. New York: New Directions, 1937.

Berger, John, "Ways of Seeing." *Ways of Seeing*, 45–65. New York: Viking, 1973.

Carpenter, Cari. *Seeing Red: Anger, Sentimentality, and American Indians*. Columbia, OH: Ohio State University Press, 2008.

Guerrilla Girls. *The Guerrilla Girls' Bedside Companion to History of Western Art*. New York: Penguin, 1998.

Guerrilla Girls. *Bitches, Bimbos, and Ballbreakers: The Guerrilla Girls' Illustrated Guide to Female Stereotypes*. New York: Penguin Books, 2003.

Haskell, Molly. *Holding My Own in No Man's Land: Women and Men and Film and Feminism*. New York: Oxford University Press, 1997.

hooks, bell. "The Oppositional Gaze: The Black Female Spectator." *Black Looks: Race and Representation*. Boston: South End Press, 1992. 115–31

Keegan, Rebecca. "Still Missing in Action Films: Women Are Underrepresented Behind and in Front of the Camera." *Los Angeles Times*, July 24, 2014. D3.

Lausen, Martha M. "It's a Man's (Celluloid) World: On-Screen Representations of Female Characters in the Top 100 Films of 2013." http://womenintvfilm.sdsu.edu/files/2013_It's_a_Man's_World_Report.pdf (accessed December 18, 2015).

Lorde, Audre. "The Uses of Anger: Women Responding to Racism." *Sister Outsider: Essays and Speeches by Audre Lorde*. Berkeley: Crossings Press, 2007. 124–33

Maruyama, Wendy. "The Tag Project: Executive Order 9066," 2012. http://thetagproject.wordpress.com and http://artgallery.sdsu.edu/exhibitions/2012_maruyama/ (accessed December 18, 2015).

Mulvey, Laura. *Visual and Other Pleasures*. Bloomington: Indiana University Press, 1989.

Pollock, Griselda. *Vision and Difference: Femininity, Feminism and Histories of Art*. London and New York: Routledge, 1988.

Satrapi, Marjane. *Persepolis*. New York: Pantheon, 2003–4.

Scott, Bonnie Kime, ed. *Gender in Modernism: New Geographies, Complex Intersections*. Urbana, IL: University of Illinois Press, 2007.

Tickner, Lisa. *The Spectacle of Women: Imagery of the Suffrage Campaign 1907–14*. Chicago and London: University of Chicago Press, 1988.

Women Make Movies. Catalog: http://www.wmm.com/filmcatalog/titleindex/browse_titles.shtml (accessed December 18, 2015).

Woolf, Virginia. *Orlando: A Biography*. 1928. San Diego: Harcourt Brace, Jovanovich, 1956.

4.1

Obasan

Joy Kogawa

There is a folder in Aunt Emily's package containing only one newspaper clipping and an index card with the words "Facts about evacuees in Alberta." The newspaper clipping has a photograph of one family, all smiles, standing around a pile of beets. The caption reads: "Grinning and Happy."

Find Jap Evacuees Best Beet Workers
　Lethbridge, Alberta, Jan. 22
　Japanese evacuees from British Columbia supplied the labour for 65% of Alberta's sugar beet acreage last year, Phil Baker, of Lethbridge, president of the Alberta Sugar Beet Growers' Association, stated today.
　"They played an important part in producing our all-time record crop of 363,000 tons of beets in 1945," he added.
　Mr. Baker explained Japanese evacuees worked 19,500 acres of beets and German prisoners of war worked 5,000 acres. The labour for the remaining 5,500 acres of Alberta's 30,000 acres of sugar beets was provided by farmers and their families. Some of the heaviest beet yields last year came from farms employing Japanese evacuees.
　Generally speaking, Japanese evacuees have developed into most efficient beet workers, many of them being better than the transient workers who cared for beets in southern Alberta before Pearl Harbor. ...

Facts about evacuees in Alberta? The fact is I never got used to it and I cannot, I cannot bear the memory. There are some nightmares from which there is no waking, only deeper and deeper sleep.

There is a word for it. Hardship. The hardship is so pervasive, so inescapable, so thorough it's a noose around my chest and I cannot move anymore. All the oil in my joints has drained out and I have been invaded by dust and grit from the fields and mud is in my bone marrow. I can't move anymore. My fingernails are black from scratching the scorching day, and there is no escape.

Aunt Emily, are you a surgeon cutting at my scalp with your folders and your filing cards and your insistence on knowing all? The memory drains down the sides of my face, but it isn't enough, is it? It's your hands in my abdomen, pulling the growth from the lining of my walls, but bring back the anesthetist turn on the ether clamp down the gas mask bring on the chloroform when will this operation be over Aunt Em?

Is it so bad?

Yes.

Do I really mind?

Yes, I mind. I mind everything. Even the flies. The flies and flies and flies from the cows in the barn and the manure pile – all the black flies that curtain the windows, and Obasan with a wad of toilet paper, spish, then with her bare hands as well, grabbing them and their shocking white eggs and the mosquitoes mixed there with the other insect corpses around the base of the gas lamp.

It's the chicken coop "house" we live in that I mind. The uninsulated unbelievable thin-as-a-cotton-dress hovel never before inhabited in winter by human beings. In summer it's a heat trap, an incubator, a dry sauna from which there is no relief. In winter the icicles drip down the inside of the windows and the ice is thicker than bricks at the ledge. The only place that is warm is by the coal stove, where we rotate like chickens on a spit, and the feet are so cold they stop registering. We eat cloves of roasted garlic on winter nights to warm up.

It's the bedbugs and my having to sleep on the table to escape the nightly attack, and the welts over our bodies. And all the swamp bugs and the dust. It's Obasan uselessly packing all the cracks with rags. And the muddy water from the irrigation ditch which we strain and settle and boil, and the tiny carcasses of water creatures at the bottom of the cup. It's walking in winter to the reservoir and keeping the hole open with the ax and dragging up the water in pails and lugging it back and sometimes the water spills down your boots and your feet are red and itchy for days. And it's everybody taking a bath in the round galvanized tub, then Obasan washing clothes in the water after and standing outside hanging the clothes in the freezing weather where everything instantly stiffens on the line.

Or it's standing in the beet field under the maddening sun, standing with my black head a sun trap even though it's covered, and lying down in the ditch, faint, and the nausea in waves and the cold sweat, and getting up and tackling the next row. The whole field is an oven and there's not a tree within walking distance. We are tiny as insects crawling along the grill and there is no protection anywhere. The eyes are lidded against the dust and the air cracks the skin, the lips crack, Stephen's flutes crack and there is no energy to sing anymore anyway.

It's standing in the field and staring out at the heat waves that waver and shimmer like see-through curtains over the brown clods and over the tiny distant bodies of Stephen and Uncle and Obasan miles away across the field day after day and not even wondering how this has come about.

There she is, Obasan, wearing Uncle's shirt over a pair of dark baggy trousers, her head covered by a straw hat that is held on by a white cloth tied under her chin. She is moving like a tiny earth cloud over the hard clay clods. Her hoe moves rhythmically up down up down, tiny as a toothpick. And over there, Uncle pauses to straighten his back, his hands on his hips. And Stephen farther behind, so tiny I can barely see him.

It's hard, Aunt Emily, with my hoe, the blade getting dull and mud-caked as I slash out the Canada thistle, dandelions, crabgrass, and other nameless nonbeet plants, then on my knees, pulling out the extra beets from the cluster, leaving just one to mature, then three hand spans to the next plant, whack whack, and down on my knees again, pull, flick flick, and on to the end of the long long row and the next and the next and it will never be done thinning and weeding and weeding and weeding. It's so hard and so hot that my tear glands burn out.

And then it's cold. The lumps of clay mud stick on my gum boots and weight my legs and the skin under the boots beneath the knees at the level of the calves grows red and hard and itchy from the flap flap of the boots and the fine hairs on my legs grow coarse there and ugly.

I mind growing ugly.

I mind the harvesttime and the hands and the wrists bound in rags to keep the wrists from breaking open. I lift the heavy mud-clotted beets out of the ground with the hook like an eagle's beak, thick and heavy as a nail attached to the top of the sugar-beet knife. Thwack. Into the beet and yank from the shoulder till it's out of the ground dragging the surrounding mud with it. Then crack two beets together till most of the mud drops off and splat, the knife slices into the beet scalp and the green top is tossed into one pile, the beet heaved onto another, one more one more one more down the icy line. I cannot tell about this time, Aunt Emily. The body will not tell.

We are surrounded by a horizon of denim-blue sky with clouds clear as spilled milk that turn pink at sunset. Pink I hear is the color of llama's milk. I wouldn't know. The clouds are the shape of our new prison walls – untouchable, impersonal, random.

There are no other people in the entire world. We work together all day. At night we eat and sleep. We hardly talk anymore. The boxes we brought from Slocan are not unpacked. The King George/Queen Elizabeth mugs stay muffled in the *Vancouver Daily Province*. The cameraphone does not sing. Obasan wraps layers of cloth around her feet and her torn sweater hangs unmended over her sagging dress.

Down the miles we are obedient as machines in this odd ballet without accompaniment of flute or song.

"Grinning and happy" and all smiles standing around a pile of beets? That is one telling. It's not how it was.

4.2
The Tag Project: Executive Order 9066

Wendy Maruyama

4.3

Do Women Have to be Naked to Get into the Met. Museum?

Guerrilla Girls

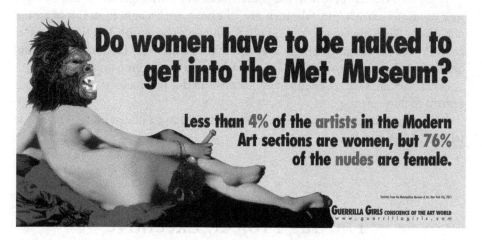

4.4

The Mythic Mannish Lesbian: Radclyffe Hall and the New Woman

Esther Newton

I hate games! I hate role-playing! It's so ludicrous that certain lesbians, who despise men, become the exact replicas of them!
[Anonymous interview in *The Gay Report*, ed. Karla Jay and Allen Young]

Because the proposition that lesbianism is an intensified form of female bonding has become a belief, thinking, acting, or looking like a man contradicts lesbian feminism's first principle: the lesbian is a "woman-identified woman."[1] What to do, then,

---

[1]   Two key texts are Radicalesbians, "The Woman Identified Woman," reprinted in *Radical Feminism*, ed. Anne Koedt, Ellen Levine, and Anita Rapone (New York: Quadrangle, 1973), pp. 240–45; and Adrienne Rich, "Compulsory Heterosexuality and Lesbian Existence," *Signs: Journal of Women in Culture and Society* 5, no. 4 (Summer 1980): 631–60. The best analysis of how these ideas have evolved and of their negative consequences for the feminist movement is Alice Echols, "The New Feminism of Yin and Yang," in *Powers of Desire*, ed. Ann Snitow, Christine Stansell, and Sharon Thompson (New York: Monthly Review Press, 1983), pp. 439–59.

with that figure referred to, in various times and circumstances, as the "mannish lesbian," the "true invert," the "bull dagger," or the "butch"? You see her in old photographs or paintings with legs solidly planted, wearing a top hat and a man's jacket, staring defiantly out of the frame, her hair slicked back or clipped over her ears; or you meet her on the street in T-shirt and boots, squiring a brassily elegant woman on one tattooed arm. She is an embarrassment indeed to a political movement that swears it is the enemy of traditional gender categories and yet validates lesbianism as the ultimate form of femaleness.

Out of sight, out of mind! "Butch and femme are gone," declares one lesbian author, with more hope than truth.[2] But what about those old photographs? Was the mannish lesbian a myth created by "the [male] pornographic mind"[3] or by male sexologists intent on labeling nineteenth-century feminists as deviant? Maybe the old photographs portray a few misguided souls – or perhaps those "premovement" women thought men's ties were pretty and practical?

In the nineteenth century and before, individual women passed as men by dressing and acting like them for a variety of economic, sexual, and adventure-seeking reasons. Many of these women were from the working class.[4] Public, *partial* cross-dressing among bourgeois women was a late nineteenth-century development. Earlier isolated instances of partial cross-dressing seem to have been associated with explicit feminism (e.g., French writer George Sand and American physician Mary Walker), although most nineteenth-century feminists wore traditional women's clothing. From the last years of the century, cross-dressing was increasingly associated with "sexual inversion" by the medical profession. Did the doctors invent or merely describe the mannish lesbian? Either way, what did this mythic figure signify, and to whom? In addressing these questions, my paper explores and speculates on the historical relationships between lesbianism, feminism, and gender.

One of the central figures in this debate is British author Radclyffe Hall (1880–1943). Without question, the most infamous mannish lesbian, Stephen Gordon, protagonist of *The Well of Loneliness* (1928), was created not by a male pornographer, sexologist, legislator, or novelist but by Hall, herself an "out" and militantly tie-wearing lesbian. And *The Well*, at least until 1970, was *the*

[2] Sasha Gregory Lewis, *Sunday's Women* (Boston: Beacon Press, 1979), p. 42.

[3] Andrea Dworkin, *Pornography and Silence: Culture's Revenge against Nature* (New York: Harper & Row, 1981), p. 219.

[4] On passing women, see San Francisco Lesbian and Gay History Project, *"She Even Chewed Tobacco"*: *Passing Women in Nineteenth-Century America* (1983), slide-tape distributed by Iris Films, Box 5353, Berkeley, California 94705; Jonathan Katz, *Gay American History: Lesbians and Gay Men in the U.S.A.* (New York: Thomas Y. Crowell, 1976), pp. 209–80.

lesbian novel.[5] Why is it that *The Well* became famous rather than all the others? Why does this novel make so many lesbian feminists and their allies squirm?[6]

Unable to wish Radclyffe Hall away, sometimes even hoping to reclaim her, our feminist scholars have lectured, excused, or patronized her. Radclyffe Hall, they declare, was an unwitting dupe of the misogynist doctors' attack on feminist romantic friendships. Or, cursed with a pessimistic temperament and brainwashed by Catholicism, Hall parroted society's condemnation of lesbians. The "real" Radclyffe Hall lesbian novel, this argument frequently continues, the one that *ought* to have been famous, is her first, *The Unlit Lamp* (1924). Better yet, Virginia Woolf's *Orlando* (1928) should have been the definitive lesbian novel. Or Natalie Barney's work, or anything but *The Well*.[7]

Heterosexual conservatives condemn *The Well* for defending the lesbian's right to exist; lesbian feminists condemn it for presenting lesbians as different from women in general. But *The Well* has continuing meaning to lesbians because it confronts the stigma of lesbianism – as most lesbians have had to live it. Maybe Natalie Barney, with her fortune and her cast-iron ego, or safely married Virginia Woolf were able to pooh-pooh the patriarchy, but most lesbians have had to face being called or at least feeling like freaks. As the Bowery bum represents all that is most feared and despised about drunkenness, the mannish lesbian, of whom Stephen Gordon is the most famous prototype, has symbolized the stigma of lesbianism and so continues to move

---

[5] "Most of us lesbians in the 1950s grew up knowing nothing about lesbianism except Stephen Gordon's swagger," admits Blanche Wiesen Cook, herself a critic of Hall; see Cook's "'Women Alone Stir My Imagination': Lesbianism and the Cultural Tradition," *Signs* 4, no. 4 (Summer 1979): 719–20. Despite Stephen Gordon's aristocratic trappings, her appeal transcended geographic and class barriers. We know that *The Well* was read early on by American lesbians of all classes (personal communication with Liz Kennedy from the Buffalo Oral History Project [1982]; and see Vern Bullough and Bonnie Bullough, "Lesbianism in the 1920s and 1930s: A Newfound Study," *Signs* 2, no. 4 [Summer 1977]: 895–904, esp. 897). *The Well* has been translated into numerous languages. According to Una Troubridge, in the 1960s it was still steadily selling over a hundred thousand copies a year in America alone; Troubridge was still receiving letters of appreciation addressed to Hall almost twenty years after Hall's death (Una Troubridge, *The Life and Death of Radclyffe Hall* [London: Hammond, Hammond & Co., 1961]). Even today, it sells as much as or more than any other lesbian novel, in straight and women's bookstores (personal communication with Amber Hollibaugh [1983], who has worked at Modem Times Bookstore [San Francisco], Djuna Books, and Womanbooks [New York City]).

[6] Hall deserves censure for her possible fascist sympathies, but this is not the focus of feminist attacks on her. In any case, such sympathies developed after she wrote *The Well*; see Troubridge, pp. 118–24.

[7] For the anti-*Well* approach, see Cook; Lillian Faderman and Ann Williams, "Raddyffe Hall and the Lesbian Image," *Conditions* 1, no. 1 (April 1977): 31–41; Catharine R. Stimpson, "Zero Degree Deviancy: The Lesbian Novel in English," in *Writing and Sexual Difference*, ed. Elizabeth Abel (Chicago: University of Chicago Press, 1982), pp. 245–60; Lillian Faderman, *Surpassing the Love of Men* (New York: William Morrow & Co., 1981), pp. 322–23; Vivian Gornick, "The Whole Radclyffe Hall: A Pioneer Left Behind," *Village Voice* (June 10–16, 1981). Only Inez Martinez, whose approach is quite different from mine, defends Hall: see "The Lesbian Hero Bound: Radclyffe Hall's Portrait of Sapphic Daughters and Their Mothers," *Journal of Homosexuality* 8, nos. 3/4 (Spring/Summer 1983): 127–37.

a broad range of lesbians.[8] A second reason for *The Well*'s continuing impact, which I will explore briefly at the close of this paper, is that Stephen Gordon articulated a gender orientation with which an important minority of lesbians still actively identify.

By "mannish lesbian" (a term I use because it, rather than the contemporary "butch," belongs to the time period I am studying) I mean a figure who is defined as lesbian *because* her behavior or dress (and usually both) manifest elements designated as exclusively masculine. From about 1900 on, this cross-gender figure became the public symbol of the new social/sexual category "lesbian." Some of our feminist historians deplore the emergence of the mannish lesbian, citing her association with the medical model of pathology. For them, the nineteenth century becomes a kind of lesbian Golden Age, replete with loving, innocent feminist couples.[9] From the perspective of Radclyffe Hall's generation, however, nineteenth-century models may have seemed more confining than liberating. I will argue that Hall and many other feminists like her embraced, sometimes with ambivalence, the image of the mannish lesbian and the discourse of the sexologists about inversion primarily because they desperately wanted to break out of the asexual model of romantic friendship. Two questions emerge from this statement of the problem. First, why did twentieth-century women whose primary social and intimate interest was other women wish their relationships to become explicitly sexual? Second, why did the figure of the mannish lesbian play the central role in this development?

* * *

The structure and ideology of the bourgeois woman's gender-segregated world in the nineteenth century have been convincingly described.[10] As British and American women gained access to higher education and the professions, they did so in all-female institutions and in relationships with one another that were intense, passionate, and committed. These romantic friendships characterized the first generation of "New Women" – such as Jane Addams, Charlotte Perkins Gilman, and Mary Wooley – who were born in the 1850s and 1860s, educated in the 1870s and 1880s, and flourished from the 1890s through the First World War. They sought personal and economic independence by rejecting their mothers' domestic roles. The battle to be autonomous was the battle to stay single *and* to separate from the family sphere. Ironically, they turned to romantic friendships as the alternative, replicating the female world of love and commitment in the new institutional settings of colleges and settlement houses.

---

[8]   Many lesbians' connection to the mannish lesbian was and is painful. The relation of any stigmatized group to the figure that functions as its symbol and stereotype is necessarily ambiguous. Even before lesbian feminism, many lesbians hastened to assure themselves and others that they were not "like that." Lesbians who could pass for straight (because they were married or appeared feminine) often shunned their butch sisters. I have dealt with these concepts at length in *Mother Camp: Female Impersonators in America* (Chicago: University of Chicago Press, 1979); I argue that the effeminate man is the stigma bearer for gay men.

[9]   See esp. Faderman.

[10]   See Carroll Smith-Rosenberg, "The Female World of Love and Ritual," *Signs* 1, no. 1 (Autumn 1975): 1–30; and Faderman. On the contradictions within the romantic friendship system, see Martha Vicinus, "'One Life to Stand Beside Me': Emotional Conflicts of First-Generation College Women in England," *Feminist Studies* 8, no. 3 (Fall 1982): 602–28.

Whether or not these women touched each other's genitals or had orgasms together, two things seem clear: their relationships were a quasi-legitimate alternative to heterosexual marriage, and the participants did not conceive of them as sexual. Their letters generally do not use the acknowledged sexual language – medical, religious, or pornographic – of the nineteenth century. Nor do the letters exhibit shame, in an era when lust was considered dirty and gross. On the contrary, the first generation had nothing to hide because their passionate outpourings were seen as pure and ennobling.

The bourgeois woman's sexuality proper was confined to its reproductive function; the uterus was its organ. But as for lust, "the major current in Victorian sexual ideology declared that women were passionless and asexual, the passive objects of male sexual desire."[11] Most bourgeois women and men believed that only males and déclassé women were sexual. Sex was seen as phallic, by which I mean that, conceptually, sex could only occur in the presence of an imperial and imperious penis. Working women and women of color's low status as well as their participation in the public sphere deprived them of the feminine purity that protected bourgeois women from males and from deriving sexual pleasure. But what "pure" women did with each other, no matter how good it felt, could not be conceived as sexual within the terms of nineteenth-century romantic discourse. Insofar as first-generation feminists were called sexual deviants, it was because they used their minds at the expense of their reproductive organs.

* * *

The second generation of New Women were born in the 1870s and 1880s and came of age during the opening decades of the twentieth century. This was an extraordinarily distinguished group. Among them we count critics of the family and political radicals Margaret Sanger and Crystal Eastman; women drawn to new artistic fields, such as Berenice Abbot and Isadora Duncan; and lesbian writers such as Gertrude Stein, Willa Cather, Margaret Anderson, Natalie Barney, and Radclyffe Hall. For them, autonomy from family was, if not a given, emphatically a right. Hall's first novel, *The Unlit Lamp* (1924; hereafter *The Lamp*) is a sympathetic analysis of the first generation from the perspective of the second. The novel portrays a devouring mother using the kinship claims of the female world to crush her daughter's legitimate bid for autonomy.[12] Hall understands that, for the first generation, economic and social separation from the family and home was the first and necessary condition of freedom.

* * *

[11] George Chauncey, Jr., "From Sexual Inversion to Homosexuality: Medicine and the Changing Conceptualization of Female Deviance," *Salmagundi*, nos. 58/59 (Fall 1982–Winter 1983), pp. 114–45, esp. 117. He has reached the same conclusion I have regarding the "necessary" masculinity of the early lesbian persona.

[12] For a related approach, *see* Carolyn Burke, "Gertrude Stein, the Cone Sisters, and the Puzzle of Female Friendship," in Abel, ed. (n. 7, above), pp. 221–42. Gertrude Stein shared the second generation's frustration with "daughters spending a lifetime in freeing themselves from family fixations" (p. 223).

For many women of Radclyffe Hall's generation, sexuality – for itself and as a symbol of female autonomy – became a preoccupation. These women were, after all, the "sisters" of D. H. Lawrence and James Joyce. For male novelists, sexologists, and artists rebelling against Victorian values, sexual freedom became the cutting edge of modernism. Bourgeois women like Hall had a different relation to modernist sexual freedom, for in the Victorian terms of the first generation, they had no sexual identity to express. Women of the second generation who wished to join the modernist discourse and be twentieth-century adults needed to radically reconceive themselves.

That most New Women of the first generation resented and feared such a development, I do not doubt. But many women of the second welcomed it, cautiously or with naive enthusiasm. (One has only to think of Virginia Woolf's thrilled participation in Bloomsbury to see what I mean.) They wanted not simply male professions but access to the broader world of male opportunity. They drank, they smoked, they rejected traditional feminine clothing, and lived as expatriates, sometimes with disastrous results. But if modernism and the new sex ideas entailed serious contradictions for women, many wrote daring novels and plunged into psychoanalysis and promiscuity anyway. After all, this was what the first generation had won for them – the tenuous right to try out the new ideas and participate in the great social movements of the day.

It was in the first two decades of the twentieth century in Britain, with perhaps a ten-year lag in the United States, that due to both external attack and internal fission the old feminist movement began to split along the heterosexual/homosexual divide that is ancestral to our own. If women were to develop a lustful sexuality, with whom and in what social context were they to express it? The male establishment, of course, wanted women to be lusty with men. A basic tenet of sexual modernism was that "normal" women had at least reactive heterosexual desire.[13] The sex reformers attacked Victorian gender segregation and promoted the new idea of companionate marriage in which both women's and men's heterosexual desires were to be satisfied.[14] Easier association with men quickly sexualized the middle-class woman, and by the 1920s the flapper style reflected the sexual ambience of working-class bars and dance halls. The flapper flirted with being "cheap" and "fast," words that had clear sexual reference.

The New Woman's social field was opening up, becoming more complex, and potentially more lonely. Thus, along with their desire to be modern, our bourgeois lesbian ancestors had another powerful reason to embrace change. Before they could find one another, they had to become visible, at least to each other. What they needed was a new vocabulary built on the radical idea that women apart from men could have autonomous sexual feeling.

* * *

[13]   See Paul Robinson, *The Modernization of Sex* (New York: Harper & Row, 1976), pp. 2, 3, and chap. l.
[14]   Christina Simmons, "Companionate Marriage and the Lesbian Threat," *Frontiers* 4, no. 3 (Fall 1979): 54–59.

"I just concluded that I had ... a dash of the masculine (I have been told more than once that I have a masculine mind ...)," Frances Wilder had confessed to Carpenter in 1915, explaining her "strong desire to caress & fondle" a female friend.[15] Like most important historical developments, the symbolic fusion of gender reversal and homosexuality was overdetermined. God himself had ordained gender hierarchy and heterosexuality at the Creation. The idea that men who had sex with other men were like women was not new. But in the second half of the nineteenth century, the emerging medical profession gave scientific sanction to tradition; homosexual behavior, the doctors agreed, was both symptom and cause of male effeminacy. The masculine female invert was perhaps an analogous afterthought. Yet the mannish lesbian proved a potent persona to both the second generation of New Women and their antifeminist enemies. I think that her image came to dominate the discourse about female homosexuality, particularly in England and America, for two reasons. First, because sexual desire was not considered inherent in women, the lesbian was thought to have a trapped male soul that phallicized her and endowed her with active lust. Second, gender reversal became a powerful symbol of feminist aspirations, positive for female modernists, negative for males regardless of whether they were conservatives or modernists.[16]

The true invert was a being between categories, neither man nor woman, a "third sex" or "trapped soul." Krafft-Ebing, Ellis, and Freud all associated this figure with female lust and with feminist revolt against traditional roles; they were at best ambivalent, at worst horrified, by both.[17] But some second-generation feminists, such as Frances Wilder, Gertrude Stein, and Vita Sackville-West, associated themselves with important aspects of the "third sex" persona. None did so as unconditionally and – this must be said – as bravely as Radclyffe Hall did by making the despised mannish lesbian the hero of *The Well of Loneliness*, which she defended publicly against the British government. Hall's creation, Stephen Gordon, is a double symbol, standing for the New Woman's painful position between traditional political and social categories, and for the lesbian struggle to define and assert an identity.

In *The Well*, Stephen Gordon's parents want a son; when a daughter is born her father names her Stephen and permits her much of the freedom boys enjoy. She grows up resembling her father physically and emotionally, despising feminine pursuits and clothing. In her late teens she rejects a sympathetic male suitor because she has no sexual feeling for him. At twenty she develops a passion for a neighbor's wife, who ultimately betrays Stephen to save her own reputation. In the aftermath,

---

[15]   Ruth F. Claus, "Confronting Homosexuality: A Letter from Frances Wilder," *Signs* 2, no. 4 (Summer 1977): 931.

[16]   Sandra Gilbert has developed this idea in the context of modernist literature in "Costumes of the Mind: Transvestism as Metaphor in Modern Literature," in Abel, ed. (n. 7 above), pp. 193–220.

[17]   Freud's analysis was by far the most sophisticated. He rejected the trapped-soul paradigm and distinguished between "choice of object" and "sexual characteristics and sexual attitude of the subject." However, his insights were distorted by his antifeminism and his acceptance of a biological base for gender. See esp. "The Psychogenesis of a Case of Homosexuality in a Woman," in *Freud: Sexuality and the Psychology of Love*, ed. Philip Rieff (New York: Collier Books, 1963), pp. 133–59.

Stephen's mother forces Stephen to leave Morton, the family estate, and Stephen discovers, by reading Krafft-Ebing's *Psychopathia Sexualis* in her dead father's library, that she is an "invert," an identity she instantly but painfully accepts.

During World War I, Stephen works in an ambulance unit and falls in love with Mary, who is young, innocent, and "normal." On holiday together after the armistice, Stephen is tormented by moral scruples. Hesitant to lure Mary into an outcast life and fearful of rejection, she struggles to remain chaste. But Mary, "no coward and no weakling," forces a confrontation; they become lovers, abandoning themselves to "what can be the most relentless of human emotions," passionate sexual love (p. 312).[18] But life in Paris, where they make a home, becomes increasingly problematic. Stephen's absorption in her writing leaves Mary bored and unhappy. Both hate being excluded from bourgeois heterosexual society. Finally, to release Mary, Stephen pretends to have an affair; Mary reluctantly leaves with Stephen's old suitor, Martin, and Stephen is left alone.

Even newborn, Stephen's body is mythically masculine: "Narrow-hipped and wide shouldered" (p. 13). She grows and her body becomes "splendid," "supple," "quick"; she can "fence like a man"; she discovers "her body for a thing to be cherished … since its strength could rejoice her" (p. 58). But as she matures, her delight degenerates into angst. She is denied male privilege, of course, in spite of her masculine body. But her physical self is also fleshly symbol of the femininity Stephen categorically rejects. Her body is not and cannot be male; yet it is not traditionally female. Between genders and thus illegitimate, it represents Every New Woman, stifled after World War I by a changed political climate and reinforced gender stereotypes. But Hall also uses a body between genders to symbolize the "inverted" sexuality Stephen can neither disavow nor satisfy. Finding herself "no match" for a male rival, the adolescent Stephen begins to hate herself. In one of Hall's most moving passages Stephen expresses this hatred as alienation from her body:

> That night she stared at herself in the glass; and even as she did so, she hated her body with its muscular shoulders, its small compact breasts, and its slender flanks of an athlete. All her life she must drag this body of hers like a monstrous fetter imposed on her spirit. This strangely ardent yet sterile body. … She longed to maim it, for it made her feel cruel: it was so white, so strong and so self-sufficient; yet withal so poor and unhappy a thing that her eyes filled with tears and her hate turned to pity. She began to grieve over it, touching her breasts with pitiful fingers, stroking her shoulders, letting her hands slip along her straight thighs – Oh, poor and most desolate body! [P. 187]

Cross-dressing for Hall is not a masquerade. It stands for the New Woman's rebellion against the male order and, at the same time, for the lesbian's desperate struggle to be and express her true self. Two years exiled from Morton, Stephen, now her own woman with a profession, wears tailored jackets, has nicotine-stained fingers, and

---

[18]   All page numbers cited in the text are from Radclyffe Hall, *The Well of Loneliness* (New York: Pocket Books, 1950).

keeps her hair cropped "close like a man's."[19] No matter how "wrong" she seems to the world, Stephen herself grows "fond of her hair" (p. 210).

The New Woman's modernity and aspiration to male privilege already had been associated with cross-dressing in *The Lamp*. But in *The Well*, Hall, like the sexologists, uses cross-dressing and gender reversal to symbolize lesbian sexuality. Unlike the sexologists, however, Hall makes Stephen the subject and takes her point of view against a hostile world. Though men resented Stephen's "unconscious presumption," Hall defends Stephen's claim to what is, in her fictional universe, the ultimate male privilege: the enjoyment of women's erotic love. The mythic mannish lesbian proposes to usurp the son's place in the Oedipal triangle.[20]

For modern readers, by this point in the novel the nature of Stephen's feeling is evident. But writing in 1928, Hall had to go farther. She shows us Sir Phillip reading sexologist Karl Heinrich Ulrichs and making notes in the margins. Later, after her disastrous passion for a scheming American woman, Stephen reads Krafft-Ebing in her dead father's library and recognizes herself as "flawed in the making."

A high price to pay for claiming a sexual identity, yes. But of those who condemn Hall for assuming the sexologists' model of lesbianism I ask, just how was Hall to make the woman-loving New Woman a sexual being? For example, despite Hall's use of words like "lover" and "passion" and her references to "inversion," her lawyer actually defended *The Well* against state censorship by trying to convince the court that "the relations between women described in the book represented a normal friendship." Hall "attacked him furiously for taking this line, which appeared to her to undermine the strength of the convictions with which she had defended the case. His plea seemed to her, as her solicitor commented later, 'the unkindest cut of all' and at their luncheon together she was unable to restrain 'tears of heartbroken anguish.'"[21]

How could the New Woman lay claim to her full sexuality? For bourgeois women, there was no developed female sexual discourse; there were only male discourses – pornographic, literary, and medical – *about* female sexuality. To become avowedly sexual, the New Woman had to enter the male world, either as a heterosexual on male terms (a flapper) or as – or with – a lesbian in male body drag (a butch).

Ideas, metaphors, and symbols can be used for either radical or conservative purposes.[22] By endowing a biological female with a masculine self, Hall both questions the inevitability of patriarchal gender categories *and* assents to it. The mannish

[19]   For the New Woman of the twenties, cutting off traditionally long hair was a daring act with enormous practical and symbolic implications. It was never a neutral act.

[20]   My use of Freud's concept indicates my conviction that it does begin to explain sexual desire, at least as it operates in our culture. Hall rejected or ignored Freud, presumably because of the implication, which so many drew from his work, that homosexuality could be "cured" (see Faderman and Williams [n. 7 above], p. 41, n. 11).

[21]   Vera Brittain, *Radclyffe Hall: A Case of Obscenity?* (New York: A. S. Barnes & Co., 1969), p. 92.

[22]   The sexologists' discourse, itself hostile to women, "also made possible the formation of a 'reverse' discourse: homosexuality began to speak in its own behalf, to demand that its legitimacy or 'naturality' be acknowledged, often in the same vocabulary, using the same categories by which it was medically disqualified" (Michel Foucault, *The History of Sexuality*, vol. 1, *An Introduction* [New York: Vintage Books, 1980], p. 102).

lesbian should not exist if gender is natural. Yet Hall makes her the breathing, suffering hero (not the villain or clown) of a novel. Stephen not only survives social condemnation, she also argues her own case. But she sacrifices her legitimacy as a woman and as an aristocrat. The interpersonal cost is high, too: Stephen loses her mother and her lover, Mary. *The Well* explores the self-hatred and doubt involved in defining oneself as a "sexual deviant." For in doing so, the lesbian accepts an invidious distinction between herself and heterosexual women.

Men have used this distinction to condemn lesbians and to intimidate straight women. The fear and antagonism between us has certainly weakened the modem feminist movement. And that is why lesbian feminists (abetted by some straight feminists) are intent on redefining lesbianism as "woman-identification," a model that, not incidentally, puts heterosexual feminists at a disadvantage.[23] Hall's vision of lesbianism as sexual difference and as masculinity is inimical to lesbian feminist ideology.

Like Hall, I see lesbianism as sexual difference. But her equation of lesbianism with masculinity needs not condemnation, but expansion. To begin with, we need to accept that whatever their ideological purposes, Hall and the sexologists were describing something real. Some people, then and now, experience "gender dysphoria," a strong feeling that one's assigned gender as a man or a woman does not agree with one's sense of self.[24] This is not precisely the same thing as wanting power and male privilege – a well-paid job, abortion on demand, athletic prowess – even though the masculine woman continues to be a symbol of feminist aspirations to the majority outside the movement. Masculinity and femininity are like two different

[23] Superficially, cultural feminism reunites lesbians and straight women under the banner of "female values." As Echols points out, hostility still surfaces "as it did at the 1979 Women Against Pornography conference where a lesbian separatist called Susan Brownmiller a 'cocksucker.' Brownmiller retaliated by pointing out that her critic 'even dresses like a man'" (Echols [n. 1 above], p. 41).

[24] Sexologists often use the concept of "gender dysphoria syndrome" synonymously with "transsexualism" to describe the "pathology" of people who apply for gender reassignment surgery. Of course the effort to describe and treat transsexualism medically has been awkward since gender is a cultural construct, not a biological entity. My broader use of "gender dysphoria" is in agreement with some sexologists who limit the word "transsexual" to people who actually have had surgery to alter their bodies. Gender dysphoria, then, refers to a variety of difficulties in establishing conventional (the doctors say "adequate" or "normal") gender identification; intense pain and conflict over masculinity and femininity is not limited to people who request reassignment surgery. See Jon K. Meyer and John Hoopes, "The Gender Dysphoria Syndromes," *Plastic and Reconstructive Surgery* 54 (October 1974): 447. Female-to-male transsexuals appear to share many similarities with lesbian butches. The most impressive difference is the rejection or acceptance of homosexual identity. Compare *The Well* to the lives described in Ira B. Pauly, "Adult Manifestations of Female Transsexualism," in *Transsexualism and Sex Reassignment*, ed. Richard Green and John Money (Baltimore: Johns Hopkins University Press, 1969), pp. 59–87. Gender dysphoria could very fruitfully be compared with anorexia nervosa, a more socially acceptable and increasingly common female body-image problem. As feminists, we need a much more sophisticated vocabulary to talk about gender. Sexologists are often appallingly conservative, but they also deal with and try to explain important data. See, e.g., John Money and Anke A. Ehrhardt, *Man & Woman, Boy & Girl* (Baltimore: Johns Hopkins University Press, 1972). For a radical scholarly approach, see Suzanne J. Kessler and Wendy McKenna, *Gender: An Ethnomethodological Approach* (New York: John Wiley & Sons, 1978). One of the best recent pieces on gender reversal is Pat Califia, "Gender-Bending: Playing with Roles and Reversals," *Advocate* (September 15, 1983).

languages. Though each of us knows both, most suppress one system and express only the other.[25] Many lesbians, like Stephen Gordon, are biological females who grow up speaking parts of the "wrong" gender language.

Obviously, the more narrow and rigid gender categories are, the more easily one can feel "out of role." And, of course, if there were no more gender categories, gender dysphoria would disappear (as would feminism). However, feminist critiques of traditional gender categories do not yet resolve gender dysphoria because, first, we have made little impact on the deep structures of gender and, second, it appears that individual gender identity is established in early childhood. Although gender dysphoria exists in some simple societies,[26] it may be amplified by the same sociohistorical processes – radical changes in the economy, in family structure and function, and in socialization – that have given rise to feminism. Why should we as feminists deplore or deny the existence of masculine women or effeminate men? Are we not against assigning specific psychological or social traits to a particular biology? And should we not support those among us, butches and queens, who still bear the brunt of homophobia?

Hall's association of lesbianism and masculinity needs to be challenged not because it doesn't exist, but because it is not the only possibility. Gender identity and sexual preference are, in fact, two related but separate systems; witness the profusion of gender orientations (which are deeply embedded in race, class, and ethnic experience) to be found in the lesbian community. Many lesbians *are* masculine; most have composite styles; many are emphatically feminine. Stephen Gordon's success eclipsed more esoteric, continental, and feminine images of the lesbian, such as Renée Vivien's decadent or Colette's bisexual. The notion of a feminine lesbian contradicted the congenital theory that many homosexuals in Hall's era espoused to counter demands that they undergo punishing "therapies." Though Stephen's lovers in *The Well* are feminine and though Mary, in effect, seduces Stephen, Hall calls her "normal," that is, heterosexual. Even Havelock Ellis gave the "womanly" lesbian more dignity and definition. As a character, Mary is forgettable and inconsistent, weakening the novel and saddling Hall with an implausible ending in which Stephen "nobly" turns Mary over to a man. In real life, Hall's lover Una Troubridge did not go back to heterosexuality even when Hall, late in her life, took a second lover.

But the existence of a lesbian who did not feel somehow male was apparently unthinkable for Hall. The "womanly" lesbian contradicted the convictions that sexual desire must be male and that a feminine woman's object of desire must be a man. Mary's real story has yet to be told.[27]

Division of Social Science
State University of New York College at Purchase

[25] See Money and Ehrhardt, pp. 18–20.

[26] Harriet Whitehead, "The Bow and the Burden Strap: A New Look at Institutionalized Homosexuality in Native North America," in *Sexual Meanings: The Cultural Construction of Gender and Sexuality*, ed. Sherry B. Ortner and Harriet Whitehead (Cambridge: Cambridge University Press, 1981), pp. 80–115.

[27] Two impressive beginnings are Joan Nestle, "Butch-Fem Relationships," and Amber Hollibaugh and Cherríe Moraga, "What We're Rollin' Around in Bed With," both in *Heresies 12* 3, no. 4 (1981): 21–24, 58–62. The latter has been reprinted in Snitow, Stansell, and Thompson, eds. (n. 2 above), pp. 394–405.

4.5

Shakespeare's Sister

Virginia Woolf

Perhaps now it would be better to give up seeking for the truth, and receiving on one's head an avalanche of opinion hot as lava, discoloured as dishwater. It would be better to draw the curtains; to shut out distractions; to light the lamp; to narrow the enquiry and to ask the historian, who records not opinions but facts, to describe under what conditions women lived, not throughout the ages, but in England, say in the time of Elizabeth.

For it is a perennial puzzle why no woman wrote a word of that extraordinary literature when every other man, it seemed, was capable of song or sonnet. What were the conditions in which women lived, I asked myself; for fiction, imaginative work that is, is not dropped like a pebble upon the ground, as science may be; fiction is like a spider's web, attached ever so lightly perhaps, but still attached to life at all four corners. Often the attachment is scarcely perceptible; Shakespeare's plays, for instance, seem to hang there complete by themselves. But when the web is pulled askew, hooked up at the edge, torn in the middle, one remembers that these webs are not spun in mid-air by incorporeal creatures, but are the work of suffering human beings, and are attached to grossly material things, like health and money and the houses we live in.

I went, therefore, to the shelf where the histories stand and took down one of the latest, Professor Trevelyan's *History of England*. Once more I looked up Women, found "position of," and turned to the pages indicated. "Wife-beating," I read, "was a recognised right of man, and was practised without shame by high as well as low. ... Similarly," the historian goes on, "the daughter who refused to marry the gentleman of her parents' choice was liable to be locked up, beaten and flung about the room, without any shock being inflicted on public opinion. Marriage was not an affair of personal affection, but of family avarice, particularly in the 'chivalrous' upper classes. ... Betrothal often took place while one or both of the parties was in the cradle, and marriage when they were scarcely out of the nurses' charge." That was about 1470, soon after Chaucer's time. The next reference to the position of women is some two hundred years later, in the time of the Stuarts. "It was still the exception for women of the upper and middle class to choose their own husbands, and when the husband had been assigned, he was lord and master, so far at least as law and custom could make him. Yet even so," Professor Trevelyan concludes, "neither Shakespeare's women nor those of authentic seventeenth-century memoirs, like the Verneys and the Hutchinsons, seem wanting in personality and character." Certainly, if we consider it, Cleopatra must have had a way with her; Lady Macbeth, one would suppose, had a will of her own; Rosalind, one might conclude, was an attractive girl. Professor Trevelyan is speaking no more than the truth when he remarks that Shakespeare's women do not seem wanting in personality and character. Not being a historian, one might go even further and say that women have burnt like beacons in all the works of all the poets from the beginning of time – Clytemnestra, Antigone, Cleopatra, Lady Macbeth, Phèdre, Cressida, Rosalind, Desdemona, the Duchess of Malfi, among the dramatists; then among the prose writers: Millamant, Clarissa, Becky Sharp, Anna Karenina, Emma Bovary, Madame de Guermantes – the names flock to mind, nor do they recall women "lacking in personality and character." Indeed, if woman had no existence save in the fiction written by men, one would imagine her a person of the utmost importance; very various; heroic and mean; splendid and sordid; infinitely beautiful and hideous in the extreme; as great as a man, some think even greater. But this is woman in fiction. In fact, as Professor Trevelyan points out, she was locked up, beaten and flung about the room.

A very queer, composite being thus emerges. Imaginatively she is of the highest importance; practically she is completely insignificant. She pervades poetry from cover to cover; she is all but absent from history. She dominates the lives of kings and conquerors in fiction; in fact she was the slave of any boy whose parents forced a ring upon her finger. Some of the most inspired words, some of the most profound thoughts in literature fall from her lips; in real life she could hardly read, could scarcely spell, and was the property of her husband.

It was certainly an odd monster that one made up by reading the historians first and the poets afterwards – a worm winged like an eagle; the spirit of life and beauty in a kitchen chopping up suet. But these monsters, however amusing to the imagination, have no existence in fact. What one must do to bring her to life was to think poetically and prosaically at one and the same moment, thus keeping in touch with fact – that she is Mrs. Martin, aged thirty-six, dressed in blue, wearing a black hat and brown shoes; but not losing sight of fiction either – that she is a vessel in which all sorts of spirits and forces are coursing and flashing perpetually. The moment, however, that one tries this method with the Elizabethan woman, one branch of illumination fails; one is held up by the scarcity of facts. One knows nothing detailed, nothing perfectly true and substantial about her. History scarcely mentions her. And I turned to Professor Trevelyan again to see what history meant to him. I found by looking at his chapter headings that it meant –

"The Manor Court and the Methods of Open-field Agriculture ... The Cistercians and Sheep-farming ... The Crusades ... The University ... The House of Commons ... The Hundred Years' War ... The Wars of the Roses ... The Renaissance Scholars ... The Dissolution of the Monasteries ... Agrarian and Religious Strife ... The Origin of English Sea-power ... The Armada ..." and so on. Occasionally an individual woman is mentioned, an Elizabeth, or a Mary; a queen or a great lady. But by no possible means could middle-class women with nothing but brains and character at their command have taken part in any one of the great movements which, brought together, constitute the historian's view of the past. Nor shall we find her in any collection of anecdotes. Aubrey hardly mentions her. She never writes her own life and scarcely keeps a diary; there are only a handful of her letters in existence. She left no plays or poems by which we can judge her. What one wants, I thought – and why does not some brilliant student at Newnham or Girton supply it? – is a mass of information; at what age did she marry; how many children had she as a rule; what was her house like; had she a room to herself; did she do the cooking; would she be likely to have a servant? All these facts lie somewhere, presumably, in parish registers and account books; the life of the average Elizabethan woman must be scattered about somewhere, could one collect it and make a book of it. It would be ambitious beyond my daring, I thought, looking about the shelves for books that were not there, to suggest to the students of those famous colleges that they should rewrite history, though I own that it often seems a little queer as it is, unreal, lop-sided; but why should they not add a supplement to history? calling it, of course, by some inconspicuous name so that women might figure there without impropriety? For one often catches a glimpse of them in the lives of the great, whisking away into the background, concealing, I sometimes think, a wink, a laugh, perhaps a tear. And, after all, we have lives enough of Jane Austen; it scarcely seems necessary to consider again the influence of the tragedies of Joanna Baillie upon the poetry of Edgar Allan Poe; as for myself, I should not mind if the homes and haunts of Mary Russell Mitford were closed to the public for a century at least. But what I find deplorable, I continued, looking about the bookshelves again, is that nothing is known about women before the eighteenth century. I have no model in my mind to turn about this way and that. Here am I asking why women did not write poetry in the Elizabethan age, and I am not sure how they were educated; whether they were taught to write; whether they had sitting-rooms to themselves; how many women had children before they were twenty-one; what, in short, they did from eight in the morning till eight at night. They had no money evidently; according to Professor Trevelyan they were married whether they liked it or not before they were out of the nursery, at fifteen or sixteen very likely. It would have been extremely odd, even upon this showing, had one of them suddenly written the plays of Shakespeare, I concluded, and I thought of that old gentleman, who is dead now, but was a bishop, I think, who declared that it was impossible for any woman, past, present, or to come, to have the genius of Shakespeare. He wrote to the papers about it He also told a lady who applied to him for information that cats do not as a matter of fact go to heaven, though they have, he added, souls of a sort. How much thinking those old gentlemen used to save one! How the borders of ignorance shrank back at their approach! Cats do not go to heaven. Women cannot write the plays of Shakespeare.

Be that as it may, I could not help thinking, as I looked at the works of Shakespeare on the shelf, that the bishop was right at least in this; it would have been impossible, completely and entirely, for any woman to have written the plays of Shakespeare in the age of Shakespeare. Let me imagine, since facts are so hard to come by, what would have happened had Shakespeare had a wonderfully gifted sister, called Judith, let us say. Shakespeare himself went, very probably – his mother was an heiress – to the grammar school, where he may have learnt Latin – Ovid, Virgil and Horace – and the elements of grammar and logic. He was, it is well known, a wild boy who poached rabbits, perhaps shot a deer, and had, rather sooner than he should have done, to marry a woman in the neighbourhood, who bore him a child rather quicker than was right. That escapade sent him to seek his fortune in London. He had, it seemed, a taste for the theatre; he began by holding horses at the stage door. Very soon he got work in the theatre, became a successful actor, and lived at the hub of the universe, meeting everybody, knowing everybody, practising his art on the boards, exercising his wits in the streets, and even getting access to the palace of the queen. Meanwhile his extraordinarily gifted sister, let us suppose, remained at home. She was as adventurous, as imaginative, as agog to see the world as he was. But she was not sent to school. She had no chance of learning grammar and logic, let alone of reading Horace and Virgil. She picked up a book now and then, one of her brother's perhaps, and read a few pages. But then her parents came in and told her to mend the stockings or mind the stew and not moon about with books and papers. They would have spoken sharply but kindly, for they were substantial people who knew the conditions of life for a woman and loved their daughter – indeed, more likely than not she was the apple of her father's eye. Perhaps she scribbled some pages up in an apple loft on the sly, but was careful to hide them or set fire to them. Soon, however, before she was out of her teens, she was to be betrothed to the son of a neighbouring woolstapler. She cried out that marriage was hateful to her, and for that she was severely beaten by her father. Then he ceased to scold her. He begged her instead not to hurt him, not to shame him in this matter of her marriage. He would give her a chain of beads or a fine petticoat, he said; and there were tears in his eyes. How could she disobey him? How could she break his heart? The force of her own gift alone drove her to it. She made up a small parcel of her belongings, let herself down by a rope one summer's night and took the road to London. She was not seventeen. The birds that sang in the hedge were not more musical than she was. She had the quickest fancy, a gift like her brother's, for the tune of words. Like him, she had a taste for the theatre. She stood at the stage door; she wanted to act, she said. Men laughed in her face. The manager – a fat, loose-lipped man – guffawed. He bellowed something about poodles dancing and women acting – no woman, he said, could possibly be an actress. He hinted – you can imagine what. She could get no training in her craft. Could she even seek her dinner in a tavern or roam the streets at midnight? Yet her genius was for fiction and lusted to feed abundantly upon the lives of men and women and the study of their ways. At last – for she was very young, oddly like Shakespeare the poet in her face, with the same grey eyes and rounded brows – at last Nick Greene the actor-manager took pity on her; she found herself with child by that gentleman and so – who shall measure the heat and violence of the poet's heart when caught and tangled in a woman's body? – killed herself one winter's night and lies buried at some crossroads where the omnibuses now stop outside the Elephant and Castle.

   That, more or less, is how the story would run, I think, if a woman in Shakespeare's day had had Shakespeare's genius. But for my part, I agree with the deceased bishop, if such he was – it is unthinkable that any woman in Shakespeare's day should have had Shakespeare's genius. For genius like Shakespeare's is not born among labouring, uneducated, servile people. It was not born in England among the Saxons and the Britons. It is not born today among the working classes. How, then, could it have been born among women whose work began, according to Professor Trevelyan, almost before they were out of the nursery, who were forced to it by their parents and held to it by all the power of law and custom? Yet genius of a sort must have existed among women as it must have existed among the working classes. Now and again an Emily Bronte or a Robert Burns blazes out and proves its presence. But certainly it never got itself on to paper. When, however, one reads of a witch being ducked, of a woman possessed by devils, of a wise woman selling herbs, or even of a very remarkable man who had a mother, then I think we are on the track of a lost novelist, a suppressed poet, of some mute and inglorious Jane Austen, some Emily Bronte who dashed her brains out on the moor or mopped and mowed about the highways crazed with the torture that her gift had put her to. Indeed, I would venture to guess that Anon, who wrote so many poems without signing them, was often a woman. It was a woman Edward Fitzgerald, I think, suggested who made the ballads and the folk-songs, crooning them to her children, beguiling her spinning with them, or the length of the winter's night.

This may be true or it may be false – who can say? – but what is true in it, so it seemed to me, reviewing the story of Shakespeare's sister as I had made it, is that any woman born with a great gift in the sixteenth century would certainly have gone crazed, shot herself, or ended her days in some lonely cottage outside the village, half witch, half wizard, feared and mocked at. For it needs little skill in psychology to be sure that a highly gifted girl who had tried to use her gift for poetry would have been so thwarted and hindered by other people, so tortured and pulled asunder by her own contrary instincts, that she must have lost her health and sanity to a certainty. No girl could have walked to London and stood at a stage door and forced her way into the presence of actor-managers without doing herself a violence and suffering an anguish which may have been irrational – for chastity may be a fetish invented by certain societies for unknown reasons – but were none the less inevitable. Chastity had then, it has even now, a religious importance in a woman's life, and has so wrapped itself round with nerves and instincts that to cut it free and bring it to the light of day demands courage of the rarest. To have lived a free life in London in the sixteenth century would have meant for a woman who was poet and playwright a nervous stress and dilemma which might well have killed her. Had she survived, whatever she had written would have been twisted and deformed, issuing from a strained and morbid imagination. And undoubtedly, I thought, looking at the shelf where there are no plays by women, her work would have gone unsigned. That refuge she would have sought certainly. It was the relic of the sense of chastity that dictated anonymity to women even so late as the nineteenth century. Currer Bell, George Eliot, George Sand, all the victims of inner strife as their writings prove, sought ineffectively to veil themselves by using the name of a man. Thus they did homage to the convention, which if not implanted by the other sex was liberally encouraged by them (the chief glory of a woman is not to be talked of, said Pericles, himself a much-talked-of man), that publicity in women is detestable. Anonymity runs in their blood. The desire to be veiled still possesses them. They are not even now as concerned about the health of their fame as men are, and, speaking generally, will pass a tombstone or a signpost without feeling an irresistible desire to cut their names on it, as Alf, Bert or Chas. must do in obedience to their instinct, which murmurs if it sees a fine woman go by, or even a dog, Ce chien est à moi....

I told you in the course of this paper that Shakespeare had a sister; but do not look for her in Sir Sidney Lee's life of the poet. She died young – alas, she never wrote a word. She lies buried where the omnibuses now stop, opposite the Elephant and Castle. Now my belief is that this poet who never wrote a word and was buried at the crossroads still lives. She lives in you and in me, and in many other women who are not here tonight, for they are washing up the dishes and putting the children to bed. But she lives; for great poets do not die; they are continuing presences; they need only the opportunity to walk among us in the flesh. This opportunity, as I think, it is now coming within your power to give her. For my belief is that if we live another century or so – I am talking of the common life which is the real life and not of the little separate lives which we live as individuals – and have five hundred a year each of us and rooms of our own; if we have the habit of freedom and the courage to write exactly what we think; if we escape a little from the common sitting-room and see human beings not always in their relation to each other but in relation to reality; and the sky, too, and the trees or whatever it may be in themselves; if we look past Milton's bogey, for no human being should shut out the view; if we face the fact, for it is a fact, that there is no arm to cling to, but that we go alone and that our relation is to the world of reality and not only to the world of men and women, then the opportunity will come and the dead poet who was Shakespeare's sister will put on the body which she has so often laid down. Drawing her life from the lives of the unknown who were her forerunners, as her brother did before her, she will be born. As for her coming without that preparation, without that effort on our part, without that determination that when she is born again she shall find it possible to live and write her poetry, that we cannot expect, for that would be impossible. But I maintain that she would come if we worked for her, and that so to work, even in poverty and obscurity, is worth while.

4.6

Creative Expressions

Maythee Rojas

Cartoonist Lela Lee has made a career out of being angry. It started with getting mad at the Spike and Mike's Sick and Twisted Festival of Animation she attended as a college sophomore. Leaving the controversial yet widely popular film venue, Lee was incensed by the number of racist and misogynist animated shorts that were featured. "I did not enjoy any of those cartoons," she recalled. "They were all making fun of ... ethnic people, and they were sexist and even though it's a cartoon, it's still not funny to me." Her protracted fuming led a friend to challenge her to create something different. The result was a simple, marker-drawn cartoon she titled "First Day at

School." Featuring an outspoken, young female character dubbed the "angry little Asian girl," the short made it clear that Lee was upset by a lot more than the festival.

The cartoon follows her character's arrival at a new school, where she is greeted by a classroom of all-white peers and a clueless teacher who introduces her as an "oriental." After the young girl tells her that the correct term is "Asian," the teacher remarks on her surprisingly "good English." What happens next is now considered a trademark in Lee's early work. A very angry little Asian girl replies, "I was born here, you stupid dipshit! Don't you know anything about immigration? Read some history books, you stupid ignoramus!" Later at home, when her parents confront her about her less than polite comments, the (still) angry little Asian girl looks up from her afternoon snack only to add, "Aw fuck off!"

Although Lee now admits that the angry little Asian girl, whom she has since named Kim, is really a kind of alter ego that allows Lee to speak out against injustice, including that which her own parents often forced her to accept as a child, she was initially embarrassed by the cartoon's content. Consequently, it was not until years later that Lee decided to develop the character. She eventually produced a five-episode video that addressed a variety of anger-inciting issues around being Asian and a woman. In her videos, Lee used the outspoken Kim to discuss such diverse topics as dominant standards of beauty, female sexuality, the model minority myth, and violence against women. Each episode portrayed Kim confronting stereotypes and defying the double passivity typically imposed on Asian women. In particular, her shocking responses refuted not only the immediate situations she faced, but also the history of invisibility and silence that has plagued many women of Asian descent.

In 1998, Lee's collection of shorts made its screen debut, and ironically, Spike and Mike's Sick and Twisted Festival of Animation acquired its exhibition rights. The increased interest in the quirky character led Lee to follow up with a website that featured a weekly comic strip and a line of T-shirts. Even in its early stage, the site received as many as one million visitors in a single month. Lee's angry little Asian girl also sparked mixed reactions among Asians and Asian Americans. Many lauded her efforts to break the stereotype of the quiet, docile Asian woman or the cute Hello Kitty accessory-carrying girl. Others were dismayed by the foul-mouthed language and occasionally crude images. In general, the angry little Asian girl got people talking. However, when Lee decided to venture into making a real profit from her unconventional ideas, she ran into a conflict that many artists of color face when they attempt to break into mainstream popular culture.

Seeking investors and media outlets that might feature her cartoons, Lee was repeatedly turned down because no one believed there was a large enough Asian consumer market. Ultimately, Lee responded by expanding her cast of characters and reintroducing her comic strip as the "angry little girls." Kim now shares the page with Deborah, Maria, Xyla, Wanda, and Pat (a boy). The new characters, whose ethnicities include African American and Latina, are still feisty, but the earlier edgy, sociopolitical commentary has become gradually subdued.

Politicizing Pop

While it can be defined in numerous ways, popular culture is usually understood as contemporary cultural expressions that carry mass-market appeal because they engage the broadest audiences possible. Highly influenced by the media, popular culture is also closely tied to capitalism through the vast production of commodities that it encourages. Some people dismiss popular culture for its celebration of the common while others embrace it specifically for its amusement value. In addition, some individuals see popular culture as a critical lens through which to examine the concrete issues that drive our concept of what is deemed superficial in our society.

During the 2008 presidential election, Republican candidate John McCain ran several ads using figures such as [Britney] Spears and Paris Hilton to critique his opponent's popularity. Similarly, both McCain and Barack Obama used various mass media outlets such as MTV, Facebook, and late-night talk shows to boost their appeal. In fact, pop culture became one of their primary sites of battle. Race, class, gender, and sexuality did not remain outside of that struggle either. Incendiary news programs such as those on the Fox television network employed the slang phrase "baby mama" to negatively characterize the frequently forthright Michelle Obama. Used most often to identify a single mother, the term's appropriation into mainstream culture exposed its racist and classist undertones when it was applied to Obama. In a similar manner, a *New Yorker* magazine cover mixing the counterculture image of the 1960s Black Panthers with current musings about Muslims turned a possible satire of the right-wing criticism President Obama received about his cultural background into another form of attack. Indeed, when we consider the powerful role that popular culture plays in shaping current social thought, cultural theorist Stuart Hall's 1981 assertion rings perhaps more true now than ever: "Popular culture is one of the sites where this struggle for and against a culture of the powerful is engaged: it is also the stake to be won or lost in that struggle. It is the arena of consent and resistance."

The double edge of "consent and resistance" in popular culture is largely what makes it such an ambiguous tool of expression for people of color. Ideas and images about ethnic communities created and circulated by the dominant culture not only serve to establish stereotypes, or what Chicana scholars Mary Romero and Michelle Habell-Pallán call "conceptual blueprints," they are also inevitably a source for rebellion. Lee's angry little Asian girl cartoon subverted the shy lotus blossom "blueprint" that had been drawn out for Asian women by directly addressing this dominant discourse about them. Similarly, many other artists of color have used subculture niches within mainstream outlets to create new visions of their realities.

Creating Rage

In her 1981 foundational essay "The Uses of Anger: Women Responding to Racism," Audre Lorde writes, "Women responding to racism is women responding to anger; the anger of exclusion, of unquestioned privilege, of racial distortions, of silence, ill-use, stereotyping, defensiveness, misnaming, betrayal, and co-optation." Twenty-eight years later, many women of color, and black women in particular, find themselves still responding to these problems, only now they must also answer to critiques of the anger they have expelled in addressing them. The stereotype of the angry black woman is a staple in mainstream pop culture. In fact, reality shows such as *The Apprentice* and MTV's *Real World/Road Rules Challenge* got so much leverage out of their two most famous angry black female characters, Omarosa Manigault-Stallworth and Coral Smith, that they brought them back to stir up more trouble in subsequent seasons. Similarly, including a bitchy black antagonist has become almost de rigueur for most films and television series featuring at least one black actress. Consider, for example, how common the sight of a neck-rolling, trash-talking black female supporting character is in contrast to the depiction of a complex, internally conflicted black female lead.

Although one might expect this problem to be the result of an entertainment industry that lacks cultural sensitivity or diversity, projects developed by African Americans fare little better. For instance, despite Mo'Nique's attempts to dispel other stereotypes about black women (her reality shows that address body image and social etiquette deserve some credit), few African American films have cast the actress/comedian in roles in which she is not forced to upbraid one or more of her fellow actors for some insignificant reason. Similarly, who can forget Pam Grier playing the gun-toting, revenge-seeking Coffy in the 1970s blaxploitation films that made her a star? Even earlier, the character of Sapphire Stevens in the television adaptation of *Amos 'n' Andy* that ran from 1951 to 1953 solidified the formulaic role of the quarrelsome, hen-pecking black wife. Whether played for comedic relief or to enhance the dramatic tension, the image of the angry black woman has long overshadowed the actual political rage of black women.

Yet black female artists have endeavored to accurately represent the complexity of their emotions. In her chilling 1939 rendition of "Strange Fruit," Billie Holiday captures both the horror and outrage with which violence against the black community is accepted as naturally as the coming of spring. Singing "Southern trees bear a strange fruit/Blood on the leaves and blood at the root," Holiday's voice reverberates with a stark honesty that met with staunch resistance when she tried to record the song. Fearing financial retaliation for the song's blunt antilynching message, most record producers passed on the option to distribute it. It took Holiday's dogged perseverance and personal investment to finally see it produced. The pain that it brought, however, never quite faded. While the song eventually became a standard in her repertoire, legend has it that she cried each time after singing it. Holiday's "Strange Fruit" provides us with a glimpse into the depth of emotion that Lorde describes.

Nina Simone's "Mississippi Goddamn" leaves no one guessing about the emotions behind it. Written by Simone in 1963, at the height of the civil rights movement, "Mississippi Goddamn" spells out the final moments of frustration felt by a people faced with an endless string of injustices. Alternating between singing and talking directly to her audience, Simone recounts the numerous sites of offenses: Alabama, where a black church was bombed and four young girls were killed; Tennessee, where the U.S. Commission on Civil Rights met unsuccessfully to address the country's race problems (and where Martin Luther King Jr. was later killed in 1968); and finally, Mississippi, where activist Medgar Evers was gunned down in his driveway while still clutching the NAACP T-shirts he had brought home that night that read JIM CROW MUST GO. Simone's overwhelming response to all these events in succession is the same: Goddamn! Her song unleashes the fury of pain and disappointment at being told to "go slow" and not protest in light of all these assaults. Addressing the rage that is dangerously building up within the community, she bluntly predicts: "Oh but this whole country is full of lies/You're all gonna die and die like flies." Much more than an angry black woman caricature, Nina Simone is the brave messenger of the urgent action required to keep a nation from imploding.

While black women may hold the reigning stereotype, they are certainly not alone in having their passion misconstrued. With their legitimate anger dismissed as evidence of their supposed savagery, Native American women have also struggled to have their protests heard. As scholar Cari Carpenter notes in *Seeing Red: Anger, Sentimentality, and American Indians*, stereotypes of anger have historically served to suppress the resistance of marginalized groups. Arguing that race and gender affect how anger is interpreted, Carpenter sees the expression of anger in Native American women's writing as a response to the denial and loss of human rights. Anger, she contends, is a reaction to a lack of entitlement and is "intimately linked to the possession of self, of land, of nation." Although Carpenter limits most of her discussion to 19th-century Native American writers, her arguments seem equally alive in the works of contemporary artists such as singer and poet Joy Harjo.

In "I Give You Back," from the poetry collection *She Had Some Horses*, Harjo personifies fear as a "beloved and hated twin" who has suppressed her rage against the rape and slaughter of her community. To release it, she finds, she must holistically embrace the multitude of emotions she has previously kept at bay. In particular, she must acknowledge how her justified anger has been displaced by an oppressive fear. Later in the collection, Harjo returns to this theme in the title poem. She describes a woman who possesses "horses." The horses carry scars ("maps drawn of blood"), lack reflection ("threw rocks at glass houses"), act fatalistically ("waited for destruction"), and yet remain vulnerably innocent ("danced in their mothers' arms"). Using these horses as a metaphor, Harjo suggests that her protagonist is kept incapacitated by the feelings that propel her into contradictory, self-destructive actions. To escape this vicious cycle, Harjo's female protagonist must take action. She must get angry. Both in this poem and the former, Harjo lobbies for Native American women to reappropriate the emotions that dominant culture has distorted and to reassume the agency that has been stolen from them. To be free, she proposes, one's anger must be one's own.

Mitsuye Yamada seeks a similar strategy when she urges Asian American women to discourage the invisibility that is frequently imposed on them because of their race and gender. "We must remember that one of the most insidious ways of keeping women and minorities powerless is to let them only talk about harmless and inconsequential subjects, or let them speak freely and not listen to them with serious intent," she argues in an essay in which she discloses her own previous complicity in promoting the image of a quiet, submissive Asian woman. "We need to raise our voices a little more, even as they say to us 'This is so uncharacteristic of you.'" Yamada's point about expectations is what makes the anger expressed by Asian American female artists such as Lela Lee so provocative. While black and Native American women are criticized for their anger, Asian American women are altogether denied its possession. Imagine then the magnitude of what Kristina Wong accomplishes in her audacious website, Big Bad Chinese Mama.com, when she decides to not just raise her voice but to outright yell.

In addition to her stage performances such as *Wong Flew Over the Cuckoo's Nest,* Wong runs a website that directly confronts the pornographic industry that targets Asian women. Set up as a fake mail-order bride site, Big Bad Chinese Mama addresses the male voyeur seeking "sweet Asian girls." Wong advertises the website in fetish chat rooms and alongside masseuse ads in local newspapers. She also has the site's addresses linked to search engines so that it comes up when someone is looking for Asian pornography. As Wong explains in the site's "manifesto" section, titled "Resistance as Living: Giving Revolution a Sense of Humor - OR - Why I Tricked Thousands of Nasty Porn Seeking Guys to Come to my Fake Mail Order Bride Site, Only to Get a Fist in Their Face," her decision to create Big Bad Chinese Mama came while she was a student at UCLA. Tired of holding conversations about oppression with everyone but the actual oppressor, and admitting to herself that she was not cut out to be the traditional take-it-to-the streets activist, she chose instead to use humor and the Internet to channel her anger at the popularized image of the pretty, meek Asian girl who also conveniently happens to be an exotic sex vixen. In the process, Wong hoped to initiate a dialogue with the men who seek out this paradoxical cliché.

Wong's site features pictures and biographies of real Asian women who, instead of posing seductively for potential clients as they might in a pornography website, are striking back, literally. They wave fists, kick groins, make ugly faces, and offer more than a few choice words to would-be Asian fetish seekers. In the "FUQ" (frequently unasked questions, acronym pun intended) section, Wong fields questions that male clients would likely ask about Asian mail-order brides. The responses are anything but accommodating or polite. Wong does not hold back in expressing her anger at the sexual perversions that she believes surround the desire for an Asian woman within this context. However, she also uses the opportunity to educate site visitors about other related issues that feed into racist and sexist ideas about Asian women. For instance, in response to "Do your brides speak English?" Wong answers: "You fucking dumbshit. Why wouldn't they speak English? Don't you know that the Asian Diaspora is over 150 years old in America? Not to mention the fact that the fuck faces who designed the education system in America left little room for the multicultural experience to thrive and be shared (Sorry, but the lesson plan on the first Thanksgiving doesn't count)."

Like Lee's, Wong's approach to using popular culture to address political topics can have mixed results, and not everyone may see it in a positive light. However, Lee and Wong are both part of a growing number of young Asian American women who are taking suggestions such as Yamada's to heart. They also join others such as comedian Margaret Cho, who broke several barriers when she received her own television program, *American Girl*, in 1994. Cho was unabashedly candid years later when she documented the failure of the series and her subsequent breakdown in *I'm the One That I Want* (1999), a stand-up show (and later book and concert-film) in which she detailed the difficulties she experienced in the entertainment industry because of her weight and ethnicity. Cho's honest admissions, which fluctuate between anger and pain and yet allow for humor, created a forum to publically address the complex experiences of Asian American women specifically, and women of color generally, within greater mainstream culture. They also laid bare the costs of succumbing to such pressures to play the wide-eyed ingenue, the sexy vixen, or the model minority. When Cho released her 2002 show, *Notorious CHO*, in which she addressed her bisexuality, she broke yet another taboo: an admission that not all Asian women are interested in men.

In more recent times, the foreign women of color needing rescue by the United States have become those from the Middle East. Soon after the 9/11 attacks, the Bush administration and the general media began focusing intensely on the oppressive practices against women in Muslim countries. In particular, the expectations for women to cover their hair with veils, or in some cases, wear full body burqas, drew wide criticism and concern. *Beneath the Veil*, a documentary that detailed how women in Afghanistan were prohibited from working, going to school, or being unaccompanied in public first aired on CNN one month before the attacks. At the time, it drew very little interest from the government, the public, or the media. However, when CNN decided to run it twice on September 22 and 23, five-and-one-half million viewers tuned in. In the following days, when Bush pressed Congress for support in the United States' efforts against the Taliban, and later Iraq, he frequently referred to the need to defend women's rights in those countries. Similarly, Feminist Majority Foundation founder and former NOW president Eleanor Smeal posited the attack on the United States in direct relation to the treatment of women in Afghanistan. As she told the *Los Angeles Times*, "These women were the first casualties of the war against the United States."

The United States' vested interest in employing the image of the burqa-clad woman as a symbol for its intervention bears some question. While Muslim countries such as Iraq and Afghanistan are targeted as oppressors, others that maintain profitable relationships with the United States are not. As Maureen Dowd, a columnist for the *New York Times*, asked, "What does it matter if Saudi women can't drive, as long as American women can keep driving their SUVs?" Similarly, why has the United States not taken a more active interest in freeing Muslim women from their religion's oppressive practices in the past? Or, for that matter, what has it done to reduce violence against women at home?

In her graphic novel, and later animated film, *Persepolis*, Marjane Satrapi illustrates her experience as a young adult living in Iran during the country's 1979–1987 revolution. As a result of the Iranian revolution in which the ruling monarch was overthrown, the country was pulled into a long period of widespread repression.

Academic institutions were shut down or censored, borders were closed, protesters were either exiled or imprisoned, and women were forced to adopt the veil. Satrapi captures these experiences in a rich narrative that reveals what these changes meant for Iranian women. While she takes a firm stand against the misogyny surrounding the forced use of the veil, she also describes a personally affirming relationship with the Islamic faith. Satrapi's story avoids facile generalizations about Islam and focuses instead on the shortsighted nature of fundamentalism, which leaves no place for intellectual freedom. Consequently, she questions the purpose behind targeting women for their sexuality. Her exploration of Marxism, feminism, and personal agency suggests that Iranian women did not need saving so much as the entire country needed assistance in removing the revolution's corrupt political government, which hid behind distortions of Islam. However, countries such as the United States and Great Britain avoided interfering at the time. The financial ties they had established long ago with Iran and other countries in the surrounding area precluded their involvement. As Satrapi's father, who is portrayed as a loving and supportive man in her works, concludes, "As long as there is oil in the Middle East, we will never have peace."

Bodily Expressions

A final aspect to consider in the cultural work produced by women of color is the exploration and use of their bodies as primary sources of inspiration. While histories of exploitation and mistreatment abound, sexuality has also served as a means of expression and empowerment. Many women of color artists have succeeded in reverting the male gaze (through which women are objectified by the way in which men depict them) as well as the subjugating imprint of colonialism by not just acknowledging their sexuality, but also by making it the focus of their creations.

Photographer Laura Aguilar's provocative images are a case in point. Serving as the primary model for her work, Aguilar transforms social expectations of the female nude when she photographs herself. Aguilar is a large woman most would categorize as obese. Conventional wisdom would assume her body is unfit to display and unlikely to evoke an erotic response. However, the freedom Aguilar exacts in her photography has just the opposite effect. In a nature series in which she engages the desert landscape, Aguilar merges her naked body with the open spaces around her. The full roundness of her back becomes a smooth boulder resting against gravel and dirt. The thickness of her breasts and stomach sloped over either side of her body as she stands bent over in a wooded path become earthy mounds of sensual comfort for the woman balanced on her back. With herself as the object, Aguilar undoes her objectification as a woman. As reviewer A. M. Rousseau notes, "[Aguilar] makes public what is most private. By this risky act she transgresses familiar images of representation of the human body and replaces stereotypes with images of self-definition. She reclaims her body for herself." As a Chicana lesbian, Aguilar reclaims in her work a sexuality that is often erased within heteronormative representations of female nudity. Admitting her personal investment in Aguilar's work for the range and complexity of Chicana lesbian desire that it offers, cultural critic Yvonne Yarbro-Bejarano adds, "The desire that flows through [her art] does not limit itself to the sexual: It is for social justice, community, and representation in all its meanings."

Aguilar's photography also recalls the works of other Latinas who have sought to deconstruct shallow sexual stereotypes of Latina women. Cuban American artist Ana Mendieta uses photography, video, sculpture, and performance to capture the symbiotic relationship between women and nature. In several works, she employs mud, sand, and other natural materials to trace her bodily imprint into the landscape. Sometimes, her work suggests a peaceful coexistence with her surroundings; at other times, it emphasizes the unnatural violence thrust upon the female body by external forces.

References

Angry Little Girls! www.angrylittlegirls.com. Accessed July 6, 2009.

Beneath the Veil. Directed by Cassian Harrison. Independent Television News, 2001.

Carpenter, Cari. *Seeing Red: Anger, Sentimentality, and American Indians*. Columbus: Ohio State University, 2008.

Habell-Pallán, Michelle, and Mary Romero, eds. *Latinola Popular Culture*. New York: New York University, 2002.

Hall, Stuart. "Notes on Deconstructing 'The Popular.'" In Raphael Samuel, ed., *People's History and Socialist Theory*. Boston: Routledge and K. Paul, 1981, pp. 227–240.

Harjo, Joy. *She Had Some Horses*. New York: Thunder's Mouth, 1983.

I'm the One That I Want. Written by Margaret Cho. Directed by Lionel Coleman. Cho Taussig Productions, 2000.

"Interview with Lela Lee: Creator of Angry Little Asian Girl and Angry Little Girls." *indieRag.com*, June 8, 2001. www.indierag.com/content/interviews/010606lelalee.html. Accessed July 6, 2009.

Jones, Vanessa E. "The Angry Black Woman." *The Boston Globe*, April 20, 2004. www.boston.com/news/globe/living/articles/2004/04/20/the_angry_black_woman. Accessed July 6, 2009.

Lorde, Audre. "The Uses of Anger: Women Responding to Racism." In *Sister Outsider: Essays and Speeches*. Freedom, CA: The Crossing Press, 1984, pp. 124–133.

McMorris, Christine McCarthy. "Grappling with Islam: Bush and the Burqa." *Religion and the News*, 5.1, 2002. www.trincoll.edu/depts/csrpl/RINVol5No1/Bush%20burqa.htm. Accessed July 6, 2009.

Mendieta, Ana, and Gloria Moure. *Ana Mendieta*. Barcelona: Ediciones Poligrafa, 1996.

Noguchi, Irene. "'Asian Girl': Comic Strip of a Different Stripe." *Washington Post*, August 27, 2001, p. C01.

Notorious CHO. Written by Margaret Cho. Directed by Lorene Machado. Cho Taussig Productions, 2002.

Persepolis. Directed by Vincent Paronnaud and Marjane Satrapi. 2.4.7 Films, 2007.

Rousseau, A. M. "The Empress Has No Clothes." www.amrousseau.com/articles/photometro10.html. Accessed July 6, 2009.

Satrapi, Marjane. *The Complete Persepolis*. New York: Pantheon, 2003.

Simone, Nina. "Mississippi Goddamn." *Nina Simone in Concert*. Philips Records, 1964.

"Strange Fruit." Independent Lens. www.pbs.org/independentlens/strangefruit/film.html. Accessed July 6, 2009.

Wong, Kristina. Big Bad Chinese Mama. www.bigbadchinesemama.com. Accessed July 6, 2009.

Yamada, Mitsuye. "Invisibility Is an Unnatural Disaster: Reflections of an Asian American Woman." In Cherríe Moraga and Gloria Anzaldúa, eds., *This Bridge Called My Back: Writings by Radical Women of Color* (2nd ed.) New York: Kitchen Table, 1983, pp. 35–40.

Yarbro-Bejarano, Yvonne. "Laying It Bare: The Queer/Colored Body in Photography by Laura Aguilar." In Carla Trujillo, ed., *Living Chicana Theory*. Berkeley, CA: Third Woman, 2007, pp. 277–305.

4.7

Beauty and the Beast of Advertising

Jean Kilbourne

"You're a Halston woman from the very beginning," the advertisement proclaims. The model stares provocatively at the viewer, her long blonde hair waving around her face, her bare chest partially covered by two curved bottles that give the illusion of breasts and a cleavage. The average American is accustomed to blue-eyed blondes seductively touting a variety of products. In this case, however, the blonde is about five years old.

Advertising is an over $100 billion a year industry and affects all of us throughout our lives. We are each exposed to over 2,000 ads a day, constituting perhaps the most powerful educational force in society. The average adult will spend one and a half years of his/her life watching television commercials. But the ads sell a great deal more than products. They sell values, images, and concepts of success and worth, love and sexuality, popularity and normalcy. They tell us who we are and who we should be. Sometimes they sell addictions.

Advertising's foundation and economic lifeblood is the mass media, and the primary purpose of the mass media is to deliver an audience to advertisers, just as the primary purpose of television programs is to deliver an audience for commercials.

Adolescents are particularly vulnerable, however, because they are new and inexperienced consumers and are the prime targets of many advertisements. They are in the process of learning their values and roles and developing their self-concepts. Most teenagers are sensitive to peer pressure and find it difficult to resist or even question the dominant cultural messages perpetuated and reinforced by the media. Mass communication has made possible a kind of nationally distributed peer pressure that erodes private and individual values and standards.

But what does society, and especially teenagers, learn from the advertising messages that proliferate in the mass media? On the most obvious level they learn the stereotypes. Advertising creates a mythical, WASP-oriented world in which no one is ever ugly, overweight, poor, struggling or disabled either physically or mentally (unless you count the housewives who talk to little men in toilet bowls, animated germs in drains or muscle-bound giants clad in white clothing). And it is a world in which people talk only about products.

Housewives or Sex Objects

The aspect of advertising most in need of analysis and change is the portrayal of women. Scientific studies and the most casual viewing yield the same conclusion: women are shown almost exclusively as housewives or sex objects.

The housewife, pathologically obsessed by cleanliness and lemon-fresh scents, debates cleaning products with herself and worries about her husband's "ring around the collar."

The sex object is a mannequin, a shell. Conventional beauty is her only attribute. She has no lines or wrinkles (which would indicate she had the bad taste and poor judgment to grow older), no scars or blemishes – indeed, she has no pores. She is thin, generally tall and long-legged, and, above all, she is young. All "beautiful" women in advertisements (including minority women), regardless of product or audience, conform to this norm. Women are constantly exhorted to emulate this ideal, to feel ashamed and guilty if they fail, and to feel that their desirability and lovability are contingent upon physical perfection.

Creating Artificiality

The image is artificial and can only be achieved artificially (even the "natural look" requires much preparation and expense). Beauty is something that comes from without; more than one million dollars is spent every hour on cosmetics. Desperate to conform to an ideal and impossible standard, many women go to great lengths to manipulate and change their faces and bodies. A woman is conditioned to view her face as a mask and her body as an object, as *things* separate from and more important than her real self, constantly in need of alteration, improvement, and disguise. She is made to feel dissatisfied with and ashamed of herself, whether she tries to achieve "the look" or not. Objectified constantly by others, she learns to objectify herself. (It is interesting to note that one in five college-age women has an eating disorder.)

"When *Glamour* magazine surveyed its readers in 1984, 75 percent felt too heavy and only 15 percent felt just right. Nearly half of those who were actually under-weight reported feeling too fat and wanting to diet. Among a sample of college women, 40 percent felt overweight when only 12 percent actually were too heavy," according to Rita Freedman in her book *Beauty Bound*.

There is evidence that this preoccupation with weight begins at ever-earlier ages for women. According to a recent article in *New Age Journal*, "even grade-school girls are succumbing to stick-like standards of beauty enforced by a relentless parade of wasp-waisted fashion models, movie stars and pop idols." A study by a University of California professor showed that nearly 80 percent of fourth-grade girls in the Bay Area are watching their weight.

A recent *Wall Street Journal* survey of students in four Chicago-area schools found that more than half the fourth-grade girls were dieting and three-quarters felt they were overweight. One student said, "We don't expect boys to be that handsome. We take them as they are." Another added, "But boys expect girls to be perfect and beautiful. And skinny."

Dr Steven Levenkron, author of *The Best Little Girl in the World*, the story of an anorexic, says his blood pressure soars every time he opens a magazine and finds an ad for women's fashions. "If I had my way," he said, "every one of them would have to carry a line saying, 'Caution: this model may be hazardous to your health.'"

Women are also dismembered in commercials, their bodies separated into parts in need of change or improvement. If a woman has "acceptable" breasts, then she must also be sure that her legs are worth watching, her hips slim, her feet sexy, and that her buttocks look nude under her clothes ("like I'm not wearin' nothin'"). This image is difficult and costly to achieve and impossible to maintain (unless you buy the product) – no one is flawless and everyone ages. Growing older is the great taboo. Women are encouraged to remain little girls ("because innocence is sexier than you think"), to be passive and dependent, never to mature. The contradictory message – "sensual, but not too far from innocence" – places women in a double bind; somehow we are supposed to be both sexy and virginal, experienced and naïve, seductive and chaste. The disparagement of maturity is, of course, insulting and frustrating to adult women, and the implication that little girls are seductive is dangerous to real children.

Influencing Sexual Attitudes

Young people also learn a great deal about sexual attitudes from the media and from advertising in particular. Advertising's approach to sex is pornographic: it reduces people to objects and de-emphasizes human contact and individuality. This reduction of sexuality to a dirty joke and of people to objects is the real obscenity of the culture. Although the sexual sell, overt and subliminal, is at a fevered pitch in most commercials, there is at the same time a notable absence of sex as an important and profound human activity.

There have been some changes in the images of women. Indeed, a "new woman" has emerged in commercials in recent years. She is generally presented as superwoman, who manages to do all the work at home and on the job (with the help of a product, of course, not of her husband or children or friends), or as the liberated woman, who owes her independence and self-esteem to the products she uses. These new images do not represent any real progress but rather create a myth of progress, an illusion that reduces complex sociopolitical problems to mundane personal ones.

Advertising images do not cause these problems, but they contribute to them by creating a climate in which the marketing of women's bodies – the sexual sell and dismemberment, distorted body image ideal and children as sex objects – is seen as acceptable.

This is the real tragedy, that many women internalize these stereotypes and learn their "limitations," thus establishing a self-fulfilling prophecy. If one accepts these mythical and degrading images, to some extent one actualizes them. By remaining unaware of the profound seriousness of the ubiquitous influence, the redundant message and the subliminal impact of advertisements, we ignore one of the most powerful "educational" forces in the culture – one that greatly affects our self-images, our ability to relate to each other, and effectively destroys any awareness and action that might help to change that climate.

4.8

Pop and Circumstance: Why Pop Culture Matters

Andi Zeisler

In the past decade or two, feminism and popular culture have become more closely entwined than ever before. This can in part be chalked up to the growing interest in cultural studies as an academic discipline and the resulting number of academic papers, conferences, and books devoted to feminist analyses of various facets of pop. (The field of studies devoted to *Buffy the Vampire Slayer* alone is proof that feminist cultural studies is no passing fad.) But it can also be explained by the fact that, well, there's a whole lot more popular culture to watch, read, examine, and deconstruct. Television networks are continually expanding their programming slates, and many in the past few years have switched to a year-round programming schedule that makes the phrase "summer rerun" nearly obsolete. Print magazines such as *Bust, Entertainment Weekly, Radar*, and *Bitch* are interested in pop culture as common language and as genuine pleasure. And the Internet teems with blogs, e-zines, and social-networking sites that not only dissect existing pop culture but create their own.

There are feminist issues that seem, it's true, more immediately vital than whether TV or movie characters are reflecting the lives of real women. There are the continuing problems of the gap between men's and women's wages, of glass ceilings and tacit sex discrimination in the workplace. There is the need to combat violence against girls and women and promote sexual autonomy. There are ongoing battles, both individual and collective, against limiting cultural definitions of "mother" and "wife." There's the fact that the Equal Rights Amendment, first proposed in 1923, has as of this writing still not been ratified by the United States Congress – meaning that under the U.S. Constitution women are not equal to men. And there are even broader, more global, and more complex issues of what it means to be a woman, a feminist, and a seeker of human and civil rights. But like the disintegrating line between high and low culture, the distinctions between political and pop have also all but disappeared. Pop culture informs our understanding of political issues that on first glance seem to have nothing to do with pop culture; it also makes us see how something meant as pure entertainment can have everything to do with politics.

I first heard the term "male gaze" in high school, and it sent me back to my seven-year-old self, watching Burt Reynolds watch that naked woman in the shower. I got angry all over again. It seems that for many women, a formative experience with that uncomfortable gaze – maybe in an issue of *Playboy*, maybe in an oil painting in a museum – becomes a defining moment. The male gaze affects how women view pop culture and how we view ourselves. And the concept of the male gaze itself is one that's crucial to understanding why reforming and reframing popular culture is a feminist project.

What is the male gaze? Put simply, it's the idea that when we look at images in art or on screen, we're seeing them as a man might – even if we are women – because those images are constructed to be seen by men. John Berger's 1972 fine-art monograph *Ways of Seeing* didn't coin the phrase, but it did describe the gendered nature of looking this way: "*Men act* and *women appear*. Men look at women. Women watch themselves being looked at. This determines not only most relations between men and women but also the relation of women to themselves. The surveyor of women in herself is male: the surveyed female. Thus she turns herself into an object – and most particularly an object of vision: a sight."

A year or two later, Laura Mulvey took this concept further in what's become a well-known work of psychoanalytic film theory, "Visual Pleasure and Narrative Cinema." In talking about the way narrative film reinforces the gender of the film's viewer using a sequence of "looks," Mulvey drew on Freudian psychoanalysis. She wrote that the male unconscious, which, according to Freud's theories, is consumed with a fear of castration, deals with that fear by seeking power over women, who represent the castrating figure. So by positioning women as nothing more than objects to be looked at, sexualized, and made vulnerable, the male unconscious reassures itself that, really, it has nothing to fear from women. As Mulvey put it:

> In a world ordered by sexual imbalance, pleasure in looking has been split between active/male and passive/female. The determining male gaze projects its phantasy on to the female figure which is styled accordingly. In their traditional exhibitionist role women are simultaneously looked at and displayed, with their appearance coded for strong visual and erotic impact so that they can be said to connote to-be-looked-at-ness. Woman displayed as sexual object is the leit-motif of erotic spectacle: from pin-ups to strip-tease, from Ziegfeld to Busby Berkeley she holds the look, plays to and signifies male desire.

Despite the clunkiness of the phrase "to-be-looked-at-ness," Mulvey pinpointed the way that images of women onscreen (and, by extension, on television, in magazines, on billboards …) seek to align viewers of any gender with the male gaze. So it makes sense that many girls and women grow up seeing images of girls and women the way men do – the images themselves are simply constructed that way. The mother figure is sexless; the cheerleader is hypersexual. The girl alone in her house is a potential victim, the man coming to the door an obvious rapist. Seeing the visual cues of the male gaze, in turn, affects how women understand images of other women on screen.

What "Visual Pleasure and Narrative Cinema" didn't suggest, however, is that perhaps there is a corresponding female gaze that informs how women see images of both themselves and of men and affects the images they themselves create. This, of course, had largely to do with the fact that female screenwriters and directors were few and far between at the time Mulvey was writing – and, in many places, remain so. Since the 1975 publication of Mulvey's article, feminist and cultural critics have responded to it – both directly and indirectly – with essays and books that attempt to define a female gaze and parse the many ways in which images of women can be claimed as powerful and even subversive. And many more authors, filmmakers, musicians, and artists have made work that takes on the male gaze directly, flipping the script on the likes of Berger and Mulvey with imagery that is unsettling in its confrontation of the looker.

The Commerce Connection

In examining how feminism has informed pop culture and vice versa, it's instructive to look at the way the evolution of the women's movement has been mirrored in pockets of popular culture. This evolution has almost never been linear; as with women's experiences as a whole, many representations of women in pop culture have stayed stubbornly behind the curve of liberation expectations. But others have changed with the times, alternately gratifying and frustrating the women who watch carefully, looking for accurate portrayals of who they are and can be.

In 1970s pop culture, for example, women were no longer just playing the role of the sweet, pliant housewife. They were going to work (*The Mary Tyler Moore Show*), getting divorced (*An Unmarried Woman*), having abortions (*Maude*), standing up for injustice (*Norma Rae*), and rocking hard (bands such as Heart and Fanny). They were also talking to each other, and in some cases, to men such as daytime talk-show host Phil Donohue, about their increasingly politicized personal decisions and debates. Not all women portrayed in pop culture were doing these things, of course – but both individual women and the media paid attention to the ones who were, because – like it or not – they were upending conventional notions of what women could and should do. In the 1980s, there were TV characters who seemed to be striving for feminist ideals, but for most of them – as it was for women in the real world – it was almost impossible to be feminist superwomen in a world that was still stubbornly unequal. There were Kate and Allie on the sitcom of the same name, two women who pooled their resources in the wake of divorce, raising their children together in what was both a clever housing arrangement and, more impor-tant, a necessary solution to working single motherhood. There were Murphy

Brown and Molly Dodd, single working women grappling with having power in the professional sphere even as their single status was assumed to plague them. There was working-class mother and worker Roseanne, blithely snarking and cursing her way through the monotony of dead-ends jobs and ungrateful children on her titular sitcom. (Jennifer Reed's essay "Roseanne: A 'Killer Bitch' for Generation X" in the 1997 book *Third Wave Agenda: Being Feminist, Doing Feminism* proclaimed that Roseanne "voices the inevitable rage that comes when the knowledge created by feminist thinking and action encounters the intractability of oppressive forces.") At the movies, there were madcap comedies about women who stood up to discrimination in the workplace (*9 to 5*) and even more madcap takes on housewifery (*The Incredible Shrinking Woman, Freaky Friday*); there were princess narratives about hookers with hearts of gold (*Pretty Woman*) and cautionary tales about the perils of female sexual agency (*Fast Times at Ridgemont High*). And in music, there was MTV, which made a handful of women into rock stars while relegating countless others to a background in which they writhed, half-naked and faceless, for the better part of a decade.

The 1980s also saw female action heroes sidling up to their historically male counterparts; even if viewers didn't regard the onscreen ass-kicking undertaken by characters such as Ellen Ripley of the *Alien* series or Sarah Connor of the *Terminator* movies as putting feminist theory into practice, these characters were nevertheless expanding the definition of what women could do onscreen and validating individual women who longed to see other females doing more in the face of danger than looking pretty. For all of these women, feminism was a work in progress.

In the early 1990s, music was a primary site in which women were challenging the roles that the industry had constructed for them, and performers from Hole's Courtney Love to Meshell Ndegeocello to Fiona Apple were rattling the walls of music's girl ghettos and calling out the forces, both personal and institutional, that wanted to hold them back. And in the 2000s, pop culture is a stew of progressivism and backlash: On one TV network, a woman might be the president of the United States; on another, she's effusing that being a Pussycat Doll is the dream of a lifetime. *New York Times* columnist Maureen Dowd asserts that women want to be saved from their ambition, and the next day a righteous clutch of bloggers debate the point furiously. Feminism – that is, explicit references to the women's liberation movement – as reflected in popular culture might charitably be described as a funhouse-mirror view: You can discern the basic construction, but the overall effect is grotesquely distorted to maximize its worst features.

When pop culture presents feminism to the public via mainstream media, the results are mixed at best. For many women, this means that it's important to examine representations of women and agency in the expected places (network television, major labels), but it's even more important to start scouting the margins – the blogs, the underground publishing collectives, the tiny bedroom record labels – for alternatives and to begin creating them ourselves. Parsing feminism and pop culture is not as easy as looking vigilantly for what's "good" (that is, feminist) in pop culture and calling out what's "bad" (antifeminist and regressive).

Pop culture has always been about commerce, and feminism and pop culture will always be uneasy bedfellows in a larger culture that remains conflicted (to say the very least) about how much power, agency, and autonomy women should have. A significant chunk of the advertising industry has always been devoted to reaching women, and in most cases its messages have instructed women to be on guard, lest they compromise their most important quality: their looks. Lucky Strike magazine ads from as far back as 1928 touted the appetite-suppressing qualities of smoking; ones for Camay soap in that same decade warned women that "The Eyes of Men … The Eyes of Women Judge your Loveliness Every Day." (There's that darned male gaze again.) As the decades progressed, women were sold products to combat every-thing from halitosis and "intimate odor" to dry hair and naked toenails with copy that was about as subtle as a sharp stick in the eye. In her 1985 book, *Femininity*, Susan Brownmiller wrote of this state of affairs, "Because she is forced to concentrate on the minutiae of her bodily parts, a woman is never free of self-consciousness. She is never quite satisfied, and never secure, for desperate, unending absorption in the drive for perfect appearance – call it feminine vanity – is the ultimate restriction on freedom of mind."

The women's movement, however, gave advertising a new way to interact with women: namely, by speaking to them in the language of liberation. Advertisements still told women that their hair needed to be shinier and their bodies more toned for bikini season – they just did so more sneakily. From Virginia Slims' famous "You've come a long way, baby" campaign to "new woman" perfumes such as Charlie and Enjoli to Nike's "Just Do It" tagline in the 1980s and 1990s, corporations saw femi-nism as a fail-safe marketing tool and sought to link their products with images of strong, inspiring, and – of course – beautiful women. Advertising has increasingly capitalized on women's shifting status in society and culture, using riffs on feminist slogans and sly references to landmark liberations to sell everything from running shoes to diet frozen pizzas to diamond rings. But is it liberation or co-optation? And does one necessarily cancel out the other? If feminist ideology and discourse are simply plugged into existing models, and if the basic message – in this instance, the message to buy stuff – remains the same, is it feminism? Furthermore, when this advertising sits alongside contradictory content – as it might in a magazine such as *Teen Vogue*, in which articles on the dangers of eating disorders immediately pre-cede fashion spreads peopled with rail-thin models – what message does that send? The very fact that pop culture depends on commerce for its reach and influence is what makes any association with feminism just a little bit suspect.

But Isn't Pop Culture Supposed to Be Fun?

An important point to make in any survey of women, feminism, and popular culture is that their intersections aren't simply ones of bloodless inquiry and pointed criti-cism. Popular culture is inescapable – it's all around us and getting more so every day. (If you want proof, try keeping a running tally, on a normal day in your life, of how many advertisements you see, how many websites you visit, how many TV shows, movies, or books you hear referenced in daily conversation, how many songs you hear snippets of in passing.) But pop culture is so powerful precisely because it can be so very engaging and pleasurable. What's better than going to a new action movie with friends after a long week of work, classes, or both? What's more satisfying than bouncing along to your new favorite song on your headphones? And I personally know many people (fine, I'm one of them) who look forward to a long plane ride for the sole reason that the time can be passed by digging into an issue of *Vanity Fair* or *Us Weekly*. Pop culture can be social, it can be secret, and it can be frivolous – but it can't be denied. The pleasure of consuming pop culture makes critiquing it one of the more challenging projects for feminists. Unlike eliminating the wage gap or securing reproductive autonomy for every woman, the relationship between feminism and pop culture has no finite, ultimate goal. There are many individual activists who use pop culture as a way to discuss women's rights – such as Jean Kilbourne, whose *Killing Us Softly* film series looks at images of women in advertising and its skewed lens on violence, love, and success, or Ani DiFranco, the independent singer-songwriter whose straightforward lyrics consistently address feminist issues. But there's no one success in the ongoing feminist project of critiquing and reforming pop culture that would cause women to high-five each other and say, "Yep, we're done here. All fixed."

What's Your Favorite Pop Culture Moment Ever?

"Sassy. Sigh. I remember being a tween and looking through my older sister's Seventeen and YM *magazines and just not getting them. I thought the hope chest ads were hokey. I thought the fashions were lame. I wanted* Seventeen's *'Sex and Your Body' column to be scandalous – or at least interesting – and was disappointed on every count. Then* Sassy *appeared, and I felt like it was talking to me. I got it. I saw myself in it. I devoured it monthly. I wrote my undergraduate senior thesis on it. I went to work there for almost a year as an unpaid intern. I got into teen magazines because of it, hoping to make changes from within. I care about feminism and pop culture because of it. I wrote a book for teen girls about decoding media messages and beauty ideals because of it. It shaped my identity, my career path, my critical-thinking skills, and my passions." –* Audrey

"I'm always moved by movies about women and sports. My mother and I saw the movie A League of Their Own *together and I remember there was one scene where I started crying and I looked over at my mother and she was crying too. I can watch that movie and* Bend It Like Beckham *over and over. In both movies, the moments when the girls realize that they have this talent that's completely unrelated to expectations of them as women always ring true, and I love reaffirming that feeling in myself by watching them." –* Donna

"A friend of mine in New York told me about this singer named Ani DiFranco and duped me a cassette tape of her first recording. It was just so raw and intense – it actually made me uncomfortable at first, but I started listening to it every single night on my headphones. It was the first time I had heard a girl use the word cunt – there was a line in one of her songs that went My cunt

is built like a wound that won't heal. That was like, whoa. That line repeated in my head for days. It was just the most brave and honest thing I had ever heard in a song. It's insane when I think about it now, but I actually stopped seeing a guy because I played him the tape and he just shrugged and was like, It's okay, but her voice is annoying. I haven't listened to Ani DiFranco in years, but that tape definitely made an impact." – Francesca

"My most profound moment was watching Thelma and Louise *with members of my college feminist collective (we were called Downer Feminist Council – terrible name) the summer in between my junior and senior years. We had this sense of great possibility and power that was connected to rage – like being pissed off was going to get me somewhere that felt really free. The next year, working at Ms. magazine, I fell for a woman who had a similar fixation on Callie Khouri's opus. I now see it as a particular moment in history – we were women nurtured on second wave feminist critiques of sexism, we were emerging from the fog of the backlash, we shrugged off those shackles and got wind of power and now what were we going to do? I think that film helped to usher in the sensibility of the third wave – Thelma and Louise go on their journey, raising their consciousness, but they don't get away. ... We younger viewers started from their point of departure, and we didn't have to sacrifice ourselves to be free, or at least more free."* – Jennifer

"K.d. lang on the cover of Vanity Fair *magazine. That was hot. I realize now that it was some kind of lesbian fantasy aimed at guys – Cindy Crawford was giving k.d. a shave, in high heels and a bathing suit. But as a just-out lesbian, I really felt like, here is an icon who isn't ambiguous or closeted. I had it on my wall for a whole semester."* – Liz

"When I saw Girls Town *at a film festival with director Jim McKay in attendance, I was blown away by seeing a multiracial cast portray teenage girls in both a realistic and hopeful manner. I couldn't believe I was watching these strong characters bond with each other, critique racism and their treatment by men, and carry out retribution against rapists. Not only did they avoid death at the end of the film (unlike* Thelma and Louise*), they carried on with their lives with integrity and respect for each other. It was such a complicated and hopeful picture of teenage girls' lives and relationships. And it was directed by a white man who was smart enough to realize he couldn't do justice to the story without women's input; the young women in the film helped write it and improvised much of their own dialogue. It gave the film its realistic feel and showed how powerful collaborative feminist projects involving all genders can be."* – Wendy

So what could a feminist reclamation of – or just an improvement on – pop culture look like? Well, let's start with Hollywood: With more feminist directors, producers, screenwriters, and network heads, perhaps women would stop being relegated to wife-and-girlfriend roles in action movies. Perhaps parts created for women of color would be not only more plentiful but also less stereotypical. Perhaps the juiciest roles for women – the ones that garner them attention, accolades, and little gold men – would be something other than, as Shirley MacLaine famously put it, "hookers, victims, and doormats." That time, as of today, seems far off: In the fall of 2007, film-industry columnist Nikki Finke leaked an internal studio missive from Warner Bros.' president of production, Jeff Robinov, announcing that the studio would no longer be making films with female leads. In a less-than-robust rebuttal, the studio issued a statement via the industry magazine *Variety*: "Contrary to recent reports in the blogosphere, Warner Bros. is still committed to women."

Then there's television. It's a little too simple to say that in a more feminist pop culture, we wouldn't see women in bikinis competing with each other to win a diamond ring from a man they've known for ten minutes, or looping around stripper poles on nearly every cable channel, or wearing tiny matching dresses and smiling toothy, Vaselined smiles while holding briefcases full of money. But it's certain that we wouldn't see quite so many of them.

What else would look different? Well, female musicians wouldn't be encouraged to sex up their images for major-label deals or coverage in music magazines or on MTV. Female comedians would have as many sitcom deals as their male counterparts, and if some yahoo sent up the inevitable cry of "But women aren't funny!" there'd be a plethora of people ready to prove him wrong. The term "chick lit" wouldn't exist to describe/denigrate books written by women that happen to be about relationships.

Some people used to think that having more women in positions of power at publishing houses, movie studios, record companies, and TV networks would make a difference. Yet even when women have held these positions of influence, their companies still produce plenty of material that demeans, objectifies, and insults women. Case in point: Sheila Nevins, as the president of HBO's documentary and family programming, produced many incredible, award-winning documentaries, but she's also responsible for the channel's recent obsession with glamorizing sex work, executive-producing HBO's series about strippers (*G-String Divas*), about porn stars (*Pornucopia: Going Down in the Valley*), and about prostitutes (*Cathouse; Cathouse 2: Back in the Saddle*). There's simply no mandate that a woman, by virtue of being in power, will make choices that will elevate all women or that other women will automatically approve of. Getting one or two seats for women at the proverbial table won't guarantee that the face of pop culture becomes one that's friendlier to women; it's simply one part of a larger push for women to be more proactive, more unapologetic, and more determined to make spaces in pop culture that represent all the dimensions of women's lives. But in the meantime, there's nothing wrong with loving, consuming, and creating pop culture with an eye toward how it can be better: smarter, less insulting to women (and men, for that matter), more diverse, and less hell-bent on perpetuating ugly and unhelpful stereotypes. And understanding more about feminism and pop culture's long, difficult, and occasionally fruitful relationship is a good way to start.

Sources

Berger, John. *Ways of Seeing*. London: British Broadcasting Company and Penguin Books, 1972, p. 47.

Brownmiller, Susan. *Femininity*. New York: Ballantine Books, 1985, p. 51.

Dowd, Maureen. *Are Men Necessary? When Sexes Collide*. New York: Putnam, 2005.

Falwell, Jerry. *The 700 Club*. (CBN), September 13, 2001.

Finke, Nikki, "Hollywood's He-Man Woman Haters Club." *L.A. Weekly*, Wednesday, October 17, 2007.

Levy, Ariel. *Female Chauvinist Pigs: Women and the Rise of Raunch Culture*. New York: Free Press, 2005, pp. 89–91.

McGinn, Daniel. "Marriage by the Numbers." *Newsweek, June* 5, 2006.

Mulvey, Laura, "Visual Pleasure and Narrative Cinema." *Screen* 16.3, 1975. In Laura Mulvey, *Visual and Other Pleasures*. Bloomington: Indiana University Press, 1989.

Reed, Jennifer. "Roseanne: A 'Killer Bitch' for Generation X." In Leslie Heywood and Jennifer Drake, eds. *Third Wave Agenda: Being Feminist, Doing Feminism*. Minneapolis: University of Minnesota Press, 1997, p. 123.

Thompson, Anne. "Warner Bros. Still Committed to Women." Variety.com, October 9, 2007.

5

Sexualities and Genders

By Susan E. Cayleff

Contents

Original publication details: 5.1 Maiana Minahal, "poem on trying to love without fear" from *Color of Violence: The Incite! Anthology*, ed. Incite! Women of Color against Violence, pp. 267–69. Cambridge, MA: South End Press, 2006. Reproduced with permission of Maiana Minahal. 5.2 Audre Lorde, "Uses of the Erotic: The Erotic as Power" from *Sister Outsider: Essays and Speeches*, pp. 53–59. Freedom, CA: Crossing Press, 1984. Reproduced with permission of Abner Stein Agency. 5.3 "The Happiest Day of My Life" from *Dear Sisters: Dispatches from the Women's Liberation Movement*, ed. Rosalyn Baxandall and Linda Gordon New York: Basic Books, 2000, p. 163. Reproduced with permission of Perseus Books Group. 5.4 Heather Corinna, "An Immodest Proposal" from *Yes Means Yes: Visions of Female Sexual Power and a World without Rape*, ed. Jaclyn Friedman and Jessica Valenti, pp. 179–86. Berkeley, CA: Seal Press, 2008. Reproduced with permission of Perseus Books Group, Jaclyn Friedman, and Jessica Valenti. 5.5 Kathy Peiss, "'Charity Girls' and City Pleasures: Historical Notes on Working-Class Sexuality, 1880–1920" from *Powers of Desire: the Politics of Sexuality*, ed. Ann Snitow, Christine Stansell, and Sharon Thompson, pp. 74–87. New York: Monthly Review, 1983. Reproduced with permission of Monthly Review Press. (continued on page 196)

Women in Culture: An Intersectional Anthology for Gender and Women's Studies, Second Edition.
Edited by Bonnie Kime Scott, Susan E. Cayleff, Anne Donadey, and Irene Lara.
© 2017 John Wiley & Sons, Ltd. Published 2017 by John Wiley & Sons, Ltd.

This chapter promotes an understanding of the culturally constructed nature of lesbian, gay, bisexual, transgender, and queer sexualities, gender identities, heterosexual privilege, intersex lives, and homophobia and transphobia. It redefines desire and the erotic across sexualities. It also dismantles previous conceptions and claims that there are only two sexes, that heterosexuality is the norm, and that one is either/or (female/male; lesbian/straight). The existence of bisexuality and two/twin spirit identities in Native American communities belies these ideas, as Will Roscoe highlights in *Changing Ones: Third and Fourth Genders in Native North America*. There are numerous ways people express their desire and their identities.

Authors in this section provide definitions, lived experiences, physiological and medical information, and cultural interpretations that define and limit human behavior and identities. Several definitions will help students understand the meaning of these terms. Many people presume that sex and gender are the same when in fact they are not; they are systems that interact, as cultural anthropologist Gayle Rubin claims. One definition of sex is that it refers to the biological organs one is born with and how those are "read" by attending medical personnel, or the sexual act itself. Gender means how one identifies and "performs/presents" oneself in the society. This allows for women who appear biologically female to choose to act and see themselves as not stereotypically female, feminine, or heterosexual. Some choose to present as masculine, non-binary, and/or gender-nonconforming. This also includes people who are female identified but whose organs may not conform to stereotypical female biological criteria.

Original publication details: 5.6 Indiana University Empowerment Workshop, "When you Meet a Lesbian: Hints for the Heterosexual Woman." Public domain. 5.7 Gay and Lesbian Speakers' Bureau, "Heterosexuality Questionnaire." The Heterosexuality Questionnaire has been used in SpeakOUT's speaker training curriculum since it was called the Gay and Lesbian Speakers' Bureau. Established in 1972, SpeakOUT is now the oldest LGBTQIA speakers' bureau in the United States. 5.8 Judith Lorber and Lisa Jean Moore, "Aligning Bodies, Identities, and Expressions: Transgender Bodies" from *Gendered Bodies: Feminist Perspectives*, pp. 118–21. New York: Oxford University Press, 2011. Reproduced with permission of Oxford University Press. 5.9 R.W. Connell, "Masculinity Politics on a World Scale" from *Masculinities*, 2nd ed., pp. 260–65. Berkeley, CA: University of California Press, 2005. Reproduced with permission of University of California Press. 5.10 Prentis Hemphill, "Brown Boi Health Manifesto" from *Freeing Ourselves: A Guide to Health and Self Love for Brown Bois*, pp. 118–19. Brown Boi Project, 2011. Reproduced with permission of Brown Boi Project.

Our culture also erroneously assumes that there are only two sexes: female and male. We now know there are people with XXY chromosomes, not just XX (female) or XY (male). Intersex people, born with aspects of both typical female and male organs, also contradict this belief. It is also untrue that biological women or men are only attracted to members of the opposite sex and/or portray themselves as stereotypically feminine or masculine. Another popular misunderstanding is that sex and eroticism are synonymous. In fact, sex acts are often distinct from eroticism. The latter means spiritual, mental, or sensual feelings that are aroused that may or may not involve an act of intimacy. If we fail to understand these differences we can un/willingly engage in homo and trans* phobic attitudes (beliefs that presume the desirability/normalcy of heterosexuality and then deem same-sex, trans*, or gender-nonconforming desire/intimacy as wrong and bad) and behavior to devalue and condemn lesbian, gay, bisexual, transgender, queer and questioning, and intersex people.

Empowerment

Four of our authors argue that eroticism, sexual desire, and self-defined pleasure are key components to diverse women's sexual satisfaction. In fact, this self-defined pleasure is a power that women have – if they recognize their ability to pursue, define, and embrace it.

In her eloquent piece "poem on trying to love without fear" (2006), Maiana Minahal offers a moving monologue about seeking empowerment. As a Filipina-American woman she faces her fear of familial rejection as she realizes she is a lesbian. This fear nearly paralyzes her trust in her own desire, her ability to act autonomously, and her willingness to express her love to another woman. This theme resonates for many lesbian and gay, bisexual, transgender, queer, questioning, intersex, and female identified people. One's self-knowledge is suppressed for fear of being rejected. Her plea to be able to love without fear resonates for people who feel forced to hide central aspects of themselves. Yet this piece provides opportunity for empowerment: Minahal's recognition of this silencing opens the dialogue and consciousness for her to reclaim and identify her own path in life. It is an *emerging* empowerment and a frequent part of the "coming out" experience. This process often takes time, self-reflection, and the willingness to risk things we once thought secure (family, friends, and cultural approval). Another key element is the need to identify community that shares similar identities and beliefs. These life factors are privileges that heterosexual women and men take for granted. Minahal also raises important questions about how race impacts gender, sexuality, and self-realization, something also done by David Newman, in *Identities and Inequalities*. To feel rejected by one's family as a person of color takes on additional meaning when one may already feel marginalized by a racist dominant society.

Audre Lorde, a self-identified Black lesbian, argues in *Uses of the Erotic* (1984) that all women, on a deeply female and spiritual plane, have the power, often unexpressed and unrecognized, to embrace and enjoy eroticism. She extends the definition of the erotic because girls and women are taught that fulfillment is achieved through intimacy with males – many women deny this potential in themselves. She emphasizes the spiritual and holistic aspect of eroticism as a life force. The antithesis of this erotic power is pornography, which largely portrays women as forced, objectified, and of little value except to please men. This power can be reclaimed by listening to our knowledge of ourselves instead of what we are taught to do. This empowering and creative force can be threatening to some. Lorde's claim has been criticized by some for generalizing that all women possess this power. This is known as essentialism – when we attribute a trait to all women based on their biological/cultural identities. These responses are not innate, as Lorde argues, but rather culturally constructed (a result of our gendered upbringings and cultural norms). This critique does not diminish the value of Lorde's powerful assertions.

Heather Corinna's "An Immodest Proposal" (2008) poses similar issues. In a budding relationship between two teens, the girl willingly engages in an erotic and sexual relationship with her boyfriend. As their relationship progresses to intercourse, she finds their encounters pleasurable but not sexually or erotically fulfilling. Despite their attempts to communicate honestly, his pleasure is at the center of their relationship and she convinces herself that things will change over time. What is missing for her is desire and passion. Like Lorde, Corinna argues that female fulfillment is as important to women as it is to men: it is an innate right during intimacy. It is not something that will hopefully emerge later. It needs to be a fundamental part of all intimacy – and, as Lorde says, it doesn't necessarily come from heterosexual contact. Another author that offers valuable insights on this topic of teen girls' sexuality is Deborah Tolman, in *Dilemmas of Desire*.

The Brown Boi Project works to empower brown bois (biological females of color who may or may not identify as female) who embrace their masculine identities and trans* and gender-nonconforming bodies. The members of the collective say this can be done through self-knowledge, like-minded community, self-love, and meaningful health care. Many more authors offer insights for transgender people and lesbians of color: Mira Alexis P. Ofreneo's "Tomboys and Lesbians: The Filipino Female Homosexual and Her Identity Development Process" and Huma Ahmed Ghosh's edited "Lesbians, Sexuality, and Islam" are both valuable. The path-breaking work of Judith Halberstam's *Female Masculinity* is vital in understanding the *fluidity* of gender expressions and sexual desires, as is Lisa M. Diamond's *Sexual Fluidity*.

Theories and behavior that seek empowerment for lesbian, heterosexual, trans*, and gender-nonconforming women/bois are frequently resisted by men who stand to benefit from maintaining their privileged positions. Kathy Peiss's historical study of "'Charity Girls' and City Pleasures" (1983) explores the trend among working-class ethnic girls who traded sexual favors in urban settings between 1880 and 1920. They were unable to afford the niceties and excitement of urban entertainment: amusement parks, dance halls, and the theatre. They defined their own willingness to trade their sexualities: they gave sexual favors to men who treated them to a night out. One could argue this is a form of empowerment, yet these working-class urban girls were in a sociopolitical climate that disempowered them along gender and economic lines. This article raises the complex issue of choice and agency in a context in which there are so few viable alternatives. The trading of sexual favors altered the meaning of premarital sex, the use of sexualized language, and women's ability to "choose" their behaviors. At the same time, this increased commodified sexuality led to heightened sexual harassment. In retrospect we could also argue that it devalued both female and male intimacy, and women's authentic pursuit of self-defined pleasure.

Redefining Genders, Identities and Sexual Binaries

As mentioned earlier, patriarchy, heterosexual privilege, and heteronormativity (the belief that all things heterosexual are normal, desirable, inherently right, and should be rewarded) are challenged by some trans*women, lesbians, and heterosexual women. Those who are gender-nonconforming challenge this limiting binary (female/male; heterosexual/gay; black/white) of what female and male "look like" and how they are read by cisgender people (those whose assigned sex at birth corresponds with their gender expression and identity). Gender-nonconformists reject the either/or view and assert their own definitions and performances of sexual/erotic identities on a *continuum*. This is very unsettling for many people who find the predictable safety and privilege they garner threatened.

Four sources in this chapter examine the pressures applied to extract appearance and behavior appropriate to our assigned sex. People who won't or can't fit into these tidy categories are gay men, transgender, non-binary, intersex, and, other authors argue, lesbian. These complexities are detailed in "When You Meet a Lesbian, Hints for the Heterosexual Woman," and the "Heterosexuality Questionnaire." Lorber and Moore's "Aligning Bodies, Identities, and Expressions" (2006/2011) focuses on female-to-male (FTM) (now called transwomen) and male-to-female (MTF) (now called transmen), at times hormonally and surgically altered, people. The use of *trans** signifies the inclusion of people on the entire spectrum of gender identities. Transgender people, they argue, "feel that their bodies do not match their true gender identity" (138). There is no one way that people respond to this realization. Some embrace their masculinities, femininities, and/or gender non-binary status without altering their bodies. Some take hormones and/or seek "top" and/or "bottom" surgery and others choose to live as gender-stereotypical women or men. The Brown Boi Project (2011) realizes the complexities of these choices and the need for vibrant support, self-respect, and healthy spiritual and mental choices. Issues of race complicate this self-realization because they are themselves inherently loaded with both privilege and oppression. These are themes that Urvashi Vaid discusses in *Irresistible Revolution*. Lorber and Moore assert being viewed as either a masculine woman or an effeminate man makes one vulnerable to societal rejection, fear, and violence. Thus the necessity for support and other forms of self- and societal worth are crucial. We now realize that gender-nonconforming people face these issues as well.

Transgender people, as well as those born intersex, challenge the traditional sex and at times gender binary. The Intersex Society of North America (2015) provides crucial information on the issues its members face. We all encounter constant pressure to conform to the sex/gender we have been assigned at birth, and intersex activists work to gain recognition that female/male is an inadequate view of human life. The forms we fill out, public bathrooms, and much else ask us to identify as either female or male on a regular basis:

activist efforts are afoot to add transgender to that choice list. These expectations of con-
formity reflect cisgender and heterosexual privilege. Kate Bornstein and S. Bear Bergman
explore these issues well in their edited *Gender Outlaws: The Next Generation*.

In recognition of these fluid identities, sexual assignment of intersex babies would
cease and adults could be themselves without having to choose a category, a necessary
step according to the Intersex Society. Intersex and transgender people who live as
female or male find themselves living on the boundaries and hiding, hoping not to be
detected; like multiracial people, they experience an insider/outsider status.

Gender queerness also subverts static categories. Fluid choices are shown through
behavior, language (preferred name and pronoun choice), and appearance-based factors:
hair, clothing, jewelry, and makeup. Embracing these identities comes with a price, Judith
Lorber and Lisa Jean Moore argue: transmen often gain economic privilege as men, and
find their feminist identities compromised. Race and social class complicate this further.
Chicano men's queerness is explored in Adelaida R. Del Castillo and Gibran Guido's edited
Queer in Aztlán. Only white heterosexual men are privileged through race, gender, and
sexual orientations.

R. W. Connell's "Masculinities" (1995/2005) asserts that globally many men are rejecting
and have rejected their privilege. When Connell authored this piece he identified as male;
Connell now identifies as a transsexual woman. Men's rejection of male privilege was due in
large part to feminist resistance to their patriarchal (and we can add heterosexual) power.
She allows that cross-culturally men have higher incomes and greater participation in the
labor force, own the vast amount of property, and enjoy more institutional power as well as
sexual and embedded cultural privilege (authority). Amidst this glum picture for women,
she notes the impact of international feminist groups who have changed these social orders
once thought immutable. As a result, a disruption in the world gender order has been
occurring among men who willingly scrutinize and challenge their own privilege and sometimes embrace pro-feminist politics: this is discussed in the introduction to Chapter 8. Yet
global resistance from most men works to reaffirm their hegemonic (nearly absolute)
patriarchal power. Despite Connell's optimism, the backlash posed by conservative politics
is powerful. This is an argument made by Susan Faludi in *Backlash*, where she demonstrates
that American women's progress in the 1990s was met with institutionalized repression.
Whether we agree with her early assertions or not, Connell says this shift is notable and will
inform future gendered relations.

Lesbian Identities and Heterosexual Normativity

Lesbians are gender outlaws as well. They can't or won't have men as their primary
sexual/affectional partners. Debates continue as to whether lesbianism is a matter of
choice or biologically determined (born that way). Many choose to center their emotional, spiritual, and mental wellbeing with other lesbians, thus rejecting heteronormativity and male dominance. We now know that some who identify as lesbians do this in
a non-static way: they can, at various life moments, choose sex with men but still maintain
their lesbian identities.

Yet rejecting cultural constructions of gender often finds lesbians confronted with questions and perceptions about their abnormality and falling short of heterosexual ideals. This resonates with Laura Hershey's writing in Chapter 6. Two brief and thought-provoking pieces, "When You Meet a Lesbian" and "Heterosexuality Questionnaire" (1972), both assert the uniqueness of lesbian identities and the need for them to be respected as whole persons, not compared to a "preferable" heterosexual life, or mined for explanations of cause, stereotypes, uninformed decisions, or lack of heterosexual knowledge. Both of these pieces insist that lesbians be respected and not bombarded with heterosexually privileged inquiries, assumptions, and ignorance. Do not, they proclaim, assume she is attracted to you, assert your own heterosexuality as a shield, ask what caused her lesbianism, desire her silence about her life, trivialize her experience, or presume that she wants to be a man.

Approaching lesbians with a heterosexual lens is also inappropriate. The Gay and Lesbian Speakers' Bureau that designed the "Heterosexuality Questionnaire" gives numerous examples of this practice that pathologizes lesbian existence and identity. Searching for causes of lesbianism, fear of seduction by lesbians, accusations of flaunting lesbian sexuality, presumptions about unstable relationships, questioning sexual fulfillment, and presumed molestation are insidious and damaging stereotypical inquiries that are both offensive and uninformed. A few sources are invaluable on lesbian life: Elizabeth Kennedy and Madeline D. Davis' *Boots of Leather, Slippers of Gold* is a groundbreaking work on lesbian communities; Bonnie Zimmerman's (ed.) *The Encyclopedia of Lesbian Histories and Cultures* offers a comprehensive global perspective on these and countless other lesbian issues, Catrióna Rueda Esquibel's *With Her Machete in Her Hand: Reading Chicana Lesbians* is a literary analysis focused on Chicana lesbian experiences, while Craig Loffin's *Letters to ONE* explores life in the United States in the 1950s and 1960s for lesbians and gay men.

What these redefinitions and challenges to patriarchal gender binaries share, according to these authors, as well as those who wrote the Brown Boi Health Manifesto, is a dramatic shift away from a monolithic (one desirable way of being) definition of what is right, normal, or desirable as human gender and sexual expressions. It is a human responsibility to move beyond self-serving definitions and learn and respect these continuums without perpetuating derogatory attitudes, economic privileges, patriarchal power and authority, or homo- and trans*phobic violence-based attitudes.

Discussion Questions

1. How does race complicate one's being LGBTQI (lesbian, gay, bisexual, transgender, queer or questioning, and intersex), gender-nonconforming or gender queer?
2. According to Corinna and Lorde, desire and passion are fundamental parts of women's erotic sexuality. Do you agree? Why or why not?
3. Peiss explains how working-class ethnic women traded sexual favors to enjoy the pleasures of city life. Do women still do this today? If yes, what factors fuel this?
4. Connell argues that globally some men are adopting feminist politics and reconsidering their privilege. Give three examples that support this – and three examples that contradict this.

5. How do transgender, intersex, gender-nonconforming, non-binary, and gender-queer people complicate our previous ideas about what it means to be female and male?

6. Why do the Brown Bois choose to focus on the needs and concerns of biological women of color who may or may not identify as female? What factors in our society make a race-based focus desirable?

7. How does Minahal's poem demonstrate the assertions made in the two readings "When You Meet a Lesbian" and "Heterosexuality Questionnaire"?

8. How can cisgender and heterosexual people work with the lesbian, gay, bisexual, transgender, queer, and intersex communities as allies? What specific steps can they take?

9. Thinking of your readings on lesbian life and experiences, why are these issues so disturbing and threatening to many Americans?

References

Beemyn, Genny, and Sue Rankin. *The Lives of Transgender People*. New York: Columbia University Press, 2011.

Bornstein, Kate, and S. Bear Bergman. *Gender Outlaws: The Next Generation*. Berkeley, CA: Seal Press, 2010.

Del Castillo, Adelaida R., and Gibran Güido, eds. *Queer in Aztlán: Chicano Male Recollections of Consciousness and Coming Out*. San Diego, CA: Cognella, 2014.

Diamond, Lisa M. *Sexual Fluidity: Understanding Women's Love and Desire*. Cambridge, MA: Harvard University Press, 2008.

Esquibel, Catrióna Rueda. *With Her Machete in Her Hand: Reading Chicana Lesbians*. Austin, TX: University of Texas Press, 2006.

Faludi, Susan. *Backlash: The Undeclared War against American Women*. New York: Crown, 1991.

Ghosh, Huma Ahmed. "Lesbians, Sexuality, and Islam." *Journal of Lesbian Studies*, Special Issue: Lesbians, Sexuality and Islam, edited by Huma Ahmed Ghosh. 16.4 (2012): 377–81.

Halberstam, Judith. *Female Masculinity*. Durham: Duke University Press, 1998.

Hemphill, Prentis. "Brown Boi Health Manifesto." *Freeing Ourselves: A Guide to Health and Self Love for Brown Bois*, Brown Boi Project, 2011. 118–19.

Intersex Society of North America. "What's the Difference between Being Transgender or Transsexual and Having an Intersex Condition?" http://www.isna.org/faq/transgender (accessed December 18, 2015).

Kennedy, Elizabeth, and Madeline D. Davis. *Boots of Leather, Slippers of Gold: The History of a Lesbian Community*. New York: Rutledge, 1993.

Loffin, Craig M. *Letters to ONE: Gay and Lesbian Voices from the 1950s and 1960s*. Albany: SUNY Press, 2012.

Newman, David. *Identities and Inequalities: Exploring the Intersections of Race, Class, Gender, and Sexuality*. New York: McGraw Hill, 2011.

Ofreneo, Mira Alexis P. "Tomboys and Lesbians: The Filipino Female Homosexual and Her Identity Development Process." *Philippine Journal of Psychology* 36.1 (2003): 26–52.

Roscoe, Will. 1998. *Changing Ones: Third and Fourth Genders in Native North America*. New York: Palgrave Macmillan, 2000.

Shrage, Laurie, *"You've Changed": Sex Reassignment and Personal Identity*. New York: Oxford University Press, 2009.

Rubin, Gayle S. *Deviations: A Gayle Rubin Reader*. Durham, NC: Duke University Press, 2011.

Tolman, Deborah L. *Dilemmas of Desire: Teenage Girls Talk About Sexuality*. Cambridge, MA: Harvard University Press, 2002.

Vaid, Urvashi. *Irresistible Revolution: Confronting Race, Class and the Assumption of LGBT Politics*. New York: Magnus Books, 2012.

Zimmerman, Bonnie, ed. *The Encyclopedia of Lesbian Histories and Cultures*. New York: Garland, 2000.

5.1

poem on trying to love without fear
Maiana Minahal

dedicated to Shu Hung and Sheila Quinlan, makers of the documentary on queer women of color, "Does Your Mother Know?"

well
i'm not stupid
i'm not blind
just scared
scared to say
i love you
scared you won't
love me
cuz at thirteen
when i told my manong*
i like girls
he turned away
from my face
scared
so then i asked a boy to prom
my mom n pop said
good girls don't
but bad girls do
so which are you
scared so i
shut the door
shut love out
of my house
n never let
never let
anyone in
to love me

* manong – older brother

n maybe they're scared too
cuz love hurts too much
hurts like children
like sisters who leave home
like me
hurts like funerals
old age
hurts like funerals
old age
disease
suicide

n i'm not crazy
i'm not bitter/but
this is not just a poem
it's me
naked on the page
these are not just words

n there are times
when i want to love without fear
i just want to love without fear
don't you?

and i hear people say
what if we really are alone
in this world
what if
none of it/matters
well
let's suppose
they're right
let's suppose
my mom n pop
want the one thing
i can't give
let's suppose
i need to hear
what my brothers
won't say
let's suppose
they're right

let's suppose
that right and wrong
is as black and white
as heaven and hell
or good and evil
n even if it all ends
in nothing

does that change
anything
like your flesh
my blood
our need
for love

n i'm not stupid
i'm not blind
just scared
scared to say
i love you
scared you won't
love me
but
i want to love
without fear
i said
i want to love
without fear
don't
you?

5.2

Uses of the Erotic: The Erotic as Power*

Audre Lorde

There are many kinds of power, used and unused, acknowledged or otherwise. The erotic is a resource within each of us that lies in a deeply female and spiritual plane, firmly rooted in the power of our unexpressed or unrecognized feeling. In order to perpetuate itself, every oppression must corrupt or distort those various sources of power within the culture of the oppressed that can provide energy for change. For women, this has meant a suppression of the erotic as a considered source of power and information within our lives.

We have been taught to suspect this resource, vilified, abused, and devalued within western society. On the one hand, the superficially erotic has been encouraged as a sign of female inferiority; on the other hand, women have been made to suffer and to feel both contemptible and suspect by virtue of its existence.

It is a short step from there to the false belief that only by the suppression of the erotic within our lives and consciousness can women be truly strong. But that strength is illusory, for it is fashioned within the context of male models of power.

* Paper delivered at the Fourth Berkshire Conference on the History of Women, Mount Holyoke College, August 25, 1978. Published as a pamphlet by Out & Out Books (available from The Crossing Press).

As women, we have come to distrust that power which rises from our deepest and nonrational knowledge. We have been warned against it all our lives by the male world, which values this depth of feeling enough to keep women around in order to exercise it in the service of men, but which fears this same depth too much to examine the possibilities of it within themselves. So women are maintained at a distant/inferior position to be psychically milked, much the same way ants maintain colonies of aphids to provide a life-giving substance for their masters.

But the erotic offers a well of replenishing and provocative force to the woman who does not fear its revelation, nor succumb to the belief that sensation is enough.

The erotic has often been misnamed by men and used against women. It has been made into the confused, the trivial, the psychotic, the plasticized sensation. For this reason, we have often turned away from the exploration and consideration of the erotic as a source of power and information, confusing it with its opposite, the pornographic. But pornography is a direct denial of the power of the erotic, for it represents the suppression of true feeling. Pornography emphasizes sensation without feeling.

The erotic is a measure between the beginnings of our sense of self and the chaos of our strongest feelings. It is an internal sense of satisfaction to which, once we have experienced it, we know we can aspire. For having experienced the fullness of this depth of feeling and recognizing its power, in honor and self-respect we can require no less of ourselves.

It is never easy to demand the most from ourselves, from our lives, from our work. To encourage excellence is to go beyond the encouraged mediocrity of our society is to encourage excellence. But giving in to the fear of feeling and working to capacity is a luxury only the unintentional can afford, and the unintentional are those who do not wish to guide their own destinies.

This internal requirement toward excellence which we learn from the erotic must not be misconstrued as demanding the impossible from ourselves nor from others. Such a demand incapacitates everyone in the process. For the erotic is not a question only of what we do; it is a question of how acutely and fully we can feel in the doing. Once we know the extent to which we are capable of feeling that sense of satisfaction and completion, we can then observe which of our various life endeavors bring us closest to that fullness.

The aim of each thing which we do is to make our lives and the lives of our children richer and more possible. Within the celebration of the erotic in all our endeavors, my work becomes a conscious decision – a longed-for bed which I enter gratefully and from which I rise up empowered.

Of course, women so empowered are dangerous. So we are taught to separate the erotic demand from most vital areas of our lives other than sex. And the lack of concern for the erotic root and satisfactions of our work is felt in our disaffection from so much of what we do. For instance, how often do we truly love our work even at its most difficult?

The principal horror of any system which defines the good in terms of profit rather than in terms of human need, or which defines human need to the exclusion of the psychic and emotional components of that need – the principal horror of such a system is that it robs our work of its erotic value, its erotic power and life appeal and fulfillment. Such a system reduces work to a travesty of necessities, a duty by which we earn bread or oblivion for ourselves and those we love. But this is tantamount to blinding a painter and then telling her to improve her work, and to enjoy the act of painting. It is not only next to impossible, it is also profoundly cruel.

As women, we need to examine the ways in which our world can be truly different. I am speaking here of the necessity for reassessing the quality of all the aspects of our lives and of our work, and of how we move toward and through them.

The very word *erotic* comes from the Greek word *eros*, the personification of love in all its aspects – born of Chaos, and personifying creative power and harmony. When I speak of the erotic, then, I speak of it as an assertion of the lifeforce of women; of that creative energy empowered, the knowledge and use of which we are now reclaiming in our language, our history, our dancing, our loving, our work, our lives.

There are frequent attempts to equate pornography and eroticism, two diametrically opposed uses of the sexual. Because of these attempts, it has become fashionable to separate the spiritual (psychic and emotional) from the political, to see them as contradictory or antithetical. "What do you mean, a poetic revolutionary, a meditating gunrunner?" In the same way, we have attempted to separate the spiritual and the erotic, thereby reducing the spiritual to a world of flattened affect, a world of the ascetic who aspires to feel nothing. But nothing is farther from the truth. For the ascetic position is one of the highest fear, the gravest immobility. The severe abstinence of the ascetic becomes the ruling obsession. And it is one not of self-discipline but of self-abnegation.

The dichotomy between the spiritual and the political is also false, resulting from an incomplete attention to our erotic knowledge. For the bridge which connects them is formed by the erotic – the sensual – those physical, emotional, and psychic expressions of what is deepest and strongest and richest within each of us, being shared: the passions of love, in its deepest meanings.

Beyond the superficial, the considered phrase, "It feels right to me," acknowledges the strength of the erotic into a true knowledge, for what that means is the first and most powerful guiding light toward any understanding. And understanding is a handmaiden which can only wait upon, or clarify, that knowledge, deeply born. The erotic is the nurturer or nursemaid of all our deepest knowledge.

The erotic functions for me in several ways, and the first is in providing the power which comes from sharing deeply any pursuit with another person. The sharing of joy, whether physical, emotional, psychic, or intellectual, forms a bridge between the sharers which can be the basis for understanding much of what is not shared between them, and lessens the threat of their difference.

Another important way in which the erotic connection functions is the open and fearless underlining of my capacity for joy. In the way my body stretches to music and opens into response, hearkening to its deepest rhythms, so every level upon which I sense also opens to the erotically satisfying experience, whether it is dancing, building a bookcase, writing a poem, examining an idea.

That self-connection shared is a measure of the joy which I know myself to be capable of feeling, a reminder of my capacity for feeling. And that deep and irreplaceable knowledge of my capacity for joy comes to demand from all of my life that it be lived within the knowledge that such satisfaction is possible, and does not have to be called *marriage*, nor *god*, nor *an afterlife*.

This is one reason why the erotic is so feared, and so often relegated to the bedroom alone, when it is recognized at all. For once we begin to feel deeply all the aspects of our lives, we begin to demand from ourselves and from our life-pursuits that they feel in accordance with that joy which we know ourselves to be capable of. Our erotic knowledge empowers us, becomes a lens through which we scrutinize all aspects of our existence, forcing us to evaluate those aspects honestly in terms of their relative meaning within our lives. And this is a grave responsibility, projected from within each of us, not to settle for the convenient, the shoddy, the conventionally expected, nor the merely safe.

During World War II, we bought sealed plastic packets of white, uncolored margarine, with a tiny, intense pellet of yellow coloring perched like a topaz just inside the clear skin of the bag. We would leave the margarine out for a while to soften, and then we would pinch the little pellet to break it inside the bag, releasing the rich yellowness into the soft pale mass of margarine. Then taking it carefully between our fingers, we would knead it gently back and forth, over and over, until the color had spread throughout the whole pound bag of margarine, thoroughly coloring it.

I find the erotic such a kernel within myself. When released from its intense and constrained pellet, it flows through and colors my life with a kind of energy that heightens and sensitizes and strengthens all my experience.

We have been raised to fear the *yes* within ourselves, our deepest cravings. But, once recognized, those which do not enhance our future lose their power and can be altered. The fear of our desires keeps them suspect and indiscriminately powerful, for to suppress any truth is to give it strength beyond endurance. The fear that we cannot grow beyond whatever distortions we may find within ourselves keeps us docile and loyal and obedient, externally defined, and leads us to accept many facets of our oppression as women.

When we live outside ourselves, and by that I mean on external directives only rather than from our internal knowledge and needs, when we live away from those erotic guides from within ourselves, then our lives are limited by external and alien forms, and we conform to the needs of a structure that is not based on human need, let alone an individual's. But when we begin to live from within outward, in touch with the power of the erotic within ourselves, and allowing that power to inform and illuminate our actions upon the world around us, then we begin to be responsible to ourselves in the deepest sense. For as we begin to recognize our deepest feelings, we begin to give up, of necessity, being satisfied with suffering and self-negation, and with the numbness which so often seems like their only alternative in our society. Our acts against oppression become integral with self, motivated and empowered from within.

In touch with the erotic, I become less willing to accept powerlessness, or those other supplied states of being which are not native to me, such as resignation, despair, self-effacement, depression, self-denial.

And yes, there is a hierarchy. There is a difference between painting a back fence and writing a poem, but only one of quantity. And there is, for me, no difference between writing a good poem and moving into sunlight against the body of a woman I love.

This brings me to the last consideration of the erotic. To share the power of each other's feelings is different from using another's feelings as we would use a kleenex. When we look the other way from our experience, erotic or otherwise, we use rather than share the feelings of those others who participate in the experience with us. And use without consent of the used is abuse.

In order to be utilized, our erotic feelings must be recognized. The need for sharing deep feeling is a human need. But within the european-american tradition, this need is satisfied by certain proscribed erotic comings-together. These occasions are almost always characterized by a simultaneous looking away, a pretense of calling them something else, whether a religion, a fit, mob violence, or even playing doctor. And this misnaming of the need and the deed give rise to that distortion which results in pornography and obscenity – the abuse of feeling.

When we look away from the importance of the erotic in the development and sustenance of our power, or when we look away from ourselves as we satisfy our erotic needs in concert with others, we use each other as objects of satisfaction rather than share our joy in the satisfying, rather than make connection with our similarities and our differences. To refuse to be conscious of what we are feeling at any time, however comfortable that might seem, is to deny a large part of the experience, and to allow ourselves to be reduced to the pornographic, the abused, and the absurd.

The erotic cannot be felt secondhand. As a Black lesbian feminist, I have a particular feeling, knowledge, and understanding for those sisters with whom I have danced hard, played, or even fought. This deep participation has often been the forerunner for joint concerted actions not possible before.

But this erotic charge is not easily shared by women who continue to operate under an exclusively european-american male tradition. I know it was not available to me when I was trying to adapt my consciousness to this mode of living and sensation.

Only now, I find more and more women-identified women brave enough to risk sharing the erotic's electrical charge without having to look away, and without distorting the enormously powerful and creative nature of that exchange. Recognizing the power of the erotic within our lives can give us the energy to pursue genuine change within our world, rather than merely settling for a shift of characters in the same weary drama.

For not only do we touch our most profoundly creative source, but we do that which is female and self-affirming in the face of a racist, patriarchal, and anti-erotic society.

5.3

The Happiest Day of My Life

the happiest
day of my life
was when J discovered
my clitoris

5.4

An Immodest Proposal

Heather Corinna

Right now, just down the street from you, two teenagers are having sex for the first time, and it's exactly as we wish that first experience to be.

Our ingenue loves her boyfriend of over a year, and he's always made her feel good about herself. He's a good guy; he cares about her and demonstrates that care in actions as well as in words. Her parents like him, though they were initially concerned this was too serious a relationship. They felt better as they watched him encourage her to apply for the colleges she had the most interest in, even though some of them would have meant a separation, or some big compromises on his end. They're not thrilled about the two of them having a sexual relationship, but they're realistic in their understanding that young people usually become sexual at some point, and if their daughter is going to be, they feel comforted it will be with a boy who loves her. They haven't ever discussed this directly with her, but they haven't said they were opposed, either.

He's never forced or pressured her into anything. He *has* often made his sexual interest clear as the relationship has developed – he's a normal teenage boy, after all – but has been equally clear that he doesn't want to push her into something he wants but she isn't ready for, and is happy to wait for her when it comes to any given sexual activity. After the first time he kissed her, they had the extended makeout sessions on the couch, the furtive first touches that he initiated but she allowed and often even enjoyed. Even when she was nervous at first, she'd always end up feeling closer to him. Once they'd been together long enough for her to feel more secure, they tried some fingering for her, some hand jobs and blow jobs for him. He usually asked before putting his hands inside her pants or shirt – and she was wary, but agreed – and he usually asked if she'd provide him with oral or manual sex. When he wasn't asking outright, it was because he'd either move his hands inside her pants – looking at her face to be sure she wasn't saying no – or move her hands to his pants, gesturing with his head that oral sex for him would be nice, hoping she knew him well enough to know she didn't have to do it. The times she declined any of this, or looked like it wasn't really okay, he backed off without argument and held her afterward so she knew he wasn't angry.

With any of this, he usually reaches orgasm, and while she doesn't, what he does sometimes feels good. She hasn't said much about that because she figures it's just something you get to over time. Once, he asked if there was something else he could do that she liked. She said no, because it was a question she didn't have the answer to – she didn't know what she liked or might like just yet. He was her first partner, after all.

He's made clear he loves her, and they've been together a long time, so isn't it right to take things to the next level and have real sex? She's not feeling quite there yet – and she's particularly nervous about moving to things where her clothes come off, worried about how he'll perceive her body. Sometimes it happens when they start to go further in the kinds of almost-sex they're having, but she's put the brakes on and he's been cool about it, even though he's felt frustrated. She went with a friend to a clinic to get on the pill, for whenever it does happen; even though they agree they'll also use condoms, she wants to be extra safe. She's also worried about bleeding – enough of her friends have said they did – but is just hoping that it doesn't happen to her or, if it does, that he won't notice.

Soon enough – and before she's really 100 percent about all this – his parents are going out of town. Who knows when that'll happen again; they don't get a lot of opportunities for extended time alone. If now's not the right time, when will be? She says she'll stay over when his parents are gone, which is her way of saying, albeit indirectly, that she'll have sex with him. The evening comes around, and they spend some awkward time at the house – impending sex the big elephant in the room – both unsure of how to initiate or talk about it. After watching a movie and sharing a pizza, they eventually head to his bedroom, where they engage in a few other sexual activities before going ahead with intercourse. It's fairly brief – he gets off, she doesn't, but that's normal enough the first time, which is probably why he doesn't ask her if she did and why she doesn't say anything about it – and it hurt a little, but it wasn't terribly painful like she was expecting. She feels like she was just lying there, and wasn't sure what she was supposed to do, but he doesn't seem to think it was a problem. Afterward, they do feel closer, and she's really glad she did It with him. They talk, both agree that it was special and that they're feeling good about it, and drift into sleep. Tomorrow morning, before she goes home, he'll make clear that his feelings for her have grown, and that she gave him a gift that he values greatly and doesn't take for granted. When he drops her off, they'll say, "I love you" and mean it, and she'll feel lucky and loved.

Sound familiar? It's a pretty common ideal for sexual initiation. It isn't all fairytale, either: In the last decade I've worked with teens and sexuality, I've heard many versions of this scenario, from young women reporting what they feel and wish for, and what adults and peers tell them is a remarkably positive first time.

On the surface, it looks pretty good. The guy is a good guy. The girl wasn't forced into anything she was opposed to or strongly did not want. They moved forward only when she gave consent, and her consent was always sought out in some way. They were safe and smart with regard to pregnancy and infections, and while it was not exactly blissful for her, it wasn't terribly painful, either. He didn't change his behavior toward her afterward; in fact, it made them feel closer, and they're both glad they chose each other. It'll be a good memory for them, whether they're together ten years from now or not. All in all, it fits most ideals of what a positive first sexual experience should be.

But something monumental is missing from this picture.

If it takes you a minute to find what it is, don't feel bad. After all, the missing piece isn't just missing from *this* picture; it's missing from nearly every common idea and ideal about sex and women. It's been missing for so long, plenty of us don't even see the giant void that sits smack in the middle of these pretty first-time fantasies.

The black hole in that scenario is her *desire*.

Nowhere do we see a strong, undeniable sexual desire, deep, dizzy sexual pleasure, or earnest, equal sexual satisfaction on her part. It makes no appearance in a sexual script many would posit as an ideal initiation. We heard her say yes, but we never once saw her beg the question herself. We saw her yes as the answer to someone else's desire, rather than as an affirmation of her own. Her yes is uncertain, but sexual desire – whether or not we choose to act on it – is certain, unmistakable, and persistent.

If I'd told you that same story and swapped the roles, you might have felt like you were reading speculative fiction. If *she* were feeling sexually frustrated – if we thought it a given that she feels strong urges for sex (she's a normal teenage girl, after all) – if things weren't moving fast enough for *her*, if *he* were the reluctant or slow-moving partner, if *she* were the one initiating, *she* were getting off, *he* were the one who felt okay about it because at least it didn't hurt ... what planet does *that* happen on? We, as a culture, still tend to consider even a woman's yes to a man's sexual invitation revolutionary. That's unsurprising, of course. This is a world where women still frequently are not asked for consent, are often raped or coerced, still engage in sex with partners out of feelings of duty or obligation, usually have our sexuality depicted in grossly inaccurate ways by men and other women alike, and independent female sexual desire and earnest sexual enjoyment are not only disbelieved, in some circles, but are even "scientifically" contested. And for many women, just finding a partner – the first time at bat, no less – who fully seeks and supports her consent, and accepts any nonconsent, is indeed monumental. We, validly, consider such women lucky.

But consent – our mere yes – is ground zero. While there are a lot of positives in a script like this one, and basics that many women, young and old, still do not have or cannot count on, many of those positives are but a Band-Aid on a wound, a best-case scenario in substandard conditions, making the most we can out of an incomplete set of materials. They're a paint-by-numbers version of Van Gogh's *Starry Night*, in which they forgot to include a pot of yellow paint.

The patriarchal roots of all this are a pit stop, not a conclusion. In case they're not as obvious as the nose on your face, or you feel the need for a quick review, here are the CliffsNotes. We've got more than a few millennia in which women's sexuality has usually been considered but an adjunct of male sexuality. We've got our whole documented, celebrated human history of men as a ruling class taking command of their own sexuality and women's sexuality alike (even when that sexuality has nothing to do with them); we've got women often having no voice when it comes to what men do to their bodies and call sex – or, when they're allowed that voice, they're allowed it only within the limited window of male desire. We've got road-weary miles of history that considers women's sexuality linked solely to reproduction and marriage, while men are allowed and encouraged to have a sexuality that exists separately from their reproductive processes and spousal arrangements. We have the endlessly tiresome arguments based in Darwinian theory or biochemistry trying to show us that this absence of women's pleasure in the equation of sex has nothing to do with social conditioning or gender status, but with the "fact" that women do not actually experience real, physical desire.

We've long idealized or enabled the romance-novel script of ravishment: reluctant women and passive girls seduced by strong partners. While we're slowly coming around to the notion that violent force is not romantic, and that rape is not sex but assault, "gentle persuasion" is still swoon-worthy stuff. The young woman who is provided with a sexual awakening by a paternal male partner remains an ideal, common fantasy *or* a profound sense of anxiety if those roles can't be performed adequately for or by women and men alike.

The chastity belts of yesteryear are on display in our museums; those of the current day live on the mutilated genitals of poor African women and rich American women alike; in sex education curricula and the tiresome continuance of good girl/bad girl binaries; in households where a male partner has a hard drive full of porn everyone knows is there (and in his head during sex), while his female other makes sure her vibrator is well hidden and resists asking her partner to use it during sex together, for fear of making him feel insecure.

And all of this and more has gone on for so long and been so widespread that what should be the simple given of our yes often seems an unattainable ideal.

That is the work of ages to try to undo or revise. It's a monumental tangle, so it's going to take monumental work and time to untangle. But I don't want to find us trapped by it, especially when getting to the good stuff is about more than just rectifying and repairing an ugly, tired history.

What if her foundation looked like this: Her family recognized that serious or casual, long-term or short, all wanted sexual relationships have value, and that whatever risks of negatives we take with sex are offset by the possibility of great positives? Academic contests, college applications, and sports tryouts aren't seen as things to avoid simply because they may have unsatisfactory outcomes: We recognize that risking hurt or disappointment for something that may be beneficial is often worthwhile. What if her family felt the same way about their daughter's experiences with sex? What if rather than nurturing an environment of sexual passivity or silence, her parents provided her with a safe space for sex, active help and encouragement with birth control and sexual health, and direct discussion about sexuality, including her own sexual desires – not just her desires for emotional closeness or security, but masturbation, anatomy, and body image, and the ways in which sex is often unrealistically presented by peers and media? What if her parents spoke to her about their own early sexual experiences realistically, both their joys and their bummers, and what they've figured out about sex since then?

5.5

"Charity Girls" and City Pleasures: Historical Notes on Working-Class Sexuality, 1880–1920

Kathy Peiss

Here Kathy Peiss describes an urban subculture of young women who orchestrated their premarital social lives in the street, dance hall, theater, and at work, places that did not exist for their rural or immigrant mothers, or that would have been out of bounds for them. Since Peiss's sources only record one moment in the life cycles of these "charity girls," we cannot know how enduring were their exuberance and adventurous social experimentation. How successfully did they avoid pregnancy? How soon did they marry and how drastically did marriage alter their social independence? We do know that because they earned money and lived in a large city, these working-class women had an unprecedented freedom to enter the marketplace of pleasures, where they bargained for still more with the coin of female sexual allure. The meaning of premarital sex, the social manner of sex and its language, the pool of potential partners – all these the factory girls helped transform in one generation. One result was an enlarged area of opportunity for women to choose, to play; another was the creation of new arenas for their sexual harassment.

Uncovering the history of working-class sexuality has been a particularly intractable task for recent scholars. Diaries, letters, and memoirs, while a rich source for studies of bourgeois sexuality, offer few glimpses into working-class intimate life. We have had to turn to middle-class commentary and observations of working people, but these accounts often seem hopelessly moralistic and biased. The difficulty with such sources is not simply a question of tone or selectivity, but involves the very categories of analysis they employ. Reformers, social workers, and journalists viewed working-class women's sexuality through middle-class lenses, invoking sexual standards that set "respectability" against "promiscuity." When applied to unmarried women, these categories were constructed foremost around the biological fact of premarital virginity, and secondarily by such cultural indicators as manners, language, dress, and public interaction. Chastity was the measure of young women's respectability, and those who engaged in premarital intercourse, or, more importantly, dressed and acted as though they had, were classed as promiscuous women or prostitutes. Thus labor investigations of the late nineteenth century not only surveyed women's wages and working conditions, but delved into the issue of their sexual virtue, hoping to resolve scientifically the question of working women's respectability.[1]

Nevertheless, some middle-class observers in city missions and settlements recognized that their standards did not always reflect those of working-class youth. As one University Settlement worker argued, "Many of the liberties which are taken by tenement boys and girls with one another, and which seem quite improper to the 'up-towner,' are, in fact, practically harmless."[2] Working women's public behavior often seemed to fall between the traditional middle-class poles: they were not truly promiscuous in their actions, but neither were they models of decorum. A boarding-house matron, for example, puzzled over the behavior of Mary, a "good girl": "The other night she flirted with a man across the street," she explained. "It is true she dropped him when he offered to take her into a saloon. But she does go to picture shows and dance halls with 'pick up' men and boys."[3] Similarly, a city missionary noted that tenement dwellers followed different rules of etiquette, with the observation: "Young women sometimes allow young men to address them and caress them in a manner which would offend well-bred people, and yet those girls would indignantly resent any liberties which they consider dishonoring."[4] These examples suggest that we must reach beyond the dichotomized analysis of many middle-class observers and draw out the cultural categories created and acted on by working women themselves. How was sexuality "handled" culturally? What manners, etiquette, and sexual style met with general approval? What constituted sexual respectability? Does the polarized framework of the middle class reflect the realities of working-class culture?

Embedded within the reports and surveys lie small pieces of information that illuminate the social and cultural construction of sexuality among a number of working-class women. My discussion focuses on one set of young, white working women in New York City in the years 1880 to 1920. Most of these women were single wage earners who toiled in the city's factories, shops, and department stores, while devoting their evenings to the lively entertainment of the streets, public dance halls, and other popular amusements. Born or educated in the United States, many adopted a cultural style meant to distance themselves from their immigrant roots and familial traditions. Such women dressed in the latest finery, negotiated city life with ease, and sought intrigue and adventure with male companions. For this group of working women, sexuality became a central dimension of their emergent culture, a dimension that is revealed in their daily life of work and leisure.[5]

These New York working women frequented amusements in which familiarity and intermingling among strangers, not decorum, defined normal public behavior between the sexes. At movies and cheap theaters, crowds mingled during intermissions, shared picnic lunches, and commented volubly on performances. Strangers at Coney Island's amusement parks often involved each other in practical jokes and humorous escapades, while dance halls permitted close interaction between unfamiliar men and women. At one respectable Turnverein ball, for example, a vice investigator described closely the chaotic activity in the barroom between dances:

> Most of the younger couples were hugging and kissing, there was a general mingling of men and women at the different tables, almost everyone seemed to know one another and spoke to each other across the tables and joined couples at different tables, they were all singing and carrying on, they kept running around the room and acted like a mob of lunatics let lo[o]se.[6]

As this observer suggests, an important aspect of social familiarity was the ease of sexual expression in language and behavior. Dances were advertised, for example, through the distribution of "pluggers," small printed cards announcing the particulars of the ball, along with snatches of popular songs or verse; the lyrics and pictures, noted one offended reformer, were often "so suggestive that they are absolutely indecent."[7]

The heightened sexual awareness permeating many popular amusements may also be seen in working-class dancing styles. While waltzes and two-steps were common, working women's repertoire included "pivoting" and "tough dances." While pivoting was a wild, spinning dance that promoted a charged atmosphere of physical excitement, tough dances ranged from a slow shimmy, or shaking of the hips and shoulders, to boisterous animal imitations. Such tough dances as the grizzly bear, Charlie Chaplin wiggle, and the dip emphasized bodily contact and the suggestion of sexual intercourse. As one dance investigator commented, "What particularly distinguishes this dance is the motion of the pelvic portions of the body."[8] In contrast, middle-class pleasure-goers accepted the animal dances only after the blatant sexuality had been tamed into refined movement. While cabaret owners enforced strict rules to discourage contact between strangers, managers of working-class dance halls usually winked at spieling, tough dancing, and unrestrained behavior.[9]

Other forms of recreation frequented by working-class youth incorporated a free and easy sexuality into their attractions. Many social clubs and amusement societies permitted flirting, touching, and kissing games at their meetings. One East Side youth reported that "they have kissing all through pleasure time, and use slang language, while in some they don't behave nice between [sic] young ladies."[10] Music halls and cheap vaudeville regularly worked sexual themes and suggestive humor into comedy routines and songs. At a Yiddish music hall popular with both men and women, one reformer found that "the songs are suggestive of everything but what is proper, the choruses are full of double meanings, and the jokes have broad and unmistakable hints of things indecent."[11] Similarly, Coney Island's Steeplechase amusement park, favored by working-class excursionists, carefully marketed sexual titillation and romance in attractions that threw patrons into each other, sent skirts flying, and evoked instant intimacy among strangers.[12]

In attending dance halls, social club entertainments, and amusement resorts, young women took part in a cultural milieu that expressed and affirmed heterosocial interactions. As reformer Belle Israels observed, "No amusement is complete in which 'he' is not a factor."[13] A common custom involved "picking up" unknown men or women in amusement resorts or on the streets, an accepted means of gaining companionship for an evening's entertainment. Indeed, some amusement societies existed for this very purpose. One vice investigator, in his search for "loose" women, was advised by a waiter to "go first on a Sunday night to 'Hans'l & Gret'l Amusement Society' at the Lyceum 86th Str & III Ave, there the girls come and men pick them up."[14] The waiter carefully stressed that these were respectable working women, not prostitutes. Nor was the pickup purely a male prerogative. "With the men they 'pick up,'" writer Hutchins Hapgood observed of East Side shop girls, "they will go to the theater, to late suppers, will be as jolly as they like."[15]

The heterosocial orientation of these amusements made popularity a goal to be pursued through dancing ability, willingness to drink, and eye-catching finery. Women who would not drink at balls and social entertainments were often ostracized by men, while cocktails and ingenious mixtures replaced the five-cent beer and helped to make drinking an acceptable female activity. Many women used clothing as a means of drawing attention to themselves, wearing high-heeled shoes, fancy dresses, costume jewelry, elaborate pompadours, and cosmetics. As one working woman sharply explained, "If you want to get any notion took of you, you gotta have some style about you."[16] The clothing that such women wore no longer served as an emblem of respectability. "The way women dress today they all look like prostitutes," reported one rueful waiter to a dance hall investigator, "and the waiter can some times get in bad by going over and trying to put some one next to them, they may be respectable women and would jump on the waiter."[17]

Underlying the relaxed sexual style and heterosocial interaction was the custom of "treating." Men often treated their female companions to drinks and refreshments, theater tickets, and other incidentals. Women might pay a dance hall's entrance fee or carfare out to an amusement park, but they relied on men's treats to see them through the evening's entertainment. Such treats were highly prized by young working women; as Belle Israels remarked, the announcement that "he treated" was "the acme of achievement in retailing experiences with the other sex."[18]

   Treating was not a one-way proposition, however, but entailed an exchange relationship. Financially unable to reciprocate in kind, women offered sexual favors of varying degrees, ranging from flirtatious companionship to sexual intercourse, in exchange for men's treats. "Pleasures don't cost girls so much as they do young men," asserted one saleswoman. "If they are agreeable they are invited out a good deal, and they are not allowed to pay anything." Reformer Lillian Betts concurred, observing that the working woman held herself responsible for failing to wangle men's invitations and believed that "it is not only her misfortune, but her fault; she should be more attractive."[19] Gaining men's treats placed a high premium on allure and personality, and sometimes involved aggressive and frank "overtures to men whom they desire to attract," often with implicit sexual proposals. One investigator, commenting on women's dependency on men in their leisure time, aptly observed that "those who are unattractive, and those who have puritanic notions, fare but ill in the matter of enjoyments. On the other hand those who do become popular have to compromise with the best conventional usage."[20]

Many of the sexual patterns acceptable in the world of leisure activity were mirrored in the workplace. Sexual harassment by employers, foremen, and fellow workers was a widespread practice in this period, and its form often paralleled the relationship of treating, particularly in service and sales jobs. Department store managers, for example, advised employees to round out their meager salaries by finding a "gentleman friend" to purchase clothing and pleasures. An angry saleswoman testified, for example, that "one of the employers has told me, on a $6.50 wage, he don't care where I get my clothes from as long as I have them, to be dressed to suit him."[21] Waitresses knew that accepting the advances of male customers often brought good tips, and some used their opportunities to enter an active social life with men. "Most of the girls quite frankly admit making 'dates' with strange men," one investigator found. "These 'dates' are made with no thought on the part of the girl beyond getting the good time which she cannot afford herself."[22]

   In factories where men and women worked together, the sexual style that we have seen on the dance floor was often reproduced on the shop floor. Many factories lacked privacy in dressing facilities, and workers tolerated a degree of familiarity and roughhousing between men and women. One cigar maker observed that his workplace socialized the young into sexual behavior unrestrained by parental and community control. Another decried the tendency of young boys "of thirteen or fourteen casting an eye upon a 'mash.'" Even worse, he testified, were the

   many men who are respected – when I say respected and respectable, I mean who walk
   the streets and are respected as working men, and who would not under any
   circumstances offer the slightest insult or disrespectful remark or glance to a female in
   the streets, but who, in the shops, will whoop and give expressions to "cat calls" and a
   peculiar noise made with their lips, which is supposed to be an endearing salutation.[23]

In sexually segregated workplaces, sexual knowledge was probably transmitted among working women. A YWCA report in 1913 luridly asserted that "no girl is more 'knowing' than the wage-earner, for the 'older hands' initiate her early through the unwholesome story or innuendo."[24] Evidence from factories, department stores, laundries, and restaurants substantiates the sexual consciousness of female workers. Women brought to the workplace tales of their evening adventures and gossip about dates and eligible men, recounting to their co-workers the triumphs of the latest ball or outing. Women's socialization into a new shop might involve a ritualist exchange about "gentlemen friends." In one laundry, for example, an investigator repeatedly heard this conversation:

"Say, you got a feller?"
"Sure. Ain t you got one?"
"Sure."[25]

Through the use of slang and "vulgar" language, heterosexual romance was expressed in a sexually explicit context. Among waitresses, for example, frank discussion of lovers and husbands during breaks was an integral part of the work day. One investigator found that "there was never any open violation of the proprieties but always the suggestive talk and behavior." Laundries, too, witnessed "a great deal of swearing among the women." A 1914 study of department store clerks found a similar style and content in everyday conversation:

> While it is true that the general attitude toward men and sex relations was normal, all the investigators admitted a freedom of speech frequently verging upon the vulgar, but since there was very little evidence of any actual immorality, this can probably be likened to the same spirit which prompts the telling of risqué stories in other circles.[26]

In their workplaces and leisure activities, many working women discovered a milieu that tolerated, and at times encouraged, physical and verbal familiarity between men and women, and stressed the exchange of sexual favors for social and economic advantages. Such women probably received conflicting messages about the virtues of virginity, and necessarily mediated the parental, religious, and educational injunctions concerning chastity, and the "lessons" of urban life and labor. The choice made by some women to engage in a relaxed sexual style needs to be understood in terms of the larger relations of class and gender that structured their sexual culture.

Most single working-class women were wage-earners for a few years before marriage, contributing to the household income or supporting themselves. Sexual segmentation of the labor market placed women in semi-skilled, seasonal employment with high rates of turnover. Few women earned a "living wage," estimated to be $9.00 or $10.00 a week in 1910, and the wage differential between men and women was vast. Those who lived alone in furnished rooms or boarding houses consumed their earnings in rent, meals, and clothing. Many self-supporting women were forced to sacrifice an essential item in their weekly budgets, particularly food, in order to pay for amusements. Under such circumstances, treating became a viable option. "If my boy friend didn't take me out," asked one working woman, "how could I ever go out?"[27] While many women accepted treats from "steadies," others had no qualms about receiving them from acquaintances or men they picked up at amusement places. As one investigator concluded, "The acceptance on the part of the girl of almost any invitation needs little explanation when one realizes that she often goes pleasureless unless she does accept 'free treats.'"[28] Financial resources were little better for the vast majority of women living with families and relatives. Most of them contributed all of their earnings to the family, receiving only small amounts of spending money, usually 25¢ to 50¢ a week, in return. This sum covered the costs of simple entertainments, but could not purchase higher priced amusements.[29]

Moreover, the social and physical space of the tenement home and boarding house contributed to freer social and sexual practices. Working women living alone ran the gauntlet between landladies' suspicious stares and the knowing glances of male boarders. One furnished-room dweller attested to the pressure placed on young, single women: "Time and again when a male lodger meets a girl on the landing, his salutation usually ends with something like this: 'Won't you step into my place and have a glass of beer with me?'"[30]

The tenement home, too, presented a problem to parents who wished to maintain control over their daughters' sexuality. Typical tenement apartments offered limited opportunities for family activities or chaperoned socializing. Courtship proved difficult in homes where families and boarders crowded into a few small rooms, and the "parlor" served as kitchen, dining room, and bedroom. Instead, many working-class daughters socialized on streetcorners, rendezvoused in cafes, and courted on trolley cars. As one settlement worker observed, "Boys and girls and young men and women of respectable families are almost obliged to carry on many of their friendships, and perhaps their lovemaking, on tenement stoops or on street corners."[31] Another reformer found that girls whose parents forebade men's visits to the home managed to escape into the streets and dance halls to meet them. Such young women demanded greater independence in the realm of "personal life" in exchange for their financial contribution to the family. For some, this new freedom spilled over into their sexual practices.[32]

The extent of the sexual culture described here is particularly difficult to establish, since the evidence is too meager to permit conclusions about specific groups of working women, their beliefs about sexuality, and their behavior. Scattered evidence does suggest a range of possible responses, the parameters within which most women would choose to act and define their behavior as socially acceptable. Within this range, there existed a subculture of working women who fully bought into the system of treating and sexual exchange, by trading sexual favors of varying degrees for gifts, treats, and a good time. These women were known in underworld slang as "charity girls," a term that differentiated them from prostitutes because they did not accept money in their sexual encounters with men. As vice reformer George Kneeland found, they "offer themselves to strangers, not for money, but for presents, attention, and pleasure, and most important, a yielding to sex desire."[33] Only a thin line divided these women and "occasional prostitutes," women who slipped in and out of prostitution when unemployed or in need of extra income. Such behavior did not result in the stigma of the "fallen woman." Many working women apparently acted like Dottie: "When she needed a pair of shoes she had found it easy to 'earn' them in the way that other girls did." Dottie, the investigator reported, was now known as a respectable married woman.[34]

Such women were frequent patrons of the city's dance halls. Vice investigators note a preponderant number of women at dances who clearly were not prostitutes, but were "game" and "lively"; these charity girls often comprised half or more of the dancers in a hall. One dance hall investigator distinguished them with the observation, "Some of the women ... are out for the coin, but there is a lot that come in here that are charity."[35] One waiter at La Kuenstler Klause, a restaurant with music and dancing, noted that "girls could be gotten here, but they don't go with men for money, only for good time." The investigator continued in his report, "Most of the girls are working girls, not prostitutes, they smoke cigarettes, drink liquers and dance dis.[orderly] dances, stay out late and stay with any man, that pick them up first."[36] Meeting two women at a bar, another investigator remarked, "They are both supposed to be working girls but go out for a good time and go the limit."[37]

Some women obviously relished the game of extracting treats from men. One vice investigator offered to take a Kitty Graham, who apparently worked both as a department store clerk and occasional prostitute, to the Central Opera House at 3 A.M.; he noted that "she was willing to go if I'd take a taxi; I finally coaxed her to come with me in a street car."[38] Similarly, Frances Donovan observed waitresses "talking about their engagements which they had for the evening or for the night and quite frankly saying what they expected to get from this or that fellow in the line of money, amusement, or clothes."[39] Working women's manipulation of treating is also suggested by this unguarded conversation overheard by a journalist at Coney Island:

> "What sort of a time did you have?"
> "Great. He blew in $5 on the blow-out."
> "You beat me again. My chump only spent $2.50."[40]

These women had clearly accepted the full implications of the system of treating and the sexual culture surrounding it.

While this evidence points to the existence of charity girls – working women defined as respectable, but who engaged in sexual activity – it tells us little about their numbers, social background, working lives, or relationships to family and community. The vice reports indicate that they were generally young women, many of whom lived at home with their families. One man in a dance hall remarked, for example, that "he sometimes takes them to the hotels, but sometimes the girls won't go to [a] hotel to stay for the night, they are afraid of their mothers, so he gets away with it in the hallway."[41] While community sanctions may have prevented such activity within the neighborhood, the growth of large public dance halls, cabarets, and metropolitan amusement resorts provided an anonymous space in which the subculture of treating could flourish.

Notes

1. See, for example, Carroll D. Wright, *The Working Girls of Boston* (1889; New York: Arno Press, 1969).
2. "'Influences in Street Life," University Settlement Society *Report* (1900), p. 30.
3. Marie S. Orenstein, "How the Working Girl of New York Lives," New York State, Factory Investigating Commission, *Fourth Report Transmitted to Legislature*, February 15, 1915, Senate Doc. 43, val. 4, app. 2 (Albany: J. B. Lyon Co., 1915), p. 1697.
4. William T. Elsing, "Life in New York Tenement-Houses as Seen by a City Missionary," *Scribner's* 11 (June 1892): 716.
5. For a more detailed discussion of these women, and further documentation of their social relations and leisure activities, see my dissertation, "Cheap Amusements: Gender Relations and the Use of Leisure Time in New York City, 1880 to 1920," Ph.D. diss., Brown University, 1982.
6. Investigator's Report, Remey's, 917 Eighth Ave., February 11, 1917, Committee of Fourteen Papers, New York Public Library Manuscript Division, New York.
7. George Kneeland, *Commercialized Prostitution in New York City* (New York: The Century Co., 1913), p. 68; Louise de Koven Bowen, "Dance Halls," *Survey* 26 (3 July 1911): 384.
8. Committee on Amusements and Vacation Resources of Working Girls, two-page circular, in Box 28, "Parks and Playgrounds Correspondence," Lillian Wald Collection, Rare Book and Manuscripts Library, Columbia University, New York.
9. See, for example, Investigator's Report, Princess Cafe, 1206 Broadway, January 1, 1917; and Excelsior Cafe, 306 Eighth Ave., December 21, 1916, Committee of Fourteen Papers. For an excellent discussion of middle- and upper-class leisure activities, see Lewis A. Erenberg, *Steppin' Out: New York Nightlife and the Transformation of American Culture, 1890–1930* (Westport, Conn.: Greenwood Press, 1981).
10. "Social Life in the Streets," University Settlement Society *Report* (1899), p. 32.
11. Paul Klapper, "The Yiddish Music Hall," *University Settlement Studies* 2, no. 4 (1905): 22.
12. For a description of Coney Island amusements, see Edo McCullough, *Good Old Coney Island; A Sentimental Journey into the Past* (New York: Charles Scribner's Sons, 1957), pp. 309–13; and Oliver Pilot and Jo Ransom, *Sodom by the Sea: An Affectionate History of Coney Island* (Garden City, N.J.: Doubleday, 1941).
13. Belle Lindner Israels, "The Way of the Girl," *Survey* 22 (3 July 1909): 486.
14. Investigator's Report, La Kuenstler Klause, 1490 Third Ave., January 19, 1917, Committee of Fourteen Papers.
15. Hutchins Hapgood, *Types from City Streets* (New York: Funk and Wagnalls, 1910), p. 131.
16. Clara Laughlin, *The Work-A-Day Girl. A Study of Some Present Conditions* (1913; New York: Arno Press, 1974), pp. 47, 145. On working women's clothing, see Helen Campbell, *Prisoners of Poverty: Women Wage-Earners, Their Trades and Their Lives* (1887; Westport, Conn.: Greenwood Press, 1970), p. 175; "What It Means to Be a Department Store Girl as Told by the Girl Herself," *Ladies Home Journal* 30 (June 1913): 8; "A Salesgirl's Story," *Independent* 54 (July 1902): 1821. Drinking is discussed in Kneeland, *Commercialized Prostitution*, p. 70; and Belle Israels, "Diverting a Pastime," *Leslie's Weekly* 113 (27 July 1911): 100.
17. Investigator's Report, Weimann's, 1422 St. Nicholas Ave., February 11, 1917, Committee of Fourteen Papers.
18. Israels, "Way of the Girl," p. 489; Ruth True, *The Neglected Girl* (New York: Russell Sage Foundation, 1914), p. 59.

19. "A Salesgirl's Story," p. 1821; Lillian Betts, *Leaven in a Great City* (New York: Dodd, Mead, 1902), pp. 251–52.

20. New York State, Factory Investigating Commission, *Fourth Report*, vol. 4, pp. 1585–86; Robert Woods and Albert Kennedy, *Young Working-Girls: A Summary of Evidence from Two Thousand Social Workers* (Boston: Houghton Mifflin, 1913), p. 105.

21. New York State, Factory Investigating Commission, *Fourth Report*, vol. 5, p. 2809; see also Sue Ainslie Clark and Edith Wyatt, *Making Both Ends Meet: The Income and Outlay of New York Working Girls* (New York: Macmillan, 1911), p. 28. For an excellent analysis of sexual harassment, see Mary Bularzik, *Sexual Harassment at the Workplace: Historical Notes* (Somerville, Mass.: New England Free Press, 1978).

22. Consumers' League of New York, *Behind the Scenes in a Restaurant: A Study of 1017 Women Restaurant Employees* (n.p., n.p., 1916), p. 24; Frances Donovan, *The Woman Who Waits* (1920; New York: Arno Press, 1974), p. 42.

23. New York Bureau of Labor Statistics, *Second Annual Report* (1884), pp. 153, 158; *Third Annual Report* (1885), pp. 150–51.

24. Report of Commission on Social Morality from the Christian Standpoint, Made to the 4th Biennial Convention of the Young Women's Christian Associations of the U.S. A., 1913, Records File Collection, Archives of the National Board of the YWCA of the United States of America, New York, N.Y.

25. Clark and Wyatt, *Making Both Ends Meet*, pp. 187–88; see also Dorothy Richardson, *The Long Day, in Women at Work*, ed. William L. O'Neill (New York: Quadrangle, 1972); Amy E. Tanner, "Glimpses at the Mind of a Waitress," *American Journal of Sociology* 13 (July 1907): 52.

26. Committee of Fourteen in New York City, *Annual Report for 1914*, p. 40; Clark and Wyatt, *Making Both Ends Meet*, p. 188; Donovan, *The Woman Who Waits*, pp. 26, 80–81.

27. Esther Packard, "Living on Six Dollars a Week," New York State, Factory Investigating Commission, *Fourth Report*, vol. 4, pp. 1677–78. For a discussion of women's wages in New York, see ibid., vol. 1, p. 35; and vol. 4, pp. 1081, 1509. For an overview of working conditions, see Barbara Wertheimer, *We Were There: The Story of Working Women in America* (New York: Pantheon Books, 1977), pp. 209–48.

28. Packard, "Living on Six Dollars a Week," p. 1685.

29. New York State, Factory Investigating Commission, *Fourth Report*, vol. 4, pp. 1512–13, 1581–83; True, *Neglected Girl*, p. 59.

30. Marie Orenstein, "How the Working Girl of New York Lives," p. 1702. See also Esther Packard, *A Study of Living Conditions of Self-Supporting Women in New York City* (New York: Metropolitan Board of the YWCA, 1915).

31. "Influences in Street Life," p. 30; see also Samuel Chotzinoff, *A Lost Paradise* (New York: Knopf, 1955), p. 81.

32. On the rejection of parental controls by young women, see Leslie Woodcock Tentler, *Wage-Earning Women: Industrial Work and Family Life in the United States, 1900–1930* (New York: Oxford University Press, 1979), pp. 110–13. For contemporary accounts, see True, *Neglected Girl*, pp. 54–55, 62–63, 162–63; Lillian Betts, "Tenement House Life and Recreation," *Outlook* (11 February 1899): 365.

33. "Memoranda on Vice Problem: IV. Statement of George J. Kneeland," New York State, Factory Investigating Commission, *Fourth Report*, v.1, p. 403. See also Committee of Fourteen, *Annual Report* (1917), p. 15, and *Annual Report* (1918), p. 32; Woods and Kennedy, *Young Working-Girls*, p. 85.

34. Donovan, *The Woman Who Waits*, p. 71; on occasional prostitution, see U.S. Senate, *Report on the Condition of Women and Child Wage-Earners in the United States*, U.S. Sen. Doc. 645, 61st Cong., 2nd Sess. (Washington, D.C.: GPO), vol. 15, p. 83; Laughlin, *The Work-A-Day Girl*, pp. 51–52.

35. Investigator's Report, 2150 Eighth Ave., January 12, 1917, Committee of Fourteen Papers.

36. Investigator's Report, La Kuenstler Klause, 1490 Third Ave., January 19, 1917, Committee of Fourteen Papers.

37. Investigator's Report, Bobby More's, 252 W. 31 Street, February 3, 1917, Committee of Fourteen Papers.

38. Investigator's Report, Remey's, 917 Eighth Ave., December 23, 1916, Committee of Fourteen Papers.

39. Donovan, *The Woman Who Waits*, p. 55.

40. Edwin Slosson, 'The Amusement Business,' *Independent* 57 (21 July 1904): 139.

41. Investigator's Report, Clare Hotel and Palm Gardens/McNamara's, 2150 Eighth Ave., January 12, 1917, Committee of Fourteen Papers.

5.6

When You Meet a Lesbian: Hints for the Heterosexual Woman

Indiana University Empowerment Workshop

- Do not run screaming from the room … this is rude.
- If you must back away, do so slowly and with discretion.
- Do not assume she is attracted to you.
- Do not assume she is not attracted to you.
- Do not assume you are not attracted to her.
- Do not expect her to be as excited about meeting a heterosexual as you may be about meeting a lesbian … she was probably raised by them.
- Do not immediately start talking about your boyfriend or husband in order to make it clear that you are straight … she probably already knows.
- Do not tell her that it is sexist to prefer women, that people are people, that she should be able to love everybody. Do not tell her that men are as oppressed by sexism as women and women should help men fight their oppression. These are common fallacies and should be treated as such.
- Do not invite her someplace where there will be men unless you tell her in advance. She may not want to be with them.
- Do not ask her how she got that way … Instead, ask yourself how you got that way.
- Do not assume that she is dying to talk about being a lesbian.
- Do not expect her to refrain from talking about being a lesbian.
- Do not trivialize her experience by assuming it is a bedroom issue only. She is a lesbian 24 hours a day.

- Do not assume that because she is a lesbian that she wants to be treated like a man.
- Do not assume that her heart will leap with joy if you touch her arm (condescendingly? flirtatiously? power-testingly?). It makes her angry.
- If you are tempted to tell her that she is sick and is taking the easy way out … Think about that … Think about that *real* hard.

5.7

Heterosexuality Questionnaire
Gay and Lesbian Speakers' Bureau

The following list of questions has been circulating among the gay and lesbian communities for some time. We gratefully acknowledge the anonymous person(s) who created it and present it here as an example of inverting the question.

1. What do you think caused your heterosexuality?
2. When and how did you first decide that you were a heterosexual?
3. Is it possible your heterosexuality is just a phase you might grow out of?
4. Is it possible your heterosexuality stems from a neurotic fear of others of the same sex?
5. If you've never slept with a person of the same sex and enjoyed it, is it possible that all you need is a good gay lover?
6. To whom have you disclosed your heterosexual tendencies? How did they react?
7. Why do you heterosexuals feel compelled to seduce others into your lifestyle?
8. Why do you insist on flaunting your heterosexuality? Can't you just be what you are and keep it quiet?
9. Would you want your children to be heterosexual, knowing the problems they'd face?
10. A disproportionate majority of child molesters are heterosexual. Do you consider it safe to expose your children to heterosexual teachers?
11. Even with all the societal support marriage receives, the divorce rate is spiralling. Why are there so few stable relationships among heterosexuals?
12. Why do heterosexuals place so much emphasis on sex?
13. Considering the menace of overpopulation, how could the human race survive if everyone was heterosexual like you?
14. Could you trust a heterosexual therapist to be objective? Don't you fear s/he might be inclined to influence you in the direction of her/his leaning?
15. How can you become a whole person if you limit yourself to compulsive, exclusive heterosexuality? Shouldn't you at least try to develop your natural, healthy homosexual potential?
16. There seem to be very few happy heterosexuals. Techniques have been developed to help you change if you really want to. Have you considered aversion therapy?

5.8

Aligning Bodies, Identities, and Expressions: Transgender Bodies

Judith Lorber and Lisa Jean Moore

Gendered norms and expectations pressure all of us to create gender-appropriate bodies, and most of us work hard to comply most of the time. Western societies do not have third genders or sexes, as some other societies do (Herdt 1994). We expect people to be "women" or "men," "female" or "male," not "other." We organize society on a two-gender system that most people believe is based on a clear-cut two-sex biology with a clear path to the "appropriate" or socially acceptable gendered body. The way we interact with others of the same or different gender reflects the "natural attitude," which assumes that there are two and only two sexes, that everyone is naturally one sex or the other no matter how they dress or act and will be that sex from birth to death, and that you can't really change your "natural" sex (Kessler and McKenna 1978, 113–114). Those who believe that sex differences are biological believe that most gendered behavior emerges from this biology. The gendered social order and the many processes that go into the production of gender differences are not seen as powerful forces that shape bodies, identities, and behavior. In actuality, not only is biological sex not the ultimate determinant of gendered bodies and behavior, but some people construct gendered bodies that do not fit the sex declared at their birth.

Birth sex, the pronouncement of a newborn's (or fetus's) biological sex by birth attendants or sonograms is the foundation of the subsequent gender socialization of individuals. That is, those who are assigned male at birth are called boys and are supposed to feel, behave, and look masculine. The same process is supposed to turn female babies into feminine girls. But throughout our lives, many of us resist the gendered expectations of our original sex categorization at birth by varying our gendered expressions. For instance, a woman might wear a man's suit; a girl might play on the boys' football team. Quite often, these actions, or transgressions from the normative, are open to social commentary or ridicule to remind the person of the breach of gendered expectations. In October 2009, a female Mississippi high school senior, Ceara Sturgis, was barred from appearing in the yearbook because she wore a tuxedo in her senior photo (Adams 2009). A National Honors Society student and an out lesbian, Ceara was attempting to wear clothing that made her feel comfortable. This act of dressing was so transgressive to her community's gender norms that she was rendered invisible.

Breaching gendered expectations through our embodied activities is something many of us do to varying degrees without questioning the veracity of our birth sex. The term for those who live in the sex assigned at birth is *cis-sexual;* their social status is *cis-gender.*[1] There are people though who do question the truth of their birth sex and who wish to live in a way that more truthfully represents who they are. What do we do about people who feel that they are boys when their birth certificate says female, or girls when their birth certificate says male?

Political theorist Paisley Currah suggests that since the early 1990s, the term "transgender" has become most commonly used to describe people in the United States whose gender identity or gender expression does not conform to social expectations for their birth sex (Currah 2006). Historian Susan Stryker defines transgender people as those

> ... who move away from the gender they were assigned at birth, people who cross over (trans-) the boundaries constructed by their culture to define and contain that gender. Some people move away from their birth-assigned gender because they feel strongly that they properly belong to another gender in which it would be better for them to live; others want to strike out toward some new location, some space not yet clearly defined or concretely occupied; still others simply feel the need to get away from the conventional expectations bound up with gender that were initially put upon them. (2008, 1)

Transgender is a complicated concept because it refers to both people whose gender identity doesn't conform to the expectations of their birth sex, and it also refers to practices of non-conforming gender expression. Prior to the 1990s, the term transsexual was more commonly used, and sometimes the terms are used interchangeably. Transsexual is also used, most often, to describe a transgender person who uses medical methods, hormones or surgery, to transform their bodies.

MTFs, or transwomen, are individuals who were assigned male at birth but live their lives as women. FTMs, or transmen, are individuals who were assigned female at birth but live their lives as men. For transgender people, the pressure to make their bodies congruent with their chosen gender is reinforced in myriad small and constant ways. Some may take hormones to bring about some physical changes. Some do only "top surgery" and leave their genitalia intact. Many legally change their gender status to their chosen gender, and most change their appearance and the way they dress, talk, and act. They may also change their first names to be more culturally appropriate to their chosen gender.

Like all of us, transgender people want to be accepted as full-fledged members of their gender community. Forms that require individuals to place themselves in M or F boxes make indicating gender compulsory; the information that is required is exclusively binary and presumably permanent. To change this identity legally means changing one's birth certificate in societies that have that documentation. Birth certificates are "breeder documents" because they are the basis of all other identity documentation, such as passports. One's legal identity, as testified to by one's birth certificate, establishes whose child you are, where you were born, how old you are, and your sex. A transgender person must jump through many bureaucratic hoops in order to have identity documents that match their gender expression and identity. In some jurisdictions, you cannot change your birth certificate at all, and in other jurisdictions, genital surgery is required to change this certification (Currah and Moore 2009).

Reconstructing Bodies

There are various surgical and hormonal methods transsexual people use to construct bodies that will fit the norms for their chosen gender. Sometimes, what is changed are genitalia and usually secondary sex characteristics that result from hormonal input at puberty. Together, these are often called "sex changes" and the process "sex reassignment." There is not a one shot, or a one-size-fits-all surgical procedure for transsexual people. As anthropologist Eric Plemons (2010) has written:

> If we were to believe the childhood lesson that what makes boys boys and what makes girls girls are penises and vaginas respectively, it would follow that changing sex was primarily a genital affair. In fact, medical interventions meant to change sex involve hormonal as well as surgical interventions. Further, the category "sex reassignment surgery" describes a whole host of procedures that include operations on the genitalia but are not limited to them. Though any of these operations may be performed for a number of conditions, these operations (including genital restructuring) are only considered "sex reassignment" when they are performed on a person who has been diagnosed as transsexual. In addition to genital and chest reconstructions, male-to-female transsexuals may have operations to raise the pitch of their voice or to shave down a prominent Adam's apple, to reconstruct their hair patterns, or to soften their jaw line or brow. Female-to-male transsexuals may choose to have operations to produce a more square jaw line or prominent brow, or may have implants that approximate more defined musculature, such as pectoral or calf implants.

Despite the multiple ways individuals may modify their bodies, "many people transition using only hormones and/or non-genital surgeries (such as double mastectomies for transgender men, breast implants for transgender women). Others transition and live full-time in their new genders without any body modification at all" (Currah and Moore 2009, 125). Still others modify their bodies outside of the parameters of the binary gender system posited by medical professionals (Spade 2003), by circumventing the medical industrial complex or not ascribing to the medicalized narrative that is required to receive care.

The public tends to be extremely curious about the details of transgender transformations. In the following excerpt, Julia Serano, a male-to-female transgender, examines the sensationalism surrounding the physical transitions of transsexual people and their sex reassignment surgeries. In this piece, Serano illustrates through media analysis and personal reflection on her own transition how the cultural obsession with surgical details confirms how obsessed we are with preserving assumptions and stereotypes about sex and gender.

Before and After: Class and Body Transformation*

Julia Serano

Independent scholar and artist

Transsexual lives are full of obstacles – childhood isolation, denial, depression, coming out, and managing our gender difference in a less than hospitable world. We have to navigate the legal limbo that surrounds what "sex" appears on our driver's licenses and passports, which restrooms we can safely use, and who we are allowed to marry. Many of us face workplace discrimination, police harassment, and the constant threat of violence. Yet the media focuses very little on any of this. Instead, TV shows and documentaries about transsexuals tend to focus rather exclusively on one particular aspect of our lives: our physical transitions.

Such transition-focused programs always seem to follow the same format, which includes rigorous discussions of all of the medical procedures involved (hormones, surgeries, electrolysis, etc.) and plenty of the requisite before-and-after shots. Before I transitioned, I found these programs predictable and formulaic, but I also found them helpful to a certain extent. As someone who had often thought about changing my sex, they gave me a certain understanding of what I might be able to expect if I were to pursue such a path myself. But of course, I was a demographic anomaly. Clearly these shows were being made by and for people who did not identify with the trans person in the program and who were not contemplating sex reassignment themselves. Back then, I never really questioned why a non-trans audience might be so interested in the minutiae of the transitioning process and trans-related medical procedures.

Now, after five years of living as an out transsexual, I have come to realize that these documentaries and TV programs reveal an even deeper underlying compulsion on the part of many cis-sexual people, one that goes way beyond natural curiosity, to dwell almost exclusively on the physical aspects of the transition process when contemplating transsexuality. Like most transsexuals, I have scores of anecdotes that highlight this tendency: During the question and answer session at a literary event, after reading a piece about the murder of trans woman Gwen Araujo, I was asked by an audience member if I had any electrolysis done on my face; after I did a workshop for college students on binary gender norms and the way we project our ideals about gender onto other people, a young woman asked me several questions about whether or not I'd had a "sex change operation"; after creating switchhitter.net, my coming-out-as-trans Web site, I received an angry email from a stranger complaining that I did not put any before-and-after pictures up on the site, as if the 3,700-word question and answer section and the 4,500-word mini-autobiography describing my experiences being trans wasn't sufficient for that person to fully grasp my transsexuality – he needed to see the changes firsthand.

*   Excerpted from Julia Serano, *Whipping Girl: A Transsexual Woman on Sexism and the Scapegoating of Femininity*, pp. 53–59, 61–64. Copyright © 2007 by Julia Serano. Published by Seal Press. Reprinted with permission.

Of course, it's not just strangers who ask to see before-and-after shots of me. When friends, colleagues, or acquaintances find out that I am trans, it is not uncommon for them to ask if I have any "before" pictures they can see, as if I just so happen to keep a boy photo of myself handy, you know, just in case. I usually respond by telling them that before I transitioned I looked exactly like I do now, except that I was a boy. They never seem particularly satisfied with that answer.

These days, whenever people ask me lots of questions about my previous male life and the medical procedures that helped facilitate my transition to female, I realize that they are making a desperate and concerted effort to preserve their own assumptions and stereotypes about gender, rather than opening their minds up to the possibility that women and men do not represent mutually exclusive categories. When they request to see my "before" photos or ask me what my former name was, it is because they are trying to visualize me as male in order to anchor my existence in my assigned sex. And when they focus on my physical transition, it is so they can imagine my femaleness as a product of medical science rather than something that is authentic, that comes from inside me.

I know that many in the trans community believe that these TV shows and documentaries following transsexuals through the transition process serve a purpose, offering us a bit of visibility and the rare chance to be depicted on TV as something other than a joke. But in actuality, they accomplish little more than reducing us to our physical transitions and our anatomically "altered" bodies. In other words, these programs objectify us. And while it has become somewhat customary for trans people to allow the media to use our "before" pictures whenever we appear on TV, this only enables the cis-sexual public to continue privileging our assigned sex over our subconscious sex and gender identity. If we truly want to be taken seriously in our identified sex, then we must not only refuse to indulge cis-sexual people's compulsion to pigeonhole us in our assigned sex, but call them out on the way that they continuously objectify our bodies while refusing to take our minds, our persons, and our identities seriously.

Critical Summary

Multiple genders, sexes, and sexualities show that the conventional categories are not universal or essential, nor are the social processes that produce dominance and subordination. Border crossers and those living on borders have opened a social dialogue over the power of categories, and their resistances, refusals, and transgressions have encouraged political activism.

The goals and political uses of community and identity have not been uniform. Those whose bodies don't conform to norms – hefty, tall women and short, slender men – don't want to change their bodies or their gender; they want gender norms to expand. Some MTFs and FTMs modify their bodies surgically and hormonally and walk, talk, dress, and gesture convincingly in order to embody femininity or masculinity. Like most of us, they support rather than challenge the gendered social order. Other trans gender people have mixed gender presentations, or want to live openly as "transgender."

What would happen if a third category – "transgender" – was added to the familiar two? Rather than weakening the power of categories to control heterogeneous and diverse lives, the establishment of another category starts the cycle of boundary definition and border disputes all over again. New categories also enter the political arena with demands for social recognition and distribution of rewards and privileges. Older identity-based political groups of gays, lesbians, transgender, and intersexed people argue that the new groups undercut their claims of discrimination and siphon off economic resources.

As this chapter demonstrates, all gendered bodies to varying degrees must engage with the larger gendered social order. Transgender people are often forced to account for themselves in deeply private ways or in humiliating detail. This act of accounting for oneself demonstrates the depths of social expectations of our gendered bodies and how our culture reproduces gender binaries. By learning about the experiences of transgender people, we can better understand the ways *all* gendered bodies are produced at the intersections of the material and the symbolic, the flesh and the self.

Note

1. The terms come from the Latin prefix *cis*, meaning "on the same side." Contrasted to *trans*, *cis* refers to the alignment of gender identity with assigned gender.

References and Recommended Readings

Adams, Ross. 2009. "Senior Yearbook Photo Causes Controversy." WJTV.COM. http://www2.wjtv.com/jtv/news/local/article/senior_yearbook_photo_causes_controversy/43650/.

Ames, Jonathan (ed.). 2005. *Sexual Metamorphosis: An Anthology of Transsexual Memoirs*. New York: Vintage.

Bernstein, Fred A. 2004. "On Campus, Rethinking Biology 101." *New York Times*, Sunday Styles,7March.http://www.nytimes.com/2004/03/07/style/on-campus-rethinking-biology-101.html?sec=health.

Bettcher, Talia, and Ann Garry. 2009. "Transgender Studies and Feminism: Theory, Politics and Gendered Realities." Special Issue of *Hypatia*. 24 (3).

Bornstein, Kate. 1994. *Gender Outlaw: On Men, Women and the Rest of Us*. New York: Routledge.

Broadus, Kylar. 2006. "The Evolution of Employment Discrimination Protections for Transgender People," in *Transgender Rights*, edited by Paisley Currah, Richard Juang, and Shannon Price Minter. Minneapolis: University of Minnesota Press.

Brown, Patricia Leigh. 2005. "A Quest for a Restroom That's Neither Men's Room Nor Women's Room." *New York Times*, 4 March, A14.

Butler, Judith. 2001. "Doing Justice to Someone: Sex Reassignment and Allegories of Transsexuality." *GLQ: A Journal of Lesbian and Gay Studies* 7: 621–636.

Califia, Pat. 1997. *Sex Changes: The Politics of Transgenderism*. San Francisco CA: Cleis Press.

Connell, Raewyn. 2009. "Accountable Conduct: 'Doing Gender' in Transsexual and Political Retrospect. *Gender & Society* 23: 104–111.

Cromwell, Jason. 1999. *Transmen and FTMs: Identities, Bodies, Genders, and Sexualities*. Chicago: University of Chicago Press.

Currah, Paisley. 2006. "Gender Pluralisms Under the Transgender Umbrella," in *Transgender Rights*, edited by Paisley Currah, Richard M. Juang, and Shannon Price Minter. Minneapolis: University of Minnesota Press.

Currah, Paisley. 2009. "The Transgender Rights Imaginary," in *Feminist and Queer Legal Theory: Intimate Encounters, Uncomfortable Conversations*, edited by Martha Albertson Fineman, Jack E. Jackson, and Adam P. Romero. Surrey, UK: Ashgate Press.

Currah, Paisley, and Lisa Jean Moore. 2009. "'We Won't Know Who You Are': Contesting Sex Designations on New York City Birth Certificates." *Hypatia: Journal of Feminist Philosophy* 24: 113–135.

Denny, Dallas (ed.). 1997. *Current Concepts in Transgender Identity*. New York: Garland Publishing.

Devor, Holly [Aaron Devor]. 1989. *Gender Blending: Confronting the Limits of Duality*. Bloomington: Indiana University Press.

Devor, Holly [Aaron Devor]. 1997. *FTM: Female-to-Male Transsexuals in Society*. Bloomington: Indiana University Press.

Dozier, Raine. 2005. "Beards, Breasts, and Bodies: Doing Sex in a Gendered World." *Gender & Society* 19: 297–316.

Ekins, Richard, and Dave King. 2006. *The Transgender Phenomenon*. London: Sage.

Epstein, Julia, and Kristina Straub (eds.). 1991. *Body Guards: The Cultural Politics of Gender Ambiguity*. New York: Routledge.

Feinberg, Leslie. 1996. *Transgender Warriors: Making History from Joan of Arc to Dennis Rodham*. Boston: Beacon Press.

Gamson, Joshua G. 1995. "Must Identity Movements Self-Destruct? A Queer Dilemma." *Social Problems* 42: 390–407.

Gamson, Joshua G. 1997. "Messages of Exclusion: Gender, Movements, and Symbolic Boundaries." *Gender & Society* 11: 178–199.

Gamson, Joshua G. 1998. *Freaks Talk Back: Tabloid Talk Shows and Sexual Nonconformity*. Chicago: University of Chicago Press.

Girshick, Lori B. 2008. *Transgender Voices: Beyond Women and Men*. Lebanon, NH: University Press of New England.

Halberstam, Judith. 1998. *Female Masculinity*. Durham, NC: Duke University Press.

Hale, C. Jacob. 1998. "Consuming the Living, Dis(re)membering the Dead in the Butch/FTM Borderlands." *Journal of Gay and Lesbian Studies* 4: 311–348.

Hausman, Bernice L. 1995. *Changing Sex: Transsexualism, Technology, and the Idea of Gender*. Durham, NC: Duke University Press.

Herdt, Gilbert (ed.). 1994. *Third Sex, Third Gender: Beyond Sexual Dimorphism in Culture and History*. New York: Zone Books.

Heyes, Cressida J. 2003. "Feminist Solidarity after Queer Theory: The Case of Transgender." *Signs* 28: 1093–1120.

Hines, Sally. 2005. "'I am a Feminist but …': Transgender Men and Women and Feminism," in *Different Wavelengths: Studies of the Contemporary Women's Movement*, edited by Jo Reger. New York: Routledge.

Hines, Sally. 2007. "(Trans)Forming Gender: Social Change and Transgender Citizenship." *Sexualities* 7: 345–362.

Jacobs, Sue-Ellen, Wesley Thomas, and Sabine Lang (eds.). 1997. *Two-Spirit People: Native American Gender Identity, Sexuality, and Spirituality.* Urbana: University of Illinois Press.

Kessler, Suzanne J., and Wendy McKenna. 1978. *Gender: An Ethnomethodological Approach.* Chicago: University of Chicago.

Lorber, Judith. 1999. "Crossing Borders and Erasing Boundaries: Paradoxes of Identity Politics." *Sociological Focus* 32: 355–369.

Lorber, Judith. 2001. "It's the 21st Century – Do You Know What Gender You Are?" in *An International Feminist Challenge to Theory*, edited by Marcia Texler Segal and Vasilikie Demos, *Advances in Gender Research*, V.5, Greenwich, CT: JAI Press.

Mason-Schrock, Douglas. 1996. "Transsexuals' Narrative Construction of the True Self." *Social Psychology Quarterly* 59: 176–192.

Meyerowitz, Joanne. 2002. *How Sex Changed: A History of Transsexuality* in *the United States.* Cambridge, MA: Harvard University Press.

Middlebrook, Diane Wood. 1998. *Suits Me: The Double Life of Billy Tipton.* Boston: Houghton Mifflin.

Najmabadi, Afsaneh. 2005. *Women with Mustaches and Men without Beards: Gender and Sexual Anxieties of Iranian Modernity.* Berkeley, CA: University of California Press.

Namaste, Viviane. 2000. *Invisible Lives: The Erasure of Transsexual and Transgendered People.* Chicago: University of Chicago Press.

Pfeffer, Carla A. 2010. "Women's Work? Women Partners of Transgender Men Doing Housework and Emotion Work." *Journal of Marriage and Family* 72: 165–183.

Plemons, Eric. 2010. "Envisioning The Body in Relation: Finding Sex, Changing Sex," in *The Body Reader: Essential Social and Cultural Readings*, edited by Lisa Jean Moore and Mary Kosut. New York: New York University Press.

Prosser, Jay. 1998. *Second Skin: The Body Narratives of Transsexuality.* New York: Columbia University Press.

Raymond, J. G. 1979. *The Transsexual Empire: The Making of the She-male.* Boston: Beacon.

Roen, Katrina. 2002. "'Either/Or' and 'Both/Neither': Discursive Tensions in Transgender Politics." *Signs* 27: 501–522.

Rubin, Gayle S. 1992. "Of Catamites and Kings: Reflections on Butch, Gender, and Boundaries," in *The Persistent Desire: A Femme-Butch Reader*, edited by Joan Nestle. Boston: Allyson Publications.

Schilt, Kristen, and Laurel Westbrook. 2009. "Doing Gender, Doing Heteronormativity: 'Gender Normals,' Transgender People, and the Social Maintenance of Heterosexuality." *Gender & Society* 23: 440–464.

Schrock, Douglas, Lori Reid, and Emily M. Boyd. 2005. "Transsexuals' Embodiment of Womanhood." *Gender & Society* 19: 317–335.

Scott-Dixon, Krista. 2006. *Trans/Feminisms: Transfeminist Voices Speak Out.* Toronto: Sumach Press.

Spade, Dean. 2003. "Resisting Medicine/Remodeling Gender." *Berkeley Women's Law Journal* 18: 15–37.

Stone, Sandy. 1991. "The Empire Strikes Back: A Posttranssexual Manifesto," in *Body Guards: The Cultural Politics of Gender Ambiguity*, edited by Julia Epstein and Kristina Straub. New York: Routledge.

Stryker, Susan. 2008. *Transgender History.* Berkeley, CA: Seal Press.

Stryker, Susan, and Stephen Whittle. 2006. *The Transgender Studies Reader*. New York: Routledge.

Valentine, David. 2007. *Imagining Transgender: An Ethnography of Category*. Durham, NC: Duke University Press.

Vidal-Ortiz, Salvador. 2009. "The Figure of the Transwoman of Color Through the Lens of Doing Gender." *Gender & Society* 23: 99–103.

West, Candace, and Sarah Fenstermaker. 1995. "Doing Difference." *Gender & Society* 9: 8–37.

West, Candace, and Don Zimmerman. 1987. "Doing Gender." *Gender & Society* 1: 125–151.

Wickman, J. 2001. *Transgender Politics: The Construction and Deconstruction of Binary Gender in the Finnish Transgender Community*. Åbo, Finland: Åbo Akademi University Press.

Wilchins, Ricky Anne. 1997. *Read My Lips: Sexual Subversion and the End of Gender*. New York: Firebrand Books.

Winerip, Michael. 2009. "Anything He Can Do, She Can Do." *New York Times*, Sunday Styles, 15 November, 2.

5.9

Masculinity Politics on a World Scale

R. W. Connell

The world gender order mostly privileges men over women. Though there are many local exceptions, there is a patriarchal dividend for men collectively, arising from higher incomes, higher labour force participation, unequal property ownership, greater access to institutional power, as well as cultural and sexual privilege. This has been documented by international research on women's situation (Taylor 1985, Valdés and Gomáriz 1995), though its implications for men have mostly been ignored. The conditions thus exist for the production of a hegemonic masculinity on a world scale – that is to say, a dominant form of masculinity that embodies, organizes and legitimates men's domination in the world gender order as a whole.

The inequalities of the world gender order, like the inequalities of local gender orders, produce resistance. The main pressure for change has come from an international feminist movement (Bulbeck 1998). International cooperation among feminist groups goes back at least a century, though it is only in recent decades that a women's movement has established a strong presence in international forums. Mechanisms such as the 1979 Convention on the Elimination of all forms of Discrimination Against Women, and the 1975–85 United Nations Decade for Women, placed gender inequality on the diplomatic agenda. The follow-up 1995 Beijing Conference agreed on a detailed 'Platform for Action', providing for international action on issues ranging from economic exclusion, women's health, and violence against women, to girls' education.

Equally important is the circulation of ideas, methods and examples of action. The presence of a worldwide feminist movement, and the undeniable fact of a worldwide debate about gender issues, has intensified cultural pressure for change. In Japan, for instance, a range of women's organizations existed before 1970, but a new activism was sparked by the international Women's Liberation movement

(Tanaka 1977). This was reflected in cultural genres such as girls' fiction and comic books with images of powerful women. Men, and men's cultural genres, gradually responded – sometimes with marked hostility. Ito (1992), tracing these changes, argues that the older patterns of Japanese 'men's culture' have collapsed, amid intensified debate about the situation of men. However, no new model of masculinity has become dominant.

With local variations, a similar course of events has occurred in many developed countries. Challenge and resistance, plus the disruptions involved in the creation of a world gender order, have meant many local instabilities in gender arrangements. They include:

- contestation of all-male networks and sexist organizational culture as women move into political office, the bureaucracy and higher education (Eisenstein 1991),
- the disruption of sexual identities that produced 'queer' politics and other challenges to gay identities in metropolitan countries (Seidman 1996),
- the shifts in the urban intelligentsia that produced profeminist politics among heterosexual men (Pease 1997),
- media images of 'the new sensitive man', the shoulder-padded businesswoman, and other icons of gender change.

One response to such instabilities, on the part of groups whose power or identity is challenged, is to reaffirm local gender hierarchies. A masculine fundamentalism is, accordingly, an identifiable pattern in gender politics. In South Africa, the paramilitary Afrikaner Weerstandsbeweging (AWB) movement led by Eugene Terre Blanche, attempts to mobilize Afrikaner men against the post-apartheid regime. A cult of masculine toughness is interwoven with open racism; weapons are celebrated and women are explicitly excluded from authority (Swart 2001). There are obvious similarities to the militia movement in the United States documented by Gibson (1994) and more recently discussed by Kimmel (2004). Tillner (2000), discussing masculinity and racism in central Europe, notes evidence that it is not underprivileged youth as such who are recruited to racism. Rather, it is young men oriented to dominance, an orientation that plays out in gender as well as race.

These fundamentalist reactions against gender change are spectacular, but are not, I consider, the majority response among men. There is considerable survey evidence for acceptance of gender change, i.e. a swing of popular attitudes towards gender equality. This change of attitudes, however, need not result in changed practices. For instance, Fuller remarks that despite changes of opinion among Peruvian men,

> the realms in which masculine solidarity networks are constructed that guarantee access to networks of influence, alliances, and support are reproduced through a masculine culture of sports, alcohol consumption, visits to whorehouses, or stories about sexual conquests. These mechanisms assure a monopoly of, or, at least, differential access by men to the public sphere and are a key part of the system of power in which masculinity is forged. (Fuller 2001: 325)

I would argue that this practical recuperation of gender change is a more wide-spread, and more successful, form of reaction among men than masculine funda-mentalism is. Such recuperation is supported by neo-liberalism. Through the market agenda, the patriarchal dividend to men is defended or restored, without an explicit masculinity politics in the form of a mobilization of men.

Within the global arena of international relations, the international state, multi-national corporations and global markets, there is nevertheless a deploy-ment of masculinities. Two models of the state of play in this arena have recently been offered.

One is the model of transnational business masculinity. This has replaced older local models of bourgeois masculinity, which were more embedded in local organizations and local conservative cultures. In global arenas, transnational business masculinity has had only one major contender for hegemony in recent decades, the rigid, control-oriented masculinity of the military, and its variant in the military-style bureaucratic dictatorships of Stalinism. With the collapse of Stalinism and the end of the Cold War, the more flexible, calculative, egocentric masculinity of the new capitalist entrepreneur holds the world stage. The political leadership of the major powers, through such figures as Clinton, Schröder and Blair, for a while conformed to this model of masculinity, working out a non-threat-ening accommodation with feminism.

Transnational business masculinity is not homogeneous. A Confucian var-iant, based in East Asia, has a stronger commitment to hierarchy and social consensus. A secularized-Christian variant, based in North America, has more hedonism and individualism, and greater tolerance for social conflict. In certain arenas there is already conflict between the business and political leaderships embodying these forms of masculinity. Such conflicts have arisen over 'human rights' versus 'Asian values', and over the extent of trade and investment liberalization.

Focusing more on international politics than on business, Hooper (1998) suggests a somewhat different pattern of hegemony in the masculinities of global arenas. A tough, power-oriented masculinity predominates in the arena of diplomacy, war and power politics – distanced from the feminized world of domesticity, but also distinguished from other masculinities, such as those of working-class men, subordinated ethnic groups, wimps and homosexuals. This is not just a matter of pre-existing masculinity being expressed in international politics. Hooper argues that international politics is a primary site for the construction of masculinities, for instance in war, or through continuing security threats.

Hooper further argues that recent globalization trends have 'softened' hege-monic masculinity in several ways. Ties with the military have been loosened, with a world trend towards demilitarization – the total numbers of men in world armies have fallen significantly since the Cold War. Men are now more often positioned as consumers, and contemporary management gives more emphasis to traditionally 'feminine' qualities such as interpersonal skills and teamwork.

Hooper also comments on the interplay of North American with Japanese corporate culture, noting some borrowing in both directions in the context of global re-structuring.

Though the softening of hegemonic masculinity described by Hooper (1998), Niva (1998) and Messner (1993) is real enough, it does not mean the obliteration of 'harder' masculinities. The election of George W. Bush to the presidency, the political aftermath of the attack on the World Trade Centre in New York, and the re-mobilization of nationalism and military force in the United States culminating in the attack on Iraq in 2003, show that hard-line political leadership is still possible in the remaining superpower. It has never gone away in China. Bush's distinctive combination of US nationalism, religiosity, support for corporate interests and rejection of alternative points of view is not, perhaps, an easily exported model of masculinity. But local equivalents can be forged elsewhere.

If these are the contenders for hegemony, they are not the only articulations of masculinity in global forums. The international circulation of 'gay' identities is an important indication that non-hegemonic masculinities may operate in global arenas. They can find political expression, for instance around human rights and AIDS prevention (Altman 2001).

Another political alternative is provided by counter-hegemonic movements opposed to the current world gender order and the groups dominant in it. They are sometimes associated with the promotion of new masculinities, but also address masculinity as an obstacle to the reform of gender relations. The largest and best known are the pro-feminist men's groups in the USA, with their umbrella group NOMAS (National Organization of Men Against Sexism) which has been active since the early 1980s (Cohen 1991). More globally oriented is the 'White Ribbon' campaign, originating in Canada as a remarkably successful mobilization to oppose men's violence against women, and now working internationally (Kaufman 1999).

Such movements, groups or reform agendas exist in many countries, including Germany (*Widersprüche* 1995), Britain (Seidler 1991), Australia (Pease 1997), Mexico (Zingoni 1998), Russia (Sinelnikov 2000), India (Kulkarni 2001) and the Nordic countries (Oftung 2000). The spectrum of issues they address is well illustrated by the conference of the Japanese men's movement in Kyoto in 1996. This conference included sessions on youth, gay issues, work, child rearing, bodies, and communications with women, as well as addressing the topic of the globalization of the men's movement (Menzu Senta 1997).

References

Altman, Dennis. 2001. *Global Sex*. Chicago: University of Chicago Press.

Bulbeck, Chilla. 1998. *Re-Orienting Western Feminisms: Women's Diversity in a Postcolonial World*. Cambridge: Cambridge University Press.

Cohen, Jon. 1991. 'NOMAS: Challenging male supremacy'. *Changing Men*, 10th Anniversary Issue, Winter/Spring: 45–6.

Eisenstein, Hester. 1991. *Gender Shock: Practising Feminism on Two Continents*. Sydney: Allen & Unwin.

Fuller, Norma. 2001. 'The social construction of gender identity among Peruvian men'. *Men and Masculinities* 3: 316–31.

Gibson, James William. 1994. *Warrior Dreams: Paramilitary Culture in Post-Vietnam America*. New York: Hill & Wang.

Hooper, Charlotte. 1998. 'Masculinist practices and gender politics: the operation of multiple masculinities in international relations'. pp. 28–53 in *The 'Man' Question in International Relations*, ed. Marysia Zalewski and Jane Parpart. Boulder: Westview.

Ito, Kimio, 1992. 'Cultural change and gender identity trends in the 1970s and 1980s'. *International Journal of Japanese Sociology* 1: 79–98.

Kaufman, Michael, ed. 1999. 'Men & violence'. *International Association for Studies of Men Newsletter* 6, special issue.

Kimmel, Michael S. 2004. 'Globalization and its mal(e)contents: the gendered moral and political economy of terrorism'. In *Handbook of Research on Men and Masculinities*, ed. M. Kimmel, J. Hearn and R. W. Connell. Thousand Oaks: Sage.

Kulkarni, Mangesh. 2001. 'Reconstructing Indian masculinities'. *Gentleman* (Mumbai), May 2001.

Menzu Senta [Men's Centre Japan]. 1997. *Otokotachi no watashisagashi* [How are men seeking their new selves?]. Kyoto: Kamogawa.

Messner, Michael A. 1993. '"Changing men" and feminist politics in the United States'. *Theory and Society* 22: 723–37.

Niva, Steve. 1998. 'Tough and tender: new world order masculinity and the Gulf War'. pp. 109–28 in *The 'Man' Question in International Relations*, ed. Marysia Zalewski and Jane Parpart. Boulder: Westview Press.

Oftung, Knut. 2000. 'Men and gender equality in the Nordic countries'. pp. 143–62 in *Male Roles, Masculinities and Violence: A Culture of Peace Perspective*, ed. Ingeborg Breines, Robert Connell and Ingrid Eide. Paris: UNESCO Publishing.

Pease, Bob. 1997. *Men and Sexual Politics: Towards a Profeminist Practice*. Adelaide: Dulwich Centre.

Seidler, Victor J. ed. 1991. *Achilles Heel Reader: Men, Sexual Politics and Socialism*. London: Routledge.

Seidman, Steven, ed. 1996. *Queer Theory/Sociology*. Oxford: Blackwell.

Sinelnikov, Andrei. 2000. 'Masculinity *à la russe*: gender issues in the Russian federation today'. pp. 201–9 in *Male Roles, Masculinities and Violence: A Culture of Peace Perspective*, ed. Ingeborg Breines, Robert Connell and Ingrid Eide. Paris: UNESCO Publishing.

Swart, Sandra. 2001. '"Man, gun and horse": hard right Afrikaner masculine identity in post-apartheid South Africa'. pp. 75–89 in *Changing Men in Southern Africa*, ed. Robert Morrell. Pietermaritzburg: University of Natal Press.

Tanaka, Kazuko. 1977. *A Short History of the Women's Movement in Modern Japan*. 3rd edn. Japan: Femintern Press.

Taylor, Debbie. 1985. 'Women, an analysis'. pp. 1–98 in *Women, A World Report*, New Internationalist. London: Methuen.

Tillner, Georg. 2000. 'The identity of dominance: masculinity and xenophobia'. pp. 53–9 in *Male Roles, Masculinities and Violence: A Culture of Peace Perspective*, ed. Ingeborg Breines, Robert Connell and Ingrid Eide. Paris: UNESCO Publishing.

Valdés, Teresa and Enrique Gomáriz. 1995. *Latin American Women: Compared Figures*. Santiago: Instituto de la Mujer and FLACSO.

Widersprüche. 1995. Special issue: 'Männlichkeiten', no. 56/7.

Zingoni, Eduardo Liendro. 1998. 'Masculinidades y violencia desde un programa de acción en México'. pp. 130–6 in *Masculinidades y Equidad de Género en América Latina*, ed. Teresa Valdés and José Olavarría. Santiago: FLACSO/UNFPA.

5.10

Brown Boi Health Manifesto
Prentis Hemphill

Every individual should have the chance to live a healthy life. In this current historical moment, this includes, but is not limited to, affordable and comprehensive healthcare, culturally grounded and holistic services, food security, accessible sites for physical activity, and community infrastructure and networks to facilitate healing. Recent research has shown us that poor communities and communities of color systematically lack many, if not all, of these health indicators. What this means is that our communities have fewer opportunities to make the choices that improve the quality and length of our lives.

In the mainstream, health is used to fuel a billion dollar industry more concerned with the aesthetics of the "perfect form" than with nurturing the development of healthy people and communities. In pursuit of this perfection, many of our communities are made invisible in the media – our bodies and our relationships are unimagined and devalued. If we are seen, it is often in stereotypical shadows and one-dimensional representations.

This flattening and marginalization of our experiences and lives requires that we take a stand for health in the service of social change. Accordingly, we elect to seek an understanding of health that can hold our many gender expressions, sexes, varied abilities, and spectrum of sizes. We know that health in its true definition refers to healing and nurturing of places both physical and spiritual. We choose to engage in this process of reclamation with generosity for ourselves and our communities and continue to develop our skills to distinguish between that which harms us and that which gives us strength.

Our Bodies are Our Own – Our Worth is Immeasurable

We recognize through our relationships with ourselves and in building community the disparate values placed on our bodies in a society that oppresses on the basis of race, sex, gender, class, sexual orientation, ability, and size. As individuals and communities existing at the cross-section of multiple oppressions, we first reclaim our true selves from internalized stories of inferiority or gender superiority and celebrate the immeasurable value of all our lives. We will work to take back our decision making power from those who do not hold our best interests at heart. And through these excavations, we will carve out in ourselves the capacity for greater choices and love.

Health is a Relationship with Oneself. A Journey

We release the idea that "healthy" is a place where we can arrive. We know that health is a lifelong journey with ourselves, of listening to and respecting the needs of our bodies and minds, of noticing and modifying harmful behaviors, and of setting goals for ourselves grounded in acceptance.

Individual and Community Transformation and Self-determination

We move toward healthier living with generosity for ourselves and an unflinching dedication to growth, inclusion, and transformation. We recognize the creativity and ancient wisdom our communities hold and seek to unearth these lessons that have been hidden. We are working toward profound social change knowing that there are no disposable people or communities. We all need to be here.

– *Prentis Hemphill*

6

Body Politics

By Susan E. Cayleff

Contents

Original publication details: 6.1 Janice Mirikitani, "Recipe" from *Shedding Silence*, p. 20. Berkeley: Celestial Arts, 1987. Reproduced with permission of Janice Mirikitani. 6.2 Rose Weitz, "A History of Women's Bodies" from *The Politics of Women's Bodies: Sexuality, Appearance, Behavior*, ed. Rose Weitz, pp. 3–11. New York: Oxford University Press, 2003. Reproduced with permission of Oxford University Press. 6.3 Gloria Steinem, "If Men Could Menstruate" from *Ms Magazine*, October 1978, p. 110. Reproduced with permission of Gloria Steinem. 6.4 Laura Hershey, "Women and Disability and Poetry (Not Necessarily in That Order)," Jan 26, 2010, from www.laurahershey.com. Reproduced with permission of R. Stephens. 6.5 Morrie Turner, "Do we call you handicapped?" *Wee Pals*, 8–3, 1981. Reproduced with permission from Creators Syndicate International for the artist. 6.6 Eric Anderson, "Maintaining Masculinity: Homophobia at Work" from *In the Game: Gay Athletes and the Cult of Masculinity*, pp. 25–30. Albany: SUNY Press, 2005. Reproduced with permission of State University of New York Press. 6.7 Judith Ortiz Cofer, "The Story of My Body" from *The Latin Deli: Prose and Poetry*, pp. 135–46. Athens: University of Georgia Press, 1993. Reproduced with permission of University of Georgia Press. 6.8 Maysan Haydar, "Veiled Intentions: Don't Judge a Muslim Girl by her Covering" from *Body Outlaws: Rewriting the Rules of Beauty and Body Image*, ed. Ophira Edut, pp. 258–65. Emeryville, CA: Seal Press, 2003. Reproduced with permission of Perseus Books Group.

Women in Culture: An Intersectional Anthology for Gender and Women's Studies, Second Edition.
Edited by Bonnie Kime Scott, Susan E. Cayleff, Anne Donadey, and Irene Lara.
© 2017 John Wiley & Sons, Ltd. Published 2017 by John Wiley & Sons, Ltd.

This chapter identifies cultural pressures and institutionalized oppressions that alienate women from our bodies. It offers strategies for reclaiming the body and healing the mind/body/spirit split typical of Western thought. The readings in this section offer historical and contemporary insights into how the norms of able-bodied persons and heteronormativity (defined as the presumption that heterosexuality is ideal and normal), as well as Westernized ideals of beauty, have been taught and institutionalized. These same dictates valorize masculinities that arose alongside culturally constructed ideals of femininities. These led to homophobia (fear and hatred of homosexuals) among hetero-sexuals, particularly men. Such norms supported emerging capitalism because they centered the nuclear family, reproduction, and consumer culture.

This chapter addresses diverse bodies of color, gender, disabilities, and masculinities. Cross-culturally the male body is seen as the baseline measure of the desirable body. It is presumed to be biologically, politically, and intellectually ideal (Barker-Benfield). Hence women's bodies are often defined, controlled, and legislated in ways that support key cultural institutions of patriarchal power, nation-state authority, able-bodiedness, and heterosexual and racialized privilege.

Based on ideas of "normalcy and desirability," women's sexualities – and their bodies – are used to reaffirm imbalances of power between men and women. Yet rejection of oppressive cultural ideals and institutions can challenge and disorder these same power relations. Forms of bodily resistance and empowerment emerge when women reclaim and combat constricting definitions imposed, created, and internalized by us. This was demonstrated early on by Nancy F. Cott's "Passionlessness". This means realizing our primary source of power does not come from attractiveness, as Mirikitani shows in "Recipe." It means giving voice to disabled bodily experiences, understanding Muslim worthiness, rejecting Anglo-as-norm beauty ideals, and challenging the idea that woman's value lies in our heterosexual desirability to men.

Historical Overview: The Male Body as Ideal

Rose Weitz's overview in "A History of Women's Bodies" (1998/2003) traces legal traditions that defined women's bodies as male property. This assigned them a status less than men's since our bodies were seen as inferior. Women's sexuality was also problematic: African American women pre- and post- American slavery (largely abolished in 1865) were deemed hypersexual, animalistic, and incapable of being raped. Such "controlling images" (Collins 69) served to justify their continuing sexual oppression by white men. During that era, middle-class Euro-American women's bodies were diametrically opposed to those of African American women (Washington) and considered frail and asexual (Smith-Rosenberg) except when conceiving children, a theme resonant in Charlotte Perkins Gilman's "The Yellow Wallpaper," which is discussed in Chapter 8. These beliefs, and the laws that enforced them, changed only when women's activism, education, and employment opportunities challenged their assigned emotional and physical frailty. Physicians, as self-appointed cultural experts, had the power to name and control women's bodies and sexualities: this is seen through the use of gynecological surgeries performed on white middle-class women (to revert them to their proper roles) (Barker-Benfield) and the class- and race-bound belief that working-class and ethnic women and women of color were robust and suffered little ill health.

In the early twentieth century (and into the present) medical opinions still held sway, but industrialization needed female factory workers. Unsafe conditions led to protective labor laws for women only, but these were soon seen as counterproductive to women's enfranchisement (1920 in the United States) because they curtailed allowable jobs for working and middle-class women on the basis of health and morality (Lehrer). These laws were abandoned soon thereafter. By the mid-twentieth century women's legal and political status remained woefully inadequate, giving rise to the "Second wave" of feminism that sought shared familial duties, legal parity, and the end of the sexual double standard. Across these centuries, American women were presumed and pressured to be heterosexual (Rich) and able-bodied and expected to be physically appealing in appearance: standards that were based on Euro-American middle-class norms. The backlash against feminism created a fetal rights movement that fostered anti-abortion activism (after the passage of Roe v. Wade in 1973) (Roth). This modern-day control of women's bodies impedes women's bodily autonomy and is now a site of organized resistance.

What is deemed normal and desirable for female and male bodies is examined again in "If Men Could Menstruate" (1978) by *Ms. Magazine* co-founder, feminist activist, spokesperson, and author Gloria Steinem. Written during the height of the Second wave of feminism (1960s–1970s), it asserts that menstruation is read as physical and emotional weakness in girls and women. She humorously speculates that if men, instead of women, could magically menstruate it would be recast as a positive, proud, and desirable event. Tellingly, she invokes the names of elite male athletes as those most suitable to pitch the products as they are deemed to embody masculinity at its finest. In her piece she demonstrates that menstrual cultural taboos are directly related to their being a female experience. Male menstruation, she argues, would justify male privilege in social institutions as well as interpersonal relations. In short, whatever the male body does is preferable, healthy, and normal, and justifies socioeconomic privilege. Hershey's "Women and Disability" takes this analysis further. Disability, she says, is also deemed abnormal and compounded by gender.

A fourth author discusses how masculinity is created and maintained in juxtaposition to hegemonic femininity. Eric Anderson's "Maintaining Masculinity: Homophobia at Work," (2005) focuses on the social policing conducted by boys and men on each other within athletic spaces. Like Weitz and Steinem, Anderson explores how social institutions, cultural expectations, and gendered ideals script behavior. Being a "real boy" (or man) means rejecting all things feminine, including emotions and any female spaces or interests. Athleticism is the ultimate proof of masculinity and offers social privileges – prime among them protection from being labeled sissy, or homosexual. Ironically, athletic boys, because they have more masculine capital, are more able to transcend gendered boundaries since their heterosexual virility is rarely questioned. This dovetails with mid nineteenth-century middle-class Euro-American values that likened male physical fitness and virility with the ability to succeed as a wage-earner, father, and citizen. In Anderson's observed "jock-ocracy" anti-gay pejoratives are routinely used to motivate males into better performance. "Faggot" becomes the ultimate insult used to induce fiercer competitiveness, while misogynist terms also re-enforce a male-only space, superiority, and desirability. As Kimmel argues in Chapter 1, in sports, the male body reigns supreme. This raises interesting questions about perceptions of and difficulties faced by gender-nonconforming female athletes such as Brittney Griner of the Women's National Basketball Association (WNBA); Jason Collins, of the NBA, an active player when he came out as gay in 2013; and NFL recruit Michael Sam who came out as gay in 2014.

Constructing and Identifying Female Bodily Ideals

Culturally specific racial, social class, heteronormative, and able-bodied hierarchies and privileging construct and co-create bodily ideals for women and female-identified people. These ideals have been defined and promulgated in large part by medical, psychological, and media "experts." Barbara Ehrenreich and Deidre English's *For Her Own Good: 150 Years of the Expert's Advice to Women* demonstrates the dangers of this symbiotic relationship. Kim Chernin developed this further in "Obsession: Reflections on the Tyranny of Slenderness," which was an important early analysis that examines the conflation of thinness and the desirability of heterosexual women. Women co-created these ideals; thus interlocking social and personal limitations are attributed to fatness, not societal constraints. In more recent years, the once widely held belief that thinness was valued only by white middle- and upper-class women has been challenged, although research demonstrates that it is primarily white middle-class women who teach their daughters to engage in fat talk that makes the shame and stigma explicit. Mimi Nichter observed this in *Fat Talk: What Girls and Their Parents Say about Dieting*. Yet young African American girls and Latinas are also impacted by its prevalence. This ties in directly with eating disorders. The academic field of Fat Studies, best explicated in Rothblum and Solovay's *The Fat Studies Reader*, further politicizes fatness and rejects the baseline definitions of healthy weight as creations of a medical profession once again positioning as arbiter of women's health and desirability. Naomi Wolf's *The Beauty Myth* continues this line of thinking: she directly connects some American women's feminist empowerment since the 1970s with a concerted sociopolitical cultural backlash. It aims to limit and curtail female empowerment through relentless pursuit of self-beautification.

Narrating Our Lives: Resistance and Re-Creation

Diverse women have identified, struggled with, and resisted the debilitating effects of these oppressive strictures and ideologies. Through telling our stories, as Mirikitani, Cofer, Haydar, and Hershey do, we give voice to lived realities, increase feminist dialogue amongst ourselves, and combat dominant ideals. Earlier and influential authors of this genre included the Personal Narrative Group's *Interpreting Women's Lives*, Carolyn G. Heilburn's *Writing a Woman's Life*, and Joanne M. Braxton's *Black Women Writing Autobiography*. For women of color, some have felt silenced by their own communities and the mainstream feminist movement. More recently, Audrey Kerr explores how Black women have given voice to their lives in "What Becomes of the Colored Girl?" Here, "Recipe," by Janice Mirikitani (1987), poetically reveals how round (or Western) eyes are sought and constructed. It is a disturbing rendition of a private self-performed alteration of indigenous features in pursuit of acceptability. In her telling of this ritual, she asks readers to find its meaning for themselves. Several years later, Judith Ortiz Cofer's "The Story of My Body" (1993) chronicles her adolescence as a white girl growing up in Puerto Rico. She became aware that she was seen as brown when her family moved to the United States. Her negotiation of race and racism portrays pain, self-realization, and intersectional identities. Her size (height and weight) made her an undesirable athletic teammate and contributed to her bodily alienation. In her homeland she and her mother fit Latina views of stereotypical beauty, but these did not translate to her white-dominated American context. As her family moved across borders and geographical regions within the Americas, shifting definitions of self-image, aesthetics, place, and people determined her perceived value. She was seen at one time as exotic, a form of "othering" non-white women. Yet she resisted these constraints by focusing on her studies, and later her writings, as the true value of her personhood.

Maysan Haydar's "Veiled Intentions: Don't Judge a Muslim Girl by Her Covering" (2003), like Ortiz Cofer's work, details her negotiation of Western and traditional female ideals. Her first wearing of the *hijab* (headscarf) was not motivated by commitment to tradition, politics, or self-assertion. Yet as she became an adult she embraced the *hijab* because she saw it as de-objectifying women. This co-exists amiably alongside her other distinctly Americanized views and personal circumstances. She critiques American condemnation of veiling that associates it with Muslim males' oppression of women. Rather, she sees it as resistance to American women's obsession with standardized/commodified beauty. For Haydar, the modesty that the headscarf symbolizes translates into more respect from men. Yet in a racist American culture it is sometimes read and conflated with anti-Islamic sentiments as backward, terrorist (post- 9/11), or fundamentalist. For her, the issue is one of choice and personal freedom, not culturally constructed limitations.

Laura Hershey's essay "Women and Disability and Poetry (Not Necessarily in that Order)" (2010) grapples with the too-often binary debate: Are disabilities experienced primarily as biological conditions or as political/policy limitations forced on a minority group? She is writing 20 years after the Americans with Disabilities Act (1990) was passed. Originally created for wounded soldiers, it became a turning point for disability rights. Hershey suggests disabled women shed this dualism and work for both: name feelings and daily experiences while working for social justice. Poetry, she believes, offers the perfect bridge to give voice to political outrage alongside nuanced personal experience. Hershey died less than a year after writing her provocative essay. Mia Mingus, a queer disabled woman of color, offers valuable insights from an intersectional perspective. Some now prefer the term "differently abled" to disabled, since it removes the sense of loss and "being less." Others suggest using "people first" language and using terms such as "people with disabilities" (Snow).

Through autobiography, and self-determination, these authors are all finding voice by reinterpreting women's worth – and challenging gendered, racial, bodily, heterosexual, and social class norms.

Discussion Questions

1. How do historical, Western interpretations of women's bodies inform current day beliefs?
2. How does taking the male body as the measure of health and desirability impact women's opportunities, status, and self-perceptions? What are contemporary examples of this?
3. How do race and nationality compound gendered expectations of the ideal body?
4. According to Anderson and Ortiz Cofer, why are athletics and sporting spaces (gyms, playgrounds, competitive sports fields and courts, and so on) so often proving grounds for female and male value?
5. How does capitalism exacerbate ideals of women's worthiness? What role does consumption play in beauty?
6. In the writings by Ortiz Cofer, Haydar, Mirikitani, Weitz, and Hershey, how do women's intersectional identities complicate standards of race, desirability, able-bodiedness, and "normalcy"?
7. Our culture largely presumes that romantic heterosexual love and marriage are ideal. How do medical opinions, consumer culture, beauty standards, and able-bodiedness contribute to this heteronormativity?
8. In the pieces by Steinem and Haydar, how do women – through their material bodies – resist being "othered?"
9. What does autobiographical writing allow women to do?
10. According to Weitz, Steinem, and Hershey, what role has feminism played in redefining women's bodies and value?
11. What have been limitations of feminist reinterpretations of women's bodies and value?

References

Barker-Benfield, G. J. *The Horrors of the Half-Known Life: Male Attitudes towards Women and Sexuality in Nineteenth Century America*. New York: Harper and Row, 1976.

Braxton, Joanne M. *Black Women Writing Autobiography*. Philadelphia: Temple University Press, 1989.

Chernin, Kim. *The Obsession: Reflections on the Tyranny of Slenderness*. New York: Harper and Row, 1981.

Collins, Patricia Hill. "Mammies, Matriarchs, and Other Controlling Images." *Black Feminist Thought: Knowledge, Consciousness, and the Politics of Empowerment*, 2nd ed. New York: Routledge, 2000. 69-96.

Cott, Nancy F. "Passionlessness: An Interpretation of Victorian Sexual Ideology 1790–1850." *Signs* 4.2 (Winter 1978): 219–36.

Ehrenreich, Barbara, and Deidre English. *For Her Own Good: 150 Years of the Experts' Advice to Women*. New York: Anchor Books, 1978.

Heilbrun, Carolyn G. *Writing a Woman's Life*. New York: Ballantine Books, 1979.

Kerr, Audrey. "What Becomes of the Colored Girl? Black Women, Autobiography and Womanist Theology." *Quodibet Journal* 2.3 (Summer 2000). http://www.quodlibet.net/articles/kerr-autobiography.shtml (accessed December 18, 2015).

Lehrer, Susan. *Origins of Protective Labor Legislation for Women, 1905–1925*. New York: SUNY University Press, 1987.

Mingus, Mia. "Feeling the Weight: Some Beginning Notes on Disability, Access, and Love." 2012. https://leavingevidence.wordpress.com/2012/05/08/feeling-the-weight-some-beginning-notes-on-disability-access-and-love/(accessed December 18, 2015).

Nichter, Mimi. *Fat Talk: What Girls and Their Parents Say about Dieting*. Cambridge, MA: Harvard University Press, 2000.

Personal Narratives Group, eds. *Interpreting Women's Lives: Feminist Theory and Personal Narratives*. Bloomington, IN: University of Indiana Press, 1989.

Rich, Adrienne. "Compulsory Heterosexuality and Lesbian Existence." *Signs* 5.4 (Summer 1980): 631–60.

Roth, Rachel. *Making Women Pay: The Hidden Cost of Fetal Rights*. New York: Cornell University Press, 2003.

Rothblum, Esther, and Sandra Solovay, eds. *The Fat Studies Reader*. New York: New York University Press, 2009.

Smith-Rosenberg, Carroll. "Puberty to Menopause: The Cycle of Femininity in Nineteenth-Century America." *Feminist Studies,* Special Double Issue: Women's History 1.3/4 (Winter/Spring 1974): 58–72.

Snow, Kathie. "Examples of People First Language." 2009. www.disabilityisnatural.com (accessed December 18, 2015).

Washington, Harriet A. *Medical Apartheid: The Dark History of Medical Experimentation on Black Americans from Colonial Times to the Present*. New York: Doubleday, 2006.

Wolf, Naomi. *The Beauty Myth: How Images of Beauty Are Used Against Women*. New York: William Morrow, 1991.

6.1

Recipe

Janice Mirikitani

Round Eyes

Ingredients: scissors, Scotch magic transparent tape,
eyeliner – water based, black.
Optional: false eyelashes.

Cleanse face thoroughly.

For best results, powder entire face, including eyelids.
　　(lighter shades suited to total effect desired)

With scissors, cut magic tape 1/16″ wide, 3/4″–1/2″ long –
depending on length of eyelid.

Stick firmly onto mid-upper eyelid area
　　(looking down into handmirror facilitates finding adequate surface)

If using false eyelashes, affix first on lid, folding any
excess lid over the base of eyelash with glue.

Paint black eyeliner on tape and entire lid.

Do not cry.

6.2
A History of Women's Bodies
Rose Weitz

Throughout history, ideas about women's bodies have played a dramatic role in either challenging or reinforcing power relationships between men and women. We can therefore regard these ideas as political tools in an ongoing political struggle. This article presents a brief history of women's bodies, looking at how ideas about the female body have changed over time in western law and biological theory.

Beginning with the earliest written legal codes, and continuing nearly to the present day, the law typically has defined women's bodies as men's property. In ancient societies, women who were not slaves typically belonged to their fathers before marriage and to their husbands thereafter. For this reason, Babylonian law, for example, treated rape as a form of property damage, requiring a rapist to pay a fine to the husband or father of the raped woman, but nothing to the woman herself. Similarly, marriages in ancient societies typically were contracted between prospective husbands and prospective fathers-in-law, with the potential bride playing little if any role.

Women's legal status as property reflected the belief that women's bodies were inherently different from men's in ways that made women both defective and dangerous. This belief comes through clearly in the writings of Aristotle, whose ideas about women's bodies formed the basis for "scientific" discussion of this topic in the west from the fourth century B.C. through the eighteenth century (Martin 1987; Tuana 1993). Aristotle's biological theories centered around the concept of heat. According to Aristotle, only embryos that had sufficient heat could develop into fully human form. The rest became female. In other words, woman was, in Aristotle's words, a "misbegotten man" and a "monstrosity" – less than fully formed and literally half-baked. Building on this premise, Galen, a highly influential Greek doctor, later declared that women's reproductive organs were virtually identical to men's, but were located internally because female embryos lacked the heat needed for those organs to develop fully and externally. This view remained common among doctors until well into the eighteenth century.

Lack of heat, classical scholars argued, also produced a plethora of other deficiencies in women, including a smaller stature, a frailer constitution, a less developed brain, and emotional and moral weaknesses that could endanger any men who fell under women's spell. These ideas later would resonate with ideas about women embedded in Christian interpretations of Mary and Eve. Christian theologians argued that Eve caused the fall from divine grace and the expulsion from the Garden of Eden by succumbing when the snake tempted her with the forbidden fruit. This "original sin" occurred, these theologians argued, because women's nature made them inherently more susceptible to sexual desire and other passions of the flesh, blinding them to reason and morality and making them a constant danger to men's souls. Mary avoided the pitfalls of passion only by remaining virginal. Such ideas later would play a large role in fueling the witch-craft hysteria in early modern Europe and colonial America. Women formed the vast majority of the tens of thousands of people executed as witches during these centuries because both Protestants and Catholics assumed that women were less intelligent than men, more driven by sexual passions, and hence more susceptible to the Devil's blandishments (Barstow 1994).

By the eighteenth century, women's legal and social position in the western world had changed little. When the famous English legal theorist, Sir William Blackstone, published his encyclopedic codification of English law in 1769, non-slave women's legal status still remained closer to that of property than to that of non-slave men. According to Blackstone, "By marriage, the husband and wife are one person in the law; that is, the very being and legal existence of the woman is suspended during the marriage, or at least is incorporated into that of her husband under whose wing, protection and cover she performs everything" (1904, 432). In other words, upon marriage a woman experienced "civil death," losing any rights as a citizen, including the right to own or bestow property, make contracts or sue for legal redress, hold custody of minor children, or keep any wages she earned. Moreover, as her "protector," a husband had a legal right to beat his wife if he believed it necessary, as well as a right to her sexual services. These principles would form the basis of marital law in the United States from its founding.

Both in colonial America and in the United States for its first eighty-nine years, slave women *were* property. Moreover, both the law and contemporary scientific writings often described African-American women (and men) as animals, rather than humans. Consequently, neither slave women nor slave men held any rights of citizenship. By the same token, female African-American slaves were completely subject to their white masters. Rape was common, both as a form of "entertainment" for white men and as a way of breeding more slaves, since the children of slave mothers were automatically slaves, regardless of their fathers' race. Nor did African-American women's special vulnerability to rape end when slavery ended.

Both before and after the Civil War, the rape of African-American women was explained, if not justified, by an ideology that defined African Americans including African-American women, as animalistically hypersexual, and thus responsible for their own rapes (Gilman 1985; Giddings 1995). For example, an article published by a white southern woman on March 17, 1904 in a popular periodical, the *Independent*, declared:

> Degeneracy is apt to show most in the weaker individuals of any race; so Negro women evidence more nearly the popular idea of total depravity than the men do. They are so nearly lacking in virtue that the color of a Negro woman's skin is generally taken (and quite correctly) as a guarantee of her immorality. … I sometimes read of a virtuous Negro woman, hear of them, but the idea is absolutely inconceivable to me.

These ideas about sexuality, combined with ideas about the inherent inferiority of African Americans, are vividly reflected in the 1861 Georgia penal code. That code left it up to the court whether to fine or imprison men who raped African-American women, recommended two to twenty years' imprisonment for white men convicted of raping white women, and mandated the death penalty for African-American men convicted of raping white women (Roberts 1990, 60). Moreover, African-American men typically were lynched before being brought to trial if suspected of raping a white woman, while white men were rarely convicted for raping white women and probably never convicted for raping African-American women.

For both free and slave women in the United States, the legal definition of women's bodies as men's property experienced its first serious challenges during the nineteenth century. In 1839, Mississippi passed the first Married Women's Property Act. Designed primarily to protect family farms and property from creditors rather than to expand the rights of women (Speth 1982), the law gave married women the right to retain property they owned before marriage and wages they earned outside the home. By the end of the nineteenth century, similar laws had been passed in all the states.

Also during the nineteenth century, both white and African-American women won the right to vote in Wyoming, Utah, Colorado, and Idaho, and a national suffrage campaign took root. Beginning with Oberlin College in 1833, a growing number of colleges began accepting women students, including free African-American women, with more than five thousand women graduating in 1900 alone (Flexner 1974, 232). At the same time, the industrial revolution prompted growing numbers of women to seek paid employment. By 1900, the U.S. census listed more than five million women as gainfully employed outside the home (Flexner 1974, 250). This did not reflect any significant changes in the lives of African-American women – who had worked as much as men when slaves and who often worked full-time post-slavery (Jones 1985) – but was a major change for white women.

Each of these changes challenged the balance of power between men and women in American society. In response to these challenges, a counterreaction quickly developed. This counterreaction combined new "scientific" ideas with older definitions of women's bodies as ill or fragile to argue that white middle-class women were unable to sustain the responsibilities of political power or the burdens of education or employment.

Ideas about middle-class women's frailty drew heavily on the writings of Charles Darwin, who had published his groundbreaking *On the Origin of Species* in 1872 (Tuana 1993). As part of his theory of evolution, Darwin argued that males compete for sexual access to females, with only the fittest succeeding and reproducing. As a result, males continually evolve toward greater "perfection." Females, on the other hand, need not compete for males, and therefore are not subject to the same process of natural selection. Consequently, in any species, males are more evolved than females. In addition, Darwin argued, females must expend so much energy on reproduction that they retain little energy for either physical or mental development. As a result, women remain subject to their emotions and passions: nurturing, altruistic, and child-like, but with little sense of either justice or morality.

Darwin's theories meshed well with Victorian ideas about middle-class white women's sexuality, which depicted women as the objects of male desire, emphasized romance and downplayed female sexual desire, and reinforced a sexual double standard. Middle-class women were expected to have passionate and even romantic attachments to other women, but these attachments were assumed to be emotional, rather than physical. Most women who had "romantic friendships" with other women were married to men, and only those few who adopted male clothing or behavior were considered lesbians (Faderman 1981). Lesbianism became more broadly identified and stigmatized only in the early twentieth century, when women's entry into higher education and the workforce enabled some women to survive economically without marrying, and lesbianism therefore became a threat to male power.

With women's increasing entry into education and employment, ideas about the physical and emotional frailty of women – with their strong echoes of both Christian and Aristotelian disdain for women and their bodies – were adopted by nineteenth-century doctors as justifications for keeping women uneducated and unemployed. So, for example:

> The president of the Oregon State Medical Society, F. W. Van Dyke, in 1905, claimed that hard study killed sexual desire in women, took away their beauty, and brought on hysteria, neurasthenia [a mental disorder], dyspepsia [indigestion], astigmatism [a visual disorder], and dysmenorrhea [painful menstruation]. Educated women, he added, could not bear children with ease because study arrested the development of the pelvis at the same time it increased the size of the child's brain, and therefore its head. The result was extensive suffering in childbirth by educated women (Bullough and Voght 1984, 32).

Belief in the frailty of middle-class women's bodies similarly fostered the epidemic rise during the late nineteenth century in gynecological surgery (Barker-Benfield 1976; Longo 1984). Many doctors routinely performed surgery to remove healthy ovaries, uteruses, or clitorises, from women who experienced an extremely wide range of physical and mental symptoms – including symptoms such as rebelliousness or malaise which reflected women's constrained social circumstances more than their physical health. These operations were not only unnecessary but dangerous, with mortality rates of up to thirty-three percent (Longo 1984).

Paradoxically, at the same time that scientific "experts" emphasized the frailty of middle-class white women, they emphasized the robustness of poorer women, both white and nonwhite. As Jacqueline Jones (1985, 15) explains:

> Slaveholders had little use for sentimental platitudes about the delicacy of the female constitution. … There were enough women like Susan Mabry of Virginia, who could pick 400 or 500 pounds of cotton a day (150 to 200 pounds was considered respectable for an average worker) to remove from a master's mind all doubts about the ability of a strong, healthy woman field worker. As a result, he conveniently discarded his time-honored Anglo-Saxon notions about the type of work best suited for women.

Similar attitudes applied to working-class white women. Thus, Dr. Lucien Warner, a popular medical authority, could in 1874 explain how middle-class women were made frail by their affluence, while "the African negress, who toils beside her husband in the fields of the south, and Bridget [the Irish maid], who washes and scrubs and toils in our homes at the north, enjoy for the most part good health, with comparative immunity from uterine disease" (cited in Ehrenreich and English 1973, 12–13).

At any rate, despite the warnings of medical experts, women continued to enter both higher education and the paid workforce. However, although education clearly benefited women, entering the workforce endangered the lives and health of many women due to hazardous working conditions.

Although male workers could hope to improve their working conditions through union agitation, this tactic was far less useful for women, who more often worked in non-unionized jobs, were denied union membership, or were not interested in joining unions. As a result, some feminists began lobbying for protective labor laws that would set maximum working hours for women, mandate rest periods, and so on (Erickson 1982). In 1908, the U.S. Supreme Court first upheld such a law in *Muller v. Oregon*. Unfortunately, it soon became clear that protective labor laws hurt women more than they helped, by bolstering the idea that female workers were inherently weaker than male workers.

Twelve years after the *Muller* decision, in 1920, most female U.S. citizens finally won the right to vote in national elections. (Most Asian-born and Native American women, however, were ineligible for citizenship, and most African-American women – like African-American men – were prevented from voting through legal and illegal means.) Unfortunately, suffrage largely marked the close of decades of feminist activism rather than the start of any broader reforms in women's legal, social, or economic positions.

By the 1960s, women's status had hardly changed. For example, although the four-teenth amendment (passed in 1868) guaranteed equal protection under the law for all U.S. citizens, not until 1971, in *Reed v. Reed*, did the Supreme Court rule that differential treatment based on sex was illegal. Similarly, based still on Blackstone's interpretation of women's legal position and the concept of women as men's prop-erty, until the 1970s courts routinely refused to prosecute wife batterers unless they killed their wives, and not until 1984 did any court convict a man for raping a woman to whom he was married and with whom he still legally resided.

Recognition of these and other inequities led to the emergence of a new feminist movement beginning in the second half of the 1960s (Evans 1979). In its ear-liest days, this movement adopted the rhetoric of liberalism and the civil rights movement, arguing that women and men were morally and intellectually equal and that women's bodies were essentially similar to men's bodies. The (unsuccessful) attempts to pass the Equal Rights Amendment, which stated that "equality of rights under the law shall not be denied or abridged by the United States or any state on account of sex," reflected this strain of thinking about gender.

The goal of these liberal feminists was to achieve equality with men within exist-ing social structures – for example, to get men to assume a fair share of child-care responsibilities. Soon, however, some feminists began questioning whether achiev-ing equality within existing social structures would really help women, or whether women would be served better by radically restructuring society to create more humane social arrangements – for example, establishing communal living arrange-ments in which child care could be more broadly shared rather than trying to allocate child-care responsibilities more equitably within a nuclear family. Along with this questioning of social arrangements came questions about the reality not only of sex differences but also of the categories "male" and "female."

In contrast, a more recent strand of feminist thought, known as "cultural femi-nism," has re-emphasized the idea of inherent differences between men and women. Unlike those who made this argument in the past, however, cultural feminists argue that women's bodies (as well as their minds and moral values) are *superior* to men's. From this perspective, women's ability to create human life makes women (especially mothers) innately more pacifistic, loving, moral, creative, and life-affirming than men (e.g., Daly 1978). For the same reason, some feminists, such as Susan Griffin (1978), now argue that women also have an inherently deeper connection than men to nature and to ecological concerns. (Ironically, many in the antiabortion movement and on the far right use rhetoric similar to that of cultural feminists to argue that women belong at home.)

Despite the differences among feminists in ideology and tactics, all share the goal of challenging accepted ideas about women's bodies and social position. Not surpris-ingly, as the modern feminist movement has grown, a backlash has developed that has attempted to reinforce more traditional ideas (Faludi 1991). This backlash has taken many forms, including (1) increasing pressure on women to control the shape of their bodies, (2) attempts to define premenstrual and postmenopausal women as ill, and (3) the rise of the anti-abortion and "fetal rights" movements.

Throughout history, women have experienced social pressures to maintain acceptable appearances. However, as Susan Faludi (1991), Naomi Wolf (1991), and many others have demonstrated, the backlash against modern feminism seems to have increased these pressures substantially. For example, the average weight of both Miss America winners and *Playboy* centerfolds has decreased steadily since 1978, even though the average height has increased (Wiseman et al. 1992). Current appearance norms call for women to be not only painfully thin, but muscular and buxom – qualities that can occur together only if women spend vast amounts of time on exercise, money on cosmetic surgery, and emotional energy on diet (Seid 1989).

The backlash against feminism also has affected women's lives by stimulating calls for the medical control of premenstrual women. Although first defined in the 1930s, the idea of a "premenstrual syndrome" (PMS) did not garner much attention either inside or outside medical circles until the 1970s. Since then, innumerable popular and medical articles have argued that to function at work or school, women with PMS need medical treatment to control their anger and discipline their behaviors. Similarly, many doctors now believe that menopausal women need drugs to maintain their sexual attractiveness and to control their behavior and emotions.

Finally, the backlash against feminism has restricted women's lives by encouraging the rise of the antiabortion and "fetal rights" movements. Prior to the twentieth century, abortion was generally considered both legally and socially acceptable, although dangerous.* By the mid-twentieth century, abortion had become a safe medical procedure, but was legal only when deemed medically necessary. Doctors were deeply divided, however, regarding when it was necessary, with some performing abortions only to preserve women's lives and others doing so to preserve women's social, psychological, or economic well-being (Luker 1984). To protect themselves legally, beginning in the 1960s, those doctors who favored more lenient indications for abortion, along with women who considered abortion a right, lobbied heavily for broader legal access to abortion. This lobbying culminated in 1973 when the U.S. Supreme Court ruled, in *Roe v. Wade*, that abortion was legal in most circumstances. However, subsequent legislative actions and Court decisions (including the 1976 Hyde Amendment and the Supreme Court's 1989 decision in *Webster v. Reproductive Health Services*) have reduced legal access to abortion substantially, especially for poor and young women.

Embedded in the legal battles over abortion is a set of beliefs about the nature of women and of the fetus (Luker 1984). On one side stand those who argue that unless women have an absolute right to control their own bodies, including the right to abortion, they will never attain fully equal status in society. On the other side stand those who argue that the fetus is fully human and that women's rights to control their bodies must be subjugated to the fetus's right to life.

This latter belief also underlies the broader social and legal pressure for "fetal rights." For example, pregnant women around the country – almost all of them

---

* Editor's note: abortion was illegal for slave women.

nonwhite and poor – have been arrested for abusing alcohol or illegal drugs while pregnant, on the grounds that they had no right to expose their fetuses to harmful substances. Others – again, mostly poor and nonwhite – have been forced to have cesarean sections against their will. In these cases, the courts have ruled that fetuses' interests are more important than women's right to determine what will happen to their bodies – in this case, the right to refuse invasive, hazardous surgery – and that doctors know better than mothers what is in a fetus's best interests. Still other women have been denied jobs by employers who have argued that hazardous work conditions might endanger a pregnant worker's fetus; these employers have ignored evidence that the same conditions would also damage men's sperm and thus any resulting fetuses.

In sum, throughout history, ideas about women's bodies have centrally affected the strictures within which women live. Only by looking at the embodied experiences of women, as well as at how those experiences are socially constructed, can we fully understand women's lives, women's position in society, and the possibilities for resistance against that position.

References

Barker-Benfield, G. J. 1976. *The Horrors of the Half-Known Life: Male Attitudes Towards Women and Sexuality in Nineteenth-Century America*. New York: Harper.

Barstow, Anne Llewellyn. 1994. *Witchcraze: A New History of the European Witch Hunts*. San Francisco: Pandora.

Blackstone, Sir William. 1904. *Commentaries on the Laws of England in Four Books*. vol. 1 edited by George Sharswood. Philadelphia: Lippincott.

Bullough, Vern and Martha Voght. 1984. Women, menstruation, and nineteenth-century medicine. In *Women and Health in America: Historical Readings*, edited by Judith Walzer Leavitt. Madison: University of Wisconsin Press.

Daly, Mary. 1978. *Gyn/Ecology: The Metaethics of Radical Feminism*. Boston: Beacon.

Darwin, Charles. 1872. *On the Origin of Species*. Akron, OH: Werner.

Ehrenreich, Barbara, and Deirdre English. 1973. *Complaints and Disorders: The Sexual Politics of Sickness*. Old Westbury, NY: Feminist Press.

Erickson, Nancy S. 1982. Historical background of "protective" labor legislation: Muller v. Oregon. In *Women and the Law: A Social Historical Perspective*. Vol. 2, edited by D. Kelly Weisberg. Cambridge, MA: Schenkman.

Evans, Sara M. 1979. *Personal Politics: The Roots of Women's Liberation in the Civil Rights Movement and the New Left*. New York: Vintage.

Faderman, Lillian. 1981. *Surpassing the Love of Men: Romantic Friendship and Love Between Women from the Renaissance to the Present*. New York: William Morrow.

Faludi, Susan. 1991. *Backlash: The Undeclared War Against American Women*. New York: Crown.

Flexner, Eleanor. 1974. *Century of Struggle: The Women's Rights Movement in the United States*. New York: Atheneum.

Giddings, Paula. 1995. The last taboo. In *Words of Fire: An Anthology of African-American Feminist Thought*, edited by Beverly Guy-Sheftall. New York: New Press.

Gilman, Sander. 1985. Black bodies, white bodies: Toward an iconography of female sexuality in late nineteenth-century art, medicine, and literature. In *"Race," Writing, and Difference*, edited by Henry Louis Gates. Chicago: University of Chicago Press.

Griffin, Susan. 1978. *Woman and Nature: The Roaring Inside Her*. New York: Harper.

Jones, Jacqueline. 1985. *Labor of Love, Labor of Sorrow: Black Women, Work, and the Family from Slavery to the Present*. New York: Basic.

Longo, Lawrence D. 1984. The rise and fall of Battey's operation: A fashion in surgery. In *Woman and Health in America*, edited by Judith Walzer Leavitt. Madison: University of Wisconsin Press.

Luker, Kristin. 1984. *Abortion and the Politics of Motherhood*. Berkeley: University of California Press.

Martin, Emily. 1987. *The Woman in the Body: A Cultural Analysis of Reproduction*. Boston: Beacon.

Roberts, Dorothy E. 1990. The future of reproductive choice for poor women and women of color. *Women's Rights Law Reporter* 12(2):59–67.

Seid, Roberta Pollack. 1989. *Never Too Thin: Why Women Are at War with Their Bodies*. Englewood Cliffs, NJ: Prentice Hall.

Speth, Linda E. 1982. The Married Women's Property Acts, 1839–1865: Reform, reaction, or revolution? In *Women and the Law: A Social Historical Perspective*. Vol. 2, edited by D. Kelly Weisberg. Cambridge, MA: Schenkman.

Tuana, Nancy. 1993. *The Less Noble Sex: Scientific, Religious, and Philosophical Conceptions of Woman's Nature*. Bloomington: Indiana University Press.

Wiseman, Claire V., James J. Gray, James E. Mosimann, and Anthony H. Ehrens. 1992. Cultural expectations of thinness in women: An update. *International Journal of Eating Disorders* 11:85–89.

Wolf, Naomi. 1991. *The Beauty Myth: How Images of Beauty Are Used Against Women*. New York: William Morrow.

6.3

If Men Could Menstruate

Gloria Steinem

A white minority of the world has spent centuries conning us into thinking that a white skin makes people superior – even though the only thing it really does is make them more subject to ultraviolet rays and to wrinkles. Male human beings have built whole cultures around the idea that penis-envy is "natural" to women – though having such an unprotected organ might be said to make men vulnerable and the power to give birth makes womb-envy at least as logical.

In short, the characteristics of the powerful, whatever they may be, are thought to be better than the characteristics of the powerless – and logic has nothing to do with it.

What would happen, for instance, if suddenly, magically, men could menstruate and women could not?

The answer is clear – menstruation would become an enviable boast-worthy, masculine event:

Men would brag about how long and how much.

Boys would mark the onset of menses, that longed-for proof of manhood, with religious ritual and stag parties.

Congress would fund a National Institute of Dysmenorrhea to help stamp out monthly discomforts.

Sanitary supplies would be federally funded and free. (Of course, some men would still pay for the prestige of commercial brands such as John Wayne Tampons, Muhammad Ali's Rope-a-dope Pads, Joe Namath Jock Shields – "For Those Light Bachelor Days" and Robert "Baretta" Blake Maxi-Pads.)

Military men, right-wing politicians, and religious fundamentalists would cite menstruation ("*men*-struation") as proof that only men could serve in the Army ("you have to give blood to take blood"), occupy political office ("can women be aggressive without that steadfast cycle governed by the planet Mars?"), be priests and ministers ("how could a woman give her blood for our sins?"), or rabbis ("without the monthly loss of impurities, women remain unclean").

Male radicals, left-wing politicians, and mystics, however, would insist that women are equal, just different and that any woman could enter their ranks if only she were willing to self-inflict a major wound every month ("you *must* give blood for the revolution"), recognize the preeminence of menstrual issues, or subordinate her selfness to all men in their Cycle of Enlightenment.

Street guys would brag ("I'm a three-pad man") or answer praise from a buddy ("Man, you lookin' *good*.") by giving fives and saying, "Yeah, man, I'm on the rag!"

TV shows would treat the subject at length. ("Happy Days": Richie and Potsie try to convince Fonzie that he is still "The Fonz," though he has missed two periods in a row.) So would newspapers. (SHARK SCARE THREATENS MENSTRUATING MEN. JUDGE CITES MONTHLY STRESS IN PARDONING RAPIST.) And movies. (Newman and Redford in "Blood Brothers"!)

Men would convince women that intercourse was *more* pleasurable at "that time of the month." Lesbians would be said to fear blood and therefore life itself – though probably only because they needed a good menstruating man.

Of course, male intellectuals would offer the most moral and logical arguments. How could a woman master any discipline that demanded a sense of time, space, mathematics, or measurement, for instance, without that in-built gift for measuring the cycles of the moon and planets – and thus for measuring anything at all? In the rarefied fields of philosophy and religion, could women compensate for missing the rhythm of the universe? Or for their lack of symbolic death-and-resurrection every month?

Liberal males in every field would try to be kind: the fact that "these people" have no gift for measuring life or connecting to the universe, the liberals would explain, should be punishment enough.

And how would women be trained to react? One can imagine traditional women agreeing to all these arguments with a staunch and smiling masochism.

("The ERA would force housewives to wound themselves every month": Phyllis Schlafly. "Your husband's blood is as sacred as that of Jesus – and so sexy, too!" Marabel Morgan.) Reformers and Queen Bees would try to imitate men, and *pretend* to have a monthly cycle. All feminists would explain endlessly that men, too, needed to be liberated from the false idea of Martian aggressiveness, just as women needed to escape the bonds of menses-envy. Radical feminists would add that the oppression of the nonmenstrual was the pattern for all other oppressions. ("Vampires were our first freedom fighters.") Cultural feminists would develop a bloodless imagery in art and literature. Socialist feminists would insist that only under capitalism would men be able to monopolize menstrual blood.

In fact, if men could menstruate, the power justifications could probably go on forever.

If we let them.

6.4
Women and Disability and Poetry
(Not Necessarily in That Order)
Laura Hershey

I've recently been following a conversation, on various web forums, about women and disability and poetry (not necessarily in that order). This discussion was partly catalyzed by Jennifer Bartlett's essay on feminist poetry on the blog delirious hem. In her essay, Bartlett writes about some of the prejudices and mistreatment that she's faced as a woman with cerebral palsy. She also conveys her sense of betrayal that feminist political and literary movements have failed to take seriously, or even notice, disabled women's issues. Bartlett also asks for comments on the intersections between gender oppression and disability oppression, and between feminism and disability rights.

From there, the discussion has migrated in various directions, including onto a listserv about women and poetry to which I subscribe. Interestingly, some tension has developed between people who view disability as a social construct, in which social barriers turn impairments into liabilities and limitations, and those who want their experiences of bodily suffering to be acknowledged. A related argument concerns the distinction between "disability" (conceived as stable, nonmedical, political) and "disease" (disruptive, painful, personal).

None of these arguments are new to me. For decades, the disability community has squabbled over the extent to which disabilities are experienced as inherent problematic biological conditions, or strictly as a social minority status. We've also debated whether to distinguish sharply between disease and disability, resisting their conflation as a symptom of medical colonization of our lives; or to embrace chronic and acute illness as another dimension of the disability experience.

These are, for the most part, dynamic and healthy debates. By questioning and challenging each other, we clarify our understanding of this complex phenomenon called disability.

Dichotomies can become destructive, though. Each side's insistent purity may eclipse the other side's valid insights. Arguments can become dogmatic, squeezing out smaller truths incompatible with the larger position. I've felt these struggles as part of my own intellectual and political development. I'm adamant about the role of external architectural and policy barriers in limiting our opportunities, far more than our disabilities themselves do. I go so far as to sport the slogan, "Cure Society, Not Me." On the other hand, I know there are aspects of my disability that entail real physical hardship. I reject clichés like "suffers from spinal muscular atrophy," and yet there are times – during respiratory distress, for example – when I have to grant that I do suffer, quite apart from the stresses imposed by social structures. And then there are times when it's not either/or, but both/and – when political and architectural structures interact in varied and complex ways with my body's weaknesses, strengths, hungers and responses.

For individuals as well as for communities, both tools are necessary: a political framework for articulating one's relationship to the broader world; and a free, true voice for conveying what wells up from within.

This is why we need poetry. Ultimately, dichotomies can't be resolved by turning up the volume, drowning out disagreements and inconsistencies. To get anywhere near a truthful representation of our lives, we need nuance, texture, color, smell. We need open-ended questions, unexpected answers, unlikely combinations. We need prickly, messy, mundane details, rendered in words as fresh as rainfall. We need the wheeling narrative, the dust-flecked sunlit lyric. We need to gasp, giggle, moan and groan, curse and pray. We need to fulfill the "task" that Virginia Woolf assigned to poets, in her 1932 essay "Letter to a Young Poet" – "to find the relation between things that seem incompatible yet have a mysterious affinity, to absorb every experience that comes your way fearlessly and saturate it completely so that your poem is a whole, not a fragment."

Woolf was right. Life can send us overwhelmingly disparate incidents and sensations. One day's events call for righteous indignation, the next day's loss brings tears. And the day after that? Just a day, when nails must be trimmed, skin sponged of sweat, linens changed, prescriptions refilled. It's up to us as women to take care of business, to name feelings, to lead the charge toward justice. Likewise, it's up to us as poets "to absorb every experience... fearlessly." Onto this fragmented life, so sundered by the demands of survival and by competing analyses, we pour artistic integrity, "saturate it completely so that your poem is a whole."

Women with disabilities, especially, live with all kinds of contradictory experiences. Here are just a few:

* Our lives are largely invisible to the media, to policymakers, and even to many nondisabled feminists; and yet individually we sometimes feel so conspicuous with our obvious differences.

* Like other women, we don't want to be sexually objectified or exploited, but we do resent it when we are seen as asexual.
* Many of us need hands-on support for daily living, and we also bear responsibilities for supporting children, elders, disabled friends; and although we both give and receive care, society recognizes only our care needs, not our caregiving.
* We would like to earn money and respect using our skills and knowledge, but we are too often kept out of the workplace by discrimination, physical barriers, inflexible schedules, and the fear of losing life-sustaining benefits when reporting earned income.

Why should anyone else care about these particular concerns? More to the point, why would anyone want to publish or read poetry written from the perspective a woman living with disability? In the conversation referenced above, several poets reported having their work dismissed by colleagues or editors as mere "disease poetry," with the implication that such writing is confessional, self-indulgent, parochial.

If poetry cannot stretch the imagination to share in another's experience, then what can? I urge all of us, myself included, to ignore any insinuation that our female disabled lives can interest no one but ourselves. Our experiences are as valid as anyone else's, and our interpretations of our own experiences are certainly more valid than other people's projections onto us.

And truly, much of the material of our lives transcends demographics. What could be more universal than having a body, and enduring that body's vicissitudes, answering its demands, discovering its pleasures? I face particular obstacles, from stairs to stares, in maneuvering my body through the world; and writing about these obstacles may illuminate our social spaces in new ways. Who has not, at one time or another, felt imperfect and ostracized? Or felt perfect and accepted, having finally found community?

All of these are part of my experience as a disabled woman. This is the stuff of my poetry.

6.5

Do We Call You Handicapped?

Morrie Turner

6.6

Maintaining Masculinity: Homophobia at Work

Eric Anderson

Once a social space is created for or claimed by men, the maintenance of that space is collectively policed by the social sanctions placed on men's identities and behaviors as a whole. Consequently, the construction of masculinity is reproduced through the policing of both collective social space (such as sport) and an individual's gendered behaviors. Divergence from the stated and unstated masculine behaviors is interpreted as subversive, for transgression undermines the desired level of masculine cohesion in the maintenance of patriarchy. Men are, therefore, ever vigilant in maintaining individual masculinity through near-total homosocial patrolling, as they are under the constant scrutiny of other men.

Sociologist Michael Kimmel (1994, 128) maintains that other men "watch us, rank us, and grant or deny our acceptance into the realm of manhood."[1] This homosocial policing is evident from early childhood, as Barrie Thorne (1999) has shown that elementary school playgrounds have been shown to be highly contested social terrains in which children explicitly define an activity or group as gendered.[2] Social sanctions already serve their purpose of intimidating boys from transgressing gendered space (or behavior) by the second grade, as boys begin to adhere to the mandates of orthodox masculinity modeled to them by older males.

Primarily fearing gay stigma, boys (gay and straight) rigidly police their gendered behaviors to best approximate orthodox masculinity, something Pollack (1999) describes as attempting to be "a real boy." He suggests that, in an attempt to displace homosexual suspicion, boys at a very young age learn not to ask for help, hide weakness, and disguise fear or intimidation. They learn that they must fight when challenged and that they must sacrifice their bodies for the sake of the team. Pollack (1999, 6) calls these mechanisms a "boy code," which he maintains "puts boys and men into a gender straight-jacket that constrains not only them but everyone else, reducing us all as human beings, and eventually making us strangers to ourselves and to one another."[3]

McGuffey and Rich (1999) show that those who cross the boundary (especially boys who move into female space) risk being ostracized and accused of being a sissy or like a girl, or being (directly) accused of homosexuality.[4] Thus, transgression is met with the violent language of homophobic and misogynistic discourse. Terms like *fag* are employed to police and pressure the individual to devalue their behaviors and return to conventional masculinized space and/or behaviors, thereby securing men's privilege over women as a whole.

Athleticism is the primary axis of masculine stratification among school-aged boys, even though athleticism (or the ability to physically dominate others in sport) has little practical value in modern society outside the athletic arena. The most athletic boys occupy the top positions within the masculine hierarchy and the least athletic the bottom. Michael Messner says that, "Every elementary or high school male knows that the more athletic you are, the more popular you are" (1992, 152). High status boys stand to gain considerably from the hierarchy as they earn social prestige and secure resources for themselves. This hierarchy is maintained in high school and university cultures.

Boys with the most masculine capital are provided with many social privileges, including near immunity from homosexual suspicion. This effect is largely a product of the association between athleticism and masculinity. Because masculine capital is achieved through athleticism, and because masculinity is thought to be incompatible with homosexuality, it follows that athletes must not be homosexual. Another way to examine this is to say that the better the athlete is – and the more masculine the sport he plays – the less homosexual suspicion there is about him. Consequently, football players are provided near immunity from homosexual suspicion, while band members are inundated with it. From the top of the hill, the male is able to marginalize others, by using homonegative discourse, and his derision is legitimated because he has earned the respect of peers.

Surprisingly, boys at the top of the masculine hierarchy are actually provided more leeway to transgress the rigid gender boundaries, because few other boys would be willing to challenge their sexuality for fear of social or physical reprisal. For example, the masculine elite boys on elementary school playgrounds have been shown to possess more freedom in transgressing norms in the form of (temporarily) playing so-called girl games. This phenomenon is also found when it comes to homoerotic activities between heterosexual men. The more masculine capital one possesses, the more homoerotic activity they seem able to engage in without having their sexuality questioned. For example, Michael Robidoux's (2001) ethnographic research on semi-professional hockey players shows that they are permitted homosocial play that many would code as homoerotic. Both in Robidoux's and my research, this homoerotic play was expressed on a number of levels. For example, it was found in towel-snapping and wrestling, but it was also found in more homoerotic activities as well. Robidoux found that hockey players often grabbed each other's testicles, and I found this among water polo players as well. Additionally, I found that in my ethnography of heterosexual male cheerleaders, and in my own experience as a collegiate coach, there was a great deal of mock intercourse between heterosexual men. Kirby Schroeder has even found homoerotic expression to be compulsory among men in a military college.[5]

This phenomena illustrates why, when a popular and well-muscled volleyball player accepted my challenge and came to one of my classes dressed in drag, he was met with positive laughter and commendations of his bravery, but when an unknown 115-pound nonathletic male came to the same course in drag (a different quarter), he was received with cold stares and indifference. It is precisely this ironic juxtaposition, that football players are theorized to be able to slap each other on the butt and be thought straight despite it.

Although athleticism has little practical value for men once they disengage from the sporting arena (particularly as masculinity becomes more scripted in professional occupations in later stages of life), the jock identity may be maintained, or the individual may publicly recall his youthful sporting accomplishments in order to influence his level of masculine capital. In other words, masculine glory in one's youth can sometimes be tapped to influence one's perception among peers in the future. I call this the Al Bundy syndrome, after the television sitcom character who proclaims his middle-age masculinity not by virtue of his current athletic prowess, but rather because he once played high school football.

While the masculine hierarchy is mainly built via athleticism, consistent association with femininity or things considered to be consistent with gay males are important determinants in the downgrading of one's masculine capital, whether the association is real or perceived. Sociologist David Plummer points out that an accusation of homosexuality is the primary manner in which to verbally marginalize another male. He maintains that homophobic terms come into currency in elementary school, even though the words may not yet have sexual connotations. Still, he posits that these terms are far from indiscriminate as they tap a complex array of meanings that he says are precisely mapped in peer cultures (2001, 2).

Young boys who slip out of their bounded zones may be able to recoup some of their masculinity and be reabsorbed back into the masculine arena by deflecting the suspicion of homosexuality onto another boy. A higher status boy, for example, who transgresses gender boundaries, might call a lower status boy a fag in an attempt to displace suspicion.[6] By negatively talking about and excluding members who are presumed gay, boys are delineating their public heterosexuality, while collectively endorsing hegemonic masculinity (McGuffey and Rich 1999, 822). In such a manner, the marginalized attempt to gain power and control by marginalizing another, almost as if it were a game of "tag, you're it" with the "it" being the label of homosexuality. More so, in certain highly masculinized social locations, demonstrating one's heterosexuality is not sufficient enough to maintain an unambiguous heterosexual masculinity. In these locations, such as within football culture, it is also important to show opposition and intolerance toward homosexuality (Curry 1991).

Because homosexuality is equated with femininity, in order to avoid accusations of homosexuality, boys must vigilantly adhere to behaviors coded as the opposite of feminine at all times, something also described as fem-phobia (Bailey 2003). Should boys transgress these boundaries, they are quickly reminded of their transgression through a litany of homophobic and misogynistic scripts. Sociologists McGuffey and Rich show, for example, a case in which older boys observed a seven-year-old crying and said that he will "probably be gay when he grows up." To these young boys, being soft and/or emotional is a quality associated with females, and a boy possessing such characteristics must subsequently be gay (1999, 81).

In this manner homosexual accusation marginalizes boys, and their status as a marginalized boy is then naturalized through their association with other marginalized people. Olympic gold medalist Mark Tewksbury (who came out after retiring from swimming in 1998) says that at the age of fourteen, when a baseball flew by him, he elicited a characteristically feminine scream that prompted other boys to call him a fag. He said, "Within hours fag was written on my locker, and from then on out I was labeled the fag in school."

Highlighting the vicious nature of homophobic discourse and the use of stigma in the policing of masculine behavior, once a boy is labeled as gay, few other boys will associate with him. The stigma of homosexuality brings with it a guilt-by-association fear that the stigma will rub off onto those not already marginalized. In this aspect homosexuality is looked upon as a contaminant, similar to the childhood notion of cooties. For example, Tewksbury told me that once he was labeled a fag, his classmates turned against him, alienating him, for fear of association with a known deviant. Similarly, after I came out of the closet as an openly gay high school coach my athletes were frequently perceived as gay because they had a gay coach. Also illustrating the contaminant effect, McGuffey and Rich quote a nine-year-old boy yelling, "I don't care if I have to sit out the whole summer 'cause I'm not going to let that faggot touch me!" (1991, 81). Making boys contaminated in this way sends a strong warning to the other boys not to act like a girl, or they too will be isolated and ostracized by their male peers.

The homosocial patrolling may continue into adulthood, especially in the athletic arena. It has, for example, been discovered that in adult male figure skaters, "kind of feminine" is a phrase used to police the boundaries of acceptable heterosexual behavior (Adams 1993), and my research on collegiate heterosexual male cheerleaders finds both homosocial and institutional policing of men's behaviors designed to distance men from homosexuality. For example, in one cheerleading association, certain dance movements or stunts are considered too feminine and are therefore associated with the stigma of homosexuality (Anderson 2004).

Because homophobic and misogynistic discourse is used to police masculine behaviors, the terms that are most commonly employed are *faggot, fag, pussy,* and *wuss.*[7] None of this is to say, however, that these are the only derogatory terms males use in derision of each other. Certainly, they use a variety of terms related to sex and biology. Michael Messner maintains that these forms of homophobic discourse are also connected to misogyny.

> In short, though children obviously do not intend it, through this sort of banter they teach each other that sex, whether of the homosexual or heterosexual kind, is a relational act of domination and subordination. The "men" are the ones who are on top, in control, doing the penetrating and fucking. Women, or penetrated men, are subordinate, degraded, and dehumanized objects of sexual aggression. (2002, 33)

This is just one manner in which homophobia also serves as a form of sexism.[8]

Homophobic language is also used as a way to motivate males into increased performance. Openly gay (retired) professional baseball player Billy Bean first heard the word *faggot* used to "motivate" in the fourth grade.

What, exactly was a faggot? How did faggots run? Clearly, it wasn't a good thing. It was probably the worst thing imaginable. It equaled weakness and timidity, everything a budding, insecure jock wanted to avoid.

Bean continued by saying that he has heard every coach he has ever had since the fourth grade use the term, even through the professional leagues. "As motivational strategy, it was effective. Coaches invoked the terms again and again. Players responded, almost reflexively raising their intensity level" (2003, 107). Similarly, a gay high school swimmer told me:

> I just grew up hearing the word fag all the time. I didn't really know what it meant, but I was damn sure that whatever it was I wasn't going to be one of them. I think I learned that it had to do with not acting like a girl and stuff early on, but by the time I was in maybe sixth grade, I knew that it meant that you weren't supposed to be attracted to guys; which was fine for me at the time, because I wasn't. Or at least I didn't know I was. But by the time I hit high school – it was a different story.

Homophobic discourse is used indiscriminately against any boy who acts in discord with masculine behaviors, whether he is gay or not. In fact, many straight athletes tell me that they questioned their sexuality because of the labeling of their feminine behavior. Matt, a heterosexual runner told me, "I used to think maybe I am gay. People called me gay all the time, so I really had to stop and question, am I?"

As a working hypothesis I maintain that while both homophobic and misogynistic discourse are used to establish dominance of men over women and men over other men, homophobic discourse is more effective in marginalizing other men because, unlike terms associated with femininity, a boy can actually *be* gay. While I frequently hear from heterosexual men that the litany of homophobic discourse led them to question their sexuality, I've yet to meet a male who questioned his sex as a result of being called a misogynistic term.

Notes

1. For a very good account of the relationship between masculinity and homophobia, see Kimmel (1994).
2. Barrie Thorne's *Gender Play* provides a thoughtful ethnography of boys and girls and how they are not simply passive agents of top-down socialization, like sex-role theory maintains. Rather, Thorne showed that boys and girls maintain considerable agency in the construction of normative gender practices.
3. Further research would have to be conducted to see if the reduction in homophobia at the national level has trickled down to elementary school children.
4. Shawn McGuffey and Lindsey Rich (1999) document elementary school-aged children and their use of homophobia to police masculine behaviors and construct peer hierarchies even before they know what homosexuality is.

5. Graduate student Kirby Schroeder, at the University of Chicago, is working on a dissertation in which he examines compulsory homosexuality amongst heterosexual men at a military college. Michael Robidoux (2001) has written an excellent ethnography of hockey players and the construction of masculinity.
6. This is similar to the findings of Hondagneu-Sotelo and Messner (1994) or Majors (1990), who both found that marginalized men may display masculine bravado in an attempt to act powerful when actually in a state of powerlessness.
7. For an excellent article on the subject, see Plummer (1999).
8. For an excellent discussion on the use of homophobia as a tool of sexism, see Suzanne Pharr (1997).

References

Adams, M.L. 1993. To be an ordinary hero: Male figure skaters and the ideology of gender. In T. Haddad (Ed.), *Men and Masculinities*. Toronto: Canadian School Press.

Anderson, Eric. 2004. *Masculine identities of male nurses and cheerleaders: Declining homophobia and the emergence of inclusive masculinity*. Dissertation, University of California, Irvine.

Bailey, Michael J. 2003. *The man who would be queen: The science of gender-bending and transsexualism*. Washington DC: Joseph Henry Press.

Bean, Billy with Bull, Chris. 2003. *Going the other way: Lessons from a life in and out of major-league baseball*. New York: Marlowe and Company.

Curry, Timothy. 1991. Fraternal bonding in the locker room: A profeminist analysis of talk about competition and women. *Sociology of Sport Journal*, 8(2): 119–35.

Hondagneu-Sotelo, Pierrete and Messner, Michael. 1994. Gender display and men's power. In H. Brod and M. Kaufman (Eds.), *Theorizing masculinities* (200–18). Thousand Oaks, CA: Sage.

Kimmel, Michael. 1994. Masculinity as homophobia: Fear, shame, and silence in the construction of gender identity. In H. Brod and M. Kaufman (Eds.), *Theorizing Masculinities*. Thousand Oaks, CA: Sage.

Majors, Richard. 1990. Cool pose: Black masculinity and sport. In Michael Messner and Donald Sabo (Eds.), *Sport, men and the gender order*. Champaign, IL: Human Kinetics.

McGuffey, Shawn and Rich, Lindsey. 1999. Playing in the gender transgression zone: Race, class, and hegemonic masculinity in middle childhood. *Gender & Society*, 13(5): 608–10.

Messner, Michael. 1992. *Power at Play: Sports and the problem of masculinity*. Boston: Beacon Press.

Messner, Michael. 2002. *Taking the field: Women, men, and sports*. Minneapolis: University of Minnesota Press.

Pharr, Suzanne. 1997. Homophobia: *A weapon of sexism*. Berkeley, CA: Chardon Press.

Plummer, David. 2001. Policing manhood: New theories about the social significance of homophobia. In C. Wood (Ed.), *Sexual positions: An Australian view*. Melbourne: Hill of Content/Collins.

Pollack, William. 1999. *Real boys: Rescuing our sons from the myth of boyhood*. New York: Henry Holt and Company.

Robidoux, Michael. 2001. *Men at Play: A working understanding of professional hockey*. Quebec: McGill-Queen's University Press.

Thorne, Barrie. 1999. Girls and boys together. .. but mostly apart: Gender arrangements in elementary school. In Michael Kimmel and Michael Messner (Eds.), *Men's lives*, 4th ed. Boston: Allyn and Bacon.

6.7
The Story of My Body
Judith Ortiz Cofer

Migration is the story of my body.

– Víctor Hernández Cruz

Skin

I was born a white girl in Puerto Rico but became a brown girl when I came to live in the United States. My Puerto Rican relatives called me tall; at the American school, some of my rougher classmates called me Skinny Bones, and the Shrimp because I was the smallest member of my classes all through grammar school until high school, when the midget Gladys was given the honorary post of front row center for class pictures and scorekeeper, bench warmer, in P.E. I reached my full stature of five feet in sixth grade.

I started out life as a pretty baby and learned to be a pretty girl from a pretty mother. Then at ten years of age I suffered one of the worst cases of chicken pox I have ever heard of. My entire body, including the inside of my ears and in between my toes, was covered with pustules which in a fit of panic at my appearance I scratched off my face, leaving permanent scars. A cruel school nurse told me I would always have them – tiny cuts that looked as if a mad cat had plunged its claws deep into my skin. I grew my hair long and hid behind it for the first years of my adolescence. This was when I learned to be invisible.

Color

In the animal world it indicates danger: the most colorful creatures are often the most poisonous. Color is also a way to attract and seduce a mate. In the human world color triggers many more complex and often deadly reactions. As a Puerto Rican girl born of "white" parents, I spent the first years of my life hearing people refer to me as *blanca*, white. My mother insisted that I protect myself from the intense island sun because I was more prone to sunburn than some of my darker, *trigueño* playmates. People were always commenting within my hearing about how my black hair contrasted so nicely with my "pale" skin. I did not think of the color of my skin consciously except when I heard the adults talking about complexion. It seems to me that the subject is much more common in the conversation of mixed-race peoples than in mainstream United States society, where it is a touchy and sometimes even embarrassing topic to discuss, except in a political context. In Puerto Rico I heard many conversations about skin color. A pregnant woman could say, "I hope my baby doesn't turn out *prieto*" (slang for "dark" or "black") "like my husband's grandmother, although she was a good-looking *negra* in her time." I am a combination of both, being olive-skinned – lighter than my mother yet darker than my fair-skinned father. In America, I am a person of color, obviously a Latina. On the Island I have been called everything from a *paloma blanca*, after the song (by a black suitor), to *la gringa*.

My first experience of color prejudice occurred in a supermarket in Paterson, New Jersey. It was Christmastime, and I was eight or nine years old. There was a display of toys in the store where I went two or three times a day to buy things for my mother, who never made lists but sent for milk, cigarettes, a can of this or that, as she remembered from hour to hour. I enjoyed being trusted with money and walking half a city block to the new, modern grocery store. It was owned by three good-looking Italian brothers. I liked the younger one with the crew-cut blond hair. The two older ones watched me and the other Puerto Rican kids as if they thought we were going to steal something. The oldest one would sometimes even try to hurry me with my purchases, although part of my pleasure in these expeditions came from looking at everything in the well-stocked aisles. I was also teaching myself to read English by sounding out the labels in packages: L&M cigarettes, Borden's homogenized milk, Red Devil potted ham, Nestle's chocolate mix, Quaker oats, Bustelo coffee, Wonder bread, Colgate toothpaste, Ivory soap, and Goya (makers of products used in Puerto Rican dishes) everything – these are some of the brand names that taught me nouns. Several times this man had come up to me, wearing his blood-stained butcher's apron, and towering over me had asked in a harsh voice whether there was something he could help me find. On the way out I would glance at the younger brother who ran one of the registers and he would often smile and wink at me.

It was the mean brother who first referred to me as "colored." It was a few days before Christmas, and my parents had already told my brother and me that since we were in Los Estados now, we would get our presents on December 25 instead of Los Reyes, Three Kings Day, when gifts are exchanged in Puerto Rico. We were to give them a wish list that they would take to Santa Claus, who apparently lived in the Macy's store downtown – at least that's where we had caught a glimpse of him when we went shopping. Since my parents were timid about entering the fancy store, we did not approach the huge man in the red suit. I was not interested in sitting on a stranger's lap anyway. But I did covet Susie, the talking schoolteacher doll that was displayed in the center aisle of the Italian brothers' supermarket. She talked when you pulled a string on her back. Susie had a limited repertoire of three sentences: I think she could say: "Hello, I'm Susie Schoolteacher," "Two plus two is four," and one other thing I cannot remember. The day the older brother chased me away, I was reaching to touch Susie's blonde curls. I had been told many times, as most children have, not to touch anything in a store that I was not buying. But I had been looking at Susie for weeks. In my mind, she was my doll. After all, I had put her on my Christmas wish list. The moment is frozen in my mind as if there were a photograph of it on file. It was not a turning point, a disaster, or an earth-shaking revelation. It was simply the first time I considered – if naively – the meaning of skin color in human relations.

I reached to touch Susie's hair. It seems to me that I had to get on tiptoe, since the toys were stacked on a table and she sat like a princess on top of the fancy box she came in. Then I heard the booming "Hey, kid, what do you think you're doing!" spoken very loudly from the meat counter. I felt caught, although I knew I was not doing anything criminal. I remember not looking at the man, but standing there, feeling humiliated because I knew everyone in the store must have heard him yell at me. I felt him approach, and when I knew he was behind me, I turned around to face the bloody butcher's apron. His large chest was at my eye level. He blocked my way. I started to run out of the place, but even as I reached the door I heard him shout after me: "Don't come in here unless you gonna buy something. You PR kids put your dirty hands on stuff. You always look dirty. But maybe dirty brown is your natural color." I heard him laugh and someone else too in the back. Outside in the sunlight I looked at my hands. My nails needed a little cleaning as they always did, since I liked to paint with watercolors, but I took a bath every night. I thought the man was dirtier than I was in his stained apron. He was also always sweaty – it showed in big yellow circles under his shirt-sleeves. I sat on the front steps of the apartment building where we lived and looked closely at my hands, which showed the only skin I could see, since it was bitter cold and I was wearing my quilted play coat, dungarees, and a knitted navy cap of my father's. I was not pink like my friend Charlene and her sister Kathy, who had blue eyes and light brown hair. My skin is the color of the coffee my grandmother made, which was half milk, *leche con café* rather than *café con leche*. My mother is the opposite mix. She has a lot of café in her color. I could not understand how my skin looked like dirt to the supermarket man.

I went in and washed my hands thoroughly with soap and hot water, and borrowing my mother's nail file, I cleaned the crusted watercolors from underneath my nails. I was pleased with the results. My skin was the same color as before, but I knew I was clean. Clean enough to run my fingers through Susie's fine gold hair when she came home to me.

Size

My mother is barely four feet eleven inches in height, which is average for women in her family. When I grew to five feet by age twelve, she was amazed and began to use the word tall to describe me, as in "Since you are tall, this dress will look good on you." As with the color of my skin, I didn't consciously think about my height or size until other people made an issue of it. It is around the preadolescent years that in America the games children play for fun become fierce competitions where everyone is out to "prove" they are better than others. It was in the playground and sports fields that my size-related problems began. No matter how familiar the story is, every child who is the last chosen for a team knows the torment of waiting to be called up. At the Paterson, New Jersey, public schools that I attended, the volleyball or softball game was the metaphor for the battlefield of life to the inner city kids – the black kids versus the Puerto Rican kids, the whites versus the blacks versus the

Puerto Rican kids; and I was 4 F, skinny, short, bespectacled, and apparently impervious to the blood thirst that drove many of my classmates to play ball as if their lives depended on it. Perhaps they did. I would rather be reading a book than sweating, grunting, and running the risk of pain and injury. I simply did not see the point in competitive sports. My main form of exercise then was walking to the library, many city blocks away from my barrio.

Still, I wanted to be wanted. I wanted to be chosen for the teams. Physical education was compulsory, a class where you were actually given a grade. On my mainly all A report card, the C for compassion I always received from the P.E. teachers shamed me the same as a bad grade in a real class. Invariably, my father would say: "How can you make a low grade for *playing games?*" He did not understand. Even if I had managed to make a hit (it never happened) or get the ball over that ridiculously high net, I already had a reputation as a "shrimp," a hopeless nonathlete. It was an area where the girls who didn't like me for one reason or another – mainly because I did better than they on academic subjects – could lord it over me; the playing field was the place where even the smallest girl could make me feel powerless and inferior. I instinctively understood the politics even then; how the *not* choosing me until the teacher forced one of the team captains to call my name was a coup of sorts – there, you little show-off, tomorrow you can beat us in spelling and geography, but this afternoon you are the loser. Or perhaps those were only my own bitter thoughts as I sat or stood in the sidelines while the big girls were grabbed like fish and I, the little brown tadpole, was ignored until Teacher looked over in my general direction and shouted, "Call Ortiz," or, worse, "Somebody's *got* to take her."

No wonder I read Wonder Woman comics and had Legion of Super Heroes daydreams. Although I wanted to think of myself as "intellectual," my body was demanding that I notice it. I saw the little swelling around my once-flat nipples, the fine hairs growing in secret places; but my knees were still bigger than my thighs, and I always wore long- or half-sleeve blouses to hide my bony upper arms. I wanted flesh on my bones – a thick layer of it. I saw a new product advertised on TV. Wate-On. They showed skinny men and women before and after taking the stuff, and it was a transformation like the ninety-seven-pound-weakling-turned-into-Charles-Atlas ads that I saw on the back covers of my comic hooks. The Wate-On was very expensive. I tried to explain my need for it in Spanish to my mother, but it didn't translate very well, even to my ears – and she said with a tone of finality, eat more of my good food and you'll get fat – anybody can get fat. Right. Except me. I was going to have to join a circus someday as Skinny Bones, the woman without flesh.

Wonder Woman was stacked. She had a cleavage framed by the spread wings of a golden eagle and a muscular body that has become fashionable with women only recently. But since I wanted a body that would serve me in P.E., hers was my ideal. The breasts were an indulgence I allowed myself. Perhaps the daydreams of bigger girls were more glamorous, since our ambitions are filtered through our needs, but I wanted first a powerful body. I daydreamed of leaping up above the gray landscape of the city to where the sky was clear and blue, and in anger and self-pity, I fantasized about scooping my enemies up by their hair from the playing fields and dumping them on a barren asteroid. I would put the P.E. teachers each on their own rock in space too, where they would be the loneliest people in the universe, since I knew they had no "inner resources," no imagination, and in outer space, there would be no air for them to fill their deflated volleyballs with. In my mind all P.E. teachers have blended into one large spiky-haired woman with a whistle on a string around her neck and a volleyball under one arm. My Wonder Woman fantasies of revenge were a source of comfort to me in my early career as a shrimp.

I was saved from more years of P.E. torment by the fact that in my sophomore year of high school I transferred to a school where the midget, Gladys, was the focal point of interest for the people who must rank according to size. Because her height was considered a handicap, there was an unspoken rule about mentioning size around Gladys, but of course, there was no need to say anything. Gladys knew her place: front row center in class photographs. I gladly moved to the left or to the right of her, as far as I could without leaving the picture completely.

Looks

Many photographs were taken of me as a baby by my mother to send to my father, who was stationed overseas during the first two years of my life. With the army in Panama when I was born, he later traveled often on tours of duty with the navy. I was a healthy, pretty baby. Recently, I read that people are drawn to big-eyed round-faced creatures, like puppies, kittens, and certain other mammals and marsupials, koalas, for example, and, of course, infants. I was all eyes, since my head and body, even as I grew older, remained thin and small-boned. As a young child I got a lot of attention from my relatives and many other people we met in our barrio. My mother's beauty may have had something to do with how much attention we got from strangers in stores and on the street. I can imagine it. In the pictures I have seen of us together, she is a stunning young woman by Latino standards: long, curly black hair, and round curves in a compact frame. From her I learned how to move, smile, and talk like an attractive woman. I remember going into a bodega for our groceries and being given candy by the proprietor as a reward for being *bonita*, pretty.

I can see in the photographs, and I also remember, that I was dressed in the pretty clothes, the stiff, frilly dresses, with layers of crinolines underneath, the glossy patent leather shoes, and, on special occasions, the skull-hugging little hats and the white gloves that were popular in the late fifties and early sixties. My mother was proud of my looks, although I was a bit too thin. She could dress me up like a doll and take me by the hand to visit relatives, or go to the Spanish mass at the Catholic church, and show me off. How was I to know that she and the others who called me "pretty" were representatives of an aesthetic that would not apply when I went out into the mainstream world of school?

In my Paterson, New Jersey, public schools there were still quite a few white children, although the demographics of the city were changing rapidly. The original waves of Italian and Irish immigrants, silk-mill workers, and laborers in the cloth industries had been "assimilated." Their children were now the middle-class parents of my peers. Many of them moved their children to the Catholic schools that proliferated enough to have leagues of basketball teams. The names I recall hearing still ring in my cars: Don Bosco High versus St. Mary's High, St. Joseph's versus St. John's. Later I too would be transferred to the safer environment of a Catholic school. But I started school at Public School Number 11. I came there from Puerto Rico, thinking myself a pretty girl, and found that the hierarchy for popularity was as follows: pretty white girl, pretty Jewish girl, pretty Puerto Rican girl, pretty black girl. Drop the last two categories; teachers were too busy to have more than one favorite per class, and it was simply understood that if there was a big part in the school play, or any competition where the main qualification was "presentability" (such as escorting a school visitor to or from the principal's office), the classroom's public address speaker would be requesting the pretty and/or nice-looking white boy or girl. By the time I was in the sixth grade, I was sometimes called by the principal to represent my class because I dressed neatly (I knew this from a progress report sent to my mother, which I translated for her) and because all the "presentable" white girls had moved to the Catholic schools (I later surmised this part). But I was still not one of the popular girls with the boys. I remember one incident where I stepped out into the playground in my baggy gym shorts and one Puerto Rican boy said to the other: "What do you think?" The other one answered: "Her face is OK, but look at the toothpick legs." The next best thing to a compliment I got was when my favorite male teacher, while handing out the class pictures, commented that with my long neck and delicate features I resembled the movie star Audrey Hepburn. But the Puerto Rican boys had learned to respond to a fuller figure: long necks and a perfect little nose were not what they looked for in a girl. That is when I decided I was a "brain." I did not settle into the role easily. I was nearly devastated by what the chicken pox episode had done to my self-image. But I looked into the mirror less often after I was told that I would always have scars on my face, and I hid behind my long black hair and my books.

After the problems at the public school got to the point where even nonconfrontational little me got beaten up several times, my parents enrolled me at St. Joseph's High School. I was then a minority of one among the Italian and Irish kids. But I found several good friends there – other girls who took their studies seriously. We did our homework together and talked about the Jackies. The Jackies were two popular girls, one blonde and the other red-haired, who had women's bodies. Their curves showed even in the blue jumper uniforms with straps that we all wore. The blonde Jackie would often let one of the straps fall off her shoulder, and although she, like all of us, wore a white blouse underneath, all the boys stared at her arm. My friends and I talked about this and practiced letting our straps fall off our shoulders. But it wasn't the same without breasts or hips.

My final two and a half years of high school were spent in Augusta, Georgia, where my parents moved our family in search of a more peaceful environment. There we became part of a little community of our army-connected relatives and friends. School was yet another matter. I was enrolled in a huge school of nearly two thousand students that had just that year been forced to integrate. There were two black girls and there was me. I did extremely well academically. As to my social life, it was, for the most part, uneventful – yet it is in my memory blighted by one incident. In my junior year, I became wildly infatuated with a pretty white boy. I'll call him Ted. Oh, he was pretty: yellow hair that fell over his forehead, a smile to die for – and he was a great dancer. I watched him at Teen Town, the youth center at the base where all the military brats gathered on Saturday nights. My father had retired from the navy, and we had all our base privileges – one other reason we had moved to Augusta. Ted looked like an angel to me. I worked on him for a year before he asked me out. This meant maneuvering to be within the periphery of his vision at every possible occasion. I took the long way to my classes in school just to pass by his locker, I went to football games, which I detested, and I danced (I too was a good dancer) in front of him at Teen Town – this took some fancy footwork, since it involved subtly moving my partner toward the right spot on the dance floor. When Ted finally approached me, "A Million to One" was playing on the jukebox, and when he took me into his arms, the odds suddenly turned in my favor. He asked me to go to a school dance the following Saturday. I said yes, breathlessly. I said yes, but there were obstacles to surmount at home. My father did not allow me to date casually. I was allowed to go to major events like a prom or a concert with a boy who had been properly screened. There was such a boy in my life, a neighbor who wanted to be a Baptist missionary and was practicing his anthropological skills on my family. If I was desperate to go some-where and needed a date, I'd resort to Gary. This is the type of religious nut that Gary was: when the school bus did not show up one day, he put his hands over his face and prayed to Christ to get us a way to get to school. Within ten minutes a mother in a station wagon, on her way to town, stopped to ask why we weren't in school. Gary informed her that the Lord had sent her just in time to find us a way to get there in time for roll call. He assumed that I was impressed. Gary was even good-looking in a bland sort of way, but he kissed me with his lips tightly pressed together. I think Gary probably ended up marrying a native woman from wherever he may have gone to preach the Gospel according to Paul. She probably believes that all white men pray to God for transportation and kiss with their mouths closed. But it was Ted's mouth, his whole beautiful self, that concerned me in those days. I knew my father would say no to our date, but I planned to run away from home if necessary. I told my mother how important this date was. I cajoled and pleaded with her from Sunday to Wednesday. She listened to my arguments and must have heard the note of desperation in my voice. She said very gently to me: "You better be ready for disappointment." I did not ask what she meant. I did not want her fears for me to taint my happiness. I asked her to tell my father about my date. Thursday at breakfast my father looked at me across the table with his eyebrows together. My mother looked at him with her mouth set in a straight line. I looked down at my bowl of cereal. Nobody said anything. Friday I tried on every dress in my closet. Ted would be picking me up at six on Saturday: dinner and then the sock hop at school. Friday night I was in my room doing my nails or something else in preparation for Saturday (I know I groomed myself nonstop all week) when the telephone rang. I ran to get it. It was Ted. His voice sounded funny when he said my name, so funny that I felt compelled to ask: "Is something wrong?" Ted blurted it all out without a preamble. His father had asked who he was going out with. Ted had told him my name. "Ortiz? That's Spanish, isn't it?" the father had asked. Ted had told him yes, then shown him my picture in the yearbook. Ted's father had shaken his head. No. Ted would not be taking me out. Ted's father had known Puerto Ricans in the army. He had lived in New York City while studying architecture and had seen how the spics lived. Like rats. Ted repeated his father's words to me as if I should understand *his* predicament when I heard why he was breaking our date. I don't remember what I said before hanging up. I do recall the darkness of my room that sleepless night and the heaviness of my blanket in which I wrapped myself like a shroud. And I remember my parents' respect for my pain and their gentleness toward me that weekend. My mother did not say "I warned you," and I was grateful for her understanding silence.

In college, I suddenly became an "exotic" woman to the men who had survived the popularity wars in high school, who were now practicing to be worldly: they had to act liberal in their politics, in their lifestyles, and in the women they went out with. I dated heavily for a while, then married young. I had discovered that I needed stability more than social life. I had brains for sure and some talent in writing. These facts were a constant in my life. My skin color, my size, and my appearance were variables – things that were judged according to my current self-image, the aesthetic values of the times, the places I was in, and the people I met. My studies, later my writing, the respect of people who saw me as an individual person they cared about, these were the criteria for my sense of self-worth that I would concentrate on in my adult life.

6.8
veiled intentions: don't judge a muslim girl by her covering

maysan haydar

O Prophet! Tell thy wives and daughters and the
believing women that they should cast their outer
garments over their persons. That is most convenient
that they should be known and not be molested.

— The Quran, Chapter 33, Verse 59

And say to the believing women that they should
lower their gaze and guard their modesty: that they
should not display their beauty and ornaments except

what ordinarily appears thereof; that they
should draw their veils over their bosoms and not
display their beauty ...

– The Quran, Chapter 24, Verse 30–31

I have a confession to make.

I've been covering my hair, as is prescribed for Muslim women, since I was twelve years old. And while there are many good reasons for doing so, I wasn't motivated by a desire to be different, to honor tradition or to make a political statement.

I wanted the board game Girl Talk.

When girls from our small, Midwestern Muslim community donned their first *hijab* (headscarf), their families rewarded them with parties and monetary gifts. At twelve, I wasn't nearly as physically developed as a Muslim girl is supposed to be when she starts covering, but I desperately wanted Girl Talk. I knew that if I announced my intention to begin veiling in the board game aisle at Kmart, I could ask for anything and receive it.

My choice of Girl Talk as reward for taking on a religious responsibility is amusing to me now, because it's so antithetical to what veiling is supposed to represent. Girl Talk was the ultimate slumber party game, where players performed gags or revealed embarrassing secrets, then got to choose from four kinds of fortune cards as a prize. My favorite cards hooked me up with the class president, the football captain or a hunky lifeguard who saved me from drowning. And I still have a sheet of "zit stickers," which were meant to punish gamers who failed to share their dirt.

Now that I'm twenty-five and have worn a veil for more than half my life, I can admit to this shallow beginning, which is so far from my reason for veiling today. As an adult, I embrace the veil's modesty, which allows me to be seen as a whole person instead of a twenty-piece chicken dinner. In spite of the seeming contradictions of my life – I'm married to a white man who was raised Catholic, I love heavy metal, I consider myself a feminist, and I sport a few well-disguised piercings – I follow my religion's standard of modesty and appearance. It's only now, after comparing my turbulent teen experiences with those of other women, that I can fully appreciate how much of a saving grace this small piece of cloth was.

Much to my chagrin, many Americans see veiling as an oppressive tool forced on Muslim women by the men in our culture. Yet, the practice of covering hair and body is a choice for many women – and it is not specific to Islam. All the monotheistic religions (Christianity, Judaism and Islam) advocate modesty in dress, though the interpretation of "modesty" varies greatly. Ironically, the population that spends millions on beauty products, plastic surgery and self-help guides is the same one that takes pity on me for being so "helpless" and "oppressed." On a New York City bus a couple weeks ago, I sat with another woman, also veiled, but wearing a traditional *jilbab* (a cloak that women wear over their clothing). A girl two seats over remarked to her friend, while flipping her hair for effect, that she couldn't understand how we could dress this way. "Me, I got to be *free*."

To my eyes, her idea of freedom involved a complicated hairstyle, loads of makeup and jeans she probably had to sew herself into. If anything, I would find that ensemble more caging, more oppressive and more painful than clothes that allow me to walk in front of construction sites confidently, with minimal risk of harassment. (Construction workers may feel obligated to say something to every passing woman, but I often get things like "I like your skirt!" or "Girl, I would marry you!" – harmless compared to the degradation I've heard many women complain about.)

As for freedom, my parents have a healthy understanding of Islam, especially the Quranic verse "Let there be no compulsion in religion" (2:256). Having been raised in religiously different homes themselves (Mom: very liberal, European-minded, not so religious; Dad: religious, culturally structured gender roles and expectations), they only practiced traditions that they understood, accepted and believed. Thus, my mother knew the best way to introduce veiling to me was to emphasize its feminist, forward-thinking reasons: Covering removes that first level of being judged, of being assessed based on my measurements, and it absolves me of the need or desire to be wanted solely for my looks. My choice of Girl Talk didn't showcase a deep understanding of that idea. But reflecting back, I see that wearing a scarf greatly influenced how people viewed me and my goals, before I could ever appreciate that it was having that effect.

In high school, my interactions with the opposite sex were different than the norm. If I hadn't yet been inclined to deal with boys in an unpressured, ungiggly, un-made-up way, the scarf shoved me in that direction. So, without being given handbooks or informative flyers about how they should curb their posturing and come-ons, guys sensed that they should treat me with respect.

I didn't watch boys and girls learn about each other from the sidelines. I have many rich friendships with men, and over the years a good number of them have made a go at becoming "more than friends." I didn't participate in dating games, but I was flattered by the attention, especially since I knew I was being liked for who I was beyond my body. What made me attractive was my ability to relate to everyone in a very natural way, without all the confusing sexual pressure. The weirdness that normally clouds boy-girl interactions was lifted, because most guys automatically assumed I wasn't available for dating. Of course, girls deserve to be treated with respect no matter what they wear. But since we live in a world of mixed messages, I got to bypass a lot of damaging experiences.

The veil bestowed other experiences upon me that I wouldn't quite classify as negative, but definitely educational. Like anyone else who's visibly different from the norm, I encountered ridiculous ideas about what a covered person should be, do and enjoy. If someone overheard me talking about my interests, which included karate and skateboarding, I grew to enjoy their disbelief and shock. I didn't pick my hobbies to prove that stereotypes are often false, but it was nice to make people reconsider their notions of a Muslim girl.

Moving to New York City right after college and living alone was the most affirming thing I've done to solidify my resolve and truly understand what veiling means. Here, for the first time, people believed that I was wearing a scarf because I wanted to, not because my family coerced me into it. On the other hand, New York exemplifies what's wrong with our image-obsessed society. I worked for a couple of magazines and saw the way women acted out to draw attention to themselves. It was especially apparent at my anything-goes dot-com job, where women showed up to work in backless halter tops and were fawned over by male coworkers.

And now, as I write this I can watch women subjugate themselves on reality dating shows. On a show about aspiring models I heard a woman say that her greatest goal would be to appear in *Stuff* magazine. I can't imagine centering my life on something as fleeting and meaningless as being admired simply for my body.

You might assume that because Muslim women traditionally don't display our bodies, we don't hold them as important or feel connected to them – or that we don't value ourselves as sexual beings. Guess again. While our degree of modesty is high, the value Muslim women place on the bodies underneath our veils is higher. In Sunday school, girls are taught that our bodies are beautiful ("God is beautiful and loves beauty" is a *hadith,* or saying, of the prophet Muhammad) and that they're so valuable that they're only meant to be shared in an intimate relationship: husband and wife, mother and baby, among women and in clinical or safe spaces (for example, with your doctor, among family members). Historically, the most severe-looking coverings used to be limited to the richest women in Arab society; being swathed in so much cloth was regarded as a sign of status.

People who have written about being in the secluded quarters of Arab homes or at their parties often express surprise at the degree to which these cloaked women maintain themselves via fitness, style and decadent rituals. (Let's not even get started on the body hair-removal process in the Middle East.) I'm not one for creams and blushes, but I understand that there are women who enjoy the beauty process, and I see no harm in indulging it for the right reasons. Feminist author Geraldine Brooks, in her book *Nine Parts of Desire*, quotes women across the Middle East who extol the virtues of prettying up for their loved ones. To me, this demonstrates that Western priorities are out of line: American women spend hours getting ready for strangers to see them but don't give the same effort to those who see them in intimate settings.

As for the variation in Muslim women's dress, it demonstrates the wide-ranging interpretations of modesty. I often get asked what the most "right" version is: the Afghani *burqah,* the Iranian *chador,* the Pakistani *salwar kameez,* the Arab *jilbab* or a sweatshirt and jeans. The short answer is that the recommendations for modesty are to be interpreted and applied at the discretion of the woman picking her clothes.

All through high school, I wore a *jilbab* exclusively, because I didn't have to spend any effort worrying about what was in season or what I would be expected to wear to fit in. I now cover my hair, but generally wear jeans and a long-sleeved shirt. My once-strict interpretation of modesty has been adapted to my urban lifestyle. Is wearing an *abaya* (the head-to-toe gown that completely covers the wearer) and a face veil a good idea in New York City? Probably not, since the *abaya* would likely get stuck in a subway door or pick up the dust off any floor you glide across. But not wearing an *abaya* in Saudi Arabia would probably make getting around very difficult for a woman.

It's utopic and ridiculous to assert that looks don't matter and that by veiling I'm avoiding the messiness – particularly after September 11th. Now some people hold their breath a bit longer, assuming I'm a fundamentalist or wondering if I'm there to cause them harm. I sense people studying me on the trains, reading the cover of the book in my hand and trying to gauge if I'm one of "us" or one of "them." I grapple with the frustration that I can't reassure everyone individually that my goals have everything to do with social justice and nothing to do with holy war. But I have seen suspicions fade in the eyes of the pregnant woman to whom I've given my subway seat, or the Hasidic man whose elbow I've taken to help him up the stairs.

Though many of the stereotypes and incorrect assumptions people had while I was growing up still prevail (that Muslim equals backwards/oppressed/fundamentalist/terrorist), current events have pedestrians describing their secondhand "expertise" of Islam – the history of Wahhabi Islam, the export of Sayyid Qutb and the Muslim Brotherhood's ideas – or trying to argue that the Quranic requirements for modesty don't include veiling. It's much harder to explain why I cover to those who think they have a full understanding of the culture and the faith than those whose "knowledge" of the Middle East is limited to *Aladdin* and *hummus*.

I do appreciate the status Islam and the Middle East have in the news these days – the interest has generated new scholarship on Arabia's history and anthropology and on Islamic law, all of which I'm interested in and am relieved is being researched. This research includes a pool of female scholars reexamining Islamic texts with a feminist lens, and separating actual religious commands from their long-held, culturally laden interpretations, which often smack of patriarchy.

Forcing women to veil or unveil usually has the opposite effect. When I attended elementary school in Saudi Arabia and flew home to Michigan each summer, a parade of women swathed in black *abayas* would head to the airplane bathrooms once we were safely in the air and emerge wearing short, tight ensembles. Conversely, banning the veil in Syria and Turkey sparked a resurgence in its popularity.

The question of veiling comes up once someone finds out that I've married into a family that celebrates Christmas, with my full participation. "If you have a daughter, what will she wear?" they ask. I haven't yet cracked a pregnancy or parenting book, but I hope that my policy will be similar to the egalitarian way I was raised. If she wants to, she can; if she doesn't want to, then she won't. It's far more important for her to respect herself, her body and her life.

At the heart of my veiling is personal freedom. I dress this way because it has made it easier to get through adolescent phases and New York City streets with no self-loathing, body hang-ups or sexual harassment. I wish more women emerged unscathed; no one should suffer for what they look like or what they wear.

7

Reproductive and Environmental Justice

By Bonnie Kime Scott

Contents

Original publication details: 7.1 Meridel le Sueur, "Sequel to Love" from *Writing Red: An Anthology of American Women Writers*, ed. Charlotte Nekola and Paula Rabinowitz, pp. 36–38. New York: Feminist Press, 1987. 7.2 Loretta J. Ross, Sarah L. Brownlee, Dazon Dixon Diallo, Luz Rodriquez, and SisterSong Women of Color Reproductive Health Project, "Just Choices: Women of Color, Reproductive Health and Human Rights" from *Policing the National Body: Sex, Race, and Criminalization. A Project of the Committee on Women, Population, and the Environment*, ed. Jael Silliman and Anannya Bhattacharjee, pp. 154–60, 168–74. Cambridge, MA: South End Press, 2002. Reproduced with permission of Loretta J. Ross. 7.3 Etobssie Wako and Cara Page. "Depo Diaries and the Power of Stories" from *Telling Stories to Change the World: Global Voices on the Power of Narrative to Build Community and Make Social Justice Claims*, ed. Rickie Solinger, Madeline Fox, and Kayhan Irani, pp. 101–07. New York: Routledge, 2008. Reproduced with permission of Taylor & Francis Group LLC. *(continued on page 280)*

Women in Culture: An Intersectional Anthology for Gender and Women's Studies, Second Edition.
Edited by Bonnie Kime Scott, Susan E. Cayleff, Anne Donadey, and Irene Lara.
© 2017 John Wiley & Sons, Ltd. Published 2017 by John Wiley & Sons, Ltd.

The reproductive capacity of life on earth may inspire wonder but it also occasions alarm when we consider threats to the reproductive wellbeing of female humans, as well as human degradation of the natural environment that sustains all forms of life. The readings in this chapter help us assess cultural narratives that have equated women with nature, ranking them in a hierarchy below men and culture, and seeking to control them through the dominant discourses of gender, heterosexuality, race, and science, which are reflected in colonial, economic, and religious doctrines. Women have worked to change the narrative, ministering to their own educational needs, as did the Boston Women's Health Collective when, in the late 1960s, it began developing the self-help book *Our Bodies, Ourselves*. As exemplified in this chapter's readings, women of color have been prominent leaders in both conceptualizing and leading movements for reproductive and environmental justice, not just in the United States, but also throughout the world. Thanks to feminist and ecofeminist work, women have the means to question previous logics of controlling women and nature, and they gain the potential to care for their bodies, communities, and the non-human members of the natural world in mutually beneficial ways. The cover of this textbook features Chicana artist Linda Vallejo's painting *Sacred Oaks: Moonlight* (2002). This representation of the endangered California oak set against a luminous sky was created at a time when she was "investigating humanity's valuable and fundamental relationship to the natural world, and conversely, the destruction of the human spirit as nature is destroyed." Among her influences were "the great Spanish artists Picasso, Goya, and Dalí; Turner's immense and glorious skies; the brilliant coloration of the Mexican muralists Rivera and Siqueiros; the sensual power of Georgia O'Keeffe's landscapes; indigenous philosophy and symbolism; and the endearing beauty and eternalness of nature" ("Artist's Statement").

Original publication details: 7.4 Karen J. Warren, "Women, People of Color, Children, and Health" and "Women and Environmental Justice" from *Ecofeminist Philosophy: A Western Perspective on What It Is and Why It Matters*, pp. 10–16, 18–19. Lanham, MD: Rowman & Littlefield, 2000. Reproduced with permission of Rowman & Littlefield Publishing Group LLC. 7.5 Ynestra King, "Healing the Wounds: Feminism, Ecology, and the Nature/Culture Dualism from *Reweaving the World: The Emergence of Ecofeminism*, ed. Irene Diamond and Gloria Feman Orenstein, pp. 106–21. San Francisco: Sierra Club Books, 1990. Reproduced with permission of Ynestra King. 7.6 Vandana Shiva, "Mad Cows and Sacred Cows," excerpts from *Stolen Harvest: The Hijacking of the Global Food Supply*, pp. 57–78. Cambridge, MA: South End Press, 2000. 7.7. Favianna Rodriguez, "Green our Communities! Plant Urban Gardens." Reproduced with permission of Favianna Rodriguez. 7.8 Greta Gaard, "Toward a Queer Ecofeminism", "Sexualizing Nature, Naturalizing Sexuality" from *New Perspectives on Environmental Justice: Gender, Sexuality, and Activism*, ed. Rachel Stein, pp. 21–29. New Brunswick, NJ: Rutgers University Press, 2004.

Approaching Reproductive Wellbeing from the Grassroots

Through both fiction and the collection of women's own stories, feminist writers enable us to hear voices of women disempowered by medical and other social authorities that seek to decide their reproductive lives for them. An advocate for women and the working class, Meridel le Sueur, provides the first person account of a young white working-class woman who is being coerced into her own sterilization in the short story "Sequel to Love" (1935/1987), set in the United States during the 1930s Depression era. This story, told in her regional and class dialect, reveals that she has been working for minimum wages since the age of 12. She has taken pleasure in her wages, and in her sexual life, and she at one time held hopes of settling on a farm, as promised by the father of her first child. Instead, figures of authority, an anonymous "they," have tried to limit her options and remove her pleasures. After having a second baby, she finds herself incarcerated in a mental institution until she agrees to sterilization. Both of her babies have been taken away. Her story illustrates the power of the eugenic theory of the day. Aiming to "improve" the genetic composition of the people, eugenicists suggested that poor people (as well as ethnic/racial minorities, homosexuals, and people with disabilities) were psychologically unfit to bear and raise children. Still, le Sueur's protagonist displays strong reasons for her ongoing resistance.

In "Depo Diaries and the Power of Stories" (2008), women's health advocate Etobssie Wako and Black queer feminist organizer Cara Page share the first person accounts of women who are still affected by a modern-day version of eugenics. As revealed by the activist work of the Committee on Women, Population, and the Environment, medical authorities have been especially aggressive in administering Depo Provera, an injected form of birth control, to poor women and women of color. The assumption is that they cannot be relied upon to employ other methods of birth control, even if they choose to limit their families. The Committee empowers women who have suffered from Depo Provera by sharing their stories. Though these firsthand accounts offer some praise for the convenience and privacy of the method, they repeatedly report short- and long-term negative effects, including depression, weight gain, loss of libido, tumors, and thyroid disorders, as well as painful ovulation and periods, once the drugs are discontinued. Offenses of the medical community include the failure of doctors to provide information on side effects of this method of birth control, and the basic arrogance of physicians who make decisions directed at the population control of queer women and women of color. In addition to sharing the stories of Depo Provera's effects, the Committee conducts research on alternative methods of birth control and abortion, disseminating this information electronically on their website.

A second example of women of color organizing strategically to promote reproductive health comes from the SisterSong Women of Color Reproductive Health Project, as presented by advocates Loretta J. Ross, Sarah L. Brownlee, Dazon Dixon Diallo, and Luz Rodriquez. In "Just Choices: Women of Color, Reproductive Health and Human Rights" (2002), they reframe arguments for women's reproductive health in public policy debates, starting with the priorities of grassroots women. Challenges include the marginality of reproductive health issues in the traditional organizations of people of color, and the difficulty of working with mainstream women's health organizations such as NARAL (the National Abortion and Reproductive Rights Action League) and Planned Parenthood. The emphasis of these mainstream organizations had been on "choice" as relates to abortion; there is further concern that their drives for inclusiveness might diminish funding that would otherwise go to women of color organizations. Additional challenges come from environmentalists who advocate population control as a corrective for environmental degradation, faith-based initiatives encouraged during the George W. Bush era, and the dependency of many anti-poverty programs upon Catholic Charities, which will not collaborate with any organization having a pro-choice agenda. Not only abortion rights, but a whole array of health concerns interest SisterSong, starting with attending to basic problems such as reproductive tract infections. For its own discourse, SisterSong adopts the language of human rights, which resonates with the history of civil rights, and operates well in an international legal arena.

Ecofeminist Approaches to Environmental Justice

Women have been making a difference in environmental study since they began collecting fossils and illustrating natural history volumes in the eighteenth century. In American regionalist author Sara Orne Jewett's short story "A White Heron" (1886), a young girl challenges the mass slaughter of birds by a young collector whose methods are comparable to those of famed artist John James Audubon. With her book *The Silent Spring,* American biologist and ecologist Rachel Carson braved the harsh criticism of male authorities to sound the alarm against chemical pesticides in the 1960s (PBS). Mindful of an ancient legend, in 1974 women of the Chipko Movement in India hugged trees to prevent lumberjacks from felling their essential community resource. The term "ecofeminist" dates back only to the mid-1970s, but it is increasingly a part of feminist vocabulary. "Healing the Wounds: Feminism, Ecology, and the Nature/Culture Dualism," by American ecofeminist and activist Ynestra King, appeared in the groundbreaking ecofeminist volume *Reweaving the World: The Emergence of Ecofeminism* (Diamond and Orenstein 1990). King critiques the hierarchical thinking that has long been accepted as rational, attributing it to "white Western male systems of hatred of all that is natural and female, people of color and working class." Dismantling the nature/culture oppositional binary, she describes giving birth as a natural process culturally handled; mothering is not a natural given, but is a complex social process. Woman, seen not as a passive being in nature, but as a social and historical agent, can reconnect and reconcile humans with nature. By insisting upon social agency, King differs from the spiritual and natural affiliations of what some term "cultural feminists." Some of them, such as Carol P. Christ and Raine Eisler, are represented alongside her in *Reweaving the World*, its very title a metaphor evocative of feminine craft. Among the social agents King salutes are the members of the Chipko movement and feminists who have reappropriated childbirth by demedicalizing the process. She calls for continuing scientific critique and seeking of alternate ways of knowing the world without dominating it. King envisions women assuming the stewardship of evolution, accomplished by bridging dualisms and connecting the social evolution of humans to the ongoing evolution of the planet.

In "Women, People of Color, Children, and Health" (2000), ecofeminist philosopher Karen J. Warren points out harmful human environmental practices that disproportionately affect women of color and children. These causes and their effects vary depending upon the region of the world: women who cook indoors with materials such as wood, straw, and dung suffer from high rates of respiratory disease; residents of the industrial world are more apt to develop chemical sensitivity to PCBs, industrial pollutants, and pesticides (the latter consumed by children in more dangerous amounts); inner city children are more likely to be exposed to lead paint in older buildings. In the United States, for example, race is a factor in the location of hazardous waste sites, many of which are near Indian Reservations, and petrochemical industrial sites, such as the dominantly African American community of Richmond, California, across the bay from San Francisco. Navajo women whose communities are situated near uranium mines are subjected to unique risks from radioactivity and water impurities, leading to an increased rate of miscarriage and birth defects. There are also enduring psychosocial effects from environmental disasters such as the 1989 Exxon Valdez oil spill. Even the setting aside of lands for national parks threatens land claims of Native Americans, as demonstrated in recent Canadian planning.

American film-maker and educator Judith Helfand combines humor with grave concerns in *Blue Vinyl*, a 2002 documentary of her quest for sustainable siding for her parent's suburban home in Long Island, New York. Through grassroots interviews conducted in manufacturing centers from Louisiana to Venice, Italy, she exposes negative health impacts of the production and eventual disposal of the highly profitable and widely used substance polyvinyl chloride (PVC).

All of these local examples make nature a feminist issue on an international scale, while demonstrating the art of advocacy and the importance of independent research.

In "Mad Cows and Sacred Cows" (2000), Indian environmental activist Vandana Shiva describes the sustainable system of animal husbandry long practiced by women in India, home of the sacred cow. Shiva is outspokenly vegetarian and recommends a diet that derives healthy amounts of protein from legumes, while it spares India's cows from slaughter. In contrast, she denounces Western practices of the green (agricultural) and white (dairy) revolutions that have depleted the environment to satisfy the growing demand for a diet of meat and artificially high yields of milk. The large scale of these operations puts small producers, many of them women, out of a profession. Indian women have tended small numbers of cattle and other domestic animals, processing their dairy products and using their manure as fuel or fertilizer – sustaining organic soil, down to the levels of worms and bacteria. In contrast, Western factory farms have altered the grass-based diet of the herbivore, introducing animal remains to their diet, with the disastrous effect of BSE (bovine spongiform encephalopathy), or "mad cow disease." The use of bovine growth formula to increase milk production also undermines the health of animals. The meat industry reduces the diversity of cattle stock by selecting for high meat and dairy yields. A further burden is imposed by government policies and interna-tional agreements that permit the exporting of polluting industries to the Third World and admit junk food chains, whose menus promote the consumption of meat. Instead, she argues, we should bring our world view closer to the treatment of the cow as sacred. Sharing Shiva's quest for a more respectful attitude toward animals, ecofemi-nists Josephine Donovan and Carol J. Adams, (working in the tradition of feminist psychologist Carol Gilligan's *In a Different Voice*) have defined a feminist care tradition in animal ethics. Science and technology scholar Donna Haraway speaks of "naturecultures" and has theorized the co-evolution of animals, particularly dogs, along with humans. The late Australian ecofeminist, Val Plumwood, in questioning the valuation placed on human reasoning, salutes animals for finely tuned ecological knowledges that escape the human.

American ecofeminist, film-maker, and activist Greta Gaard works to bring ecofemi-nist and queer theory together as a coalition in her essay "Toward a Queer Ecofeminism" (2004/2014). Like Ynestra King, she challenges the dominating Western tradition of dualistic, hierarchical thinking, in this case questioning the conflicting binary of reason (seen as masculine) versus the erotic (seen as feminine). She notes the additional irony that homosexual acts are considered crimes against nature, the very entity that mascu-line culture dominates in the traditional scheme. Much of the essay presents an anal-ysis of Christian rhetoric. Gaard begins by pointing out the original asceticism of the early Christian cult, and ways that it fit into hierarchical modes of thought found in its Roman context. She finds that the rhetoric of Christianity (often deployed in colonial contexts) naturalizes the intersectional oppression of women, queers, and nature, pre-senting this as something ordained by God. Historical examples include: the Inquisition, in which heretics were persecuted for their permissiveness of homoeroticism; the elim-ination of homosexual practices and transgender people from American Indian com-munities as they were converted to Christianity; and the discouraging of female equality found in pre-colonial cultures, which were feminized in the conquering nations' nationalist discourse. The removal of these oppressions leads toward a recovery of nature in all its variety. Much of this, quite naturally, is queer, erotic, and affirmative.

Discussion Questions

1. How have racial, colonial, and religious doctrines intersected to result in oppressive doctrines affecting reproductive and environmental justice?
2. Note ways that what is "natural" has been determined by homophobic attitudes toward sexuality.
3. How have white women's organizations and those of women of color differed in framing their arguments for women's reproductive health?
4. How are the health of the environment and women's reproductive rights linked in a positive way in our readings? In what ways might environmental arguments be problematic to reproductive rights?

5. Do you find some of our authors divided on the form of feminist approach they take to reproductive and environmental justice? How do the views differ?
6. What evidence do you have of negative attitudes toward women's erotic pleasures in our readings?
7. Why is it important to think locally as well as globally about issues concerning the health of women and the environment? Give some examples of local actions and situations.

References

Blue Vinyl. Dir. Daniel B. Gold and Judith Helfand. New Video, 2002. https://www.youtube.com/watch?v=Amz5RzVYpLo (accessed December 18, 2015).

Boston Women's Health Collective. *Our Bodies, Ourselves*. New York: Simon and Schuster, 1973.

Carson, Rachel. *Silent Spring*. Boston: Houghton Mifflin, 1962.

Committee on Women, Population, and the Environment. http://www.cwpe.org (accessed December 18, 2015).

Diamond, Irene, and Gloria Feman Orenstein, eds. *Reweaving the World: The Emergence of Ecofeminism*. San Francisco: Sierra Club Books, 1990.

Donovan, Josephine. "Caring to Dialogue: Feminism and the Treatment of Animals." *The Feminist Care Tradition in Animal Ethics*. Ed. Josephine Donovan and Carol J. Adams. New York: Columbia University Press, 2007. 360–69.

Gilligan, Carol. *In a Different Voice: Psychological Theory and Woman's Development*. Cambridge, MA: Harvard University Press, 1982.

Haraway, Donna. *When Species Meet*. Minneapolis: University of Minnesota Press, 2008.

Jewett, Sarah Orne. "A White Heron." 1886. *The Selected Best Stories of Sarah Orne Jewett*, selected and arranged with a preface by Willa Cather, Vol. 2. Boston and New York: Houghton Mifflin, 1925. 1–25.

Plumwood, Val. *Environmental Culture: The Ecological Crisis of Reason*. London: Routledge, 2002.

Rachel Carson's Silent Spring. PBS "The American Experience" Series, 1993. https://www.youtube.com/watch?v=ekDeG-BJYnE (accessed December 18, 2015).

Sistersong website: http://www.sistersong.net (accessed December 18, 2015).

Vallejo, Linda. *Women in Culture*: Artist's Statement. Email communication, October 27, 2015.

7.1

Sequel to Love

Meridel le Sueur

I am in the place where they keep the feeble-minded at Faribault. This place is full of girls moanen' and moanen' all night so I can't get no sleep in to speak of.

They won't let me out of here if I don't get sterilized. I been cryin' for about three weeks. I'd rather stay here in this hole with the cracked ones than have that done to me that's a sin and a crime. I can't be sleepin' hardly ever any night yet I'd stay right here than have that sin done to me because then I won't be in any pleasure with a man and that's all the pleasure I ever had. Workers ain't supposed to have any pleasure and now they're takin' that away because it ain't supposed to be doin' anybody any good and they're afraid I'll have another baby.

I had one baby and I named her Margaret after myself because I was the only one had her. I had her at the Salvation Army home.

Pete and me had her but Pete never married me. He was always at the library after he lost his job.

Pete said he had a place on a farm. I guess he had a farm then and he said he would take me out there and give me red cheeks and we would have a cute kid.

I been workin' in the five and ten since I was twelve because I was big and full for my age. Before the New Deal we got eight dollars dependin' on if a girl was an old girl or a new one and extra girls got $6.25 a week for fifty-four hours work, but if you only worked fifty hours you got thirteen cents an hour. I hear from my girl friends it's different now and they cut down the girls a lot and a girl there now has got to do the work of two. That's what I hear. I ain't worked there now for a year and a half.

Peter used to meet me after work on Seventh there, and we used to go to a show or walkin' or to the park, and he used to tell me these things. He was a good talker and I guess he meant it. He never made the depression, although you'd think it the way people talk about him.

Gee, the baby Pete and me had was pretty! Red cheeks and kind of curly hair. I would like to of kept her right good. I hated havin' her and was sure I was going to die off, but after I seen her I would have liked to of kept her good.

When I had her I was missen' all the shows in town and I was mad. They had to strap me down to nurse her and I had to stay there so long that I was even missen' them when they come to the fifteen centers and after that you have to go a long ways out to see them.

But where I got mixed up with the charities was about havin' this baby. One month I missed and got nervous and went to a doctor and he wouldn't do nothin' because I didn't have no money. I went to three like that, and then one give me some pills and I took one and it made my ears ring so I was afraid to take any more. I cried for about two days but I didn't take no more pills.

I went to another doctor and he told me I was goin' to have a baby and I come out and went up to a corner of the hall and began to cry right there with everybody goin' by and a crowd come around. I thought you got to be quiet or you'll get arrested now so I was quiet and went on downstairs but I was shakin' and the sweat was comin' off me.

My girl friend tooken me home with her and told me I better go on and have it because to get rid of it would cost about one hundred dollars.

My father is a garbage collector and he wouldn't be ever makin' that much.

I swan that summer I don't know where I was goin' all the time. I kept lookin' in all the parks for him because I thought he was goin' to skip town and when I see him he hollered at me that he didn't have no money to skip.

I went to the clinic and they told me to eat lots of oranges and milk for my baby. My girl friend didn't have no work and her and me went out lookin' for food all the time because she kept tellin' me I had to eat for two now.

I kept lookin' and lookin' for Pete and lookin' for somethin' to eat. When I could see Pete seems like I could rest. I would follow him to the library and sit in the park until he come out and I would feel alright.

We kept lookin' for food. We walked miles and miles askin' at restaurants for food. I got an awful hankerin' for spice cakes. Seems like I would putnear die without spice cakes. Sometimes we would walk clean over town lookin' and lookin' for spice cakes.

I thought I was goin' to die when I had my baby … I was took to the Salvation Home and had it there but I didn't like it none there and they had to strap me down to make me nurse the baby. Seems like there is a law a mother's got to nurse her baby.

I wanted to keep the baby but they wouldn't let me. My dad wanted to keep it, even, and my sister's got twelve kids and she wanted it. Even then it was such a cute kid. Kind of curly hair. But they rented it out to a woman and now they got me here.

My dad spent about fifty dollars with lawyers to keep me out but it ain't no good. They got me here until I have that operation.

I got a letter from Pete and he says you got no business to be there; you ain't dumb. Miss Smith that comes here to talk me into havin' an operation says I like men too much, that they can't let me get out at all.

I like men. I ain't got any other pleasure but with men. I never had none. I got to lay here every night, listenin' to the moanen' and thinkin' are they crazy, and my dad keeps saying to have it done it will be alright, that I won't get old or anything too soon. It ain't a natural thing that it should be done to a young girl.

I might know a man sometime with a job and getting along pretty, and why shouldn't I have a baby if it was alright so the Salvation Army wouldn't take care of me or anything and I wouldn't bother them? Like before, which wasn't our fault because I believe what Pete said to me about the farm and all.

We had a cute kid, an awful bright kid, Miss Smith says it sure is a cute kid, an awful bright kid alright.

They keep sayin' I like men but why shouldn't I like men, why shouldn't a girl like a man? But for us girls that work for our livin' we ain't got no right to it and I was gettin' seven dollars at the five and ten and that seems to be all I got a right to, my measly seven dollars, and they're firin' girls all the time now so I wouldn't get that back, even.

They don't want us to have nothin'.

Now they want to sterilize us so we won't have that.

They do it all the time and the police follow a girl around and the police women follow you around to see if you're doin' anything and then they nab you up and give you a lot of tests and send you here and do this to you.

They don't want us to have nothin', alright.

Pete and me sure had a cute kid, but we'll never see it any more.

Now I'm locked up here with the feeble-minded.

7.2

Just Choices: Women of Color, Reproductive Health and Human Rights

*Loretta J. Ross, Sarah L. Brownlee, Dazon Dixon Diallo,
Luz Rodriquez, and SisterSong Women of Color
Reproductive Health Project*

A New Organizing Strategy

This essay will address issues of reproductive health for women of color in the United States and offer a case study of the SisterSong Women of Color Reproductive Health Project, a collective that seeks to advocate for the reproductive health rights of women of color. SisterSong was founded to organize women of color and establish a plan of action for addressing the reproductive health needs of our communities. SisterSong works to secure adequate funding in order to mobilize significant numbers of grassroots women; it also aims to develop a public policy advocacy agenda and to cooperate rather than compete with other pro-choice and women's health organizations. While interested in broad reproductive health issues, SisterSong focuses mainly on reproductive tract infections (RTIs). This focus on RTIs is a response to the failure of mainstream reproduction rights organizations to pay attention to the impact they have had on women of color.

The sixteen organizations involved in SisterSong are using their histories and experiences in organizing their communities. Their goal is to develop and apply human rights standards to reproductive health education and services for women of color. SisterSong strongly advocates for the reframing of the reproductive health movement in terms of human rights. It defines the right to health, including the right to reproductive health, as a human right that should be protected in the United States.

Reproductive Tract Infections

In 1987, the International Women's Health Coalition (IWHC) formulated the concept of "reproductive tract infections" (RTIs) to draw attention to a serious, neglected aspect of women's sexual and reproductive health, and to stimulate development of the necessary health services and technologies, information dissemination, and wider program efforts. RTIs affect the ovaries, fallopian tubes, uterus, cervix, vagina, and external genitalia. They affect both men and women, but are more common among women.[1]

There are three known types of RTIs that are grouped by cause of infection:

1. Sexually transmitted diseases (STDs) are caused by bacterial or viral infections such as gonorrhea, genital warts, chlamydia, syphilis, and HIV.
2. Endogenous infections result from an overgrowth of microorganisms (bacteria, yeast) that are normally present in the reproductive tract and are not normally transmitted sexually.
3. Iatrogenic infections result from medical procedures such as improper insertion of an IUD, unsafe childbirth/obstetric practices, and unsafe abortions.[2]

There is a culture of silence about reproductive tract infections that affect women around the world because many diseases can be transmitted through sexual intercourse, which is often considered a taboo subject that is also complicated by the subordination of women in nearly every culture. The taboo of non-heterosexual intercourse also makes addressing RTIs in communities of color a challenge. Many women spend years suffering in silence:

> [R]eproductive ill health is different from other forms of ill health because of the centrality of intimate human behaviors. Human sexual and reproductive behaviors are heavily dependent on social relationships, on custom, tradition, and taboo. It is therefore inevitable that social groups and individuals with the least power, with the most limited ability to make decisions, with the most constrained capacities for choice, will suffer the major portion of the burden of ill health results from these behaviors and relationships.[3]

These diseases include viral infections (genital herpes and warts), other diseases related to bacteria or similar organisms (syphilis, gonorrhea, chlamydia, vaginosis), or fungal or protozeal infections (candiasis or trichomoniasis). Women can also be infected by the insertion of unclean materials into the vagina to prevent pregnancy or induce abortion, by unsafe childbirth techniques, and by female circumcision. However, there is growing awareness about the importance of RTIs because of the discovery that RTIs increase the risk of HIV transmission.[4]

RTIs kill thousands of women each year through their association with cervical cancer, unsafe deliveries, and septic abortions.[5] They can cause emotional distress, pain, and marital discord. The economic costs to society include the loss of women's productivity and the expense of treating the severest consequences of RTIs, such as pelvic inflammatory disease (PID). RTIs received the greatest media attention with the advent of AIDS. Each year, 12 million people in the United States become infected with a sexually transmitted disease.[6] Roughly a quarter of infections occur among young people, between the ages of 15 to 19 years.[7]

The high rate of RTIs among women is associated with a number of interrelated sociocultural, biological, and economic factors, including poverty, the low social status of women, low educational levels, racism, rapid urbanization, and local customs.[8] These multiple factors often reduce women's decision-making power over their own sexuality, and constrain their ability to seek quality reproductive health care.

Women's health advocates around the world have been addressing some of these issues, and identifying what can be done locally, nationally, and globally to bring awareness and action to improving women's reproductive health. To the extent that RTIs have been recognized as a public health issue, they have been approached as diseases to be mapped by epidemiologists, prevented through public education, and cured by health professionals. Yet these conventional approaches are not working; RTIs are rampant in many countries, and their prevalence is increasing.

Women of color have raised a number of new questions regarding RTIs, including the ways in which women of color are vulnerable to them, and how they experience their infections personally and culturally. They have also begun to question how they can protect their sexual and reproductive health in the context of power imbalances in their private lives and in their public encounters.

Appropriate health services for women, particularly marginalized women (such as poor women, women of color, rural women, and lesbians) have always posed a challenge for modern Western medicine. Typically, medical approaches within the United States cling to the assumption that there exists a universal treatment for all women in all cases for reproductive health problems.[9] Rarely is enough priority given to individually tailored health care which takes into account the environment in which women live, although there has been a recent resurgence of health care that does not strictly adhere to Western medical models.

US studies estimate that of 36 million women of color, almost a fourth are uninsured, with limited or no access to quality health care.[10] These 36 million women of color are 46 percent Black, 38 percent Hispanic, 13 percent Asian and Pacific Islander, and 3 percent American Indian/Alaska Native women. Women of color are more than a fourth (27 percent) of all American women.[11] Studies also show that many women of color do not have preventive health screenings tests such as Pap smears, which are critical in early detection of RTIs.[12] While researchers attribute these findings to financial, cultural, and informational causes, the absence of data on women of color has produced inadequate and sometimes inappropriate policies and programs as reported by the Office of Research on Women's Health at the National Institutes of Health.

The SisterSong Model

In an attempt to promote research and advocacy on reproductive health issues faced by women of color, and to ensure appropriate medical treatment of women of color, women of color organizations in the United States, including Puerto Rico and Hawaii, collaborated in collecting reproductive health data, sharing experiences in treatment and prevention, and addressing societal factors that impact the reproductive health of women of color. In 1997 and 1998, the Latina Roundtable on Health and Reproductive Rights convened meetings for sixteen women of color organizations (four Native American, four African-American, four Latina/ Hispanic, four Asian-American/Pacific Islander) and eventually formed the SisterSong: Women of Color Reproductive Health Project, with Ford Foundation funding.[13]

The foundation selected the participating organizations with input and advice from organizers who work on reproductive health issues. The meetings and continued consultations identified common concerns and needs in reproductive health, and served as the catalyst for each of the sixteen groups to formulate a plan on prevention and early treatment of RTIs in their respective communities. The groups also recognized the lack of coordinated and effective efforts among women's and children's health initiatives in their communities, and the impact of biased health policies on poor women.

The collective includes a diverse set of organizations working on reproductive health issues as direct services providers and/or as advocates. Among the reproductive health issues addressed by the collective are midwifery, AIDS services, abortion and contraceptive services, clinical research, health rights advocacy, sexually transmitted diseases, and reproductive tract infections.

In order to address identified concerns and achieve its goals, SisterSong formed four mini-communities within the main body of the collective. Each mini-community was established in order to maintain the representation of the cultural experience and sensitivity of each ethnic group. Each mini-community consists of four grassroots organizations, including at least one national, one state, and two local organizations from that ethnic group. This format maintains commitment to the ability of grassroots organizations to effectively reach a diverse group of women.

One organization from each mini-community was chosen to perform as the "anchor organization" in order to facilitate and coordinate the communications, efforts, and contributions of the respective mini-community. Together the four anchor organizations formed the collective coordinating body assuming the administrative duties of the collective. Their responsibilities include maintaining cohesion between the mini-communities and the main body of the collective as well as advancing the organization's overall agenda – the reduction of RTIs among women of color and thereby the improvement of reproductive health.

The process for planning and implementing a three-year program included the development of a collective vision, which identified basic needs, leadership issues, resources, and common ground within the collective. Several themes emerged during the process. There is a general deficiency of knowledge in communities of color across the country about RTIs and there is a dearth of current, accurate, and culturally sensitive research. In addition, there is a lack of funding to institute programs and increase awareness about RTIs. Linguistic and attitudinal issues usually create barriers to accessing information and services. Women often experience challenges in communicating health needs and concerns to sex partners. Traditional medical analyses fail to include the social and economic conditions – often experienced as human rights violations – that inhibit women from obtaining adequate health care.

Initial Program Findings

At a 1998 symposium in Savannah, Georgia, members of SisterSong identified various barriers which impede their work on RTIs in communities of color. Many programs providing physical and mental health care to women are inappropriate and discriminatory. For example, Asian-Americans have been documented to underuse mental health services. The trauma due to war (for example, torture, starvation, rape, forced labor, and witnessing murder), leaving one's homeland, and resettling in another land often results in unique medical conditions, such as psychosomatic or non-organic blindness reported among Cambodian women 40 years of age or older.[14]

In addition, many providers lack the cultural competency to provide a safe and accessible environment for women of color to pursue good health care and make sound health decisions. Another barrier addressed was the overall lack of awareness and sensitivity of heath care providers and consumers of all their human rights, and the lack of adequate information concerning contraceptive choices, reproductive tract infections, and specific behavioral patterns that increase risk.

SisterSong's first step was to create an opportunity for shared learning through the mutual exchange of health information from each ethnic group. For example, data available from the Centers for Disease Control was frequently incomplete and/or inconsistent in meeting the needs of the women in the collective. The aggregated data frequently failed to identify the particular details of population subsets, like indigenous Pacific Islanders or grouping immigrant Black women with African-Americans. By working with researchers from the Centers for Disease Control, the Office of Minority Health, and the National Institutes of Health, SisterSong began the process of identifying the research and advocacy needs of women of color.

The outcome of the symposium has allowed SisterSong to develop education, outreach, and advocacy strategies that increase awareness of reproductive health issues among women of color, inform practitioners of more appropriate treatment, and advocate for more effective legislation regarding women's health. Other findings include the following:

- Approximately 77 percent of women with HIV/AIDS are women of color. In 1996, African-American women were 56 percent of reported US female AIDS cases; another 20 percent were Hispanic women. HIV infection is the third leading cause of death among all women age 25–44, and the leading cause among African-American women of that age group. These women tend to be young, poor, and tend to live in distressed urban neighborhoods.[15]
- The Public Health Service's Office on Women's Health reported that less than 1 percent of Asian/Pacific Islanders and American Indian/Alaska Native women have HIV/AIDS, but the highest rate of increase in new HIV/AIDS cases in recent years occurred among these two groups of women.[16]
- Occupational hazards pose a significant health threat to women of color. Disproportionate numbers of Latina and Asian/Pacific Islanders are employed in farming, forestry, fishing, and service occupations that hold higher risk for occupational diseases and injuries. Inhalation, absorption, ingestion, and repetitive movements of assembly-type activities may cause these illnesses.[17]
- Asian/Pacific Islander women have the lowest screening rate for cervical cancer, second only to American Indian women. Fifty-five percent of Asian Pacific Islanders, compared to 43 percent of Latinas, and 37 percent of African-Americans were unscreened in 1995.[18]

Reconceptualizing the Human Rights Framework

Global structural adjustment policies imposed by the World Bank on developing countries have resulted in cuts in social services, fees for public services, privatization, and the removal of subsidies for food, medicines, clean water, and transportation. In the United States, welfare reform is, in effect, acting as a structural adjustment program. A high level of poverty forces thousands of girls and women to sell their bodies as a means of survival.[19] Sadly enough, even in monogamous relationships, women's sexuality becomes their only bargaining tool for survival. Violence against women also tends to increase poverty, risks of STDs, unintended pregnancies, drug and alcohol abuse, and mental illness.

The lack of effective coordinated efforts to ensure the health of women and children, and for the prevention of STDs and HIV, represents an extreme challenge to the vision of SisterSong. The need for policy changes is apparent in states where schools provide only abstinence-based sex education and where women are forced to receive spousal or parental permission for reproductive medical procedures such as abortion or contraception. A solution to many of these challenges is a reconceptualization of reproductive health in terms of human rights.

Organizations concerned with reproductive health issues in the United States are increasingly drawing inspiration and tools from the international human rights movement, and those working within a traditional human rights framework are gradually including issues related to reproductive health. Women, particularly women of color, have spearheaded this rearticulation of the human rights framework in the United States.

Through the application of human rights education, SisterSong began to reconceptualize the human rights framework in the United States, particularly in its applicability to health care problems. The organizations joined other social justice activists in demanding that the United States be held accountable to an internationally applied standard of human rights. This new generation of human rights activists has called attention to significant human rights violations committed against women of color by local, state, and federal governments as well as private citizens and institutions.

Because of inherent limits in the United States Constitution, which seeks to protect the civil and political rights of individuals, the United States lacks a sufficient legal framework within which women of color may have safe and reliable access to health care. This results from the law's denial of the importance of and obligation to achieve economic, social, and cultural human rights which emphasize group or collective needs. While individual human rights are nearly universally accepted, collective or group rights remain extremely controversial.

Liberal human rights interpretations often do not recognize that equality of opportunity is an illusion in a society based on competitive individualism in which one ethnic group (whites) has social, political, and economic advantages in relationship to other ethnic groups (people of color). Thus, individualistic rights frameworks often neglect the importance of group rights of ethnicity and culture.[20] For example, while an individual African-American may have the legal freedom and the financial means to purchase a home in any community, that potential buyer must be protected from racial discrimination against African-Americans as a group, in order to enjoy that individual right.

Parental consent laws, for-profit health care, welfare reform policies, and immigration policies impact women's health choices and detrimentally affect the quality of care available. In order to ensure access to health care and treatment, and to address the intersection of class, race, and gender that affects women of color, a comprehensive human rights–based approach is necessary.

This new and comprehensive, human rights–based reproductive health agenda challenges the traditional American liberal human rights framework, by giving economic, social, and cultural rights the same consideration given to civil and political rights. The United States government has an obligation to provide an environment in which policies, laws, and practices enable women to realize their reproductive rights, and to refrain from creating conditions that compromise or restrict such rights.

In 1994, the Cairo International Conference on Population and Development (ICPD) acknowledged that reproductive rights are human rights. It called on countries to ensure the reproductive rights of all individuals; to provide the information and means to decide the number, spacing, and timing of children; and to uphold the rights to have the highest standard of sexual and reproductive health, and to make sexual and reproductive decisions free of discrimination, coercion, and violence.

The World Conference Against Racism, Racial Discrimination, Xenophobia and Related Intolerance held in South Africa in August 2001 offered an opportunity to increase awareness about reproductive health issues for women of color and to identify those human rights violations women of color face around the world. The United States government failed to significantly participate in the conference, but it also denied that its policies discriminated against women of color. Further, the United States claimed that historical patterns of racism, colonialism, and genocide have no contemporary impact on the health of women of color.

Despite this intransigence, many women of color participated in the World Conference Against Racism to help develop concrete recommendations for regional and international measures to combat all forms of racial and gender oppression. Women of color recognized the fundamental, interlinked relationship between individual and collective human rights. They understood that individual human rights of women of color cannot be protected without the protection of the collective rights of all people of color.

There are many challenges associated with the awesome task of making domestic, regional, and international human rights mechanisms responsive to the needs of women of color in the United States. Not only has the United States denied the applicability of human rights to domestic policies, it has also prevented broad applicability and coverage of the few human rights treaties it has ratified by attaching exemptions to the treaties that prevent their justiciability in United States courts.

Opponents to women's human rights have also created an artificial dichotomy between "needs" and "rights" by claiming that a human rights–based approach to health is an elite Western imposition designed to counter a "needs-based" approach. These critics ignore the reality that rights are born out of needs: rights are legal articulations of claims upon governments to meet human needs and protect human freedoms. Instead of a rights/needs hierarchy there is, in fact, a rights/needs symbi-osis.[21] Despite tremendous opposition by critics and the US government's failure time and again to ratify treaties linking health and human rights, women of color have not been dissuaded from continuing their advocacy. Women organizers and trainers are beginning to increase human rights awareness among reproductive rights and women's health activists around the world. In the United States, many have yet to recognize women's human rights as a framework within which reproductive rights activists can find greater solidarity.

The incorporation of human rights instruments such as the Convention to End All Forms of Discrimination Against Women (CEDAW) should be a goal for the reproductive freedom movement. For example, CEDAW recognizes the ability of a woman to control her own fertility as fundamental to the full enjoyment of her human rights, including her right to health care and to family planning. It also addresses the obligations of the United States government to proactively tackle social, cultural, or traditional discrimination against women. CEDAW defines any law that restricts women's access to a range of family planning options as discrimi-natory. Despite the potential it holds, CEDAW remains one of the twenty-three human rights treaties the United States has yet to ratify.

Conclusion

SisterSong has made a promising beginning by bringing together women of color to address reproductive tract infections in the United States. Grassroots groups retain a great role, allowing SisterSong to build a wide-reaching, national collective. The Ford Foundation has taken a monumental step by funding a unique collaboration like SisterSong. The creative approach of SisterSong has increased the capacity of member organizations to access educational materials, services, and programs previously unavailable.

While organizations involved in the SisterSong collective face many barriers, through collaboration the collective has increased its potential. However, there still remain many challenges. Globalization is making socioeconomic conditions worse around the world and policy makers are increasingly turning to quick fixes to com-plex problems. Population control efforts are back with a vengeance and many liberal feminist organizations remain focused on abortion issues only. An even more troubling trend is the collaboration between international women's rights organiza-tions and population control organizations. As Asoka Bandarage of the Committee on Women, Population, and the Environment notes:

> As fertility control is presented increasingly as the means for women's empowerment, feminist criticisms of coercion and experimentation within family planning programs get softened; the resurgence of eugenics associated with the growth of new productive technologies gets overlooked; and the social structural roots of women's subordination and the global crisis tend to be forgotten.[22]

All these challenges make the mission of organizations like SisterSong all the more urgent. The need to highlight the inextricable link between health and human rights is pressing. This is not a battle against diseases only; it is a battle against poverty, homelessness, inadequate health care, and the denial of human rights.

Notes

1. Native American Women's Health Education Resource Center, "Focus Group Report 2: The Current Status of Reproductive Health Awareness Among Young Native American Women" (1999), 6.
2. Ibid.
3. Tomris Turmen, "Reproductive Rights: How to Move Forward?" *Health and Human Rights International Journal*, Vol. 4, No.2, (2000), 32.
4. Leslie Doyal, *What Makes Women Sick: Gender and the Political Economy of Health* (New Brunswick, NJ: Rutgers University Press), 77.
5. National Institutes of Health, *Women of Color Health Data Book* (1998), 79.
6. Centers for Disease Control and Prevention, Office of Women's Health (1999), www.cdc.gov.
7. Sexually Transmitted Disease Information Center, "What Teens Should Know and Don't (But Should) Know About Sexually Transmitted Diseases," *The Journal of the American Medical Association* (March 8, 1999).
8. Doyal, *What Makes Women Sick*, 75.
9. Gena Corea, *The Hidden Malpractice: How American Medicine Mistreats Women*, Updated ed. (New York: Harper Colophon Books, 1985), 79.
10. US Census Bureau, "Income and Poverty Status of Americans Improve" (1996).
11. National Institutes of Health, *Women of Color Health Data Book* (1998), 1.
12. Ibid., vii.
13. A complete listing of the member organizations of the SisterSong Collective from 1998–2001 is in the Appendix.
14. National Institutes of Health, *Women of Color Health Data Book* (1998), 20.
15. National Institute of Allergy and Infectious Disease, National Institutes of Health, "Women and HIV" (April 1997).
16. US Public Health Service Office on Women's Health, "The Health of Minority Women" (1996).
17. US Office of Occupational Safety and Health, *1993 Handbook on Women Workers: Trends and Issues* (1994).
18. "Women's Health: Choices and Challenges," *The Commonwealth Fund Quarterly*, Special issue (1996).
19. Kamala Kempadoo and Jo Doezema, *Global Sex Workers: Rights, Resistance and Redefinition* (New York: Routledge Press, 1998), 17.
20. William Felice, *Taking Suffering Seriously: The Importance of Collective Human Rights* (Albany, NY: SUNY Press, 1996), 35.
21. Ibid.
22. Asoka Bandarage, "Political Environments. A New and Improved Population Control Policy" (Committee on Women, Population and the Environment, 1994).

7.3

Depo Diaries and the Power of Stories

Etobssie Wako and Cara Page

Depo Diaries: A National Storytelling Project came out of our need to understand our own experiences with the adverse effects of birth control. We needed to highlight the ways that the medical community and others enforce systemic and coercive reproductive practices, relying on racist, ableist, heterosexist, and classist assumptions. Over generations, these assumptions continue to marginalize the health needs and quality of care of poor women, women of color, queer women, and women with disabilities. The Committee on Women, Population, and the Environment (CWPE) has been working for over fifteen years against policies that target certain women as the root cause of all global social ills. CWPE has been working against policies that subject certain women to unethical testing of contraceptives, involuntary sterilization, and reproductive control. We seek to promote women's rights to safe, voluntary birth control and abortion, and we strive for a reorientation of contraceptive technology that is safe, non-invasive, affordable, and woman-controlled. In addition, CWPE is committed to the principle that self-determination for all women can only come by addressing the intersections of oppressions and the impacts of these oppressions on our emotional, physical, and spiritual well-being.

In the early 1900s under the guise of promoting "good breeding" and "building a better race" of Americans, or what was known as "eugenics," a number of state laws and programs targeted certain women for sterilization, including Native American women, African American women, Latina women, poor women, and women with mental and developmental disabilities. By mid-century, when most official, abusive sterilization practices had been dismantled (if not wholly abandoned or discredited), or had been taken over by regulated private practices less easily monitored, government-funded public health clinics began distributing systemic hormonal birth controls which often had adverse, long-term effects on women and girls.

Late in the twentieth century, in 1992, the Food and Drug Administration (FDA) approved Depo-Provera, a synthetic hormonal contraceptive. Women's health activists mounted campaigns against the approval because they were concerned about evidence that Depo caused severe depression, breast cancer, cervical cancer, higher HIV/AIDS susceptibility, excessive bleeding, weight change, and osteoporosis, among other health impacts. These activists were also concerned that Depo would probably be mass-marketed to clinics and doctors as an easy and cost-effective product to administer to females in poor communities and communities of color. Indeed, studies have determined that this is how health professionals – including many who likely believe that women in these communities ought to practice "population control" – have used Depo-Provera.

Vision for the Stories

At the INCITE! Color of Violence III Conference in New Orleans, Louisiana in the Spring of 2005, CWPE led a workshop called "The Tactics of C.R.A.C.K. & Other Methods of Eugenics & Population Control." The workshop defined certain birth control practices as strategies and acts of violence against women of color. Approximately thirty women of African, Asian, Middle Eastern, and Latina descent attended the workshop. Almost all of the women had either used Depo-Provera or had family members who were using it. Many of the women reported that no one had warned them about the full range of possible long-term effects of Depo-Provera, but many told about the results they had seen and felt. For example, women from rural, African American, southern communities noted that three generations of women in their families had been using Depo and had experienced serious side effects.

As women began to tell their stories in the workshop, it turned out that almost everyone had experienced an adverse side effect, but each woman had chosen to keep quiet – and isolated – about these matters in her life because of communal and religious taboos regarding sex and sexuality. Many women discussed feeling shame about their own bodies. Each woman thought there was something wrong only with herself. Most never linked their depression, their weight gain, or their extreme hair loss to the birth control they were using.

The workshop was intended to be a way of sharing information and generating some strategic planning about how to respond to – and dismantle – twenty-first-century eugenics. But the event took on a life of its own, becoming a transformative experience in which the participants told their own stories of Depo in a context of personal and political liberation. One woman after another told her story about and against reproductive injustice. We learned from this powerful process that using a model of storytelling to demand change and build public education around the dangers of such commonly known birth controls as Depo-Provera needed to come from the stories of our lived experiences.

Speaking Out of Isolation

Since the Depo Diaries initiative began in 2006, we have received stories from across the world. Some stories praise the convenience and privacy of Depo-Provera. But most speak about the pain and isolation women experience while using the hormonal contraceptive. The narratives differ drastically from one another but at the same time, they are deeply connected by the ways that the writers express their experiences of disempowerment and the helplessness that follows. The stories also share this theme: many within the healthcare system seem ready to wholly disregard the physical, mental, and spiritual welfare of Depo users. Women report that navigating the healthcare systems has felt treacherous and dangerous, a voyage marked by hostility, dismissal, and a general contempt for their voices and experiences. The Depo Diaries initiative challenges this culture of enforced silence. It is built on the idea that when these women tell their stories, when all the stories are collected, a new power is born in that accumulation of narratives and in that collective voice. These stories take us out of isolation and grant us an opportunity to promote systemic change for our well-being and for the sustainability of our communities.

From Ontario, Canada

I originally asked for my tubes to be tied; however, the doctor went on and on about how I was too young for that. I was twenty-nine and had two children and was a single mom. I thought I was quite capable of deciding if I wanted more children or not, but the doctor kept arguing with me and told me how great Depo-Provera was. In the doctor's office I went to, the doctor always took the vial containing the Depo out of its box and neither the box nor the pamphlet with the side effects was given to me. Later that changed when I started asking to keep the boxes.

At first, the negative side effects were not noticeable. I totally lost my period and spotted at any time. The longer I used Depo, the more the side effects came out. First was the vaginal dryness and decrease in libido which caused much friction between my partner and me (no pun intended). Then I just started getting more and more tired, the longer I was on it, but the doctor dismissed this. He said I was a single mom with young children and that I was getting older (but not old enough to choose to have my tubes tied!).

Then I started forgetting things, getting irritable, getting shakes, etc. Soon, I had experienced about 80 percent of the negative side effects I read about on a particular site bashing Depo. I feel Depo triggered my thyroid disease although this illness is in my family. Once my thyroid resolved itself, I stupidly went back on Depo. I kept going back to the doctor and telling her that I felt like my thyroid was acting up again, and she kept testing it and saying it was fine. After a year of this, she started looking at me like I was crazy and offered me depression meds. I felt helpless. She thought I was going crazy, and I couldn't convince her that I was not.

After seeing that anti-Depo website and all the complaints, I was very relieved. I started crying so hard, I could hardly read the more than 300 complaints. After that I stopped using Depo. Immediately I began to feel better. The headaches went away. Irritability went away. My sex drive came back. My period came back. However!!!! I still have never felt like I got back to the way I used to feel before Depo even though I have not been using it for over a year.

The two things that feel like they have never resolved themselves are first, that I have problems remembering things (for example, sometimes it takes me ten minutes to remember how to spell a simple word) and second, I am always tired, although not as tired as I felt on Depo.

Anyway, thanks for listening. I really hope they do something to warn people about the side effects because my experience was awful. And one more thing! I asked over and over again to be monitored by the doctor, in the same way that women are when they take the birth control pill, and my doctor's office kept acting like they were too busy, and it wasn't necessary. I had one half-assed pap test done the whole time I was on Depo, and that was only because I demanded it. I would change doctor's offices immediately if I could, but there is a shortage in Brampton, where I live. People even have to take their newborns to walk-in clinics, and they get a different doctor every time for their well-baby check-ups. I guess a bad doctor is better than no doctor, but I wish I could sue them for the Depo thing!

From Alabama

I was prescribed Depo by a health clinic in Alabama when I was fifteen because, they said, it would help with my terrible periods. The only side effect I was told about was that I may not have a period. I used Depo for over ten years. Now, over a year after I stopped taking Depo, I suffer from terrible migraines, depression, weight gain, IBS, fibromyalgia, loss of libido. My periods have not returned without help, and I have many more problems. This drug is toxic and should be taken off the market. I was only a child when I was put on this drug, and now I am all messed up. I have been suffering with stomach problems for the past year and have not been able to find a source of the problem. I know it is from Depo.

From Newport News, VA

My ob/gyn prescribed Depo for me after the birth of my son. I gained forty pounds between the first shot and the second shot. While I was on it, mostly I thought it was wonderful. I had no periods and seemingly no other side effects, other than the weight gain. But actually, I started having migraine headaches, and I never had them before the shot. Also, from the time I got the first shot till I got off the shot, every pap I had was abnormal. Also, after receiving the first shot, the doctor told me I was basically on my way to cervical cancer. The same ob/gyn who prescribed Depo told me I should stop it because it was aggravating the condition.

Six months after I stopped the shots, my paps became normal. But I had a myriad of other problems I never had before taking Depo. I had painful ovulations. Painful and heavy cycles. Basically, I was having the entire period in a matter of hours. After this happened two cycles in a row, the doc urged me to go back on the shot since it stopped my cycle. I did. I was on it for a year. In that year, I was constantly sick, had constant pelvic pain, sex became very painful, and my paps were back to being abnormal again. I wanted off the shot, but I was scared. I went off the shot and immediately started birth control pills, hoping to get the cycle regulated so it wouldn't be like before. It didn't help. I ended up having a full vaginal hysterectomy in August 2002.

Location Unknown

I am twenty-seven years old and have been on Depo for over five years. Two weeks after my last shot, my body literally began falling apart overnight. I have tumors on my liver and cysts on my kidneys, osteoporosis, heart palpitations, vomit constantly, hiatal hernia, chest pains, shortness of breath, rapid heart rate, insomnia, muscle and bone pain, numbness on one side of my body. I am going through menopause, have blood in my stools, and much more! I literally woke up with all these ailments. I was perfectly healthy before. After no support from the medical community, I finally found tens of thousands of women on websites experiencing these same side effects. I also found websites that contained lists of these possible side effects so that I could present it to an emergency room person and get the tests done that I needed. I am currently undergoing breast cancer detection and cervical cancer testing as well. Again, I am only twenty-seven years old, but I feel as if I am eighty. Help me give women a voice. There is no freedom of choice if there is not an awareness of potential risks. The only warning I was given was that I would probably gain five pounds.

Feel free to ask me any questions. I am about to start doing everything I can to get awareness out. I may be only one person, but I am very "spirited" and very angry that a greedy pharmaceutical company has taken away my quality of life, and potentially life itself. I am equally upset at the damage it has caused to the tens of thousands of women who are writing about their "Depo-Provera horror stories" on the web. In some cases, the damage is not reversible. These are teenagers who are now sterile, who have cancer and osteoporosis. I will use my last breath to help women become aware of the dangers and get this drug off the market. We should have freedom of choice and that means knowing the facts.

Collective Voice and Power

In telling our stories, we are speaking about our pain, our resilience, and our self-determination. We are taking back our lives by naming how our bodies are viewed and treated inside the medical industrial complex. This storytelling initiative gives women an opportunity to highlight their negative experiences against the mass marketing and mass prescription of Depo-Provera. Through telling our stories, we are claiming our right to high-quality birth control and health care, generally. The Depo storytelling initiative has become an opportunity to participate in the creative process of story sharing, personal healing, empowerment, and community building. This kind of research creates a more accurate picture of the range and kinds of side effects women are experiencing while using Depo-Provera. It also makes it possible for us to expose the ways that women's bodies are still targeted for "population control." We believe that in order to create gynecological, reproductive, and other forms of basic safety and security for women, we must make these practices visible and, in the process, transform our isolation into collective action for reproductive freedom.

Beyond telling our stories we are highlighting leaders in reproductive justice. The Depo Diaries storytelling initiative has been instrumental in identifying groups and individuals working to overcome reproductive oppression. We have a vested interest in continuing to map and document networks and community initiatives that are effectively intervening against coercive practices by producing public education, providing accessible and creative ways to research and dissemi-nate information, and other transformative approaches.

We are currently working on a DVD about women's experiences in coercive reproductive practices, and have developed a booklet which examines contraceptive technologies through a critical feminist and reproductive justice analysis. From information available on our webpage (www.cwpe.org) to community workshops and conferences, we are expanding the traditional discourse of reproductive health to incorporate the voices of marginalized communities and to offer a critical view-point that opposes these oppressive and population-based practices. We also recog-nize that there is a critical need to map stories of trans and queer women, indigenous women, women with disabilities, and immigrant and refugee women. We need to understand their particular stories of coercion and unethical testing, justified by his-torical pathologizing and the domination of bodies and communities. Through the work of Depo Diaries, we call on all of these communities for their acute knowledge about the experiences of women with healthcare systems – state, public, and private – to contribute to the work against all abusive practices.

Further Reading

Please send testimonials and/or stories of your experiences of Depo-Provera and/or other adverse effects of birth control or stories of coercive reproductive practices to: depodiaries@cwpe.org

Please contact us for further information or inquiries of trainings and workshops on using stories as tools for liberatory practice against violence and population control at: powerofstories@cwpe.org

Visit the Committee on Women, Population, and the Environment's official website for current research, actions, and campaigns against population control: www.cwpe.org

Population & Development Program of Hampshire College: http://popdev.hampshire.edu

7.4

Women, People of Color, Children, and Health *and* Women and Environmental Justice

Karen J. Warren

Women, People of Color, Children, and Health

The health of women and children, particularly in poor communities of color, is adversely and disproportionately affected by harmful human environmental prac-tices. For example, in some developing countries, women spend much of their time cooking with biomass – wood, straw, or dung – in poorly ventilated areas. They are thereby exposed to high levels of indoor pollution. As the United Nations reports in *The World's Women, 1995*, significant health risks are experienced by women who cook indoors in developing countries.

> One study in Nepal found that women cook for about five hours a day, with indoor particulate concentrations in rural areas as high as 20,000 micrograms per cubic meter. As a result, acute respiratory infections and bronchitis are said to be very common in rural areas.
>
> Nonsmoking women in India and Nepal exposed to biomass smoke have been found to have abnormally high levels of chronic respiratory diseases – with mortality rates comparable to that of heavy male smokers. The enormously high levels of women's exposure to indoor air pollution during cooking found in 15 countries of Africa and Asia indicate very significant health risks to the many women who cook indoors in developing countries.[1]

Health issues in Western countries around chemical sensitivity also affect women. There are three main ways in which chemicals can enter the body: through inhalation, ingestion, or absorption through the skin.[2] In the United States and Canada, the chemical sensitivity literature shows that human sensitivities to substances like formaldehyde are strongly gender related (two to three times the number of cases among women than men) and age dependent (children and older women are the most vulnerable). In the Great Lakes Basin ecosystem, pesticides, heavy metals, PCBs (polychlorinated biphenyls), and dioxins have been shown not only to produce reproductive impairments, cancers, and tumors in fish and mammals and deformities in insect larvae, but in human tissue as well. PCBs have contributed to adverse reproductive outcomes (including decreased sperm count in males), low birth weight, infants born with smaller head circumferences, increased rates of cancer of all types, and circulatory and immune system diseases.[3] Similarly, pesticides and industrial pollutants contribute to many types of reproductive impairment in humans, for example, difficulty conceiving, miscarriages and spontaneous abortions, sperm toxicity, and fetal/infant related health problems.[4] Due largely to their ability to cross the placenta, to bioaccumulate, and to occur as mixtures, persistent toxic chemicals pose disproportionate serious health threats to infants, mothers, and the elderly.

There are important psychosocial aspects of exposure to environmental toxins. Studies in the United States of people exposed to relatively high levels of hazardous substances in Love Canal, New York, and Three Mile Island, Pennsylvania, show the prevalence of fear and anxieties about the future health impacts of such exposure.[5] According to Tom Muir and Anne Sudar, "These impacts are exacerbated by the people's feelings that they have no control over the situation."[6] They live in homes and communities from which no escape seems financially possible. This high level of distress has been shown to be associated with significantly poorer DNA repair in lymphocytes, as compared to low-distress subjects.[7]

Take, for example, the Exxon *Valdez* case. On March 24, 1989, the Exxon *Valdez* ran aground in Prince William Sound, Alaska, spilling 11 million gallons of oil, wiping out countless numbers of birds and sea otters, and drastically affecting ecosystem function in the region. The toll on human lives has also been great. Aleut

Indian villages of Chenega Bay and Tatilek and the cities of Valdez and Cordova face increased depression and alcoholism. According to Paul Koberstein:

> In Valdez, records show the divorce rate is four times higher than before the spill. In Cordova, a state survey indicates that nearly two-thirds of the population suffers from post-traumatic stress syndrome, an emotional breakdown that typically occurs after a catastrophe or war. In Homer, demand for substance abuse programs doubled. In Kodiak, admissions to the local mental health centers increased by nearly 50 percent. In many communities, health officials are seeing increases in child abuse and neglect.[8]

Like other indigenous populations, the seventy villagers of Chenega Bay "face the paradox of good money for ruined lives. Many of them earned $2,000 a week on the spill, but the tribe lost an entire year of subsistence fishing" and untold disruptions to their traditional way of life.

While environmental disasters such as those caused by the Exxon *Valdez* affect both men and women, some environmental problems affect women more harshly. In the United States, American Indian women historically have faced unique health risks.

> A survey of households and hospitals on the Pine Ridge Reservation in South Dakota revealed that in one month in 1979, 38 percent of the pregnant women on the reservation suffered miscarriages, compared to the normal rate of between 10 and 20 percent… [there were] extremely high rates of cleft palate and other birth defects, as well as hepatitis, jaundice, and serious diarrhea. Health officials confirmed that their reservation had higher than average rates of bone and gynecological cancers.[9]

Inadequate sewage treatment facilities have led to fecal contamination of drinking and bathing water. "Tests done by government officials also showed high levels of radioactivity in the water. The reservation is downwind from old mines surrounded by uranium trailings."[10]

Children are also particularly vulnerable to toxins. According to "What's Gotten Into Our Children," published by Children Now, a California-based children's advocacy organization, some characteristics unique to children make them particularly vulnerable to environmental hazards. Children Now cites four specific areas in which children are physically more vulnerable than adults: food and water, home, schools, and outdoor play areas. Children tend to consume greater amounts of food that contain toxins, thereby multiplying the potential risk.[11] In the United States, the National Resources Defense Council (NRDC) estimates that more than half of the lifetime risk of cancer associated with pesticides on fruit is incurred before the age of six.[12] In homes and schools, hazardous products (e.g., cleaning products), and exposure to lead, radon, asbestos, and indoor air pollution (e.g., tobacco smoke, formaldehyde found in some carpeting, wallboard, and insulation) are thought to be particularly harmful to children since the same amount of exposure to children and adults is believed to produce higher concentrations in the smaller bodies of children. Outdoors, pesticides, harmful sun exposure (due to depletion of the ozone layer), air pollution, and unsafe play areas can result in serious health conditions in children (e.g., breathing certain kinds of asbestos fibers can increase the chance of developing chronic diseases, ground level ozone-caused air pollution can cause respiratory problems such as shortness of breath, coughing).

Furthermore, in the United States, over 700,000 inner-city children are suffering from lead poisoning (and the learning disabilities that result), 50 percent of whom are African, Hispanic, and Asian American.[13] While all children are at risk, poor children are at greater risk: they are more likely to live in neighborhoods with environmental hazards; poor families lack the financial resources to remove hazards from their home or purchase alternative, nonhazardous products; poor children are less likely to have access to health care for treatment; the families of poor children often lack the necessary political clout to insist on the cleanup of hazards in the neighborhood.[14] Furthermore, in Third World countries, usually over half the people are under fifteen years old. So children are a majority of any group. In increasing numbers, children are developing environmental sensitivities, allergies, and asthma (the study and treatment of which is developing into a field of its own, clinical ecology).[15]

Women and Environmental Justice

In 1987, the United Church of Christ Commission for Racial Justice published a stunning and now-classic report entitled "Toxic Waste and Race in the United States." Using sophisticated statistical analysis, the report indicated that race (not class) is the primary factor in the location of hazardous waste in the United States: Three out of every five African and Hispanic Americans (more than 15 million of the nation's 26 million African Americans, and over 8 million of the 15 million Hispanics), and over half of all Asian Pacific Islanders and American Indians, live in communities with one or more uncontrolled toxic waste sites. The nation's largest hazardous waste landfill, receiving toxins from forty-five states, is in Emelle, Alabama, which is 79.9 percent African American. Probably the greatest concentration of hazardous waste sites in the United States is on the predominately African American and Hispanic South Side of Chicago. In Houston, Texas, six of eight municipal incinerators, and all five city landfills, are located in predominately African American neighborhoods.[16]

The federal Centers for Disease Control in Atlanta, Georgia, documents that lead poisoning endangers the health of nearly 8 million inner-city, largely African American and Hispanic, children. Countless more live with crumbling asbestos in housing projects and schools. Seventy-five percent of the residents in rural areas of the southwestern United States, mainly Hispanic Americans, are drinking pesticide-contaminated water. Yet Hispanics hold only 1 percent of substantive policy-making positions at the United States Environmental Protection Agency (EPA).[17] Hispanics thereby have limited institutional input at policy-making levels to the plights of Hispanic communities affected by lead poisoning.

Women, especially poor women of color, are organizing throughout the world to fight environmental contaminations of all kinds in their communities. For example, in the United States, Mothers of East Los Angeles (MELA), founded in 1985, protested a hazardous-waste incinerator in the small city of Vernon, California. According to Dick Russell:

> Even in state-of-the-art hazardous-waste incinerators, pollutants escape through the stacks. In Vernon, the burning of an estimated 225,000 tons a year of solvents, pesticides, alcohols, oil and paint sludges, heavy metal residues, industrial liquids, and infectious wastes from hospitals would also leave some 19,000 tons of highly toxic ash, dust, and other by-products to dispose of. All this in close proximity not only to twenty-six schools, but also dozens of food-related industries.[18]

Time magazine reported the outcome of MELA's activities:

> Last week, after six years of agitation marked by four lawsuits, 16 hearings and six mile-long protest marches, the 400-strong Mothers of East L.A. passed around cookies to celebrate a major victory: cancellation of a proposed commercial incinerator they claimed could spew cancer-causing particles over the community by burning 22,500 tons of used motor oil and industrial sludge annually. Citing "political pressure" and the prospect of "interminable litigation," attorneys for Security Environmental Systems, which was to build the facility, ruefully announced "abandonment" of the project.[19]

Women often play a primary role in community environmental activism because environmental ills touch their lives in direct, immediate ways.[20] As Cynthia Hamilton writes:

> Women often play a primary role in community action because it is about things they know best. They also tend to use organizing strategies and methods that are the antithesis of those of the traditional environmental movement. Minority women in several urban areas [of the United States] have found themselves part of a new radical core of environmental activists, motivated by the irrationalities of capital-intensive growth. These individuals are responding not to "nature" in the abstract but to their homes and the health of their children…. Women are more likely to take on these issues than men precisely because the home has been defined as a woman's domain.[21]

Because of the direct impact of environmental degradation on their lives, working-class minority women organize around "very pragmatic environmental issues."[22]

The early roots of the upsurge of minority environmental activism in the United States can be found in Warren County, North Carolina, where, in 1982, the state decided to build a PCB disposal site with $2.5 million in federal monies. The EPA modified the permit to locate the site only fifteen feet above the water table (normally fifty feet is required for PCBs).[23] The area's 16,000 residents – 60 percent African American and 4 percent Native American – organized a series of marches and protests involving "a cross-section of religious leaders, farmers, educators, citizens of all races" because they felt the decision was racially motivated. The residents lost. Shortly thereafter, the U.S. General Accounting Office reported "on racial and socioeconomic characteristics of communities surrounding hazardous waste landfills in the Southeast [United States]. It found that three out of four were predominantly black and poor."[24]

Citizens for a Better Environment (CBE) released a report in 1989 on the Richmond, California, area, located sixteen miles across the bay from San Francisco and home to about 100,000 residents, about half of whom are African American. Richmond has more than 350 industrial facilities that handle hazardous chemicals, and 210 toxins are routinely emitted into the air, water, as solid waste or in industrial storage sites. According to CBE, "All of the lower income, minority neighborhoods are in the western and southern parts of Richmond where the highest concentration of petro-chemical facilities are also located."[25]

Navajo Indians are the primary workforce in the mining of uranium in the United States. According to a 1986 report, "Toxics and Minority Communities" by the Center for Third World Organizing (Oakland, California), 2 million tons of radio-active uranium tailings have been dumped on Native American lands. Reproductive organ cancer among Navajo teenagers is seventeen times the national average. Indian reservations of the Kaibab Paiutes (northern Arizona) and other tribes across the United States are targeted sites for hazardous waste incinerators, disposal, and storage facilities.[26] On July 4, 1990, the *Minneapolis Star Tribune* reported that members of the Kaibab Paiute reservation in northern Arizona were negotiating to bring about 70,000 tons of hazardous waste each year to the Kaibab Paiute reserva-tion in Northern Arizona. An incinerator would burn the waste, and the ash would be buried on tribal land. The Paiutes stand to reap $1 million a year from the waste-burning operation. The Kaibab Paiutes and other tribes are torn between the economic gains and the integrity of their land and traditional ways. "The plans are seductive on reservations where unemployment averages 40 percent."[27]

Garbage and hazardous waste firms are well aware that the majority of reserva-tions, governed by tribal leaders, do not have strict environmental regulations. "On self-governing Indian lands, where tribal councils are the authority, waste companies can avoid tough state laws and the prying eyes of county and local governments."[28] As reported by the *Christian Science Monitor*:

> Recently, over the objection of tribal members, the Rosebud Sioux Tribal Council in South Dakota signed a contract with a Connecticut-based waste disposal firm to develop a 5,000-acre garbage dump that will accept wastes from Minneapolis, Denver, and beyond. The proposed dump, located on what is thought to be an ancient Indian burial ground, is 70 miles from the site of the massacre at Wounded Knee and in the heart of the unspoiled prairie [North] Americans recently viewed in [Kevin Costner's epic drama] "Dances with Wolves." The contract states that not any existing environ-mental regulations of South Dakota are applicable and forbids the Sioux from enacting any laws to govern the waste project. What will the Sioux receive in return for receiving this waste? A little more than $1 per ton for the garbage they will be host to forever.[29]

In Canada, much of the land being proposed for parks is already claimed by original peoples. For example, Auyuittuq National Park Reserve, located on Cumerland Peninsula, Baffin Island, established as a park in 1972, was probably first inhabited about 4,000 years ago by Inuit.[30] While several native groups have proposed "joint native-government management regimes," no joint management regimes now exist in the Canadian national park system.[31] Furthermore, subjecting such land to be used as parks and a government-run management scheme raises significant concerns about whether national parks established on lands claimed by aboriginal peoples legally prejudice future land claim settlements by natives.

Conclusion

This chapter uses a feminist approach to discuss empirical women–other human Others–nature interconnections. While all humans are affected by environmental degradation, women, people of color, children, and the poor throughout the world experience environmental harms disproportionately. Nature is, indeed, a feminist issue....

Notes

1. *The World's Women, 1995: Trends and Statistics* (New York: United Nations, 1995), 49.
2. Sonia Jasso and Maria Mazorra, "Following the Harvest: The Health Hazards of Migrant and Seasonal Farm working Women," in *Double Exposure: Women's Health Hazards on the Job and at Home*, ed. Wendy Chavkin (New York: Monthly Review Press, 1984), 94.
3. See Tom Muir and Anne Sudar, "Toxic Chemicals in the Great Lakes Basin Ecosystem: Some Observations" (Burlington, Ont.: Environment Canada, 1988; unpublished).
4. Muir and Sudar, "Toxic Chemicals," 61.
5. Muir and Sudar, "Toxic Chemicals," 82.
6. Muir and Sudar, "Toxic Chemicals," 82.
7. Muir and Sudar, "Toxic Chemicals," 82.
8. Paul Koberstein, "Exxon Oil Spill Taints Lives of Aleut Indian Villagers," *The Sunday Oregonian*, 24 September 1989, A2.
9. Nicholas Freudenberg and Ellen Zaltzberg, "From Grassroots Activism to Political Power: Women Organizing Against Environmental Hazards," in *Double Exposure: Women's Health Hazards on the Job and at Home*, ed. Wendy Chavkin (New York: Monthly Review Press, 1984), 249.
10. Freudenberg and Zaltzberg, "From Grassroots Activism," 249.
11. Dana Hughes, "What's Gotten Into Our Children" (Los Angeles: Children Now, 1990), 6. (Children Now can be reached at 10951 West Pico Boulevard, Los Angeles, CA 90064.)
12. Hughes, "What's Gotten Into Our Children," 6.
13. Cynthia Hamilton, "*Women, Home, and Community*," *woman of power: a magazine of feminism, spirituality, and politics*, 20 (Spring 1991), 42.
14. Hughes, "What's Gotten Into Our Children," 35.
15. Muir and Sudar, "Toxic Chemicals," 78–9.

16. "Toxic Waste and Race in the United States: A National Report on the Racial and Socioeconomic Characteristics of Communities with Hazardous Waste Sites," 1987, Commission for Racial Justice, United Church of Christ, 105 Madison Avenue, New York, NY 10016.

17. Centers for Disease Control, Atlanta, Georgia, cited in Dick Russell, "Environmental Racism," *The Amicus Journal* (Spring 1989), 24.

18. Dick Russell, "Environmental Racism," 29.

19. "Mothers of Prevention," *Time*, 10 June 1991, 25.

20. For example, the South West Organizing Project (SWOP) has been actively involved in protesting and publicizing acts of environmental racism. (SWOP can be reached at 211 10th St. S.W., Albuquerque, NM 87102.)

21. Hamilton, "Women, Home," 43.

22. Hamilton, "Women, Home," 42.

23. Russell, "Environmental Racism," 24.

24. Russell, "Environmental Racism," 24.

25. Cited in Russell, "Environmental Racism," 25.

26. "Toxics and Minority Communities," the Center for Third World Organizing (Oakland, California), 1986.

27. "The Indian and Toxic Waste," *Minneapolis Star/Tribune*, 4 July 1990.

28. "The Indian and Toxic Waste," *Minneapolis Star/Tribune*, 4 July 1990.

29. Thomas A. Daschle, "Dances with Garbage," *Christian Science Monitor*, 14 February 1991, 18.

30. Nicholas Lawson, "Where Whitemen Come to Play," *Cultural Survival Quarterly* 13, no. 2 (1989), 54.

31. Lawson, "Where Whitemen," 56.

7.5

Healing the Wounds: Feminism, Ecology, and the Nature/Culture Dualism

Ynestra King

No part of living nature can ignore the extreme threat to life on Earth. We are faced with worldwide deforestation, the disappearance of hundreds of species of life, and the increasing pollution of the gene pool by poisons and low-level radiation. We are also faced with biological atrocities unique to modern life – the existence of the AIDS virus and the possibility of even more dreadful and pernicious diseases caused by genetic mutation. Worldwide food shortages, including episodes of mass starvation, continue to mount as prime agricultural land is used to grow cash crops to pay national debts instead of food to feed people.[1] Animals are mistreated and mutilated in horrible ways to test cosmetics, drugs, and surgical procedures. The stock-piling of ever greater weapons of annihilation and the terrible imagining of new ones continues. The piece of the pie that women have only begun to sample as a result of the feminist movement is rotten and carcinogenic, and surely our feminist theory and politics must take account of this, however much we yearn for the opportunities that have been denied to us. What is the point of partaking equally in a system that is killing us all?

The contemporary ecological crisis alone creates an imperative that feminists take ecology seriously, but there are other reasons ecology is central to feminist philosophy and politics. The ecological crisis is related to the systems of hatred of all that is natural and female by the white, male, Western formulators of philosophy, technology, and death inventions. It is my contention that the systematic denigration of working-class people and people of color, women, and animals is connected to the basic dualism that lies at the root of Western civilization. But the mind-set of hierarchy originates within human society. It has its material roots in the domination of human by human, particularly of women by men. While I cannot speak for the liberation struggles of people of color, I believe that the goals of feminism, ecology, and movements against racism and for the survival of indigenous peoples are internally related and must be understood and pursued together in a worldwide, genuinely pro-life,[2] movement.

There is at the root of Western society a deep ambivalence about life itself, about our own fertility and that of non-human nature, and a terrible confusion about our place in nature. But as the work of social ecologist Murray Bookchin demonstrates, nature did not declare war on humanity, patriarchal humanity declared war on women and on living nature.[3] ...

Ecofeminism: Beyond the Nature/Culture Dualism

Women have been culture's sacrifice to nature. The practice of human sacrifice to outsmart or appease a feared nature is ancient. And it is in resistance to this sacrificial mentality – on the part of both the sacrificer and sacrifice – that some feminists have argued against the association of women with nature, emphasizing the social dimension of traditional women's lives. Part of the work of feminism has been asserting that the activities of women, believed to be more natural than those of men, are in fact absolutely social. For example, giving birth is natural (though how it is done is very social) but mothering is an absolutely social activity.[4] In bringing up their children, mothers face ethical and moral choices as complex as those considered by professional politicians and ethicists. In the wake of feminism, women will continue to do these things, but the problem of connecting humanity to nature will still have to be acknowledged and solved. In our mythology of complementarity, men and women have led vicarious lives, where women had feelings and led instinctual lives and men engaged in the projects illuminated by reason. Feminism has exposed the extent to which it was all a lie – that's why it has been so important to feminism to establish the mindful, social nature of mothering.

It is as if women were entrusted with and have kept the dirty little secret that humanity emerges from non-human nature into society in the life of the species and the person. The process of nurturing an unsocialized, undifferentiated human infant into an adult person – the socialization of the organic – is the bridge between nature and culture. The Western male bourgeois then extracts himself from the realm of the organic to become a public citizen, as if born from the head of Zeus. He puts away childish things. He disempowers and sentimentalizes his mother, sacrificing her to nature. But the key to the historic agency of women with respect to the nature/culture dualism lies in the fact that the traditional activities of women – mothering, cooking, healing, farming, foraging – are as social as they are natural.

The task of an ecological feminism is the organic forging of a genuinely anti-dualistic, or dialectical, theory and practice. No previous feminism has addressed this problem adequately, hence the necessity of ecofeminism. Rather than succumb to nihilism, pessimism, and an end to reason and history, we seek to enter into history, to a genuinely ethical thinking – where one uses mind and history to reason from the "is" to the "ought" and to reconcile humanity with nature, within and without. This is the starting point for ecofeminism.

Each major contemporary feminist theory, liberal, social, and cultural, has taken up the issue of the relationship between women and nature. And each in its own way has capitulated to dualistic thinking. Ecofeminism takes from socialist feminism the idea that women have been *historically* positioned at the biological dividing line where the organic emerges into the social. The domination of nature originates in society and therefore must be resolved in society. Thus, it is the embodied woman as social historical agent, rather than as a product of natural law, who is the subject of ecofeminism. But the weakness of socialist feminism's theory of the person is serious from an ecofeminist standpoint. An ecological feminism calls for a dynamic, developmental theory of the person – male *and* female – who emerges out of non-human nature, where difference is neither reified nor ignored and the dialectical relationship between human and non-human nature is understood.

Cultural feminism's greatest weakness is its tendency to make the personal into the political, with its emphasis on personal transformation and empowerment. This is most obvious in the attempt to overcome the apparent opposition between spirituality and politics. For cultural feminists, spirituality is the heart in a heartless world (whereas for socialist feminists it is the opiate of the people). Cultural feminists have formed the "beloved community" of feminism – with all the power, potential, and problems of a religion. And as an appropriate response to the need for mystery and attention to personal alienation in an overly rationalized world, it is a vital and important movement. But by itself it does not provide the basis for a genuinely dialectical ecofeminist theory and practice, one that addresses history as well as mystery. For this reason, cultural/spiritual feminism (sometimes even called "nature feminism") is not synonymous with ecofeminism in that creating a gynocentric culture and politics is a necessary but not sufficient condition for ecofeminism.

Both feminism and ecology embody the revolt of nature against human domination. They demand that we rethink the relationship between humanity and the rest of nature, including our natural, embodied selves. In ecofeminism, nature is the central category of analysis. An analysis of the interrelated dominations of nature – psyche and sexuality, human oppression, and non-human nature – and the historic position of women in relation to those forms of domination is the starting point of ecofeminist theory. We share with cultural feminism the necessity of a politics with heart and a beloved community, recognizing our connection with each other – and with non-human nature. Socialist feminism has given us a powerful critical perspective with which to understand, and transform, history. Separately, they perpetuate the dualism of "mind" and "nature." Together they make possible a new ecological relationship between nature and culture, in which mind and nature, heart and reason, join forces to transform the systems of domination, internal and external, that threaten the existence of life on Earth.

Practice does not wait for theory – it comes out of the imperatives of history. Women are the revolutionary bearers of this anti-dualistic potential in the world today. In addition to the enormous impact of feminism on Western civilization, women have been at the forefront of every historical, political movement to reclaim the Earth. For example, for many years in India poor women who come out of the Gandhian movement have waged a non-violent campaign for land reform and to save the forest, called the *Chipko Andolan* (the hugging movement), wrapping their bodies around trees as bulldozers arrive. Each of the women has a tree of her own she is to protect – to steward. When loggers were sent in, one of the women said, "Let them know they will not fell a single tree without the felling of us first. When the men raise their axes, we will embrace the trees to protect them."[5] These women have waged a remarkably successful non-violent struggle, and their tactics have spread to other parts of India. Men have joined in, though the campaign was originated and continues to be led by women. Yet this is not a sentimental movement – lives depend on the survival of the forest. For most of the women of the world, interest in preservation of the land, water, air, and energy is no abstraction but a clear part of the effort to simply survive.

The increasing militarization of the world has intensified this struggle. Women and children make up 80 percent of war refugees. Lands are often burned and scarred in such a way as to prevent cultivation for many years after the battles, so that starvation and hardship follow long after the fighting has stopped.[6] And, here, too, women – often mothers and farmers – respond to necessity. They become the protectors of the Earth in an effort to eke out a small living on the land to feed themselves and their families.

There are other areas of feminist activism that illuminate an enlightened ecofeminist perspective.[7] Potentially, one of the best examples of an appropriately mediated, dialectical relationship to nature is the feminist health movement. The medicalization of childbirth in the first part of this century and, currently, the redesign and appropriation of reproduction both create new profit-making technologies for capitalism and make heretofore natural processes mediated by women into arenas controlled by men. Women offered themselves up to the ministrations of "experts," internalizing the notion that they didn't know enough and surrendering their power. They also accepted the idea that maximum intervention in and domination of nature are inherently good. But since the onset of feminism in the 1960s, women in the United States have gone quite a way in reappropriating and demedicalizing childbirth. As a result of this movement, many more women want to be told what all their options are and many choose invasive medical technologies only under unusual and informed circumstances. They do not necessarily reject these useful technologies in some cases, but they have pointed a finger at motivations of profit and control in the technologies' widespread application. Likewise, my argument here is not that feminism should repudiate all aspects of Western science and medicine. It is to assert that we should develop the sophistication to decide for ourselves when intervention serves our best interest.

Another central area of concern in which women may employ ecofeminism to overcome misogynist dualism is that of body consciousness. Accepting our own bodies just as they are, knowing how they look, feel, and smell, and learning to work with them to become healthier is a basis for cultural and political liberation. In many patriarchal cultures, women are complicit in the domination of our natural bodies, seeking to please men at any cost. Chinese foot-binding, performed by women, is a widely cited example of misogynist domination of women's bodies. But even as Western feminists condemn these practices, most of us will do anything to our bodies (yes, even feminists) to appear closer to norms of physical beauty that come naturally to about 0.2 percent of the female population. The rest of us struggle to be skinny, hairless, and, lately, muscular. We lie in the sun to get tan even when we know we are courting melanoma, especially as the accelerating depletion of the ozone layer makes "sunbathing" a dangerous sport. We submit ourselves to extremely dangerous surgical procedures. We primp, prune, douche, deodorize, and diet as if our natural bodies were our mortal enemies. Some of us living the most privileged lives in the world starve ourselves close to death for beauty, literally.

To the extent that we make our own flesh an enemy, or docilely submit ourselves to medical experts, we are participating in the domination of nature. To the extent that we learn to work with the restorative powers of our bodies, using medical technologies and drugs sparingly, we are developing an appropriately mediated relationship to our own natures. But even the women's health movement has not realized a full ecofeminist perspective.[8] It has yet to fully grasp health as an ecological and social rather than an individual problem, in which the systematic poisoning of environments where women live and work is addressed as a primary political issue. Here the community-based movements against toxic wastes, largely initiated and led by women, and the feminist health movement may meet.

A related critical area for a genuinely dialectical practice is a reconstruction of science, taking into account the critique of science advanced by radical ecology and feminism.[9] Feminist historians and philosophers of science are demonstrating that the will to know and the will to power need not be the same thing. They argue that there are ways of knowing the world that are not based on objectification and domination.[10] Here, again, apparently antithetical epistemologies, science and mysticism, can coexist. We shall need all our ways of knowing to create life on this planet that is both ecological and sustainable.

As feminists, we shall need to develop an ideal of freedom that is neither antisocial nor anti-natural.[11] We are past the point of throwing off our chains to reclaim our ostensibly free nature, if such a point ever existed. Ecofeminism is not an argument for a return to prehistory. The knowledge that women were not always dominated and that society was not always hierarchical is a powerful inspiration for contemporary women, so long as such a society is not represented as a "natural order," apart from history, to which we will inevitably return by a great reversal.

From an ecofeminist perspective, we are part of nature, but not inherently good or bad, free or unfree. There is no one natural order that represents freedom. We are *potentially* free in nature, but as human beings that freedom has to be intentionally created by using our understanding of the natural world. For this reason we must develop a different understanding of the relationship between human and non-human nature, based on the stewardship of evolution. To do this we need a theory of history where the natural evolution of the planet and the social history of the species are not separated. We emerged from non-human nature, as the organic emerged from the inorganic.

Here, potentially, we recover ontology as the ground for ethics. We thoughtful human beings must use the fullness of our sensibility and intelligence to push ourselves intentionally to another stage of evolution: one where we will fuse a new way of being human on this planet with a sense of the sacred, informed by all ways of knowing – intuitive *and* scientific, mystical *and* rational. It is the moment where women recognize ourselves as agents of history – yes, even as unique agents – and knowingly bridge the classic dualisms between spirit and matter, art and politics, reason and intuition. This is the potentiality of a *rational re-enchantment*. This is the project of ecofeminism.

At this point in history, the domination of nature is inextricably bound up with the domination of persons, and both must be addressed – without arguments over "the primary contradiction" in the search for a single Archimedes point for revolution. There is no such thing. And there is no point in liberating people if the planet cannot sustain their liberated lives, or in saving the planet by disregarding the preciousness of human existence not only to ourselves but to the rest of life on Earth.

Notes

1. One of the major issues at the United Nations Decade on Women forum held in Nairobi, Kenya, in 1985 was the effect of the international monetary system on women and the particular burdens women bear because of the money owed the "First World," particularly US economic interests, by developing countries.
2. It is one of the absurd examples of newspeak that the designation "pro-life" has been appropriated by the militarist right to support forced child bearing.
3. See especially Murray Bookchin, *The Ecology of Freedom* (Palo Alto, CA: Cheshire Books, 1982). Of the various ecological theories that are not explicitly feminist, I draw here on Bookchin's work because he articulates a historical theory of hierarchy that begins with the domination of women by men, making way for domination by race and class, and the domination of nature. Hence the term "social" ecology. *The Ecology of Freedom* presents a radical view of the emergence, and potential dissolution, of

hierarchy. Social ecology is just as concerned with relations of domination between persons as it is with the domination of nature. Hence it should be of great interest to feminists.

4. On the social, mindful nature of mothering, see the work of Sara Ruddick, especially "Maternal thinking," *Feminist Studies*, 6(2): 342–67; and "Preservative love and military destruction: some reflections on mothering and peace," in Joyce Trebilcot (ed.), *Mothering: Essays in Feminist Theory*, pp. 231–62 (Totowa, NJ: Rowman and Allanheld, 1983).

5. Catherine Caufield, *In the Rainforest*, pp. 156–8 (Chicago: University of Chicago Press, 1984).

6. See Edward Hyams, *Soil and Civilization* (New York: Harper and Row, 1976).

7. See Petra Kelly, *Fighting for Hope* (Boston: South End Press, 1984) for a practical, feminist green political analysis and program, with examples of ongoing movements and activities.

8. I am indebted to ecofeminist sociologist and environmental health activist Lin Nelson for pointing out to me why the feminist health movement is yet to become ecological.

9. See Elizabeth Fee, "Is feminism a threat to scientific objectivity?" *International Journal of Women's Studies*, 4(4): 378–92. See also Sandra Harding, *The Science Question in Feminism* (Ithaca, NY: Cornell University Press, 1986) and Evelyn Fox Keller, *Reflections on Gender and Science* (New Haven, CT: Yale University Press, 1985).

10. See, for example, Evelyn Fox Keller, *A Feeling for the Organism: the Life and Work of Barbara McClintock* (San Francisco, Freeman, 1983).

11. The cross-cultural interpretations of personal freedom of anthropologist Dorothy Lee are evocative of the possibility of such an ideal of freedom. See Dorothy Lee, *Freedom and Culture* (Englewood Cliffs, NJ: Prentice-Hall, 1959).

7.6
Mad Cows and Sacred Cows
Vandana Shiva

When I gave a speech at the Dalai Lama's 60th birthday celebration, he wrote me two beautiful lines of compassion: "All sentient beings, including the small insects, cherish themselves. All have the right to overcome suffering and achieve happiness. I therefore pray that we show love and compassion to all."[1]

What is our responsibility to other species? Do the boundaries between species have integrity? Or are these boundaries mere constructs that should be broken for human convenience? The call to "transgress boundaries" advocated by both patriarchal capitalists and postmodern feminists cannot be so simple. It needs to be based on a sophisticated and complex discrimination between different kinds of boundaries, an understanding of whom is protected by what boundaries and whose freedom is achieved by what transgressions.

In India, cows have been treated as sacred – as Lakshmi, the goddess of wealth, and as the cosmos in which all gods and goddesses reside – for centuries. Ecologically, the cow has been central to Indian civilization. Both materially and conceptually the world of Indian agriculture has built its sustainability on the integrity of the cow, considering her inviolable and sacred, seeing her as the mother of the prosperity of food systems.

According to K.M. Munshi, India's first agriculture minister after independence from the British, cows

> are not worshipped in vain. They are the primeval agents who enrich the soil—nature's great land transformers—who supply organic matter which, after treatment, becomes nutrient matter of the greatest importance. In India, tradition, religious sentiment, and economic needs have tried to maintain a cattle population large enough to maintain the cycle.[2]

By using crop wastes and uncultivated land, indigenous cattle do not compete with humans for food; rather, they provide organic fertilizer for fields and thus enhance food productivity. Within the sacredness of the cow lie this ecological rationale and conservation imperative. The cow is a source of cow-dung energy, nutrition, and leather, and its contribution is linked to the work of women in feeding and milking cows, collecting cow dung, and nurturing sick cows to health. Along with being the primary experts in animal husbandry, women are also the food processors in the traditional dairy industry, making curds, butter, ghee, and buttermilk.

Indian cattle provide more food than they consume, in contrast to those of the U.S. cattle industry, in which cattle consume six times more food than they provide.[3] In addition, every year, Indian cattle excrete 700 million tons of recoverable manure: half of this is used as fuel, liberating the thermal equivalent of 27 million tons of kerosene, 35 million tons of coal, or 68 million tons of wood, all of which are scarce resources in India. The remaining half is used as fertilizer.

Two-thirds of the power requirements of Indian villages are met by cattle-dung fuel from some 80 million cattle. (Seventy million of these cattle are the male progeny of what industrial developers term "useless" low-milk-yielding cows.) To replace animal power in agriculture, India would have to spend about $1 billion annually on gas. As for other livestock produce, it may be sufficient to mention that the export of hides, skins, and other products brings in $150 million annually.[4]

Yet this highly efficient food system, based on multiple uses of cattle, has been dismantled in the name of efficiency and development. The Green Revolution shifted agriculture's fertilizer base from renewable organic inputs to non-renewable chemical ones, making both cattle and women's work with cattle dispensable in the production of food grain. The White Revolution, aping the West's wasteful animal husbandry and dairying practices, is destroying the world's most evolved dairy culture and displacing women from their role in the dairy-processing industry.

The Green Revolution has emerged as an enemy to the White, as the high-yielding crop varieties have reduced straw production, and their byproducts are unpalatable to livestock and thus useless as fodder. Further, hybrid crops deprive the soil of nutrients, creating deficiencies in fodder and disease in livestock. The White

Revolution, in turn, instead of viewing livestock as ecologically integrated with crops, has reduced the cow to a mere milk machine. As Shanti George observes,

> The trouble is that when dairy planners look at the cow, they see just her udder; though there is much more to her. They equate cattle only with milk, and do not consider other livestock produce – draught power, dung for fertilizer and fuel, hides, skins, horn, and hooves.[5]

In India, cow's milk is but one of the many byproducts of the interdependence between agriculture and animal husbandry. There, cattle are considered agents of production in the food system; only secondarily are they viewed as producing consumable items. But the White Revolution makes milk production primary and exclusive, and according to the Royal Commission and the Indian Council of Agricultural Research, if milk production is unduly pushed up, it may indirectly affect the entire basis of Indian agriculture.[6]

Worse, trade-liberalization policies in India are leading to the slaughter of cattle for meat exports, threatening diverse, disease-resistant breeds and small farmers' integrated livestock-crop-production systems with extinction. In the United Kingdom, giant slaughterhouses and the factory farming of cattle are being called into question by the spread of "mad cow disease" (BSE – bovine spongiform encephalopathy), which has infected over 1.5 million cows in Britain. While this disease is sounding the death knell of the non-sustainable livestock economy in Britain, India's "sacred cows" are being sent to slaughterhouses to "catch up" with the beef exports and beef consumption figures of "advanced" countries. This globalization of non-sustainable and hazardous systems of food production is symptomatic of a deeper madness than that infecting U.K. cows.

Ratcheting Up the Milk Machine

As the idea of the cow-as-milk-machine runs into trouble worldwide, multinational biotech industries are promoting new miracles of genetic engineering to increase milk production, further threatening the livelihoods of small producers. Multinational corporations such as Elanco (a subsidiary of Eli Lilly), Cynamic, Monsanto, and Upjohn are all rushing to put bovine somatrophin (BST), a growth hormone commercially produced by genetic engineering, on the market, in spite of controversy about its ecological impact.[7]

When injected daily into cows, BST diverts energy to milk production. Cows may get emaciated if too much energy is diverted to produce milk. And, as in all other "miracles" of modern agricultural science, the gain in milk production is contingent upon a number of other factors, such as use of industrial feed and a computerized feeding program.[8] Finally, women's traditional role in caring for cows and processing milk falls into the hands of men and machines.

The use of genetically engineered BST, or bovine growth hormone (BGH), is leading to major consumer resistance and a demand for the labeling of milk, which the biotechnology industry actively opposes. The European Union has voted against the labeling of genetically engineered products, and Monsanto has sued U.S. farmers who label their milk "BGH-free." Democracy is thus stifled by "free trade."

The inherent violence of the White Revolution lies in its treatment of the needs of small farmers and of living resources as dispensable if they produce the wrong thing in the wrong quantity. The same global commoditization processes that render Indian cattle "unproductive" (even when, considered holistically, they are highly productive) simultaneously dispense with European cattle for being overproductive. Annihilating diverse livestock destroys knowledge on how to protect and conserve living resources as sources of life. This protection is replaced by the protection of the profits of rich farmers and the control of agribusiness.

Crops as Food for All

In ecological agricultural cultures, technologies and economies are based on an integration between crops and animal husbandry. The wastes of one provide nutrition for the other, in mutual and reciprocal ways. Crop byproducts feed cattle, and cattle waste feeds the soils that nourish the crops. Crops do not just yield grain, they also yield straw, which provides fodder and organic matter. Crops are thus food for humans, animals, and the many organisms in the soil. These organically fed soils are home to millions of microorganisms that work and improve the soil's fertility. Bacteria feed on the cellulose fibers of straw that farmers return to the soil. In each hectare, between 100 and 300 kilograms of amoebas feed on these bacteria, making the lignite fibers available for uptake by plants. In each gram of soil, 100,000 algae provide organic matter and serve as vital nitrogen fixers. In each hectare are one to two tons of fungi and macrofauna such as arthropods, mollusks, and field mice. Rodents that bore under the fields aerate the soil and improve its water-holding capacity. Spiders, centipedes, and insects grind organic matter from the surface of the soil and leave behind enriching droppings.[9]

Soils treated with farmyard manure have from 2 to 2.5 times as many earthworms as untreated soils. These earthworms contribute to soil fertility by maintaining soil structure, aeration, and drainage and by breaking down organic matter and incorporating it into the soil. According to Charles Darwin, "It may be doubted whether there are many other animals which have played so important a part in the history of creatures."[10]

The little earthworm working invisibly in the soil is actually a tractor, fertilizer factory, and dam combined. Worm-worked soils are more water-stable than unworked soils, and worm-inhabited soils have considerably more organic carbons and nitrogen. By their continuous movement through soils, earthworms aerate the soil, increasing the air volume in soil by up to 30 percent. Soils with earthworms drain four to ten times faster than soils without earthworms, and their water-holding capacity is 20 percent higher. Earthworm casts, or droppings, which can consist of up to 36 tons per acre per year, contain carbon, nitrogen, calcium, magnesium, potassium, sodium, and phosphorous, promoting the microbial activity essential to soil fertility.

Industrial-farming techniques would deprive these diverse species of food sources and instead assault them with chemicals, destroying the rich biodiversity in the soil and with it the basis for the renewal of soil fertility.

The Intensive Livestock Economy

Europe's intensive livestock economy requires seven times the area of Europe in other countries for the production of cattle feed.[11] These "shadow acres" necessary for feed production are in fact an extensive use of resources. While this feed-production system does not conserve acres, the concentration of animals in unlivable spaces does save space. The efficiency question that the intensive livestock industry is always asking is, "How many animals can be crammed into the smallest space for the least cost and the greatest profit?"[12]

In a complementary system of agriculture, the cattle eat what the humans cannot. They eat straw from the crops and grass from pastures and field boundaries. In a competitive model such as the livestock industry, grain is diverted from human consumption to intensive feed for livestock. It takes two kilograms of grain to produce one kilogram of poultry, four kilograms of grain to produce one kilogram of pork, and eight kilograms of grain to produce one kilogram of beef.

Cows are basically herbivores. The biomass they eat is digested in the rumen, the huge first chamber of the four stomachs of the cow. The livestock industry has increased cows' milk and meat production by giving them intensive, high-protein feed concentrate, an inappropriate diet since cows need roughage. One of the methods developed by the livestock industry to circumvent this need for roughage is by feeding them plastic pot-scrubbing pads. The scrubbing pads remain in the rumen for life.[13]

Robbing cattle of the roughage they need does not merely treat them unethically; it also does not reduce the acreage needed to feed the cows, since the concentrate comes from grain that could have fed people. The shift from a cooperative, integrated system to a competitive, fragmented one creates additional pressures on scarce land and grain resources. This in turn leads to non-sustainability, violence to animals, and lower productivity when all systems are assessed.

Breaking Boundaries: Transforming Herbivores into Cannibals

As food for animals from farms disappears, animal feed is based increasingly on other sources, including the carcasses of dead animals. This is how the conditions for the mad-cow-disease epidemic were created. BSE infection, known as "scrapie" in sheep, typically bores into the brain and the nervous system and does not show itself as a disease until the infected animals are adults. Infected cows are nervous and shaky, and rapidly descend into dementia and death. Dissection of affected cows shows that their brains have disintegrated and are full of holes. In humans, this disease is called Creutzfeldt-Jakob disease, named after two German doctors.

The first case of BSE in the United Kingdom was confirmed in November 1986. By 1988, more than 2,000 cases of BSE had been confirmed. By August 1994, there were 137,000 confirmed cases, more than six times the number predicted by the government in their "worst case scenario."

The epidemic spread by feeding healthy cattle the remains of infected cattle. In 1987, 1.3 million tons of animal carcasses were processed into animal feed by "rendering plants." The largest portion of the animal material processed, 45 percent, came from cows. Pigs contributed 21 percent, poultry 19 percent, and sheep 15 percent. This created 350,000 tons of meat and bone meal and 230,000 tons of tallow.[14] Sheep infected with scrapie were thus fed to cows, which contracted BSE, and their carcasses were again fed to cattle. By 1996, more than 1.6 million cattle had become victims of BSE.

British farmers, increasingly dependent on industrial cattle feed, demanded that the sources of cattle feed be labeled, but the feed industry has denied farmers' and consumers' "right to know." Instead, the feed industry has been labeling its feed on the basis of its chemical constitution, thus camouflaging its biological sources.

McDonaldization

Globalization has created the McDonaldization of world food, resulting in the destruction of sustainable food systems. It attempts to create a uniform food culture of hamburgers. The mad-cow-disease epidemic tells us something of the costs hidden in this food culture and food economy.

In 1994, Pepsi Food, Ltd., was given permission to start 60 restaurants in India: 30 each of Kentucky Fried Chicken (KFC) and Pizza Hut. The processed meats and chicken offered at these restaurants have been identified by the U.S. Senate as sources of the cancers that one American contracts every seven seconds. The chicken, which would come from an Indian firm called Venky's, would be fed on a "modern" diet of antibiotics and other drugs, such as arsenic compounds, sulfa drugs, hormones, dyes, and nitrofurans. Still, many chickens are riddled with disease, in particular chicken cancer (leukosis). They can also carry salmonellosis, which does not die with ordinary cooking.

Both KFC and Pizza Hut have guaranteed that they will generate employment. However, according to studies conducted by the Ministry of Environment on other meat industries, Al-Kabeer[15] has displaced 300,000 people from their jobs, while employing only 300 people at salaries ranging from Rs. 500 to Rs. 2,000 per month. Venky's chicken has not employed one extra person after getting the contract for chicken supply from KFC and Pizza Hut. In fact, the company is being encouraged to mechanize further rather than use human labor.

Junk-food chains, including KFC and Pizza Hut, are under attack from major environmental groups in the United States and other developed countries because of their negative environmental impact. Intensive breeding of livestock and poultry for such restaurants leads to deforestation, land degradation, and contamination of water sources and other natural resources. For every pound of red meat, poultry, eggs, and milk produced, farm fields lose about five pounds of irreplaceable top soil. The water necessary for meat breeding comes to about 190 gallons per animal per day, or ten times what a normal Indian family is supposed to use in one day, if it gets water at all.

KFC and Pizza Hut insist that their chickens be fed on maize and soybean. It takes 2.8 kilograms of corn to produce one pound of chicken. Egg-layers also need 2.6 pounds of corn and soybean. Nearly seven pounds of corn and soybean are necessary to produce one pound of pork. Overall, animal farms use nearly 40 percent of the world's total grain production. In the United States, nearly 70 percent of grain production is fed to livestock.

Maize, though not a major food crop in India, has traditionally been grown for human consumption. Land will be diverted from production of food crops for humans to production of maize for chicken. Thirty-seven percent of the arable land in India will be diverted toward such production. Were all the grain produced consumed directly by humans, it would nourish five times as many people as it does after being converted into meat, milk, and eggs, according to the Council for Agricultural Science and Technology.

The food culture of India is as diverse as its ecosystems and its people, who use a variety of cereals, pulses, and vegetables as well as cooking methods to suit every need and condition. However, advertising is already having a negative impact on Indians' food and drink patterns. No longer are homemade snacks and lime juice or buttermilk offered to guests; instead, chips and aerated soft drinks are.

Reversing the McDonaldization of the World

"What man does to the web of life, he does to himself." How we relate to other species will determine whether the third millennium will be an era of disease and devastation, and of exclusion and violence, or rather a new era based on peace and non-violence, health and well-being, inclusiveness and compassion.

Unsustainable outcomes are the inevitable result of the deepening of patriarchal domination over ways of knowing and relating non-violently to what have been identified as "lesser species," including women. But sustainability can be created by an inclusive feminism, an ecological feminism, in which the freedom of every species is linked to the liberation of women, in which the tiniest life form is recognized as having intrinsic worth, integrity, and autonomy.

Women of our generation especially have to decide whether to protect the knowledge and wisdom of our grandmothers in the maintenance of life or whether to allow global corporations to push most species to extinction, mutilate and torture those that are found profitable, and undermine the health and well-being of the earth and its communities.

The mad cow, as a product of border crossings, is a "cyborg" in Donna Haraway's brand of "cyborg" feminism.[16] According to Haraway, "I'd rather be a cyborg than a goddess."[17] In India, the cow is Lakshmi, the goddess of wealth. Cow dung is worshipped as Lakshmi because it is the source of renewal of the earth's fertility through organic manuring. The cow is sacred because it is at the heart of the sustainability of an agrarian civilization. The cow as goddess and cosmos symbolizes care, compassion, sustainability, and equity.

From the point of view of both cows and people, I would rather be a sacred cow than a mad one.

Notes

1. Special issue on "Reverence for Life," *Quarterly Monitor*, No. 13, New Delhi: Research Foundation for Science, Technology and Natural Resource Policy.
2. K.M. Munshi, "Towards Land Transformation," Government of India, Ministry of Food and Agriculture, 1951.
3. In India, cattle use 29 percent of the organic matter, 22 percent of the energy, and 3 percent of the protein provided to them, in contrast to 9, 7, and 5 percent respectively in the United States' intensive cattle industry. Shanti George, *Operation Flood*, Delhi: Oxford University Press, 1985, p. 31.
4. Shanti George, p. 31.
5. Shanti George, p. 30.
6. Shanti George, p. 59.
7. "Buttercup Goes on Hormones," *The Economist*, May 9, 1987.
8. B. Kneen, "Biocow," *Ram's Horn: Newsletter of the Nutrition Policy Institute*, Toronto, Ontario, No. 40, May 1987.
9. Claude Bourguignon, Address at ARISE workshop, Auroville, India, April 1995.
10. Charles Darwin, "The Formation of Vegetable Mould through the Action of Worms with Observations on their Habits," London: Faber and Faber, 1927.
11. "Sustainable Europe," Friends of the Earth (International), 1995.
12. David Coats, *Old MacDonald's Factory Farm*, New York: Continuum, 1989, p. 73.
13. Trials indicated that steers fed 100 percent concentrate plus pot scrubbers grew at approximately the same rate as cattle fed 85 percent concentrate with 15 percent roughage. S. Loerch, "Efficiency of plastic pot scrubbers as a replacement for roughage in high concentrate cattle diets," *Journal of Animal Science*, No. 60, 1991, pp. 2321–28.
14. Richard W. Lacey, *Mad Cow Disease: The History of BSE in Britain*, Channel Islands: Cypsela Publications Limited, 1994, p. 32.
15. Shiva cites this as "One of the largest export-oriented slaughterhouses... in Andhra Pradesh."
16. Donna Haraway, "A Manifesto for Cyborgs: Science, Technology, and Socialist Feminism in the 1980s," *Socialist Review*, Vol. 80, pp. 65–108.
17. Donna Haraway, "A Manifesto for Cyborgs."

7.7

Green our Communities! Plant Urban Gardens

Favianna Rodriguez

7.8

Toward a Queer Ecofeminism

Greta Gaard

Although many ecofeminists acknowledge heterosexism as a problem, a systematic exploration of the potential intersections of ecofeminist and queer theories has yet to be made. By interrogating social constructions of the "natural," the various uses of Christianity as a logic of domination, and the rhetoric of colonialism, this essay finds those theoretical intersections and argues for the importance of developing a queer ecofeminism.

Progressive activists and scholars frequently lament the disunity of the political left in the United States. Often characterized as a "circular firing squad," the left or progressive movement has been known for its intellectual debates and hostilities, which have served to polarize many groups that could be working in coalition: labor activists, environmentalists, civil rights activists, feminists, animal rights activists, indigenous rights activists, and gay/lesbian/bisexual/transgender (GLBT) activists. Meanwhile, it is observed, the conservative right in the United States has lost no time in recognizing the connections among these various liberatory movements and has launched a campaign (most recently articulated in the "Contract with America") to ensure their collective annihilation. As a result, the future of progressive organizing may well depend on how effectively scholars and activists can recognize and articulate our many bases for coalition. In theory and in practice, ecofeminism has already contributed much to this effort.

At the root of ecofeminism is the understanding that the many systems of oppression are mutually reinforcing. Building on the socialist feminist insight that racism, classism, and sexism are interconnected, ecofeminists recognized additional similarities between those forms of human oppression and the oppressive structures of speciesism and naturism. An early impetus for the ecofeminist movement was the realization that the liberation of women – the aim of all branches of feminism – cannot be fully effected without the liberation of nature, and, conversely, the liberation of nature so ardently desired by environmentalists will not be fully effected without the liberation of women: conceptual, symbolic, empirical, and historical linkages between women and nature as they are constructed in Western culture require feminists and environmentalists to address these liberatory efforts together if we are to be successful (Warren 1991). To date, ecofeminist theory has blossomed, exploring the connections among many issues: racism, environmental degradation, economics, electoral politics, animal liberation, reproductive politics, biotechnology, bioregionalism, spirituality, holistic health practices, sustainable agriculture, and others. Ecofeminist activists have worked in the environmental justice movement, the Green movement, the antitoxics movement, the women's spirituality movement, the animal liberation movement, and the movement for economic justice. To continue and build on these efforts toward coalition, I would like to explore in this essay the connection between ecofeminism and queer theory.

"We have to examine how racism, heterosexism, classism, ageism, and sexism are *all* related to naturism," writes ecofeminist author Ellen O'Loughlin (1993, 148). Chaia Heller elaborates: "Love of nature is a process of becoming aware of and unlearning ideologies of racism, sexism, heterosexism, and ableism so that we may cease to reduce our idea of nature to a dark, heterosexual, 'beautiful' mother" (1993, 231). But as Catriona Sandilands astutely comments, "It is not enough simply to add 'heterosexism' to the long list of dominations that shape our relations to nature, to pretend that we can just 'add queers and stir'" (1994, 21).[1] Unfortunately, it is exactly this approach that has characterized ecofeminist theory to date, which is the reason I believe it is time for queers to come out of the woods and speak for ourselves.[2]

The goal of this essay is to demonstrate that to be truly inclusive, any theory of ecofeminism must take into consideration the findings of queer theory; similarly, queer theory must consider the findings of ecofeminism. To this end, I will examine various intersections between ecofeminism and queer theory, thereby demonstrating that a democratic, ecological society envisioned as the goal of ecofeminism will, of necessity, be a society that values sexual diversity and the erotic.

Sexualizing Nature, Naturalizing Sexuality

The first argument linking ecofeminism and queer theory is based on the observation that dominant Western culture's devaluation of the erotic parallels its devaluations of women and of nature; in effect, these devaluations are mutually reinforcing. This observation can be drawn from ecofeminist critiques that describe the normative dualisms, value-hierarchical thinking, and logic of domination that together characterize the ideological framework of Western culture. As Karen Warren explains, value dualisms are ways of conceptually organizing the world in binary, disjunctive terms, wherein each side of the dualism is "seen as exclusive (rather than inclusive) and oppositional (rather than complementary), and where higher value or superiority is attributed to one disjunct (or, side of the dualism) than the other" (1987, 6). Val Plumwood's 1993 critique of Western philosophy pulls together the most salient features of these and other ecofeminist critiques in what she calls the "master model," the identity that is at the core of Western culture and that has initiated, perpetuated, and benefited from Western culture's alienation from and domination of nature. The master identity, according to Plumwood, creates and depends on a "dualized structure of otherness and negation" (1993, 42). Key elements in that structure are the following sets of dualized pairs:

culture	/	nature
reason	/	nature
male	/	female
mind	/	body (nature)
master	/	slave
reason	/	matter (physicality)
rationality	/	animality (nature)
reason	/	emotion (nature)
mind, spirit	/	nature
freedom	/	necessity (nature)
universal	/	particular
human	/	nature (nonhuman)
civilized	/	primitive (nature)
production	/	reproduction (nature)
public	/	private
subject	/	object
self	/	other (Plumwood 1993, 43)

Plumwood does not claim completeness for the list. In the argument that follows, I will offer a number of reasons that ecofeminists must specify the linked dualisms of white/nonwhite, financially empowered/impoverished, heterosexual/queer, and reason/the erotic.[3]

Ecofeminists have uncovered a number of characteristics about the interlocking structure of dualism. First, ecofeminist philosophers have shown that the claim for the superiority of the self is based on the difference between self and other as manifested in the full humanity and reason that the self possesses but the other supposedly lacks. This alleged superiority of the self, moreover, is used to justify the subordination of the other (Warren 1990, 129; Plumwood 1993, 42–47). Next, ecofeminists have worked to show the linkages within the devalued category of the other, demonstrating how the association of qualities from one oppressed group with another serves to reinforce their subordination. The conceptual linkages between women and animals, women and the body, or women and nature, for example, all serve to emphasize the inferiority of these categories (Adams 1990; 1993). But while all categories of the other share these qualities of being feminized, animalized, and naturalized, socialist ecofeminists have rejected any claims of primacy for one form of oppression or another, embracing instead the understanding that all forms of oppression are now so inextricably linked that liberation efforts must be aimed at dismantling the system itself.

There is a theoretical gap, however, when we find that those few ecofeminists who do mention heterosexism in their introductory lists of human oppressions have still not taken the dualism of heterosexual/queer forward to be analyzed in the context of their lists of dualized pairs, and consequently into the theory being developed. In some cases, the same could be said for the dualism of white/nonwhite. This omission is a serious conceptual error, for the heterosexual/queer dualism has affected Western culture through its "ineffaceable marking" of these normative dualisms, according to queer theorist Eve Kosofsky Sedgwick (1990, 11). In her book *Epistemology of the Closet*, Sedgwick finds that these normative dualisms (or "symmetrical binary oppositions") "actually subsist in a more unsettled and dynamic tacit relation according to which, first, term B is not symmetrical with but subordinated to term A; but, second, the ontologically valorized term A actually depends for its meaning on the simultaneous subsumption and exclusion of term B; hence, third, the question of priority between the supposed central and the supposed marginal category of each dyad is irresolvably unstable, an instability caused by the fact that term B is constituted as at once internal and external to term A" (1990, 10). Sedgwick's findings bear a neat resonance with Plumwood's theorizing of the linking postulates that connect such dualisms both "horizontally" (one member of a dyad with the other) and "vertically" (groups of dyads with each other; my terms). These linking postulates include

1. Backgrounding, in which the master relies on the services of the other and simultaneously denies his dependency;
2. Radical exclusion, in which the master magnifies the differences between self and other and minimizes the shared qualities;

3. Incorporation, in which the master's qualities are taken as the standard, and the other is defined in terms of her possession or lack of those qualities;
4. Instrumentalism, in which the other is constructed as having no ends of her own, and her sole purpose is to serve as a resource for the master;
5. Homogenization, in which the dominated class of others is perceived as uniformly homogeneous (Plumwood 1993, 42–56).[4]

Queers experience backgrounding, radical exclusion, incorporation, and homogenization. As Sedgwick argues, the heterosexual identity is constituted through a denied dependency on the homosexual/queer identity (backgrounding). In terms of radical exclusion, queers find that the erotic (a particularly perverse erotic) is projected onto queer sexuality to such a degree that this quality is seen as the only salient feature of queer identities. When queers come out, heterosexuals frequently conclude they know everything there is to know about us once they know our sexuality. In terms of incorporation, it is clear that heterosexuality and its associated gender identities are taken as the standard in dominant Western culture, and queers are defined primarily in relation to that standard, and our failure to comply with it.

But the problem of oppression based on sexuality is not limited to the heterosexual/queer dualism. As queer theorists have shown, the larger problem is the erotophobia of Western culture, a fear of the erotic so strong that only one form of sexuality is overtly allowed, only in one position, and only in the context of certain legal, religious, and social sanctions (Hollibaugh 1983, 1989; Rubin 1989). The oppression of queers may be described more precisely, then, as the product of two mutually reinforcing dualisms: heterosexual/queer, and reason/the erotic.

As Plumwood has ably demonstrated, Western culture's oppression of nature can be traced back to the construction of the dominant human male as a self fundamentally defined by its property of reason, and the construction of reason as definitionally opposed to nature and all that is associated with nature, including women, the body, emotions, and reproduction (Plumwood 1993). Feminists have also argued that women's oppression in Western culture is characterized by our association with emotion, the body, and reproduction, and feminists have responded to these associations in different ways. Some have rejected these associations and attempted to align themselves with the public male sphere of rationality (liberal feminists); others have reversed the valuation and embraced these associations while devaluing the male rational culture (cultural feminists). In contrast, ecofeminists have argued for a "third way," one that rejects the structure of dualism and acknowledges both women and men as equal parts of culture and nature (Warren 1987; King 1989; Plumwood 1993; Gruen 1993; Gaard 1994). As a logical development of ecofeminism, a queer ecofeminist theory would build on these analyses using both queer theory and feminist theories about the oppression of the erotic. Though the reason/erotic dualism seems to be an aspect of the original culture/nature dualism, the heterosexual/queer dualism is a fairly recent development, as it is only in the past century that the concept of homosexual and heterosexual identities has developed (Smith 1989; Katz 1990). A queer ecofeminist perspective would argue that the reason/erotic and heterosexual/queer dualisms have now become part of the master identity, and that dismantling these dualisms is integral to the project of ecofeminism.

Bringing these dualisms into the list of self/other and culture/nature dualisms offered by Plumwood is one step toward queering ecofeminism. With this added perspective, ecofeminists would find it very productive to explore "vertical" associations on either side of the dualisms: associations between reason and heterosexuality, for example, or between reason and whiteness as defined in opposition to emotions and nonwhite persons; or associations between women, nonwhite persons, animals, and the erotic. From a queer ecofeminist perspective, then, we can examine the ways queers are feminized, animalized, eroticized, and naturalized in a culture that devalues women, animals, nature, and sexuality. We can also examine how persons of color are feminized, animalized, eroticized, and naturalized. Finally, we can explore how nature is feminized, eroticized, even queered.

The critical point to remember is that each of the oppressed identity groups, each characteristic of the other, is seen as "closer to nature" in the dualisms and ideology of Western culture. Yet queer sexualities are frequently devalued for being "against nature." Contradictions such as this are of no interest to the master, although they have been of great interest to feminists and queer theorists alike, who have argued that it is precisely such contradictions that characterize oppressive structures (Frye 1983; Mohr 1988; Sedgwick 1990).

Before launching into a discussion of queer sexualities as both "closer to nature" and "crimes against nature," it is crucial to acknowledge that sexuality itself is a socially constructed phenomenon that varies in definition from one historical and social context to another. As scholars of queer history have shown, there was no concept of a homosexual identity in Western culture before the late nineteenth century (Faderman 1981; Greenberg 1988; Katz 1990; Vicinus 1993). Until then, people spoke (or did not speak) of individual homosexual acts, deviance, and sodomy; the persons performing those acts were always presumed to be "normal" (the word "heterosexual" had no currency). Those homosexual acts were castigated as sinful excesses, moral transgressions of biblical injunctions.

The shift from seeing homosexual behavior as a sin to seeing it as a "crime against nature" began during the seventeenth century. As early as 1642, ministers in the American colonies began referring to the "unnatural lusts of men with men, or women with women," "unnatural acts," and acts "against nature" (Katz 1983, 43). "After the American Revolution," however, "the phrase 'crimes against nature' increasingly appeared in the statutes, implying that acts of sodomy offended a natural order rather than the will of God" (D'Emilio and Freedman 1988, 122). The natural/unnatural distinction had to do with procreation, but even "natural" acts leading to procreation could be tainted by lust and thus not free from sin. Procreative lust was preferable to "unnatural" lust, however (Katz 1983, 43). Finally, a third shift in the definition of homosexuality occurred toward the end of the nineteenth century. Through the work of sexologists such as Havelock Ellis, Magnus Hirschfeld, and Richard von Krafft-Ebing, the sexual invert became a recognizable identity, and the origins of sexual inversion were believed to lie in an individual's psychology. The word heterosexual first appeared in American medical texts in the early 1890s, but not in the popular press until 1926 (Katz 1983, 16).[5]

Today, nearly thirty years after the Stonewall rebellion, which launched the movement for gay liberation, the definition of queer identities is still evolving. "Homosexual" has changed to "gay," and "gay" to "gay and lesbian"; bisexuals have become more vocal; and most recently, transgender liberation has also reshaped queer communities, changes that have prompted many organizations to replace "gay and lesbian" with "gay/lesbian/bisexual/transgendered" or simply "queer" in their self-definitions. The recognition of varying sexual identities and practices has inspired a rereading of not only straight history or queer history but the history of sexuality itself. Based on these historical developments, queer theorists have determined that queer sexualities (both practices and identities) have been seen as transgressive in at least three categories: as acts against biblical morality, against nature, or against psychology. Thus, queer sexualities have been seen as a moral problem, a physiological problem, or a psychological problem (Pronk 1993). Though all three arguments are used against all varieties of queer sexuality today, the "crime against nature" argument stands out as having the greatest immediate interest for ecofeminists.

Queer theorists who explore the natural/unnatural dichotomy find that "natural" is invariably associated with "procreative." The equation of "natural" with "procreative" should be familiar to all feminists, for it is just this claim that has been used in a variety of attempts to manipulate women back into compulsory motherhood and the so-called women's sphere. From a historical perspective, the equation of woman's "true nature" with motherhood has been used to oppress women just as the equation of sexuality with procreation has been used to oppress both women and queers. The charge that queer sexualities are "against nature" and thus morally, physiologically, or psychologically depraved and devalued would seem to imply that nature is valued – but as ecofeminists have shown, this is not the case. In Western culture, just the contrary is true: nature is devalued just as queers are devalued. Here is one of the many contradictions characterizing the dominant ideology. On the one hand, from a queer perspective, we learn that the dominant culture charges queers with transgressing the natural order, which in turn implies that nature is valued and must be obeyed. On the other hand, from an ecofeminist perspective, we learn that Western culture has constructed nature as a force that must be dominated if culture is to prevail. Bringing these perspectives together indicates that the "nature" queers are urged to comply with is none other than the dominant paradigm of heterosexuality – an identity and practice that is itself a cultural construction, as both feminists and queer theorists have shown (Chodorow 1978; Foucault 1980; Rich 1986).

There are many flaws in the assertion that queer sexualities are "unnatural." First among them is that such an assertion does not accurately reflect the variety of sexual practices found in other species. For example, female homosexual behavior has been found in chickens, turkeys, chameleons, and cows, while male homosexual behavior has been observed in fruit flies, lizards, bulls, dolphins, porpoises, and apes (Denniston

1965; Pattatucci and Hamer 1995). An examination of insect sexual behavior reveals that the female scorpion kills the male after mating, the black widow spider eats the male after mating, and the praying mantis may eat the male while mating. Some animals are hermaphrodites (snails, earthworms), while other species are entirely female (toothcarp). Mating behavior also varies across mammal species. "Some pairs mate for life (jackals), some are promiscuous (zebras, most whales, chimpanzees). In some species, males and females travel together in herds, packs, or prides (musk ox, wolves, lions); in others, family groups are the basic unit (coyotes, gibbons); in others, males and females spend most of their time in same-sex groups and get together only for mating (hippopotamuses); in still others, all are loners who seek out members of their species only for the purpose of procreation (pandas)" (Curry 1990, 151).

The equation of "natural" sexual behavior with procreative purposes alone is conclusively disproven by both the evidence of same-sex behaviors and the observations of sexual activity during pregnancy, which have been reported for chimpanzees, gorillas, rhesus macaques, stumptailed macaques, Japanese monkeys, and golden lion tamarins (Pavelka 1995). In his study of the bonobo (pygmy chimpanzee), a species that, together with the chimpanzee, is the nearest relative to *Homo sapiens,* Frans de Waal (1995) found that sexual behavior served a variety of reproductive and nonreproductive functions. In effect, research on nonhuman primate sexual behavior indicates that nonhuman primates "engage in sexual activity far more than they need to from a reproductive point of view and thus much of their sexuality is nonreproductive" (Pavelka 1995, 22). As Jane Curry concludes, "If we look to nature for models of human behavior, we are bound, are we not, to value tolerance and pluralism" (1990, 154). This, however, is the second flaw in the assertion that queer sexualities are "unnatural"; norms for one species cannot be derived from the behaviors and seeming norms of other species.

By attempting to "naturalize" sexuality, the dominant discourse of Western culture constructs queer sexualities as "unnatural" and hence subordinate. As Jeffrey Weeks writes in *Against Nature,* "appeals to nature, to the claims of the natural, are among the most potent we can make. They place us in a world of apparent fixity and truth. They appear to tell us what and who we are, and where we are going. They seem to tell us the truth" (1991, 87). Arguments from "nature," as feminist philosophers of science have repeatedly argued, are frequently used to justify social norms rather than to find out anything new about nature (Bleier 1984; Fausto-Sterling 1985; Hubbard et al. 1982; Keller 1985; Lowe and Hubbard 1983). Attempts to naturalize one form of sexuality function as attempts to foreclose investigation of sexual diversity and sexual practices and to gain control of the discourse on sexuality. Such attempts are a manifestation of Western culture's homophobia and erotophobia.

Returning to the list of dualisms that ecofeminists have shown to characterize Western culture, and examining how qualities are distributed across each side of the disjuncts to enhance that disjunct's superiority (that is, the association of culture, men, and reason) or subordination (the association of nature, women, and the erotic), we can see that the eroticization of nature emphasizes its subordination. From a queer ecofeminist perspective, then, it becomes clear that liberating women requires liberating nature, the erotic, and queers. The conceptual connections among the oppressions of women, nature, and queers make this need particularly clear.

Notes

Written during my 1995–1996 sabbatical and originally published in Hypatia (winter 1997), published by Indian University Press, this essay responds to social justice questions in both theory and activism. As an ecofeminist member of the Green Party, I had listened to the distress of Lavender Greens who felt alienated by our premature presidential candidate, Ralph Nader, whose cavalier responses to questions about queer rights undermined the four pillars of the Green movement. (Nader has since become more educated on this issue and many queers see him as an ally.) Three years after the passage of Proposition 2 in Colorado, Lavender Greens from Boulder and Denver were still quick to detect any lack of commitment to their human rights at the August 1995 presidential nominating convention of the U.S. Greens, and some debated whether to stay in the movement or withdraw in order to spend more time working directly on civil rights. As members of a queer caucus within the Greens, we were holistic, multi-issue activists with a clear "first emergency" of survival as gays, lesbians, bisexuals, and transgendered people fighting for our lives and our rights – and yet we had developed no argument for explaining our conflicting commitments to other Greens. What we needed, I felt, was a clear, systematic exploration of the potential intersections of ecofeminist and queer theories. By interrogating social constructions of the "natural," the various uses of Christianity as a logic of domination, and the rhetoric of colonialism, this essay exposes those theoretical intersections and argues for the importance of developing queer ecofeminisms.

In 2003, progressives of all kinds still struggle to build a cohesive movement capable of confronting corporate globalization, defending environmental justice, and reclaiming the earth. They ask each other, "Why can't we sustain the kind of unity in diversity that we saw in Seattle, at the 1999 World Trade Organization protests?" And they are given an answer over and over again – but are these progressive activists really listening? What is it that prevents progressives from working together?

As part of the national "Rolling Thunder Down Home Democracy Tour" intended to energize and unite progressives of all types on Labor Day 2002, the St. Paul Area Trades and Labor Assembly hosted a Labor Day Picnic on Harriet Island, inviting activists and pundits of local and national fame to converse on panels and mobilize participants. Author Barbara Ehrenreich joined Mark Ritchie from the Institute for Agriculture and Trade Policy, Larry Weiss of Minnesota's Fair Trade Coalition, former legislator Tom Hayden, Senator Paul Wellstone, poet and indigenous activist John Trudell, and over a thousand activists committed to social and environmental justice. During the panel discussion on "Building a Progressive Movement," a woman from the audience challenged the three privileged male panelists – Cornel West, a scholar in history and African American studies from Princeton; Joel Rogers, founder of the New Party; and Tom Hayden, activist and former legislator – to put their progressive democratic theory into practice by refusing speaking invitations unless they were assured that other places on their panels would be given to less dominant groups such as women of color, gays and lesbians, and youth. Cornel West, whose talk had focused on the importance of building a multigenerational movement, replied that what was most important on these panels was the democratic ideology of the speakers, and not the specific features of their embodiment. Here, as a community, we lost another practice opportunity for "Building a Progressive Movement," and the audience discussion dissolved into shouting after West's reply.

The conceptual, economic, and historic links between the oppression of queers, people of color, and the earth can readily be detected using the analytic frameworks of ecofeminism, environmental justice, and other inclusive movements for a radical, economic, and ecological democracy. Yet these movements fall short, in practice, of delivering the democracy they espouse in theory. This essay is still as urgently relevant in 2003 as it was when it was written in 1995.

1. The May 1994 special issue of the Canadian journal *UnderCurrents* was the first to address the topic of "Queer Nature." In addition to Sandilands, two other contributors to this special issue explicitly recognize a relationship between ecofeminism and queer theory. In "Lost Landscapes and the Spatial Contextualization of Queerness," Gordon Brent Ingram writes that "an understanding of the intensifying juncture of environmentalism, radical ecology, ecofeminism, and queer theory is becoming crucial for the expansion of political activism in the coming decade" (5). And J. Michael Clark compares ecofeminism and ecotheology in his essay, "Sex, Earth, and Death in Gay Theology," asserting that "we can construct a gay ecotheological analysis in contradistinction to primarily male 'deep ecology' and as a further extension of ecofeminism" (34). The essays in the special issue initiate explorations of a queer ecofeminist geography and a queer ecofeminist theology, respectively; none, however, develops the connections between queer theory and ecofeminism.

2. I use the term queer as a shorthand for gay/lesbian/bisexual/transgender, but I use more specific terms as the context warrants. I use first-person plural pronouns when speaking of queers (us and we) to make my subject position clear. I am fully aware that queer is a contested term, generally popular among urban, under forty, academic queers, but generally unpopular among rural, over forty, community-based people; again, I use the term to reflect my own situatedness in a particular historical moment and geographic and cultural location.

3. Two definitions are in order. First, I define the dualism as heterosexual/queer rather than heterosexual/homosexual in order to reference and to emphasize the many and various combinations of gender and sexual identity that are constructed as aberrant under the hegemony of heterosexuality; I do not believe that a dualism of monosexualities (hetero/ homo) captures my meaning quite as precisely. Second, by erotic I refer not exclusively to sexuality but also in a more general way to sensuality, spontaneity, passion, delight, and pleasurable stimulation; I also expect the erotic to be variously defined in accordance with specific historical and cultural contexts.

4. I use the pronoun his for the master self and her for the subordinated other because these identities are gendered; I do not mean, however, to essentialize either position. Many privileged women benefit from participating in various structures of oppression, and many men are subordinated through those structures.

5. According to Smith, the word homosexual was coined in 1869 by a little-known Hungarian doctor, Karoly Maria Benkert (1989, 112); according to Katz, heterosexual was first used publicly in Germany in 1880 (1990, 12). In the United States, the words heterosexual and homosexual were first used in 1892 by a Chicago medical doctor, James G. Kiernan (Katz 1990, 14).

References

Abramson, Paul R., and Steven D. Pinkerton, eds. 1995. *Sexual Nature/Sexual Culture*. Chicago: University of Chicago Press.

Adams, Carol. 1990. *The Sexual Politics of Meat: A Feminist-Vegetarian Critical Theory*. New York: Continuum.

Adams, Carol. 1993. "The Feminist Traffic in Animals." In Gaard 1993.

Bleier, Ruth. 1984. *Science and Gender: A Critique of Biology and Its Theories on Women*. New York: Pergamon Press.

Chodorow, Nancy. 1978. *The Reproduction of Mothering: Psychoanalysis and the Sociology of Gender*. Berkeley: University of California Press.

Curry, Jane. 1990. "On Looking to Nature for Women's Sphere." In *And a Deer's Ear, Eagle's Song and Bear's Grace: Animals and Women,* ed. Theresa Corrigan and Stephanie Hoppe. San Francisco: Cleis Press.

De Waal, Frans B. M. 1995. "Sex as an Alternative to Aggression in the Bonobo." In Abramson and Pinkerton 1995.

D'Emilio, John, and Estelle B. Freedman. 1988. *Intimate Matters: A History of Sexuality in America*. New York: Harper and Row.

Denniston R. H. 1965. "Ambisexuality in Animals." In *Sexual Inversion: The Multiple Roots of Homosexuality,* ed. Judd Marmor. New York: Basic Books.

Faderman, Lillian. 1981. *Surpassing the Love of Men: Romantic Friendship and Love between Women from the Renaissance to the Present*. New York: William Morrow.

Fausto-Sterling, Anne. 1985. *Myths of Gender: Biological Theories about Women and Men*. New York: Basic Books.

Foucault, Michel. 1980. *The History of Sexuality*. Vol. 1, An Introduction. New York: Vintage Books.

Frye, Marilyn. 1983. "Oppression." In *The Politics of Reality*. Trumansburg, N.Y.: Crossing Press.

Gaard. Greta. 1994. "Misunderstanding Ecofeminism." *Z papers* 3, no 1: 20–24.

Gaard. Greta, ed. 1993. *Ecofeminism: Women, Animals, Nature*. Philadelphia: Temple University Press.

Greenberg, David F. 1988. *The Construction of Homosexuality*. Chicago: University of Chicago Press.

Gruen, Lori. 1993. "Dismantling Oppression: An Analysis of the Connection between Women and Animals." In Gaard 1993.

Heller, Chaia. 1993. "For the Love of Nature: Ecology and the Cult of the Romantic." In Gaard 1993.

Hollibaugh, Amber. 1983. "The Erotophobic Voice of Women." *New York Native* 7 (Sept. 26–Oct. 9): 33.

Hollibaugh, Amber. 1989. "Desire for the Future: Radical Hope in Passion and Pleasure." In Vance 1989.

Hubbard, Ruth, Mary Sue Henifin, and Barbara Fried, eds. 1982. *Biological Woman: The Convenient Myth*. Cambridge, Mass.: Schenkman Publishing Co.

Katz, Jonathan Ned. 1983. *Gay/Lesbian Almanac: A New Documentary*. New York: Harper and Row.

Katz, Jonathan Ned. 1990. "The Invention of Heterosexuality." *Socialist Review* 20, no. 1 (Jan.–Feb.): 7–34.

Keller, Evelyn Fox. 1985. *Reflections on Gender and Science.* New Haven: Yale University Press.

King, Ynestra. 1989. "The Ecology of Feminism and the Feminism of Ecology." In *Healing the Wounds: The Promise of Ecofeminism*, ed. Judith Plant. Philadelphia: New Society Publishers.

Lowe, Marion, and Ruth Hubbard, eds. 1983. *Woman's Nature: Rationalizations of Inequality.* New York: Pergamon Press.

Mohr, Richard D. 1988. *Gays/Justice: A Study of Ethics, Society, and Law.* New York: Columbia University Press.

O'Loughlin, Ellen. 1993. "Questioning Sour Grapes: Ecofeminism and the United Farm Workers Grape Boycott." In Gaard 1993.

Pattatucci, Angela M. L., and Dean H. Hamer. 1995. "The Genetics of Sexual Orientation: From Fruit Flies to Humans." In Abramson and Pinkerton 1995.

Pavelka, Mary S. McDonald. 1995. "Sexual Nature: What Can We Learn from a Cross-species Perspective?" In Abramson and Pinkerton 1995.

Plumwood, Val. 1993. *Feminism and the Mastery of Nature.* New York: Routledge.

Pronk, Pim. 1993. *Against Nature? Types of Moral Argumentation Regarding Homosexuality.* Trans. John Vriend. Grand Rapids: William B. Eerdmans.

Rich, Adrienne. 1986. "Compulsory Heterosexuality and Lesbian Existence." In *Blood, Bread, and Poetry.* New York: W. W. Norton.

Rubin, Gayle. 1989. "Thinking Sex: Notes for a Radical Theory of the Politics of Sexuality." In Vance 1989.

Sandilands, Catriona. 1994. "Lavender's Green? Some Thoughts on Queer(y)ing Environmental Politics." *Undercurrents* (May): 20–24.

Sedgwick, Eve Kosofsky. 1990. *Epistemology of the Closet.* Berkeley: University of California Press.

Smith, John H. 1989. "Abulia: Sexuality and Diseases of the Will in the Late Nineteenth Century." *Genders* 6 (fall): 102–24.

Vance, Carole S., ed. 1989. *Pleasure and Danger: Exploring Female Sexuality.* London: Pandora Press.

Vicinus, Martha. 1993. "'They wonder to which sex I belong': The Historical Roots of the Modern Lesbian Identity." In *The Lesbian and Gay Studies Reader,* ed. Henry Abelove, Michele Aina Barale, and David M. Halperin. New York: Routledge.

Warren, Karen J. 1987. "Feminism and Ecology: Making Connections." *Environmental Ethics* 9, no. 1: 3–21.

Warren, Karen J. 1990. "The Power and the Promise of Ecological Feminism." *Environmental Ethics* 12, no. 2: 125–46.

Warren, Karen J. 1991. "Feminism and the Environment: An Overview of the Issues." *APA Newsletter on Feminism and Philosophy* 90, no. 3: 108–16.

Weeks, Jeffrey. 1991. *Against Nature: Essays on History, Sexuality, and Identity.* London: Rivers Oram Press.

8

Violence and Resistance

By Anne Donadey

Contents

Original publication details: 8.1 Charlotte Perkins Gilman, "The Yellow Wallpaper," 1892. Public domain. 8.2 Carol Bohmer and Andrea Parrot, "Scope of the Problem" from *Sexual Assault on Campus: The Problem and the Solution*, pp. 18–40. New York: Lexington Books, 1993. Reproduced with permission of Rowman & Littlefield. 8.3 Colleen Jamison, "Sexual Assault Prevention Tips Guaranteed to Work!" from http://feminally.tumblr.com/post/168208983/sexual-assault-prevention-tips-guaranteed-to-work (posted Aug. 21, 2009). 8.4 Martha R. Mahoney, "Legal Images of Battered Women: Redefining the Issue of Separation," from *Michigan Law Review*, 90.1 (Oct. 1991), pp. 1–19. Reproduced with permission of Martha R. Mahoney and Michigan Law Review. 8.5 Alicia Gaspar de Alba and Georgina Guzmán, "Feminicidio: The 'Black Legend' of the Border" from *Making a Killing: Femicide, Free Trade, and La Frontera*, ed. Alicia Gaspar de Alba with Georgina Guzmán, pp. 1–11. Austin: University of Texas Press, 2010. Reproduced with permission of University of Texas Press. 8.6 Cheryl Chase, "Hermaphrodites with Attitude: Mapping the Emergence of Intersex Political Activism" from *GLQ: A Journal of Lesbian and Gay Studies*, 4.2 (1998), pp. 189–203, 208–11. Reproduced with permission of Duke University Press. 8.7 Andrea Smith, "Heteropatriarchy and the Three Pillars of White Supremacy: Rethinking Women of Color Organizing" from *Color of Violence: The Incite! Anthology*, ed. Incite! Women of Color against Violence, pp. 66–73. Cambridge, MA: South End Press, 2006. Reproduced with permission of A. Smith.

Women in Culture: An Intersectional Anthology for Gender and Women's Studies, Second Edition.
Edited by Bonnie Kime Scott, Susan E. Cayleff, Anne Donadey, and Irene Lara.
© 2017 John Wiley & Sons, Ltd. Published 2017 by John Wiley & Sons, Ltd.

The need to find ways to address violence against women was one of the forces behind the rise of feminism. Feminists contributed the important understanding that sexualized violence against women is motivated more by a desire for power than by sexual desire. In her famous essay "Compulsory Heterosexuality and Lesbian Existence," Jewish American author Adrienne Rich discusses how male dominance, even violence, in heterosexual relationships is viewed as normal and heterosexual pleasure is linked to violence, while lesbian love is ironically seen as sick and deviant (40, 42). As readings in Chapters 4 and 6 demonstrate, stereotypical representations of women are often violent and coercive. Female subordination and sexual violence are eroticized in our heteronormative culture (Catharine MacKinnon in Rich, "Compulsory Heterosexuality" 43). In their documentary films, white anti-violence activist Jackson Katz and African American former football player and film-maker Byron Hurt demonstrate that violent masculinity is a cultural norm that includes sexual violence against women; it also promotes homophobia and is linked to power and control. In Chapter 6, Eric Anderson makes a related argument focusing on men in sports. Katz argues that we need to change definitions of masculinity in order to transform the culture of violence. Besides elucidating the systemic conditions leading to violence against women, feminists have thus also proposed avenues of resistance to this violence.

Violence

Suzanne Pharr, a white lesbian feminist and anti-racist activist, defines oppression as a norm that maintains its control through institutional and economic power, backed up by violence and the threat of violence. As a way of enforcing oppression, violence always includes an institutional, system-wide aspect and an interpersonal one, as is made clear in this chapter's readings. Most physical and sexual violence is committed by men. Individual men inflict violence on individual women in order to control them. Lesbians, gay men, and transgender people are often victims of hate crimes, sometimes due to their sexual orientation, sometimes due to their transgressive or nonconforming gender presentation (see Chapter 5). Working-class transgender people of color are at even greater risk for violence. Violence against women and children occurs in all strata of society and in all cultures; it can happen to feminists and non-feminists alike, and contributes to keeping women in secondary positions in society. For too many women and children, home is often no safer than the streets. Incest and intimate partner violence often force women and children into poverty and homelessness in Western nations. What feminists have called a pervasive rape culture blames the victim and normalizes violence against women (Buchwald et al.). Women are expected to enforce such oppressions upon other women and upon ourselves through our internalization of sexist rules and because we sometimes stand to benefit from participating in patriarchal structures. This is what Turkish feminist scholar Deniz Kandiyoti has called "bargaining with patriarchy." From mothers who demean their daughters (or daughters-in-law) to women who lure unsuspecting girls into the sex trafficking industry, women also perpetuate violence against other women (as the powerful opening of Chicana film-maker Lourdes Portillo's documentary film *Señorita Extraviada* makes very clear). Finally, as law professor and feminist and labor activist Martha R. Mahoney elucidates in "Legal Images of Battered Women" (1991), institutions such as the legal system seem to be organized in such a way as to let perpetrators go unpunished by trivializing the violence and blaming women for the abuse.

As masculinities theorist Michael S. Kimmel explained in Chapter 1, hegemonic masculinity props itself up by demeaning women and feminine men; aggression is the only emotion Western society deems appropriate for men. Carol Bohmer, a US-based New Zealand scholar and lawyer, and academic Andrea Parrot, demonstrate in "Scope of the Problem" (1993) how the confluence of these two factors creates a situation in which groups of men in highly hegemonic masculinist organizations such as college fraternities and team sports are more likely to sexually assault women. There is also a higher incidence of sexual and relationship violence against women in the police forces as well as in the military, especially during war time. In situations of domestic violence, the likelihood of female death increases if men have access to guns. The likelihood of intimate partner violence increases if the perpetrator is intoxicated. The connection between drinking and violence against women clarifies why the nineteenth-century temperance movement seeking to ban alcohol in the United States was part of the feminist movement (Buhle). Bohmer and Parrot explain that in US colleges, first-year female students are the group most at risk for acquaintance rape (by far the most common form of rape), especially at the beginning of the school year, before they have had a chance to establish a support system. The institutions (universities, fraternities, sports teams, the police, and the military) tend to protect the perpetrators and try to shield themselves from lawsuits by discouraging women from reporting these crimes. Bohmer and Parrot's analysis, as well as the statistics they provide, unfortunately remains accurate today.

Society encourages female behaviors that can, ironically, put women more at risk, such as seeking men (the primary source of violence against women) for protection against violence, identifying with the perpetrator and wanting to help him, trusting that a man they know would not exert violence against them (Bohmer and Parrot), dis-identifying with the image of the battered woman, denying the extent of the intimate partner violence they have experienced, and denying that they are victims of relationship violence (Mahoney).

Violence against women is often also part of other forms of oppression. In her essay "Heteropatriarchy and the Three Pillars of White Supremacy," academic and activist Andrea Smith (2006) discusses three different types of institutional violence that white supremacy (or white dominance) uses to establish and maintain itself: slavery/capitalism, genocide/colonialism, and Orientalism/war. In the United States, the first aspect has been used particularly against African Americans, the second against Native peoples, and the third against immigrants of color (especially Latinos, Asians, and Arab Americans). Smith's essay was published in the important book collection *Color of Violence*, which focuses on the centrality of State violence in the lives of women of color and proposes new anti-violence strategies. Smith argues that the US empire depends on imposing heteropatriarchy (the societal norm of heterosexual coupling in which the man has more power than the woman) and that therefore, any attempt at decolonization must include women's and LGBT (lesbian, gay, bisexual, and transgender) liberation as well. Violence against women and the purposeful diminishing of women's and queer people's status are part and parcel of the colonial project.

An excellent example of how sexual violence has been used against African Americans to enforce white supremacy is provided by Danielle McGuire's intersectional study of the US Civil Rights movement.[1] McGuire definitively demonstrates that Black women in general were at the center of the Civil Rights movement. She notes that in her role as secretary of a local branch of the NAACP (National Association for the Advancement of Colored People), Rosa Parks (best known for refusing to give up her seat on a Montgomery, Alabama, bus to a white passenger in 1955) had a long history of documenting white male sexualized violence against Black women. This went back to 1944, several decades before rape became a central part of the feminist agenda in the early 1970s. Beginning in the nineteenth century, Black women such as Anna Julia Cooper, Ida B. Wells-Barnett, and others have spoken out publicly against sexualized violence and analyzed its role as a foundational part of maintaining white supremacy (McGuire xvii–xix, 227). African American activist-scholars Angela Davis and bell hooks similarly demonstrated that the myth of the Black male rapist of white women was created in the post-Reconstruction US South to justify violence against Black men, hide the reality of white male sexual depredations against Black women, and create a regime of terror used to maintain segregation and white supremacy. That lynchings of Black men (accused of such crimes as having looked at a white woman) by mobs of enraged white men in the South in the nineteenth and twentieth centuries often included genital mutilation, demonstrates that "sexual violence sat at the core of white supremacy" (McGuire 47), not only for Black women, but for Black men as well. Intraracial sexual violence (sexual violence among people of the same racial or ethnic background), the most common form of violence, also becomes hidden under the myth of the Black male rapist, which shields white male perpetrators from scrutiny at the same time that it makes it harder for women of color to speak out. The need to attend to the issue of sexual violence within the Black, Latino, and American Indian communities is addressed in African American film-maker Aishah Simmons's *No! The Rape Documentary* and by Inés Hernández-Avila in Buchwald et al.

Rape is a form of social control that has often been used on a large scale as a weapon of war, in particular in contexts of ethnic cleansing. Wars also tend to create an influx of refugees and displaced persons, the majority of whom are women and children whose refugee status places them at heightened risk for violence, including sexual violence. The same goes with spaces of globalized capitalism such as export processing zones, which draw many rural women who find themselves alone and vulnerable there, as discussed by Ehrenreich and Hochschild in Chapter 2. In their essay "*Feminicidio*" (2010), Chicana lesbian feminist author Alicia Gaspar de Alba and Chicana scholar Georgina Guzmán examine a particularly egregious and systemic case, that of the serial killing of hundreds of poor young Mexican mestizas (mixed-race) and indigenous women working in *maquiladoras* (partially US-owned plants taking advantage of lax labor laws and access to a cheap, docile workforce) in Ciudad Juárez, Mexico, south of the Texas border city of El Paso. The term that feminists have created to describe killings of women just because they are women is "femicide" (*feminicidio* in Spanish). Gaspar de Alba and Guzmán discuss the fact that the killers have been operating – and continue to operate – with impunity since 1993 and that neither Mexico nor the United States has worked very hard to solve these crimes, in part because the victims are members of several devalued groups who are conveniently seen as prostitutes and blamed for their fate. In Portillo's film *Señorita Extraviada*, one of the testifying women accuses police officers of being the perpetrators.

As Gaspar de Alba and Guzmán demonstrate, negative representations of victimized women in the media and society contribute to the State's inaction. In her article on domestic violence, Martha Mahoney also starts from this perspective but adds that stereotypical representations of victimized women and of domestic violence in the legal system also specifically contribute to the State's inability to right the wrongs done to survivors of intimate partner violence. She highlights that the prevalence of intimate partner violence, which is estimated to affect close to half of American women, is hidden by the legal profession's emphasis on the most severe cases. Echoing Rich's insight regarding how society normalizes male violence in heterosexual relationships, Mahoney argues that the over-representation of the most extreme cases of intimate partner violence makes it hard for the legal system and the broader society, as well as the women who are on the receiving end of the abuse, to even identify their situations as cases of intimate partner violence. Mahoney relies on the voices of survivors of domestic violence (including her own) to flesh out her theories and call the legal system, as well as the broader society, to go beyond their denial of the extent of the problem and redefine the terms of analysis.

Not all violence is physical in nature. The classic 1892 feminist short story "The Yellow Wallpaper," penned by US white middle-class author, editor, and economist Charlotte Perkins Gilman, illustrates the psychological violence that patriarchal society does to women, even in the absence of physical violence. The story chronicles a female narrator's descent into madness as a response to her alienating conditions of isolation and enclosure in a sparsely furnished upstairs room of her home, as prescribed by her husband after the birth of their son. That the husband is a medical doctor is no accident given the long history of how Western doctors medicalized childbirth and infantilized women in the process (Rich, *Of Woman Born* 128–55). The narrator's individual situation reflects a wider situation for women, caught in a pattern of oppressive conditions reminiscent of Marilyn Frye's analogy of women's oppression as a bird cage (see Chapter 1). As the narrator descends from postpartum depression into psychosis, she begins hallucinating and seeing a woman (her double), who then multiplies into a large number of women, trapped behind the "bars" of the yellow wallpaper in her bedroom. As feminist critics Sandra M. Gilbert and Susan Gubar have argued in their famous analysis of nineteenth-century British and Anglo-American feminist literature *The Madwoman in the Attic*, "patriarchal socialization literally makes women sick, both physically and mentally" (53). Like patriarchy, the wallpaper "pattern" "strangles" and traps its victims. Gilman is often associated with First-wave feminism (see Chapter 3).

Some forms of medical violence are specifically directed at people who do not fit the male/female binary or the heterosexual norm. In her article "Hermaphrodites with Attitude," Cheryl Chase (1998) discusses a specific case of institutional violence, which is visited upon intersex children (people born with ambiguous genitals or sexual characteristics of both sexes) in the United States. The medical establishment pushes parents to approve so-called corrective surgeries in order to ensure that the children will fit in one of the two binary boxes that govern gender in our culture. Ninety percent of the surgeries create female bodies, and children are generally not told about their medical history. As teens and adults, they often suffer from severe emotional trauma and sexual dysfunction. Chase, an intersex person who now uses the name Bo Laurent, highlights both the oppressive nature of medical surgeries on intersex infants and children and the resistance of intersex people to this violence done to their bodies and spirits. Humor is often a strategy of resistance, as seen in the title of Chase's essay: "Hermaphrodites with Attitude" references the medical term used to describe intersex people – which is no longer in use today – and makes fun of it by mentioning that these objects of medical attention have an attitude, making a statement about intersex people reclaiming their agency and subjectivity away from the medical field.

Resistance

The "Sexual Assault Prevention Tips," by anonymous Internet activist Feminally (2009), also uses humor and the strategy of reversal to criticize the fact that prevention tips are usually addressed to women and that they mostly recommend that victims, rather than perpetrators, curtail our behaviors in order to avoid rape. Instead, this feminist version of the list makes the point that men are the ones that can – and should – stop sexually assaulting women. The myth of an uncontrollable male sex drive serves to ensure male sexual right of access to women by presenting it as a natural need, thus enforcing the expectation of women's sexual availability (Rich, "Compulsory Heterosexuality" 46–49). Radical feminist Kathleen Barry criticized this myth early on, calling it a case of "arrested sexual development" that passes itself off as normal for men (Barry, quoted in Rich, "Compulsory Heterosexuality" 48). A number of male allies have taken up the task of "transforming a rape culture" (Buchwald et al.) and offering alternative definitions of masculinity (see Bucholtz; Douglas and Nuriddin (also featured in Simmons); Hurt; Katz; and Messner, Kimmel, Madhubuti, and Stoltenberg in Buchwald et al.). There are many resources on the Web for developing violence-free relationships and "navigating consent" (Scarleteen).

Feminist critiques and activism have been instrumental in creating legal concepts protecting women from various forms of "sexual terrorism" (Sheffield). Sexual terrorism is defined as a continuum of violence and threat of violence against women that includes marital rape and battering as well as sexual harassment, and whose goal it is to keep women in subordinate roles to men. The United Nations' 1993 Declaration on the Elimination of Violence against Women includes "[p]hysical, sexual and psychological violence occurring in the family, ... the general community, ... and ... perpetrated or condoned by the State." Influenced by feminist definitions, the Declaration acknowledges that violence against women has both an interpersonal and an institutional component.

When women are trapped in an interpersonal situation of psychological violence from which they see no way out, such as that experienced by the narrator in Gilman's "The Yellow Wallpaper," their resistance may take less positive forms. Many feminist critics have pointed out that illness can become one of very few avenues open to women to resist paralyzing circumstances created by patriarchy. The story's narrator madly yet methodically starts ripping out the wallpaper in the hopes of freeing the women and herself. While she appears partially victorious in that she is able to interrupt the smooth patriarchal functioning for a short time and disrupt her husband's sense of medical authority and control (like a Victorian lady, he faints at the improper sight of the shredded wallpaper in the room and his wife crawling around in it), we are left to speculate on whether any of these events actually occurred or are part of her delusions, and what the future might hold for her.

Gilman's story was an influential critique of the patriarchal aspects of the rest cure that was often prescribed by doctors for depressed and/or "disorderly" women at the time. She mentions in a later essay that the doctor who had prescribed this cure for her changed his practice after reading her story ("Why I Wrote"). Although the story's ending is rather bleak, its afterlife may have had an unexpected impact that testifies to the importance of literature as a form of activism. Similarly, Gaspar de Alba and Guzmán demonstrate how, in the absence of State response to femicides, artists and scholars have used print and visual media to raise awareness about the femicides and demand action, highlighting the power of the visual arts to make people care by having them identify with the nameless victims.

Chase's search for answers and community led her to associate with already existing activist groups such as radical lesbian feminism and the transgender liberation movement. She created the Intersex Society of North America (ISNA), a major support and information group whose main platform is the elimination of surgeries on intersex infants, in 1993. ISNA works through alliances with journalists and scholars (some of whom are well-known feminists such as Anne Fausto-Sterling) as well as transgender, queer, and gay and lesbian activist groups. Unfortunately, alliances with mainstream feminist groups have been more difficult to accomplish, in part because the mainstream feminist movement focuses on women and the existence of intersex people questions the stability of that category.

Finally, Smith also discusses the importance of alliance politics. She argues that in order to be more effective in their struggle against multiple forms of oppression, people of color from various groups need to take into account the fact that slavery, genocide, and war all function in somewhat different ways and that therefore, strategies of resistance against them must differ as well. For example, civil rights struggles that demand full inclusion for African Americans within the nation-state are very different from decolonial Native struggles to separate from the nation-state and establish tribal sovereignty (see also Chapters 3 and 9). Activists must be able to acknowledge, understand, and support different groups' social justice goals in order to create viable, more effective alliances.

Discussion Questions

1. What factors contribute to acquaintance rape, according to Bohmer and Parrot?
2. According to Smith, what are some of the connections between empire and heteropatriarchy and between State (institutional) and interpersonal violence? How does Gaspar de Alba and Guzmán's essay illustrate these connections? Can you think of other examples?
3. In "The Yellow Wallpaper," what factors contribute to the narrator's feelings of being caged in? Can you identify examples of the husband's psychological violence and belittling of his wife? How do you interpret the end of the story?
4. According to Mahoney, why is it important for an analysis of domestic violence to go beyond the question of "why didn't she leave"? Why has the criminal justice system tended to blame women for the abuse? What are some of the reasons why women in "bad" relationships do not recognize themselves in the stereotype of the battered woman?
5. In what ways does Gaspar de Alba and Guzmán's essay highlight the power of the arts and humanities to contribute to activism for social change? Can you think of other examples?
6. How does the existence of intersex people complicate the idea that sex is biological and that gender is a social construct? How does Chase demonstrate that sex is a social construct in this context?
7. What does the inclusion of Chase's and Mahoney's personal stories add to their arguments? What makes this inclusion particularly persuasive?

Note

1. We thank Adisa Alkebulan for bringing this intersectional approach to the Civil Rights movement to our attention.

References

Bucholtz, Jeffrey S. We End Violence. http://www.weendviolence.com/about_us_who_we_are.html (accessed December 18, 2015).

Buchwald, Emilie, Pamela Fletcher, and Martha Roth, eds. 1993. *Transforming a Rape Culture*. Minneapolis, MN: Milkweed Editions, 2005.

Buhle, Mari Jo. *Women and American Socialism, 1780–1920*. Urbana: University of Illinois Press, 1981.

Davis, Angela Y. "Rape, Racism, and the Myth of the Black Rapist." *Women, Race and Class*. New York: Vintage, 1981. 172–201.

Douglas, Ulester, and Sulaiman Nuriddin. Men Stopping Violence. http://www.menstoppingviolence.org/about/team (accessed December 18, 2015).

Gilbert, Sandra M., and Susan Gubar. 1979. *The Madwoman in the Attic: The Woman Writer and the Nineteenth-Century Literary Imagination*. New Haven, CT: Yale University Press, 2000.

Gilman, Charlotte Perkins. "Why I Wrote The Yellow Wallpaper." *The Forerunner* October 1913. http://csivc.csi.cuny.edu/history/files/lavender/whyyw.html (accessed December 18, 2015).

hooks, bell. "Reflections on Race and Sex." *Yearning: Race, Gender, and Cultural Politics*. Boston, MA: South End Press, 1990. 57–64.

Hurt, Byron, dir., prod., and writer. *Hip-Hop: Beyond Beats and Rhymes*. DVD. 61 mins. Northampton, MA: Media Education Foundation, 2006.

Incite! Women of Color against Violence. *Color of Violence: The Incite! Anthology*. Cambridge, MA: South End Press, 2006.

Kandiyoti, Deniz. "Bargaining with Patriarchy." *Gender and Society* 2.3 (1988): 274–90.

Katz, Jackson. *Tough Guise: Violence, Media, and the Crisis in Masculinity*. Dir. Sut Jhally. DVD. Abridged version. 57 mins. Northampton, MA: Media Education Foundation, 2002.

McGuire, Danielle L. *At the Dark End of the Street: Black Women, Rape, and Resistance – A New History of the Civil Rights Movement from Rosa Parks to the Rise of Black Power*. New York: Knopf, 2010.

Pharr, Suzanne. 1997. *Homophobia: A Weapon of Sexism*, 2nd ed. Berkeley, CA: Chardon. http://suzannepharr.org/wp/wp-content/uploads/2008/01/homophobiaaweaponofsexismcondensed.pdf (accessed December 18, 2015).

Portillo, Lourdes, dir. and prod. *Señorita Extraviada* [Missing Young Woman]. Independent Television Service, Xochitl Films, and Center for Independent Documentary. VHS. 74 mins. New York: Women Make Movies, 2001.

Rich, Adrienne. 1980. "Compulsory Heterosexuality and Lesbian Existence." *Blood, Bread and Poetry: Selected Prose 1979–1985*. New York: Norton, 1986. 23–75.

Rich, Adrienne. 1976. *Of Woman Born: Motherhood as Experience and Institution*. New York: Norton, 1986.

Scarleteen: Sex Ed for the Real World. "Driver's Ed for the Sexual Superhighway: Navigating Consent." (written November 18, 2010, updated January 9, 2014). http://www.scarleteen.com/article/abuse_assault/drivers_ed_for_the_sexual_superhighway_navigating_consent (accessed December 18, 2015).

Sheffield, Carole J. "Sexual Terrorism." *Women: A Feminist Perspective*. Ed. Jo Freeman. 5th ed. Mountain View, CA: Mayfield, 1995. 1–21.

Simmons, Aishah Shahidah, dir. *No! The Rape Documentary*. AfroLez Productions. DVD. 94 mins. San Francisco, CA: California Newsreel, 2006.

United Nations. "Declaration on the Elimination of Violence against Women." 1993. http://www.un-documents.net/a48r104.htm (accessed December 18, 2015).

8.1

The Yellow Wallpaper

Charlotte Perkins Gilman

It is very seldom that mere ordinary people like John and myself secure ancestral halls for the summer.

A colonial mansion, a hereditary estate, I would say a haunted house, and reach the height of romantic felicity – but that would be asking too much of fate!

Still I will proudly declare that there is something queer about it.

Else, why should it be let so cheaply? And why have stood so long untenanted?

John laughs at me, of course, but one expects that in marriage.

John is practical in the extreme. He has no patience with faith, an intense horror of superstition, and he scoffs openly at any talk of things not to be felt and seen and put down in figures.

John is a physician, and *perhaps* – (I would not say it to a living soul, of course, but this is dead paper and a great relief to my mind –) *perhaps* that is one reason I do not get well faster.

You see he does not believe I am sick!

And what can one do?

If a physician of high standing, and one's own husband, assures friends and relatives that there is really nothing the matter with one but temporary nervous depression – a slight hysterical tendency – what is one to do?

My brother is also a physician, and also of high standing, and he says the same thing.

So I take phosphates or phosphites – whichever it is, and tonics, and journeys, and air, and exercise, and am absolutely forbidden to "work" until I am well again.

Personally, I disagree with their ideas.

Personally, I believe that congenial work, with excitement and change, would do me good.

But what is one to do?

I did write for a while in spite of them; but it *does* exhaust me a good deal – having to be so sly about it, or else meet with heavy opposition.

I sometimes fancy that in my condition if I had less opposition and more society and stimulus – but John says the very worst thing I can do is to think about my condition, and I confess it always makes me feel bad.

So I will let it alone and talk about the house.

The most beautiful place! It is quite alone, standing well back from the road, quite three miles from the village. It makes me think of English places that you read about, for there are hedges and walls and gates that lock, and lots of separate little houses for the gardeners and people.

There is a *delicious* garden! I never saw such a garden – large and shady, full of box-bordered paths, and lined with long grape-covered arbors with seats under them.

There were greenhouses, too, but they are all broken now.

There was some legal trouble, I believe, something about the heirs and co-heirs; anyhow, the place has been empty for years.

That spoils my ghostliness, I am afraid, but I don't care – there is something strange about the house – I can feel it.

I even said so to John one moonlight evening, but he said what I felt was a *draught,* and shut the window.

I get unreasonably angry with John sometimes. I'm sure I never used to be so sensitive. I think it is due to this nervous condition.

But John says if I feel so, I shall neglect proper self-control; so I take pains to control myself – before him, at least, and that makes me very tired.

I don't like our room a bit. I wanted one downstairs that opened on the piazza and had roses all over the window, and such pretty old-fashioned chintz hangings! but John would not hear of it.

He said there was only one window and not room for two beds, and no near room for him if he took another.

He is very careful and loving, and hardly lets me stir without special direction.

I have a schedule prescription for each hour in the day; he takes all care from me, and so I feel basely ungrateful not to value it more.

He said we came here solely on my account, that I was to have perfect rest and all the air I could get. "Your exercise depends on your strength, my dear," said he, "and your food somewhat on your appetite; but air you can absorb all the time." So we took the nursery at the top of the house.

It is a big, airy room, the whole floor nearly, with windows that look all ways, and air and sunshine galore. It was nursery first and then playroom and gymnasium, I should judge; for the windows are barred for little children, and there are rings and things in the walls.

The paint and paper look as if a boys' school had used it. It is stripped off – the paper – in great patches all around the head of my bed, about as far as I can reach, and in a great place on the other side of the room low down. I never saw a worse paper in my life.

One of those sprawling flamboyant patterns committing every artistic sin.

It is dull enough to confuse the eye in following, pronounced enough to constantly irritate and provoke study, and when you follow the lame uncertain curves for a little distance they suddenly commit suicide – plunge off at outrageous angles, destroy themselves in unheard of contradictions.

The color is repellant, almost revolting; a smouldering unclean yellow, strangely faded by the slow-turning sunlight.

It is a dull yet lurid orange in some places, a sickly sulphur tint in others.

No wonder the children hated it! I should hate it myself if I had to live in this room long.

There comes John, and I must put this away, – he hates to have me write a word.

******

We have been here two weeks, and I haven't felt like writing before, since that first day.

I am sitting by the window now, up in this atrocious nursery, and there is nothing to hinder my writing as much as I please, save lack of strength.

John is away all day, and even some nights when his cases are serious.

I am glad my case is not serious!

But these nervous troubles are dreadfully depressing.

John does not know how much I really suffer. He knows there is no *reason* to suffer, and that satisfies him.

Of course it is only nervousness. It does weigh on me so not to do my duty in any way!

I meant to be such a help to John, such a real rest and comfort, and here I am a comparative burden already!

Nobody would believe what an effort it is to do what little I am able, – to dress and entertain, and order things.

It is fortunate Mary is so good with the baby. Such a dear baby!

And yet I *cannot* be with him, it makes me so nervous.

I suppose John never was nervous in his life. He laughs at me so about this wall-paper!

At first he meant to repaper the room, but afterwards he said that I was letting it get the better of me, and that nothing was worse for a nervous patient than to give way to such fancies.

He said that after the wall-paper was changed it would be the heavy bedstead, and then the barred windows, and then that gate at the head of the stairs, and so on.

"You know the place is doing you good," he said, "and really, dear, I don't care to renovate the house just for a three months' rental."

"Then do let us go downstairs," I said, "there are such pretty rooms there."

Then he took me in his arms and called me a blessed little goose, and said he would go down to the cellar, if I wished, and have it whitewashed into the bargain.

But he is right enough about the beds and windows and things.

It is an airy and comfortable room as any one need wish, and, of course, I would not be so silly as to make him uncomfortable just for a whim.

I'm really getting quite fond of the big room, all but that horrid paper.

Out of one window I can see the garden, those mysterious deep-shaded arbors, the riotous old-fashioned flowers, and bushes and gnarly trees.

Out of another I get a lovely view of the bay and a little private wharf belonging to the estate. There is a beautiful shaded lane that runs down there from the house. I always fancy I see people walking in these numerous paths and arbors, but John has cautioned me not to give way to fancy in the least. He says that with my imaginative power and habit of story-making, a nervous weakness like mine is sure to lead to all manner of excited fancies, and that I ought to use my will and good sense to check the tendency. So I try.

I think sometimes that if I were only well enough to write a little it would relieve the press of ideas and rest me.

But I find I get pretty tired when I try.

It is so discouraging not to have any advice and companionship about my work. When I get really well, John says we will ask Cousin Henry and Julia down for a long visit; but he says he would as soon put fireworks in my pillow-case as to let me have those stimulating people about now.

I wish I could get well faster.

But I must not think about that. This paper looks to me as if it *knew* what a vicious influence it had!

There is a recurrent spot where the pattern lolls like a broken neck and two bulbous eyes stare at you upside down.

I get positively angry with the impertinence of it and the everlastingness. Up and down and sideways they crawl, and those absurd, unblinking eyes are everywhere.

There is one place where two breadths didn't match, and the eyes go all up and down the line, one a little higher than the other.

I never saw so much expression in an inanimate thing before, and we all know how much expression they have! I used to lie awake as a child and get more entertainment and terror out of blank walls and plain furniture than most children could find in a toy-store.

I remember what a kindly wink the knobs of our big, old bureau used to have, and there was one chair that always seemed like a strong friend.

I used to feel that if any of the other things looked too fierce I could always hop into that chair and be safe.

The furniture in this room is no worse than inharmonious, however, for we had to bring it all from downstairs. I suppose when this was used as a playroom they had to take the nursery things out, and no wonder! I never saw such ravages as the children have made here.

The wall-paper, as I said before, is torn off in spots, and it sticketh closer than a brother – they must have had perseverance as well as hatred.

Then the floor is scratched and gouged and splintered, the plaster itself is dug out here and there, and this great heavy bed which is all we found in the room, looks as if it had been through the wars.

But I don't mind it a bit – only the paper.

There comes John's sister. Such a dear girl as she is, and so careful of me! I must not let her find me writing.

She is a perfect and enthusiastic housekeeper, and hopes for no better profession. I verily believe she thinks it is the writing which made me sick!

But I can write when she is out, and see her a long way off from these windows.

There is one that commands the road, a lovely shaded winding road, and one that just looks off over the country. A lovely country, too, full of great elms and velvet meadows.

This wallpaper has a kind of sub-pattern in a different shade, a particularly irritating one, for you can only see it in certain lights, and not clearly then.

But in the places where it isn't faded and where the sun is just so – I can see a strange, provoking, formless sort of figure, that seems to skulk about behind that silly and conspicuous front design.

There's sister on the stairs!

******

Well, the Fourth of July is over! The people are all gone and I am tired out. John thought it might do me good to see a little company, so we just had mother and Nellie and the children down for a week.

Of course I didn't do a thing. Jennie sees to everything now.

But it tired me all the same.

John says if I don't pick up faster he shall send me to Weir Mitchell in the fall.

But I don't want to go there at all. I had a friend who was in his hands once, and she says he is just like John and my brother, only more so!

Besides, it is such an undertaking to go so far.

I don't feel as if it was worth while to turn my hand over for anything, and I'm getting dreadfully fretful and querulous.

I cry at nothing, and cry most of the time.

Of course I don't when John is here, or anybody else, but when I am alone.

And I am alone a good deal just now. John is kept in town very often by serious cases, and Jennie is good and lets me alone when I want her to.

So I walk a little in the garden or down that lovely lane, sit on the porch under the roses, and lie down up here a good deal.

I'm getting really fond of the room in spite of the wallpaper. Perhaps *because* of the wallpaper.

It dwells in my mind so!

I lie here on this great immovable bed – it is nailed down, I believe – and follow that pattern about by the hour. It is as good as gymnastics, I assure you. I start, we'll say, at the bottom, down in the corner over there where it has not been touched, and I determine for the thousandth time that I *will* follow that pointless pattern to some sort of a conclusion.

I know a little of the principle of design, and I know this thing was not arranged on any laws of radiation, or alternation, or repetition, or symmetry, or anything else that I ever heard of.

It is repeated, of course, by the breadths, but not otherwise.

Looked at in one way each breadth stands alone, the bloated curves and flourishes – a kind of "debased Romanesque" with *delirium tremens* – go waddling up and down in isolated columns of fatuity.

But, on the other hand, they connect diagonally, and the sprawling outlines run off in great slanting waves of optic horror, like a lot of wallowing seaweeds in full chase.

The whole thing goes horizontally, too, at least it seems so, and I exhaust myself in trying to distinguish the order of its going in that direction.

They have used a horizontal breadth for a frieze, and that adds wonderfully to the confusion.

There is one end of the room where it is almost intact, and there, when the crosslights fade and the low sun shines directly upon it, I can almost fancy radiation after all, – the interminable grotesques seem to form around a common centre and rush off in headlong plunges of equal distraction.

It makes me tired to follow it. I will take a nap I guess.

******

I don't know why I should write this.

I don't want to.

I don't feel able.

And I know John would think it absurd. But I *must* say what I feel and think in some way – it is such a relief!

But the effort is getting to be greater than the relief.

Half the time now I am awfully lazy, and lie down ever so much.

John says I mustn't lose my strength, and has me take cod liver oil and lots of tonics and things, to say nothing of ale and wine and rare meat.

Dear John! He loves me very dearly, and hates to have me sick. I tried to have a real earnest reasonable talk with him the other day, and tell him how I wish he would let me go and make a visit to Cousin Henry and Julia.

But he said I wasn't able to go, nor able to stand it after I got there; and I did not make out a very good case for myself, for I was crying before I had finished.

It is getting to be a great effort for me to think straight. Just this nervous weakness I suppose.

And dear John gathered me up in his arms, and just carried me upstairs and laid me on the bed, and sat by me and read to me till it tired my head.

He said I was his darling and his comfort and all he had, and that I must take care of myself for his sake, and keep well.

He says no one but myself can help me out of it, that I must use my will and self-control and not let any silly fancies run away with me.

There's one comfort, the baby is well and happy, and does not have to occupy this nursery with the horrid wallpaper.

If we had not used it, that blessed child would have! What a fortunate escape! Why, I wouldn't have a child of mine, an impressionable little thing, live in such a room for worlds.

I never thought of it before, but it is lucky that John kept me here after all, I can stand it so much easier than a baby, you see.

Of course I never mention it to them any more – I am too wise, – but I keep watch of it all the same.

There are things in that paper that nobody knows but me, or ever will.

Behind that outside pattern the dim shapes get clearer every day.

It is always the same shape, only very numerous.

And it is like a woman stooping down and creeping about behind that pattern. I don't like it a bit. I wonder – I begin to think – I wish John would take me away from here!

******

It is so hard to talk with John about my case because he is so wise, and because he loves me so.

But I tried it last night.

It was moonlight. The moon shines in all around just as the sun does.

I hate to see it sometimes, it creeps so slowly, and always comes in by one window or another.

John was asleep and I hated to waken him, so I kept still and watched the moon-light on that undulating wallpaper till I felt creepy.

The faint figure behind seemed to shake the pattern, just as if she wanted to get out.

I got up softly and went to feel and see if the paper *did* move, and when I came back John was awake.

"What is it, little girl?" he said, "Don't go walking about like that – you'll get cold."

I thought it was a good time to talk, so I told him that I really was not gaining here, and that I wished he would take me away.

"Why, darling!" said he, "our lease will be up in three weeks, and I can't see how to leave before.

"The repairs are not done at home, and I cannot possibly leave town just now. Of course if you were in any danger, I could and would, but you really are better, dear, whether you can see it or not. I am a doctor, dear, and I know. You are gaining flesh and color, your appetite is better, I feel really much easier about you."

"I don't weigh a bit more," said I, "nor as much; and my appetite may be better in the evening when you are here, but it is worse in the morning when you are away!"

"Bless her little heart!" said he with a big hug, "she shall be as sick as she pleases! But now let's improve the shining hours by going to sleep, and talk about it in the morning!"

"And you won't go away?" I asked gloomily.

"Why, how can I, dear? It is only three weeks more and then we will take a nice little trip of a few days while Jennie is getting the house ready. Really dear you are better!"

"Better in body perhaps –" I began, and stopped short, for he sat up straight and looked at me with such a stern, reproachful look that I could not say another word.

"My darling," said he, "I beg of you, for my sake and for our child's sake, as well as for your own, that you will never for one instant let that idea enter your mind! There is nothing so dangerous, so fascinating, to a temperament like yours. It is a false and foolish fancy. Can you not trust me as a physician when I tell you so?"

So of course I said no more on that score, and we went to sleep before long. He thought I was asleep first, but I wasn't, and lay there for hours trying to decide whether that front pattern and the back pattern really did move together or separately.

******

On a pattern like this, by daylight, there is a lack of sequence, a defiance of law, that is a constant irritant to a normal mind.

The color is hideous enough, and unreliable enough, and infuriating enough, but the pattern is torturing.

You think you have mastered it, but just as you get well underway in following, it turns a back-somersault and there you are. It slaps you in the face, knocks you down, and tramples upon you. It is like a bad dream.

The outside pattern is a florid arabesque, reminding one of a fungus. If you can imagine a toadstool in joints, an interminable string of toadstools, budding and sprouting in endless convolutions – why, that is something like it.

That is, sometimes!

There is one marked peculiarity about this paper, a thing nobody seems to notice but myself, and that is that it changes as the light changes.

When the sun shoots in through the east window – I always watch for that first long, straight ray – it changes so quickly that I never can quite believe it.

That is why I watch it always.

By moonlight – the moon shines in all night when there is a moon – I wouldn't know it was the same paper.

At night in any kind of light, in twilight, candlelight, lamplight, and worst of all by moonlight, it becomes bars! The outside pattern I mean, and the woman behind it is as plain as can be.

I didn't realize for a long time what the thing was that showed behind, that dim sub-pattern, but now I am quite sure it is a woman.

By daylight she is subdued, quiet. I fancy it is the pattern that keeps her so still. It is so puzzling. It keeps me quiet by the hour.

I lie down ever so much now. John says it is good for me, and to sleep all I can.

Indeed he started the habit by making me lie down for an hour after each meal.

It is a very bad habit I am convinced, for you see I don't sleep.

And that cultivates deceit, for I don't tell them I'm awake – O no!

The fact is I am getting a little afraid of John.

He seems very queer sometimes, and even Jennie has an inexplicable look.

It strikes me occasionally, just as a scientific hypothesis, – that perhaps it is the paper!

I have watched John when he did not know I was looking, and come into the room suddenly on the most innocent excuses, and I've caught him several times *looking at the paper!* And Jennie too. I caught Jennie with her hand on it once.

She didn't know I was in the room, and when I asked her in a quiet, a very quiet voice, with the most restrained manner possible, what she was doing with the paper – she turned around as if she had been caught stealing, and looked quite angry – asked me why I should frighten her so!

Then she said that the paper stained everything it touched, that she had found yellow smooches on all my clothes and John's, and she wished we would be more careful!

Did not that sound innocent? But I know she was studying that pattern, and I am determined that nobody shall find it out but myself!

******

Life is very much more exciting now than it used to be. You see I have something more to expect, to look forward to, to watch. I really do eat better, and am more quiet than I was.

John is so pleased to see me improve! He laughed a little the other day, and said I seemed to be flourishing in spite of my wall-paper.

I turned it off with a laugh. I had no intention of telling him it was *because* of the wall-paper – he would make fun of me. He might even want to take me away.

I don't want to leave now until I have found it out. There is a week more, and I think that will be enough.

******

I'm feeling ever so much better! I don't sleep much at night, for it is so interesting to watch developments; but I sleep a good deal in the daytime.

In the daytime it is tiresome and perplexing.

There are always new shoots on the fungus, and new shades of yellow all over it. I cannot keep count of them, though I have tried conscientiously.

It is the strangest yellow, that wall-paper! It makes me think of all the yellow things I ever saw – not beautiful ones like buttercups, but old foul, bad yellow things.

But there is something else about that paper – the smell! I noticed it the moment we came into the room, but with so much air and sun it was not bad. Now we have had a week of fog and rain, and whether the windows are open or not, the smell is here.

It creeps all over the house.

I find it hovering in the dining-room, skulking in the parlor, hiding in the hall, lying in wait for me on the stairs.

It gets into my hair.

Even when I go to ride, if I turn my head suddenly and surprise it – there is that smell!

Such a peculiar odor, too! I have spent hours in trying to analyze it, to find what it smelled like.

It is not bad – at first, and very gentle, but quite the subtlest, most enduring odor I ever met.

In this damp weather it is awful, I wake up in the night and find it hanging over me.

It used to disturb me at first. I thought seriously of burning the house – to reach the smell.

But now I am used to it. The only thing I can think of that it is like is the *color* of the paper! A yellow smell.

There is a very funny mark on this wall, low down, near the mopboard. A streak that runs round the room. It goes behind every piece of furniture, except the bed, a long, straight, even *smooch,* as if it had been rubbed over and over.

I wonder how it was done and who did it, and what they did it for. Round and round and round – round and round and round – it makes me dizzy!

******

I really have discovered something at last.

Through watching so much at night, when it changes so, I have finally found out.

The front pattern *does* move – and no wonder! The woman behind shakes it!

Sometimes I think there are a great many women behind, and sometimes only one, and she crawls around fast, and her crawling shakes it all over.

Then in the very bright spots she keeps still, and in the very shady spots she just takes hold of the bars and shakes them hard.

And she is all the time trying to climb through. But nobody could climb through that pattern – it strangles so; I think that is why it has so many heads.

They get through, and then the pattern strangles them off and turns them upside down, and makes their eyes white!

If those heads were covered or taken off it would not be half so bad.

******

I think that woman gets out in the daytime!

And I'll tell you why – privately – I've seen her!

I can see her out of every one of my windows!

It is the same woman, I know, for she is always creeping, and most women do not creep by daylight.

I see her in that long shaded lane, creeping up and down. I see her in those dark grape arbors, creeping all around the garden.

I see her on that long road under the trees, creeping along, and when a carriage comes she hides under the blackberry vines.

I don't blame her a bit. It must be very humiliating to be caught creeping by daylight!

I always lock the door when I creep by daylight. I can't do it at night, for I know John would suspect something at once.

And John is so queer now, that I don't want to irritate him. I wish he would take another room! Besides, I don't want anybody to get that woman out at night but myself.

I often wonder if I could see her out of all the windows at once.

But, turn as fast as I can, I can only see out of one at one time.

And though I always see her, she *may* be able to creep faster than I can turn!

I have watched her sometimes away off in the open country, creeping as fast as a cloud shadow in a high wind.

******

If only that top pattern could be gotten off from the under one! I mean to try it, little by little.

I have found out another funny thing, but I shan't tell it this time! It does not do to trust people too much.

There are only two more days to get this paper off, and I believe John is beginning to notice. I don't like the look in his eyes.

And I heard him ask Jennie a lot of professional questions about me. She had a very good report to give.

She said I slept a good deal in the daytime.

John knows I don't sleep very well at night, for all I'm so quiet!

He asked me all sorts of questions, too, and pretended to be very loving and kind.

As if I couldn't see through him! Still, I don't wonder he acts so, sleeping under this paper for three months.

It only interests me, but I feel sure John and Jennie are secretly affected by it.

******

Hurrah! This is the last day, but it is enough. John is to stay in town over night, and won't be out until this evening.

Jennie wanted to sleep with me – the sly thing! but I told her I should undoubtedly rest better for a night all alone.

That was clever, for really I wasn't alone a bit! As soon as it was moonlight and that poor thing began to crawl and shake the pattern, I got up and ran to help her.

I pulled and she shook, I shook and she pulled, and before morning we had peeled off yards of that paper.

A strip about as high as my head and half around the room.

And then when the sun came and that awful pattern began to laugh at me, I declared I would finish it to-day!

We go away to-morrow, and they are moving all my furniture down again to leave things as they were before.

Jennie looked at the wall in amazement, but I told her merrily that I did it out of pure spite at the vicious thing.

She laughed and said she wouldn't mind doing it herself, but I must not get tired.

How she betrayed herself that time!

But I am here, and no person touches this paper but me, – not *alive!*

She tried to get me out of the room – it was too patent! But I said it was so quiet and empty and clean now that I believed I would lie down again and sleep all I could; and not to wake me even for dinner – I would call when I woke.

So now she is gone, and the servants are gone, and the things are gone, and there is nothing left but that great bedstead nailed down, with the canvas mattress we found on it.

We shall sleep downstairs to-night, and take the boat home to-morrow.

I quite enjoy the room, now it is bare again.

How those children did tear about here!

This bedstead is fairly gnawed!

But I must get to work.

I have locked the door and thrown the key down into the front path.

I don't want to go out, and I don't want to have anybody come in, till John comes.

I want to astonish him.

I've got a rope up here that even Jennie did not find. If that woman does get out, and tries to get away, I can tie her!

But I forgot I could not reach far without anything to stand on!

This bed will *not* move!

I tried to lift and push it until I was lame, and then I got so angry I bit off a little piece at one corner – but it hurt my teeth.

Then I peeled off all the paper I could reach standing on the floor. It sticks horribly and the pattern just enjoys it! All those strangled heads and bulbous eyes and waddling fungus growths just shriek with derision!

I am getting angry enough to do something desperate. To jump out of the window would be admirable exercise, but the bars are too strong even to try.

Besides I wouldn't do it. Of course not. I know well enough that a step like that is improper and might be misconstrued.

I don't like to *look* out of the windows even – there are so many of those creeping women, and they creep so fast.

I wonder if they all come out of that wall-paper as I did?

But I am securely fastened now by my well-hidden rope – you don't get *me* out in the road there!

I suppose I shall have to get back behind the pattern when it comes night, and that is hard!

It is so pleasant to be out in this great room and creep around as I please!

I don't want to go outside. I won't, even if Jennie asks me to.

For outside you have to creep on the ground, and everything is green instead of yellow.

But here I can creep smoothly on the floor, and my shoulder just fits in that long smooch around the wall, so I cannot lose my way.

Why there's John at the door!

It is no use, young man, you can't open it!

How he does call and pound!

Now he's crying for an axe.

It would be a shame to break down that beautiful door!

"John dear!" said I in the gentlest voice, "the key is down by the front steps, under a plantain leaf!"

That silenced him for a few moments.

Then he said – very quietly indeed, "Open the door, my darling!"

"I can't," said I. "The key is down by the front door under a plantain leaf!"

And then I said it again, several times, very gently and slowly, and said it so often that he had to go and see, and he got it of course, and came in. He stopped short by the door.

"What is the matter?" he cried. "For God's sake, what are you doing!"

I kept on creeping just the same, but I looked at him over my shoulder.

"I've got out at last," said I, "in spite of you and Jane. And I've pulled off most of the paper, so you can't put me back!"

Now why should that man have fainted? But he did, and right across my path by the wall, so that I had to creep over him every time!

8.2

Scope of the Problem
Carol Bohmer and Andrea Parrot

Most people, including those who have experienced it, have trouble understanding sexual assault. This is especially true if the victim and assailant are acquainted, are friends, or are dating. Many of the common questions about sexual assault on a college campus will be addressed in this chapter.

Who Are the Victims of Campus Sexual Assault?

The case that follows includes many of the elements common to cases of sexual assault on campus. In this case the victim did report the sexual assault to the campus authorities, but she was manipulated into not pursuing legal or judicial authorities.

Ellen, a first-year student, went to several parties the first Saturday of the fall semester. She had a lot to drink over the course of the evening. She was then taken by one of the men she had met at one of the parties to his residence hall, where there was a toga party under way. They both dressed in sheets and drank more alcohol at the residence hall party. Ellen passed out, and when she gained consciousness, she discovered his penis in her mouth.

Ellen was a typical victim of campus sexual assault in that she was female, a freshman in college, and had been drinking alcohol. Victims of rape may be men or women of any age; however, they are usually females between the ages of fifteen and twenty-four. Most of them are of college age, an age when they are dating most frequently (Koss et al., 1987). Most sexual assaults occur between acquaintances, frequently on dates. The sexual assault victims we will be discussing in this book are most often college women between seventeen and twenty-one. It is possible for men to be raped by male assailants – or, more rarely, by female assailants – but because the vast majority of acquaintance rapes involve male assailants and female victims, this book will primarily focus on this type of sexual assault.

The two most important determining factors regarding whether a date rape will occur are the number of men a woman dates (Burkhart and Stanton, 1985), and the degree of intoxication of those men (Polonko et al., 1986). The first factor is based on probability of exposure, in part because it is impossible to tell a date rapist by the way he looks, and in part because women are socialized to ignore cues that may indicate that some men are a threat. For example, if a man calls a woman a derogatory name (such as "bitch") or continues to tease her when she asks him to stop, he is harassing her and is likely to exploit her. If he harasses, exploits, and/or objectifies her in a non-sexual situation, he is likely to do so in a sexual situation as well. Most women are socialized to put up with harassment, however, because saying something assertive is considered contrary to proper feminine behavior. The more times a woman experiences harassing kinds of behavior, the more they become part of her social environment, and the more she learns to "grin and bear it."

Some sexual assault victims have such low self-esteem that they feel that they are worthless without a relationship, and that it is better to be associated with any man than no man at all. This attitude is also enforced in American culture. The victim may say, "As soon as he gets to know the real me, he will fall in love with me, and will stop doing that. He will change for me." Or she may say, "I know he did something to me that I didn't like, but that is all I deserve." The victim may have watched her father harass or assault her mother, making her believe that this is the way adult sexual relationships are supposed to be. She may even have been sexually assaulted as a child; forced sexual experiences may be the only kind of sexual relationships she knows. Some victims may not want to believe that someone they love could do anything as terrible as rape them, so these victims may define the sexual assault as their own fault rather than believe that their boyfriends are rapists. For example, a victim may say, "I got him so excited that he couldn't stop himself."

With regard to the second factor, the more intoxicated a man is, the greater the likelihood that he will ignore a woman's protests or be unable to interpret her words and actions as she intended them. This is especially true if she does not want to have sex but he does, which is a common pattern in acquaintance sexual assaults.

While visiting from another institution, John got drunk at a fraternity party and raped a woman at the party. His friends, who were fraternity brothers, helped to get her drunk and then encouraged the assault by cheering him on. After the party the woman filed a complaint with the college administration, but because the alleged rapist was not a student at the college, the administration was not able to do anything to him.

Studies have not consistently indicated any female personality traits that make a woman more likely to become a date or acquaintance rape victim. Our research indicates that the typical scenario of sexual assault on a college campus includes the woman's drinking at a party (especially a fraternity party) and playing drinking games, a situation where she has been given a drink in which the alcohol has been disguised as punch. First-year college students are most likely to become the victims of sexual assault while in college (Koss et al., 1987). Sexual assault, however, can and does also happen in other circumstances.

Sexual assault victims sometimes have sex again with their assailant. In many cases in which the victim has sex with the assailant again, the latter was the boyfriend of the victim. The victim may believe that, although he did force her to have sex, he will treat her better and not rape her once he really gets to know what a wonderful person she is (and, presumably, falls in love with her). Only after repeated sexual assaults over time does she realize that he will not change, and so she ends the relationship.

Neil Gilbert, a professor of social work at Stanford University, believes that if a woman does not know that what has happened to her is rape, then it is not rape (Collison, 1992). This type of attitude is probably pervasive among the administrations of some colleges. Gilbert cites FBI statistics, which consist disproportionately of reports of stranger rape, to prove that the 20 to 25 percent estimate of sexual assaults on female college students is inflated. The FBI estimates that fewer than one in ten stranger rapes are actually reported to them, however, and data from national studies suggest that fewer than one in one hundred acquaintance rapes are reported to the police (Burkhart, 1983; Parrot, 1992). Because most rapes and sexual assaults that occur in college are between acquaintances, they are not likely to be reported to the police or even the college administration. This is especially true if administrators have made it clear to victims that they don't believe sexual assault happens on their campus.

Who Are the Assailants?

Approximately 5 to 8 percent of college men know that raping acquaintances is wrong, but choose to do it because they know the odds of their being caught and convicted are very low (Koss et al., 1987; Koss, 1992; Hannan and Burkhart, 1994). There is a larger group of men who rape acquaintances but do not believe it is rape. They often believe they are acting in the way men are "supposed to act" – that "no" really means "maybe," and "maybe" really means "yes." Once a case becomes public, several other women often come forth who are willing to testify that the assailant sexually assaulted them as well, even though the other women had not pressed charges themselves. This was the case in the William Kennedy Smith trial, although the three women who also claimed to have been raped by him were not permitted to testify.

Some studies have compared the incidence of sexual assault among various groups of men. One study indicated that 35 percent of fraternity men reported having forced someone to have sexual intercourse. This figure was significantly higher than for members of student government (9 percent) or men not affiliated with other organizations (11 percent) (Garrett-Gooding and Senter, 1987). Based on an FBI survey, basketball and football players from NCAA colleges were reported to the police for committing sexual assault 38 percent more often than the average for males on college campuses (Hoffman, 1986).

The men who are most likely to rape in college are fraternity pledges (Bird, 1991; Koss, 1991). It is unclear whether this is because either forced sexual intercourse or sexual intercourse under any circumstances is a condition of pledging, or because the pledges are trying to act in a way that they believe the brothers will admire. The process of pledging a fraternity often desensitizes men to behaviors that objectify women, and it also creates a "groupthink" mentality (Sanday, 1990). As a result, once men become pledges or fraternity members, some of them may commit a sexual assault to be "one of the brothers." All of these factors, plus the heavy alcohol consumption that occurs in fraternities, contribute to the likelihood that a sexual assault will occur on campus. Not all fraternity pledges who abuse alcohol, however, actually commit sexual assault. Conversely, women should not automatically feel safe with a man who is not in a fraternity and who is a teetotaler.

> Tom sexually assaulted Carol, the girlfriend of one of his fraternity brothers. Carol passed out from drinking too much at a fraternity party, and Tom had sex with her while she was unconscious in her boyfriend's bedroom. When she started moaning her boyfriend's name during the rape, Tom panicked and went to get the boyfriend, encouraging him to have sex with her so that if she regained consciousness, she would see him instead of Tom. Friends of Carol saw Tom leave the room and then reappear with her boyfriend, who he pushed into the room. Tom, however, had inadvertently left his tie in the bed, which was seen as evidence that he had been there with Carol. Tom was subsequently convicted of sexual assault by the campus judicial board.

The likelihood to commit a sexual assault also increases if men choose to live in all-male living units when co-educational units are also available. In fact, men who elect to live in all-male residences often do so in order to be able to behave in a violent or antisocial way, such as punching walls or getting drunk and vomiting in the hallways. There is significantly more damage done in all-male living units than on male floors of co-educational residences for this reason (Walters et al., 1981).

Another group at risk for committing rape in college are athletes competing in such aggressive team sports as football, lacrosse, and hockey. Athletes are most likely to sexually assault after a game, when they are out either celebrating a win or drowning their sorrows after a loss. Drinking parties are frequently part of the post-game ritual, with female fans helping the athletes celebrate or commiserating with them. The likelihood of a sexual assault is greatest at this point if a female "groupie" appears to be "throwing herself" at an athlete with the intent of being seen with him or because she wants to be his friend. The athlete may be unable to distinguish between her desire for friendship and his perception that she is throwing herself at him because she wants sex. Further, he may believe that this is what he deserves as a result of his "star" status. There have been many celebrated cases of high school, college, and professional athletes who were successfully charged with rape or sexual assault by college and civil authorities.

Assailants are not limited to fraternity members and athletes, however, and the vast majority of fraternity men and athletes do not rape. The rate is higher among these two groups because of their position of privilege on campus, and because of their involvement with alcohol. The characteristics that are most important in determining if a man will become an acquaintance rapist are macho attitudes, antisocial behavior, and abuse of alcohol (either on a regular basis, or through binge experiences) (Malamuth and Dean, 1991; Rapaport and Posey, 1991). Athletes and fraternity men may exhibit some or all of these traits.

> Bill, a fraternity pledge, was a virgin at the time he was pledging. He was told by the brothers that they did not accept virgins into their house, and so he would have to do something about his virginity status. When he protested that he did not have a girlfriend, he was told that he should bring a girl to their fraternity formal, and the brothers would do the rest. He invited a very naïve first-year student, Lori, to the party. Once there, she was given punch spiked with grain alcohol. When Lori blacked out, Bill took her to the bedroom of one of the brothers, put a condom on, and forced her to have sex over her feeble protests. She was also a virgin at the time, and she became pregnant because the condom broke during the rape.

Different Types of Campus Sexual Assault and Rape

Each different type of sexual assault has specific characteristics and problems associated with it. Campus sexual assaults vary by the status of the victim (student, faculty, staff, visitor, and so on), the status of the assailant, the number of assailants involved, and the degree of acquaintanceship between those involved. Rape or sexual assault on college campuses may be committed by an acquaintance or a stranger; most typically, the assailant is someone the victim knows. For the purposes of this book we have defined *campus sexual assault* as assault cases in which at least one of the people involved is associated with the institution.

Sexual Assault of a Member of the College Community by a Stranger from Outside the Campus Community

We probably hear about this type of sexual assault more often than any other. Women are much more likely to report a sexual assault in which they are seen as having little or no culpability. Therefore, victims are more likely to report a sexual assault to the police or campus authorities if they do not know the assailant, do not share the same friends, and consequently do not receive any pressure from friends or acquaintances to keep quiet so the assailant's life will not be "ruined." Stranger rape usually occurs more in urban than rural areas because of higher crime rates in urban areas.

> On the night of January 2, 1989, a female employee of the University of Southern California was attacked near the school's credit union building by an unknown man who dragged her into some bushes, where she was beaten, stabbed, robbed, and raped. The attack lasted forty minutes, during which time no one came to the woman's aid. She was rescued by two passersby, who scared off the assailant and then helped her to walk to the security office about a block away. It turned out that only one security officer was in the field at the time of the attack. Six months before the attack, there was a report that identified the building as a security risk, but no one had ever followed up on the report's recommendations, which included increasing the lighting and cutting back the bushes.
>
> A young woman at Clarkson University was assaulted while walking home through an isolated area behind the field house. A fire watchman who was inside the field house reported it to another fire watchman who was on patrol on another part of campus. The watchman in the car came to the building to investigate. He came upon two people having what he believed to be consensual sex. He called the other fire watchman and they were unsure of how to respond. When they went to check the scene again, they found the woman alone, bloody, and unconscious. They then called the village police, who responded and apprehended the man after he had raped and beaten the woman. She later died in the hospital. Clarkson College was sued and settled out of court. The college has subsequently hired a director of campus safety with a law enforcement background and has dramatically upgraded the training for its campus safety personnel (Cooper, 1992).

Sexual assault by a stranger (other than a student) from within the campus community is more likely in large campus communities than on smaller campuses, where most people tend to know each other. These rapes may be between students and faculty, administrators, or college staff members or visitors to the campus community.

Rape by a Student Unknown to the Victim

This type of sexual assault is also more common in larger schools, and may happen in circumstances such as after the assailant notices the victim in a bar or at a large party. It may also occur if a woman has a "bad" reputation, passes out at a party after drinking alcohol, and is used sexually by male students who are strangers to the victim. In some instances, the victim is in a presumably safe place but is attacked by a stranger who has gained access based on false pretenses (for example, posing as a student or pizza delivery person). It is typical in gang rape that at least some of the assailants are strangers to the victim.

In 1986, Lehigh freshman Jeannie Clery was raped, sodomized, and murdered while sleeping in her bed at 6.00 a.m. That night another student, who had been drinking and who did not know her, entered her residence hall through three automatically locking doors that were propped open, entered her room, and sexually assaulted and strangled her. Her parents sued the university for failing to provide a safe environment for their daughter and for violation of "foreseeable action." They settled for an undisclosed sum, and in addition, they committed Lehigh to extensive improvements in dormitory security.

Acquaintance Rape and Sexual Assault

"Acquaintance rape" and "date rape" are not legal categories; the term *rape* usually applies to any forced intercourse, regardless of the degree of acquaintance. We are using the terms *acquaintance rape* and *date rape* for clarity of understanding in a sociological rather than a legal sense.

Amy, a senior in high school, was visiting her sister, Jill (a first-year student), for the weekend at a small liberal arts college. They went to a lacrosse game, and Jill had a party in her room afterward. One of the lacrosse players, Adam, attended the party after the game, and Amy spent over an hour with him there. Amy and Adam both got drunk and went into an adjoining room during the party for about an hour. When they emerged, he went home, and Amy told Jill that Adam had raped her. Amy and Jill reported the event to the authorities, and Adam was suspended. Adam sued the college on the grounds that the campus policy explicitly stated that the college community would protect its students, but it said nothing about protecting visitors. (Parrot and Bechhofer, 1991)

Acquaintance sexual assaults are by far the most common type of rape both on and off the campus; however, they are rarely reported to authorities. Date rape (the most common type on college campuses) and acquaintance rape are estimated to happen to one-fifth of college women, whereas one-quarter of college women will experience either attempted or completed forced sex (Koss et al., 1987). These sexual assaults happen most often during the woman's first year, although a victim may also experience further episodes later on. Sexual assaults often happen to victims in the first week of college, before they know the social "rules." At colleges where first-year students live on campus and then must move off campus during their sophomore year, however, the incidence increases when students no longer have the protection of the structured college living environment (Parrot and Lynk, 1983; Parrot, 1985).

What Happens When Victims Report to Campus or Criminal Authorities

Even when victims do report to the police, they are frequently disbelieved or blamed. This phenomenon was seen in the William Kennedy Smith case, in which the victim did report being raped. Although this case was not a campus sexual assault, the issues are similar; because it was so highly publicized, we will use it as an example for purposes of illustration. Patricia Bowman's character was called into question; she was criticized for being in a bar drinking, for going to his home voluntarily, and for using poor judgment. The same things happen when campus sexual assault victims report to the campus authorities. But in the campus system, because rules of evidence are more flexible than in the criminal courts, victims are also often asked inappropriate questions about their sexual behavior (for example, "Do you have oral sex with all the men you date? Do you like it?").

In most acquaintance sexual assault cases, the victim is usually blamed by her peers and her support system. Martha Burt (1991) found that a majority of Americans think that at least half of all rape reports are false and that they are invented by women to retaliate against men who have wronged them. Many people believe that the charge of acquaintance rape or gang rape occurs because a woman feels guilty after a sexual encounter with a man and cries "rape" in order to ease her conscience. The fact is that only 2 percent of rape reports prove to be intentionally reported falsely to the police (Brownmiller, 1975).

> Mary, a graduate student, was raped by another student in her apartment and reported the assault to the police. (Because the rape was not on college property, it was not within the jurisdiction of that particular college.) The district attorney accepted the case and was preparing it for trial. In order to obtain information from the alleged assailant about another crime, however, the district attorney offered the assailant a plea bargain, and the latter received a light sentence. Mary was very angry and disappointed at having been denied the right to "have her day in court" or to see the man sentenced to what she considered an appropriate penalty. At least in her case, however, the assailant was sentenced for some offense and as a result will have a criminal record.

Many victims find it cathartic and healing to tell their stories in court and to play a role in their assailant's punishment. But a plea bargain is often negotiated for a lesser charge, and the victim feels cheated when the assailant pleads guilty to a much less serious crime than that which he committed against her.

The low reporting and conviction rates are generally characteristic of what are called *simple rapes:* those with no violence, a single attacker, and no other crime committed at the time (Estrich, 1987). Acquaintance rapes are usually simple rapes. The report and criminal conviction rates are much higher in the case of aggravated rapes, but those are far less likely than simple rapes to take place, especially on a college campus. Therefore, more assailants may be punished if acquaintance rape cases are heard by the college judicial board or officer, because the campus system can operate under different rules of evidence. Campus judicial processes are able to find more defendants guilty of sexual assault violations, all other things being equal, than the criminal courts, provided that the system is well designed and administered. The most serious penalty that may be administered in the campus system, however, is expulsion from the institution, which is not comparable to the loss of liberty that may follow a guilty verdict in the criminal justice system.

In many cases of sexual assault reported to the criminal justice system, the case is not accepted by the district attorney or indicted by the grand jury, which may make the victim feel powerless or very angry, especially if she wants to see her assailant behind bars. Victims who report their assaults to the campus criminal judicial system often also experience anger, frustration, and disappointment. For example, victims may be told that their case is not eligible for action by the campus judicial system because it occurred outside of the jurisdiction of the system. Other cases may fail because the victim is not taken seriously by law enforcement officials or campus officials, or because of long delays, among other reasons.

If the case is handled within a campus system, the result may be an acquittal. Although on some campuses, the cases of campus sexual assault that are brought to the judicial body for hearing almost always result in a guilty verdict, this is not universally the case. The outcome depends, in large part, on the thoroughness of the investigation and the mind-set of the administrator(s) hearing the case. The way the campus code is written may also make a guilty verdict very difficult. Alternatively, there may not be enough evidence to convict the defendant, even when the rules of evidence are more flexible.

Even if the defendant is found guilty, he may receive an extremely light sentence (for example, thirty hours of community service). Additionally, the victim often has to face harassment by other students on campus who believe that she was not really raped, that it was her fault, that she is ruining the assailant's life, or that it was not "that big a deal." She may also be harassed by the assailant or his friends, especially if the former is a member of a fraternity that stands to be sanctioned if he is found guilty. Fear of this kind of harassment is more likely if the victim is on a small campus, where students tend to know almost everyone and everything that occurs on campus. All of these factors may contribute to reluctance on the part of women to report campus sexual assault....

Public Attitudes about Acquaintance Rape

The role of public opinion in general and the influence of highly publicized cases of sexual assault in particular help to shape the way campus sexual assault is viewed. This book is about the problem of campus sexual assault in general, and those cases resulting in civil suits are but one small segment of the cases that occur. Case studies that did not occur on a college campus, involving the campus judicial process, or result in civil litigation are also included here if they are celebrated and have played a major role in developing societal attitudes about acquaintance rape. Examples of such cases include the William Kennedy Smith and Mike Tyson rape trials and the confirmation hearings for Clarence Thomas's appointment to the Supreme Court. Each of these events took place within a 12-month period early in the 1990s and were instrumental in shaping public opinion about "real rape" and attitudes blaming the victim.

We have learned a great deal about how the American public views rape, sexual assault, and sexual harassment involving acquaintances from cases that have received wide publicity. The victim is held to a higher standard than is the assailant; her testimony must be perfectly consistent and impeccable. She is blamed for her behavior if she has been drinking, and for not being able to stop him. His drinking behavior, on the other hand, excuses his sexual needs. ("He couldn't stop himself"; "He got carried away.")

Most people in our culture are socialized to believe rape myths. Rape myths allow us to believe that a "real rape" is one in which a victim is raped by a stranger who jumps out of the bushes with a weapon, and in which she fought back, was beaten and bruised, reported the event to the police, and had medical evidence collected immediately. In a "real rape," the victim has never had sex with the assailant before, is preferably a virgin, was not intoxicated, was not wearing seductive clothing, and has a good reputation. If a rape occurred under these circumstances, most people would agree that the woman was indeed raped. Unfortunately, acquaintance sexual assaults contain few, if any, of those elements. In many acquaintance rape situations the victim had been drinking, did voluntarily go with the man to his apartment or room, was not threatened with a weapon, did not fight back, did not report the event to the police immediately, did not have medical evidence collected, and may have even had sex with the assailant voluntarily before.

In many of the highly publicized cases of 1990 and 1991, the verdict was simply based on the man's word against the woman's. It is a matter of whom we believe and why. Societal messages have suggested that men must always be ready and willing to have sex, that a woman who says "no" never means it, and that sex is a man's right if he spent money on the date (Muehlenhard et al., 1985). Some men also feel that a woman is asking for sex if she gets drunk, goes to a man's apartment, or asks him over to hers. These ideas are in stark contrast to the legal definitions of rape and sexual assault in the United States. Most states have laws that define rape as a situation in which sexual intercourse is forced on one person by another against the victim's will and without the victim's consent, or if the victim submits out of fear for his or her safety or life. In theory, the victim does not have to say "no" more than once, and does not have to explain why he or she wants the offender to stop. Many people, however, do not believe that an event was rape if the woman is not bruised and hysterical, and if the offender was not a stranger (Burt, 1980; Johnson, 1985). Legally, these factors do not have to be present for a sexual assault to have occurred.

In some cases, members of society believe that the victim should have known better, such as in the Mike Tyson case. Even though Tyson was convicted of rape and sexual assault, the behavior of his victim, Desiree Washington, was still questioned, and victim-blaming statements were abundant. Many of the following comments were made by people who disbelieved the victim. Why did she go up to his hotel room unescorted? She must have known of his reputation. He was reported as having sexually harassed beauty pageant contestants earlier that day, and she surely must have seen that. In reality, most women have a hard time believing that men they know would hurt them if they have never hurt them before. If attacked, women often have a difficult time defending themselves against most men. In the case of the former heavyweight boxing champion of the world, she could never have fought her way out if he behaved inappropriately.

Tyson's reputation as a man who had previously been involved in sexual violence was very different than that of William Kennedy Smith, who was a physician and a member of a very influential family. Desiree Washington's background (as a pillar of the community, an upstanding member of her church, and a member of the National Honor Society) was very different from that of Smith's accuser, Patti Bowman. Bowman had obviously had sex before (because she was a mother) and was drinking in a bar where she met Smith. Undoubtedly, racial factors were also a likely contributor to Tyson's conviction, in contrast to the acquittal in the William Kennedy Smith trial.

The public often assumes that victims will make false accusations for some kind of personal gain. Anita Hill was accused of making up charges against Clarence Thomas because she was either a woman scorned, emotionally imbalanced, looking for a movie or book contract and a way to become famous, or a pathological liar. Patricia Bowman, the woman who accused William Kennedy Smith of rape, was portrayed as a "wild girl" with a "taste for glitz" by the media. Sexual assault and rape victims are often charged by public opinion with trying to ruin a man's life; when a public figure is charged, the victim is viewed as being out for fame and fortune as well.

College students are aware of news events of this nature, and one can assume that they are influenced by them. Potential rapists may believe that they can rape with impunity as long as they choose the right kind of victim. Victims are likely to have learned the lesson that there are many factors, unrelated to the sexual assault, that will have bearing on whether their cases will be treated seriously. If victims do decide to report the assault, they must know that their chances of a conviction are not good, and that their chances of being further harassed and blamed are high. Current and highly publicized cases will undoubtedly have an important impact on the number of sexual assaults committed and the number of cases reported to authorities, both on and off the campus.

References

Bird, L. (1991) "Psycho-social and environmental predictors of sexually assaultive attitudes and behaviors among American college men," PhD dissertation at the University of Arizona.

Brownmiller, S. (1975) *Against Our Will: Men, Women and Rape* (New York: Simon and Schuster).

Burkhart, B. (1983) "Acquaintance rape statistics and prevention," paper presented at the Acquaintance Rape and Prevention on Campus Conference in Louisville, KY.

Burkhart, B. R. and Stanton, A. L. (1985) "Sexual aggression in acquaintance relationships," in G. Russel (ed.), *Violence in Intimate Relationships* (New York: Spectrum Press).

Burt, M. (1980) "Cultural myths and supports for rape," *Journal of Personality and Social Psychology*, 38: 217–30.

Burt, M. (1991) "Rape myths and acquaintance rape," in A. Parrot and L. Bechhofer (eds), *Acquaintance Rape: the Hidden Crime*, pp. 26–40 (New York: John Wiley & Sons).

Collison, M. (1992) "A Berkeley scholar clashes with feminists over validity of their research on date rape," *Chronicle of Higher Education*, February 26.

Cooper, Dean (1992) Personal communication from the dean of students, Clarkson College, October 15.

Estrich, S. (1987) *Real Rape: How the Legal System Victimizes Women Who Say No* (Cambridge, MA: Harvard University Press).

Garrett-Gooding, J. and Senter, R. (1987) "Attitudes and acts of sexual aggression on a university campus," *Sociological Inquiry*, 59: 348–71.

Hannan, K. E. and Burkhart, B. (1994) "The typography of violence in college men: frequency, and comorbidity of sexual and physical aggression," *Journal of College Student Psychotherapy*.

Hoffman, R. (1986) "Rape and the college athlete: part one," *Philadelphia Daily News*, March 17, p. 104.

Johnson, K. M. (1985) *If You are Raped* (Holmes Beach, FL: Learning Publications).

Koss, M. (1991) Keynote address presented at the First International Conference on Sexual Assault on Campus, Orlando, FL.

Koss, M. (1992) "Alcohol, athletics, and the fraternity rape connection," paper presented at the Second International Conference on Sexual Assault on Campus, Orlando, FL.

Koss, M. P., Gidicz, C. A., and Wisniewski, N. (1987) "The scope of rape: incidence and prevalence of sexual aggression and victimization in a national sample of higher education students," *Journal of Consulting and Clinical Psychology*, 55(2): 162–70.

Malamuth, N. and Dean, C. (1991) "Attraction to sexual aggression," in A. Parrot and L. Bechhofer (eds), *Acquaintance Rape: the Hidden Crime* (New York: John Wiley & Sons).

Muehlenhard, C. L., Friedman, D. E., and Thomas, C. M. (1985) "Is date rape justifiable? The effects of dating activity, who initiated, who paid, and man's attitudes toward women," *Psychology of Women Quarterly*, 9(3): 297–310.

Parrot, A. (1985) "Comparison of acquaintance rape patterns among college students in a large co-ed university and a small women's college," paper presented at the Annual Meeting of the Society for the Scientific Study of Sex, San Diego, CA.

Parrot, A. (1992) "A comparison of male and female sexual assault victimization experiences involving alcohol," paper presented at the Annual Meeting of the Society for the Scientific Study of Sex, San Diego, CA.

Parrot, A. and Bechhofer, L. (eds) (1991) *Acquaintance Rape: the Hidden Crime* (New York: John Wiley & Sons).

Parrot, A. and Lynk, R. (1983) "Acquaintance rape in a college population," paper presented at the Eastern Regional Meeting of the Society for the Scientific Study of Sex, Philadelphia, PA.

Polonko, K., Parcell, S., and Teachman, J. (1986) "A methodological note on sexual aggression," paper presented at the National Convention of the Society for the Scientific Study of Sex, St Louis, MO.

Rapaport, K. R. and Posey, D. (1991) "Sexually coercive college males," in A. Parrot and L. Bechhofer (eds), *Acquaintance Rape: the Hidden Crime* (New York: John Wiley & Sons).

Sanday, P. (1990) *Fraternity Gang Rape* (New York: New York University Press).

Walters, J., McKellar, A., Lipton, M., and Karme, L. (1981) "What are the pros and cons of coed dorms?" *Medical Aspects of Human Sexuality*, 15(8): 48–56.

8.3

Sexual Assault Prevention Tips
Feminally

1. Don't put drugs in people's drinks in order to control their behavior.
2. When you see someone walking by themselves, leave them alone!
3. If you pull over to help someone with car problems, remember not to assault them!
4. NEVER open an unlocked door or window uninvited.
5. If you are in an elevator and someone else gets in, DON'T ASSAULT THEM!
6. USE THE BUDDY SYSTEM! If you are not able to stop yourself from assaulting people, ask a friend to stay with you while you are in public.
7. Always be honest with people! Don't pretend to be a caring friend in order to gain the trust of someone you want to assault. Consider telling them you plan to assault them. If you don't communicate your intentions, the other person may take that as a sign that you do not plan to rape them.
8. Don't forget: you can't have sex with someone unless they are awake!
9. Carry a whistle! If you are worried you might assault someone "accidentally" you can hand it to the person you're with so they can blow it if you do.
10. **Don't assault people**.

8.4

Legal Images of Battered Women
Martha R. Mahoney

.../I found an announcement/not the woman's bloated body in the river/ floating not the child bleeding in the 59th street corridor/not the baby broken on the floor/

"there is some concern that alleged battered women might start to murder their husbands and lovers with no immediate cause"[1]

I am writing about women's lives. Our lives, like everyone's, are lived within particular cultures that both reflect legal structures and affect legal interpretation. Focusing on domestic violence, this article describes an interrelationship between women's lives, culture, and law. This relationship is not linear (moving from women's lives to law, or from law to life) but interactive: cultural assumptions about domestic violence affect substantive law and methods of litigation in ways that in turn affect society's

---

[1]   Ntozake Shange, *With No Immediate Cause, in* FAMILY VIOLENCE: POEMS ON THE PATHOLOGY 66, 67 (Mary McAnally ed., 1982).

perceptions of women; both law and societal perceptions affect women's understanding of our own lives, relationships, and options; our lives are part of the culture that affects legal interpretation and within which further legal moves are made. Serious harm to women results from the ways in which law and culture distort our experience.

The courtroom is the theater in which the dramas of battered women have been brought to public attention. Trials like that of Francine Hughes, whose story became the book and movie *The Burning Bed,*[2] create a cultural and legal spotlight that has in some ways benefited women by increasing public knowledge of the existence of domestic violence. However, the press has emphasized sensational cases that have a high level of terrorism against women and a grotesque quality of abuse.[3] These cases come to define a cultural image of domestic violence, and the women in these cases define an image of battered women.

These images disguise the commonality of violence against women. Up to one half of all American women – and approximately two thirds of women who are separated or divorced – report having experienced physical assault in their relationships.[4] However, litigation and judicial decisionmaking in cases of severe violence reflect implicit or explicit assumptions that domestic violence is rare or exceptional.

For actors in the courtroom drama, the fiction that such violence is exceptional allows denial of the ways in which domestic violence has touched their own lives. Perhaps most damagingly, the fiction of exceptionality also increases the capacity of women to deny that the stories told in the publicized courtroom dramas have anything to do with our own lives. Therefore, it limits the help we may seek when we encounter trouble, the charges we are willing to file, our votes as jurors when charges have been filed by or against others, and our consciousness of the meaning of the struggles and dangers of our own experience.

Although domestic violence is important in many areas of legal doctrine, including family law and torts, the criminal justice system places the greatest pressures on cultural images of battered women. The self-defense cases in which women kill their batterers are small in number compared to the overall universe of domestic violence, yet they are highly emotionally charged as well as highly publicized. In many states, the right to expert testimony on behalf of these defendants has been won through much dedicated feminist litigation.[5] The justification for admitting expert testimony is determined in large part by cultural

---

[2]   FAITH MCNULTY, THE BURNING BED (1980).

[3]   *See* Julie Blackman, *Emerging Images of Severely Battered Women and the Criminal Justice System,* 8 BEHAVIORAL SCI. & L. 121 (1990). Women who kill their batterers are likely to have experienced extremely severe violence during the course of their marriages. *See* ANGELA BROWNE, WHEN BATTERED WOMEN KILL (1987).

[4]   For discussion of the estimates of the incidence of domestic violence in the United States, see *infra* text accompanying notes 27–35.

[5]   *See, e.g.,* State v. Kelly: *Amicus Briefs,* 9 WOMEN'S RTS. L. REP. 245 (1986).

perceptions of women and of battering; therefore, many points made by experts respond to just these cultural perceptions.[6]

Yet the expert testimony on battered woman syndrome and learned helplessness can interact with and perpetuate existing oppressive stereotypes of battered women.[7]

Academic expertise on women has thus become crucial to the legal explanation of women's actions and the legal construction of women's experience. Psychological analysis, in particular, has responded to the sharp demand for explanation of women's actions in the self-defense cases.[8] Yet the sociological and psychological literature still reflect some of the oppressive cultural heritage that has shaped legal doctrines.[9] Even when expertise is developed by feminists who explain that women act rationally under circumstances of oppression, courts and the press often interpret feminist expert testimony through the lens of cultural stereotypes, retelling a simpler vision of women as victims too helpless or dysfunctional to pursue a reasonable course of action.[10] These retold stories affect other areas of law, such as custody cases, which share the problems of professional evaluation of women and the incorporation of cultural stereotypes.[11] The portrait of battered women as pathologically weak – the court's version of what feminists have told them – therefore holds particular dangers for battered women with children.

---

[6] *See, e.g.*, State v. Kelly, 478 A.2d 364, 378 (N.J. 1984) ("[Expert testimony] is aimed at an area where the purported common knowledge of the jury may be very much mistaken ... an area where expert knowledge would enable the jurors to disregard their prior conclusions as being common myths rather than common knowledge.") A telling example of the relationship between the *need* for expert testimony and the *points* made by experts is the issue of women's "failure" to leave violent relationships. Many cases review the jury's common-sense belief that women can and will leave violent relationships freely. The experts explain the women's incapacity and failure as a function of many factors, especially the psychology of abused women and traditionalism about the family. *See, e.g.*, People v. Torres, 488 N.Y.S.2d 358, 361–62 (Sup. Ct. 1985); State v. Kelly, 478 A.2d 364, 370–73.

[7] *See* Elizabeth M. Schneider, *Describing and Changing: Women's Self-Defense Work and the Problem of Expert Testimony on Battering*, 9 WOMEN'S RTS. L. REP. 19 (1986); Lenore Walker, *A Response to Elizabeth M. Schneider's* Describing and Changing, 9 Women's Rts. L. Rep. 223–25 (1986).

[8] For example, see three recent books on this subject: JULIE BLACKMAN, INTIMATE VIOLENCE (1989); CYNTHIA GILLESPIE, JUSTIFIABLE HOMICIDE (1989); LENORE WALKER, TERRIFYING LOVE (1989).

[9] *Compare* R. EMERSON DOBASH & RUSSELL DOBASH, VIOLENCE AGAINST WIVES 193–99 (1979) (describing traditional psychological approaches) *and* EDWARD GONDOLF & ELLEN FISHER, BATTERED WOMEN AS SURVIVORS: AN ALTERNATIVE TO TREATING LEARNED HELPLESSNESS 13–15 (1988) (describing psychological views of women as masochistic) *with* DOBASH & DOBASH, *supra*, 211–26 (criticizing the legal system).

[10] Schneider, *supra* note 7 at 198.

[11] In contested custody decisions, for example, women are also at risk that either too little strength *or* too much strength may be held against them. *See generally* PHYLLIS CHESLER, MOTHERS ON TRIAL: THE BATTLE FOR CHILDREN AND CUSTODY (1986). Therefore, the portrait of battered women as pathologically weak – the courts' version of what feminists have told them – may disserve battered mothers seeking custody. Myra Sun & Elizabeth Thomas, *Custody Litigation on Behalf of Battered Women*, 21 CLEARINGHOUSE REV. 563, 570 (1987); Laura Crites & Donna Coker, *What Therapists See That Judges May Miss*, Judges J., Spring 1988, at 8, 13 (1988).

Legal pressures thus distort perceptions of violence in ways that create real problems for women. Many of us cannot recognize our experience in the cultural picture that develops under the influence of legal processes. The consequence is that we understand ourselves less, our society less, and our oppression less, as our capacity to identify with battered women diminishes ("I'm not like *that*"). Before the feminist activism of the early 1970s brought battering to public attention, society generally denied that domestic violence existed. Now, culturally, we know what it is, and we are sure it is not us.

Recent feminist work on battering points to the struggle for power and control – the *batterer's quest for control* of the woman – as the heart of the battering process. Case law and the popular consciousness that grows from it have submerged the question of control by psychologizing the recipient of the violence[12] or by equating women's experience of violence with men's experience.[13] We urgently need to develop legal and social explanations of women's experience that illuminate the issue of violence as part of the issue of power, rather than perpetuating or exacerbating the images that now conceal questions of domination and control.

As one example of a strategic effort to change both law and culture, this article proposes that we seek to redefine in both law and popular culture the issue of women's separation from violent relationships.[14] The question "why didn't she leave?" shapes both social and legal inquiry on battering; much of the legal reliance on academic expertise on battered women has developed in order to address this question. At the moment of separation or attempted separation – for many women, the first encounter with the authority of *law*[15] – the batterer's quest for control often becomes most acutely violent and potentially lethal.[16] Ironically, although the proliferation of shelters and the elaboration of statutory structures facilitating the grant of protective orders[17] vividly demonstrate both socially and legally the dangers attendant on separation, a woman's "failure" to permanently separate from a violent relationship is still widely held to be mysterious and in

---

[12] See GONDOLF & FISHER, *supra* note 9, at 1–3 (describing "psychologizing" of domestic violence).

[13] See Phyllis Crocker, *The Meaning of Equality for Battered Women Who Kill in Self-Defense*, 8 HARV. WOMEN'S L.J. 121 (1985); *see also* GILLESPIE, *supra* note 9, at 115–17 (discussing women's and men's differing experiences of violence in layperson's terms).

[14] Redefining separation must include rethinking many assumptions – that it is the woman's job to separate from a battering relationship, that separation is the appropriate choice for all women when violence first occurs within a relationship, that appropriate separation is an immediate and final break rather than the process of repeated temporary separations made by many women – as well as identifying the violent assault on women's attempts to separate.

[15] These encounters may take many forms, including the attempt to have a violent partner arrested, the filing of a temporary restraining order or legal separation, or the rush to find legal counsel because the partner has threatened to take custody of the children.

[16] See Desmond Ellis, *Post-Separation Woman Abuse: The Contribution of Lawyers as "Barracudas," "Advocates," and "Counsellors,"* 10 INTL. J.L. & PSYCHIATRY 403, 408 (1987). Many authors note the dangers of this period. *See, e.g.,* GILLESPIE, *supra* note 8, at 150–52; ANN JONES, WOMEN WHO KILL 298–99 (1980).

[17] GONDOLF & FISHER, *supra* note 9, at 1.

need of explanation, an indicator of *her* pathology rather than her batterer's. We have had neither cultural names nor legal doctrines specifically tailored to the particular assault on a woman's body and volition that seeks to block her from leaving, retaliate for her departure, or forcibly end the separation. I propose that we name this attack "separation assault."

Separation assault is the common though invisible thread that unites the equal protection suits on enforcement of temporary restraining orders, the cases with dead women that appear in many doctrinal categories, and the cases with dead men – the self-defense cases. As with other assaults on women that were not cognizable until the feminist movement named and explained them,[18] separation assault must be identified before women can recognize our own experience and before we can develop legal rules to deal with this particular sort of violence. Naming one particular aspect of the violence then illuminates the rest: for example, the very concept of "acquaintance rape" moves consciousness away from the stereotype of rape (assault by a stranger)[19] and toward a focus on the woman's volition (violation of her will, "consent"). Similarly, by emphasizing the urgent control moves that seek to prevent the woman from ending the relationship, the concept of separation assault raises questions that inevitably focus additional attention on the ongoing struggle for power and control in the relationship.

Because of the interactive relationships between law and culture in this area, law reform requires such an approach to simultaneously reshape cultural understanding. Separation assault is particularly easy to grasp because it responds to prevailing cultural and legal inquiry ("why didn't she leave") with a twist emphasizing the batterer's violent quest for control. However, meaningful change requires rethinking the entire relationship of law and culture in the field of domestic violence and developing many approaches to revealing power and control. Otherwise, since separation assault is so resonant with existing cultural stereotypes, it may be understood as justifying or excusing the woman's failure to leave rather than challenging and reshaping legal and social attitudes that now place this burden on the woman.

To illustrate the contrast between women's lives and legal and cultural stereotypes, and to accomplish a translation between women's lives and law, this article offers narratives and poems from the lives of survivors of domestic violence, and a few from

---

[18] An example is "date rape." Sexual harassment is another such example. In her book *Sexual Harassment of Working Women*, Catharine MacKinnon defined sexual harassment in terms of power and inequality ("sexual harassment … refers to the unwanted imposition of sexual requirements in the context of a relationship of unequal power") and argued that sexual harassment was sex discrimination. CATHARINE MACKINNON, SEXUAL HARASSMENT OF WORKING WOMEN 1, 4 (1979). Within a decade, this argument had transformed both sex discrimination law and cultural understanding of sexual harassment.

[19] SUSAN ESTRICH, REAL RAPE 3–4 (1987).

the stories of non-survivors, as part of its analysis and argument.[20] Seven women's stories have come to me through their own accounts.[21] Five of these have at some time identified themselves as battered women.[22] Three of these women were Stanford Law School students or graduates; another was an undergraduate student at Stanford. One was an acquaintance in a support group. One is black, the rest are white. All but two were mothers when the violence occurred. Though our class backgrounds vary, only one was a highly educated professional before the battering incidents described, but several have acquired academic degrees since the marriages ended. The other women's voices in this paper are drawn from identified published sources.

One of these stories is my own. I do not feel like a "battered woman."[23] Really, I want to say that I am not, since the phrase conjures up an image that fails to describe either my marriage or my sense of myself. It is a difficult claim to make for several reasons: the gap between my self-perceived competence and strength and my own image of battered women, the inevitable attendant loss of my own denial of painful experience, and the certainty that the listener cannot hear such a claim without filtering it

[20]   Particularly thoughtful input has come from Kim Hanson and Donna Coker. This citation form is deliberately chosen and consistent with the method of the article. Each citation credits the woman with an original thought or contribution that has not appeared in a form suitable for conventional citation as this article goes to press.

There are three reasons for my choice of citation form. The first is honesty: when other women who have not yet published scholarly work have offered me so much of their best thought – and it has become so deeply part of my own best thought – I must either falsely claim their ideas as my own or credit them as they spoke. The second reason is methodological: much of feminist theory, and much of the strength women draw upon for survival, grows out of conversations with each other. This is, for example, the fundamental method of consciousness-raising. *See, e.g.,* Ronnie Lichtman, *Consciousness Raising – 1970, in* THE FEMALE EXPERIENCE 456 (Gerda Lerner ed., 1977). For a discussion of consciousness-raising and its role in feminist method, see, *e.g.,* Christine A. Littleton, *Feminist Jurisprudence: The Difference Method Makes,* 41 Stan. L. Rev. 751 (1989) (reviewing CATHARINE MACKINNON, FEMINISM UNMODIFIED (1987)).

Finally, the third reason for citing women's conversations is political: women may not have published their thoughts because of constraints on their time and effort imposed by uniquely womanly responsi-bilities. This article had its roots in conversations between Kim Hanson and myself, neighbors in family student housing, when I was a first-year and she a third-year law student at Stanford. Our children played together, and we talked around them over the back fence, encountering each other while hanging laundry, while carrying groceries in from the car. This work is in part the product of that shared work and thought. Since then, Kim has litigated for a major law firm, started her own firm, become known as a battered women's advocate, and remarried. She has had two more babies since we first met. I hope some day she writes her own articles. Until then, I acknowledge her thought in my work as a way of acknowledging her *work* as part of my own.

[21]   These are women who talked with me or sought me out for help over the past several years. One was my next-door neighbor at Stanford; another sought me out during my second year of law school, six months after I gave a talk for incoming women students about emotional reactions to the materials in casebooks. When I relate these women's stories, I do not include specific citations.

[22]   Most did not generally use the term when describing themselves.

[23]   This term labels the woman instead of the process or the man. I would prefer some term that lets us discuss stereotyping without hopelessly dooming the discourse from the start. However, I think it is important to overcome our fear of the stigma and stereotype that come with the term "battered woman," so I accept it for this paper.

through a variety of derogatory stereotypes.[24] However, the definitions of battered women have broad contours, at least some of which encompass my experience and the experiences of the other strong, capable women whose stories are included here.

In fact, women often emphasize that they do not fit their own stereotypes of the battered woman:

> The first thing I would tell you is that very little happened. I am not one of those women who stayed and stayed to be beaten. It is very important to me not to be mistaken for one of them, I wouldn't take it. Besides, I never wanted to be the one who tells you what it was really like.

The rejection of stereotypes, the fear of being identified with these stereotypes, is expressed by lesbian women as well as heterosexual women:

> First I want you to know that I am an assertive and powerful woman. I do not fit my stereotype of a battered woman. I am telling you this because I *never* thought it could happen to me. Most lesbians I know who have been battered impress me with their presence and strength. None of them fit my stereotype. Do not think that what happened to me could not happen to you.[25]

Although there is relatively little published material on lesbian battering, this literature can shed light on the ways in which we conceptualize the battering process. Although lesbian battering is similar to heterosexual battering, the analysis of lesbian battering is unique in two ways that are significant for this paper: it has been generated entirely by feminist activists, and it has developed in isolation from the legal system. Therefore, it provides one clue to the question, "[W]hat would this ... landscape look like if women had constructed it for ourselves?"[26] ...

Violence and The Ordinary Lives of Women

The Prevalence of Violence and the Phenomenon of Denial

> Most people I have known who have been abused in marriage have come out – once burned, twice shy. But that doesn't mean fire's not hot. But people treat marriage and relationships and love, in our society, as if fire's not hot.

[24] I fear derogatory stereotypes of myself and of my ex-husband and of that marriage. *See* Liz Kelly, *How Women Define Their Experiences of Violence, in* FEMINIST PERSPECTIVES ON WIFE ABUSE 114, 116 (Kersti Yllo & Michele Bograd eds., 1988) (meaning of terms like "rape" and "battering" often taken for granted).

[25] Arlene Istar, *The Healing Comes Slowly, in* NAMING THE VIOLENCE: SPEAKING OUT ABOUT LESBIAN BATTERING 163, 164 (Kerry Lobel ed., 1986) [hereinafter NAMING THE VIOLENCE].

[26] Christine A. Littleton, *Women's Experience and the Problem of Transition: Perspectives on Male Battering of Women*, 1989 U. Chi. Legal F. 23, 30 (1989) (paraphrasing Heather R. Wishik, *To Question Everything: The Inquiries of Feminist Jurisprudence*, 1 BERKELEY WOMEN'S L.J. 64, 75 (1985) ("In an ideal world, what would this woman's life situation look like, and what relationship, if any, would the law have to this future life situation?")).

Statistics show that domestic violence is extremely widespread in American society. Exact figures on its incidence are difficult to come by. Some studies have counted incidents of violence by or against either spouse regardless of context and found a nearly equal incidence of violence by men and women.[27] Other studies show that women are far more frequently victimized than men,[28] and that women's violence is almost always in self-defense and generally less severe than their partner's.[29] The most conservative figures estimate that women are physically abused in twelve percent of all marriages,[30] and some scholars estimate that as many as fifty percent[31] or more[32] of all women will be battering victims at some point in their lives. Accurate estimates are difficult,[33] in part because of the likelihood of underreporting.[34] However, using any of these estimates, marriages that include violence against the woman represent a relatively widespread phenomenon in our society.[35]

[27] MURRAY A. STRAUS ET AL., BEHIND CLOSED DOORS: VIOLENCE IN THE AMERICAN FAMILY (1980).

[28] In New Jersey, wives or girlfriends were victims in 85% of all reported domestic violent offenses. Gail A. Goolkasian, *Confronting Domestic Violence: A Guide for Criminal Justice Agencies, in* U.S. DEPT. OF JUSTICE REP. (1986).

[29] Daniel G. Saunders, *Wife Abuse, Husband Abuse, or Mutual Combat? A Feminist Perspective on the Empirical Findings, in* FEMINIST PERSPECTIVES ON WIFE ABUSE, *supra* note 24, at 90, 103–08.

[30] STRAUS ET AL., *supra* note 27, at 36.

[31] LENORE WALKER, THE BATTERED WOMAN 19 (1979) [hereinafter LENORE WALKER]. The 50% estimate is weighed and accepted by Christine A. Littleton. Littleton, *supra* note 26, at 28 n. 19. For the reasons articulated by Littleton, and from the stories told to me by women, the 50% figure seems reasonable to me as well.

[32] JENNIFER B. FLEMING, STOPPING WIFE ABUSE 155 (1979), *quoted in Achieving Equal Justice for Victims of Domestic Violence, in* ADVISORY COMM. ON GENDER BIAS IN THE COURTS, CALIFORNIA JUDICIAL COUNCIL, ACHIEVING EQUAL JUSTICE FOR WOMEN AND MEN IN THE COURTS pt. 6, at 3 (draft Mar. 23, 1990) [hereinafter *Achieving Equal Justice*] (estimating 60% of married women experience domestic violence at some time during their marriages); SISTERHOOD IS GLOBAL, 703 (Robin Morgan ed., 1984) (50%–70% of women experience battering during marriage).

[33] The incidence of domestic violence is hard to determine, in part because it takes place within the home, and in part because the many studies in the field present statistical information that is not directly comparable with that in other studies. Some focus on the number of women who are victims of spouse abuse: estimates of women physically abused by husbands or boyfriends in the United States range from 1.5 million, BROWNE, *supra* note 3, at 5, to 3–4 million, Mary Pat Bryger, *Domestic Violence: The Dark Side of Divorce*, FAM. ADVOCATE, Summer 1990, at 48. Straus, Gelles, and Steinmetz studied violence against spouses of either gender and found that more than 1.7 million Americans at some time faced a spouse wielding a knife or gun. STRAUS ET AL., *supra* note 27, at 34.

[34] BROWNE, *supra* note 3, at 4–5 (citing studies by Straus, Gelles, and Steinmetz and the Louis Harris organization). Self-reports may undercount significantly. *See generally* DIANA E. RUSSELL, RAPE IN MARRIAGE 96–101 (1982) (reviewing statistical techniques and results of several surveys on domestic violence).

[35] Stating violence is normal does not mean it is normative or culturally accepted, as it once was. See DOBASH & DOBASH, *supra* note 9, at 48–74, for a discussion of violence that was historically part of control of women within marriage. Violence against women was an early focus of feminist protest and efforts at reform. By the mid-nineteenth century, contrary to some popular stereotypes, wifebeating was already considered "a disreputable, seamy practice"; it was illegal in most states by the 1870s. LINDA GORDON, HEROES OF THEIR OWN LIVES: THE POLITICS AND HISTORY OF FAMILY VIOLENCE 255 (1988). Although today domestic violence is indeed "disreputable," that does not mean that it has disappeared in fact – only that the commonality of its occurrence in normal marriage is widely denied.

Although these statistics are widely reproduced, there is little social or legal recognition that domestic violence has touched the lives of many people in this society and must be known to many people. Judicial opinions, for example, treat domestic violence as aberrant and unusual: "a unique and almost mysterious area of human response and behavior,"[36] "beyond the ken of the average lay [person]."[37] This radical discrepancy between the "mysterious" character of domestic violence and repeatedly gathered statistics reflects massive denial throughout society and the legal system.

Denial is a defense mechanism well recognized in psychology that protects people from consciously knowing things they cannot bear to reckon with at the time. A powerful if undiscussed force affecting the evolution of the law and litigation on battered women, denial exists at both the societal and individual levels. Societal denial amounts to an ideology[38] that protects the institution of marriage by perpetuating the focus on individual violent actors, concealing both the commonality of violence in marriage and the ways in which state and society participate in the subordination of women.

"Societal" denial – albeit within a smaller, more consciously self-defined society – also slowed recognition of lesbian battering. Although many lesbian activists helped start the battered women's movement, battering did not emerge as an internal problem in the consciousness of the lesbian community until years after the movement had begun.[39] This collective denial of internal violence was based, in part, on the reluctance to let go of an ideal of lesbian relationships and community, a "lesbian utopia – a nonviolent, fairly androgynous, often separatist community struggling for social justice and freedom for ourselves and other oppressed people."[40]

However, there are important differences between the ideological defense of marriage and the defense of lesbian utopia. The differences lie in the way power is vested in one partner of a marriage at the time of marriage by society, law, and tradition, fitting heterosexual battering into a historic framework of oppression and domination *of* women *by* men. Marriage is an institution which underlies many – perhaps most – other social, political, and economic relations, and to that end many elements of society have a stake in defending it. Because of oppression of lesbians and exclusion from many social structures – for example, lesbians

---

[36] *See, e.g.,* Sinns v. State, 283 S.E.2d 479, 481 (Ga. 1981) (explaining Smith v. State, 277 S.E.2d 678 (Ga. 1980)).

[37] *See, e.g.,* Ibn-Tamas v. United States, 407 A.2d 626, 634 (D.C. 1983).

[38] JURGEN HABERMAS, KNOWLEDGE AND HUMAN INTERESTS 311 (Jeremy J. Shapiro trans., 1971), *quoted in* James Ptacek, *Why Do Men Batter Their Wives?, in* FEMINIST PERSPECTIVES ON WIFE ABUSE, *supra* note 24, at 155 ("From everyday experiences we know that ideas serve often enough to furnish our actions with justifying motives in place of the real ones. What is called rationalization at this level is called ideology at the level of collective action.").

[39] *See, e.g.,* Lydia Walker, *Battered Women's Shelters and Work with Battered Lesbians, in* NAMING THE VIOLENCE, *supra* note 25, at 73 (describing her work in a battered women's project, her work with battered lesbians, and her difficulty in facing the violence she had experienced in her own relationships with women).

[40] Barbara Hart, *Preface* to NAMING THE VIOLENCE, *supra* note 25, at 9, 13.

cannot marry in [many parts of] the United States – the dream at stake was less central to the surrounding society but, poignantly, at least equally central to lesbian self-definition and community.

The ideology that protects the institution of marriage and the state's participation in subordinating women is consistent with the findings of James Ptacek's study of batterers.[41] Ptacek found that both batterers and the criminal justice system tended to blame women for their abuse and deny or trivialize the violence involved.[42] These excuses and justifications are ideological in nature: "At the individual level, they obscure the batterer's self-interest in acting violently; *at the societal level, they mask the male domination underlying violence against women.* Clinical and criminal justice responses to battering are revealed as ideological in the light of their collusion with batterers' rationalizations."[43]

This ideology pervades the courtroom as well as other areas of the criminal justice system. It shapes legal events in several ways: it affects the individual consciousness of the actors in the courtroom,[44] the doctrinal questions that are the legal framework of each action, and the options to avoid legal confrontation and the resources individuals bring into the courtroom. Especially troublesome, this ideology which denies oppression has had a profound impact on the development of explanations of women's experience and behavior that can fit within the conceptual structure of the law.[45]

It is likely that a number of people present in any court will have some personal experience of domestic violence.[46] Using the conservative estimate that domestic violence occurs in one quarter of households,[47] at least four of the fifteen or more

---

[41] See generally Ptacek. *supra* note 38. A New York judge told the state's Task Force on Women in the Courts that, when a woman gives up an attempt to separate, judges either smile (thinking they have brought the couple back together), or snicker. The snickering response is based on their perception "that the woman who accepts this violent behavior and reconciles with the man[,] even if she reconciles in a split but doesn't pursue the case, isn't worthy of our respect because she does not respect herself. ..." New York Task Force on Women in the Courts, *Report of the New York Task Force on Women in the Courts*, 15 FORDHAM URB. L.J. 11, 36–37 (1986–1987).

[42] Ptacek, supra note 38, at 141–149 (batterers), 154–55 (criminal justice system).

[43] *Id.* at 155 (emphasis added).

[44] See *infra* text accompanying notes 46–49 (discussing experience of battering among courtroom participants).

[45] For example, if the batterers' position is essentially identical with the perspective of the criminal justice system, and both fit with an ideology that protects marriage, then the "common-sense" position in any courtroom will tend to favor men. Therefore, women will need experts to explain their lives; men will not. *See, e.g.,* Littleton, *supra* note 26, at 35 (all women, not only battered women, may appear alien from a male perspective).

[46] Violence in our personal lives has existed for everyone in varying degrees. The magnitude of the damage and turmoil is the real crux of the problem. If individuals on the panel are afraid of their own feelings about having been battered, then perhaps they will not be open to the battered woman's feelings. Some will have battered someone themselves and will struggle to justify their own actions. Roberta K. Thyfault et al., *Battered Women in Court: Jury and Trial Consultants and Expert Witnesses, in* DOMESTIC VIOLENCE ON TRIAL: PSYCHOLOGICAL AND LEGAL DIMENSIONS OF FAMILY VIOLENCE 55, 62 (Daniel J. Sonkin ed., 1987).

[47] See *supra* notes 27–35 and accompanying text.

actors in an average criminal action – jurors, judge, and attorneys – probably will have experienced or committed at least one domestic assault.[48] Similarly, in custody suits, the judge and the attorneys – *and* the social workers and psychologists who are performing evaluations of the parents – have this statistical likelihood of having experienced or committed violence. Therefore, the atmosphere in the courtroom will not reflect mere ignorance, nor merely the broad social stereotypes which courts generally recognize can be a problem.[49] Rather, the response to and evaluation of the case before them will also include the unseen and unspoken ties that bind these participants to the fabric of their own lives, their parents' lives, and their children's.

Social workers and psychologists play an important role in this process. Our legal system – like the rest of society – has to a large extent entrusted these professionals with the definition of what is normal and functional. Despite the statistics on the epidemic incidence of domestic violence, there is almost no legal or social science scholarship that describes an author's experience of violence[50] or even indicates that the author has had any such experience.[51] It is unlikely that a disinterested body of social scientists is doing all this research. However, scholars may be reluctant to indicate their own experience because they fear intellectual marginalization[52] or familial repercussions. Scholarly fears of marginalization probably reflect some acceptance of stereotypes of battered women; certainly, they reflect caution about the power and danger of stereotyping by others.

This silence among professionals and scholars is one intersection between individual denial and an ideology of societal denial. This is where one of the lenses through which we see the world is constructed: if scholars are silent for "personal" reasons, their "professional" silence then perpetuates the social stereotypes that construct battered women as different, exceptional, "other." Ultimately, the denial of personal experience of domestic violence in social science literature and forensic testimony permits continued societal blindness to the implications of the statistics these same experts gather and employ.[53]

---

[48] Overrepresentation of the middle class in the courtroom would not change this estimate. Domestic violence occurs across class lines. LENORE WALKER, *supra* note 31, at 19.

[49] *See, e.g.*, State v. Kelly, 478 A.2d 364, 378 (N.J. 1984) (jurors may hold "common myths").

[50] The exceptions here are Robin West, who discusses her own experience of battering, Robin L. West, *The Difference in Women's Hedonic Lives: A Phenomenological Critique of Feminist Legal Theory,* 3 WIS. WOMEN'S L.J. 81, 98–99 (1987); and Terry Davidson, who discusses being the child of a wife beater, TERRY DAVIDSON, CONJUGAL CRIME: UNDERSTANDING AND CHANGING THE WIFEBEATING PATTERN 14–15, 131–54 (1978).

[51] *But see* Jan E. Stets' preface to her excellent study, JAN E. STETS, DOMESTIC VIOLENCE AND CONTROL v (1988) (research on domestic violence brought understanding of violence she witnessed and experienced while growing up).

[52] *See, e.g.*, West, *supra* note 50, at 99 (describes grappling with this anxiety but goes on to discuss her own experience).

[53] Conversation with Kim Hanson, 1989 ("As long as you don't speak out, you're part of the conspiracy of silence.").

Individual denial protects the images of self and marriage held by individual women and men, as well as being the mechanism through which much societal denial operates. This is true elsewhere as it is in the courtroom: people need to know that their own marriages are sound, therefore it is important to know that they (or their wives) do not "stay" in the relationship; they "are" in the relationship. Their own relationships define what is normal and appropriate; it is appropriate for their own relationships to continue. The battered woman *must* be different. Therefore, the question "why did she stay?" commonly finds answers that attempt to explain difference: "because she had children" or "because she was frightened" or "because she became pathologically helpless" – not, significantly, because I/you/we "stayed" too.

Do we "stay," or are we simply married? Writing this article forced me to grapple with my own image of battered women, my "credentials" in claiming this identity, and my experience of marriage. As I worked, I found similar conceptions of self and marriage in several of the women who spoke with me. These women described their marriages as "bad" or "unhappy" and then went on to recount attacks that were almost murderous – threats with guns and knives, partial strangling, deliberately running into a woman with a car:

> I tried to nurse John [her colicky baby], but Ed screamed that I was trying to poison him. I said, "OK, I'll get you a bottle." I had to kneel down by the microwave, and Ed pushed me over, so that I fell over. So I put the bottle in the micro and stood up, and finished microwaving the bottle, put the nipple on, and gave it to Ed. ... Ed began screaming almost incoherently, and grabbed John, and started to storm back out to the car with him.
>
> At this point I got worried. The first time [earlier that night, when her husband first stormed out and drove around with the baby] I thought he was angry because I had yelled, and I felt guilty ... it didn't seem that aberrant. But screaming about poison when I tried to nurse him, knocking me over ... it just seemed like there was something wrong. I said, "You're welcome to leave, but you can't take John. I don't think you're all there."
>
> He pushed past. I stood in front of the car. He drove into me. I tried to go over the hood of the car, hit the pavement quite hard, and blacked out for a minute. When I came to, he had turned the car around, he was like a foot from me, and he was saying "get up, or I'll drive over you."
>
> [Her husband had "scared himself ... realized he had gone too far" and gave her the baby to nurse. They finally fell asleep.] Next morning, Ed had gone to work. I couldn't move, I couldn't move my legs. I remember thinking, I'm going to die. [The baby] is going to wake up next to a corpse ... When I look back, there was so much rage in that thought [at the colicky baby as well as the husband]. ... I had a very hard time functioning. I was able to make it to the bathroom, but the tunnel vision seemed worse.

Women often discussed the relationship at length before they mentioned any violence. Finally, I began to understand that the violence against these women seemed shocking to me – and the violence against me seemed shocking to them – precisely because we heard each other's reports of violence isolated from the context of the marriages. For ourselves, on the other hand, the daily reality of the marriages – none of which included daily or even weekly violent episodes – defined most of our memories and retrospective sense of the relationship: these were "bad" marriages, not ordeals of physical torture. We resisted defining the entire experience of marriage by the episodes of violence that had marked the relationship's lowest points. Our understanding of marriage, love, and commitment in our own lives – as well as our stereotypes of battered women – shaped our discussion.

This question of the line between "normal" marriage and violent marriage is a common one. One activist social worker recounts that when she speaks on domestic violence in any forum, someone *always* asks why women "stay." She says, "When should she have left? At what point? Maybe the time she watched while he smashed up the furniture?" A silence, a shock of recognition, falls over the audience. It is, relatively speaking, *normal* for a woman to watch a man smash up the furniture. Many of the women in the room have seen something like it – and called it "marriage," and not "staying."[54]

Denial conditions women's perceptions of our own relationships and need for assistance. An extreme example is a woman who founded a shelter for battered women; although her husband was beating her during this period, she never identified with the women she sought to help:

> I just thought that the incidents of violence that I – in order to be a battered woman you had to be really battered. I mean OK, I had a couple of bad incidents, but mostly it was pretty minor, in inverted commas, "violence." I didn't see myself in that category, as a battered woman at all.[55]

Similarly, women may fail to perceive armed attacks that do not result in injury as physical abuse – or indeed fail to so perceive anything other than an archetypal brutal beating:

> I don't know what I'd have done if I had to live with what [I assume] you did. My marriage wasn't physically abusive, but there was emotional abuse. My husband had a pistol ... he did pull his gun on me. ...

This may happen even when the woman calls for help:

> When I finally called the Battered Women's Center for help, I was just looking for advice – my husband had threatened to move back in without my consent while I was recovering from a Cesarian section. ... He said "you can't stop me." ... I told the counselor that I was just looking for a referral, as I didn't qualify for their help because my marriage had not been violent, although I had left after he attacked me with a loaded shotgun. There was a tiny pause, and then she said gently: "We classify that as extreme violence."

---

[54] Conversation with Donna Coker, 1989 (discussing four years of activist feminist social work with battered women in Honolulu).

[55] Kelly, *supra* note 24, at 114, 123–24.

Other aspects of women's denial of oppression within ordinary marriage also affect our perception of battered women. Battered women interviewed by social workers often say they felt a responsibility to support their children's relationship with their father because "he's really good with the children."[56] This is not dissimilar to statements by women in nonviolent relationships – or relationships they do not perceive as violent. Women often admit when pressed that they are actually describing a father who is loving with a child when he chooses to interact with it, even if that interaction happens seldom, yet insist on the value of his presence in the children's lives. However, this is a parallel that makes many women uncomfortable: how could a batterer be like their husband? Similarly, although sexual abuse is often a part of domestic violence, many battered women who did not experience sexual abuse describe sex as having been "the only good thing about the marriage."[57] Women who are in relationships of unequal power that are not violent must also find sexual pleasure under conditions of inequality, yet they may not wish to recognize the similarity in experience.

The literature on battering notes, clinically and sometimes with condescending undertones, that women tend to "perceive" the onset of violence as atypical.[58] Of course, the *onset* of violence *is* atypical, and therefore our perceptions are in many ways appropriate.[59] Yet we may ignore danger signals and early attacks because we believe that the "battered-ness" is a characteristic of the woman – a characteristic we do not have – rather than a characteristic of her partner or a symptom of a dynamic in the relationship. Denial creates and reinforces the perceptions (1) that battered women are weak, (2) that we are not weak, and (3) that therefore we are safe.

Finally, individual denial leads women to minimize the pain and oppressiveness of our experiences while we continue to live with them. This is also a familiar dynamic in women's relationships; yet if violence is what we are minimizing, we face great costs and dangers.

> That session in the hospital when I had been married one month, and the nurse came and sat on the bed and said she had heard I didn't care if I went home for Christmas.... The truth was, I couldn't face what I was going home to. I instinctively knew it was very bad to lie about this but I couldn't bear to tell the truth. It was too humiliating. I didn't tell her anything. To my friends, I said I fell down. I did not intend to cover for him but for myself ... for the confusion and humiliation ... for finding myself in this unbelievable position.

---

[56] Conversation with Donna Coker, *supra* note 54.

[57] *Id.; see also* Lenore Walker's discussion of her difficulty understanding the reports of sexual pleasure among the battered women she interviewed. LENORE WALKER, *supra* note 31, at 108–12.

[58] BROWNE, *supra* note 3, at 85.

[59] The initial violent episode is not treated as though it signals the beginning of a violent relationship. It is treated as an isolated, exceptional event, which is what one would expect it to be treated as. Only in retrospect does the woman begin to examine the first violent act more broadly, seeking signs that "she should have noticed...." The evidence is that there has never been any violence before, that the husband rejects this behavior in principle.... There is no reason to expect the violence to be repeated. DOBASH & DOBASH, *supra* note 9, at 95–96.

This woman's images of battered women and herself make her position "unbelievable." Her response, based on these images, is to disguise her experience. She allows her husband to avoid the censure of family and friends in order to protect *herself* from their opinions, setting up the possibility of more such lies in the future because the image itself has not been confronted, and making it likely that she will minimize her own pain in order to maintain silence.[60]

The cumulative effect of this denial has been very destructive for women. We have difficulty recognizing ourselves and our experience on the continuum of violence and power in which we actually live. To the extent that we cannot recognize ourselves, we are hindered in formulating an affirmative vision in which our integrity is protected. Although much of this article emphasizes legal aspects of the related forces of law, society, and academia at work in the field of battered women, I believe that the ways in which women are divided from each other – and deprived of the capacity to understand our own experience in relation to other women – are ultimately most important.

---

[60] Battered women tend to minimize the history of assault against them and the pain they have suffered. *See* Julie Blackman, *Potential Uses for Expert Testimony: Ideas Toward the Representation of Battered Women Who Kill*, 9 WOMEN'S RTS. L. REP. 227, 228–29 (1986).

8.5

Feminicidio: The "Black Legend" of the Border

Alicia Gaspar de Alba and Georgina Guzmán

Femicide is the killing of women qua women, often condoned by, if not sponsored, by the state and/or by religious institutions.
　　　　　　　　　　　　　– Jill Radford and Diana E. H. Russell, eds.,
　　　　　　　　　　　　　　　Femicide: The Politics of Woman Killing

The Black Legend (Spanish: La Leyenda Negra) is the depiction of Spain and Spaniards as bloodthirsty and cruel, intolerant, greedy, and fanatical.
　　　　　　　　　　　　　　　　　　　　　　　　– Wikipedia

Just because I published a novel called *Desert Blood: The Juárez Murders* (2005) does not mean the Juárez murders are fiction. Since May 1993, over five hundred women and girls have been found brutally murdered on the El Paso/Juárez border, and thousands more have been reported missing and remain unaccounted for, making this the longest epidemic of femicidal violence in modern history. The victims are known colloquially as "*las inditas del sur*," the little Indian girls from the south of Mexico – poor, dark-skinned, and indigenous-looking – who have arrived alone and disenfranchised in Ciudad Juárez to work at a twin-plant *maquiladora* and earn dollars to send back home. Not all of the victims are rural, not all of them are outsiders to the border metropolis, not all of them worked at a *maquiladora,* lived alone, or had indigenous features. But most of them are Mexican, impoverished, and young. And all of them are female, the victims of this particular crime wave.[1]

There was a time when no one knew about the Juárez femicides, as these crimes have come to be called to signify the misogyny of the perpetrators. There was a time when little coverage could be found in newspapers or on television shows or on the Internet about what was happening in Juárez to poor, young, Mexican women. Nowadays, we know too much, and yet we continue to know nothing. In the process of learning; reading; researching; raising consciousness; signing petitions; writing stories, poetry, and music; making art; organizing conferences; and collecting anthologies, there are only two things that have changed. The number of victims continues to grow. And now the Juárez femicides have become a legend, the "black legend" of the border.

The Mexican government's new line, after years of inept investigations and covert maneuvers to derail progress on any of the cases, is that the femicides are nothing but an invention of some crazy feminists and the attention-grabbing mothers of a few dead prostitutes, a way of making Juárez look like a modern-day incarnation of the Spanish Inquisition out to hunt down, torture, and sacrifice young women, an image that city officials and merchants say is spoiling tourism to the city.[2]

Despite these negations of history, you have, by now, probably heard of the gendered death toll in Ciudad Juárez. You already know that between 1993 and 2008, more than five hundred poor Mexican women and girls, some as young as five, some in their sixties and seventies, were violently slain in Ciudad Juárez, across the border from El Paso, Texas. You know that their bodies were found strangled, mutilated, dismembered, raped, stabbed, torched, or so badly beaten, disfigured, or decomposed that the remains have never been identified. You know that many bore the signature of serial killers: the bodies half-clothed, hands tied behind their backs, evidence of rape, genital mutilation. You know that a majority of the victims shared the same physical profile: predominantly between the ages of twelve and twenty-three, young, slim, petite, dark-haired, and dark-skinned. You know that their brutalized bodies were dumped in deserted lots around Juárez as well as in landfills, motels, downtown plazas, and busy city intersections. You may even know that bodies were found inside trash dumpsters, brick ovens, vats of acid, and abandoned cars, as well as on train tracks, under beds in hotel rooms, and across the street from a police station or the headquarters of the Maquiladora Association. You know, perhaps, that the victims are also called "*maqui-locas,*" assumed to be *maquiladora* workers living *la vida loca,* or *una vida doble,* of a border metropolis, coded language for prostitution.

In fact, you may know quite a bit about these dead women because, first of all, the bodies have been accruing since 1993, and, second, we now have a plethora of cultural products about the femicides. Since 1999, for example, a repertoire of songs has emerged from artists as diverse as Tori Amos, At the Drive-In, Lila Downs, Los Tigres del Norte, and Los Jaguares.[3] For online video fans, there are over twenty short films available on YouTube alone, including one by Amnesty International.[4]

Beyond the early documentaries, such as "Maquila: A Tale of Two Mexicos" (2000) and Lourdes Portillo's "Señorita Extraviada" (2001), which alone helped raise consciousness about the crimes all over the world, we now also have two Hollywood films,[5] one pulp Mexican film,[6] and at least three new documentaries.[7]

In print, other than my mystery novel and a collection of poetry about the murdered women of Juárez by Marjorie Agosín, we have a new fictionalized first-person account of life in the "capital city of murdered women,"[8] as well as two book-length journalistic accounts,[9] and a monograph.[10]

In the academic world, numerous panels have been presented at conferences such as the American Studies Association, the Modern Language Association, the National Association for Chicana and Chicano Studies, and MALCS (Mujeres Activas en Letras y Cambio Social). New Mexico State University, UCLA, Ohio State University, the University of Texas at El Paso, the University of Nebraska, and Stanford University (to name a few) have all hosted conferences and symposia dedicated specifically to the Juárez femicides. And this is not to mention all of the writers, visual artists, and performance artists on both sides of the border who have lent their talents to a massive binational outrage over these crimes and the continued impunity granted the perpetrators.[11] Coupled with the investigative reports of major newspapers and television news shows across the country as well as across the world and the denunciations of organizations like Amnesty International, the Organization of American States, and the World Court, all of these cultural efforts have contributed to what you have learned about the femicides.

But there is another reason you know something about the dead daughters of Juárez. You know about them because they *are* dead, because they *are* part of this sensational, unresolved heinous crime wave that has taken the public by storm and has suddenly put this border on the radar of every human rights organization in the known universe. Ironically, the main signifier of their lives is a corpse half-buried in a sand dune. As Marjorie Agosín says in a poem from her collection about the murdered women of Juárez, *Secrets in the Sand*, "All we know about them/is their death" (25).

We did not know anything about these "*muchachas del sur*" (girls from the south) when they were alive, did not even realize they *were* alive or that they were living in such squalid and inhumane conditions just a stone's throw from El Paso, working at their mind-numbing, carpal tunnel–warping factory jobs, going to school some of them, struggling to support children or parents, to find a decent place to live in a squatter colony with no electricity, no running water, no sewage system, no paved streets, no city services whatsoever. Nothing about them was of any interest to us until they died, and even then, it took over three hundred bodies piling up over ten years and the noisy interventions of First World celebrities like Eve Ensler, Jane Fonda, Sally Field, and Christine Lahti (who in 2004 led us through the V-Day march in Juárez, which drew a crowd of thousands from both sides of the border) for us to really pay attention to the presence of these women in our midst. I myself – native of that very border, with family living on both sides of the Córdoba Bridge – did not find out about the crimes until 1998, five years after the bodies began piling up in the desert, when I read a story called "The Maquiladora Murders," by Sam Quiñones in the May/June issue of *Ms.* magazine.

Reading the story enraged me, not only because these crimes were happening right across the border from my hometown of El Paso and because very little about them had been reported in any major U.S. newspaper, or even the local papers of El Paso and Las Cruces, but also because, as a scholar of border studies and gender studies, as a native of that very place on the map in which the femicides were happening at a rate of two per month, I too had been caught in the web of silence that surrounds these crimes.

What was at the root of the silence? Surely such a crime spree would sell newspapers, if nothing else. In 1999, my search for media coverage on the femicides resulted in only a handful of stories. Other than the Sam Quiñones article in *Ms.*, I found an earlier piece by Debbie Nathan in *The Nation*, a piece in the *Los Angeles Times*, one in the *New York Times*, and a two-part, multiple-page-spread in the *Washington Post*. On television, only two news shows, *20/20* and *60 Minutes*, had broadcast exposés. After those eight bodies were discovered in a cotton field in November 2001, the U.S. media swarmed over the story, and suddenly we were reading about the Juárez femicides not only in the newspapers, but also in periodicals that ranged from left to right of the political scale: the *Utne Reader, Mother Jones, People*, and the *Texas Observer*. These were all signs of interest, finally, in a tragedy that has been accruing bones since 1993.

Nowadays, of course, the Internet and YouTube provide access to stories about the femicides worldwide, but when I first started my research after reading Quiñones's exposé, the Worldwide Web had precious little. I found a link to a story done by the BBC in London, another link to the Frontera NorteSur digest from Las Cruces, and, finally, a link to the now-defunct Sagrario Consortium (or Fundación Sagrario), named after one of the victims, Sagrario González Flores (daughter of Paula Flores, who has been very active in the mothers' struggle to end the femicides in Juárez ...). My research assistant in 1999 was informed by a reference librarian at the El Paso Public Library that the murders were "Juárez news, not El Paso news," and so the *El Paso Times* did not cover them. Media coverage in Mexican periodicals between 1993 and 1998, on the other hand, constituted a three-inch-thick archive of information.

Where were the academics, I wondered? Where were the Mexican, Chicana/o, and Latino/a academics, particularly those working on labor issues, immigration policy, the North American Free Trade Agreement (NAFTA), or the abuse and exploitation of women workers on the border? Why were they, especially my U.S. colleagues, not bringing their time, energy, and resources to this issue? Why was there so little scholarship on the crimes?[12] Was it fear or apathy that defined the silence?

In an effort to break that silence on the U.S. side of the border, I decided to write a mystery novel about the crimes – based on research and on what I knew from having grown up in that precise, paradoxical place on the map – to inform the broadest-possible English-speaking public about the femicides. When the novel was finished, I (with the help of a handful of students) organized an international conference called "The Maquiladora Murders, Or, Who Is Killing the Women of Juárez?" at UCLA in the fall of 2003, under the aegis of the Chicano Studies Research Center and co-sponsored by Amnesty International. We brought together scholars, journalists, artists, activists, writers, forensic investigators, policy specialists, as well as mothers of the victims in a series of roundtable discussions and presentations. Cong. Hilda Solís, actor Eve Ensler, and then–University of California regent Dolores Huerta all gave keynote speeches. There were literary and dramatic presentations; a multimedia student exhibition of written, aural, and visual materials collected in a yearlong undergraduate research internship on the crimes; and a special altar of ceramic pieces by the San Antonio–based MujerArtes collective commemorating the lives and losses of the Juárez women. The pieces were sold at a silent auction, the full proceeds of which were donated to the nongovernmental organizations of the mothers who attended the conference.[13] The purpose of the conference was to facilitate more scholarly inquiry into the crimes and, in particular, to examine the social, political, economic, and cultural infrastructure in which the crimes were multiplying like another form of toxic waste on the border.

The conference was held during the Mexican Days of the Dead, October 31–November 2, and more than fifteen hundred people from across Los Angeles, the United States, Mexico, and Europe attended. The conference generated twelve resolutions that echoed the demands of Mexican NGOs and policy makers in the United States for a binational task force that would help bring an end to the crimes and justice to the murdered women and their families. The resolutions became the "¡Ni Una Más!" petition, which called for an "End [to] Violence against Women and Children in Juárez and Chihuahua" and was addressed to both the U.S. and Mexican governments (it is still available online).[14]

Our conference logo, designed by Chicana digital artist Alma López,[15] was called *Coyolxauhqui's Tree of Life,* both to commemorate the primordial dismembered daughter of Aztec mythology, who was slashed to pieces by her brother, the War God, Huitzilopochtli, and to reconstitute her many pieces into a whole self.[16] My intention as the organizer of the conference was not only to raise consciousness about the crimes and provide a forum for discussing, analyzing, and taking action against the binational silence that had protected the perpetrators for so long, but also to re-member the sacrificed daughters of Juárez. I wanted to focus not so much on "who is killing them" as on, as Alma López's digital image suggests, how we could reassemble the pieces of the puzzle of their deaths to help us understand why they died and why they were killed with such viciousness directed at the brown female body. López's image suggests two other key questions: What war gods are being served by their deaths? and What "mother" or "father" are the killers – these modern-day Huitzilopochtlis who are wielding their own fiery serpents against their sisters – protecting?

There is so much we do not know. We do not know why there is a binational task force that includes immigration officers, Border Patrol agents, FBI agents, and police on both sides of the border – engaged in the collective task of trying to solve the pernicious problem of *car theft* – but not a similar binational effort to stop this epidemic of femicides. We do not know what role El Paso plays in either the investigation of the crimes or the protection of the perpetrators. We do not know how Mexico punishes sex crimes. We do not know, even, how many victims there actually are. Were there 254 murdered women in 2002, which is the statistic provided by the Juárez rape crisis shelter, Casa Amiga, or 320, which is the number reported by *El Paso Times* journalist Diana Washington Valdez, based on her own investigative research? Amnesty International's 2003 report on the Juárez murders, "Intolerable Killings: Ten Years of Abductions and Murders in Ciudad Juárez and Chihuahua,"[17] concludes that 370 young women and girls had been killed on that border since 1993, "of which at least 137 were sexually assaulted prior to death." As reported in a Mexico City paper, the Chihuahua state government's response was that the Amnesty findings were "partial, slanted, distorted, and tendentious," and that the information presented in the report was both "inconsistent and decontextualized."[18]

Another thing we do not know: Can the DNA-testing techniques employed by the Chihuahua state authorities be trusted? In a shocking revelation by a group of Argentine anthropologists and forensics experts who came to Juárez in 2005 to lend their expertise to the DNA investigations – the same team "which gained fame by using advanced DNA-study techniques to identify people killed in Argentina's 'dirty war' of the 1970s"[19] – the mothers of two of those eight victims found in the cotton field in November 2001 learned that the remains they had been given were not those of their daughters.

Today, activists assert that the body count (that is to say, the found bodies, not the missing ones, which number in the thousands) has now exceeded five hundred. While attention has focused on the tangible murders, cases in which bodies have been discovered, the actual number of victims may be more than twice as high.[20]

Why have we not been made aware of their existence; why did they have to die for us to see them? Because they were women? Because they were poor, brown, young women? Because they were so low on the social totem pole that we all tacitly agreed the most polite thing we could do was to ignore them?

The essays and *testimonios* in *Making a Killing* make it difficult for us to continue to ignore the victims, or the murders, or the political, geographic, and economic context in which the crimes keep happening. Collectively, these essays are an intervention in the Freirian notion of *concientización*, offering as they do academic and personal reflection on a variety of factors that produce and sanction this gendered violence on an increasingly globalized U.S.-Mexico border, as well as analyses of actions being taken both to protest femicide and also to transform the social discourse that sees the victims as responsible for manufacturing their own deaths.

Readers will note that the numbers do not match in any of the essays in this book; the body count is always different. Indeed, that is one of the major issues with these crimes. There has been no systematic accounting of the victims or accountability by the authorities, which results in only more confusion, more impunity for the perpetrators, and less chance of resolution. Despite the discrepancy in the numbers, however, the contributors all agree with the activists and NGOs that have been working on these cases that the numbers given by "official" channels are much lower than the actual body count.

Who can hate these powerless women so much? What is it about them that they hate? What is so threatening about their presence on the border? What accounts for this level of misogyny? Is the poor brown female really an endangered species on the U.S.-Mexico border? What specific threats does she pose to the society, the economy, and the culture of the border? How can we explain the silence that continues to protect the perpetrators and haunt the mothers and families of the victims? What specific actions have been taken and must be taken to protest the impunity with which these crimes are committed, which is as much a signature of the criminals as of the authorities who refuse to bring justice to the daughters of Juárez? How do we put an end to the femicides?

Notes

1. These crimes should not be confused with "narco-killings," which are crimes committed in the turf-and-power struggles of local drug cartels and which target mainly male victims.
2. North of the border, U.S. lawmakers' only response to this increased gender-targeted border violence has been to tighten homeland security measures. A resolution was introduced to the House of Representatives by Rep. Hilda Solís (D-CA) in 2003, and a similar one was introduced in the Senate by Sen. Jeff Bingaman (D-NM) in 2004 "to express sympathy for the families of the victims" and to get the U.S. government involved in a binational task force to address the crimes. The votes necessary for passage of the legislation were slow in coming, but in May 2006, Amnesty International reported that the joint resolution had at last been passed in the House. "Congress has now unanimously called on the secretary of state and the U.S. ambassador to Mexico to take specific steps to ensure that addressing these horrendous murders becomes a part of the U.S.-Mexico bilateral agenda." See http://www.amnestyusa.org/violence-against-women/page.do?id=1011012.
3. "Juárez," by Tori Amos on the album *To Venus and Back* (Atlantic, 1999); "Invalid Litter Department," CD single by At the Drive-In (EMI International, 2001); "La Niña de la Maquiladora," by Lila Downs on the album *The Border/La Línea* (Narada World, 2001); "Las Mujeres de Juárez," by Los Tigres del Norte on the album *Pacto de Sangre* (Fonovisa, 2004); "Madera," by Los Jaguares on the album *Crónicas de un Laberinto* (Sony International, 2005).
4. See www.youtube.com/watch?v=o5mlgmqy9oI&mode=related&search=.
5. HBO's *The Virgin of Juárez* (2006), directed by Kevin James Dobson and starring Minnie Driver; *Bordertown* (2007), directed by Gregory Nava and starring Jennifer López, Antonio Banderas, Martin Sheen, and Sonia Braga. In February 2009, Paramount released a Mexican production titled *Backyard/Traspatio,* written by Sabina Berman, directed by Carlos Carrera *(The Crime of Padre Amaro),* and starring Jimmy Smits.
6. *Las Muertas de Juárez,* directed by Enrique Murillo (Laguna Productions, 2002).

7. *Bajo Juárez: A City Devouring Its Girls,* directed by Alejandra Sánchez Orozco and José Antonio Cordero (Indymedia, 2006); *On the Edge: Femicide in Ciudad Juárez,* directed by Steve Hise (Illegal Art, 2006); and *Border Echoes,* directed by Lorena Méndez (Documentary Films, 2006).

8. See *Desert Blood: The Juárez Murders,* by Alicia Gaspar de Alba (Houston: Arte Público Press, 2005); *Secrets in the Sand: The Young Women of Ciudad Juárez,* by Marjorie Agosín, trans. Celeste Kostopulos-Cooperman (New York: White Pine Press, 2006); *If I Die in Juárez,* by Stella Pope Duarte (Tempe: University of Arizona Press, 2007).

9. See Diana Washington Valdez, *Cosecha de mujeres: Safari en el desierto mexicano* (Mexico City: Océano, 2005); and Theresa Rodríguez et al., *The Daughters of Juárez: A True Story of Serial Murder South of the Border* (New York: Atria Books, 2007).

10. See Melissa Wright, *Disposable Women and Other Myths of Global Capitalism* (New York: Routledge, 2006).

11. To name a few artists: Coco Fusco, Rubén Amavisca, Alma López, Laura Molina, Rigo Maldonado, Victoria Delgadillo, Daisy Tonantzin, Ester Hernández, Yreina Cervántez, Consuelo Flores, and Favianna Rodríguez.

12. For some of the earliest scholarship on the femicides, see Melissa Wright, "The Dialectics of Still Life: Murder, Women, and the Maquiladoras," *Public Culture* 11.3 (1999): 453–474; and "A Manifesto against Femicide," *Antipode* 33.3 (July 2001): 550–566; Rosa Linda Fregoso, "Voices without Echo: The Global Gendered Apartheid," *Emergences* 10.1 (May 2000): 137–155; Julia Monárrez-Fragoso, "La cultura del feminicidio en Juárez, 1993–1999," *Frontera Norte* 12.23 (January–June 2000): 87–118. For early pre-NAFTA scholarship on the *maquiladora* industry, see Norma Iglesias Prieto, *La flor más bella de la maquiladora* (Tijuana: Secretaría de Educación Pública, Centro de Estudios Fronterizos, El Colegio de la Frontera Norte, 1985). For early feminist scholarship on sex crimes, see Jane Caputi, "The Sexual Politics of Murder," *Gender and Society* 3.4 (December 1989): 437–456.

13. MujerArtes is a collective of elderly community ceramicists affiliated with the Esperanza Peace and Justice Center in San Antonio, Texas. Working under the direction of Verónica Castillo, MujerArtes created a community altar entitled *Lamento por las Mujeres de Juárez* (Elegy for the Women of Juárez), which included Verónica Castillo's *Maquilando Mujeres: Árbol de la Muerte* (Milling Women: Tree of Death) and twenty-six other pieces of ceramic art – plates, plaques, sculptures, and trees of life depicting scenes of violence, innocence, and mourning. *Lamento* opened as an exhibition at the Esperanza Center in July 2003 and was later transported to and installed at UCLA's Fowler Museum of Cultural History in the fall of 2003 as part of the museum's special exhibition on the Mexican cultural tradition of "trees of life," which featured the work of Verónica Castillo's family. The silent auction generated a $5,000 donation from MujerArtes to Amigos de las Mujeres de Juárez, which divided the funds among the victims' families that the group represents.

14. Access the petition at http://www.petitiononline.com/NiUnaMas/petition.html. As of June 28, 2007, four and a half years after the petition went online, it had garnered 10,700 votes from supporters from Europe, Latin America, and the United States.

15. See Jane Caputi's Afterword: Goddess Murder and Gynocide in Ciudad Juárez," *Making a Killing: Femicide, Free Trade, and La Frontera,* ed. Alicia Gaspar de Alba with Georgina Guzmán (Austin, TX: University of Texas Press, 2010, 279–94) for a detailed deconstruction of the image.

16. The story of Coyolxauhqui, the Moon Goddess, links to the story of Coatlicue, her mother and the mother of all the gods, and is taken from the Florentine Codex. While Coatlicue was performing her ritual sweeping of a temple on the hill of Coatepec, she mystically became impregnated by a ball of falling feathers that she nestled to her breast. This pregnancy enraged Coyolxauhqui and her four hundred brothers and sisters – the stars – who made plans to attack and kill their mother on the hill of Coatepec. Coyolxauhqui, whose name means "the goddess of the bells on her cheeks," is the female warrior who led her siblings to their mother to mount the attack in response to feeling disgraced by their mother's unexplained pregnancy. Just as Coyolxauhqui and her siblings arrived, Coatlicue gave birth to the full-grown God of the Sun and God of War, Huitzilopochtli. Huitzilopochtli promised his mother that he would protect her from his sister's wrath. He armed himself with the Xiuhcoatl, the Fiery Serpent, and stopped his sister from killing their mother by decapitating Coyolxauhqui and hurling her body down the hill to smash into many pieces at the bottom. Huitzilopochtli then defeated the other siblings and claimed his title as the supreme ruler of the Aztecs, the God of War.

17. For an updated list of femicides in Juárez between 2004 and 2006, see the Web site of the Washington Office for Latin America (WOLA) at http://www.wola.org/publications/updated_list_of_murders_of_women_in_juarez_and_chihuahua_city.

18. See "Ciudad Juárez: Gobierno de Chihuahua desacreditó informe de AI," *Mujeres Hoy* (August 15, 2003), available online on the Nuestras Hijas de Regreso a Casa Web site, http://www.mujeresdejuarez.org.

19. Theresa Braine, "Argentine Experts Study Juárez Murder Remains," *Women's eNews* (April 16, 2006), http://womensenews.org/story/crime-policylegislation/060416/argentine-experts-study-juarez-murder-remains.

20. By 2003, copycat killings had started to crop up in other border cities such as Nogales, Matamoros, Mexicali, and Nuevo Laredo, and also in Chihuahua City, where over one hundred women and girls have been slain in the "Juárez style."

8.6
Hermaphrodites with Attitude: Mapping the Emergence of Intersex Political Activism

Cheryl Chase

The insistence on two clearly distinguished sexes has calamitous personal consequences for the many individuals who arrive in the world with sexual anatomy that fails to be easily distinguished as male or female. Such individuals are labeled "intersexuals" or "hermaphrodites" by modern medical discourse.[1] About one in a hundred births exhibits some anomaly in sex differentiation,[2] and about one in two thousand is different enough to render problematic the question "Is it a boy or a girl?"[3] Since the early 1960s, nearly every major city in the United States has had a hospital with a standing team of medical experts who intervene in these cases to assign – through drastic surgical means – a male or female status to intersex infants. The fact that this system for preserving the boundaries of the categories male and female has existed for so long without drawing criticism or scrutiny from any quarter indicates the extreme discomfort that sexual ambiguity excites in our culture. Pediatric genital surgeries literalize what might otherwise be considered a theoretical operation: the attempted production of normatively sexed bodies and gendered subjects through constitutive acts of violence. Over the last few years, however, intersex people have begun to politicize intersex identities, thus transforming intensely personal experiences of violation into collective opposition to the medical regulation of bodies that queer the foundations of heteronormative identifications and desires.

Hermaphrodites: Medical Authority and Cultural Invisibility

Many people familiar with the ideas that gender is a phenomenon not adequately described by male/female dimorphism and that the interpretation of physical sex differences is culturally constructed remain surprised to learn just how variable sexual anatomy is.[4] Though the male/female binary is constructed as natural and presumed to be immutable, the phenomenon of intersexuality offers clear evidence to the contrary and furnishes an opportunity to deploy "nature" strategically to disrupt heteronormative systems of sex, gender, and sexuality. The concept of bodily sex, in popular usage, refers to multiple components including karyotype (organization of sex chromosomes), gonadal differentiation (e.g., ovarian or testicular), genital morphology, configuration of internal reproductive organs, and pubertal sex characteristics such as breasts and facial hair. Because these characteristics are expected to be concordant in each individual – either all male or all female – an observer, once having attributed male or female sex to a particular individual, assumes the values of other unobserved characteristics.[5]

Because medicine intervenes quickly in intersex births to change the infant's body, the phenomenon of intersexuality is today largely unknown outside specialized medical practices. General public awareness of intersex bodies slowly vanished in modern Western European societies as medicine gradually appropriated to itself the authority to interpret – and eventually manage – the category which had previously been widely known as "hermaphroditism." Victorian medical taxonomy began to efface hermaphroditism as a legitimated status by establishing mixed gonadal histology as a necessary criterion for "true" hermaphroditism. By this criterion, both ovarian and testicular tissue types had to be present. Given the limitations of Victorian surgery and anesthesia, such confirmation was impossible in a living patient. All other anomalies were reclassified as "pseudo-hermaphroditisms" masking a "true sex" determined by the gonads.[6]

With advances in anesthesia, surgery, embryology, and endocrinology, however, twentieth-century medicine moved from merely labeling intersexed bodies to the far more invasive practice of "fixing" them to conform with a diagnosed true sex.

The techniques and protocols for physically transforming intersexed bodies were developed primarily at Johns Hopkins University in Baltimore during the 1920s and 1930s under the guidance of urologist Hugh Hampton Young. "Only during the last few years," Young enthused in the preface to his pioneering textbook, *Genital Abnormalities*, "have we begun to get somewhere near the explanation of the marvels of anatomic abnormality that may be portrayed by these amazing individuals. But the surgery of the hermaphrodite has remained a terra incognita." The "sad state of these unfortunates" prompted Young to devise "a great variety of surgical procedures" by which he attempted to normalize their bodily appearances to the greatest extents possible.[7]

Quite a few of Young's patients resisted his efforts. One, a "'snappy' young negro woman with a good figure" and a large clitoris, had married a man but found her passion only with women. She refused "to be made into a man" because removal of her vagina would mean the loss of her "meal ticket," namely, her husband.[8] By the 1950s, the principle of rapid postnatal detection and intervention for intersex infants had been developed at Johns Hopkins with the stated goal of completing surgery early enough so that the child would have no memory of it.[9] One wonders whether the insistence on early intervention was not at least partly motivated by the resistance offered by adult intersexuals to normalization through surgery. Frightened parents of ambiguously sexed infants were much more open to suggestions of normalizing surgery, while the infants themselves could of course offer no resistance whatever. Most of the theoretical foundations justifying these interventions are attributable to psychologist John Money, a sex researcher invited to Johns Hopkins by Lawson Wilkins, the founder of pediatric endocrinology.[10] Wilkins's numerous students subsequently carried these protocols to hospitals throughout the United States and abroad.[11] Suzanne Kessler notes that today Wilkins and Money's protocols enjoy a "consensus of approval rarely encountered in science."[12]

In keeping with the Johns Hopkins model, the birth of an intersex infant today is deemed a "psychosocial emergency" that propels a multidisciplinary team of intersex specialists into action. Significantly, they are surgeons and endocrinologists rather than psychologists, bioethicists, representatives from intersex peer support organizations, or parents of intersex children. The team examines the infant and chooses either male or female as a "sex of assignment," then informs the parents that this is the child's "true sex." Medical technology, including surgery and hormones, is then used to make the child's body conform as closely as possible to that sex.

The sort of deviation from sex norms exhibited by intersexuals is so highly stigmatized that the likely prospect of emotional harm due to social rejection of the intersexual provides physicians with their most compelling argument to justify medically unnecessary surgical interventions. Intersex status is considered to be so incompatible with emotional health that misrepresentation, concealment of facts, and outright lying (both to parents and later to the intersex person) are unabashedly advocated in professional medical literature.[13] Rather, the systematic hushing up of the fact of intersex births and the use of violent techniques to normalize intersex bodies have caused profound emotional and physical harm to intersexuals and their families. The harm begins when the birth is treated as a medical crisis, and the consequences of that initial treatment ripple out ever afterward. The impact of this treatment is so devastating that until just a few years ago, people whose lives have been touched by intersexuality maintained silence about their ordeal. As recently as 1993, no one publicly disputed surgeon Milton Edgerton when he wrote that in forty years of clitoral surgery on intersexuals, "not one has complained of loss of sensation, *even when the entire clitoris was removed.*"[14]

The tragic irony is that, while intersexual anatomy occasionally indicates an underlying medical problem such as adrenal malfunction, ambiguous genitals are in and of themselves neither painful nor harmful to health. Surgery is essentially a destructive process. It can remove and to a limited extent relocate tissue, but it cannot create new structures. This technical limitation, taken together with the framing of the feminine as a condition of lack, leads physicians to assign 90 percent of anatomically ambiguous infants as female by excising genital tissue. Members of the Johns Hopkins intersex team have justified female assignment by saying, "You can make a hole, but you can't build a pole."[15] Positively heroic efforts shore up a tenuous masculine status for the remaining 10 percent assigned male, who are subjected to multiple operations – twenty-two in one case[16] – with the goal of straightening the penis and constructing a urethra to enable standing urinary posture. For some, the surgeries end only when the child grows old enough to resist.[17]

Children assigned to the female sex are subjected to surgery that removes the troubling hypertrophic clitoris (the same tissue that would have been a troubling micropenis if the child had been assigned male). Through the 1960s, feminizing pediatric genital surgery was openly labeled "clitorectomy" and was compared favorably to the African practices that have been the recent focus of such intense scrutiny. As three Harvard surgeons noted, "Evidence that the clitoris is not essential for normal coitus may be gained from certain sociological data. For instance, it is the custom of a number of African tribes to excise the clitoris and other parts of the external genitals. Yet normal sexual function is observed in these females."[18] A modified operation that removes most of the clitoris and relocates a bit of the tip is variously (and euphemistically) called clitoroplasty, clitoral reduction, or clitoral recession and is described as a "simple cosmetic procedure" to differentiate it from the now infamous clitorectomy. However, the operation is far from benign. Here is a slightly simplified summary (in my own words) of the surgical technique – recommended by Johns Hopkins Surgeons Oesterling, Gearhart, and Jeffs – that is representative of the operation:

> They make an incision around the phallus, at the corona, then dissect the skin away from its underside. Next they dissect the skin away from the dorsal side and remove as much of the corpora, or erectile bodies, as necessary to create an "appropriate size clitoris." Next, stitches are placed from the pubic area along both sides of the entire length of what remains of the phallus; when these stitches are tightened, it folds up like pleats in a skirt, and recesses into a concealed position behind the mons pubis. If the result is still "too large," the glans is further reduced by cutting away a pie-shaped wedge.[19]

For most intersexuals, this sort of arcane, dehumanized medical description, illustrated with close-ups of genital surgery and naked children with blacked-out eyes, is the only available version of *Our Bodies, Ourselves*. We as a culture have relinquished to medicine the authority to police the boundaries of male and female, leaving intersexuals to recover as best they can, alone and silent, from violent normalization.

My Career as a Hermaphrodite: Renegotiating Cultural Meanings

I was born with ambiguous genitals. A doctor specializing in intersexuality deliberated for three days – sedating my mother each time she asked what was wrong with her baby – before concluding that I was male, with a micropenis, complete hypospadias, undescended testes, and a strange extra opening behind the urethra. A male birth certificate was completed for me, and my parents began raising me as a boy. When I was a year and a half old my parents consulted a different set of experts, who admitted me to a hospital for "sex determination." "Determine" is a remarkably apt word in this context, meaning both "to ascertain by investigation" and "to cause to come to a resolution." It perfectly describes the two-stage process whereby science produces through a series of masked operations what it claims merely to observe. Doctors told my parents that a thorough medical investigation would be necessary to determine (in the first sense of that word) what my "true sex" was. They judged my genital appendage to be inadequate as a penis, too short to mark masculine status effectively or to penetrate females. As a female, however, I would be penetrable and potentially fertile. My anatomy having been relabeled as vagina, urethra, labia, and outsized clitoris, my sex was determined (in the second sense) by amputating my genital appendage. Following doctors' orders, my parents then changed my name, combed their house to eliminate all traces of my existence as a boy (photographs, birthday cards, etc.), changed my birth certificate, moved to a different town, instructed extended family members no longer to refer to me as a boy, and never told anyone else – including me – just what had happened. My intersexuality and change of sex were the family's dirty little secrets.

At age eight, I was returned to the hospital for abdominal surgery that trimmed away the testicular portion of my gonads, each of which was partly ovarian and partly testicular in character. No explanation was given to me then for the long hospital stay or the abdominal surgery, nor for the regular hospital visits afterward, in which doctors photographed my genitals and inserted fingers and instruments into my vagina and anus. These visits ceased as soon as I began to menstruate. At the time of the sex change, doctors had assured my parents that their once son/now daughter would grow into a woman who could have a normal sex life and babies. With the confirmation of menstruation, my parents apparently concluded that that prediction had been borne out and their ordeal was behind them. For me, the worst part of the nightmare was just beginning.

As an adolescent, I became aware that I had no clitoris or inner labia and was unable to orgasm. By the end of my teens, I began to do research in medical libraries, trying to discover what might have happened to me. When I finally determined to obtain my medical records, it took me three years to overcome the obstruction of the doctors whom I asked for help. When I did obtain them, a scant three pages, I first learned that I was a "true hermaphrodite" who had been my parents' son for a year and a half and who bore a name unfamiliar to me. The records also documented my clitorectomy. This was the middle 1970s, when I was in my early twenties. I had come to identify myself as lesbian, at a time when lesbianism and a biologically based gender essentialism were virtually synonymous: men were rapists who caused war and environmental destruction; women were good and would heal the earth; lesbians were a superior form of being uncontaminated by "men's energy." In such a world, how could I tell anyone that I had actually possessed the dreaded "phallus"? I was no longer a woman in my own eyes but rather a monstrous and mythical creature. Because my hermaphroditism and long-buried boyhood were the history behind the clitorectomy, I could never speak openly about that or my consequent inability to orgasm. I was so traumatized by discovering the circumstances that produced my embodiment that I could not speak of these matters with anyone.

Nearly fifteen years later, I suffered an emotional meltdown. In the eyes of the world, I was a highly successful businesswoman, a principal in an international high tech company. To myself, I was a freak, incapable of loving or being loved, filled with shame about my status as a hermaphrodite and about my sexual dysfunction. Unable to make peace with myself, I finally sought help from a psychotherapist, who reacted to each revelation about my history and predicament with some version of "no, it's not" or "so what?" I would say, "I'm not really a woman," and she would say, "Of course you are. You look female." I would say, "My complete withdrawal from sexuality has destroyed every relationship I've ever entered." She would say, "Everybody has their ups and downs." I tried another therapist and met with a similar response. Increasingly desperate, I confided my story to several friends, who shrank away in embarrassed silence. I was in emotional agony, feeling utterly alone, seeing no possible way out. I decided to kill myself.

Confronting suicide as a real possibility proved to be my personal epiphany. I fantasized killing myself quite messily and dramatically in the office of the surgeon who had cut off my clitoris, forcibly confronting him with the horror he had imposed on my life. But in acknowledging the desire to put my pain to some use, not to utterly waste my life, I turned a crucial corner, finding a way to direct my rage productively out into the world rather than destructively at myself. I had no conceptual framework for developing a more positive self-consciousness. I knew only that I felt mutilated, not fully human, but that I was determined to heal. I struggled for weeks in emotional chaos, unable to eat or sleep or work. I could not accept my image of a hermaphroditic body any more than I could accept the butchered one the surgeons left me with. Thoughts of myself as a Frankenstein's monster patchwork alternated with longings for escape by death, only to be followed by outrage, anger, and a determination to survive. I could not accept that it was just or right or good to treat any person as I had been treated – my sex changed, my genitals cut up, my experience silenced and rendered invisible. I bore a private hell within me, wretchedly alone in my condition without even my tormentors for company. Finally, I began to envision myself standing in a driving storm but with clear skies and a rainbow visible in the distance. I was still in agony, but I was beginning to see the painful process in which I was caught up in terms of revitalization and rebirth, a means of investing my life with a new sense of authenticity that possessed vast potentials for further transformation. Since then, I have seen this experience of movement through pain to personal empowerment described by other intersex and transsexual activists.[20]

I slowly developed a newly politicized and critically aware form of self-understanding. I had been the kind of lesbian who at times had a girlfriend but who had never really participated in the life of a lesbian community. I felt almost completely isolated from gay politics, feminism, and queer and gender theory. I did possess the rudimentary knowledge that the gay rights movement had gathered momentum only when it could effectively deny that homosexuality was sick or inferior and assert to the contrary that "gay is good." As impossible as it then seemed, I pledged similarly to affirm that "intersex is good," that the body I was born with was not diseased, only different. I vowed to embrace the sense of being "not a woman" that I initially had been so terrified to discover.

I began searching for community and consequently moved to San Francisco in the fall of 1992, based entirely on my vague notion that people living in the "queer mecca" would have the most conceptually sophisticated, socially tolerant, and politically astute analysis of sexed and gendered embodiment. I found what I was looking for in part because my arrival in the Bay Area corresponded with the rather sudden emergence of an energetic transgender political movement. Transgender Nation (TN) had developed out of Queer Nation, a post-gay/lesbian group that sought to transcend identity politics. TN's actions garnered media attention – especially when members were arrested during a "zap" of the American Psychiatric Association's annual convention when they protested the psychiatric labeling of transsexuality as mental illness. Transsexual performance artist Kate Bornstein was introducing transgender issues in an entertaining way to the San Francisco gay/lesbian community and beyond. Female-to-male issues had achieved a new level of visibility due in large part to efforts made by Lou Sullivan, a gay FTM activist who had died an untimely death from HIV-related illnesses in 1991. And in the wake of her underground best-selling novel, *Stone Butch Blues,* Leslie Feinberg's manifesto *Transgender Liberation: A Movement Whose Time Has Come* was finding a substantial audience, linking transgender social justice to a broader progressive political agenda for the first time.[21] At the same time, a vigorous new wave of gender scholarship had emerged in the academy.[22] In this context, intersex activist and theoretician Morgan Holmes could analyze her own clitorectomy for her master's thesis and have it taken seriously as academic work.[23] Openly transsexual scholars, including Susan Stryker and Sandy Stone, were visible in responsible academic positions at major universities. Stone's "*Empire* Strikes Back: A

Posttranssexual Manifesto" refigured open, visible transsexuals not as gender conformists propping up a system of rigid, binary sex but as "a set of embodied texts whose potential for productive disruption of structured sexualities and spectra of desire has yet to be explored."[24]

Into this heady atmosphere, I brought my own experience. Introduced by Bornstein to other gender activists, I explored with them the cultural politics of intersexuality, which to me represented yet another new configuration of bodies, identities, desires, and sexualities from which to confront the violently normativizing aspects of the dominant sex/gender system. In the fall of 1993, TN pioneer Anne Ogborn invited me to participate in a weekend retreat called the New Woman Conference, where postoperative transsexual women shared their stories, their griefs and joys, and enjoyed the freedom to swim or sunbathe in the nude with others who had surgically changed genitals. I saw that participants returned home in a state of euphoria, and I determined to bring that same sort of healing experience to intersex people.

Birth of an Intersex Movement: Opposition and Allies

Upon moving to San Francisco, I started telling my story indiscriminately to everyone I met. Over the course of a year, simply by speaking openly within my own social circles, I learned of six other intersexuals – including two who had been fortunate enough to escape medical attention. I realized that intersexuality, rather than being extremely rare, must be relatively common. I decided to create a support network. In the summer of 1993, I produced some pamphlets, obtained a post office box, and began to publicize the Intersex Society of North America (ISNA) through small notices in the media. Before long, I was receiving several letters per week from intersexuals throughout the United States and Canada and occasionally some from Europe. While the details varied, the letters gave a remarkably coherent picture of the emotional consequences of medical intervention. Morgan Holmes: "All the things my body might have grown to do, all the possibilities, went down the hall with my amputated clitoris to the pathology department. The rest of me went to the recovery room – I'm still recovering." Angela Moreno: "I am horrified by what has been done to me and by the conspiracy of silence and lies. I am filled with grief and rage, but also relief finally to believe that maybe I am not the only one." Thomas: "I pray that I will have the means to repay, in some measure, the American Urological Association for all that it has done for my benefit. I am having some trouble, though, in connecting the timing mechanism to the fuse."

ISNA's most immediate goal has been to create a community of intersex people who could provide peer support to deal with shame, stigma, grief, and rage as well as with practical issues such as how to obtain old medical records or locate a sympathetic psychotherapist or endocrinologist. To that end, I cooperated with journalists whom I judged capable of reporting widely and responsibly on our efforts, listed ISNA with self-help and referral clearinghouses, and established a presence on the Internet (http://www.isna.org). ISNA now connects hundreds of intersexuals across North America, Europe, Australia, and New Zealand. It has also begun sponsoring an annual intersex retreat, the first of which took place in 1996 and which moved participants every bit as profoundly as the New Woman Conference had moved me in 1993.

ISNA's longer-term and more fundamental goal, however, is to change the way intersex infants are treated. We advocate that surgery not be performed on ambiguous genitals unless there is a medical reason (such as blocked or painful urination), and that parents be given the conceptual tools and emotional support to accept their children's physical differences. While it is fascinating to think about the potential development of new genders or subject positions grounded in forms of embodiment that fall outside the familiar male/female dichotomy, we recognize that the two-sex/gender model is currently hegemonic and therefore advocate that children be raised either as boys or girls, according to which designation seems most likely to offer the child the greatest future sense of comfort. Advocating gender assignment without resorting to normalizing surgery is a radical position given that it requires the willful disruption of the assumed concordance between body shape and gender category. However, this is the only position that prevents irreversible physical damage to the intersex person's body, that respects the intersex person's agency regarding his/her own flesh, and that recognizes genital sensation and erotic functioning to be at least as important as reproductive capacity. If an intersex child or adult decides to change gender or to undergo surgical or hormonal alteration of his/her body, that decision should also be fully respected and facilitated. The key point is that intersex subjects should not be violated for the comfort and convenience of others.

One part of reaching ISNA's long-term goal has been to document the emotional and physical carnage resulting from medical interventions. As a rapidly growing literature makes abundantly clear (see the bibliography on our website, http://www.isna.org/bigbib.html), the medical management of intersexuality has changed little in the forty years since my first surgery. Kessler expresses surprise that "in spite of the thousands of genital operations performed every year, there are no meta-analyses from within the medical community on levels of success."[25] They do not know whether postsurgical intersexuals are "silent and happy or silent and unhappy."[26] There is no research effort to improve erotic functioning for adult intersexuals whose genitals have been altered, nor are there psychotherapists specializing in working with adult intersex clients trying to heal from the trauma of medical intervention. To provide a counterpoint to the mountains of medical literature that neglect intersex experience and to begin compiling an ethnographic account of that experience, ISNA's *Hermaphrodites with Attitude* newsletter has developed into a forum for intersexuals to tell their own stories. We have sent complimentary copies of the newsletter filled with searing personal narratives to academics, writers, journalists, minority rights organizations, and medical practitioners – to anybody we thought might make a difference in our campaign to change the way intersex bodies are managed.

ISNA's presence has begun to generate effects. It has helped politicize the growing number of intersex organizations, as well as intersex identities themselves. When I first began organizing ISNA, I met leaders of the Turner's Syndrome Society, the oldest known support group focusing on atypical sexual differentiation, founded in 1987. Turner's Syndrome is defined by an XO genetic karyotype that results in a female body morphology with nonfunctioning ovaries, extremely short stature, and a variety of other physical differences described in the medical literature with such stigmatizing labels as "web-necked" and "fish-mouthed." Each of these women told me what a profound, life-changing experience it had been simply to meet another person like herself. I was inspired by their accomplishments (they are a national organization serving thousands of members), but I wanted ISNA to have a different focus. I was less willing to think of intersexuality as a pathology or disability, more interested in challenging its medicalization entirely, and more interested still in politicizing a pan-intersexual identity across the divisions of particular etiologies in order to destabilize more effectively the heteronormative assumptions underlying the violence directed at our bodies.

When I established ISNA in 1993, no such politicized groups existed. In the United Kingdom in 1988, the mother of a girl with androgen-insensitivity syndrome (AIS, which produces genetic males with female genital morphologies) formed the AIS Support Group. The group, which initially lobbied for increased medical attention (better surgical techniques for producing greater vaginal depth, more research into the osteoporosis that often attends AIS), now has chapters in five countries. Another group, K. S. and Associates, was formed in 1989 by the mother of a boy with Klinefelter's Syndrome and today serves over one thousand families. Klinefelter's is characterized by the presence of one or more additional X chromosomes, which produce bodies with fairly masculine external genitals, above-average height, and somewhat gangly limbs. At puberty, people with K. S. often experience pelvic broadening and the development of breasts. K. S. and Associates continues to be dominated by parents, is highly medical in orientation, and has resisted attempts by adult Klinefelter's Syndrome men to discuss gender identity or sexual orientation issues related to their intersex condition.

Since ISNA has been on the scene, other groups with a more resistant stance vis-à-vis the medical establishment have begun to appear. In 1995, a mother who refused medical pressure for female assignment for her intersex child formed the Ambiguous Genitalia Support Network, which introduces parents of intersexuals to each other and encourages the development of pen-pal support relationships. In 1996, another mother who had rejected medical pressure to assign her intersex infant as a female by removing his penis formed the Hermaphrodite Education and Listening Post (HELP) to provide peer support and medical information. Neither of these parent-oriented groups, however, frames its work in overtly political terms. Still, political analysis and action of the sort advocated by ISNA has not been without effect on the more narrowly defined service-oriented or parent-dominated groups. The AIS Support Group, now more representative of both adults and parents, noted in a recent newsletter,

Our first impression of ISNA was that they were perhaps a bit too angry and militant to gain the support of the medical profession. However, we have to say that, having read [political analyses of intersexuality by ISNA, Kessler, Fausto-Sterling, and Holmes], we feel that the feminist concepts relating to the patriarchal treatment of intersexuality are extremely interesting and do make a lot of sense. After all, the lives of intersexed people are stigmatized by the cultural disapproval of their genital appearance, [which need not] affect their experience as sexual human beings.[27]

Other more militant groups have now begun to pop up. In 1994, German intersexuals formed both the Workgroup on Violence in Pediatrics and Gynecology and the Genital Mutilation Survivors' Support Network, and Hijra Nippon now represents activist intersexuals in Japan.

Outside the rather small community of intersex organizations, ISNA's work has generated a complex patchwork of alliances and oppositions. Queer activists, especially transgender activists, have provided encouragement, advice, and logistical support to the intersex movement. The direct action group Transsexual Menace helped an ad hoc group of militant intersexuals calling themselves Hermaphrodites with Attitude plan and carry out a picket of the 1996 annual meeting of the American Academy of Pediatrics in Boston – the first recorded instance of intersex public protest in modern history.[28] ISNA was also invited to join GenderPAC, a recently formed national consortium of transgender organizations that lobbies against discrimination based on atypical expressions of gender or embodiment. More mainstream gay and lesbian political organizations such as the National Gay and Lesbian Task Force have also been willing to include intersex concerns as part of their political agendas. Transgender and lesbian/gay groups have been supportive of intersex political activism largely because they see similarities in the medicalization of these various identities as a form of social control and (especially for transsexuals) empathize with our struggle to assert agency within a medical discourse that works to efface the ability to exercise informed consent about what happens to one's own body.

Gay/lesbian caucuses and special interest groups within professional medical associations have been especially receptive to ISNA's agenda. One physician on the Internet discussion group glb-medical wrote:

The effect of Cheryl Chase's postings – admittedly, after the shock wore off – was to make me realize that THOSE WHO HAVE BEEN TREATED might very well think [they had not been well served by medical intervention]. This matters a lot. As a gay man, and simply as a person, I have struggled for much of my adult life to find my own natural self, to disentangle the confusions caused by others' presumptions about how I am/should be. But, thankfully, their decisions were not surgically imposed on me!

Queer psychiatrists, starting with Bill Byne at New York's Mount Sinai Hospital, have been quick to support ISNA, in part because the psychological principles underlying the current intersex treatment protocols are manifestly unsound. They seem almost willfully designed to exacerbate rather than ameliorate already difficult emotional issues arising from sexual difference. Some of these psychiatrists see the surgical and endocrinological domination of a problem that even surgeons and endocrinologists acknowledge to be psychosocial rather than biomedical as an unjustified invasion of their area of professional competence.

ISNA has deliberately cultivated a network of nonintersexed advocates who command a measure of social legitimacy and can speak in contexts where uninterpreted intersex voices will not be heard. Because there is a strong impulse to discount what intersexuals have to say about intersexuality, sympathetic representation has been welcome – especially in helping intersexuals reframe intersexuality in non-medical terms. Some gender theory scholars, feminist critics of science, medical historians, and anthropologists have been quick to understand and support intersex activism. Years before ISNA came into existence, feminist biologist and science studies scholar Anne Fausto-Sterling had written about intersexuality in relation to intellectually suspect scientific practices that perpetuate masculinist constructs of gender, and she became an early ISNA ally.[29] Likewise, social psychologist Suzanne Kessler had written a brilliant ethnography of surgeons who specialize in treating intersexuals. After speaking with several "products" of their practice, she, too, became a strong supporter of intersex activism.[30] Historian of science Alice Dreger, whose work focuses not only on hermaphroditism but on other forms of potentially benign atypical embodiment that become subject to destructively normalizing medical interventions (conjoined twins, for example), has been especially supportive. Fausto-Sterling, Kessler, and Dreger will each shortly publish works that analyze the medical treatment of intersexuality as being culturally motivated and criticize it as harmful to its ostensible patients.[31]

Allies who help contest the medicalization of intersexuality are especially important because ISNA has found it almost entirely fruitless to attempt direct, non-confrontational interactions with the medical specialists who themselves determine policy on the treatment of intersex infants and who actually carry out the surgeries. Joycelyn Elders, the Clinton administration's first surgeon general, is a pediatric endocrinologist with many years of experience managing intersex infants but, in spite of a generally feminist approach to health care and frequent overtures from ISNA, she has been dismissive of the concerns of intersexuals themselves.[32] Another pediatrician remarked in an Internet discussion on intersexuality: "I think this whole issue is preposterous. ... To suggest that [medical decisions about the treatment of intersex conditions] are somehow cruel or arbitrary is insulting, ignorant and misguided. ... To spread the claims that [ISNA] is making is just plain wrong, and I hope that this [on-line group of doctors and scientists] will not blindly accept them." Yet another participant in that same chat asked what was for him obviously a rhetorical question: "Who is the enemy? I really don't think it's the medical establishment. Since when did we establish the male/female hegemony?" While a surgeon quoted in a *New York Times* article on ISNA summarily dismissed us as "zealots,"[33] there is considerable anecdotal information supplied by ISNA sympathizers that professional meetings in the fields of pediatrics, urology, genital plastic surgery, and endocrinology are buzzing with anxious and defensive discussions of intersex activism. In response to the Hermaphrodites with Attitude protests at the American Academy of Pediatrics meeting, that organization felt compelled to issue the following statement to the press: "The Academy is deeply concerned about the emotional, cognitive, and body image development of intersexuals, and believes that successful early genital surgery minimizes these issues." Further protests were planned for 1997.

The roots of resistance to the truth claims of intersexuals run deep in the medical establishment. Not only does ISNA critique the normativist biases couched within most scientific practice, it advocates a treatment protocol for intersex infants that disrupts conventional understandings of the relationship between bodies and genders. But on a level more personally threatening to medical practitioners, ISNA's position implies that they have – unwittingly at best, through willful denial at worst – spent their careers inflicting a profound harm from which their patients will never fully recover. ISNA's position threatens to destroy the assumptions motivating an entire medical subspecialty, thus jeopardizing the ability to perform what many surgeons find to be technically difficult and fascinating work. Melissa Hendricks notes that Dr. Gearhart is known to colleagues as a surgical "artist" who can "carve a large phallus down into a clitoris" with consummate skill.[34] More than one ISNA member has discovered that surgeons actually operated on their genitals at no charge. The medical establishment's fascination with its own power to change sex and its drive to rescue parents from their intersex children are so strong that heroic interventions are delivered without regard to the capitalist model that ordinarily governs medical services.

Given such deep and mutually reinforcing reasons for opposing ISNA's position, it is hardly surprising that medical intersex specialists have, for the most part, turned a deaf ear toward us. The lone exception as of April 1997 is urologist Justine Schober. After watching a videotape of the 1996 ISNA retreat and receiving other input from HELP and the AIS Support Group, she suggests in a new textbook on pediatric surgery that while technology has advanced to the point that "our needs [as surgeons] and the needs of parents to have a presentable child can be satisfied," it is time to acknowledge that problems exist that "we as surgeons ... cannot address. Success in psychosocial adjustment is the true goal of sexual assignment and genitoplasty. ... Surgery makes parents and doctors comfortable, but counseling makes people comfortable too, and is not irreversible."[35]

While ISNA will continue to approach the medical establishment for dialogue (and continue supporting protests outside the closed doors when doctors refuse to talk), perhaps the most important aspect of our current activities is the struggle to change public perceptions. By using the mass media, the Internet, and our growing network of allies and sympathizers to make the general public aware of the frequency of intersexuality and of the intense suffering that medical treatment has caused, we seek to create an environment in which many parents of intersex children will have already heard about the intersex movement when their child is born. Such informed parents we hope will be better able to resist medical pressure for unnecessary genital surgery and secrecy and to find their way to a peer-support group and counseling rather than to a surgical theater.

Notes

My appreciation goes to Susan Stryker for her extensive contributions to the structure and substance of this essay.

1. Claude J. Migeon, Gary D. Berkovitz, and Terry R. Brown, "Sexual Differentiation and Ambiguity," in *Wilkins: The Diagnosis and Treatment of Endocrine Disorders in Childhood and Adolescence*, ed. Michael S. Kappy, Robert M. Blizzard, and Claude J. Migeon (Springfield, Ill.: Charles C. Thomas, 1994), 573–715.

2. Lalitha Raman-Wilms et al., "Fetal Genital Effects of First-Trimester Sex Hormone Exposure: A Meta-Analysis," *Obstetrics and Gynecology* 85 (1995): 141–48.

3. Anne Fausto-Sterling, *Body Building: How Biologists Construct Sexuality* (New York: Basic Books, forthcoming).

4. Judith Butler, *Gender Trouble: Feminism and the Subversion of Identity* (New York: Routledge, 1990); Thomas Laqueur, *Making Sex: Body and Gender from the Greeks to Freud* (Cambridge, Mass.: Harvard University Press, 1990).

5. Suzanne Kessler and Wendy McKenna, *Gender: An Ethnomethodological Approach* (New York: John Wiley and Sons, 1978).

6. Alice Domurat Dreger, "Doubtful Sex: Cases and Concepts of Hermaphroditism in France and Britain, 1868–1915," (Ph.D. diss., Indiana University, 1995); Alice Domurat Dreger, "Doubtful Sex: The Fate of the Hermaphrodite in Victorian Medicine," *Victorian Studies* (spring 1995): 336–70; Alice Domurat Dreger, "Hermaphrodites in Love: The Truth of the Gonads," *Science and Homosexualities*, ed. Vernon Rosario (New York: Routledge, 1997), 46–66; Alice Domurat Dreger, "Doctors Containing Hermaphrodites: The Victorian Legacy," *Chrysalis: The Journal of Transgressive Gender Identities* (fall 1997): 15–22.

7. Hugh Hampton Young, *Genital Abnormalities, Hermaphroditism, and Related Adrenal Diseases* (Baltimore: Williams and Wilkins, 1937), xxxix–xl.

8. Ibid., 139–42.

9. Howard W. Jones Jr. and William Wallace Scott, *Hermaphroditism, Genital Anomalies, and Related Endocrine Disorders* (Baltimore: Williams and Wilkins, 1958), 269.

10. John Money, Joan G. Hampson, and John L. Hampson, "An Examination of Some Basic Sexual Concepts: The Evidence of Human Hermaphroditism," *Bulletin of the Johns Hopkins Hospital* 97 (1955): 301–19; John Money, Joan G. Hampson, and John L. Hampson, "Hermaphroditism: Recommendations Concerning Assignment of Sex, Change of Sex, and Psychologic Management," *Bulletin of Johns Hopkins Hospital* 97 (1955): 284–300; John Money, *Venuses Penuses* (Buffalo: Prometheus, 1986).

11. Robert M. Blizzard, "Lawson Wilkins," in Kappy et al., *Wilkins*, xi–xiv.

12. Suzanne Kessler, "The Medical Construction of Gender: Case Management of Intersexual Infants," *Signs: Journal of Women in Culture and Society* 16 (1990): 3–26.

13. J. Dewhurst and D. B. Grant, "Intersex Problems," *Archives of Disease in Childhood* 59 (1984): 1191–94; Anita Natarajan, "Medical Ethics and Truth-Telling in the Case of Androgen Insensitivity Syndrome," *Canadian Medical Association Journal* 154 (1996): 568–70; Tom Mazur, "Ambiguous Genitalia: Detection and Counseling," *Pediatric Nursing* (1983): 417–22; F. M. E. Slijper et al., "Neonates with Abnormal Genital Development Assigned the Female Sex: Parent Counseling," *Journal of Sex Education and Therapy* 20 (1994): 9–17.

14. Milton T. Edgerton, "Discussion: Clitoroplasty for Clitoromegaly due to Adrenogenital Syndrome without Loss of Sensitivity (by Nobuyuki Sagehashi)," *Plastic and Reconstructive Surgery* 91 (1993): 956.

15. Melissa Hendricks, "Is It a Boy or a Girl?" *Johns Hopkins Magazine,* November 1993, 10–16.

16. John F. Stecker et al., "Hypospadias Cripples," *Urologic Clinics of North America: Symposium on Hypospadias* 8 (1981): 539–44.

17. Jeff McClintock, "Growing Up in the Surgical Maelstrom," *Chrysalis: The Journal of Transgressive Gender Identities* (fall 1997): 53–54.

18. Robert E. Gross, Judson Randolph, and John F. Crigler, "Clitorectomy for Sexual Abnormalities: Indications and Technique," *Surgery* 59 (1966): 300–308.

19. Joseph E. Oesterling, John P. Gearhart, and Robert D. Jeffs, "A Unified Approach to Early Reconstructive Surgery of the Child with Ambiguous Genitalia," *Journal of Urology* 138 (1987): 1079–84.

20. Kira Triea, "The Awakening," *Hermaphrodites with Attitude* (winter 1994): 1; Susan Stryker, "My Words to Victor Frankenstein above the Village of Chamounix: Performing Transgender Rage," *GLQ* 1 (1994): 237–54.

21. Leslie Feinberg, *Stone Butch Blues* (Ithaca, N.Y.: Firebrand, 1993); Leslie Feinberg, *Transgender Liberation: A Movement Whose Time Has Come* (New York: World View Forum, 1992).

22. See, for example, Judith Butler, *Bodies That Matter: On the Discursive Limits of "Sex"* (New York: Routledge, 1993); Butler, *Gender Trouble;* Laqueur, *Making Sex;* and Julia Epstein and Kristina Straub, eds., *Body Guards: The Cultural Politics of Gender Ambiguity* (New York: Routledge, 1991).

23. Morgan Holmes, "Medical Politics and Cultural Imperatives: Intersexuality Beyond Pathology and Erasure" (master's thesis, York University, Toronto, 1994).

24. Sandy Stone, "The *Empire* Strikes Back: A Posttranssexual Manifesto," in Epstein and Straub, *Body Guards,* 280–304, quotation on 296.

25. Suzanne Kessler, *Lessons from the Intersexed* (New Brunswick, N.J.: Rutgers University Press, forthcoming).

26. Robert Jeffs, quoted in Ellen Barry, "United States of Ambiguity," Boston *Phoenix,* 22 November 1996, 6–8, quotation on 6.

27. AIS Support Group, "Letter to America," *ALIAS* (spring 1996): 3–4.

28. Barry, "United States of Ambiguity," 7.

29. Anne Fausto-Sterling, "The Five Sexes: Why Male and Female Are Not Enough," *The Sciences* 33, no. 2 (March/April 1993): 20–25; Anne Fausto-Sterling, *Myths of Gender: Biological Theories about Women and Men,* 2d ed. (New York: Basic Books, 1985), 134–41.

30. Kessler, "The Medical Construction of Gender"; Suzanne Kessler, "Meanings of Genital Variability," *Chrysalis: The Journal of Transgressive Gender Identities* (fall 1997): 33–38.

31. Anne Fausto-Sterling, *Building Bodies: Biology and the Social Construction of Sexuality* (New York: Basic Books, forthcoming); Kessler, "Meanings of Genital Variability"; Alice Domurat Dreger, *Hermaphrodites and the Medical Invention of Sex* (Cambridge, Mass.: Harvard University Press, forthcoming).

32. "Dr. Elders' Medical History," *New Yorker,* 26 September 1994: 45–46; Joycelyn Elders and David Chanoff, From *Sharecropper's Daughter to Surgeon General of the United States of America* (New York: William Morrow, 1996).

33. Natalie Angier, "Intersexual Healing: An Anomaly Finds a Group," *New York Times,* 4 February 1996, E14.

34. Hendricks, "Is It a Boy or a Girl?" 10.

35. Justine M. Schober, "Long Term Outcomes of Feminizing Genitoplasty for Intersex," in *Pediatric Surgery and Urology: Long Term Outcomes,* ed. Pierre Mouriquant (Philadelphia: W. B. Saunders, forthcoming).

8.7

Heteropatriarchy and the Three Pillars of White Supremacy: Rethinking Women of Color Organizing

Andrea Smith

Scenario #1

A group of women of color come together to organize. An argument ensues about whether or not Arab women should be included. Some argue that Arab women are "white" since they have been classified as such in the US census. Another argument erupts over whether or not Latinas qualify as "women of color," since some may be classified as "white" in their Latin American countries of origin and/or "pass" as white in the United States.

Scenario #2

In a discussion on racism, some people argue that Native peoples suffer from less racism than other people of color because they generally do not reside in segregated neighborhoods within the United States. In addition, some argue that since tribes now have gaming, Native peoples are no longer "oppressed."

Scenario #3

A multiracial campaign develops involving diverse communities of color in which some participants charge that we must stop the black/white binary, and end Black hegemony over people of color politics to develop a more "multicultural" framework. However, this campaign continues to rely on strategies and cultural motifs developed by the Black Civil Rights struggle in the United States.

These incidents, which happen quite frequently in "women of color" or "people of color" political organizing struggles, are often explained as a consequence of "oppression olympics." That is to say, one problem we have is that we are too busy fighting over who is more oppressed. In this essay, I want to argue that these incidents are not so much the result of "oppression olympics" but are more about how we have inadequately framed "women of color" or "people of color" politics. That is, the premise behind much "women of color" organizing is that women from communities victimized by white supremacy should unite together around their shared oppression. This framework might be represented by a diagram of five overlapping circles, each marked Native women, Black women, Arab/Muslim women, Latinas, and Asian American women, overlapping like a Venn diagram.

This framework has proven to be limited for women of color and people of color organizing. First, it tends to presume that our communities have been impacted by white supremacy in the same way. Consequently, we often assume that all of our communities will share similar strategies for liberation. In fact, however, our strategies often run into conflict. For example, one strategy that many people in US-born communities of color adopt, in order to advance economically out of impoverished communities, is to join the military. We then become complicit in oppressing and colonizing communities from other countries. Meanwhile, people from other countries often adopt the strategy of moving to the United States to advance economically, without considering their complicity in settling on the lands of indigenous peoples that are being colonized by the United States.

Consequently, it may be more helpful to adopt an alternative framework for women of color and people of color organizing. I call one such framework the "Three Pillars of White Supremacy." This framework does not assume that racism and white supremacy is enacted in a singular fashion; rather, white supremacy is constituted by separate and distinct, but still interrelated, logics. Envision three pillars, one labeled Slavery/Capitalism, another labeled Genocide/Colonialism, and the last one labeled Orientalism/War, as well as arrows connecting each of the pillars together.

Slavery/Capitalism

One pillar of white supremacy is the logic of slavery. As Sora Han, Jared Sexton, and Angela P. Harris note, this logic renders Black people as inherently slaveable – as nothing more than property.[1] That is, in this logic of white supremacy, Blackness becomes equated with slaveability. The forms of slavery may change – whether it is through the formal system of slavery, sharecropping, or through the current prison-industrial complex – but the logic itself has remained consistent.

This logic is the anchor of capitalism. That is, the capitalist system ultimately commodifies all workers – one's own person becomes a commodity that one must sell in the labor market while the profits of one's work are taken by someone else. To keep this capitalist system in place – which ultimately commodifies most people – the logic of slavery applies a racial hierarchy to this system. This racial hierarchy tells people that as long as you are not Black, you have the opportunity to escape the commodification of capitalism. This helps people who are not Black to accept their lot in life, because they can feel that at least they are not at the very bottom of the racial hierarchy – at least they are not property; at least they are not slaveable.

The logic of slavery can be seen clearly in the current prison industrial complex (PIC). While the PIC generally incarcerates communities of color, it seems to be structured primarily on an anti-Black racism. That is, prior to the Civil War, most people in prison where white. However, after the thirteenth amendment was passed – which banned slavery, except for those in prison – Black people previously enslaved through the slavery system were reenslaved through the prison system. Black people who had been the property of slave owners became state property, through the convict leasing system. Thus, we can actually look at the criminalization of Blackness as a logical extension of Blackness as property.

Genocide/Colonialism

A second pillar of white supremacy is the logic of genocide. This logic holds that indigenous peoples must disappear. In fact, they must *always* be disappearing, in order to allow non-indigenous peoples rightful claim over this land. Through this logic of genocide, non-Native peoples then become the rightful inheritors of all that was indigenous – land, resources, indigenous spirituality, or culture. As Kate Shanley notes, Native peoples are a permanent "present absence" in the US colonial imagination, an "absence" that reinforces, at every turn, the conviction that Native peoples are indeed vanishing and that the conquest of Native lands is justified. Ella Shohat and Robert Stam describe this absence as "an ambivalently repressive mechanism [which] dispels the anxiety in the face of the Indian, whose very presence is a reminder of the initially precarious grounding of the American nation-state itself. ... In a temporal paradox, living Indians were induced to 'play dead,' as it were, in order to perform a narrative of manifest destiny in which their role, ultimately, was to disappear."[2]

Rayna Green further elaborates that the current Indian "wannabe" phenomenon is based on a logic of genocide: non-Native peoples imagine themselves as the rightful inheritors of all that previously belonged to "vanished" Indians, thus entitling them to ownership of this land. "The living performance of 'playing Indian' by non-Indian peoples depends upon the physical and psychological removal, even the death, of real Indians. In that sense, the performance, purportedly often done out of a stated and implicit love for Indians, is really the obverse of another well-known cultural phenomenon, 'Indian hating,' as most often expressed in another, deadly performance genre called 'genocide.'"[3] After all, why would non-Native peoples need to play Indian – which often includes acts of spiritual appropriation and land theft – if they thought Indians were still alive and perfectly capable of being Indian themselves? The pillar of genocide serves as the anchor for colonialism – it is what allows non-Native peoples to feel they can rightfully own indigenous peoples' land. It is okay to take land from indigenous peoples, because indigenous peoples have disappeared.

Orientalism/War

A third pillar of white supremacy is the logic of Orientalism. Orientalism was defined by Edward Said as the process of the West defining itself as a superior civilization by constructing itself in opposition to an "exotic" but inferior "Orient." (Here I am using the term "Orientalism" more broadly than to solely signify what has been historically named as the Orient or Asia.) The logic of Orientalism marks certain peoples or nations as inferior and as posing a constant threat to the well-being of empire. These peoples are still seen as "civilizations" – they are not property or "disappeared" – however, they will always be imaged as permanent foreign threats to empire. This logic is evident in the anti-immigration movements within the United States that target immigrants of color. It does not matter how long immigrants of color reside in the United States, they generally become targeted as foreign threats, particularly during war time. Consequently, orientalism serves as the anchor for war, because it allows the United States to justify being in a constant state of war to protect itself from its enemies.

For example, the United States feels entitled to use Orientalist logic to justify racial profiling of Arab Americans so that it can be strong enough to fight the "war on terror." Orientalism also allows the United States to defend the logics of slavery and genocide, as these practices enable the United States to stay "strong enough" to fight these constant wars. What becomes clear then is what Sora Han states – the United States is not at war; the United States *is* war.[4] For the system of white supremacy to stay in place, the United States must always be at war.

Because we are situated within different logics of white supremacy, we may misunderstand a racial dynamic if we simplistically try to explain one logic of white supremacy with another logic. For instance, think about the first scenario that opens this essay: if we simply dismiss Latino/as or Arab peoples as "white," we fail to understand how a racial logic of Orientalism is in operation. That is, Latino/as and Arabs are often situated in a racial hierarchy that privileges them over Black people. However, while Orientalist logic may bestow them some racial privilege, they are still cast as inferior yet threatening "civilizations" in the United States. Their privilege is not a signal that they will be assimilated, but that they will be marked as perpetual foreign threats to the US world order.

Organizing Implications

Under the old but still potent and dominant model, people of color organizing was based on the notion of organizing around shared victimhood. In this model, however, we see that we are victims of white supremacy, but complicit in it as well. Our survival strategies and resistance to white supremacy are set by the system of white supremacy itself. What keeps us trapped within our particular pillars of white supremacy is that we are seduced with the prospect of being able to participate in the other pillars. For example, all non-Native peoples are promised the ability to join in the colonial project of settling indigenous lands. All non-Black peoples are promised that if they comply, they will not be at the bottom of the racial hierarchy. And Black, Native, Latino, and Asian peoples are promised that they will economically and politically advance if they join US wars to spread "democracy." Thus, people of color organizing must be premised on making strategic alliances with each other, based on where we are situated within the larger political economy. Thus, for example, Native peoples who are organizing against the colonial and genocidal practices committed by the US government will be more effective in their struggle if they also organize against US militarism, particularly the military recruitment of indigenous peoples to support US imperial wars. If we try to end US colonial practices at home, but support US empire by joining the military, we are strengthening the state's ability to carry out genocidal policies against people of color here and all over the world.

This way, our alliances would not be solely based on shared victimization, but where we are complicit in the victimization of others. These approaches might help us to develop resistance strategies that do not inadvertently keep the system in place for all of us, and keep all of us accountable. In all of these cases, we would check our aspirations against the aspirations of other communities to ensure that our model of liberation does not become the model of oppression for others.

These practices require us to be more vigilant in how we may have internalized some of these logics in our own organizing practice. For instance, much racial justice organizing within the United States has rested on a civil rights framework that fights for equality under the law. An assumption behind this organizing is that the United States is a democracy with some flaws, but is otherwise admirable. Despite the fact that it rendered slaves three-fifths of a person, the US Constitution is presented as the model document from which to build a flourishing democracy. However, as Luana Ross notes, it has never been against US law to commit genocide against indigenous peoples – in fact, genocide *is* the law of the country. The United States could not exist without it. In the United States, democracy is actually the alibi for genocide – it is the practice that covers up United States colonial control over indigenous lands.

Our organizing can also reflect anti-Black racism. Recently, with the outgrowth of "multiculturalism" there have been calls to "go beyond the black/white binary" and include other communities of color in our analysis, as presented in the third scenario. There are a number of flaws with this analysis. First, it replaces an analysis of white supremacy with a politics of multicultural representation; if we just *include* more people, then our practice will be less racist. Not true. This model does not address the nuanced structure of white supremacy, such as through these distinct logics of slavery, genocide, and Orientalism. Second, it obscures the centrality of the slavery logic in the system of white supremacy, which is *based on a black/white binary*. The black/white binary is not the *only* binary which characterizes white supremacy, but it is still a central one that we cannot "go beyond" in our racial justice organizing efforts.

If we do not look at how the logic of slaveability inflects our society and our thinking, it will be evident in our work as well. For example, other communities of color often appropriate the cultural work and organizing strategies of African American civil rights or Black Power movements without corresponding assumptions that we should also be in solidarity with Black communities. We assume that this work is the common "property" of all oppressed groups, and we can appropriate it without being accountable.

Angela P. Harris and Juan Perea debate the usefulness of the black/white binary in the book *Critical Race Theory*. Perea complains that the black/white binary fails to *include* the experiences of other people of color. However, he fails to identify alternative racializing logics to the black/white paradigm.[5] Meanwhile, Angela P. Harris argues that "the story of 'race' itself is that of the construction of Blackness and whiteness. In this story, Indians, Asian Americans, and Latinos/as do exist. But their roles are subsidiary to the fundamental binary national drama. As a political claim, Black exceptionalism exposes the deep mistrust and tensions among American ethnic groups racialized as nonwhite."[6]

Let's examine these statements in conversation with each other. Simply saying we need to move beyond the black/white binary (or perhaps, the "black/non-black" binary) in US racism obfuscates the racializing logic of slavery, and prevents us from seeing that this binary constitutes Blackness as the bottom of a color hierarchy. However, this is not the *only* binary that fundamentally constitutes white supremacy. There is also an indigenous/settler binary, where Native genocide is central to the logic of white supremacy and other non-indigenous people of color also form "a subsidiary" role. We also face another Orientalist logic that fundamentally constitutes Asians, Arabs, and Latino/as as foreign threats, requiring the United States to be at permanent war with these peoples. In this construction, Black and Native peoples play subsidiary roles.

Clearly the black/white binary is central to racial and political thought and practice in the United States, and any understanding of white supremacy must take it into consideration. However, if we look at only this binary, we may misread the dynamics of white supremacy in different contexts. For example, critical race theorist Cheryl Harris's analysis of whiteness as property reveals this weakness. In *Critical Race Theory*, Harris contends that whites have a property interest in the preservation of whiteness, and seek to deprive those who are "tainted" by Black or Indian blood from these same white property interests. Harris simply assumes that the positions of African Americans and American Indians are the same, failing to consider US policies of forced assimilation and forced whiteness on American Indians. These policies have become so entrenched that when Native peoples make political claims, they have been accused of being white. When Andrew Jackson removed the Cherokee along the Trail of Tears, he argued that those who did not want removal were really white.[7] In contemporary times, when I was a non-violent witness for the Chippewa spearfishers in the late 1980s, one of the more frequent slurs whites hurled when the Chippewa attempted to exercise their treaty-protected right to fish was that they had white parents, or they were really white.

Status differences between Blacks and Natives are informed by the different economic positions African Americans and American Indians have in US society. African Americans have been traditionally valued for their labor, hence it is in the interest of the dominant society to have as many people marked "Black" as possible, thereby maintaining a cheap labor pool; by contrast, American Indians have been valued for the land base they occupy, so it is in the interest of dominant society to have as few people marked "Indian" as possible, facilitating access to Native lands. "Whiteness" operates differently under a logic of genocide than it does from a logic of slavery.

Another failure of US-based people of color in organizing is that we often fall back on a "US-centricism," believing that what is happening "over there" is less important than what is happening here. We fail to see how the United States maintains the system of oppression here precisely by tying our allegiances to the interests of US empire "over there."

Heteropatriarchy and White Supremacy

Heteropatriarchy is the building block of US empire. In fact, it is the building block of the nation-state form of governance. Christian Right authors make these links in their analysis of imperialism and empire. For example, Christian Right activist and founder of Prison Fellowship Charles Colson makes the connection between homosexuality and the nation-state in his analysis of the war on terror, explaining that one of the causes of terrorism is same-sex marriage:

> Marriage is the traditional building block of human society, intended both to unite couples and bring children into the world ... There is a natural moral order for the family ... the family, led by a married mother and father, is the best available structure for both child-rearing and cultural health. Marriage is not a private institution designed solely for the individual gratification of its participants. If we fail to enact a Federal Marriage Amendment, we can expect not just more family breakdown, but also more criminals behind bars and more chaos in our streets.[8]

Colson is linking the well-being of US empire to the well-being of the heteropatriarchal family. He continues:

> When radical Islamists see American women abusing Muslim men, as they did in the Abu Ghraib prison, and when they see news coverage of same-sex couples being "married" in US towns, we make this kind of freedom abhorrent – the kind they see as a blot on Allah's creation. We must preserve traditional marriage in order to protect the United States from those who would use our depravity to destroy us.[9]

As Ann Burlein argues in *Lift High the Cross*, it may be a mistake to argue that the goal of Christian Right politics is to create a theocracy in the United States. Rather, Christian Right politics work through the private family (which is coded as white, patriarchal, and middle class) to create a "Christian America." She notes that the investment in the private family makes it difficult for people to invest in more public forms of social connection. In addition, investment in the suburban private family serves to mask the public disinvestment in urban areas that makes the suburban lifestyle possible. The social decay in urban areas that results from this disinvestment is then construed as the result of deviance from the Christian family ideal rather than as the result of political and economic forces. As former head of the Christian Coalition, Ralph Reed, states: "The only true solution to crime is to restore the family,"[10] and

"Family break-up causes poverty."[11] Concludes Burlein, "'The family' is no mere metaphor but a crucial technology by which modern power is produced and exercised."[12]

As I have argued elsewhere, in order to colonize peoples whose societies are not based on social hierarchy, colonizers must first naturalize hierarchy through instituting patriarchy.[13] In turn, patriarchy rests on a gender binary system in which only two genders exist, one dominating the other. Consequently, Charles Colson *is* correct when he says that the colonial world order depends on heteronormativity. Just as the patriarchs rule the family, the elites of the nation-state rule their citizens. Any liberation struggle that does not challenge heteronormativity cannot substantially challenge colonialism or white supremacy. Rather, as Cathy Cohen contends, such struggles will maintain colonialism based on a politics of secondary marginalization where the most elite class of these groups will further their aspirations on the backs of those most marginalized within the community.[14]

Through this process of secondary marginalization, the national or racial justice struggle takes on either implicitly or explicitly a nation-state model as the end point of its struggle – a model of governance in which the elites govern the rest through violence and domination, as well as exclude those who are not members of "the nation." Thus, national liberation politics become less vulnerable to being coopted by the Right when we base them on a model of liberation that fundamentally challenges right-wing conceptions of the nation. We need a model based on community relationships and on mutual respect.

Conclusion

Women of color-centered organizing points to the centrality of gender politics within antiracist, anticolonial struggles. Unfortunately, in our efforts to organize against white, Christian America, racial justice struggles often articulate an equally heteropatriarchal racial nationalism. This model of organizing either hopes to assimilate into white America, or to replicate it within an equally hierarchical and oppressive racial nationalism in which the elites of the community rule everyone else. Such struggles often call on the importance of preserving the "Black family" or the "Native family" as the bulwark of this nationalist project, the family being conceived of in capitalist and heteropatriarchal terms. The response is often increased homophobia, with lesbian and gay community members construed as "threats" to the family. But, perhaps we should challenge the "concept" of the family itself. Perhaps, instead, we can reconstitute alternative ways of living together in which "families" are not seen as islands on their own. Certainly, indigenous communities were not ordered on the basis of a nuclear family structure – it is the result of colonialism, not the antidote to it.

In proposing this model, I am speaking from my particular position in indigenous struggles. Other peoples might flesh out these logics more fully from different vantage points. Others might also argue that other logics of white supremacy are missing. Still others might complicate how they relate to each other. But I see this as a starting point for women of color organizers that will allow us to reenvision a politics of solidarity that goes beyond multiculturalism, and develop more complicated strategies that can really transform the political and economic status quo.

Notes

1. Angela P. Harris, "Embracing the Tar-Baby: LatCrit Theory and the Sticky Mess of Race," in *Critical Race Theory*, eds. Richard Delgado and Jean Stefancic, 2nd ed. (Philadelphia: Temple University Press, 2000), 440–7. I also thank Sora Han and Jared Sexton for their illuminating analysis of Blackness.
2. Ella Shohat and Robert Stam, *Unthinking Eurocentrism* (London: Routledge, 1994), 118–119.
3. Rayna Green, "The Tribe Called Wannabee," *Folklore* 99, no. 1 (1988): 30–55.
4. Sora Han, *Bonds of Representation: Vision, Race and Law in Post-Civil Rights America* (Santa Cruz: University of California-Santa Cruz, 2006).
5. Juan Perea, "The Black/White Binary Paradigm of Race," in *Critical Race Theory*, Delgado and Stefancic, 2nd ed.
6. Angela P. Harris, "Embracing the Tar-Baby."
7. William McLoughlin, *Cherokees and Missionaries, 1789–1839* (Norman, OK: University of Oklahoma Press, 1995).
8. Charles Colson, "Societal Suicide," *Christianity Today* 48, no. 6 (June 2004): 72.
9. Charles Colson and Anne Morse, "The Moral Home Front," *Christianity Today* 48, no. 10 (October 2004): 152.
10. Ralph Reed, *After the Revolution* (Dallas: Word, 1990).
11. Ibid.
12. Ann Burlein, *Lift High the Cross* (Raleigh, NC: Duke University Press, 2002).
13. Andrea Smith, *Conquest: Sexual Violence and American Indian Genocide* (Cambridge, MA: South End Press, 2005).
14. Cathy Cohen, *The Boundaries of Blackness* (Chicago: University of Chicago Press, 1999).

9

Healing and Spirituality

By Irene Lara

Contents

Original publication details: 9.1 Helena María Viramontes, "The Moths" from *The Moths and Other Stories*, 2nd ed., pp. 27–34. Houston: Arte Público Press, 1995. Reproduced with permission of Arte Público Press. 9.2 Ama R. Saran, "My Guardian Spirits" from *Wings of Gauze: Women of Color and the Experience of Health and Illness*, ed. Barbara Bair and Susan E. Cayleff, pp. 23–25. Detroit: Wayne State University Press, 1993. Reproduced with permission of Wayne State University Press. 9.3 E. M. Broner, "Honor and Ceremony in Women's Rituals" from *The Politics of Women's Spirituality: Essays by Founding Mothers of the Movement*, ed. Charlene Spretnak, pp. 234–44. Reproduced with permission of Random House LLC and Frances Goldin Literary Agency, 1982. 9.4 Alifa Rifaat, "My World of the Unknown" from *Distant View of a Minaret and Other Stories*, trans. Denys Johnson-Davies, pp. 61–76. London: Quartet Books, 1983. 9.5 Inés Maria Talamantez, "Seeing Red: American Indian Women Speaking about Their Religious and Political Perspectives" from *In Our Own Voices: Four Centuries of American Women's Religious Writing*, ed. Rosemary Skinner Keller and Rosemary Radford Ruether, pp. 398–401, 406–409. San Francisco: Harper San Francisco, 1995. Reproduced with permission of Rosemary Radford Ruether. 9.6 Terry Tempest Williams, "The Clan of One-Breasted Women" from *Refuge: An Unnatural History of Family and Place*, pp. 281–90. New York: Vintage, 1992. © 1991 by Terry Tempest Williams. Reproduced with permission of Pantheon Books, an imprint of the Knopf Doubleday Publishing Group, a division of Random House LLC. *(continued on page 414)*

Women in Culture: An Intersectional Anthology for Gender and Women's Studies, Second Edition.
Edited by Bonnie Kime Scott, Susan E. Cayleff, Anne Donadey, and Irene Lara.
© 2017 John Wiley & Sons, Ltd. Published 2017 by John Wiley & Sons, Ltd.

Women's Studies has long been at the forefront of examining spirituality and healing through a critical and creative feminist lens. While "spirituality" refers to "the quality or state of being concerned with religion or religious matters," it more broadly implies "the quality or state of being spiritual," that is, relating to spirit, a vital, animating force (*Merriam-Webster*), within and beyond one's self. As conceptualized by Chicana Religious Studies scholar Lara Medina, spirituality is about the many ways people cultivate balanced relationships "with self, with others, with nature, with the universe, with the ancestors, and with the sacred source and great mystery of life and death" and includes acting on the awareness "of one's interdependence or connectedness to all that can be seen and that is unseen" (167). So while one's spiritual and religious identities may certainly go hand in hand, many contemporary writers make a distinction between the two. They associate the latter with canonical texts, fixed tenets, and hierarchical institutions and the former with a more personal, everyday relationship to "God," "Mother Earth, Hutash" (as Chumash activist Pilulaw Khus describes in this chapter), or other names for who or what they consider to have spirit and thus be sacred or divine, including humans, other elements of nature – such as revered homelands – and what Egyptian writer Alifa Rifaat expresses in her short story here as "unseen powers in the universe."

Many feminists recognize that spirituality can be oppressive and can also promote liberation. Indeed, several authors critique the ways that heteropatriarchy, imperialism, and nationalism are oftentimes reflected in dominant manifestations of the world's religions, which participate in the division of people into superior and inferior social groups and "true" believers from pagans or infidels, as well as the division of people from "God" and earth from heaven – ideologies that have been used to maintain systems of inequality. For example, in Khus's account of the colonial missionization process in California, she documents how native people were not allowed to leave the Santa Barbara Mission and were made into enslaved workers or killed. Such legacies of religiously sanctioned oppression persist and continue to be resisted by many indigenous peoples and members of religious minorities globally.

Feminists have responded to the patriarchal biases of most organized religions in a variety of ways, from revisions of religious beliefs and practices, such as E. M.

Original publication details: 9.7 Lori Arviso Alvord and Elizabeth Cohen Van Pelt, "Life out of Balance" from *The Scalpel and the Silver Bear*. pp. 59–61, 65–76. New York: Bantam, 1999. Reproduced with permission of William Morris Endeavour Entertainment and Bantam Books, an imprint of Random House, a division of Random House LLC.

Broner's in this chapter, to rejection of organized religions in favor of other spiritual practices. Jewish, Christian, and Muslim (or Islamic) feminists have all proposed reformulations of their religions, often based on arguing that a male hermeneutic tradition (tradition of interpretation) of Scriptures has ignored the more egalitarian aspects of the religion. US-based Egyptian feminist scholar Leila Ahmed demonstrates that there are at least two Islams, one textual, hierarchical, and legalistic (that of male clerics) and one ethical, egalitarian, and based on the oral tradition (an Islam of women, other marginalized groups, and more spiritual branches of Islam such as Sufism) (238–39). Moroccan feminist sociologist Fatima Mernissi pushed the reformulation of Islam even further in her memoir *Dreams of Trespass*, extending an egalitarian stance based on Islam not only to all humans, but to animals as well (35). Rifaat's story "My World of the Unknown" (1974/1983) is part of this Islamic feminist tradition. In her article on Rifaat's story, Diya Abdo explains that the short story provides a radical Islamic feminist reinterpretation in which women are seen as participating in the divine principle and female-to-female sexual relations provide both "sexual and spiritual fulfillment" (401).

Christian feminists have also reinterpreted Biblical texts in more egalitarian ways than most organized churches have. Influenced by Latin American Liberation Theology (a mixture of Catholicism and Marxism that advocates for economic justice for the poor and structural redistribution of resources), UK-based Argentinian Catholic feminist Marcella Althaus-Reid, for example, calls for Catholic ethics to be fully inclusive of expressions of queer and female sexuality, including those of poor and indigenous women. Euro-American Catholic feminist theologian Rosemary Radford Ruether's reformulations of religion include the need to heal the entire earth in a broad ecofeminist spiritual vision for justice. Several recent contributions in the field attest to ongoing engagement with such concerns, including: womanist theological perspectives largely grounded in African American cultural traditions (Floyd-Thomas), Chicana feminist perspectives that recuperate Mesoamerican indigenous worldviews and re-envision the Virgin of Guadalupe, a mestiza Marian figure, and other feminine indigenous deities or revered forces (Anzaldúa; Castillo), Native feminist theology (Smith), Asian American feminist theology (Kim), and more.

Focusing on the ways spirituality can forward social and ecological justice and foster liberation and harmony is another rich area of scholarship (e.g. Anzaldúa; Facio and Lara; Hull; Maparyan; Spretnak). As suggested by Mescalero Apache medicine woman Meredith Begay in her 1994 interview with Native American Religions scholar Inés Talamantez (Mescalero Apache and Chicana) excerpted here, being genuinely spiritual and an effective healer entails understanding "the intricacies of equalness between earth, plant, trees, rock, clouds" and humans, and acting accordingly. Similarly, Women's Studies scholarship highlights the ways holistic healing practices promote empowerment and socially equitable wellbeing in harmony with nature (echoed in Chapter 7's reproductive and environmental justice readings). It is critically aware that healing, "the process of making or becoming sound or healthy again" (*Oxford Dictionary*), is often solely associated with Western biomedical approaches that tend to focus on curing physical illness. In contrast to concentrating on the end result of whether or not one is cured, many scholars and healers offer an analysis of healing as a process of transformation that attends to the wellbeing of the whole person as a body, mind, *and* spirit situated within social, environmental, and cosmic contexts mediated by power relations. Moreover, they extend the need for healing to the non-human yet living world, such as the earth, as well as to oppressive beliefs, worldviews, behaviors, policies, and institutions that wound and create illness or "dis-ease" in personal, social, or environmental ways. Taking an intersectional approach, Women's Studies scholars ask: Who or what needs healing and why? Who or what gets in the way of healing? What does taking a spiritual approach to healing teach us?

As suggested by the authors in this chapter, a critical spiritual and healing inquiry includes examining the meaning of life and death, wellness and illness, and humans' relationships to our complex, fluid, yet "whole" selves, each other, and the social, global, natural, and spiritual cosmic worlds. Drawing on various cultural knowledges and informed by specific histories and relationships to land, these readings present female-centered visions of spirit and spirituality in relation to health and healing. They question the imposition of patriarchal, Judeo-Christian, Islamic, and/or Western biomedical and corporate dominant perspectives that are not inclusive, holistic, or just. Presupposing that all livingkind is connected and has "spirit," an invisible life force, they are recovering and (re)creating spiritual and healing practices that forward positive personal, social, and environmental change.

Ceremonies and Rituals from Women's Perspectives

Several writings touch on the significance of ceremony within women's spiritual and healing practices. Writing from a community of feminist ritualists and scholars of religion that emerged as part of the US women's movement in the 1970s (i.e., Spretnak, Christ and Plaskow), Jewish American writer E. M. Broner, for example, discusses the importance of recuperating pre-patriarchal ceremonies and the historical role of women as healers and ceremonial leaders. The restoration of these empowered women's histories goes hand in hand with remembering that before the global advent of dominant manifestations of the Abrahamic traditions – Judaism, Christianity, and Islam – in which God is represented as male, many cultures gendered God or other powerful spiritual elements of nature as feminine, dual-gendered, transgender, or non-gendered. Indeed, such belief systems persist, as depicted in Rifaat's short story featuring a feminine Djinn, a sacred spirit that can take the shape of a serpent, and in the documentation of Native American and Mesoamerican cosmologies by many scholars (e.g., Anzaldúa; Castillo; Facio and Lara; and Gunn Allen; Pérez and Smith).

In "Honor and Ceremony in Women's Rituals," Broner defines ritual as "a collective experience, repeated and sanctified" that people perform "to remind ourselves and one another that we are not alone … [that] what has happened to us is not an isolated instance." Showing how one can simultaneously maintain one's identity as a Jewish woman and creatively transgress oppressive manifestations of institutionalized Judaism, Broner shares the many corrective ceremonies in which she has participated that center women's experiences and roles, such as home birth, male circumcision, weddings, Chanukah, and the Jewish New Year. She also describes re-scripting Woman's Passover as a ceremony that addresses the exodus of women (not just men) and the value of teaching this history to one's daughters (not just sons), and reincorporates women as prophets, mothers, and ceremonial leaders. As significantly, through rewriting ritual verses, this Woman's Passover encourages critical thinking by, for example, naming "ignorance as the worst plague of all," and claiming "The one who knows not how to question, / she has no past, / she can have no present, / she can have no future / without knowing her mother, / without knowing her angers, / without knowing her questions."

Whatever one's religious or spiritual identity, ritual is a way to perform, perpetuate, and (re)create cultural and spiritual authority, as well as enact personal and collective power, healing, and transformation. Thus, all ritual is political. Women's Studies scholars ask: Who created, revised, or enacted the ceremony? For what ends? What cultural histories and ideologies undergird it? Who should or should not participate in or lead it and who decides? This question is particularly salient for Khus, who raises critical awareness about the historical appropriation of Native traditions by some whites who feel entitled to participate. Moreover, resonating with Audre Lorde's engagement with the spiritual power of the erotic discussed in Chapter 5, we ask: how does one experience power, healing, and transformation through the rituals of everyday embodied life? At least three other examples of the power of ceremony and ritual are addressed in the chapter: a collective protest performance as described by Terry Tempest Williams, Chumash ceremonies related to introducing newborn children to their community and protecting indigenous sacred places referred to by Khus, and bathing the dead in sacred water in Chicana feminist Helena María Viramontes's 1985 short story "The Moths."

Illness, Healing, and Building Community

Working from holistic, indigenous perspectives that consider how physical, emotional, spiritual, and environmental factors interweave to create health, several authors engage illness as a state of being out of balance, internally and in relationship to the social and natural world. Navajo (self-named Diné) neurosurgeon Lori Arviso Alvord analyzes "Life out of Balance" (1999) as a doctor for Indian Health Services and for her Native patients. She reflects on the ways her assimilation of the white world and Western medical training that excluded such holistic approaches has affected her life and therefore the lives of her patients. Moreover, she situates such lack of balance within the broader historical context of settler colonialism to which much illness can be traced: "… it often occurred to me that much of what we were treating were white men's diseases – syndromes and conditions the people would never have known if not for the European colonizers." Alvord recognizes that such diseases include those "caused by lifestyle changes, such as poor diet and inactivity – an indirect result of the influence of acculturation."

Adapting indigenous knowledge about this array of potential causes of illness or factors that worsen illness and can lead to death can lead one to practice preventive medicine as a patient and a healer. In the case of Alvord, she relearns from her Diné culture to be responsible for the energy that she brings to the operating room and all of her interactions with patients and fellow staff. In this context, feelings, thoughts, and words also have spirit and can have negative, as well as positive, effects. Tragically, for one of Alvord's patients, the lack of reassuring words and words uttered in anger and frustration during her operation itself may have contributed to her post-surgery stroke, which was physiologically inexplicable otherwise. Finding a way to integrate Diné philosophy with her Western medical training to "work *with* patients" instead of *on* patients, Alvord aims "to create a superior system of healing" that values good communication and elicits trust. Within a traditional Apache system of healing, Meredith Begay speaks more directly to being "an instrument for the Supreme Being" and the importance of practicing medicine "with dignity, with faith," in her interview excerpted here.

African American writer Ama R. Saran (1993) also explores the connection between healing, living in balance, and building relationships. Through a missive to her earthly "Guardian Spirits" on the dawn of her scheduled surgery, Saran takes healing into her own hands by teaching her "Beloved Sister-Friends and Brother-Friends" how to participate in her path to wellness. Aware of the joy and efficacy of healing in community and acknowledging she cannot "achieve this alone nor … intend[s] to," she calls on her friends to step up as co-healers. For example, she distinguishes between "spiritual sustenance" and "religious relics," directing her guardians to "Gift me with simple prayers, light candles, [and] hold my hand." From what can be interpreted as a womanist standpoint (as discussed in Chapter 1), Saran unabashedly outlines a total of 16 needs and reminders that attend to her body, mind, and spirit as a whole.

Euro-American writer Terry Tempest Williams also builds spiritually grounded community to forward healing. She specifically creates solidarity with other children of her generation born in Utah in the 1950s whose family members are also part of "The Clan of One-Breasted Women" (1991/1992). Situating herself among the genealogy of her mother, grandmothers, and aunts who have been afflicted with breast cancer, Williams critically reflects on the human-made sources of cancer and is compelled to take social action that raises public awareness of the lingering damage of nuclear atomic testing and holds the government accountable. In her narrative, she juxtaposes what she learned through her Mormon culture, namely to respect authority without question, with her spiritual inquiry into the reasons for such a high incidence of cancer in the lives of her family and neighbors living downwind from the Nevada atomic bomb test site. Williams is driven to independent critical thinking, research, and creating community with like-minded activists by the increasing awareness of illness and death experienced by those living in the region where rampant nuclear testing was justified by the fear of communism and its damaging effects denied or downplayed by the US government. Empowered by collective spiritual vision and drawing on Shoshone native teachings valuing all of life, she documents her act of civil disobedience trespassing into a military test site. She reconfigures both her patriarchal Mormon and national identities to make room for hard questions and to challenge injustice, for "tolerating blind obedience in the name of patriotism or religion ultimately takes our lives." Like Khus, Williams shows us how many women embody their spirituality by participating in political activism.

Death, Dying, and Rebirth

Both the granddaughter protagonist in Viramontes's "The Moths" and Williams in "The Clan of One-Breasted Women" bear witness to death, and in that witnessing become "midwi[ves] to the rebirth of … souls" (Williams). Alongside the realities of pain, suffering, sadness, grief, and injustice lay the realities of hope, love, connection, awareness, knowledge, and justice. These are all spiritual themes. Viramontes offers us the story of an unnamed fourteen-year-old granddaughter and her Abuelita, the healer or curandera in her family knowledgeable about the medicinal effects of plants, touch, and unconditional love. Although the adolescent is not a typical feminine girl, she is chosen to be her Abuelita's midwife delivering her to death. In the midst of violence at home and "unanswered prayers" at church, Abuelita, also called Mama Luna, is her refuge, making her feel "safe and guarded and not alone."

Compellingly, the author chooses moths to represent the spirit that vacates Abuelita's body upon death. In not choosing the moth's more colorful butterfly cousins, the more ubiquitous metaphor of transformation, the author does not romanticize Abuelita's cancerous death. Indeed, there is no public reckoning of the possible human causes of Abuelita's cancer, as in William's narrative, or of the seeming lack of access to health care in "The Moths," but there is healing nonetheless. Exhibiting spiritual and physical strength beyond her years, the adolescent granddaughter provides her beloved Mama Luna a dignified death. Within an indigenous worldview that recognizes the necessary duality of life and death, without judging one as necessarily good and the other bad, the symbolic moths lead readers to consider that as Abuelita dies, something is (re)born in her granddaughter as she becomes a healer of her own.

Healers, Healing, and a Decolonial Feminist Spiritual Imaginary

Highlighting close intergenerational relationships as a source of learning and teaching familial spirituality, "The Moths" describes several healing lessons. We learn about the placing of potato slices on feverish foreheads to quell high temperatures and massages with balm made of dried moth wings and Vicks or with alcohol and marijuana, folk remedies ubiquitous in many Indigenous, Latin American, and US Latino households, as well as part of herbal medicinal lore globally. Mama Luna, which means Mother Moon, represents the unconditionally loving feminine divine for the granddaughter who finds church to be a cold and lonely place. In contrast to "the frozen statues with blank eyes" the granddaughter finds at the neighborhood chapel, Mama Luna, with her one gray eye and other brown eye, is a living spirit. Following in the spiritual traditions of many cultures that treat nature with reverence and associate humans with the vast elements, the author imbues the grandmother moon with healing power. In locating the divine in humans and in the natural world, and specifically in Mexican-American females and a feminized moon, rather than apart or distinct from them, the author provides a decolonial feminist spiritual imaginary. Taken up by many writers, this anti-racist imaginary consists of images and stories from the perspectives of indigenous and other people of color's approaches to the divine that do not privilege a male God, male spiritual leadership, or a Eurocentric definition of the sacred. For example, Diya Abdo makes a parallel between Rifaat's and Chicana feminist Gloria Anzaldúa's use of the serpent as a female figure that comes from indigenous religious traditions and is positively connected to sexuality and spirituality, healing the body/spirit split.

As suggested by Aurora Levins Morales in Chapter 3, there are many ways to work toward healing oppressive omissions, distortions, and errors in the making of history and other forms of knowledge production. Embodying a decolonial feminist spirituality, she promotes the idea of adapting the positionality of a curandera, a holistic healer, as a way for researchers to develop their methodological skills and commitment to doing work that heals, such as telling "'medicinal' histories [that] seek to re-establish the connections between people and their histories," including those of spirituality and healing. Indeed, others also link the idea of healer to critical, creative, and activist activities that heal, such as Laura E. Pérez's work on Chicana artists as healers (2007) and my own work on Latina health activist-healers (Lara 2008). As several others forward throughout this collection, stories and the process of storytelling and listening can be healing in and of themselves for the critical consciousness they raise (e.g., Wako and Page in Chapter 7). Thus, in addition to acknowledging the legacy of women as recognized healers who specifically tend to restoring wellness cross-culturally, the authors in this chapter can also be considered healers for the ways they are bringing healing knowledge and creativity to the fore.

Discussion Questions

1. What do dance, song, writing, and other forms of creativity have to do with spirituality and healing? Discuss at least two examples from the chapter.
2. How does E. M. Broner transform patriarchal ritual traditions to include or center women's experiences? Why is it socially and politically important to do so?
3. Reflecting on the different types of feminism discussed in Chapter 1 and the readings in this chapter, if you were to create a feminist ritual, what would you do and why? Alternatively, think about a ritual in which you have participated and discuss how one could integrate feminist elements.
4. What metaphors of pregnancy, birth, and motherhood does Terry Tempest Williams use in her essay? Why do you think she foregrounds the protestors' identities as mothers and what are the advantages and limits of doing so?
5. In what ways do Mama Luna, Amá, and the granddaughter in "The Moths" internalize and/or challenge patriarchal and Christian approaches to spirituality and healing?
6. How are death, dying, and the duality of life and death represented in the chapter? How are these spiritual and healing themes? Discuss at least two examples.
7. How has Pilulaw Khus lived spirituality and healing given her "assignment … to protect the sacred places and to do the ceremonies" as a Chumash woman?
8. What role do intergenerational storytelling and modeling play in passing on spiritual and healing knowledge? Analyze at least two examples from the chapter.

9. In what ways are the relationships with family, friends, nature, and community that are discussed throughout the chapter sources of healing and spiritual knowledge? Analyze at least two examples from the chapter.

10. What connections does Alifa Rifaat draw between female-to-female sexual love and spirituality?

References

Abdo, Diya M. "My Qarina, My Self: The Homoerotic as Islamic Feminism in Alifa Rifaat's 'My World of the Unknown.'" *Journal of Lesbian Studies* 16.4 (2012): 398–415.

Ahmed, Leila. *Women and Gender in Islam: Historical Roots of a Modern Debate*. New Haven: Yale University Press, 1992.

Althaus-Reid, Marcella. *Indecent Theology: Theological Perversions in Sex, Gender and Politics*. London: Routledge, 2000.

Anzaldúa, Gloria E. "now let us shift … the path of conocimiento … inner work, public acts." *this bridge we call home: visions for transformation*. Ed. Gloria E. Anzaldúa and AnaLouise Keating. New York: Routledge, 2002. 540–78.

Castillo, Ana, ed. *Goddess of the Americas/La diosa de las Américas: Writings on the Virgin of Guadalupe*. New York: Riverhead, 1996.

Christ, Carol P., and Judith Plaskow, eds. *Womanspirit Rising: A Feminist Reader in Religion*. San Francisco: Harper & Row, 1979.

Gunn Allen, Paula. *The Sacred Hoop: Recovering the Feminine in American Indian Traditions*. Boston, MA: Beacon Press, 1992.

Facio, Elisa, and Irene Lara, eds. *Fleshing the Spirit: Spirituality and Activism in Chicana, Latina, and Indigenous Women's Lives*. Tucson: University of Arizona Press, 2014.

Floyd-Thomas, Stacey M. "Womanist Theology." *Liberation Theologies in the United States: An Introduction*. Ed. Stacey M. Floyd-Thomas and Anthony B. Pinn, New York: New York University Press, 2010. 37–60.

Hull, Akasha Gloria. *Soul Talk: The New Spirituality of African American Women*. Rochester, VT: Inner Traditions, 2001.

Kim, Grace Ji-Sun. "Asian American Feminist Theology." *Liberation Theologies in the United States: An Introduction*. Ed. Stacey M. Floyd-Thomas and Anthony B. Pinn. New York: New York University Press, 2010. 131–48.

Lara, Irene. "Latina Health Activist-Healers Bridging Body and Spirit." *Women and Therapy* 31.1 (Spring 2008): 21–40.

Maparyan, Layli. *The Womanist Idea*. New York: Taylor & Francis, 2012.

Medina, Lara. "Nepantla Spirituality: My Path to the Source(s) of Healing." *Fleshing the Spirit: Spirituality and Activism in Chicana, Latina, and Indigenous Women's Lives*. Ed. Elisa Facio and Irene Lara. Tucson: University of Arizona Press, 2014. 167–85.

Mernissi, Fatima. *Dreams of Trespass: Tales of a Harem Girlhood*. Reading, MA: Addison-Wesley, 1994.

Merriam-Webster.com. http://www.merriam-webster.com/dictionary/spirituality (last accessed February 7, 2016)

Oxford Dictionaries.com. http://www.oxforddictionaries.com/us/definition/american_english/healing (last accessed February 7, 2016)

Pérez, Laura E. *Chicana Art: The Politics of Spiritual and Aesthetic Altarities*. Durham, NC: Duke University Press, 2007.

Ruether, Rosemary Radford. *Gaia and God: An Ecofeminist Theology of Earth Healing.* San Francisco, CA: HarperSanFrancisco, 1992.

Ruether, Rosemary Radford. *Catholic Does Not Equal the Vatican: A Vision for Progressive Catholicism.* New York: New Press, 2008.

Spretnak, Charlene, ed. *The Politics of Women's Spirituality: Essays on the Rise of Spiritual Power Within the Feminist Movement.* New York: Anchor Books/Doubleday, 1982.

Smith, Andrea. "Native Feminist Theology." *Liberation Theologies in the United States: An Introduction.* Ed. Stacey M. Floyd-Thomas and Anthony B. Pinn. New York: New York University Press, 2010. 149–67.

9.1

The Moths

Helena María Viramontes

I was fourteen years old when Abuelita requested my help. And it seemed only fair. Abuelita had pulled me through the rages of scarlet fever by placing, removing and replacing potato slices on the temples of my forehead; she had seen me through several whippings, an arm broken by a dare-jump off Tío Enrique's toolshed, puberty, and my first lie. Really, I told Amá, it was only fair.

Not that I was her favorite granddaughter or anything special. I wasn't even pretty or nice like my older sisters and I just couldn't do the girl things they could do. My hands were too big to handle the fineries of crocheting or embroidery and I always pricked my fingers or knotted my colored threads time and time again while my sisters laughed and called me bull hands with their cute waterlike voices. So I began keeping a piece of jagged brick in my sock to bash my sisters or anyone who called me bull hands. Once, while we all sat in the bedroom, I hit Teresa on the forehead, right above her eyebrow, and she ran to Amá with her mouth open, her hand over her eye while blood seeped between her fingers. I was used to the whippings by then.

I wasn't respectful either. I even went so far as to doubt the power of Abuelita's slices, the slices she said absorbed my fever. "You're still alive, aren't you?" Abuelita snapped back, her pasty gray eye beaming at me and burning holes in my suspicions. Regretful that I had let secret questions drop out of my mouth, I couldn't look into her eyes. My hands began to fan out, grow like a liar's nose until they hung by my side like low weights. Abuelita made a balm out of dried moth wings and Vicks and rubbed my hands, shaping them back to size. It was the strangest feeling. Like bones melting. Like sun shining through the darkness of your eyelids. I didn't mind helping Abuelita after that, so Amá would always send me over to her.

In the early afternoon Amá would push her hair back, hand me my sweater and shoes, and tell me to go to Mama Luna's. This was to avoid another fight and another whipping, I knew. I would deliver one last direct shot on Marisela's arm and jump out of our house, the slam of the screen door burying her cries of anger, and I'd gladly go help Abuelita plant her wild lilies or jasmine or heliotrope or cilantro or hierbabuena in red Hills Brothers coffee cans. Abuelita would wait for me at the top step of her porch holding a hammer and nail and empty coffee cans. And although we hardly spoke, hardly looked at each other as we worked over root transplants, I always felt her gray eye on me. It made me feel, in a strange sort of way, safe and guarded and not alone. Like God was supposed to make you feel.

On Abuelita's porch, I would puncture holes in the bottom of the coffee cans with a nail and a precise hit of a hammer. This completed, my job was to fill them with red clay mud from beneath her rose bushes, packing it softly, then making a perfect hole, four fingers round, to nest a sprouting avocado pit, or the spidery sweet potatoes that Abuelita rooted in mayonnaise jars with toothpicks and daily water, or prickly chayotes that produced vines that twisted and wound all over her porch pillars, crawling to the roof, up and over the roof, and down the other side, making her small brick house look like it was cradled within the vines that grew pear-shaped squashes ready for the pick, ready to be steamed with onions and cheese and butter. The roots would burst out of the rusted coffee cans and search for a place to connect. I would then feed the seedlings with water.

But this was a different kind of help, Amá said, because Abuelita was dying. Looking into her gray eye, then into her brown one, the doctor said it was just a matter of days. And so it seemed only fair that these hands she had melted and formed found use in rubbing her caving body with alcohol and marihuana, rubbing her arms and legs, turning her face to the window so that she could watch the Bird of Paradise blooming or smell the scent of clove in the air. I toweled her face frequently and held her hand for hours. Her gray wiry hair hung over the mattress. Since I could remember, she'd kept her long hair in braids. Her mouth was vacant and when she slept, her eyelids never closed all the way. Up close, you could see her gray eye beaming out the window, staring hard as if to remember everything. I never kissed her. I left the window open when I went to the market.

Across the street from Jay's Market there was a chapel. I never knew its denomination, but I went in just the same to search for candles. I sat down on one of the pews because there were none. After I cleaned my fingernails, I looked up at the high ceiling. I had forgotten the vastness of these places, the coolness of the marble pillars and the frozen statues with blank eyes. I was alone. I knew why I had never returned.

That was one of Apá's biggest complaints. He would pound his hands on the table, rocking the sugar dish or spilling a cup of coffee and scream that if I didn't go to Mass every Sunday to save my goddamn sinning soul, then I had no reason to go out of the house, period. Punto final. He would grab my arm and dig his nails into me to make sure I understood the importance of catechism. Did he make himself clear? Then he strategically directed his anger at Amá for her lousy ways of bringing up daughters, being disrespectful and unbelieving, and my older sisters would pull me aside and tell me if I didn't get to Mass right this minute, they were all going to kick the holy shit out of me. Why am I so selfish? Can't you see what it's doing to Amá, you idiot? So I would wash my feet and stuff them in my black Easter shoes that shone with Vaseline, grab a missal and veil, and wave goodbye to Amá.

I would walk slowly down Lorena to First to Evergreen, counting the cracks on the cement. On Evergreen I would turn left and walk to Abuelita's. I liked her porch because it was shielded by the vines of the chayotes and I could get a good look at the people and car traffic on Evergreen without them knowing. I would jump up the porch steps, knock on the screen door as I wiped my feet and call Abuelita, mi Abuelita? As I opened the door and stuck my head in, I would catch the gagging scent of toasting chile on the placa. When I entered the sala, she would greet me from the kitchen, wringing her hands in her apron. I'd sit at the corner of the table to keep from being in her way. The chiles made my eyes water. Am I crying? No, Mama Luna, I'm sure not crying. I don't like going to mass, but my eyes watered anyway, the tears dropping on the tablecloth like candle wax. Abuelita lifted the burnt chiles from the fire and sprinkled water on them until the skins began to separate. Placing them in front of me, she turned to check the menudo. I peeled the skins off and put the flimsy, limp-looking green and yellow chiles in the molcajete and began to crush and crush and twist and crush the heart out of the tomato, the clove of garlic, the stupid chiles that made me cry, crushed them until they turned into liquid under my bull hand. With a wooden spoon, I scraped hard to destroy the guilt, and my tears were gone. I put the bowl of chile next to a vase filled with freshly cut roses. Abuelita touched my hand and pointed to the bowl of menudo that steamed in front of me. I spooned some chile into the menudo and rolled a corn tortilla thin with the palms of my hands. As I ate, a fine Sunday breeze entered the kitchen and a rose petal calmly feathered down to the table.

I left the chapel without blessing myself and walked to Jay's. Most of the time Jay didn't have much of anything. The tomatoes were always soft and the cans of Campbell soups had rusted spots on them. There was dust on the tops of cereal boxes. I picked up what I needed: rubbing alcohol, five cans of chicken broth, a big bottle of Pine Sol. At first Jay got mad because I thought I had forgotten the money. But it was there all the time, in my back pocket.

When I returned from the market, I heard Amá crying in Abuelita's kitchen. She looked up at me with puffy eyes. I placed the bags of groceries on the table and began putting the cans of soup away. Amá sobbed quietly. I never kissed her. After a while, I patted her on the back for comfort. Finally: "¿Y mi Amá?" she asked in a whisper, then choked again and cried into her apron.

Abuelita fell off the bed twice yesterday, I said, knowing that I shouldn't have said it and wondering why I wanted to say it because it only made Amá cry harder. I guess I became angry and just so tired of the quarrels and beatings and unanswered prayers and my hands just there hanging helplessly by my side. Amá looked at me again, confused, angry, and her eyes were filled with sorrow. I went outside and sat on the porch swing and watched the people pass. I sat there until she left. I dozed off repeating the words to myself like rosary prayers: when do you stop giving when do you start giving when do you … and when my hands fell from my lap, I awoke to catch them. The sun was setting, an orange glow, and I knew Abuelita was hungry.

There comes a time when the sun is defiant. Just about the time when moods change, inevitable seasons of a day, transitions from one color to another, that hour or minute or second when the sun is finally defeated, finally sinks into the realization that it cannot with all its power to heal or burn, exist forever, there comes an illumination where the sun and earth meet, a final burst of burning red orange fury reminding us that although endings are inevitable, they are necessary for rebirths, and when that time came, just when I switched on the light in the kitchen to open Abuelita's can of soup, it was probably then that she died.

The room smelled of Pine Sol and vomit, and Abuelita had defecated the remains of her cancerous stomach. She had turned to the window and tried to speak, but her mouth remained open and speechless. I heard you, Abuelita, I said, stroking her cheek, I heard you. I opened the windows of the house and let the soup simmer and overboil on the stove. I turned the stove off and poured the soup down the sink. From the cabinet I got a tin basin, filled it with lukewarm water and carried it carefully to the room. I went to the linen closet and took out some modest bleached white towels. With the sacredness of a priest preparing his vestments, I unfolded the towels one by one on my shoulders. I removed the sheets and blankets from her bed and peeled off her thick flannel nightgown. I toweled her puzzled face, stretching out the wrinkles, removing the coils of her neck, toweled her shoulders and breasts. Then I changed the water. I returned to towel the creases of her stretch-marked stomach, her sporadic vaginal hairs, and her sagging thighs. I removed the lint from between her toes and noticed a mapped birthmark on the fold of her buttock. The scars on her back, which were as thin as the life lines on the palms of her hands, made me realize how little I really knew of Abuelita. I covered her with a thin blanket and went into the bathroom. I washed my hands, turned on the tub faucets and watched the water pour into the tub with vitality and steam. When it was full, I turned off the water and undressed. Then I went to get Abuelita.

She was not as heavy as I thought and when I carried her in my arms, her body fell into a V. And yet my legs were tired, shaky, and I felt as if the distance between the bedroom and bathroom was miles and years away. Amá, where are you?

I stepped into the bathtub one leg first, then the other. I bent my knees slowly to descend into the water slowly so I wouldn't scald her skin. There, there, Abuelita, I said, cradling her, smoothing her as we descended, I heard you. Her hair fell back and spread across the water like eagles' wings. The water in the tub overflowed and poured onto the tile of the floor. Then the moths came. Small gray ones that came from her soul and out through her mouth fluttering to light, circling the single dull light bulb of the bathroom. Dying is lonely and I wanted to go to where the moths were, stay with her and plant chayotes whose vines would crawl up her fingers and into the clouds; I wanted to rest my head on her chest with her stroking my hair, telling me about the moths that lay within the soul and slowly eat the spirit up; I wanted to return to the waters of the womb with her so that we would never be alone again. I wanted. I wanted my Amá. I removed a few strands of hair from Abuelita's face and held her small light head within the hollow of my neck. The bathroom was filled with moths, and for the first time in a long time I cried, rocking us, crying for her, for me, for Amá, the sobs emerging from the depths of anguish, the misery of feeling half-born, sobbing until finally the sobs rippled into circles and circles of sadness and relief. There, there, I said to Abuelita, rocking us gently, there, there.

9.2
My Guardian Spirits
Ama R. Saran

October 30, 1989
4:00 a.m.

My Guardian Spirits.

My Beloved Sister-Friends and Brother-Friends, perhaps now I can lose myself in *The Temple of My Familiar,* set a fire for my spirit from the soul-sated litanies she's laid down, fling myself into her sensuous smoke, and wrap myself in her wise words.

I am going to the hospital. Northside. Monday. October 30, 1989, at 6 a.m. At 7:30 I am scheduled for:

1. Repair of an umbilical hernia (or whatever it turns out to be);
2. Removal of my last and much loved ovary; and
3. Exploratory surgery – in search of those pain-producing adhesions.

This is a critical time, primarily because this is an opportunity for my personal and spiritual instruction into healing for my fundamental, life-changing wellness.

> I cannot possibly achieve this alone nor do I intend to.
> Please know that I would … Welcome;
> I would need..........
> I would expect you to be with me in this moment:

1. Please remember how much I love the natural gifts that the earth offers up – most of all rose petals, many, many rose petals for my bed.
2. Know I need my familiar – the life and color of Africa to cover the foot of my bed.
3. Bring incense to soak my senses in.
4. Bring good reading – copies of *Vital Signs* for the nurses, assistants, doctors, and visitors to read. Lend me the love poetry of our Brother, Henry Dumas, and short stories on long and well-lived lives of brave black women. Give me Nikky's *On Wings Made of Gauze.*
5. Bring laughter – being sure to hold my hand, because it will hurt but it does heal.

6. Careful ... bring what comforts you but think of me also. I am not comforted by religious relics but spiritual sustenance. Gift me with simple prayers, light candles, hold my hand. Please don't be offended – just understand that when I am ill I can't distinguish between communion and the last rites/rights.
7. When visiting, kindly do not speak of my illness as metaphor. I do see it as such and already understand what I'm ridding myself of.
8. Know that this operation *is* a last resort for me. It is not the time to speak of alternatives. This *is* the one. I am grateful for the sister-spirit instruction on where/how/when and who to seek out. I am now using this to heal into a whole. Let's not haggle with Shoulda' and Coulda', keep those two sisters outa' my presence.
9. Bring me music – the sound of your soothing voices and instruments. Bring tapes – old Doo-Wahs, the Soulful Strings, Ferrante and Teicher, Leontyne Price and Clamma Dale.
10. My hair – brush my hair frequently and massage my scalp. I really do believe uncombed hair is a sure sign of dementia.
11. Keep me shining with almond-scented musk oil. Oil my scalp, face, arms, hands, legs, and feet. Note: I've already arranged for my manicure and pedicure before surgery.
12. Please massage me. Particularly my neck and hands and shoulders where I store all my tension and pain. Massage my back, which will ache badly from the cold steel of the surgeon's table.
13. Know this about me ... I am usually able to "appear" alert. I've been socialized to do so from my birth – a woman's way. Talk to me ... read ... sing to me but not *with* me.
14. Feed me well. Water, much water, peppermint or spearmint tea, warm lemon water. Be prepared to replace the solid food they'll insist upon. Pureed soups (potatoes, sister honey, and vegetables), clam chowder, Dick Gregory with juice would be fine.
15. Help me. Help me to walk straight and tall back into the world of wellness. Even when I protest pitifully. It's the only way to fully and quickly regain my strength.
16. Think about me. Inquire but watch the phoning. Abdominal surgery insists that every slamming door, every telephone ring, voice, clinking glass be involuntarily answered by my stomach muscles or their close kin.

I'll be hospitalized for about a week, then home. Come see about me. Help me up and back into the world gently.

> Know that I need you. ...
> Know that I love you. ...
> Know that with you I shall be well. ...

Love and Strength.
Ama R. Saran

9.3

Honor and Ceremony in Women's Rituals

E. M. Broner

Gender preceded modern religion. We were women before we were Jews, Christians, Moslems. It seems only natural, historical, and just, therefore, to make religion respond to our origins.

Preserved on tablet and stone are historical ceremonies. Women greeted the new moon, presided at births, held forth at funerals. We selected our mates and passed property on to our daughters. Ancient female gods were honored by their daughter priests in psalms. But after the gender of God was changed, all else changed. Woman became the ruled. Psalms were neither written to her nor by her. Her rights as a citizen were denied. She shrank as a human and was condemned as a deity. Gradually rites even excluded her. Looking casually for definitions, one finds today (in *Webster's New World Dictionary*) that *rite* is "a division of … churches according to the liturgy used; specifically, a patriarchate."

Many of those prepatriarchal ceremonies have survived as vestigial structures into the present, vestigial because their original meaning has been altered. The new moon ceremony is danced at the beginning of the Jewish month by male Chasidic Jews. The birthing ceremony in the Jewish religion welcomes only the birth of a boy child. The puberty ceremony welcomes only the maturation of the boy child. After death, it is the son who can mourn for his parents. Even the word *holy* in Hebrew has been reserved for males exclusively. It derived from the Akkadian name for the holy women of the temple, *kadishtu*, and has passed into Hebrew as *kadesh*, *holy*. The prayer for the dead, *kaddesh*, another form of *holy*, is uttered only by the male lips. That which is not holy is profane. Women priests were renamed temple prostitutes.

Ritual displays cultural authority. Kay Turner has observed that in patriarchal religions and the societies they influence ritual is used as "man's warrant to create and define culture and, by exclusion, a sign to women to keep in their place, a place … without the symbolic or real attributes of power."[1] The patriarchal world would remove woman from ritual.

It is my feeling that all humans mark their paths on trees, mark time with ceremony. That repetition and orderliness make for ritual. Etymologically, *rite* is from *ritual*, as is *arithmetic*. We want sums, constants. *Rhythm* is from the same root. Ritual is a collective experience, repeated and sanctified. We perform it to remind ourselves and one another that we are not alone, that we sing in chorus. We are historical, and what has happened to us is not an isolated instance. Birth has occurred before, and we women birth in a cave of women's experiences, when we are fortunate. Death has happened before, and we lament with others who have suffered losses.

The power of ritual has been explored by Barbara Myerhoff:

> All rituals are paradoxical and dangerous enterprises, the traditional and improvised, the sacred and secular. Paradoxical because rituals are conspicuously artificial and theatrical, yet designed to suggest the inevitability and absolute truth of their messages. Dangerous because when we are not convinced by a ritual we may become aware of ourselves as having made them up, thence on to the paralyzing realization that we have made up all our truths; our ceremonies, our most precious conceptions and convictions – all are mere invention.[2]

Number Our Days, Dr. Myerhoff's anthropological study of the Jewish community center for the aging in Venice, California, shows lyrically and compassionately how central ritual is to the lives of the elderly and how expectation of a ritual even prolongs their years.

If not to prolong life, but to mark it, I began creating ritual. I made ceremony out of need before knowing an anthropological definition. Nor was I aware, in the writing and performance of a ceremony, of its aftereffects. Kay Turner would define me as a "feminist ritualist." She believes women in the United States and elsewhere have "begun to claim sacred space for themselves, to create rituals … as a source of power, vision, and solidarity. …" Turner defines ritual as political: "Feminist ritual practice is currently the most important model for symbolic and, therefore, psychic and spiritual change in women."[3]

These early forms of woman worship have faded but not disappeared. We have tenuous connections with the Mother Gods – reproductions in art books, literary allusions. I have had the warm feeling of stone in my hand when I lifted a household manifestation of female deity. I do not think of those ancient women as testing our souls or as representing a body of law that governs our lives, yet we have to know of them, to know of that origin, of that beginning, *B'Reshit*, as the first section of the Bible is called. In the Beginning. If we do not know of that earliest of beginnings, we will think of the world as having begun in the Testaments. Our allusions, speech, vision have been altered by the supplanting of one mythic context for another. We attest, testify, test ourselves. The origin of *testament* is *testes, testicle,* that most holy of objects on which men swore (the Hebrew patriarchs and their servants placed their hands there and swore the sacred oath). If we must swear by the Old and New Testes, then we worship a false idol that was "erected" while others were leveled. If we do not remember our womanly origins, then we lose our images, our language, and the meaning of the cave of self.

I, being a Jew, have written ceremonies timed to the Jewish calendar. I have written a Spring exodus, a Woman's Passover Haggadah; I have worked on High Holy Day ceremonies and a revision of Chanukah. One might ask, "Isn't that acceptable to the Jewish faith then? Isn't that being a good Jew?" No, for as Cynthia Ozick has demonstrated, a woman cannot be a Jew. In her brilliant, talmudic essay, "Notes

Toward Finding the Right Question," Ozick explains that under Jewish law "women *qua* women are seen as a subdivision of humanity, not as the main class itself … the male is the norm and the female a class apart."[4] She describes sitting among women in her traditional synagogues:

> … and the rabbi speaks the word "Jew." I can be sure that he is not referring to me, for to him "Jew" means "male Jew" … When my rabbi says, "A Jew is called to the Torah," he never means me or any other living Jewish woman.

The Jewish woman has limited access for her talents as a devotional writer, for the use of her mind. Even after the Holocaust when so much was lost, Ozick notes, the loss of the intelligence of the woman is not yet counted. Since the works of the Jewish people are not the work of all the people but of half – for woman was never allowed to contribute to that pride and monument, Torah (Law) – Ozick concludes that the law "is in this respect frayed."

Creating Our Exodus From Darkness

Perhaps in disobeying one law we create another. Perhaps in changing one ceremony, we make another. The first corrective ceremony I co-created was the women's Passover.

It is written in Exodus and in the male Haggadah: "In each generation let each man look on himself as if he came forth out of Egypt." It further directs, "And thou shalt tell thy son. …" How is it possible that a ceremony in which I have participated my entire remembered life makes no mention of my coming out of Egypt, and I am not commanded to remind my daughter of the exodus? In the male Haggadah four sons ask questions on which the entire seder is structured, and these questions are answered by wise men. How is it possible that with all the formalistic and informal debate and dispute, with all the revisions to the Haggadah, not a woman is mentioned?

Passover is regarded as a Freedom Holiday. Not to women. It is the time of spring cleaning, changing of dishes, shopping for special ingredients, cooking of dishes peculiar to the holiday. It is the time when we rise from the table to tend the big dinner while the men are seated and tend to the prayer.

I and my co-author of the new ceremony, Naomi Nimrod of Haifa, met to study and revise this ceremony and its attendant customs during the spring of 1975 in Israel. As the male Haggadah begins with the child singing four questions, we began with different questions: "Why is this Haggadah different from traditional Haggadoth?" "Because this Haggadah deals with the exodus of women." We altered the second question also and the next two. Instead of asking about the bitter herbs, we asked: "Why have our mothers on this night been bitter?" "Because they did the preparation but not the ritual. They did the serving but not the conducting. They read of their fathers but not of their mothers." The question that traditionally deals with leaning back on pillows to celebrate being free men, we altered: "Why on this night do we recline?" "We recline on this night for the unhurried telling of the legacy of Miriam."

In writing women into the festival of freedom – the end of slavery, the time of crossing borders – we *named* women. We chose the first prophet of all, Miriam, as our symbol. We followed her in Torah, in commentaries, and legends. We followed her prophecy of the exodus, her safe-guarding of the baby in the bullrushes until he was rescued, her dancing on the banks of the Red Sea long afterwards, celebrating exodus, her anger when she was deprived of honor, God's punishment inflicted upon her by turning her into a leper and curing her a week later to teach her the lesson of pride. We learned the lesson well – woman large yet brought low, woman supplanted by younger brother, woman disappearing, and leaving no footprint in the desert. We used the male Haggadah as the spine of our ceremony and, within it, reincorporated women. We dug up Miriam's bones from the desert. And we asked questions.

THE SONG OF QUESTIONS

> Mother, asks the clever daughter,
> who are our mothers?
> Who are our ancestors?
> What is our history?
> Give us our name. Name our genealogy.
> Mother, asks the wicked daughter,
> if I learn my history,
> will I not be angry?
> Will I not be bitter as Miriam
> who was deprived of her prophecy?
> Mother, asks the simple daughter,
> if Miriam lies buried in sand,
> why must we dig up those bones?
> Why must we remove her from sun and stone
> where she belongs?
> The one who knows not how to question,
> she has no past,
> she can have no present,
> she can have no future
> without knowing her mother,
> without knowing her angers,
> without knowing her questions.[5]

Passover is famous for its plagues, the ten plagues visited upon the Egyptians. Women have plenty of plagues, more than ten, more than hundreds. We rewrote the plagues to make the curses come from our experiences. We used the traditional ten as our base. We used blood; the blood which filled the river of the Egyptians and choked their water supply has also choked the history of women:

BLOOD

The bleeding and bearing cycle of the female
is considered unclean by the male.
She will be killed
her blood spilled
if holy places, priests and men
are approached by bleeding women.
And so woman is forcibly removed
from power and rule because of blood.

We reinterpreted the noxious beasts:

LICE

She scratches her life
like a lice-filled head.

We named ignorance as the worst plague of all:

DARKNESS

It became pitch dark
in the history of women.
They could not see one another.
And no one stirred from where she sat.
All the lights of learning were dimmed
and the doors of the House of Study were locked.
The woman could not read.
The woman could not write,
could not take part in her community,
could not participate
in writing her own history.[6]

All the decisions Naomi Nimrod and I made while writing the Haggadah were political, for, as Turner says, ritual is political. We made linguistic changes. We changed gender from masculine to feminine. That was political. We had to rename or name woman; we had to rename Elohim, the masculine, as Shchena, the feminine form. We shook tradition, unrhymed ancient rhymes, changed rhythms of old chants. That would be our political stand. We would not write a Haggadah of the daily news. We felt our approach would ultimately be more radical and would not yellow like yesterday's headlines.

This Haggadah, which means, "Telling," has had its own telling. It was first performed in 1976 in two places simultaneously, the first Passover seder in Haifa at the home of Marcia Freedman, a member of the Israeli Parliament, where Naomi wore her cantor father's long black robes, and in New York at the apartment of Phyllis Chesler, distinguished psychologist. The women in Israel talked all night, reclined on pillows until, as in the traditional source, the cocks crowed and it was time to say the morning prayer. We twenty Mothers of the Seder gathered in Manhattan on West End Avenue. We were varied in background, age, race, sexual preference. I trembled before the group. I trembled, as Myerhoff would later explain, in fear that this ritual would fail, that all the trappings, the seder plates, the candles, I in my priestess cap, would only be symbols and would not transcend into the private sphere of their lives. I began by calling out to them:

> I bless you, I the priestess of you
> I, your mouth, your cry, your prayer, your pain,
> your connection, your separation …
> I am your scribe. I inscribe your pain.
> I am your collective soul …
> I am born through the tunnel of your collective bodies,
> yet I am old – your ancient, your memory, your ancestor.
> My tears fill cauldrons, brews, broths, seas, eyes,
> I am the mourner for you,
> I am your wake …
> I blow trumpets for you, I celebrate you,
> I laugh aloud for you …
> Trust me for I am the ghost of you.
> Look, in the shadows I walk behind you …
> Spread your legs, my daughters,
> let us give birth to one another.
> Let us cry out in birthing pain.
> Let us uncover our shame.
> Let this ceremony, let these friendships be born.

So this holiday was born and continues. On Passover 1980, we celebrated the Fifth Annual Women's Seder. Each succeeding seder has had its own special character. Each spring we become anxious to meet once again – Chesler; Letty, Robin and Abigail Pogrebin; Lily Rivlin; Bea Kreloff; I; my daughters; and other Mothers of the Seder.

When Naomi and I began work on the Women's Haggadah, we could not anticipate its reception nor the commitment of women to it. It has been read and performed by such traditionalist Jewish groups as the Pioneer women and Hadassah, as well as by Catholic nuns, and Protestant women clergy and laity seeking new ceremonies. As with all tradition, each new group that adopted it also adapted it. In 1979, one feminist seder group brought the artifacts of their lives to the table, a grandmother's fish knife, a family heirloom cooking pot, albums of foremothers. I do not believe the radicalism of the ceremony has diluted while spreading.

The holiday is anticipated as we prepare to leave the men in our families, to seclude and exclude ourselves with women in introspection, thoughtfulness, and woman's prayer.

Honoring Forms of Birthing

As exodus is universal, so is birthing, so is pairing, so is death. Women have always been present at birth, and women were there at the final exodus as the body dressers, keeners – gods of entrance and exit. Ceremony returns to ourselves as our bodies return to ourselves.

I have gone with Harriette Hartigan, a Detroit photographer, to watch a home delivery. There were no white-masked strangers, only friendly women, a child or two, and a father-to-be, who was massaging the laboring woman. Barbara was deep into her labor, and her lover rubbed her back low and to the sides when the contractions were full upon her. Barbara called to the life within: "Come down, baby." Her three-year-old, Lenay, asked, "What's Mommy doing?" Barbara said, "Mommy is working, Lenay." Lenay asked, "Why is Mommy making those sounds?" Barbara said, "Mommy is calling in a secret voice to the baby. Those are working and calling sounds." The child watched as the eye of the vagina opened wide in surprise, crowned with a head, with eyebrows, stuck on the nose. Barbara labored mightily and crooned and lullaby'd the life into birth. The midwife caught the baby. Barbara's body sweated like that of any road laborer; her hair was tangled and damp. She rose from the birthing bed, showered, and brushed her hair. I had brought champagne. We popped the cork, drank, and talked quietly about matters of birthing. We played the tape that we had made of Barbara calling to the baby, of Barbara calling out to her mother and to her lover. We were there to begin a new kind of ceremony.

I also participated in an old birthing ceremony. In January 1978, during a great snowstorm, I flew from Detroit to New York. It was Friday, the thirteenth, the day of the circumcision of Phyllis Chesler's son. Chesler knew the rabbi would speak of the son as if he were only of father born, grandfather connected, male ancestry descended, but would forget that the womb had held him. It was as we had anticipated. After the male ceremony, we women retrieved the baby and took him into the library. There we surrounded him with the magic circle of ourselves. I requested that we each bless him in our own voice, that we give him something useful and magical, a growing part of ourselves. I took out scissors and cut a lock of my hair. I taped it onto a sheet of red oaktag. Each woman present cut her hair – grey, black, blonde, brown hair. We lit candles and wished the baby courage to be the son of a feminist, courage to be lonely, to have laughter and friendship with his mother. We blew out the candles and presented the baby with this hairy card of great power. The storm had not abated, but I rose and flew through it back to Detroit.[7]

Notes

1. Kay Turner, "Contemporary Feminist Rituals," *Heresies*, no. 5, 1978, p. 21.
2. Barbara Myerhoff, *Number Our Days*, New York: E. P. Dutton, 1979, p. 86.
3. Turner, *op. cit.*
4. Cynthia Ozick, "Notes toward Finding the Right Question," *Lilith*, no. 6, 1979, pp. 19–29.

5. Some portions of this ceremony appeared in "A Woman's Passover Haggadah," by E. M. Broner and Naomi Nimrod, *Ms.*, April 1977, pp. 54–56.
6. *Ibid.*
7. For a fuller account, as well as wisdom, see Phyllis Chesler's *With Child* (New York: Thomas Y. Crowell, 1979).

9.4

My World of the Unknown

Alifa Rifaat

There are many mysteries in life, unseen powers in the universe, worlds other than our own, hidden links and radiations that draw creatures together and whose effect is interacting. They may merge or be incompatible, and perhaps the day will come when science will find a method for connecting up these worlds in the same way as it has made it possible to voyage to other planets. Who knows?

Yet one of these other worlds I have explored; I have lived in it and been linked with its creatures through the bond of love. I used to pass with amazing speed between this tangible world of ours and another invisible earth, mixing in the two worlds on one and the same day, as though living it twice over.

When entering into the world of my love, and being summoned and yielding to its call, no one around me would be aware of what was happening to me. All that occurred was that I would be overcome by something resembling a state of languor and would go off into a semi-sleep. Nothing about me would change except that I would become very silent and withdrawn, though I am normally a person who is talkative and eager to go out into the world of people. I would yearn to be on my own, would long for the moment of surrender as I prepared myself for answering the call.

Love had its beginning when an order came through for my husband to be transferred to a quiet country town and, being too busy with his work, delegated to me the task of going to this town to choose suitable accommodation prior to his taking up the new appointment. He cabled one of his subordinates named Kamil and asked him to meet me at the station and to assist me.

I took the early morning train. The images of a dream I had had that night came to me as I looked out at the vast fields and gauged the distances between the towns through which the train passed and reckoned how far it was between the new town in which we were fated to live and beloved Cairo.

The images of the dream kept reappearing to me, forcing themselves upon my mind: images of a small white house surrounded by a garden with bushes bearing yellow flowers, a house lying on the edge of a broad canal in which were swans and tall sailing boats. I kept on wondering at my dream and trying to analyse it. Perhaps it was some secret wish I had had, or maybe the echo of some image that my unconscious had stored up and was chewing over.

As the train arrived at its destination, I awoke from my thoughts. I found Kamil awaiting me. We set out in his car, passing through the local *souk*. I gazed at the mounds of fruit with delight, chatting away happily with Kamil. When we emerged from the *souk* we found ourselves on the bank of the Mansoura canal, a canal on which swans swam and sailing boats moved to and fro. I kept staring at them with uneasy longing. Kamil directed the driver to the residential buildings the governorate had put up for housing government employees. While gazing at the opposite bank a large boat with a great fluttering sail glided past. Behind it could be seen a white house that had a garden with trees with yellow flowers and that lay on its own amidst vast fields. I shouted out in confusion, overcome by the feeling that I had been here before.

'Go to that house,' I called to the driver. Kamil leapt up, objecting vehemently: 'No, no, – no one lives in that house. The best thing is to go to the employees' buildings.'

I shouted insistently, like someone hypnotized: 'I must have a look at that house.' 'All right,' he said. 'You won't like it, though – it's old and needs repairing.' Giving in to my wish, he ordered the driver to make his way there.

At the garden door we found a young woman, spare and of fair complexion. A fat child with ragged clothes encircled her neck with his burly legs. In a strange silence, she stood as though nailed to the ground, barring the door with her hands and looking at us with doltish enquiry.

I took a sweet from my bag and handed it to the boy. He snatched it eagerly, tightening his grip on her neck with his podgy, mud-bespattered feet so that her face became flushed from his high-spirited embrace. A half-smile showed on her tightly-closed lips. Taking courage, I addressed her in a friendly tone: 'I'd like to see over this house.' She braced her hands resolutely against the door. 'No,' she said quite simply. I turned helplessly to Kamil, who went up to her and pushed her violently in the chest so that she staggered back. 'Don't you realize,' he shouted at her, 'that this is the director's wife? Off with you!'

Lowering her head so that the child all but slipped from her, she walked off dejectedly to the canal bank where she lay down on the ground, put the child on her lap, and rested her head in her hands in silent submission.

Moved by pity, I remonstrated: 'There's no reason to be so rough, Mr Kamil. Who is the woman?' 'Some mad woman,' he said with a shrug of his shoulders, 'who's a stranger to the town. Out of kindness the owner of this house put her in charge of it until someone should come along to live in it.'

With increased interest I said: 'Will he be asking a high rent for it?' 'Not at all,' he said with an enigmatic smile. 'He'd welcome anyone taking it over. There are no restrictions and the rent is modest – no more than four pounds.'

I was beside myself with joy. Who in these days can find somewhere to live for such an amount? I rushed through the door into the house with Kamil behind me and went over the rooms: five spacious rooms with wooden floors, with a pleasant hall, modern lavatory, and a beautifully roomy kitchen with a large verandah overlooking vast pistachio-green fields of generously watered rice. A breeze, limpid and cool, blew, playing with the tips of the crop and making the delicate leaves move in continuous dancing waves.

I went back to the first room with its spacious balcony overlooking the road and revealing the other bank of the canal where, along its strand, extended the houses of the town. Kamil pointed out to me a building facing the house on the other side. 'That's where we work,' he said, 'and behind it is where the children's schools are.'

'Thanks be to God,' I said joyfully. 'It means that everything is within easy reach of this house – and the *souk*'s nearby too.' 'Yes,' he said, 'and the fishermen will knock at your door to show you the fresh fish they've caught in their nets. But the house needs painting and re-doing, also there are all sorts of rumours about it – the people around here believe in djinn and spirits.'

'This house is going to be my home,' I said with determination. 'Its low rent will make up for whatever we may have to spend on re-doing it. You'll see what this house will look like when I get the garden arranged. As for the story about djinn and spirits, just leave them to us – we're more spirited than them.'

We laughed at my joke as we left the house. On my way to the station we agreed about the repairs that needed doing to the house. Directly I reached Cairo I cabled my husband to send the furniture from the town we had been living in, specifying a suitable date to fit in with the completion of the repairs and the house being ready for occupation.

On the date fixed I once again set off and found that all my wishes had been carried out and that the house was pleasantly spruce with its rooms painted a cheerful orange tinge, the floors well polished and the garden tidied up and made into small flowerbeds.

I took possession of the keys and Kamil went off to attend to his business, having put a chair on the front balcony for me to sit on while I awaited the arrival of the furniture van. I stretched out contentedly in the chair and gazed at the two banks with their towering trees like two rows of guards between which passed the boats with their lofty sails, while around them glided a male swan heading a flotilla of females. Halfway across the canal he turned and flirted with them, one after the other, like a sultan amidst his harem.

Relaxed, I closed my eyes. I projected myself into the future and pictured to myself the enjoyment I would have in this house after it had been put in order and the garden fixed up. I awoke to the touch of clammy fingers shaking me by the shoulders.

I started and found myself staring at the fair-complexioned woman with her child squatting on her shoulders as she stood erect in front of me staring at me in silence. 'What do you want?' I said to her sharply. 'How did you get in?' 'I got in with this,' she said simply, revealing a key between her fingers.

I snatched the key from her hand as I loudly rebuked her: 'Give it here. We have rented the house and you have no right to come into it like this.' 'I have a lot of other keys,' she answered briefly. 'And what,' I said to her, 'do you want of this house?' 'I want to stay on in it and for you to go,' she said. I laughed in amazement at her words as I asked myself: Is she really mad? Finally I said impatiently: 'Listen here, I'm not leaving here and you're not entering this house unless I wish it. My husband is coming with the children, and the furniture is on the way. He'll be arriving in a little while and we'll be living here for such period of time as my husband is required to work in this town.'

She looked at me in a daze. For a long time she was silent, then she said: 'All right, your husband will stay with me and you can go.' Despite my utter astonishment I felt pity for her. 'I'll allow you to stay on with us for the little boy's sake,' I said to her gently, 'until you find yourself another place. If you'd like to help me with the housework I'll pay you what you ask.'

Shaking her head, she said with strange emphasis: 'I'm not a servant. I'm Aneesa.' 'You're not staying here,' I said to her coldly, rising to my feet. Collecting all my courage and emulating Kamil's determination when he rebuked her, I began pushing her in the chest as I caught hold of the young boy's hand. 'Get out of here and don't come near this house,' I shouted at her. 'Let me have all the keys. I'll not let go of your child till you've given them all to me.'

With a set face that did not flicker she put her hand to her bosom and took out a ring on which were several keys, which she dropped into my hand. I released my grip on the young boy. Supporting him on her shoulders, she started to leave. Regretting my harshness, I took out several piastres from my bag and placed them in the boy's hand. With the same silence and stiffness she wrested the piastres from the boy's hand and gave them back to me. Then she went straight out. Bolting the door this time, I sat down, tense and upset, to wait.

My husband arrived, then the furniture, and for several days I occupied myself with putting the house in order. My husband was busy with his work and the children occupied themselves with making new friends and I completely forgot about Aneesa, that is until my husband returned one night wringing his hands with fury: 'This woman Aneesa, can you imagine that since we came to live in this house she's been hanging around it every night. Tonight she was so crazy she blocked my way and suggested I should send you off so that she might live with me. The woman's gone completely off her head about this house and I'm afraid she might do something to the children or assault you.'

Joking with him and masking the jealousy that raged within me, I said: 'And what is there for you to get angry about? She's a fair and attractive enough woman – a blessing brought to your very doorstep!' With a sneer he took up the telephone, muttering: 'May God look after her!'

He contacted the police and asked them to come and take her away. When I heard the sound of the police van coming I ran to the window and saw them taking her off. The poor woman did not resist, did not object, but submitted with a gentle sadness that as usual with her aroused one's pity. Yet, when she saw me standing in tears and watching her, she turned to me and, pointing to the wall of the house, called out: 'I'll leave her to you.' 'Who?' I shouted. 'Who, Aneesa?' Once again pointing at the bottom of the house, she said: 'Her.'

The van took her off and I spent a sleepless night. No sooner did day come than I hurried to the garden to examine my plants and to walk round the house and carefully inspect its walls. All I found were some cracks, the house being old, and I laughed at the frivolous thought that came to me: Could, for example, there be jewels buried here, as told in fairy tales?

Who could 'she' be? What was the secret of this house? Who was Aneesa and was she really mad? Where were she and her son living? So great did my concern for Aneesa become that I began pressing my husband with questions until he brought me news of her. The police had learnt that she was the wife of a well-to-do teacher living in a nearby town. One night he had caught her in an act of infidelity, and in fear she had fled with her son and had settled here, no one knowing why she had betaken herself to this particular house. However, the owner of the house had been good enough to allow her to put up in it until someone should come to live in it, while some kind person had intervened on her behalf to have her name included among those receiving monthly allowances from the Ministry of Social Affairs. There were many rumours that cast doubt upon her conduct: people passing by her house at night would hear her conversing with unknown persons. Her madness took the form of a predilection for silence and isolation from people during the daytime as she wandered about in a dream world. After the police had persuaded them to take her in to safeguard the good repute of her family, she was returned to her relatives.

The days passed and the story of Aneesa was lost in oblivion. Winter came and with it heavy downpours of rain. The vegetation in my garden flourished though the castor-oil plants withered and their yellow flowers fell. I came to find pleasure in sitting out on the kitchen balcony looking at my flowers and vegetables and enjoying the belts of sunbeams that lay between the clouds and lavished my balcony with warmth and light.

One sunny morning my attention was drawn to the limb of a nearby tree whose branches curved up gracefully despite its having dried up and its dark bark being cracked. My gaze was attracted by something twisting and turning along the tip of a branch: bands of yellow and others of red, intermingled with bands of black, were creeping forward. It was a long, smooth tube, at its end a small striped head with two bright, wary eyes.

The snake curled round on itself in spiral rings, then tautened its body and moved forward. The sight gripped me; I felt terror turning my blood cold and freezing my limbs.

My senses were numbed, my soul intoxicated with a strange elation at the exciting beauty of the snake. I was rooted to the spot, wavering between two thoughts that contended in my mind at one and the same time: should I snatch up some implement from the kitchen and kill the snake, or should I enjoy the rare moment of beauty that had been afforded me?

As though the snake had read what was passing through my mind, it raised its head, tilting it to right and left in thrilling coquetry. Then, by means of two tiny fangs like pearls, and a golden tongue like a twig of *arak* wood, it smiled at me and fastened its eyes on mine in one fleeting, commanding glance. The thought of killing left me. I felt a current, a radiation from its eyes that penetrated to my heart ordering me to stay where I was. A warning against continuing to sit out there in front of it surged inside me, but my attraction to it paralysed my limbs and I did not move. I kept on watching it, utterly entranced and captivated. Like a bashful virgin being lavished with compliments, it tried to conceal its pride in its beauty, and, having made certain of captivating its lover, the snake coyly twisted round and gently, grace-fully glided away until swallowed up by a crack in the wall. Could the snake be the 'she' that Aneesa had referred to on the day of her departure?

At last I rose from my place, overwhelmed by the feeling that I was on the brink of a new world, a new destiny, or rather, if you wish, the threshold of a new love. I threw myself onto the bed in a dreamlike state, unaware of the passage of time. No sooner, though, did I hear my husband's voice and the children with their clatter as they returned at noon than I regained my sense of being a human being, wary and frightened about itself, determined about the existence and continuance of its species. Without intending to I called out: 'A snake – there's a snake in the house.'

My husband took up the telephone and some men came and searched the house. I pointed out to them the crack into which the snake had disappeared, though racked with a feeling of remorse at being guilty of betrayal. For here I was denouncing the beloved, inviting people against it after it had felt safe with me.

The men found no trace of the snake. They burned some wormwood and fumi-gated the hole but without result. Then my husband summoned Sheikh Farid, Sheikh of the Rifa'iyya order in the town, who went on chanting verses from the Qur'an as he tapped the ground with his stick. He then asked to speak to me alone and said:

'Madam, the sovereign of the house has sought you out and what you saw is no snake, rather it is one of the monarchs of the earth – may God make your words pleasant to them – who has appeared to you in the form of a snake. Here in this house there are many holes of snakes, but they are of the non-poisonous kind. They inhabit houses and go and come as they please. What you saw, though, is something else.'

'I don't believe a word of it,' I said, stupefied. 'This is nonsense. I know that the djinn are creatures that actually exist, but they are not in touch with our world, there is no contact between them and the world of humans.'

With an enigmatic smile he said: 'My child, the Prophet went out to them and read the Qur'an to them in their country. Some of them are virtuous and some of them are Muslims, and how do you know there is no contact between us and them? Let your prayer be "O Lord, increase me in knowledge" and do not be nervous. Your purity of spirit, your translucence of soul have opened to you doors that will take you to other worlds known only to their Creator. Do not be afraid. Even if you should find her one night sleeping in your bed, do not be alarmed but talk to her with all politeness and friendliness.'

'That's enough of all that, Sheikh Farid. Thank you,' I said, alarmed, and he left us.

We went on discussing the matter. 'Let's be practical,' suggested my husband, 'and stop all the cracks at the bottom of the outside walls and put wire-mesh over the windows, also paint wormwood all round the garden fence.'

We set about putting into effect what we had agreed. I, though, no longer dared to go out onto the balconies. I neglected my garden and stopped wandering about in it. Generally I would spend my free time in bed. I changed to being someone who liked to sit around lazily and was disinclined to mix with people; those diversions and rec-reations that previously used to tempt me no longer gave me any pleasure. All I wanted was to stretch myself out and drowse. In bewilderment I asked myself: Could it be that I was in love? But how could I love a snake? Or could she really be one of the daughters of the monarchs of the djinn? I would awake from my musings to find that I had been wandering in my thoughts and recalling to mind how magnificent she was. And what is the secret of her beauty? I would ask myself. Was it that I was fascinated by her multi-coloured, supple body? Or was it that I had been dazzled by that intelligent, commanding way she had of looking at me? Or could it be the sleek way she had of gliding along, so excitingly dangerous, that had captivated me?

Excitingly dangerous! No doubt it was this excitement that had stirred my feelings and awakened my love, for did they not make films to excite and frighten? There was no doubt but that the secret of my passion for her, my preoccupation with her, was due to the excitement that had aroused, through intense fear, desire within myself; an excitement that was sufficiently strong to drive the blood hotly through my veins whenever the memory of her came to me, thrusting the blood in bursts that made my heart beat wildly, my limbs limp. And so, throwing myself down in a pleasurable state of torpor, my craving for her would be awakened and I would wish for her coil-like touch, her graceful gliding motion.

And yet I fell to wondering how union could come about, how craving be quenched, the delights of the body be realized, between a woman and a snake. And did she, I wondered, love me and want me as I loved her? An idea would obtrude itself upon me sometimes: did Cleopatra, the very legend of love, have sexual intercourse with her serpent after having given up sleeping with men, having wearied of amorous adventures with them so that her sated instincts were no longer moved other than by the excitement of fear, her senses no longer aroused other than by bites from a snake? And the last of her lovers had been a viper that had destroyed her.

I came to live in a state of continuous torment, for a strange feeling of longing scorched my body and rent my senses, while my circumstances obliged me to carry out the duties and responsibilities that had been placed on me as the wife of a man who occupied an important position in the small town, he and his family being objects of attention and his house a Kaaba for those seeking favours; also as a mother who must look after her children and concern herself with every detail of their lives so as to exercise control over them; there was also the house and its chores, this house that was inhabited by the mysterious lover who lived in a world other than mine. How, I wondered, was union between us to be achieved? Was wishing for this love a sin or was there nothing to reproach myself about?

And as my self-questioning increased so did my yearning, my curiosity, my desire. Was the snake from the world of reptiles or from the djinn? When would the meet-ing be? Was she, I wondered, aware of me and would she return out of pity for my consuming passion?

One stormy morning with the rain pouring down so hard that I could hear the drops rattling on the window pane, I lit the stove and lay down in bed between the covers seeking refuge from an agonizing trembling that racked my yearning body which, ablaze with unquenchable desire, called out for relief.

I heard a faint rustling sound coming from the corner of the wall right beside my bed. I looked down and kept my eyes fixed on one of the holes in the wall, which I found was slowly, very slowly, expanding. Closing my eyes, my heart raced with joy and my body throbbed with mounting desire as there dawned in me the hope of an encounter. I lay back in submission to what was to be. No longer did I care whether love was coming from the world of reptiles or from that of the djinn, sovereigns of the world. Even were this love to mean my destruction, my desire for it was greater.

I heard a hissing noise that drew nearer, then it changed to a gentle whispering in my ear, calling to me: 'I am love, O enchantress. I showed you my home in your sleep; I called to you to my kingdom when your soul was dozing on the horizon of dreams, so come, my sweet beloved, come and let us explore the depths of the azure sea of pleasure. There, in the chamber of coral, amidst cool, shady rocks where reigns deep, restful silence lies our bed, lined with soft, bright green damask, inlaid with pearls newly wrenched from their shells. Come, let me sleep with you as I have slept with beautiful women and have given them bliss. Come, let me prise out your pearl from its shell that I may polish it and bring forth its splendour. Come to where no one will find us, where no one will see us, for the eyes of swimming creatures are innocent and will not heed what we do nor understand what we say. Down there lies repose, lies a cure for all your yearnings and ills. Come, without fear or dread, for no creature will reach us in our hidden world, and only the eye of God alone will see us; He alone will know what we are about and He will watch over us.'

I began to be intoxicated by the soft musical whisperings. I felt her cool and soft and smooth, her coldness producing a painful convulsion in my body and hurting me to the point of terror. I felt her as she slipped between the covers, then her two tiny fangs, like two pearls, began to caress my body; arriving at my thighs, the golden tongue, like an *arak* twig, inserted its pronged tip between them and began sipping and exhaling; sipping the poisons of my desire and exhaling the nectar of my ecstasy, till my whole body tingled and started to shake in sharp, painful, rapturous spasms – and all the while the tenderest of words were whispered to me as I confided to her all my longings.

At last the cool touch withdrew, leaving me exhausted. I went into a deep slumber to awake at noon full of energy, all of me a joyful burgeoning to life. Curiosity and a desire to know who it was seized me again. I looked at the corner of the wall and found that the hole was wide open. Once again I was overcome by fear. I pointed out the crack to my husband, unable to utter, although terror had once again awakened in me passionate desire. My husband filled up the crack with cement and went to sleep.

Morning came and everyone went out. I finished my housework and began roaming around the rooms in boredom, battling against the desire to surrender myself to sleep. I sat in the hallway and suddenly she appeared before me, gentle as an angel, white as day, softly undulating and flexing herself, calling to me in her bewitching whisper: 'Bride of mine, I called you and brought you to my home. I have wedded you, so there is no sin in our love, nothing to reproach yourself about. I am the guardian of the house, and I hold sway over the snakes and vipers that inhabit it, so come and I shall show you where they live. Have no fear so long as we are together. You and I are in accord. Bring a container with water and I shall place my fingers over your hand and we shall recite together some verses from the Qur'an, then we shall sprinkle it in the places from which they emerge and shall thus close the doors on them, and it shall be a pact between us that your hands will not do harm to them.'

'Then you are one of the monarchs of the djinn?' I asked eagerly. 'Why do you not bring me treasures and riches as we hear about in fables when a human takes as sister her companion among the djinn?'

She laughed at my words, shaking her golden hair that was like dazzling threads of light. She whispered to me, coquettishly: 'How greedy is mankind! Are not the pleasures of the body enough? Were I to come to you with wealth we would both die consumed by fire.'

'No, no,' I called out in alarm. 'God forbid that I should ask for unlawful wealth. I merely asked it of you as a test, that it might be positive proof that I am not imagining things and living in dreams.'

She said: 'And do intelligent humans have to have something tangible as evidence? By God, do you not believe in His ability to create worlds and living beings? Do you not know that you have an existence in worlds other than that of matter and the transitory? Fine, since you ask for proof, come close to me and my caresses will put vitality back into your limbs. You will retain your youth. I shall give you abiding youth and the delights of love – and they are more precious than wealth in the world of man. How many fortunes have women spent in quest of them? As for me I shall feed from the poisons of your desire, the exhalations of your burning passion, for that is my nourishment and through it I live.'

'I thought that your union with me was for love, not for nourishment and the perpetuation of youth and vigour,' I said in amazement.

'And is sex anything but food for the body and an interaction in union and love?' she said. 'Is it not this that makes human beings happy and is the secret of feeling joy and elation?'

She stretched out her radiant hand to my body, passing over it like the sun's rays and discharging into it warmth and a sensation of languor.

'I am ill,' I said. 'I am ill. I am ill,' I kept on repeating. When he heard me my husband brought the doctor, who said: 'High blood pressure, heart trouble, nervous depression.' Having prescribed various medicaments he left. The stupidity of doctors! My doctor did not know that he was describing the symptoms of love, did not even know it was from love I was suffering. Yet I knew my illness and the secret of my cure. I showed my husband the enlarged hole in the wall and once again he stopped it up. We then carried the bed to another corner.

After some days had passed I found another hole alongside my bed. My beloved came and whispered to me: 'Why are you so coy and flee from me, my bride? Is it fear of your being rebuffed or is it from aversion? Are you not happy with our being together? Why do you want for us to be apart?'

'I am in agony,' I whispered back. 'Your love is so intense and the desire to enjoy you so consuming. I am frightened I shall feel that I am tumbling down into a bottomless pit and being destroyed.'

'My beloved,' she said. 'I shall only appear to you in beauty's most immaculate form.'

'But it is natural for you to be a man,' I said in a precipitate outburst, 'seeing that you are so determined to have a love affair with me.'

'Perfect beauty is to be found only in woman,' she said, 'so yield to me and I shall let you taste undreamed of happiness; I shall guide you to worlds possessed of such beauty as you have never imagined.'

She stretched out her fingers to caress me, while her delicate mouth sucked in the poisons of my desire and exhaled the nectar of my ecstasy, carrying me off into a trance of delicious happiness.

After that we began the most pleasurable of love affairs, wandering together in worlds and living on horizons of dazzling beauty, a world fashioned of jewels, a world whose every moment was radiant with light and formed a thousand shapes, a thousand colours.

As for the opening in the wall, I no longer took any notice. I no longer complained of feeling ill, in fact there burned within me abounding vitality. Sometimes I would bring a handful of wormwood and, by way of jest, would stop up the crack, just as the beloved teases her lover and closes the window in his face that, ablaze with desire for her, he may hasten to the door. After that I would sit for a long time and enjoy watching the wormwood powder being scattered in spiral rings by unseen puffs of wind. Then I would throw myself down on the bed and wait.

For months I immersed myself in my world, no longer calculating time or counting the days, until one morning my husband went out on the balcony lying behind our favoured wall alongside the bed. After a while I heard him utter a cry of alarm. We all hurried out to find him holding a stick, with a black, ugly snake almost two metres long, lying at his feet.

I cried out with a sorrow whose claws clutched at my heart so that it began to beat wildly. With crazed fury I shouted at my husband: 'Why have you broken the pact and killed it? What harm has it done?' How cruel is man! He lets no creature live in peace.

I spent the night sorrowful and apprehensive. My lover came to me and embraced me more passionately than ever. I whispered to her imploringly: 'Be kind, beloved. Are you angry with me or sad because of me?'

'It is farewell,' she said. 'You have broken the pact and have betrayed one of my subjects, so you must both depart from this house, for only love lives in it.'

In the morning I packed up so that we might move to one of the employees' buildings, leaving the house in which I had learnt of love and enjoyed incomparable pleasures.

I still live in memory and in hope. I crave for the house and miss my secret love. Who knows, perhaps one day my beloved will call me. Who really knows?

9.5

From *Seeing Red: American Indian Women Speaking about Their Religious and Political Perspectives*

Inés Maria Talamantez

I don't presume to speak for the women whose voices I document in this essay. Yet I feel that their voices are also my voice, and I am in the process of understanding how to write the history that they speak about and how to describe their religious perspectives. I focus here on the voices of contemporary indigenous women. Too often we look to the old texts and feel comforted by the wisdom of those women who have now passed on. Yet there are indigenous women across this land whose religious and political perspectives can enrich us all today. The Chicano and American Indian Movement of the sixties produced writers who gave voice to our struggles and helped me to begin to find my own voice. Examining the warp and woof of a history whose tightly woven threads are not easily unraveled, I remember what a Dene weaver at the Hubbell Trading Post, Ganado, Arizona, once said to me as she sat before her loom. "Weaving," she said, "is about understanding power."

Documents

Document 1. Meredith Begay: An Apache Medicine Woman

Meredith Begay is a contemporary medicine woman, spiritual adviser, and teacher of the traditions of the Mescalero Apache Reservation in New Mexico. The following is an interview on the role of medicine in Apache culture, recorded June 1994 on a trip to collect Indian Banana for an Apache female initiation ceremony.

Inés: Meredith, you're a Medicine Woman and very much respected by your people here at the Mescalero Reservation, and you're also trying to teach people beyond Mescalero. I am interested in talking with you to find out how you deal with it. A lot of people think of Medicine Women as something from the past, except for New Agers who keep inventing Medicine Women. So I would like to know what it is you do, why you do it and what your concerns are in terms of the present Apache Traditions and some of the political issues you face in being a Medicine Woman today.

Meredith: Medicine is Traditional Indian medicine. The focal point of it is healing. To be healed, the person has to live a healthy, good life. What I feel I am doing is just being an instrument to help heal. This is what I am doing for my people to help the young children. To help them understand that there is medicine and that there is

Apache religion and that all of these cohese in order to be an Apache, a proud Indian. That's what it is. I don't profess to be the greatest medicine person. I don't profess to say that I know all medicines, *no*. I know my area; I know how far I can go with my medicines. And if somebody needs further medicine with a more stronger power I refer that person. A lot of times I have helped other people heal. I have talked to them, or sometimes they ask for herbs, so I give them herbs, but I use them holistically. I don't just give it to them in a tea form and say here, drink this – no, I don't do that. I use it holistically.

And I always stress that I am just a little person in this world trying to help my Indian people wherever they are, to help them understand that there is still good in traditional medicine and that medicine is all around us, the pharmacy is all around us, and it doesn't cost anything; it's free. It's for the people to get healed and live right. These are the things that I stress, and especially for the children I try to stress that they know their medicine, know that they have a heritage – something to be proud of and especially the Apache child. I always do this. I give them a lot of insight and teach them how to harvest medicine, when to get it, how to preserve it, and how to use it when they need it. This is what I do. But in order to become a medicine person you have to have lived the life on a reservation with Indian people. You have to know the intricacies of equalness between earth, plant, trees, rock, clouds. All of nature you have to know, have equalness with it and understand it, even the tiniest little insect. You have to understand that.

It is said that when a little black ant gets sacred pollen that has dropped to the ground, and the little ant is under you, and it gets pollen on it, it feels good. It's happy because it was blessed, and that's the way you have to be with Mother Nature. You don't over use it, and you don't under use. You equalize everything. That's the way you live. And a lot of these people that are now coming into medicine, it's not going to take one day or one night or one year to learn. It's going to take about 10, 15 years before they really understand and get to the focal point of what medicine is. You cannot practice Indian medicine at all in the United States unless you have been brought up into a particular life way. You have to have a background, people in your background, people that know how to heal, that tell you the story of the medicine, the way that it was applied, how it was used. You don't learn those things in just a matter of four days or five days. You learn it over a period of time, and then when you perform for other people, it will show.

A lot of it is fake today. You can tell the fake medicine from the real. A lot of people will copy you. Coyote copied a lot of people but he always came out at the short end of the stick. You have to do it with dignity, with faith, and if you don't have that you are not performing right. Anybody can copy a sweat; anybody can copy a ceremony or dance; anybody can copy these things, but if they don't have the essence, it's no use; it's no good; it's a waste of time; it's a waste of money; it's just a lot of hogwash – because the end result is what you look at after you've performed something. The end results show the truth. If it was good, the person will feel good when they come out of it. If it was just an act, the person will still feel the same as when they went into the healing, dance or ceremony. That's how it is, and medicine is not to be played with because since you're an instrument or something to that effect – you're an instrument for the Supreme Being – you have to do within your own realm what you can do.

Like I said, if you can't do any more than what you've done, if you've helped the person as much as you can, you refer them to the next medicine person that has a little more power or maybe a different approach. Usually your true medicine people are poor – they don't have much. They don't have much in ways of physical things, maybe they don't have a big house and cars – things like that – they are poor people. Their spirit is very, very big. They are strong, they are giving, they are kind.

But a person that goes into medicine for money, then that person is in it for me, I and myself – nobody else matters. Their attitude is, I don't care. I'm just copying so I get the money. That's their whole idea. It's not like that. A true medicine person doesn't do that, doesn't put these things ahead. A true medicine person puts the sick person or whomever needs help ahead of me, I and myself. They put it ahead, they want to help. They give all that they can give, and the end result, like I said, is what comes out after the person is either healed or half healed or is on its way to healing. So this is why there could be a lot of people out there saying I'm a medicine person, but within their own life they are going to come to a crossroads.

****

Document 3. Pilulaw Khus: Chumash Culture

Pilulaw Khus is a highly respected Chumash elder who lives in Santa Barbara, California. In the following account she analyzes Chumash culture from daily life in Chumash villages before missionization until recent struggles for recovery of the sacred site of Point Conception. She also discusses her own role within that culture.[1]

Mother Earth, Hutash, is very important to us. It is hard to understand. I'm not saying that any other nation or area of the world is less. I just know that within our nation, there is an incredible amount of power. There are amazingly powerful sacred places within the Chumash nation, and that is one of my primary jobs, that's the direction I've been given. The assignment I've been given is to protect the sacred places and to do the ceremonies. Point Conception, commonly known as Western Gate, is a very powerful place for our people, and not just our people; it also includes the stories of other native people.

When the Europeans came here, first there were the Spaniards, the military, and the priests. Secondly came the Mexican government and then the U.S. government. With each invasion our people suffered more. Within one generation, the population of our people was reduced by half: our systems were pretty much out the window. There was a well-thought-out and specific plan of genocide. Take a minute and think about it, that in one generation people were watching their world being destroyed. Their families were being pulled apart. If we went into a mission together there – because we were very spiritual people of course we were interested in this new spirituality the people were bringing – we weren't allowed to leave. We became slave labor. And, later, when our people did leave, the military was sent out to bring us back. Frequently we were killed in those raids. Think about the holocaust coming down on us, in one generation. We'd been going along for thousands and thousands and thousands of years, doing things for the most part in the same way.

When a baby was conceived that baby was beginning to be taught about people and about the baby's place within the group and the environment, and as soon as the baby was born, there would be ceremonies and there would be certain things to take care of that baby, to introduce that baby not just to the parents, but to all the people, to the environment and to the universe. And that baby would know its place, and it worked well.

The idea of changing by assimilating, by contact with others, it didn't work that much for us. We were a very integrated group. We were very satisfied with how it operated. We lived in a paradise, and so we had no real need to change a whole lot. We're still that way. We're what people might call clannish. We're not real interested in having people bringing their ways of doing things and doing it on our land. If you think about that consistency and that persistence coming through time, in that way, and that all of a sudden, something hits and everything is wiped out in one generation, that is devastation, that is holocaust. The death rate soared during that time and the birth rate dropped during that time, and that makes perfect sense to me. Who would want to bring a baby into the world when that world was no longer your own anymore? Who would want to live in that kind of situation?

When the U.S. government came in, they said okay, we want to make a treaty with you tribes, and they were really determined to take over all our land. In that treaty, the one thing we held onto (we said they could take everything if they would leave us one thing) and that was Point Conception, because it was so important. The Western Gate, that's where our spirits go through, pierce that veil and go into the next reality. And it's very important that it be left open so that we can go through.

In 1975/76, companies called Western Light and Natural Gas and Pacific Gas and Electric decided they were going to put a facility there, a big plant, and we didn't know anything about the treaties. The reason we didn't know anything was that when it got back to Washington, D.C., the politicians in California here prevailed on the officials back in D.C. to put our treaty under a seal of secrecy. This was done with about eighteen treaties here in California. So people treated in good faith with the representative of the government and believed that this was going to give some protection to the Western Gate, and the seal of secrecy allowed them to do what they want to and not live up to the conditions of the treaty. These treaties have only recently surfaced. Ours was found when we were on the occupation out there at Point Conception.

When these companies decided to put that facility out there, I had already been married, had children, divorced, and been in and out of the area. At about this time I was pulled back to Santa Barbara and started to work on an educational project, and then this occupation came up, and that was pretty much when I began to work in a more public open way. I went out in the occupation because we couldn't allow the plant to be put there. It would interfere with the spirits from this reality. We did everything the way you're supposed to do. We had lawyers, people from the

Environmental Defense Center. … We did everything, tried every legal way, but the court said this may be good for your spirituality, but the greater good is for the natural gas plant to be put there. This was crazy, not just from a spiritual point of view, but from an environmental point of view, because a lot of earthquake faults are there and seas are very rough, and they were going to be loading and off-loading these volatile fuels out there, in what they called the graveyard of ships.

So we were very innocent and naive. We said we'd go and occupy because we can't allow this to be put out there. So we were innocent, all of us, and we packed up our backpacks and sleeping bags and we went out there and we set up a sweat lodge and we sweated, and we prayed and we sat out there. We thought now they'll see we're really serious and they'll go away. But no, we ended up being out there for close to a year on that occupation, and that was an incredibly important period of time. There were people who came here to support us from all the different nations and from Alaska, Canada, Mexico, and over and over and over again, when I talked to people, they said we know of this place, that's why we've come to help you, because it's our story. We had a phenomenal amount of help out there. That was one the Native people won. They did not put their plant out there. We won that one, and it's still clean out there. Our spirits can still travel back and forth out there.

That's the way I got started on the protection of sites and battling in that way, for that particular place and that particular purpose. I feel very strongly about any place where our people were, whether it's just an ordinary village or a sacred site. Remember that at ordinary village sites people have been living there for thousands of years, and as people lived there, that place became more and more sacred. Why? Because they were birthing there, they were dying, they were doing ceremonies there, and they were going into spirits there. Their bodies were being returned to the embrace of our mother, and each time these kinds of things occur, a place becomes increasingly sacred. … I tell my children, when I die I want to go like an Indian into the mother, because she gave me my life and sustained me all my life, and it is only right that I return to her and that the life cycles can continue. Somebody is returned to the earth in that way. They go into the earth. There is a change that begins to happen in that soil, and the longer the burial stays in the earth, the more that change occurs. That person's essence permeates throughout the soil, so even the grasses, trees, flowers are all that person coming into all of that, and beyond to even the birds and animals that are there and feed are being benefited by the essence of that person.

We can't stop the ceremonies. I've received my bundle in a ceremony. I was given the opportunity to walk away from it, because once accepted I have responsibility that goes with that. I was told there would be times when no one would come, when I'd do it by myself and that's the way it is. It doesn't matter if anyone else is there, I have a responsibility to earth, to ancestors, to spirits, the universe, the people, to earth, to myself.

The way I've been taught, if someone comes here, they need to be taught. I say to non-Native, you're welcome to come here and sit by the fire. All people are connected to the earth and recognize what people are doing, the destruction. Come and be part of this, but at some point you need to give up and leave my fire and find your own ancestors, become strong and knowledgeable in your own way.

Note

1. This document is taken from Pilalau Khus's lecture to a religious studies class on myth
    and symbols at the University of California at Santa Barbara, April 7, 1994. The lecture
    was transcribed by D. Bell.

9.6
The Clan of One-Breasted Women
Terry Tempest Williams

Epilogue

I belong to a Clan of One-Breasted Women. My mother, my grandmothers, and six aunts have all had mastectomies. Seven are dead. The two who survive have just completed rounds of chemotherapy and radiation.

I've had my own problems: two biopsies for breast cancer and a small tumor between my ribs diagnosed as a "borderline malignancy."

This is my family history.

Most statistics tell us breast cancer is genetic, hereditary, with rising percentages attached to fatty diets, childlessness, or becoming pregnant after thirty. What they don't say is living in Utah may be the greatest hazard of all.

We are a Mormon family with roots in Utah since 1847. The "word of wisdom" in my family aligned us with good foods – no coffee, no tea, tobacco, or alcohol. For the most part, our women were finished having their babies by the time they were thirty. And only one faced breast cancer prior to 1960. Traditionally, as a group of people, Mormons have a low rate of cancer.

Is our family a cultural anomaly? The truth is, we didn't think about it. Those who did, usually the men, simply said, "bad genes." The women's attitude was stoic. Cancer was part of life. On February 16, 1971, the eve of my mother's surgery, I accidently picked up the telephone and overheard her ask my grandmother what she could expect.

"Diane, it is one of the most spiritual experiences you will ever encounter."

I quietly put down the receiver.

Two days later, my father took my brothers and me to the hospital to visit her. She met us in the lobby in a wheelchair. No bandages were visible. I'll never forget her radiance, the way she held herself in a purple velvet robe, and how she gathered us around her.

"Children, I am fine. I want you to know I felt the arms of God around me."

We believed her. My father cried. Our mother, his wife, was thirty-eight years old.

A little over a year after Mother's death, Dad and I were having dinner together. He had just returned from St. George, where the Tempest Company was completing the gas lines that would service southern Utah. He spoke of his love for the country, the sandstoned landscape, bare-boned and beautiful. He had just finished hiking the

Kolob trail in Zion National Park. We got caught up in reminiscing, recalling with fondness our walk up Angel's Landing on his fiftieth birthday and the years our family had vacationed there.

Over dessert, I shared a recurring dream of mine. I told my father that for years, as long as I could remember, I saw this flash of light in the night in the desert – that this image had so permeated my being that I could not venture south without seeing it again, on the horizon, illuminating buttes and mesas.

"You did see it," he said.

"Saw what?"

"The bomb. The cloud. We were driving home from Riverside, California. You were sitting on Diane's lap. She was pregnant. In fact, I remember the day, September 7, 1957. We had just gotten out of the Service. We were driving north, past Las Vegas. It was an hour or so before dawn, when this explosion went off. We not only heard it, but felt it. I thought the oil tanker in front of us had blown up. We pulled over and suddenly, rising from the desert floor, we saw it, clearly, this golden-stemmed cloud, the mushroom. The sky seemed to vibrate with an eerie pink glow. Within a few minutes, a light ash was raining on the car.

I stared at my father.

"I thought you knew that," he said. "It was a common occurrence in the fifties."

It was at this moment that I realized the deceit I had been living under. Children growing up in the American Southwest, drinking contaminated milk from contaminated cows, even from the contaminated breasts of their mothers, my mother – members, years later, of the Clan of One-Breasted Women.

It is a well-known story in the Desert West, "The Day We Bombed Utah," or more accurately, the years we bombed Utah: above ground atomic testing in Nevada took place from January 27, 1951 through July 11, 1962. Not only were the winds blowing north covering "low-use segments of the population" with fallout and leaving sheep dead in their tracks, but the climate was right. The United States of the 1950s was red, white, and blue. The Korean War was raging. McCarthyism was rampant. Ike was it, and the cold war was hot. If you were against nuclear testing, you were for a communist regime.

Much has been written about this "American nuclear tragedy." Public health was secondary to national security. The Atomic Energy Commissioner, Thomas Murray, said, "Gentlemen, we must not let anything interfere with this series of tests, nothing."

Again and again, the American public was told by its government, in spite of burns, blisters, and nausea, "It has been found that the tests may be conducted with adequate assurance of safety under conditions prevailing at the bombing reservations." Assuaging public fears was simply a matter of public relations. "Your best action," an Atomic Energy Commission booklet read, "is not to be worried about fallout." A news release typical of the times stated, "We find no basis for concluding that harm to any individual has resulted from radioactive fallout."

On August 30, 1979, during Jimmy Carter's presidency, a suit was filed, *Irene Allen v. The United States of America*. Mrs. Allen's case was the first on an alphabetical list of twenty-four test cases, representative of nearly twelve hundred plaintiffs seeking compensation from the United States government for cancers caused by nuclear testing in Nevada.

Irene Allen lived in Hurricane, Utah. She was the mother of five children and had been widowed twice. Her first husband, with their two oldest boys, had watched the tests from the roof of the local high school. He died of leukemia in 1956. Her second husband died of pancreatic cancer in 1978.

In a town meeting conducted by Utah Senator Orrin Hatch, shortly before the suit was filed, Mrs. Allen said, "I am not blaming the government, I want you to know that, Senator Hatch. But I thought if my testimony could help in any way so this wouldn't happen again to any of the generations coming up after us ... I am happy to be here this day to bear testimony of this."

God-fearing people. This is just one story in an anthology of thousands.

On May 10, 1984, Judge Bruce S. Jenkins handed down his opinion. Ten of the plaintiffs were awarded damages. It was the first time a federal court had determined that nuclear tests had been the cause of cancers. For the remaining fourteen test cases, the proof of causation was not sufficient. In spite of the split decision, it was considered a landmark ruling. It was not to remain so for long.

In April 1987, the Tenth Circuit Court of Appeals overturned Judge Jenkins's ruling on the ground that the United States was protected from suit by the legal doctrine of sovereign immunity, a centuries-old idea from England in the days of absolute monarchs.

In January 1988, the Supreme Court refused to review the Appeals Court decision. To our court system it does not matter whether the United States government was irresponsible, whether it lied to its citizens, or even that citizens died from the fallout of nuclear testing. What matters is that our government is immune: "The King can do no wrong."

In Mormon culture, authority is respected, obedience is revered, and independent thinking is not. I was taught as a young girl not to "make waves" or "rock the boat."

"Just let it go," Mother would say. "You know how you feel, that's what counts."

For many years, I have done just that – listened, observed, and quietly formed my own opinions, in a culture that rarely asks questions because it has all the answers. But one by one, I have watched the women in my family die common, heroic deaths. We sat in waiting rooms hoping for good news, but always receiving the bad. I cared for them, bathed their scarred bodies, and kept their secrets. I watched beautiful women become bald as Cytoxan, cisplatin, and Adriamycin were injected into their veins. I held their foreheads as they vomited green-black bile, and I shot them with morphine when the pain became inhuman. In the end, I witnessed their last peaceful breaths, becoming a midwife to the rebirth of their souls.

The price of obedience has become too high.

The fear and inability to question authority that ultimately killed rural communities in Utah during atmospheric testing of atomic weapons is the same fear I saw in my mother's body. Sheep. Dead sheep. The evidence is buried.

I cannot prove that my mother, Diane Dixon Tempest, or my grandmothers, Lettie Romney Dixon and Kathryn Blackett Tempest, along with my aunts developed cancer from nuclear fallout in Utah. But I can't prove they didn't.

My father's memory was correct. The September blast we drove through in 1957 was part of Operation Plumbbob, one of the most intensive series of bomb tests to be initiated. The flash of light in the night in the desert, which I had always thought was a dream, developed into a family nightmare. It took fourteen years, from 1957 to 1971, for cancer to manifest in my mother – the same time, Howard L. Andrews, an authority in radioactive fallout at the National Institutes of Health, says radiation cancer requires to become evident. The more I learn about what it means to be a "downwinder," the more questions I drown in.

What I do know, however, is that as a Mormon woman of the fifth generation of Latter-day Saints, I must question everything, even if it means losing my faith, even if it means becoming a member of a border tribe among my own people. Tolerating blind obedience in the name of patriotism or religion ultimately takes our lives.

When the Atomic Energy Commission described the country north of the Nevada Test Site as "virtually uninhabited desert terrain," my family and the birds at Great Salt Lake were some of the "virtual uninhabitants."

One night, I dreamed women from all over the world circled a blazing fire in the desert. They spoke of change, how they hold the moon in their bellies and wax and wane with its phases. They mocked the presumption of even-tempered beings and made promises that they would never fear the witch inside themselves. The women danced wildly as sparks broke away from the flames and entered the night sky as stars.

And they sang a song given to them by Shoshone grandmothers:

Ah ne nah, nah	Consider the rabbits
nin nah nah –	How gently they walk on the earth –
ah ne nah, nah	Consider the rabbits
nin nah nah –	How gently they walk on the earth –
Nyaga mutzi	We remember them
oh ne nay –	We can walk gently also –
Nyaga mutzi	We remember them
oh ne nay –	We can walk gently also –

The women danced and drummed and sang for weeks, preparing themselves for what was to come. They would reclaim the desert for the sake of their children, for the sake of the land.

A few miles downwind from the fire circle, bombs were being tested. Rabbits felt the tremors. Their soft leather pads on paws and feet recognized the shaking sands, while the roots of mesquite and sage were smoldering. Rocks were hot from the inside out and dust devils hummed unnaturally. And each time there was another nuclear test, ravens watched the desert heave. Stretch marks appeared. The land was losing its muscle.

The women couldn't bear it any longer. They were mothers. They had suffered labor pains but always under the promise of birth. The red hot pains beneath the desert promised death only, as each bomb became a stillborn. A contract had been made and broken between human beings and the land. A new contract was being drawn by the women, who understood the fate of the earth as their own.

Under the cover of darkness, ten women slipped under a barbed-wire fence and entered the contaminated country. They were trespassing. They walked toward the town of Mercury, in moonlight, taking their cues from coyote, kit fox, antelope squirrel, and quail. They moved quietly and deliberately through the maze of Joshua trees. When a hint of daylight appeared they rested, drinking tea and sharing their rations of food. The women closed their eyes. The time had come to protest with the heart, that to deny one's genealogy with the earth was to commit treason against one's soul.

At dawn, the women draped themselves in mylar, wrapping long streamers of silver plastic around their arms to blow in the breeze. They wore clear masks, that became the faces of humanity. And when they arrived at the edge of Mercury, they carried all the butterflies of a summer day in their wombs. They paused to allow their courage to settle.

The town that forbids pregnant women and children to enter because of radiation risks was asleep. The women moved through the streets as winged messengers, twirling around each other in slow motion, peeking inside homes and watching the easy sleep of men and women. They were astonished by such stillness and periodically would utter a shrill note or low cry just to verify life.

The residents finally awoke to these strange apparitions. Some simply stared. Others called authorities, and in time, the women were apprehended by wary soldiers dressed in desert fatigues. They were taken to a white, square building on the other edge of Mercury. When asked who they were and why they were there, the women replied, "We are mothers and we have come to reclaim the desert for our children."

The soldiers arrested them. As the ten women were blindfolded and handcuffed, they began singing:

> *You can't forbid us everything*
> *You can't forbid us to think –*
> *You can't forbid our tears to flow*
> *And you can't stop the songs that we sing.*

The women continued to sing louder and louder, until they heard the voices of their sisters moving across the mesa:

> *Ah ne nah, nah*
> *nin nah nah –*
> *Ah ne nah, nah*
> *nin nah nah –*
> *Nyaga mutzi*
> *oh ne nay –*
> *Nyaga mutzi*
> *oh ne nay –*

"Call for reinforcements," one soldier said.

"We have," interrupted one woman, "we have – and you have no idea of our numbers."

I crossed the line at the Nevada Test Site and was arrested with nine other Utahns for trespassing on military lands. They are still conducting nuclear tests in the desert. Ours was an act of civil disobedience. But as I walked toward the town of Mercury, it was more than a gesture of peace. It was a gesture on behalf of the Clan of One-Breasted Women.

As one officer cinched the handcuffs around my wrists, another frisked my body. She found a pen and a pad of paper tucked inside my left boot.

"And these?" she asked sternly.

"Weapons," I replied.

Our eyes met. I smiled. She pulled the leg of my trousers back over my boot.

"Step forward, please," she said as she took my arm.

We were booked under an afternoon sun and bused to Tonopah, Nevada. It was a two-hour ride. This was familiar country. The Joshua trees standing their ground had been named by my ancestors, who believed they looked like prophets pointing west to the Promised Land. These were the same trees that bloomed each spring, flowers appearing like white flames in the Mojave. And I recalled a full moon in May, when Mother and I had walked among them, flushing out mourning doves and owls.

The bus stopped short of town. We were released.

The officials thought it was a cruel joke to leave us stranded in the desert with no way to get home. What they didn't realize was that we were home, soul-centered and strong, women who recognized the sweet smell of sage as fuel for our spirits.

9.7

Life out of Balance

Lori Arviso Alvord and Elizabeth Cohen Van Pelt

This was where I was supposed to be. I was coming home richer than I had left, laden with gifts, knowledge, and state-of-the-art medical training. It was now time for me to give back to the people who had given me the opportunity to pursue my education – my tribe had footed much of the Dartmouth bill.

Atop Gallup's highest promontory stands the Gallup Indian Medical Center. The blue-and-white five-story hospital, with its wide halls and large, low windows, is characteristic of buildings the government built in the 1960s. It commands an impressive eagle's-nest view of the surrounding hills and the rust-colored bay of desert below. Like all Indian Health Service facilities, GIMC treats exclusively Native people, mostly Navajo, although some patients come from Zuni, Hopi, and other Indian pueblos.

All of the medicine practiced at IHS hospitals like GIMC is free to Indian patients, as a result of treaties between the U.S. government and Native American tribes. Sometimes people say they think that is an enormous benefit, proof that Native people are treated well in this country. As I grew accustomed to my new practice in Gallup, it often occurred to me that much of what we were treating were white men's diseases – syndromes and conditions the people would never have known if not for the European colonizers. I am referring to much more than the infamous smallpox-infected blankets. There were other diseases – tuberculosis, measles, whooping cough, and mumps. These and the malaria, yellow fever, and influenza brought by Columbus, had killed off 90 percent of all Native Americans in the New World. Still other diseases were caused by lifestyle changes, such as poor diet and inactivity – an indirect result of the influence of white people.

The ancestors of my people who migrated across the expanses of desert and mountain of the Southwest had rarely suffered from obesity, diabetes, or heart disease. Smoking-related diseases – hypertension, heart disease, lung cancer, oral cancers – did not exist either. Tobacco was used rarely and in moderation, kept in "balance." Just as many of the diseases were Western diseases, the medicine we were practicing was Western medicine, practiced in the white men's way – and the patients knew it. It seemed to me sometimes that the whole arrangement was an awkward fit.

The doctors at GIMC found their Navajo patients both confusing and compelling. Many of them worked through translators and often after their conditions were explained to them through these translators, the patients still did not seem to have a clue what was going on. And vice versa: the physicians didn't really understand the words of their patients.

****

As I learned the ropes I also noticed the unique culture of the hospital itself. The higher positions in the GIMC administration were almost all held by Anglos. The entire medical staff – with the exception of Dr. Taylor McKenzie, who was the first Navajo doctor; Dr. Valden Johnson, a Navajo anesthesiologist; and I – were non-Navajo. Roy Smith, a Navajo from Standing Rock, was our patient advocate. A strong and stocky man, with a ponytail protruding from beneath his baseball cap, Roy found ways for families to help sick members get around, arranged for rehabilitation, worked out finances, and even helped them deal with the one thing that Navajos can't stand to think about – advance directives, or living wills.

Because Navajos are so uncomfortable with death and dying, speaking to them about making a decision to end life, to stop a life-support system, was nearly impossible and had to be handled very carefully. The discomfort arises partly because of the Navajo belief in the power of language, the belief that you can "speak" something into existence. Most Navajos, for instance, would never say, "If I fall into a coma, I don't want to be kept alive." Such verbalizing would be seen as asking for it to happen.

Roy was able to finesse these problematic and culturally sensitive areas with skill and kindness. Patients responded well to his presence. And he handled the *bilagáana* administrators well, too. He was quite a talented man.

As for Dr. McKenzie, I had grown up in awe of him. He had been in practice on the rez when I was a child, and everyone knew of him. By the time I came to GIMC, however, he was nearing retirement. He rarely worked in the OR and mostly did clinic visits and a few special cases.

When I first got to GIMC I often observed Roy, Dr. McKenzie, and Valden Johnson, who was near my own age. We had our own silent code of medicine. Sometimes when we saw a brash young Anglo doctor whip through an exam gazing inappropriately, hurrying, talking loudly, cutting off the patient when they ventured to ask a question, and moving their hands over their bodies in a methodical, impersonal, irreverent fashion, we exchanged glances. I saw my own unease echoed in Roy's eyes. That was not the way to treat a Navajo person, not if you wanted the patient to respond positively, not if you wanted them to get well.

One afternoon, while removing an infected gallbladder with a colleague, Barney Nelson, I grew extremely frustrated. Cast in the blue glow of the video monitor, Barney was suctioning up a mauve pool of bile and blood in the area where we were working, while I removed the gallbladder and brought it up through a small incision in the abdomen. It was a laparoscopic procedure, in which tiny tools are used through a "keyhole" incision in the abdomen, at that time a state-of-the-art technology that I'd learned at Stanford.

The patient, a woman in her fifties named Evelyn Bitsui, had come into the hospital for gallbladder surgery. She'd arrived with her daughter, Josephine Smith, who translated for her. When I met them, Evelyn was lying on a hospital bed, waiting for her pre-op consultation. Josephine was seated beside her. Unfortunately Sue Stuart, her surgeon, had come down with the flu.

"Your doctor is sick, Evelyn," I told her. "If you want, I can perform your surgery instead of her, or you can wait and come back another day."

I waited while Josephine translated. They had traveled a long way, perhaps with some trouble, over very muddy roads, the result of hard rains the night before. It would be difficult for them just to leave and come back another day. "Think about it, and I'll come back and see you in a little while," I said.

I was called down to the OR for my first case of the day, a teenage boy who was having increasingly severe attacks of abdominal pain, caused by gallstones. Although he showed no signs of infection, he was in a lot of pain. He looked so uncomfortable, I had scheduled him as early as possible. The surgery was uneventful, and we were finished by nine o'clock.

Then I went over to 2 East, where patients are prepared for surgery, and met up with Evelyn and her daughter. Josephine was clearly worried about her mother. A deep gullied frown lay between her eyebrows, and she kept her hand on her mother's shoulder as she searched my face, as if trying to determine whether to trust me. Josephine was dressed in jeans and an Arizona State University T-shirt, but her mother's clothes, folded on her lap, were traditional: a long cotton print skirt, a matching shirt, and a pile of turquoise necklaces and bracelets. She had worn her best jewelry.

"Momma says she wants to get it over with," Josephine said.

"That's fine," I said, and smiled at her mother. I took a look at her chart. She had a past history of hypertension, back surgery, and left leg sciatica (pain caused by the sciatic nerve, which travels down the back of the leg).

Not bad for sixty years old, I thought. Evelyn was wheeled into the OR, and preparations for her surgery and anesthesia were begun. While Barney and I scrubbed up, Beth Jones, one of our nurse anesthetists, put her to sleep.

A few minutes later, when we first looked into the abdominal cavity with the laparoscope, I saw that we were in for a struggle. The gallbladder was covered with omental adhesions (fatty tissues that are attached to the stomach and colon, which frequently wrap around areas of infection and act as a defense mechanism to control and prevent the infection's spread). Often such adhesions are firmly attached to the gallbladder, so removing them can cause bleeding, which is exactly what happened as I tried to gently release Evelyn's. At first the blood squeezed out slowly from a few spots, then it flowed more heavily. It began along the edges of the omentum and became a miniwaterfall.

Barney and I controlled the bleeding, but not before the operative field was smeared with blood.

"Damn, I can't stand the sight of blood," I said. Barney laughed and handed me a suction irrigator, which washes the area with saline and suctions it back out, so we could proceed with the operation.

Ideally surgeons operate in a "bloodless field," and the very presence of blood indicates that an operation is not going smoothly. Uncontrolled bleeding is a surgical nightmare and can be life threatening. Nowadays we have many ways to stop it, and such situations are fairly rare.

Once the blood was gone, I got a fresh look at the gallbladder. It was inflamed, which made the walls thicker and harder to dissect.

I was tired, it was my third day in a row on call, my feet hurt, and under my gown and gloves, I felt very hot. The new scrub nurse, who was training for this kind of surgery, often handed us the wrong instrument or couldn't locate what we asked for at all. I was beginning to wish I hadn't volunteered to take the case.

"Not that," I snapped at the nurse at one point, and pointed with my nose at a Maryland dissector, which lay on the table beside her. "*That.*"

A few minutes later she handed me another wrong instrument. This time Marge Cleveland, the seasoned OR nurse, intervened. "Not that clamp. *That* one, the toothed grasping forceps," she said.

"I know," said the nurse in an irritated tone, handing me yet another wrong instrument.

"That's still the wrong one. Now watch it – watch it! Don't twist the end of that cable!" I said.

"I *know* that." The new nurse, a woman in her late twenties, had an edge of anger in her voice.

I located the cystic artery, dissected it free, placed metal clips on it, and divided it with miniature scissors. Then I stopped and stared at the video screen. The end of the artery had started bleeding heavily.

I took a deep breath and exhaled. I tried to suction the blood away, but nothing happened. It wasn't working. The suction system had become clogged somewhere.

"I need a bulb syringe right now," I ordered. The nurse scrambled to find one. Meanwhile I considered the possibilities: the surgical clip could have misfired from the "gun"; there might be a small posterior branching vessel that the clip had not closed around; or the vessel might have torn where the clip was placed. These possible explanations were flashing through my mind as I waited for the bulb syringe, which I needed to flush the suction tubing. When I looked up and saw that the nurse still didn't have the suction, I became angry. The blood was slowly rising and had covered the artery.

"Get one *now!*" I shouted this time, realizing that she had totally missed the fact that we were facing an emergency.

Once the suction was working again, I cleared the area of the accumulated blood. As Barney held up the end of the artery with his forceps, I placed another clip slightly lower than the first.

Yes, I thought. *That's it.* The vessel stopped bleeding.

I'd been holding my breath. I exhaled and took a gulp of fresh air. *Calm down, calm down,* I thought, peripherally aware that a combination of things – the heat of the room, my aching feet, the difficulty of the case, and the length of time I'd been operating that morning – was making even small things annoy me. As the rest of the operation refused to proceed smoothly, I found myself growling and swearing. We struggled to dissect through an inflamed plane of tissue between the wall of the gallbladder and the liver, finally freeing the gallbladder, only to encounter another struggle in bringing it out of the abdomen. I felt really hot and lightheaded. But finally, the operation was over.

Evelyn had done just fine, her vital signs had registered normal throughout, and she came out of anesthesia with no difficulty. She had not lost anywhere near enough blood to necessitate a transfusion. *Everything will be fine,* I thought. *Thank God.* Instinctively, I touched my silver bear fetish and felt its smooth, comforting shape.

But everything was not fine. Sometime during the next day, our patient had a stroke.

I will never forget the expressions of pure bewilderment on the faces of the family of Evelyn Bitsui as they stationed themselves outside the intensive care unit. Sitting in the plastic chairs in an alcove designed for temporary visitors, they held a twenty-four-hour vigil over the next few days. They brought in blankets and food and sometimes it seemed like a little campsite – the only thing missing were the tents and fires. The hours passed, the staff came and went, we had our showers, changed our clothes, ate our dinners, and slept in our own beds. But Josephine Smith, now joined by her son and husband and a small child, who must have been Evelyn's grandson, just stayed right there. They spoke to one another quietly, and each time we left the ICU, they looked up at our faces, searching for clues about Evelyn's condition.

The stroke had partially paralyzed her left side, and she had trouble breathing. For a few days she required a ventilator. When I came to speak with her, her eyes looked unfocused, and she didn't respond to my greeting or questions. It was as though she were looking right past me, at a spot somewhere over my right shoulder. She was staring so intensely, I was tempted on several occasions to turn around and see who was there. She looked right past the members of her family, too. She seemed completely unaware of their presence at her bedside.

Her children remarked that something like this had happened many years before, after her back surgery, which had left her left leg mildly weakened. Upon hearing this, we requested that details of her previous surgery be forwarded from Albuquerque. When the envelope arrived, I pored over the records and shook my head.

In spite of the computer age, physicians in the United States still do not have easy access to medical records from other hospitals, and they are often not requested unless something seems unusual. Although we knew that Evelyn had had surgery years before, neither the patient nor her family had told us that a stroke had been suspected at that time. Her head CT scan had been normal back then, but this time that was not the case – the CT showed an area of infarction to the brain. The lack of blood flow had occurred in the right middle cerebral artery in the temporal parietal region, the area that controls movement of the left arm and leg.

I felt a growing unease. The medical team did a variety of tests to look for the cause of the stroke: an ultrasound of the carotid arteries in the neck, probing for narrowing, damage to the artery walls, and blood clots, and an ultrasound of the heart, looking for abnormalities that might have caused it to develop clots and send them shooting up to the brain. Lastly, Evelyn's blood was tested to check for conditions that would make it thicken and clot easily. Every one of these studies came up normal. It was a mystery. According to all our data, there was no reason for this woman to have had a stroke. She would stay in the hospital for a week so we could assess the damage and then be discharged with a referral to a rehabilitation clinic. She might still recover a lot of her movement, but there was no way to tell just yet.

"No good deed goes unpunished," I said to Tim, using one of his famous quips and wishing, for the hundredth time, that I'd never offered to do that operation.

"That's right," he said wisely. "Remember that."

As I joked with him, an important realization dawned. I could not tell which physiological processes had conspired to bring about Evelyn's stroke, yet instinctively I knew the reason for it. This was not the "doctor" side of me. It was not the white side of me. It was the Navajo. In the pit of my stomach I knew what had happened.

Ever since I finished my surgical training, I had been developing a set of ideas about how to care for patients. The concepts I was beginning to form were bicultural, drawing heavily on a philosophy that is in essence very Navajo. To this day I keep adding to this theory and fine-tuning it. It has to do with working *with* patients to create a superior system of healing.

When I first returned to the Navajo area to work, I realized that although I had been well trained as a surgeon to perform operations, I had received minimal training in how to communicate well with patients. Evelyn was a perfect example. Evelyn had been frightened. I was not the doctor she'd known and was comfortable with. And during her surgery there'd been arguments in the OR. The new nurse assistant had not been listening, and I'd grown angry. The combination of all these variables – my anger, the nurse's inattentive and defensive posture, and Evelyn Bitsui's fear – had been a perfect setup for the complications that had arisen.

My anger had frightened me. Despite all I'd learned in medical school and during residency, a part of me remained underdeveloped. I could be quick-tempered and intolerant of people who weren't doing what I felt was a good job. Sometimes I was unable to control that anger. I didn't like to be questioned and I didn't like to be challenged. Sometimes my anger would flare up like a gasoline fire, then be gone as quickly as it had come. I could not control it, and could not live with its aftermath. I was not completely sure where it came from inside me. Many surgeons I have known have had this tendency to deal with difficult situations with anger. Had I unintentionally adopted this personality? Was it just impatience with laziness or incompetence? Was it a deeply felt, long-term anger over the deterioration of my culture that spilled into other areas of my life? I did not know. I knew that I still had many deficiencies when it came to my bedside manner and my "surgical personality." I was not the warmest person in the world because I didn't let people get too close to me. I wanted to be a better doctor, and I looked to the Navajo tradition of healing for answers.

From a Navajo standpoint, illness can be caused by an imbalance or lack of harmony in any area of a patient's life. I began to realize that *everything* a patient encounters has an impact on her. If illness could be caused by a lack of harmony, could not the same be true for wellness and the ability to heal? It made sense that if the healing environment was more "harmonious," a patient might return to wellness faster.

Why is it that some doctors do an operation right but their patients die? I asked. *Why do some procedures go so seriously wrong?* It had to do with other things besides the procedures and instruments, besides the preconditions of patients. It had to do with stress, fear, and the problems of the surgery.

After what happened with Evelyn, it became clearer to me why there were so many difficulties. I had operated on a patient I hardly knew, stepping in for another surgeon (something we all try to avoid) at the last minute, assuming that all would be well. I had not developed any bond of trust or acceptance in advance. During her operation, her body had been anything but cooperative, and I cringed when I thought of how either Evelyn or her spirit may have listened as I ranted during the surgery. She had no doubt sensed my own discomfort, fatigue, frustration, and anger. And the nurses had argued with each other. Even when patients are anesthetized, there is some evidence that they hear what goes on during surgery and respond to what is happening. Some surgeons or anesthesiologists will play music while operating. This is in part for their own enjoyment, but it also must soothe the patient.

Was the stroke Evelyn's body's response to the disharmony that had prevailed during her surgery? I would never know for sure. But I had been taught a powerful lesson, and I promised myself I would become more sensitive, work on my temper, and never let such conditions interfere with a patient's treatment again, if I could help it. I had to try harder to make sure that patients felt comfortable. Perhaps I could set up my practice so that the occasions for frustration and anger would be rare.

Or maybe, by working closer with nurses, staff, and other doctors, by trying to prevent problems before they arose, I could create greater harmony in my own surgical world, which could make things better for everyone on the team.

Before a surgeon proceeds with an operation, it is important that she obtain the patient's trust and acceptance, as is making sure that the patient wants to have the surgery done, that the doctor is not just talking them into it. They must understand the procedure that will be performed on them. And during the procedure, there should be a sense of *hózhǫ́* and beauty in the OR. My spirit and the patient's spirit can work together to make the surgery successful, I thought. They will encourage a positive outcome.

In the Navajo world traditional healers are expected to lead by example. They teach their patients to Walk in Beauty in part by Walking in Beauty themselves. There is no correlate for this practice in Western medicine. Physicians work and live under conditions of great stress, and there is little cultural expectation that they will take care of themselves or set an example for their patients. In a Western health care system the different components are under no obligation to work smoothly together. Because of this the results are widely variable; some relationships are cordial, but others can be antagonistic, if not downright hostile. If all the members of my team worked together harmoniously and in concert, I thought, and if we tried to gain the trust, respect, and understanding of the patient, we could create better surgical outcomes. We ourselves would be happier and less stressed as well.

I looked at every part of our hospital to see if we could do a better job of making our patients relaxed and comfortable. There were factors that could make all the difference in the world: at GIMC, many of the nurses were Navajo or from other tribes, as were many of the maintenance and secretarial staff. At night, when almost everyone else had gone home, it made the patients feel safe to have Navajo speakers caring for them.

Similarly, early on, I saw the benefits of a doctor speaking to patients in their own language. Ruby Billy and Rosemary Ramone, two of our surgical nurses, quietly and clearly spoke to elderly female patients about the surgery or treatment they needed in their native tongue. The difference was striking: these women's facial expressions were invariably calmer and more trusting.

A ten-year-old girl with a hernia was brought into the OR for an operation. She had a beautiful, innocent face, but fear was clearly etched in her eyes. Valden would make her unconscious by giving her a cocktail of anesthetic gases that had been designed specifically for her weight and age. Dressed in the blue scrubs over his old cowboy boots, Valden whispered reassuring Navajo words into her ear as she fell asleep: "*Ił wosh shiyázh.*" ("Go to sleep, little one"). The fear in her face dissipated.

Soon I began using bits of Navajo with my own patients. I began to say, "*Ni bid neezgai'ish?*" ("Does your stomach hurt?") I told them in their own language I would need to operate on them: "*Ni tł'izh ndeeshgizh*" ("We're going to operate on your gallbladder"). At the end of every examination I would ask "*Nabídiłkid?*" ("Do you have any questions?") The faces of the older people would relax when the person who would perform their procedures spoke to them in their own language.

10

Activism for the Future

By Susan E. Cayleff

Contents

Original publication details: 10.1 bell hooks, "Feminism: A Transformational Politic" from *Talking Back: Thinking Feminist, Thinking Black*, pp. 19–26. Boston: South End Press, 1989. 10.2 Rebekah Putnam and Carri Bennett, "If I had a hammer … I'd SMASH Patriarchy" from *Habitual Freak* zine, issue 2 (Sept 1994). 10.3 Judy Freespirit and Aldebaran, "Fat Liberation Manifesto" (1973), from *The Fat Studies Reader*, ed. Esther Rothblum and Sondra Solovay, pp. 341–42. New York: NYU Press, 2009. Reproduced with permission of NYU Press. 10.4 Jenny Morris, "Fighting Back" from *Pride against Prejudice: A Personal Politics of Disability*, pp. 169–80. London: Women's Press, 1991. Reproduced with permission of Jenny Morris. 10.5 Julie Sze, "Expanding Environmental Justice: Asian American Feminists' Contribution" from *Dragon Ladies: Asian American Feminists Breathe Fire*, ed. Sonia Shah, pp. 90–99. Boston: South End Press, 1997. Reproduced with permission of Julie Sze. 10.6 M. Jacqui Alexander, "El Mundo Zurdo and the Ample Space of the Erotic" subsection in "Remembering This Bridge, Remembering Ourselves: Yearning, Memory, and Desire" from *This Bridge We Call Home: Radical Visions for Transformation*, ed. Gloria E. Anzaldúa and AnaLouise Keating, pp. 97–103. New York: Routledge, 2002. Reproduced with permission of Taylor & Francis. *(continued on page 464)*

Women in Culture: An Intersectional Anthology for Gender and Women's Studies, Second Edition.
Edited by Bonnie Kime Scott, Susan E. Cayleff, Anne Donadey, and Irene Lara.
© 2017 John Wiley & Sons, Ltd. Published 2017 by John Wiley & Sons, Ltd.

Readings in this book have highlighted both the means of women's empowerment and their institutionalized global oppression along the lines of gender, race, sexuality, able-bodiedness, gender identity, and social class. This last set of readings show ways that Women's Studies' intersectional analyses encourage resistance and proactive leadership both locally and globally. In the face of new as well as continuing issues and challenges, these essays provide a road map to further social justice. They emphasize collective struggle rather than exclusive, one-cause one-cure thinking, and encourage attention to intersectional identities and strategies for empowerment.

hooks, in "Feminism: A Transformational Politic" (1989), argues that it is insufficient to identify patriarchy as the root cause of systems of exploitation and domination. Women have also been agents of domination and this has flourished according to social class and race. Sexism does dominate the private sphere, however, but that same sphere is (often) the source of caring bonds. Sexism, hooks argues, must be part of a larger struggle to eliminate all forms of domination: sexism, racism, and social class privilege, all of which are co-equal determinants. All of these interlocking forces must be addressed while recognizing that no one woman's experience is universal. To struggle for these goals necessitates love as a source of empowerment.

The "Fat Liberation Manifesto" (1973), written by Judy Freespirit and Aldebaran, asserts equal rights for fat people whose identities are often missing from discussions of inter-sectionality. The authors decry their mistreatment via sexism, commercialism, and medi-calization and asserts their intention to reclaim power over their bodies and our lives. But this cannot be done in isolation: the struggle for fat liberation is allied with other social justice movements against classism, racism, sexism, ageism, able-bodiedism, financial exploitation, and imperialism. It is a call to reclaim bodily definitions and ally with other liberation struggles. Interestingly, while this is the oldest document in this section, it is still one of the least covered issues in many feminist circles.

Morris, in "Fighting Back" (1991), applies these same principles to the disability rights movements. Her historical overview, which covers 1969–1990, asserts that non-disabled people's attitudes towards disabled people are more disabling than the latter's physical conditions. This echoes Hershey's arguments in Chapter 6. Like hooks, Morris states that disability

Original publication details: 10.7 AnaLouise Keating, "From Intersections to Interconnections: Lessons for Transformation *from This Bridge Called My Back: Radical Writings by Women of Color*" from *The Intersectional Approach: Transforming the Academy through Race, Class, and Gender*, ed. Michele Tracy Berger and Kathleen Guidroz, pp. 84–95. Chapel Hill: University of North Carolina Press, 2009. Reproduced with permission of University of North Carolina Press. 10.8 Sabrina Margarita Sandata, 1998, "All Sleeping Women Now Awake and Move" from *Bamboo Girl* zine, issue 7. Reproduced with permission from M. Alcantara. 10.9 Maya Angelou, "Still I Rise" from *And Still I Rise*. New York: Random House, Virago, 1978. Reproduced with permission of Penguin Random House LLC and Little Brown.

is compounded by intersectional identities: race and social class, and she includes the vital category of heterosexual privilege. For disabled people, affirmation and empowerment comes from organizational bonding with one another both nationally and internationally; this breaks down isolation and creates a better quality of life. Morris identifies key areas that disabled people have reclaimed and renamed: the right for independent living; the rejection of traditional rehabilitation; the medical model where non-disabled people speak for the disabled; and community-based self-help programs that empower the disabled. This is and must be an international movement that makes disabled people experts on their own lives and rejects the inspirational model that puts a disabled person on a pedestal. This liberation movement must – and does – generate self-definitions and collaborations with other social justice movements. Yet these bold assertions cannot obscure the reality of living with the frailty of the human body. What is needed is feeling friendly towards one's body. This echoes hooks's idea that love is necessary to succeed as a movement.

Sze, a self-identified Asian American woman, details the interlocking concerns and strategies for environmental justice in "Expanding Environmental Justice" (1997). She details the sex-segregated global workplaces where Asian women are clustered in industries with toxic materials that damage their health. She links this with global economic exploitation, anti-immigrant policies (that blame immigrants, largely of color, for environmental degradation), and dumping of toxic materials in communities of color. Like hooks and Morris, Sze asserts that social justice movements cannot work in isolation, but must mesh their efforts and strategies. She calls upon radical Asian feminists as well as labor and environmental justice activists to eradicate the forces that exploit women and nature as expendable commodities. Only through organization and resistance across borders can a safe and healthy environment emerge that values women and all working people.

M. Jacqui Alexander's "El Mundo Zurdo and the Ample Space of the Erotic" (2002) addresses the necessity for radical political people to embrace spirituality. She says that organized religion's precepts that sex and sexuality are sinful and shameful creates a "fragmented colonization" that prevents a holistic, non-hierarchical value system that values bodymindspirit wellness amidst a community. Self-healing, she says, similar to hooks's valuing of love and Morris's call for bodily acceptance, can remind us why we do political social justice work. Through this approach, we can reciprocally heal the collective self.

AnaLouise Keating's "From Intersections to Interconnections: Lessons for Transformation" (2009) gives us specific strategies to reshape and expand our analyses to create change. She revisits the lessons from Moraga and Anzaldúa's path-breaking *This Bridge Called My Back* (1981). We can redefine difference in transformative ways that embrace commonalities *and* difference into a relational approach. We must also embrace the concept of interrelatedness, realizing that what we do impacts others. Finally, we must listen with "raw openness" to create new pathways to dialogue.

Finally, Angelou's iconic poem "Still I Rise" (1978) expresses the ability of Black women to overcome a legacy of racism and oppression and assert a genuine self. She speaks of joy, self-determination, richness of personality, and visions of resistance. The poem is at once a manifesto of a survivor and of a prophet. It tells women that our spirits cannot be dominated when we individually and collectively fight against oppression. This is a perfect note on which to end this text book.

All of these lessons and directives provide workable and hopeful visions of social justice activism.

Discussion Questions

1. hooks, Morris, Alexander, and others call for the need for self-care and healing as central to social justice work. Discuss why this is vital and strategies to create it.
2. How are women's "othered" bodies marginalized and invalidated, according to the authors of the "Fat Liberation Manifesto" and "Fighting Back?" What are realistic strategies for reclaiming empowerment?
3. Why do all of the authors in this section assert that collaborative work across borders and special interests is necessary for social justice work?
4. How do the concepts and practices that Keating describes, of seeking commonalities, creating an ethics of radical interrelatedness, and listening with raw openness, shift the way you can think and act in social justice work?
5. Why is feminist anti-patriarchal analysis important? In what ways is it limited?
6. Identify a campus- or community-based issue around which you can create a movement for social change. If one already exists, join it. What skills do you bring to it? What is it you don't know? How can you be open to learning about issues that challenge your own privilege? This is not hypothetical – this is a real challenge to immerse yourself in feminist social change social justice activism!

Reference

Moraga, Cherríe, and Gloria Anzaldúa, eds. 1981. *This Bridge Called My Back: Writings by Radical Women of Color*. New York: Kitchen Table Press, 1983.

Further Reading

ACT UP NY/Women's AIDS Book Group. *Women, AIDS, and Activism*. Cambridge, MA. South End Press, 1999.

Cayleff, Susan E. and Angela LaGrotteria. "The Young Women's Studies Club: Placing Gender and Multicultural Competence at the Center." *Gender, Identity, Equity, and Violence: Multidisciplinary Perspectives Through Service Learning*, ed. Geraldine Stahly. Sterling, VA: Stylus, 2007. 121–36.

Crittendon, Danielle. "What We Tell Our Daughters." *What Our Mothers Didn't Tell Us: Why Happiness Eludes the Modern Woman*, 181–92. New York: Simon and Schuster, 2000.

Desai, Manisha. "Transnational Solidarity: Women's Agency, Structural Adjustment, and Globalization." *Women's Activism and Globalization: Linking Local Struggles and Transnational Politics*. Ed. Nancy A. Naples and Manisha Desai. New York: Routledge, 2002. 15–32.

Hancock, Ange-Marie. *Solidarity Politics for Millennials: A Guide to Ending the Oppression Olympics*. New York: Palgrave Macmillan, 2011.

Hayward, Lesley and Jennifer Drake. *Third Wave Agenda: Being Feminist Doing Feminism*. Minneapolis, MN: University of Minnesota Press, 1997.

Keating, AnaLouise. "From Intersections to Interconnections: Lessons for Transformation." *The Intersectional Approach: Transforming Women's and Gender Studies through Race, Class, and Gender*. Ed. Michele Tracy Berger and Kathleen Guidroz. Chapel Hill: University of North Carolina Press, 2009. 81–99.

Lorde, Audre. "The Transformation of Silence into Language and Action." *Sister Outsider*. Berkeley: Crossing Press, 1984. 40–45.

Morales, Aurora Levins. "Walking the Talk, Dancing to the Music: The Sustainable Activist Life." *Medicine Stories: History, Culture, and the Politics of Integrity*. Cambridge, MA: South End Press, 1998. 127–30.

Sarachild, Kathie. "Consciousness-Raising: A Radical Weapon." *Feminist Revolution*. Ed. Redstockings, Inc. New York: Random House, 1978. 144–50.

10.1

Feminism: A Transformational Politic
bell hooks

We live in a world in crisis – a world governed by politics of domination, one in which the belief in a notion of superior and inferior, and its concomitant ideology – that the superior should rule over the inferior – affects the lives of all people everywhere, whether poor or privileged, literate or illiterate. Systematic dehumanization, worldwide famine, ecological devastation, industrial contamination, and the possibility of nuclear destruction are realities which remind us daily that we are in crisis. Contemporary feminist thinkers often cite sexual politics as the origin of this crisis. They point to the insistence on difference as that factor which becomes the occasion for separation and domination and suggest that differentiation of status between females and males globally is an indication that patriarchal domination of the planet is the root of the problem. Such an assumption has fostered the notion that elimination of sexist oppression would necessarily lead to the eradication of all forms of domination. It is an argument that has led influential Western white women to feel that feminist movement should be *the* central political agenda for females globally. Ideologically, thinking in this direction enables Western women, especially privileged white women, to suggest that racism and class exploitation are merely the offspring of the parent system: patriarchy. Within feminist movement in the West, this has led to the assumption that resisting patriarchal domination is a more legitimate feminist action than resisting racism and other forms of domination. Such thinking prevails despite radical critiques made by black women and other women of color who question this proposition. To speculate that an oppositional division between men and women existed in early human communities is to impose on the past, on these non-white groups, a worldview that fits all too neatly within contemporary feminist paradigms that name man as the enemy and woman as the victim.

Clearly, differentiation between strong and weak, powerful and powerless, has been a central defining aspect of gender globally, carrying with it the assumption that men should have greater authority than women, and should rule over them. As significant and important as this fact is, it should not obscure the reality that women can and do participate in politics of domination, as perpetrators as well as victims – that we dominate, that we are dominated. If focus on patriarchal domination masks this reality or becomes the means by which women deflect attention from the real conditions and circumstances of our lives, then women cooperate in suppressing and promoting false consciousness, inhibiting our capacity to assume responsibility for transforming ourselves and society.

Thinking speculatively about early human social arrangement, about women and men struggling to survive in small communities, it is likely that the parent–child relationship with its very real imposed survival structure of dependency, of strong and weak, of powerful and powerless, was a site for the construction of a paradigm of domination. While this circumstance of dependency is not necessarily one that leads to domination, it lends itself to the enactment of a social drama wherein domination could easily occur as a means of exercising and maintaining control. This speculation does not place women outside the practice of domination, in the exclusive role of victim. It centrally names women as agents of domination, as potential theoreticians, and creators of a paradigm for social relationships wherein those groups of individuals designated as "strong" exercise power both benevolently and coercively over those designated as "weak."

Emphasizing paradigms of domination that call attention to woman's capacity to dominate is one way to deconstruct and challenge the simplistic notion that man is the enemy, woman the victim; the notion that men have always been the oppressors. Such thinking enables us to examine our role as women in the perpetuation and maintenance of systems of domination. To understand domination, we must understand that our capacity as women and men to be either dominated or dominating is a point of connection, of commonality. Even though I speak from the particular experience of living as a black woman in the United States, a white-supremacist, capitalist, patriarchal society, where small numbers of white men (and honorary "white men") constitute ruling groups, I understand that in many places in the world oppressed and oppressor share the same color. I understand that right here in this room, oppressed and oppressor share the same gender. Right now as I speak, a man who is himself victimized, wounded, hurt by racism and class exploitation is actively dominating a woman in his life – that even as I speak, women who are ourselves exploited, victimized, are dominating children. It is necessary for us to remember, as we think critically about domination, that we all have the capacity to act in ways that oppress, dominate, wound (whether or not that power is institutionalized). It is necessary to remember that it is first the potential oppressor within that we must resist – the potential victim within that we must rescue – otherwise we cannot hope for an end to domination, for liberation.

This knowledge seems especially important at this historical moment when black women and other women of color have worked to create awareness of the ways in which racism empowers white women to act as exploiters and oppressors. Increasingly this fact is considered a reason we should not support feminist struggle even though sexism and sexist oppression is a real issue in our lives as black women (see, for example, Vivian Gordon's *Black Women, Feminism, Black Liberation:*

Which Way?). It becomes necessary for us to speak continually about the convictions that inform our continued advocacy of feminist struggle. By calling attention to interlocking systems of domination – sex, race, and class – black women and many other groups of women acknowledge the diversity and complexity of female experience, of our relationship to power and domination. The intent is not to dissuade people of color from becoming engaged in feminist movement. Feminist struggle to end patriarchal domination should be of primary importance to women and men globally not because it is the foundation of all other oppressive structures but because it is that form of domination we are most likely to encounter in an ongoing way in everyday life.

Unlike other forms of domination, sexism directly shapes and determines relations of power in our private lives, in familiar social spaces, in that most intimate context – home – and in that most intimate sphere of relations – family. Usually, it is within the family that we witness coercive domination and learn to accept it, whether it be domination of parent over child, or male over female. Even though family relations may be, and most often are, informed by acceptance of a politic of domination, they are simultaneously relations of care and connection. It is this convergence of two contradictory impulses – the urge to promote growth and the urge to inhibit growth – that provides a practical setting for feminist critique, resistance, and transformation.

Growing up in a black, working-class, father-dominated household, I experienced coercive adult male authority as more immediately threatening, as more likely to cause immediate pain than racist oppression or class exploitation. It was equally clear that experiencing exploitation and oppression in the home made one feel all the more powerless when encountering dominating forces outside the home. This is true for many people. If we are unable to resist and end domination in relations where there is care, it seems totally unimaginable that we can resist and end it in other institutionalized relations of power. If we cannot convince the mothers and/or fathers who care not to humiliate and degrade us, how can we imagine convincing or resisting an employer, a lover, a stranger who systematically humiliates and degrades?

Feminist effort to end patriarchal domination should be of primary concern precisely because it insists on the eradication of exploitation and oppression in the family context and in all other intimate relationships. It is that political movement which most radically addresses the person – the personal – citing the need for transformation of self, of relationships, so that we might be better able to act in a revolutionary manner, challenging and resisting domination, transforming the world outside the self. Strategically, feminist movement should be a central component of all other liberation struggles because it challenges each of us to alter our person, our personal engagement (either as victims or perpetrators or both) in a system of domination.

Feminism, as liberation struggle, must exist apart from and as a part of the larger struggle to eradicate domination in all its forms. We must understand that patriarchal domination shares an ideological foundation with racism and other forms of group oppression, that there is no hope that it can be eradicated while these systems remain intact. This knowledge should consistently inform the direction of feminist theory and practice. Unfortunately, racism and class élitism among women has frequently led to the suppression and distortion of this connection so that it is now necessary for feminist thinkers to critique and revise much feminist theory and the direction of feminist movement. This effort at revision is perhaps most evident in the current widespread acknowledgment that sexism, racism, and class exploitation constitute interlocking systems of domination – that sex, race, and class, and not sex alone, determine the nature of any female's identity, status, and circumstance, the degree to which she will or will not be dominated, the extent to which she will have the power to dominate.

While acknowledgment of the complex nature of woman's status (which has been most impressed upon everyone's consciousness by radical women of color) is a significant corrective, it is only a starting point. It provides a frame of reference which must serve as the basis for thoroughly altering and revising feminist theory and practice. It challenges and calls us to re-think popular assumptions about the nature of feminism that have had the deepest impact on a large majority of women, on mass consciousness. It radically calls into question the notion of a fundamentally common female experience which has been seen as the prerequisite for our coming together, for political unity. Recognition of the inter-connectedness of sex, race, and class highlights the diversity of experience, compelling redefinition of the terms for unity. If women do not share "common oppression," what then can serve as a basis for our coming together?

Unlike many feminist comrades, I believe women and men must share a common understanding – a basic knowledge of what feminism is – if it is ever to be a powerful mass-based political movement. In *Feminist Theory: from Margin to Center*, I suggest that defining feminism broadly as "a movement to end sexism and sexist oppression" would enable us to have a common political goal. We would then have a basis on which to build solidarity. Multiple and contradictory definitions of feminism create confusion and undermine the effort to construct feminist movement so that it addresses everyone. Sharing a common goal does not imply that women and men will not have radically divergent perspectives on how that goal might be reached. Because each individual starts the process of engagement in feminist struggle at a unique level of awareness, very real differences in experience, perspective, and knowledge make developing varied strategies for participation and transformation a necessary agenda.

Feminist thinkers engaged in radically revisioning central tenets of feminist thought must continually emphasize the importance of sex, race, and class as factors which *together* determine the social construction of femaleness, as it has been so deeply ingrained in the consciousness of many women active in feminist movement that gender is the sole factor determining destiny. However, the work of education for critical consciousness (usually called consciousness-raising) cannot end there. Much feminist consciousness-raising has in the past focused on identifying the particular ways men oppress and exploit women. Using the paradigm of sex, race, and class means that the focus does not begin with men and what they do to women, but rather with women working to identify both individually and collectively the specific character of our social identity.

Imagine a group of women from diverse backgrounds coming together to talk about feminism. First they concentrate on working out their status in terms of sex, race, and class using this as the standpoint from which they begin discussing patriarchy or their particular relations with individual men. Within the old frame of reference, a discussion might consist solely of talk about their experiences as victims in relationship to male oppressors. Two women – one poor, the other quite wealthy – might describe the process by which they have suffered physical abuse by male partners and find certain commonalities which might serve as a basis for bonding. Yet if these same two women engaged in a discussion of class, not only would the social construction and expression of femaleness differ, so too would their ideas about how to confront and change their circumstances. Broadening the discussion to include an analysis of race and class would expose many additional differences even as commonalities emerged.

Clearly the process of bonding would be more complex, yet this broader discussion might enable the sharing of perspectives and strategies for change that would enrich rather than diminish our understanding of gender. While feminists have increasingly given "lip service" to the idea of diversity, we have not developed strategies of communication and inclusion that allow for the successful enactment of this feminist vision.

Small groups are no longer the central place for feminist consciousness-raising. Much feminist education for critical consciousness takes place in women's studies classes or at conferences which focus on gender. Books are a primary source of education which means that already masses of people who do not read have no access. The sepa-ration of grassroots ways of sharing feminist thinking across kitchen tables from the spheres where much of that thinking is generated, the academy, undermines feminist movement. It would further feminist movement if new feminist thinking could be once again shared in small group contexts, integrating critical analysis with discussion of personal experience. It would be useful to promote anew the small group setting as an arena for education for critical consciousness, so that women and men might come together in neighborhoods and communities to discuss feminist concerns.

Small groups remain an important place for education for critical consciousness for several reasons. An especially important aspect of the small group setting is the emphasis on communicating feminist thinking, feminist theory, in a manner that can be easily understood. In small groups, individuals do not need to be equally literate or literate at all because the information is primarily shared through conversation, in dialogue which is necessarily a liberatory expression. (Literacy should be a goal for feminists even as we ensure that it does not become a require-ment for participation in feminist education.) Reforming small groups would subvert the appropriation of feminist thinking by a select group of academic women and men, usually white, usually from privileged class backgrounds.

Small groups of people coming together to engage in feminist discussion, in dialectical struggle make a space where the "personal is political" as a starting point for education for critical consciousness. This can be extended to include politicization of the self that focuses on creating understanding of the ways sex, race, and class together determine our individual lot and our collective experience. It would further feminist movement if many well-known feminist thinkers would participate in small groups, critically re-examining ways their works might be changed by incorporating broader perspectives. All efforts at self-transformation challenge us to engage in ongoing, critical self-examination and reflection about feminist practice, about how we live in the world. This individual commitment, when coupled with engagement in collective discussion, provides a space for critical feedback which strengthens our efforts to change and make ourselves new. It is in this commitment to feminist principles in our words and deeds that the hope of feminist revolution lies.

Working collectively to confront difference, to expand our awareness of sex, race, and class as interlocking systems of domination, of the ways we reinforce and perpetuate these structures, is the context in which we learn the true meaning of solidarity. It is this work that must be the foundation of feminist movement. Without it, we cannot effectively resist patriarchal domination; without it, we remain estranged and alienated from one another. Fear of painful confrontation often leads women and men active in feminist movement to avoid rigorous critical encounter, yet if we cannot engage dialectically in a committed, rigorous, humanizing manner, we cannot hope to change the world. True politicization – coming to critical consciousness – is a difficult, "trying" process, one that demands that we give up set ways of thinking and being, that we shift our paradigms, that we open ourselves to the unknown, the unfamiliar. Undergoing this process, we learn what it means to struggle and in this effort we experience the dignity and integrity of being that comes with revolutionary change. If we do not change our consciousness, we cannot change our actions or demand change from others.

Our renewed commitment to a rigorous process of education for critical consciousness will determine the shape and direction of future feminist movement. Until new perspectives are created, we cannot be living symbols of the power of feminist thinking. Given the privileged lot of many leading feminist thinkers, both in terms of status, class, and race, it is harder these days to convince women of the primacy of this process of politicization. More and more, we seem to form select interest groups composed of individuals who share similar perspectives. This limits our capacity to engage in critical discussion. It is difficult to involve women in new processes of feminist politicization because so many of us think that identifying men as the enemy, resisting male domination, gaining equal access to power and privilege is the end of feminist movement. Not only is it not the end, it is not even the place we want revitalized feminist movement to begin. We want to begin as women seriously addressing ourselves, not solely in relation to men, but in relation to an entire structure of domination of which patriarchy is one part. While the struggle to eradicate sexism and sexist oppression is and should be the primary thrust of feminist movement, to prepare ourselves politically for this effort we must first learn how to be in solidarity, how to struggle with one another.

Only when we confront the realities of sex, race, and class, the ways they divide us, make us different, stand us in opposition, and work to reconcile and resolve these issues will we be able to participate in the making of feminist revolution, in the transformation of the world. Feminism, as Charlotte Bunch emphasizes again and again in *Passionate Politics*, is a transformational politics, a struggle against domination wherein the effort is to change ourselves as well as structures. Speaking about the struggle to confront difference, Bunch asserts:

> A crucial point of the process is understanding that reality does not look the same from different people's perspective. It is not surprising that one way feminists have come to understand about differences has been through the love of a person from another culture or race. It takes persistence and motivation – which love often engenders – to get beyond one's ethnocentric assumptions and really learn about other perspectives. In this process and while seeking to eliminate oppression, we also discover new possibilities and insights that come from the experience and survival of other peoples.

Embedded in the commitment to feminist revolution is the challenge to love. Love can be and is an important source of empowerment when we struggle to confront issues of sex, race, and class. Working together to identify and face our differences – to face the ways we dominate and are dominated – to change our actions, we need a mediating force that can sustain us so that we are not broken in this process, so that we do not despair.

Not enough feminist work has focused on documenting and sharing ways individuals confront differences constructively and successfully. Women and men need to know what is on the other side of the pain experienced in politicization. We need detailed accounts of the ways our lives are fuller and richer as we change and grow politically, as we learn to live each moment as committed feminists, as comrades working to end domination. In reconceptualizing and reformulating strategies for future feminist movement, we need to concentrate on the politicization of love, not just in the context of talking about victimization in intimate relationships, but in a critical discussion where love can be understood as a powerful force that challenges and resists domination. As we work to be loving, to create a culture that celebrates life, that makes love possible, we move against dehumanization, against domination. In *Pedagogy of the Oppressed*, Paulo Freire evokes this power of love, declaring:

> I am more and more convinced that true revolutionaries must perceive the revolution, because of its creative and liberating nature, as an act of love. For me, the revolution, which is not possible without a theory of revolution – and therefore science – is not irreconcilable with love ... The distortion imposed on the word "love" by the capitalist world cannot prevent the revolution from being essentially loving in character, nor can it prevent the revolutionaries from affirming their love of life.

That aspect of feminist revolution that calls women to love womanness, that calls men to resist dehumanizing concepts of masculinity, is an essential part of our struggle. It is the process by which we move from seeing ourselves as objects to acting as subjects. When women and men understand that working to eradicate patriarchal domination is a struggle rooted in the longing to make a world where everyone can live fully and freely, then we know our work to be a gesture of love. Let us draw upon that love to heighten our awareness, deepen our compassion, intensify our courage, and strengthen our commitment.

Bibliography

Bunch, Charlotte, *Passionate Politics*. New York: St. Martin's Press, 1987.
Freire, Paulo, *Pedagogy of the Oppressed*. New York: Herder and Herder, 1970.
Gordon, Vivian, *Black Women, Feminism, Black Liberation: Which Way?* Chicago: Third World Press, 1991.
hooks, bell, *Feminist Theory from Margin to Center*. New York: South End Press, 2000.

10.2
Smash Patriarchy

10.3

Fat Liberation Manifesto

Judy Freespirit and Aldebaran

1. WE believe that fat people are fully entitled to human respect and recognition.
2. WE are angry at mistreatment by commercial and sexist interests. These have exploited our bodies as objects of ridicule, thereby creating an immensely profitable market selling the false promise of avoidance of, or relief from, that ridicule.
3. WE see our struggle as allied with the struggles of other oppressed groups against classism, racism, sexism, ageism, financial exploitation, imperialism and the like.
4. WE demand equal rights for fat people in all aspects of life, as promised in the Constitution of the United States. We demand equal access to goods and services in the public domain, and an end to discrimination against us in the areas of employment, education, public facilities and health services.
5. WE single out as our special enemies the so-called "reducing" industries. These include diet clubs, reducing salons, fat farms, diet doctors, diet books, diet foods and food supplements, surgical procedures, appetite suppressants, drugs and gadgetry such as wraps and "reducing machines."

    WE demand that they take responsibility for their false claims, acknowledge that their products are harmful to the public health, and publish long-term studies proving any statistical efficacy of their products. We make this demand knowing that over 99% of all weight loss programs, when evaluated over a five-year period, fail utterly, and also knowing the extreme proven harmfulness of frequent large changes in weight.
6. WE repudiate the mystified "science" which falsely claims that we are unfit. It has both caused and upheld discrimination against us, in collusion with the financial interests of insurance companies, the fashion and garment industries, reducing industries, the food and drug industries, and the medical and psychiatric establishment.
7. WE refuse to be subjugated to the interests of our enemies. We fully intend to reclaim power over our bodies and our lives. We commit ourselves to pursue these goals together.

FAT PEOPLE OF THE WORLD, UNITE! YOU HAVE NOTHING TO LOSE.

Note

Originally Published by the Fat Underground, Los Angeles, California, November 1973. Also published in *Shadow on a Tightrope: Writings by Women on Fat Oppression*, edited by Lisa Schoenfielder and Barb Wieser, Aunt Lute Books, 1983.

10.4

Fighting Back

Jenny Morris

Disabled people throughout history have attempted to insist on their right to live and to a decent quality of life. Even those who were institutionalised under the Third Reich and killed under the Nazi Euthanasia Programme resisted. At Absberg, for example, the residents of the Abbey (an institution run by the Catholic Church for disabled people) refused to get on the bus which came to collect them to take them to the gas chambers. They were dragged and carried by force on to the bus and their resistance put to shame the nuns' and local people's helplessness as they stood by (Gallagher, 1990, pp. 138–145).

The assertion of the value of our lives runs through both our individual struggles with the non-disabled world and the collective action which disabled people have increasingly taken over the last 20 years.

Confronting Prejudice

Pam Evans describes her recognition of the assumption that her life is not worth living and the way that this assumption underlies both 'kindly' and hostile reactions to disabled people. It takes courage to confront the fact that this devaluation of our lives is the determinant of most non-disabled people's interaction with us. 'To continue to live as best we can, keeping faith with who we know ourselves to be, in the face of what society has decided we are, does take courage. But it's a quiet, unspectacular and, above all, unrecognised courage. Real courage has no witnesses and no rewards.'

Pam is also generous in her understanding of why non-disabled people so devalue us when she says, 'We should keep in mind when we are being treated in this way, that these things generate from the murkier depths of humanity and that they are not perpetuated consciously. We need to make the effort to understand that people are far more disabled by their attitudes than we are by our physical condition once we acknowledge it unreservedly.'

We have to struggle as individuals on a daily basis against other people's assumptions about us which are such an important factor in determining the quality of our lives. Some of us also have to struggle against racism, sexism or heterosexism. The isolation that Anna Mathison felt as a result of her segregation from mainstream society throughout her childhood and adolescence was compounded by the fact that she was the only Black child at her 'special' school and only one of three Black young people at college. 'I was never allowed to forget that I was a Black child,' she said. 'I remember the hatred, the unkindness. It was difficult to call it racism. It just felt like unkindness, other children being preferred over me when, for example, sweets were being given out. Just little things.'

Anna has fought against disablism and racism all her life. She has asserted herself as an independent, autonomous woman, and now has her own flat, the personal assistance that she requires to carry on her life, and is in paid employment which she enjoys. She has the strength to say, 'I feel very positive about myself and if other people don't recognise my worth then that's their problem.' She sees working with other disabled people as a priority in her life.

Many of us find that joining together with other disabled people brings a feeling of strength. However, when we take collective action together, or organise our own cultural events, we have to fight against the negative connotations of just being together in a group of disabled people. Just as to a white, predominantly racist society, a group of Black youths congregated together spells trouble, so to non-disabled people a group of disabled people are a subject of pity, fascinated repulsion and, sometimes, fear. Such an attitude is undermining and can make us feel uncomfortable about being in a group of disabled people. To overcome these feelings, however, is to feel empowered by joining together.

Rachel Cartwright describes her experience of going to a play put on by a group of learning disabled people:

> I haven't really associated with other disabled people throughout my life, but recently I've started to be involved in my local disability association and there's a strong group of learning disabled people involved in it. They put on a play about the difficulties of leaving home when you're considered to be incapable of independence – and it was brilliant. It felt so good to be in an audience of people with whom I had so much in common – in spite of our age differences and the range of disabilities – and to be listening to something which came out of the experience of being discriminated against because you're different. I remember the difficulties I had establishing an independent life for myself because of being blind but at the time I was just an isolated individual. Whereas these young people are together and angry and saying that they won't put up with it.

Over the last 10 to 15 years, an increasing number of organisations of disabled people have been formed, which have both broken down our isolation from each other and demanded that the needs associated with our physical and intellectual limitations are met in a way which ensures control over, and a better quality to, our lives.

The Independent Living Movement

The Independent Living Movement started in 1969 when a group of physically disabled hospital residents, who were attending courses at the University of California at Berkeley, organised their own class called 'Strategies for Independent Living'.

Rachel Hurst, the British delegate to Disabled People's International (an international federation of disability organisations), explained the origins of the movement when she spoke at a conference on Housing and Independent Living in 1990:

> Despite being in some ways institutionalised by the hospital, studying and living together had allowed them to form a close-knit group in which their political consciousness could grow. They realised that their need for self-determination and independence was shared by the Black and student civil rights movements which were dominating the university scene in California. And they learned from those movements as well as from each other. They learned where their real oppression lay and took strength from each other in understanding how to deal with it (L. Laurie, 1991).

These people faced much opposition in their demand for the right to live independently. There were attempts to expel two of the students from the university on the grounds that their academic goals could not be achieved and that they were not living 'suitable lives'. The students managed to prevent this happening. The principles on which their strategy for independent living was based were seen as a threat to the professionals who made their living out of disabled people's segregation. Rachel Hurst identified the three basic principles involved as: 'those who know best the needs of disabled people, and how to meet those needs, are disabled people; the needs of disabled people can best be met by comprehensive programmes which provide a variety of services; disabled people should be fully integrated into their community.'

She went on to explain how by 1972 the first Centre for Independent Living (CIL) had been established which served both disabled students at Berkeley and disabled members of the wider community. The CIL used a number of different sources of funding to enable people to get access to personal support, accessible housing, advice and information on benefits, an accessible environment, peer counselling, transport and wheelchair repairs.

In Britain where there are now seven Centres for Independent Living, the approach is less on the actual provision of services than on ensuring that local and central government provide the housing and personal and other support services necessary for independent living. The British Council of Organisations of Disabled People has an active Independent Living Forum which forms a network of all the CILs and other organisations of disabled people which are developing independent living initiatives. This forum is also part of a European Network on Independent Living which in turn participates in the Independent Living Committee of Disabled People's International. As Rachel Hurst says, these organisations are all 'rooted in the radical move away from the traditional medical and rehabilitation professionals' control over our lives to the self-help, community-based programmes which ensure our empowerment'.

When the non-disabled society has done things for us it has resulted in our segregation into special schools, residential care and our isolation within a physical, social and economic environment which does not address our needs. Disabled people and their organisations are increasingly insisting that we are the experts on disability and that if we had control over the response to our needs we would develop very different policies from the ones which currently dominate our lives.

The international dimension to the disability movement has brought strength to national movements and is a very important part of the increasing collective organising by disabled people.

Disabled People's International

The First Congress of the Disabled People's International (DPI), held in 1981, adopted a manifesto which set out the organisation's philosophical base. 'We maintain that all people are of equal value. This conviction implies that disabled people have the right to participate in every sphere of society … We therefore reject all forms of segregation and we refuse to accept lifetime isolation in special institutions' (Driedger, 1989, p. 54).

The manifesto asserted that disabled people have rights as citizens to education, rehabilitation, employment, independent living and income security. And it also stated that disabled people must have the right to influence governments and policy-makers: '… organisations of the disabled must be given decisive influence in regard to all measures taken on their behalf'.

The significance of disabled people coming together to form an international movement cannot be underestimated. Disabled people are imprisoned within institutions, constrained within inaccessible housing and obstacle-ridden physical environments, dependent on unpaid care by family members, discriminated against in the labour market. Such people lack power by virtue of their socio-economic circumstances. The foundation of Disabled People's International was about disabled people taking control over their lives.

Disabled People's International is also crucial in the struggle against organisations *for* disabled people. In most of the industrialised world, the richest and most prominent organisations working on disability are controlled by non-disabled people and their activities do much to confirm the prejudices against which we struggle. DPI itself had grown out of the conflict with Rehabilitation International, an international organisation made up mainly of (non-disabled) rehabilitation professionals. Until 1980 this was the only international organisation concerned with the needs of people with varying disabilities. Very few disabled people ever participated at its congresses until – following protests by the handful of disabled delegates at the 1976 congress – disabled people in Sweden and Canada organised to increase the number of disabled delegates to the 1980 World Congress and Delegate Assembly. The Swedish delegation put a resolution that organisations of disabled people should have at least 50 per cent of the delegates in a national delegation (which would have meant that at least 50 per cent of the delegate assembly would be composed of disabled people).

When the resolution was resoundingly defeated a meeting of the disabled delegates who were attending the congress was held. The 250 disabled people who assembled decided to form a World Congress of Citizens with Disabilities (which subsequently became Disabled People's International). As two of the Canadian delegates recalled, these disabled people – who came from all over the world – 'had a sense of their own destiny. They wanted to proclaim their rights, as citizens, to an equal voice in the decision-making of services, the policies and programs that affected them. They were no longer willing to passively accept the control of rehabilitation professionals over their lives. They demanded dignity, equality and full participation in society. They demanded release from the yoke of paternalism and charity ...' (quoted by Dreidger, 1989, p. 35).

The rehabilitation professionals at the congress reacted either with outright hostility to the idea of disabled people forming their own international organisation or with a condescending paternalism. One non-disabled delegate gave voice to this latter reaction when he wrote, 'To me, they are going through a developmental stage which resembles the adolescent or young adult in a family, who often becomes rebellious for a period of time. After this stage, an excellent partnership and relationship with the "family" evolves and life goes on better than ever.' (quoted by Dreidger, 1989, p. 37).

Against such attitudes disabled people had to assert their autonomy and attempt to take power away from the professionals who controlled not only the disability organisations but also the individual lives of disabled people.

DPI delegates from both developing and industrialised countries found that there were common elements to the struggle between organisations of and organisations for disabled people. Joshua Malinga, for example, recounted the story of the foundation of the Zimbabwean Council of Disabled People and how they were met with hostility. 'When news came out in the papers, we were branded with all sorts of names from all corners. We were called "rebels" and "ungratefuls" ... They refused to see the difference between an organisation of the disabled and one that is for the disabled. They refused to see the difference between a service organisation and a political organisation fighting for the human rights of the disabled' (DPI, 1981, p. 15).

As in many other countries, the Zimbabwean organisation of disabled people allied itself with the liberation movement. 'As soon as our majority government took over we started meeting all members of the parliament and reminding them that the struggle for liberation, which put them into power, was a struggle for social justice and that it is accepted that the justice should permeate to all communities, including the disabled' (DPI, 1981, p. 16). In South Africa, where the government refused to recognise the International Year of Disabled People, the disability rights movement which emerged in the 1980s soon realised that they had to actively oppose apartheid, both because of the natural links between the struggles of Black people and disabled people as oppressed groups and also because of the relationship between the poverty created by apartheid and the incidence of disability among Black people. As a historian of the movement said, 'The particular handicaps the majority of disabled people in South Africa face are inextricably linked with apartheid. Therefore, in challenging and dismantling these handicaps we also need to do the same to apartheid' (quoted by M. Pagel, 1988).

'Organisations of' versus 'Organisations for'

Throughout the world, non-disabled people have formed organisations which seek to provide services for disabled people. These organisations operate within a framework which assumes that disabled people are not capable of taking control of their own lives and require the services of professionals and voluntary workers, and the aid of charity. As Mike Oliver, an academic who is disabled, writes, these organisations work within 'the medical rather than a social model of disability which locates the problems faced by disabled people within the individual rather than being contingent upon social organisation' (M. Oliver, 1990, p. 115). Or, as Susan Hannaford argued, the assumption is that disabled people are the problem, just as the poor are the problem and not the society that caused poverty, and homosexuality the problem and not heterosexual mores (Hannaford, 1985, p. 82).

Organisations of disabled people, on the other hand, reject the charity and the medical models of disability, asserting that the services we require should be provided as a civil right and that it is society which disables us rather than our physical condition. Organisations for disabled people have their social origins in the surplus time and money of the wealthy and the post-war development of the professions. Organisations of disabled people have very different roots.

Martin Pagel, in his booklet on the history of the disability movement, makes links with the labour and trades union movement both internationally and in Britain. Disabled people in Britain first started to organise during the late nineteenth century. One of the first British organisations of disabled people, the National League of the Blind (founded in 1899; the British Association of the Deaf was founded in 1890), was registered as a trade union and affiliated to the Trades Union Congress.

A movement which asserts the rights of oppressed people to organise for themselves to create better social and economic conditions is bound to ally itself with other oppressed groups – whether these be based on class, race or gender – and is therefore likely to be on the left of the political spectrum. This is undoubtedly one of the reasons for the conflict between organisations of and organisations for disabled people. The latter are run by those who are from the advantaged groups in society (in the sense that they are predominantly white, non-disabled and economically advantaged) and are within a conservative charitable tradition. Governments can afford to give financial and political support to such organisations for they do not challenge social, economic or political frameworks.

Those disabled people who ally themselves with organizations *for* disabled people do so predominantly because their class position leads them to fear radical social change. Some of us may feel a sense of outrage at how such disabled people are used to give legitimacy to the organisations which do so much to oppress disabled people. We must also recognise, however, that internalised oppression exerts a tremendous influence. A disabled person who holds a position within a conservative charitable organisation has been told all their lives – as we all have – how inadequate and pitiable disabled people are. Small wonder then that such people, when asked to involve more disabled people in their organisation, commonly respond that there just isn't any capable person with the relevant expertise amongst the disabled community.

Just as some women who achieve high social and economic status take on the role of an honorary man and often do little to further the interests of other women, so some disabled people take on the role of honorary non-disabled people. They are considered to be exceptions to the rule of the inadequacy of disabled people generally. In accepting this role they do little or nothing to aid other disabled people and in giving their support to organisations *for* disabled people they do much to confirm our oppression.

The British Council of Organisations of Disabled People is the British branch of the DPI. It is made up over 80 organisations controlled by disabled people and as such it is engaged in a struggle to wrest control and resources away from the disability charities. In 1990, RADAR, the major umbrella group of the organisations for disabled people, received just under £500,000 from the Department of Health. In comparison BCODP received £30,000 – but then BCODP has an unequivocal commitment to policies such as anti-discrimination legislation which, if implemented, could have major resource implications. Such a policy is also predicated on the notion of disabled people having civil rights rather than being recipients of charity; this too constitutes a fundamental challenge to the prevailing ideology.

Racism, Sexism and Heterosexism

Disabled people and their organisations are no more exempt from racism, sexism and heterosexism than non-disabled people and their organisations. While DPI has made strenuous, and to some extent successful, efforts to ensure that developing countries are fully represented, within its constituent national organisations both women and ethnic minorities are distinctly under-represented and issues around racism, sexism and sexuality have tended to be avoided.

At a national conference held in Britain in 1990 on housing and independent living, Millie Hill addressed the issues for Black disabled people. 'Black disabled people, I have found to my cost, are a discrete and insular minority within a minority. We have been unfairly and unjustly saddled with restrictions and limitations, subjected to a history of purposeful unequal treatment and relegated to a position of political powerlessness and disenfranchisement in a society where even the label "second class citizen" seems wholly inadequate to identify our social status' (L. Laurie, 1991). The discrimination which all disabled people face, she said, is compounded for Black people by the discrimination that Black people face in areas such as employment, housing and education. The disability movement needs to address issues such as the way that services for disabled people are predominantly provided by white non-disabled people for white disabled people.

At the same conference Michael Jeewa from the Asian People with Disabilities Alliance argued that Black disabled people need, at present, to organise separately from white disabled people. This does not mean, however, that the white-dominated disability movement can abdicate its responsibility to address the interests of Black disabled people. Indeed, there are integral links between racism and the discrimination that disabled people face, as was made clear by a remark Sir Geoffrey Howe made when he was Foreign Secretary. He was responding to the demand that people from Hong Kong should be given the right of entry to Britain before the takeover of the former British colony by China in 1997. 'Any society,' he said, 'has a limit to the pace at which it can absorb people, and the more strange they are the more difficult it is to accept them.' Such a remark can be equally applied to non-disabled people's reactions to those whose physical or intellectual differences mark them off from the normal.

The disability movement also has a responsibility to address the interests of disabled women. Non-disabled academics tend to think that they are addressing such interests by highlighting how much worse off disabled women are than disabled men (and how much worse off Black disabled people are than white disabled people). There is something very offensive about this type of analysis because essentially such academics are assuming a right to define our reality – and it is predominantly a very negative reality from their point of view. We, too, must not fall into the same trap of treating issues around women and disability, race and disability, sexuality and disability (or, indeed, class and disability) as things to be 'added on' to our history, our politics and our organising. The experiences of Black and ethnic minority disabled people, disabled women and disabled gay men and lesbians are integral to the experience of being disabled. Disabled people, as a group, are made up of Black people, women, gay men and lesbians as well as of white people, men and heterosexuals. Sexism, racism and heterosexism affect us all and the struggle against them must be an integral part of any disability politics.

The Meaning of Disability

Academics and professionals play a key role in influencing the meanings which non-disabled people give to disability and in determining the policies and services which affect our lives. The models of disability which most commonly inform this role are the 'personal tragedy' and medical models of disability. Those who subscribe, consciously or unconsciously, to these models view disabled people as individuals whose experience is determined by their medical or physical condition. Someone who is blind is thus viewed as experiencing a 'personal tragedy' and it is the role of the professional to mitigate the difficulties caused by not being able to see. The individualist assumptions which are at the heart of this definition of disability also encourage a particular psychology of disability. By this I mean that disabled people's behaviour is often interpreted in terms of individual pathologies. Our justifiable anger about our oppression is interpreted as a self-destructive bitterness which arises out of a failure to 'accept' our disability. Our difficulties in getting access to the resources we need to live independently are treated as a 'lack of motivation' or similar individual inadequacies.

The medical and 'personal tragedy' models of disability and the attitudes which go with them are a very important part of the powerlessness experienced by disabled people in their relationship with those professions whose role is so important to the quality and nature of our daily lives. Disabled people – in their struggles to assert their autonomy and to counter their powerlessness – challenge these attitudes in their day-to-day contact with those who have power over us.

Bibliography

Disabled People's International, (1981), *Proceedings of the First World Congress*, DPI.

Driedger, Diane, (1989), *The Last Civil Rights Movement*, Hurst.

Gallagher, Hugh, (1990), *By Trust Betrayed: Patients, Physicians, and the Licence to Kill in the Third Reich*, Henry Holt, New York.

Hannaford, Susan, (1985), *Living Outside Inside*, Canterbury Press, Berkeley, California.

Laurie, Linda, (1991), National Conference on Housing and Independent Living, Shelter.

Oliver, Mike, (1990), *The Politics of Disablement*, Macmillan. OPCS.

Pagel, Martin, (1988), *On Our Own Behalf – an Introduction to the Self-Organisation of Disabled People*, Greater Manchester Coalition of Disabled People.

10.5

Expanding Environmental Justice: Asian American Feminists' Contribution

Julie Sze

An Asian American feminist movement for environmental justice is critical for both expanding the scope of environmental justice and for realizing a radical Asian women's politics and vision.[1] Among the social injustices that affect large numbers of Asian women in the United States and around the world are occupational health hazards, labor exploitation due to economic globalization, and anti-immigrant policies. Each of these poses an obstacle to the creation and protection of a healthy environment for Asian women.

A diversity of Asian American communities face environmental risks such as high rates of lead poisoning on the job, lack of open space, elevated exposure to military toxics, and health hazards from fish consumption.[2] A draft position paper on Asian environmental justice issues in the United States circulating within the Environmental Protection Agency (EPA) reflects a growing recognition of Asian environmental justice issues, according to Angela Chung, an environmental protection specialist from the EPA's Office of Environmental Justice.[3]

Asian women's organizing shares a number of similarities with environmental justice organizing. These similarities need to be recognized and built on to further the common goals of both movements.

The Environmental Justice Movement

Environmental justice is a social movement led by and for people of color that views environmental issues as having social, public health, economic, political, and ideological components. It thus seeks not only environmental justice but also economic, political, and cultural justice, both in the United States[4] and abroad.[5]

Early catalyzing events for environmental justice include nonviolent direct action in 1982 against the proposed siting of a hazardous waste landfill in the predominantly African American community of Warren County, North Carolina, and the 1987 publication of *Toxic Wastes and Race* by the United Church of Christ Commission for Racial Justice, which documented the disproportionate location of toxic waste sites in communities of color. Environmental justice first came to prominence when advocates documented that people of color suffer from disproportionately high effects of environmental pollution, as well as unequal protection from the state. According to the Commission on Racial Justice, three fifths of African and Hispanic Americans live in communities with uncontrolled toxic waste sites, and approximately half of all Asian/Pacific Islanders and Native Americans live in communities with uncontrolled toxic waste sites.[6] In one study, the EPA took 20 percent longer to identify Superfund sites in minority communities, and pollution in those neighborhoods resulted in fines only half as high as those in white neighborhoods.[7] Environmental justice activists attempt to remediate environmental damage and at the same time educate people of color about how power, knowledge, science, and authority are constructed.

Environmental justice repudiates elitist, racist, and classist wilderness/preservationist conceptions of the environment as being equal to "nature" – typically characterized as pristine, green space devoid of people.[8] Such conceptions often regard nature as being threatened by the sustaining activities of people in "underdeveloped" countries. Environmental justice foregrounds social categories and shifts the concept of the environment to include not just natural resources such as air, water, and land, but also public and human health concerns.

In a span of roughly 15 years, the environmental justice movement has succeeded in changing what environmentalism means. In February 1994, President Clinton signed the Executive Order on Environmental Justice, provoked by the organizing of people of color, most notably at the historic 1991 People of Color Environmental Leadership Summit, at which the Principles of Environmental Justice[9] were introduced and adopted.

One of the key contributions of the environmental justice movement has been to challenge long-held assumptions about risks and hazards. Rather than considering risks and hazards to human health and the environment in isolation, environmental justice advocates consider cumulative risks – the combination and accumulation of hazards. While individual polluting sources may not pose fatal health hazards, their cumulative effect might. Consideration of cumulative risks is particularly important in urban settings: in rural areas, toxic sites are often the result of single, egregious polluters, whereas in an urban environment, toxic pollution is more often a problem of cumulative hazards.

Environmental Justice and Asian American Women

> I live in San Jose [California]. I assemble electronics parts and boards at my company. I've been there for ten years. I was a housewife in Korea. ... We got very little training about health and safety. I have headaches, nausea, dizziness, shoulder aches, backaches. ... I see everyone with the same problems in my department. Some women have Carpal Tunnel Syndrome, high blood pressure, and kidney problems. It's difficult to learn about safety at work. ... we lose our health.[10]
>
> – Korean electronics worker

A number of initiatives by Asian American women have connected workers' rights and occupational health with environmental justice concerns. According to Pam Tau Lee of the University of California at Berkeley Labor Occupational Health Program, immigrant Asian women are disproportionately employed in hazardous industries such as the garment and the electronics/semiconductor industries. The hazards they face include exposure to toxic materials, low wages, and institutional neglect by the government, unions, employers, and consumers.[11]

Fifty-three percent of all textile workers and apparel workers in the United States are Asian women.[12] Garment workers face increased exposure to fiber particles, dyes, formaldehydes, and arsenic, leading to high rates of byssinosis and respiratory illness. Asian Americans – primarily women – comprise 43 percent of electronics workers in assembly line and operative jobs in Silicon Valley.[13] Asian and Latina immigrant women in the electronics/semiconductor industry suffer from "damage to the central nervous system, and possibly the reproductive system, as a result of using dangerous solvents to clean electronic components, as well as exposure to other chemicals," according to Lee. They suffer occupational illness at triple the rate of workers in general manufacturing.

The Asian Pacific Environmental Network (APEN) is the most prominent Asian environmental justice organization in the United States. Other organizations that work on Asian environmental justice issues include Asian Immigrant Women Advocates (AIWA), which organizes and empowers immigrant Asian garment and electronic workers, "so they can improve their living and working conditions," according to Helen Kim, an organizer from AIWA.[14]

Young Hi Shin, AIWA's executive director, gave one of two major papers presented by an Asian woman at the first People of Color Environmental Leadership Summit (the other was given by Pam Tau Lee). It is no accident that its focus was also occupational health issues – many activists argue that occupational health is the number one environmental justice concern for Asian Americans.

Both Lee and Shin helped create innovative models to educate immigrant Asian women about occupational and environmental hazards, for example, by including political education in English classes. In these classes, immigrant women practice their English by translating warning information about chemicals they are routinely exposed to at work.[15] Lee explains how trainers in the Labor Occupational Health Program use graphics and risk-mapping – which enable workers to identify health hazards through visual means – to reach diverse linguistic communities.[16]

Environmental Justice Abroad

Internationally, economic globalization necessitates further strategic alliances between radical Asian feminist, labor, and environmental justice movements. According to Lee,

> You will find women in the Philippines, Malaysia, and Japan and other parts of Asia working very hard to stop deforestation, organizing around military toxics, organizing around issues of health and safety. ... Environmental justice efforts do not confine themselves to local efforts or national ones. Environmental justice activists also work in solidarity with those in Asia, Africa, Mexico, Central and Latin America against corporate greed and profits.[17]

Poor people and people of color both here and abroad have suffered from economic globalization orchestrated by governments and corporations and supported by mainstream environmental organizations in the United States. The World Wildlife Fund, Natural Resources Defense Council, National Audubon Society, and Environmental Defense Fund all supported the North American Free Trade Agreement (NAFTA), to the outrage of labor and social justice organizations.[18] While NAFTA claims to emphasize protection of natural resources, it encourages the degradation of human life by driving down wages and work standards to maximize corporate profit.

The links between occupational health and environmental justice will become increasingly relevant as more multinational corporations move their factories to countries with little or no worker or environmental protections. Asian countries such as Indonesia, Singapore, Vietnam, South Korea, Taiwan, Thailand, and China are low-wage countries where legions of workers – mostly women – face slave-like working conditions. One of the more egregious work situations led to the deaths of 188 workers who were trapped in a fire at the Kader toy factory in Thailand in 1993.[19]

One of the leading theorists of the links between the exploitation of women, labor, and natural resources in an international development matrix is the Indian environmentalist Vandana Shiva, a leading spokesperson for radical Asian politics and environmental justice. Shiva, a physicist, philosopher, Science and Environment Advisor with The Third World Network, and Director of the Research Foundation for Science, Technology and Natural Resource Policy in Dehra Dun, India, has researched, written, and spoken extensively about how Third World women are particularly targeted in the logic of "maldevelopment" that exploits both women and nature as commodities.[20] According to Shiva,

> You really can't separate issues of ecology from feminism or from human rights or from development or from issues of ethnic and cultural diversity. ... to me, the choice ... is between environmental justice and green imperialism, between a common future for all or continued economic and environmental apartheid.[21]

Shiva is also an activist with the International Forum on Globalization and with the Chipko movement, a women's movement in the Himalayas that successfully resisted World Bank deforestation projects. The "Chipko andolan" translates literally into "hugging movement."[22] In the United States, "tree hugger" is generally a pejorative term (used by people from across the political spectrum) to describe environmentalists who care more about trees than about people. People of color often level this charge of elitism against mainstream environmental organizers. Their critique is entirely valid and necessary, but the fact that many environmental justice advocates in the United States do not know the history of this term, which emerged from an integrated struggle for both human dignity and preservation of natural resources, suggests that the links and histories of environmental justice struggles in other countries need to be highlighted.

The Anti-Immigration Assault on Asian Women

Shiva's critique of macro-level economic policies and their impact on individuals is reinforced by Cathi Tactaquin, Executive Director of the National Network for Immigrant and Refugee Rights. According to Tactaquin, in the United States, immigrants and refugees are scapegoated for various social ills, such as "stealing" jobs or "ruining" the environment. Tactaquin points out that the real global threat is from "neo-liberalism – the globalization of poverty imposed by United States policies and by international financial institutions."[23]

Environmentally based anti-immigration and zero-population movements pose a serious threat to Asian and Asian American women. A growing number of anti-immigrant and zero-population advocates argue that immigration should be limited because of environmental degradation. This argument – most developed in California – is another version of the "limited resource" argument that convinced voters in California to pass Proposition 187, an anti-immigration bill, in the fall of 1994. The "limited resource" perspective argues that finite resources – whether financial or environmental – are wasted on immigrants generally, and illegal immigrants specifically, who are purely a resource drain and make no contribution to their adopted society (regardless of the fact that they provide low-wage labor that is much used – and abused). Therefore, proponents conclude, the answer to a multitude of social and environmental problems is to reduce immigration.

For these activists, "environmentalism" is used to justify severe, punitive, and regressive calls for immigration moratoriums and changes in national immigration legislation. In 1995, Population Environment Balance, Californians for Population Stabilization, and Carrying Capacity Network called for a five-year immigration moratorium with a ceiling for all countries of 100,000 immigrants. Negative Population Growth placed advertisements in environmental magazines such as *E* and *Natural History* calling for an immigration moratorium.[24]

Anti-immigrant and zero-population advocates fuel a political and social atmosphere of hate and misinformation by pandering to the white electorate's fears

of "Third World-ification" by Latinos and Asians. The fundamental assumptions
that ground this argument are:

- More immigrants mean more environmental degradation and a lower quality
  of life.
- Population growth is the primary cause of environmental degradation, and high
  population density leads to ecological devastation.
- A rising population, fueled by immigration, is the cause of water quality and
  scarcity problems.
- Immigrants not only have higher rates of population growth, but quickly adopt
  resource-intensive lifestyles.
- The world's people of color cause overpopulation – birth rates for people of
  European descent are under control.[25]

On the contrary, the nation's single largest environmental polluter is the U.S.
military. Rich people consume more resources than poor people. The United States
has 5 percent of the world's population and uses 36 percent of the world's resources.
The average American uses energy at the rate of 3 Japanese, or 6 Mexicans, or
12 Chinese, or 33 Indians, or 147 Bangladeshis, or 422 Ethiopians.[26] Rather than
reducing wasteful consumption of natural resources by rich people generally, and of
Americans specifically, these xenophobic "environmentalists" want to reduce human
populations – specifically immigrants of color, even though immigrants are not the
primary (nor for that matter, a significant) cause of environmental degradation.

Anti-immigration environmentalists' dangerous arguments have been absorbed
by mainstream politicians. For example, Senator Reid from Nevada described the
Immigration Stabilization Act of 1994 – which called for more limits on and fewer
benefits for illegal immigration and refugees – as "one of the most important bills for
protecting the environment." According to Reid,

> As you know, our environment is beset from all sides by the problems of the gravest
> and most intractable kind: vanishing ecosystems, acid rain, global warming, ground-
> water pollution, air pollution, and dwindling wetlands and farmlands. All of these
> problems have one root cause – too many people. If we have any hope of slowing our
> country's population growth, immigration must be reduced.[27]

The Political Ecology Group is a multiracial social justice organization based in
San Francisco that fights anti-immigration and zero-population policies. It creates
and disseminates factsheets that outline the myths and facts on immigration,
population, and the environment.[28] The Political Ecology Group researches anti-
immigration groups and other allied groups, such as the Federation for American
Immigration Reform, to publicize their scapegoating statements and funding links
to right-wing eugenicist foundations.

We need to expand our efforts to educate and mobilize Asian women to assert our
right to live and work safely and productively wherever we choose.

Conclusion

Since Asian women are disproportionately affected by environmental and social injustice, we are also uniquely positioned to lead insurgent movements for justice. Our efforts pave the road for stronger domestic and international resistance against corporate and political agendas that exploit Asian women, our labor, and the natural environment.

Radical Asian women must continue to theorize about and organize around a wide range of issues, including: labor exploitation, healthcare, institutional violence, domestic violence, and cultural discrimination. Radical Asian women's movements, like environmental justice, envision multiracial, multiethnic, international/national movements for progressive social change.

International workers' rights and environmental justice movements need to share information, make organizational links, and coordinate campaigns against wage and environmental exploitation. Radical Asian women as labor organizers and environmental justice advocates need to organize across borders and recognize our common visions for justice, community-based self-determination, and a safe and healthy environment.

Notes

The ideas in this essay are my own, and do not necessarily reflect the views or position of the New York City Environmental Justice Alliance, for whom I work. I'd like to thank my Executive Director Michelle DePass, Asian Immigrant Women Advocates, Asian Pacific Environmental Network, the Political Ecology Group, EDGE: Alliance of Ethnic and Environmental Organizations, Pam Tau Lee, Lilly Lee, Angela Chung, and others for their assistance with this essay.

1. Though I reject the notion that any static or essential Asian feminist perspective exists, I believe that race- and gender-specific analysis is critical. See for example, Anthony, Carl "Why Blacks Should Be Environmentalists." *Call to Action*. Ed. Brad Erickson. San Francisco: Sierra Club Books, 1990.

2. Schaffer, Gwen. "Asian Americans Organize for Justice." *Environmental Action*, Winter 1994.

3. Telephone interview with Angela Chung.

4. Bullard, Robert. *Dumping in Dixie*. Boulder: Westview Press, 1994; Bullard, Robert, ed. *Confronting Environmental Racism*. Boston: South End Press, 1993, and *Environmental Justice and Communities of Color*. San Francisco: Sierra Club Books, 1994; Richard Hofrichter, ed. *Toxic Struggles: The Theory and Practice of Environmental Justice*. Philadelphia: New Society Publishers, 1993; Lavelle, Marianne, and Marcia Coyle. "Unequal Protection: The Racial Divide in Environmental Law" in Hofrichter, ed., *Toxic Struggles*.

5. "The Global Connection: Exploitation of Developing Countries" in Hofrichter, ed. *Toxic Struggles*.

6. United Church of Christ Commission for Racial Justice. *Toxic Wastes and Race in the United States: A National Report on the Racial and Socio-Economic Characteristics of Communities With Hazardous Waste Sites*. 1987.

7. Lavelle and Coyle, op cit.

8. Darnovsky, Marcy. "Stories Less Told: Histories of U.S. Environmentalism." *Socialist Review* (October-December 1992): 9214.

9. "Principles of Environmental Justice." Proceedings from the First National People of Color Environmental Leadership Summit. United Church of Christ, Commission for Racial Justice, 1992.

10. *Working Healthy.* Asian Immigrant Women Advocates brochure, 7.

11. Proceedings from the First National People of Color Environmental Leadership Summit United Church of Christ, Commission for Racial Justice, 1992. Lee is a former labor organizer and a board member of the Washington Office on Environmental Justice, the National Environmental Justice Advisory Council, and Asian Pacific Environmental Network.

12. Saika, Peggy. "APEN Brings Asian Pacific Perspective to Environmental Justice." Washington Office on Environmental Justice Newsletter, Summer 1995.

13. Schaffer, op cit.

14. Telephone interview with Helen Kim, 13 September 1996.

15. Schaffer, op cit.

16. Swanson, Sandra. "Can We Balance the Scales of Environmental Justice?" *Safety + Health* (October 1995).

17. Interview with Pam Tau Lee, 21 August 1996.

18. Athanasiou, Tom. *Divided Planet*. Boston: Little Brown & Co., 1996. 191.

19. Zuckoff, Mitchell. "Trapped by Poverty, Killed by Neglect." *Boston Globe* (10 July 1994).

20. Shiva, Vandana. "Women & Nature." *Environmental Ethics: Divergence & Convergence*. Ed. Armstrong and Botzier. New York: McGraw Hill, 1993, and "Development, Ecology & Women." *Healing the Wounds: The Promise of Ecofeminism*. Ed. Plant. Philadelphia: New Society Publishers, 1989.

21. Ethnic News Watch. *India Currents* 6.4 (July 31, 1992): Ml5.

22. Shiva, Vandana. *Staying Alive: Women, Ecology, and Development*. London: Zed Books, 1989. 67–77.

23. National Network For Immigrant and Refugee Rights. *Network News,* Summer 1996.

24. Loh, Penn. "Creating an Environment of Blame: Anti-Immigration Forces Seek to Woo Environmentalists." *RESIST* newsletter (December 1995): 4.

25. Political Ecology Group Immigration and Environment Campaign Organizer's Kit.

26. *Environmental Action* (Summer 1994): 15.

27. *Environmental Action* (Summer 1994): 23.

28. Political Ecology Group Immigration and Environment Campaign Organizer's Kit.

10.6

El Mundo Zurdo and the Ample Space
of the Erotic
M. Jacqui Alexander

Moraga: If the gun and the cross have been used as instruments of oppression, we must learn to use them as instruments of liberation.

Anzaldúa: And yet to act is not enough. Many of us are learning to sit perfectly still to sense the presence of the Soul and commune with Her. We are beginning to realize that we are not wholly at the mercy of circumstance ... We have come to realize we are not alone in our struggles, nor separate, nor autonomous but that we ... are connected and interdependent.

Lorde: *[T]he dichotomy between the spiritual and the political is false resulting from an incomplete attention to our erotic knowledge, for the bridge which connects them is formed by the erotic, the sensual, those physical, emotional and psychic expressions of what is deepest and strongest and richest within each of us being shared: the passion of love in its deepest meaning.*

For three years now I have been participating in ongoing meetings and discussions among a group of women and men – lesbian, gay, bisexual, transgendered, and heterosexual, of different nationalities and ages, with different cultural and spiritual affinities, including those with close relationships to the institutionalized Christian church, to learn what sex and spirit, what sexuality and spirituality taken together, might tell us about who we are. Early in this work, we found that many "secular" activists were reluctant to come out spiritually. Some reluctance came from the historical ways the Judaeo-Christian church, in particular, operated as an instrument of colonization: enforcing heterosexuality and nuclear family as the moral norm; attempting to erase the connection between sexuality and land – in Hawai'i, for instance, splitting apart the ontology of mind, body, and spirit into the particularities of (white) manliness, colonized "other," and christian religion, respectively. A more contemporary religious right had mobilized globally to advance an anti-human agenda, mistakenly attributing its authority to God. But this dominant mythologized collapse of spirituality into religion was also operating among us, another indication of the subtle internalization of dominance. We found that we had a great deal of practice coming out politically, but many were timid about coming out spiritually *as* (radical) political people. It seemed that in combining the two we were on the brink of committing heresy of a different kind.

As we moved to unite these powerful forces of sex and the spirit, we identified another kind of shared internalization. Grappling with the inherited division, we understood that it is sustained in part by an ideology steeping sex and sexuality in sin, shame, and general disavowal of the sacred. Simultaneously, this very ideology has attempted to contain all spirit and the spiritual within the structure of religion, with predictably devastating consequences. We named this process of fragmentation colonization, usually understood as a set of exploitative practices in political, ideological, and aesthetic terms, but also linked in minute ways to dualistic-hierarchical thinking: divisions among mind, body, spirit; between sacred and secular; male and female; heterosexual and homosexual; in class divisions; in divisions between the Erotic and the Divine. We saw its operation creating mono-thinking: the mistaken notion that only one kind of justice work leads to freedom. Presumably, organizing for a decent, just, living wage is not connected to anti-racist work, to anti-homophobia work, to organizing against the U.S state in Vieques. Such thinking is always premised in negation, often translated into singular explanations for oppression. Breaking down these divisions and hierarchies, indeed making ourselves whole again, became our work throughout our entire journey.

Since colonization has produced fragmentation and dismemberment at both the material and the psychic levels, the work of decolonization must make room for the deep yearning for wholeness, oftentimes expressed as a yearning to belong, a yearning both material and existential, both psychic and physical, which, when satisfied, can subvert and ultimately displace the pain of dismemberment. Because anti-colonial and left liberation movements have not understood this sufficiently in their psychology of liberation, they have not made ample political room for it. This yearning to belong cannot be confined only to membership or citizenship in community, political movement, nation, group, or belonging to a family, however constituted, although important. Indeed, we would not have come to the various political movements in which we have been engaged with such intense passion had it not been for this yearning. With the help of Bernice Johnson Reagon we recognized in this yearning a desire to reproduce home in "coalitions": our political movements were forced to bear too much of a longing for sameness as home, the limits of nationalism. But we needed to wrestle with that desire for home a bit longer, examining more closely the source of that yearning we wanted to embed in the metaphysics of political struggle, the metaphysics of life. Its source is the deep knowing that we are in fact interdependent, neither separate nor autonomous. As human beings, we have a sacred connection to one another, and this is why enforced separations wreak havoc on our souls. There is great danger, then, in living lives of segregation. Racial segregation. Segregation in politics. Segregated frameworks. Segregated, compartmentalized selves. Our oppositional politic has been necessary, but it will never sustain us; while it may give us some temporary gains (themselves becoming more ephemeral the greater the threat, which is not a reason not to fight), it can never ultimately feed that deep place within us: that space of the erotic, that space of the soul, that space of the Divine.[1]

"To sense the presence of the soul and commune with her" is what Gloria Anzaldúa has said is required in this job of excavation, this job of changing the self. It is a job. It requires work. It requires practice. It cannot be someone else's excavation easily appropriated as our own. It cannot be done as spectator or ventriloquist. It requires the work of each and every one, to unearth this desire to belong to the self *in* community as part of a radical project – not to be confused with the self-preoccupation on which individualism thrives. Self-determination is both an individual and collective project.

There is an inevitability (not passivity) in this movement toward wholeness, this work of spirit and the journey of the Soul in its vocation to reunite us with the erotic and the Divine. Whether we want it or not, it will occur. Do we dare to undertake this task of recognition intentionally, as self-reflexive human beings, open at the very core to a foundational truth? We are connected to the Divine through our connections with each other. Yet no one comes to consciousness alone, in isolation, only for oneself, or passively. It is here we need a verb – conscientize, which Paulo Freire used to underscore the fact that shifts in consciousness happen through active processes of practice and reflection. Of necessity, they occur in community. We must constantly envision this as we devise ways to practice building communities (not sameness) over and over again. We can continue holding on to a consciousness of our different locations, our understanding of the simultaneous ways dominance shapes our lives and, at the same time, water the erotic as that place of our Divine connection which can transform the ways we relate to one another.

Oftentimes when we have failed at solidarity work we *retreat*, struggling to convince ourselves that this is indeed the work we have been called upon to do. The fact is that there *is* no other work but the work of creating and re-creating ourselves within the context of community. Simply put, there is no other work. It took five hundred years, at least in this hemisphere, to solidify the division of things that belong together. It need not take us five hundred more years to move ourselves out of this existential impasse. Spirit work does not conform to the dictates of human time: But it needs our courage, revolutionary patience, and intentional shifts in consciousness allowing us to anchor the struggle for social justice within the ample space of the erotic.[2]

One of feminism's earliest lessons is that the personal is political: some of our lives' most infinitesimal details are shaped by ideological and political forces much larger than our individual selves. During a pitched battle to transform the curriculum at the New School University, where I taught five years ago, I came to appreciate another shade of this insight as the school's administration sought to make me *the* entire political struggle. With a great deal of help and a deep level of self-scrutiny I learned how a single individual could ignite a political struggle but ultimately had to be subsumed under it, simply be within it, if that struggle was to be successful. This interior work is indispensable in the journey to wholeness. Through the task force's conscious attention to the reknitting of sex and spirit and the spiritual-political work I have undertaken in my life, I have come to see that an inside change in the personal is not entirely complete if it remains at the level of a shift in ideas, or even in practice, although both are necessary. Desire is expressed most fundamentally where change takes place: at the root of our very souls, the base of the internal source of our power and yearning. Yearning and power we have been taught so much to fear. When Anzaldúa asks us to commune with the Soul, or Lorde urges us to find something our soul craves and do it, our first task is to become attentive to the soul's desire and to place ourselves in its service. It is a necessary and delicate undertaking in spirit-based politics, this joining of the sacred and secular, "to have," as Sharon Day imaged it, "the ethics of spirituality inform daily life." It requires intention, a revolutionary patience, courage, and, above all, humility. Once this work begins, the temptation to cross narrow boundaries becomes irresistible; connections, once invisible, come into full view. And I am assured that when the practice begins to bear fruit, the yearning itself is transformed.

An old man has etched himself into an ancient slab of rock deposited in a park at the end of my street in Harlem. His face comes into view only from afar, with distance, with perspective. Close up, he simply folds himself back into the stone, disappearing – pretending, perhaps, not to be there. When we do not see him does it mean he does not exist? Unlike the figures of Davis, Lee, and Jackson – patiently chiseled into the Mountain of Stone in Georgia, now pasted on the tourist bus stationed opposite the park, figures that announce themselves from far and near – this old man works in stealth, through years of weather, bringing himself into my field of vision only by the angle of my gaze and the distance from which I stand. Although I have lived for seven years on this same one-way street leading directly to this slab of stone, I had not seen him before. And yet, he is there. The challenge for me is to see him in the present and to know he's there even when I cannot see. Rocks hold memory.

Land holds memory. This is why the land and live oak trees rooted in the Georgia Sea Islands whisper in our ear when we allow ourselves to listen. The Ibo of Nigeria were captured and brought to these islands. When they arrived and saw the conditions of their capture and homelessness, they turned around, walked on water, and drowned themselves. The place, bearing the name Ibo Landing, holds the memory of that moment which still lives in the heart of every Gullah child and in the oaks' solid trunks. The live oaks will tell us these stories when we listen. And the mountains of Hawai'i will echo the ancient Kanaka Maoli belief that they are stewards, eyes, children of the land. Deep within their undulating folds draping themselves with the ease of velvet around the opulent embrace of mist and cloud, we will feel the land's ancient power to heal. Ocean will reveal the secrets that lie at the bottom of its silted deep. She requires no name before her. Neither Pacific. Atlantic. Arctic. Southern. Indian. She is simply her watery translucent self, reaching, without need for a compass, for her sisters, whomever and wherever they are. She will call you by your ancient name and you would answer because you would not have forgotten. Water always remembers.

Notes

This essay is in honor of Cherríe Moraga and Gloria Anzaldúa, who bore the original vision. It is dedicated to Gloria Wekker. Much gratitude to AnaLouise Keating for her insights and for staying close throughout this process; and to AnaLouise and Gloria Anzaldúa for their gentleness. Angela Bowen, Gloria Joseph, Gail Lewis, Mab Segrest, Jerma Jackson, Linda Carty, and Gloria Wekker have all accompanied me throughout this process and have read different versions of this essay. I relied upon them for their astute eyes, their commitment to sisterhood, their critical engagement, their desire to make our world intelligible in order to change it, and their perpetual generosity and love.

1. Chela Sandoval's original formulation of an oppositional consciousness remains very important.
2. I borrow the term *revolutionary patience* from Gloria Joseph.

10.7
Lessons for Transformation
AnaLouise Keating

Lesson #1: Making Connections Through Differences,
Seeking Commonalities

As I've already mentioned, *This Bridge Called My Back* is especially praised for its attention to differences among women. At its strongest and most provocative, however, *This Bridge* does not simply emphasize difference. Rather, it redefines difference in potentially transformative ways. While some contributors rely on status-quo stories that reinforce self-enclosed identities and rigid racialized/gendered/sexualized differences, others do not. I have been especially struck by Andrea Canaan, Mirtha Quintanales, Audre Lorde, Rosario Morales, and Gloria Anzaldúa. These writers attempt to forge alliances and coalitions that do not ignore the differences among women (and in many instances men) but instead use difference as catalysts for personal and social change. Through their explorations of difference, they enter into what Helene Lorenz describes as the "unimaginable gulfs of difference" between self and other (2002, 502). As the phrase "unimaginable gulfs" might suggest, these differences are formidable; they cannot be fully understood or entirely anticipated. At times these differences are so sharp, so profound, and so deep that they seem permanent and impossible to span.

Rather than gloss over such differences, Canaan, Quintanales, Lorde, Morales, and Anzaldúa acknowledge and explore them; risking the personal, they expose (both to themselves and to their readers) their own previously hidden fears and desires. This risk, although incredibly dangerous, is vital to community building. As Anzaldúa explains, "To bridge is to attempt community, and for that we must risk being open to personal, political, and spiritual intimacy, to risk being wounded" (2002b, 3). Making themselves vulnerable, these contributors engage in open conversations about differences. More specifically they use difference – or, more precisely, the dangerous self-exposure and exploration of differences which this exposure makes possible – to discover and/or create commonalities. Significantly, they forge commonalities without assuming that their experiences, histories, ideas, or traits are *identical* with those of others. Let me emphasize: as I use the terms, *"commonalities" and "sameness" are not synonymous*. Rather, "commonalities" indicates complex points of connection that both incorporate and move beyond sameness, similarity, and difference; commonalities acknowledge and contain difference. When defined in this complex fashion, commonalities indicate one of intersectionality's most important theoretical contributions, and the search for and invention of commonalities indicates an important methodological approach.

These tricky negotiations among sameness, similarity, and difference represent a radical departure from conventional practices. Generally, feminists and other social-justice theorists define differences oppositionally, in binary self/other terms; however, these binary configurations inadvertently reinforce an exclusionary (and often invisible) norm. As Lorde explains, we have been trained to define differences as deviations from a false standard, or what she terms the '"*mythical norm*,' which ... in america [*sic*]... is usually defined as white, thin, male, young, heterosexual, christian [*sic*], and financially secure" (1984, 116, her emphasis). This oppositional definition of difference distorts our ability to forge intricate alliances, for it compels us to define difference as "deviation" and therefore to regard all differences as shameful marks of inferiority. Driven by our shame of difference-as-deviation, we ignore, deny, and/or misname the differences among us. In a mistaken attempt to demonstrate solidarity, we hide our differences (as well as those of others) beneath a facade of sameness. But of course differences don't disappear just because we reject them. Ironically, it is often the reverse: the denied differences grow stronger as we pretend they don't exist by seeking refuge behind stereotypes, monolithic labels, and other false assumptions of sameness. Think, for instance, of the mainstream U.S. women's movement of the 1970s and early 1980s, when gender – defined in simplistic terms – was supposed to trump the many differences among women by creating an automatic (pseudo)universal female bond. As *Bridge* contributors demonstrated, this assumption of a homogeneous womanhood created new divisions.

In *This Bridge Called My Back,* writers acknowledge, express, and investigate differences, yet – *and simultaneously* – they insist on commonalities. This intertwined acknowledgment of differences and commonalities, coupled with a willingness to risk self-exposure, can revolutionize our approaches to difference. Making themselves vulnerable, *Bridge* authors draw on their personal experiences to explore the stereotypes and the limitations in identity labels. Their bold explorations challenge assumptions of sameness, demonstrating that it is not differences that divide us but rather our refusal to openly examine and discuss the differences among us. This point is worth repeating because it's so often misunderstood: Differences are not, in themselves, divisive. Rather, it's our refusal to openly acknowledge, examine, and discuss these differences that divides us.[1]

This nuanced approach to differences culminates in Anzaldúa's theory and practice of *El Mundo Zurdo*, or "The Left-Handed World." This activist theory spans Anzaldúa's career and in many ways embodies her visionary, inclusionary stance. In addition to titling the last section of *This Bridge Called My Back* "El Mundo Zurdo: The Vision," Anzaldúa included a discussion of El Mundo Zurdo in her essay, "La Prieta"; and at various points throughout her career she returned to and expanded on this theory and practice.[2] With El Mundo Zurdo, Anzaldúa proposes and enacts a spirit-inflected, visionary approach to community building that enables very different people – men and women from diverse backgrounds with a wide variety of needs and concerns – to coexist and work together to enact revolutionary change. As she explains in "La Prieta": "We are the queer groups, the people that don't belong anywhere, not in the dominant world nor completely within our own respective cultures. Combined we cover so many oppressions. But the over-whelming oppression is the collective fact that we do not fit, and because we do not fit, *we are a threat*" (1983b, 209, her emphasis).

Anzaldúa replaces conventional definitions of difference-as-opposition with a relational approach. She acknowledges that inhabitants/practitioners of El Mundo Zurdo are not all alike; their specific oppressions, solutions, and beliefs are different. She accepts these differences and uses them to create new forms of commonality: "These different affinities are not opposed to each other. In El Mundo Zurdo I with my own affinities and my people with theirs can live together and transform the planet" (1983b, 209). Joined by their rejection of the status quo and their so-called deviation from the dominant culture, inhabitants of El Mundo Zurdo create new alliances and use these alliances to transform their worlds.

Anzaldúa's theory of El Mundo Zurdo originated in her daily life when, in the late 1970s, she organized a series of poetry readings called El Mundo Surdo Reading Series[3] in San Francisco. This series was extremely diverse and included progressive people of all types: feminists, U.S. "Third World" writers, lesbians, and gay men. Unlike many other progressive social-justice activists and theorists of this time period who were uniting into identity-specific groups, Anzaldúa refused to self-segregate and insisted on creating alliances among people from a variety of different social locations. Despite the many differences among them, her El Mundo Surdo participants shared several commonalities, including their personal experiences of alienation, discrimination, and oppression; their interest in issues of social justice; their shared rejection of the status quo; their belief in the transformational power of imagination and the spoken word; and their work as creative writers and artists.

With her theory of El Mundo Zurdo, Anzaldúa demonstrates that we can seek commonalities without ignoring differences (whether in cultures, experiences, beliefs, or desires) among people. As she asserts in her preface to *this bridge we call home*, "Our goal is not to use differences to separate us from others, but neither is it to gloss over them" (2002b, 3). Anzaldúa grounds this nuanced approach in her holistic, spirit-infused worldview, which creates broader, more inclusive contexts for difference. Defining each individual as part of a larger whole, she insists on a commonality shared by "everyone/everything"; despite our many differences, we "share a category of identity wider than any social position or racial label" (2002a, 558).[4] For Anzaldúa, this shared identity category is foundational and enables her to replace the rigid boundaries imposed by status-quo stories with a relational approach.

The belief in our interrelatedness is the second lesson I explore.

Lesson #2: Forging an Ethics of Radical Interrelatedness

Because we are radically interrelated, what we think and do impacts others – all others, no matter how different or distant they seem. To be sure, this concept of interrelatedness is a key tenet of many indigenous worldviews – ranging from the Dakota belief expressed in the phrase "all my relatives" *(mitakuye owasin)*, which reminds us that we are related to all existence, to the Buddhist teaching of codependent arising, to Thich Nhat Hanh's theory of interbeing. Indeed, interdependence is even partially grasped by some nineteenth-century U.S. American transcendentalists like Ralph Waldo Emerson and Walt Whitman. However, I first saw interrelatedness embodied and lived out within the pages of *This Bridge Called My Back*: in Rosario Morales's assertion that "we are all in the same boat" (1983, 93); in Luisah Teish's belief that "my destiny is infinitely tied with that of everybody else" (Anzaldúa 1983c, 223); and in Anzaldúa's bold claim that "we have come to realize that we are not alone in our struggles nor separate nor autonomous but that we – white black straight queer female male – are connected and interdependent. We are accountable for what is happening down the street, south of the border or across the sea" (1983a, foreword). We are interrelated and interdependent – on multiple levels and in multiple ways: economically; socially, ecologically, emotionally, linguistically, physically, and spiritually. We are interlinked in every way that we can possibly imagine, as well as in ways that we cannot yet fathom. As Inés Hernández-Ávila states, "We are related to all that lives" (2002, 523).

Interconnectivity is foundational to *This Bridge Called My Back*. Indeed, I would argue that a key part of Anzaldúa's motivation for initiating this collection of writings by women of colors was her own deeply held belief in our radical interrelatedness.[5] As she writes in an unpublished draft of her 1983 foreword to the collection's second edition, she believes that "every person, animal, plant, stone is interconnected in a life and death symbiosis."[6]

I want to emphasize this lesson of radical interconnectivity because it's one that we too often forget. *This Bridge Called My Back* is so often associated with the recognition of differences that it's easy to overlook its equally important points about interrelatedness. Jacqui Alexander makes a similar observation: "In the midst of uncovering the painful fault lines of homophobia, culture, and class within different communities of belonging, [and] advancing critiques of racism within the women's movement, [*This Bridge Called My Back*] did not relinquish a vision of interdependence, of interbeing. ... Not a transcendent vision, but one rooted in transforming the dailiness of lived experience, the very ground upon which violence finds fodder" (2002, 97). As Alexander suggests, this "vision of interdependence" is not some abstract belief in an otherworldly reality to which we escape; it is, rather, deeply embedded in everyday life and impacts even our most ordinary actions and encounters.

Not surprisingly, then, positing radical interrelatedness has concrete ethical implications. Because we are all interconnected, the events and belief systems impacting other people – no matter how different and/or distant these others seem to be – affect us as well. To borrow Rosario Morales's analogy, we are all in the same boat, and we all rise or sink together. If we view ourselves as interrelated, we must consider our actions' impact on others. On the personal level, then, interconnectivity and accountability are closely intertwined – like two sides of the same coin. When we perceive ourselves as radically interrelated, we learn to self-reflect and carefully think through the implications of our words and deeds before we speak or act.

Recognition of our profound interrelatedness has revolutionized my life in ways that I'm still trying to comprehend. In my scholarship and teaching, positing interconnectivity has challenged me to reconsider my use of binary-oppositional frameworks. Like many people trained in the academy, I have honed my debate skills; I have learned to think on my feet, to quickly assess and find the weaknesses in opponents' arguments and perspectives. I focus on these weak spots as I champion my own views. Given my progressive politics, as well as my status as a woman of color in the academy, this oppositionality has seemed vital for my survival. However, after living so intimately with *This Bridge Called My Back*, working with Gloria on *this bridge we call home*, and reflecting on my personal and professional life thus far, I have come to realize that my oppositional politics have inhibited my growth, damaged my health, threatened my relationships, and harmed me in other ways.

Ironically, I arrived at this realization while editing *this bridge we call home*. Excited about the book's progress and in awe of the brilliant women and men participating in our project, Gloria and I wanted to provide a virtual space for everyone to meet and exchange ideas. To facilitate community building and dialogue, we started a listserv for all contributors. Although many contributors used the listserv to share insights and express their excitement about our project, a few people reacted violently when they learned that Gloria and I would be including contributions by people who do not identify as "women of color" in the book. The anger was visceral and shocking as several contributors expressed their intense disappointment that our new book would not provide the same type of "safe" women-of-color-only space as that provided by *This Bridge Called My Back*. I still do not fully understand the dynamics, but these reactions shifted from sorrow to aggressive anger – directed not toward the editors but instead toward each other. Instead of expressing their anger directly by confronting Gloria and me about our decision to create a radically inclusionary book, the listserv conversation took a strange detour into a volatile debate between pro-Palestinian and pro-Israeli contributors. The rhetoric grew increasingly hateful and hostile; each side treated its "Other" with total disdain, dehumanizing anyone who held an opposing view, refusing to listen and understand their Other's perspectives. It was a stunning display of oppositional energies, and it made us physically ill. As Anzaldúa writes, "The contentious debates … churned a liquid fire in our guts" (2002b, 2).

This painful clash among our contributors led me to reflect on my own oppositional politics and energies. As I carefully monitored my initial reactions, I noted my strong desire to react oppositionally, to fight back, to counter the angry words with my own anger, to meet aggression with aggression, and to give what I was receiving. Our listserv – this beautiful space designed to facilitate visionary planning and bonding – had been hijacked by a few very angry people, and I was angry in turn. I was hurt, and this wound made me furious! I wanted to point out that the hostility was misdirected and should be directed toward Gloria and me; they had been sidetracked. I wanted to scold these contributors; I wanted to remind them of *This Bridge Called My Back*'s radical vision; and I wanted to suggest that they adopt the contributors' teachings and stop judging each other so harshly. I wanted to respond by attacking those contributors who were slinging hostile words at each other. I was so mad! I composed (but did not send) many angry emails, filled with harsh words and strong critiques of the flaws in both sides' perspectives – the stereotyping, the othering, and the hate. Instead, I became physically ill and (after many discussions and much soul searching), Gloria and I decided to shut down the listserv.

My illness forced me to slow down and reflect on the angry debate. Through this reflection and conversations with Gloria, I was reminded of the limitations in oppositional strategies. Our experiences illustrated Irene Lara's assertion: "Standing in rigid opposition is a strategy for survival, but it has also killed us and will continue to sever our souls and assail our hearts. Western binary oppositions wound us in many ways. ... Feeding the interests of the dominant, these false splits keep us from ourselves, each other, and our visible and invisible world" (2002, 434).[7] Because binary oppositions have their source in the dominating culture and support its values and worldviews, our oppositional politics are not as transformative as we might assume.

Based on either/or thinking and dualistic ("us" against "them") models of identity, this binary-oppositional approach reinforces the status quo. Oppositional logic reduces our interactional possibilities to two mutually exclusive options: either our views are entirely the same *or* they are entirely different. In this either/or system, differences of opinion and differing worldviews become monolithic, rigid, and divisive. When we examine the world through this binary lens, we assume that the differences between our views and those of others are too different – too *other*, as it were – to have *anything* (of importance) in common. This assumption keeps us trapped within our existing ideas and beliefs, for it prevents us from developing new forms of knowledge and new alliances. After all, if we're so busy defending our own views, where is the room for complexity, compromise, and exchange? How can we possibly learn from social-justice theorists who hold views different from our own?

Positing radical interconnectivity, I am shifting my politics and pedagogy from oppositional to holistic approaches. In my classrooms, interdependence offers alternative epistemologies and serves as a crucial point of departure for teaching about and enacting social justice. Exposing the limitations in status-quo stories about self-enclosed identities, I invite students to examine both our radical interconnectedness and the ways this interconnectivity makes us accountable – on multiple levels and in multiple ways. This recognition, when it occurs, encourages us to develop new alliances. As Anzaldúa explains, "The knowledge that we are in symbiotic relationship to all that exists and co-creators of ideologies – attitudes, beliefs, and cultural values – motivates us to act collaboratively" (2002b, 2).

However, these collaborative actions will only succeed when we begin moving beyond binary thinking and dualistic self/other identities, which brings me to the third lesson I explore.

Lesson #3: The Importance of Listening with Raw Openness

We must listen to each other. It sounds so obvious. .. doesn't it? But we (I'm thinking here of feminist scholars and students; however, it applies to those in other social-justice disciplines as well) spend so much time "talking back" (hooks 1989) and "transforming silence into language and action" (Lorde 1984), that we seem to forget the importance of listening—opening ourselves and really *hearing* what others say. This, too, is a lesson found in *This Bridge Called My Back*. As Mitsuye Yamada reminds us, "One of the most insidious ways of keeping women and minorities

powerless is to ... let them speak freely and not listen to them with serious intent"
(1983, 40). I interpret the phrase "serious intent" to represent a type of deep listening
that takes tremendous effort and requires a willingness to be altered by the words
spoken.

Throughout *This Bridge Called My Back* contributors insist on the importance of
listening with serious intent – listening carefully, thoughtfully, and humbly, ready to
be changed by what they hear. Judit Muscovitch, for example, challenges her Anglo-
American women audience to stop tokenizing Latinas and other women of colors
and to do their own homework: they must *"read and listen"* to what women of colors
have to say (1983, 80, her emphasis). Similarly, in her "Open Letter to Mary Daly,"
Lorde implies that Daly has not read Lorde's work with an open mind, with the
desire to be altered through what she learns. Lorde asks Daly, "Do you ever really
read the work of black women? Did you ever read my words, or did you merely
finger through them for quotations?" (1983, 95). Although these examples, taken on
their own, seem to imply a unidirectional approach, where women of colors voice
their experiences and concerns as white-raced women silently hear what is said,
listening with raw openness is multidirectional. We need numerous overlapping
dialogues among all beings. We need dialogues where listeners do not judge each
other based on appearance or in other ways jump to conclusions but instead just
open up their minds and listen.

I describe this deep listening as *listening with raw openness* to underscore its difficult, potentially painful dimensions. When we listen with raw openness we make
ourselves vulnerable: we risk being wounded. Peeling back our defensive barriers, we
expose ourselves (our identities, our beliefs, and our worldviews) to change. By so
doing, we learn new, sometimes shocking truths about ourselves and others. As
Anzaldúa suggests, we open "the gate to the stranger, within and without" (2002b, 3).

Listening with raw openness begins with the belief in our interrelatedness, with
the willingness to posit and seek commonalities – defined not as sameness but as
intertwined differences and possible points of connection. It requires that we make
space for what Anzaldúa describes as "an unmapped common ground" (2002a, 570).
As the word "unmapped" suggests, this common ground cannot be narrowly labeled
or described. Resisting the certainty of precise definition, it must be created tentatively and (perhaps) temporarily, through our interactions. We posit commonalities
and step out on faith; we engage in conversations and investigate what we might
have in common as we listen to and explore each other's positions.

Like most academic sites, feminist classrooms, conferences, and listservs often
operate according to the binary-oppositional politics I described earlier in this essay.
In these situations, we can be very quick to judge each other – often in negative,
extremely harsh terms.[8] Yet these judgments are driven by overly simplistic, status-
quo thinking based on stereotypes that invite us to look at a person, label her, and
categorize her based on these labels. We assume that we fully know her position,
motivations, values, and beliefs: we *know* her ... because of her appearance and the
identity groups to which she seems to belong, because of her previous comments,
because of her overly assertive tone, or because of other such external signs. Okay,

maybe we *do* know what she'll say, but can we be certain that we will fully understand what she means? Do we thoroughly know the intentions and desires behind
her words? My point here is when we assume that we entirely know this other
person/this other group, we stop listening "with serious intent." After all, if "I know
you," then I don't need to listen to your words. I've heard them already, I've heard
them many times, and so I'll just react. I will dismiss your words and perspective
while loudly repeating my own views.

Listening with raw openness demands intellectual humility – the willingness to
embrace uncertainty, contradiction, and limitation, coupled with the willingness
to self-reflect. Our understanding is always partial and incomplete. How could it be
otherwise? To imply that we already have 100 percent accurate and complete
information and/or knowledge about another person or situation prevents intellectual growth. I believe that we should remain open to learning more, and acknowledging the possibility of limitations in our views. Through this acknowledgment, we
expand our views and enhance our learning. In my epistemology, openness to
change is one of the primary ways that new knowledge is created.

Applied to those we encounter, this intellectual humility demands that we recognize each individual's "complex personhood": every person we encounter has a
specific, highly intricate history, an upbringing and life experiences that we cannot
fully know. We don't know the forces that shaped her and, at best, we can only
partially ascertain her intentions and desires.[9] We will misunderstand, despite our
best efforts. Perhaps some misunderstanding is inevitable. Here again *This Bridge
Called My Back* is instructive. Despite the editors' desire to create an inclusionary
space for all radical women of colors, they did not fully achieve their goal. *This Bridge
Called My Back* has absences, gaps, silences, and spaces where marked but invisible
others do not appear. As Deborah Miranda (2002) notes, the collection does not
adequately represent Native women, and as Nada Elia (2002) points out, it totally
ignores women of Arab descent. There are other omissions as well. Even our best
intentions can fall short. What might we learn if we could view errors – when
acknowledged with grace – as pathways for growth, avenues that lead to fuller
understanding?

> We stand at a major threshold in the extension of consciousness, caught in the remoli-
> nos (vortices) of systemic change across all fields of knowledge. The binaries of
> colored/white, female/male, mind/body are collapsing. Living in nepantla, the overlap-
> ping space between different perceptions and belief systems, you are aware of the
> changeability of racial, gender, sexual, and other categories rendering the conventional
> labelings obsolete. Though these markings are outworn and inaccurate, those in power
> continue using them to single out and negate those who are "different" *because* of color,
> language, notions of reality, or other diversity.
>
> – GLORIA ANZALDÚA

As Anzaldúa suggests, we live at a nexus point, or what she calls *nepantla*, the
Nahuatl word meaning "in-between space." For Anzaldúa, nepantla represents an

unstable, unpredictable, precarious, and transitional space/time/epistemology lacking clear boundaries, directions, or definitions. During nepantla, our status-quo stories and comfortable self-conceptions are shattered as apparently fixed categories – whether based on gender, ethnicity/"race," sexuality, religion, nationality, or some combination of these categories and perhaps others as well – unravel. Boundaries become more permeable and begin breaking down. This loosening of previously restrictive labels, while intensely painful, can create shifts in consciousness and transgressive opportunities for change.

I find this shift in Anzaldúa's own thinking, where she transforms the oppositional politics and intersectional identities of *This Bridge Called My Back* into increasingly holistic politics and identities in her twenty-first-century writings. Thus in the above epigraph, drawn from Anzaldúa's 2002 essay, "now let us shift," Anzaldúa describes conventional identity categories as "obsolete," "outworn," and "inaccurate." As she investigates the "changeability" in these categories and labels, she questions and begins to transform the clear-cut distinctions between women "of color" and "white," asserting that "whiteness may not be applied to all whites, as some possess women-of-color-consciousness, just as some women of color bear white consciousness" (2002b, 2). I want to underscore the radical nature of Anzaldúa's provocative claim. By emphasizing consciousness, she shifts from the external (culturally-imposed racialized categories) to the internal (self-selected ways of thinking and acting). This shift, in turn, enables her to envision inclusionary communities that simultaneously draw from and move beyond the oppositional politics employed by most academics and activist scholars.

Unfortunately, however, few theorists are willing to blur boundaries and question oppositional politics in such extreme ways. Although we "deconstruct" some of our old worldviews and theories, we still cling to identity-based labels and claim the power of self-naming in the face of erasure. Look! Even in this essay – an essay designed to *interrogate* these social categories – I've only somewhat loosened my own grip on them!

Our collective resistance to change leads me to describe this current theoretical moment as a space/time of nepantla. For me, nepantla also represents a crossroads of sorts – a space/time with many options: we can remain where we are, locked within the narrow safety of status-quo stories, fixed identities, and oppositional politics. We can try to protect ourselves by actively resisting change. (After all, who knows what the future will bring, if we give up our old worldviews?) We can reinforce the existing categories, and perhaps even create a few new ones. Or, we can move in an extremely different direction. We can let go of our old worldviews and step out on faith, attempting to create the world we envision. We can question the barriers that (seem to) divide us. We can risk listening with raw openness. We can stretch feminism to new places.

To be sure, we have no maps, no clear-cut plans, and no definitive solutions. However, I am convinced that these lessons from *This Bridge Called My Back* – making connections through differences, forging an ethics of radical interconnectedness, and listening with raw openness – offer guidelines for those of us interested in stretching feminist theorizing in new directions, moving beyond intersectionality into radical interconnectivity.

Notes

I dedicate this essay to Gloria Anzaldúa and the contributors to, as well as the spirit of, *This Bridge Called My Back. Mil gracias* to the students in my Fall 2007 U.S. Women of Colors graduate course for reading and commenting on an earlier draft of this essay.

1. For specific examples of these difference-inflected commonalities, see Mirtha Quintanales's letter to Barbara Smith, "I Paid Very Hard." In it, Quintanales fearlessly explores difference while drawing parallels between her experiences as an "essentially middle-class (and white-skinned woman)" immigrant from Cuba and the experiences of women she describes as "black," "Third World," "white, poor, and working-class." See also Audre Lorde's "Open Letter to Mary Daly," where Lorde posits a series of commonalities with Daly while, simultaneously, challenging Daly to recognize profound differences among women.
2. For some of Anzaldúa's later versions of El Mundo Zurdo, see her *Interviews/Entrevistas*, "now let us shift," and "Counsels from the Firing."
3. Note the change in spelling from "El Mundo Surdo" to "El Mundo Zurdo." The shift from "s" to "z" in the word "Zurdo" occurred when *This Bridge Called My Back* was in press. Although Anzaldúa was not pleased with this alteration, eventually she accepted and adopted it. For more on this issue see her archives, located at the Nettie Lee Benson Latin American Collection at the University of Texas, Austin.
4. I explore Anzaldúa's holistic worldview in more detail in "Shifting Perspectives."
5. See for instance Anzaldúa's discussions of interconnectivity in *Interviews/Entrevistas*, especially in her interviews from the early 1980s.
6. These manuscripts can be found in the Benson Collection, University of Texas, Austin.
7. See also Jacqui Alexander: "We are in fact interdependent, neither separate nor autonomous. As human beings, we have a sacred connection to one another, and this is why enforced separations wreak havoc on our souls. There is great danger ... in living lives of segregation. Racial segregation. Segregation in politics. Segregated frameworks. Segregated, compartmentalized selves. Our oppositional politic has been necessary, but it will never sustain us; while it may give us some temporary gains ... it can never ultimately feed that deep place within us: that space of the erotic, that space of the soul, that space of the Divine" ("Remembering This Bridge," 99).
8. For discussions of these difficult classroom/conference politics, see Fernandes Cervenak et al., "Imagining Differently" and Anzaldúa's "En rapport, In Opposition."
9. I borrow the idea of complex personhood from Cervenak et al., "Imagining Differently," who borrowed it from Avery Gordon, *Ghostly Matters*.

Bibliography

Alexander, M. Jacqui. 2002. "Remembering This Bridge, Remembering Ourselves: Yearning, Memory, and Desire." In *this bridge we call home: radical visions for transformation*, edited by Gloria E. Anzaldúa and AnaLouise Keating, 81–103. New York: Routledge.

Anzaldúa, Gloria. 1983a. Foreword to *This Bridge Called My Back: Writings by Radical Women of Color*, edited by Cherríe Moraga and Gloria Anzaldúa. 2nd ed. New York: Kitchen Table: Women of Color Press.

Anzaldúa, Gloria. 1983b. "La Prieta." In *This Bridge Called My Back: Writings by Radical Women of Color*, edited by Cherríe Moraga and Gloria Anzaldúa, 198–209. 2nd ed. New York: Kitchen Table: Women of Color Press.

Anzaldúa, Gloria. 1983c. "O.K. Momma, Who the Hell Am I?: An Interview with Luisah Teish." In *This Bridge Called My Back: Writings by Radical Women of Color*, edited by Cherríe Moraga and Gloria Anzaldúa, 221–31. 2nd ed. New York: Kitchen Table: Women of Color Press.

Anzaldúa, Gloria. 2002a. "now let us shift … the path of conocimiento … inner work, public acts." In *this bridge we call home: radical visions for transformation*, edited by Gloria E. Anzaldúa and AnaLouise Keating, 540–78. New York: Routledge.

Anzaldúa, Gloria. 2002b. "(Un)natural bridges, (Un)safe spaces." In *this bridge we call home: radical visions for transformation*, edited by Gloria E. Anzaldúa and AnaLouise Keating 1–5. New York: Routledge.

Canaan, Andrea. 1983. "Brownness." In *This Bridge Called My Back: Writings by Radical Women of Color*, edited by Cherríe Moraga and Gloria Anzaldúa, 232–37. 2nd ed. New York: Kitchen Table: Women of Color Press.

Cervenak, Sarah J., Karina L. Cespedes, Caridad Souza, and Andrea Straub. 2002. "Imagining Differently: The Politics of Listening in a Feminist Classroom." In *this bridge we call home: radical visions for transformation*, edited by Gloria E. Anzaldúa and AnaLouise Keating, 341–56. New York: Routledge.

Elia, Nada. 2002. "The 'White' Sheep of the Family: But *Bleaching* Is Like Starvation." In *this bridge we call home: radical visions for transformation*, edited by Gloria E. Anzaldúa and AnaLouise Keating, 223–31. New York: Routledge.

Gordon, Avery. 1997. *Ghostly Matters: Haunting and the Sociological Imagination*. Minneapolis: University of Minnesota Press.

Hernández-Ávila, Inés. 2002. "In the Presence of Spirit(s): A Meditation on the Politics of Solidarity and Transformation." In *this bridge we call home: radical visions for transformation*, edited by Gloria E. Anzaldúa and AnaLouise Keating, 530–38. New York: Routledge.

hooks, bell. 1989. *Talking Back: Thinking Feminist, Thinking Black*. Boston: South End Press.

Keating, AnaLouise. 2005. "Shifting Perspectives: Spiritual Activism, Social Transformation, and the Politics of Spirit." In *Entre Mundos/Among Worlds: New Perspectives on Gloria E. Anzaldúa*, edited by AnaLouise Keating, 241–54. New York: Palgrave Macmillan.

Keating, AnaLouise. 2007. *Teaching Transformation: Transcultural Classroom Dialogues*. New York: Palgrave Macmillan.

Keating, AnaLouise, ed. 2000. *Interviews/Entrevistas*. New York: Routledge.

Lara, Irene. 2002. "Healing Sueños for Academia." In *this bridge we call home: radical visions for transformation*, edited by Gloria E. Anzaldúa and AnaLouise Keating, 433–38. New York: Routledge.

Lorde, Audre. 1983. "An Open Letter to Mary Daly." In *This Bridge Called My Back: Writings by Radical Women of Color*, edited by Cherríe Moraga and Gloria Anzaldúa, 94–97. 2nd ed. New York: Kitchen Table: Women of Color Press.

Lorde, Audre. 1984. *Sister Outsider*. Freedom, Calif.: Crossing Press.

Lorenz, Helene Shulman. 2002. "Thawing Hearts, Opening a Path in the Woods, Founding a New Lineage." In *this bridge we call home; radical visions for transformation*, edited by Gloria E. Anzaldúa and AnaLouise Keating, 496–506. New York: Routledge.

Miranda, Deborah A. 2002. "'What's Wrong With A Little Fantasy?' Storytelling from the (Still) Ivory Tower." In *this bridge we call home: radical visions for transformation*, edited by Gloria E. Anzaldúa and AnaLouise Keating, 192–201. New York: Routledge.

Moraga, Cherríe, and Gloria Anzaldúa, eds. 1981. *This Bridge Called My Back: Writings by Radical Women of Color*. Waterton, Mass: Persophene Press.

Moraga, Cherríe, and Gloria Anzaldúa, eds. 1983. *This Bridge Called My Back: Writings by Radical Women of Color*. 2nd ed. New York: Kitchen Table: Women of Color Press.

Morales, Rosario. 1983. "We're All in the Same Boat." In *This Bridge Called My Back: Writings by Radical Women of Color*, edited by Cherríe Moraga and Gloria Anzaldúa, 91–93. 2nd ed. New York: Kitchen Table: Women of Color Press.

Muscovitch, Judit. 1983. "'– But I Know You, American Woman.'" In *This Bridge Called My Back: Writings by Radical Women of Color*, edited by Cherríe Moraga and Gloria Anzaldúa, 79–84. 2nd ed. New York: Kitchen Table: Women of Color Press.

Quintanales, Mirtha. 1983. "I Paid Very Hard for My Immigrant Ignorance." In *This Bridge Called My Back: Writings by Radical Women of Color*, edited by Cherríe Moraga and Gloria Anzaldúa, 150–56. 2nd ed. New York: Kitchen Table: Women of Color Press.

Yamada, Mitsuye. 1983. "Invisibility is an Unnatural Disaster: Reflections of an Asian American Woman." In *This Bridge Called My Back: Writings by Radical Women of Color*, edited by Cherríe Moraga and Gloria Anzaldúa, 35–40. 2nd ed. New York: Kitchen Table: Women of Color Press.

10.8
All Sleeping Women Now Awake and Move

10.9
Still I Rise
Maya Angelou

You may write me down in history
With your bitter, twisted lies,
You may trod me in the very dirt
But still, like dust, I'll rise.

Does my sassiness upset you?
Why are you beset with gloom?
'Cause I walk like I've got oil wells
Pumping in my living room.

Just like moons and like suns,
With the certainty of tides,
Just like hopes springing high,
Still I'll rise.

Did you want to see me broken?
Bowed head and lowered eyes?
Shoulders falling down like teardrops,
Weakened by my soulful cries.

Does my haughtiness offend you?
Don't you take it awful hard
'Cause I laugh like I've got gold mines
Diggin' in my own back yard.

You may shoot me with your words,
You may cut me with your eyes,
You may kill me with your hatefulness,
But still, like air, I'll rise.

Does my sexiness upset you?
Does it come as a surprise
That I dance like I've got diamonds
At the meeting of my thighs?

Out of the huts of history's shame
I rise
Up from a past that's rooted in pain
I rise
I'm a black ocean, leaping and wide,
Welling and swelling I bear in the tide.

Leaving behind nights of terror and fear
I rise
Into a daybreak that's wondrously clear
I rise
Bringing the gifts that my ancestors gave,
I am the dream and the hope of the slave.
I rise
I rise

I rise.

Glossary

Agency   Ways that members of targeted/non-dominant groups, who are often represented just as oppressed and victimized, find large and small means to set their own course and make their own decisions, even when their options are limited.

Anti-Semitism   Fear and hatred of Jewish people, traditions, and culture.

Binary oppositions   See hierarchical binary oppositions.

Brown bois   Biological females of color who may or may not identify as female, who embrace their masculine identities and trans* and gender-nonconforming bodies.

Chicana   A politicized, historically conscious Mexican-American girl or woman.

Cisgender   People whose sense of gender identity and expression or presentation of gender matches their sex assigned at birth (e.g., an individual assigned female who identifies as a woman).

Class   A political system that creates different social group access to economic, educational, cultural, health, environmental, and other resources.

Classism   The systematic oppression of working class and poor people by those who own or control resources. It is perpetuated by ideologies that rank people according to their economic status (income and wealth), job, level of education, and family background or connections. Classism marks poor or poorer people as inherently less intelligent, and more likely to be lazy, immoral, untrustworthy, and

Women in Culture: An Intersectional Anthology for Gender and Women's Studies, Second Edition.
Edited by Bonnie Kime Scott, Susan E. Cayleff, Anne Donadey, and Irene Lara.
© 2017 John Wiley & Sons, Ltd. Published 2017 by John Wiley & Sons, Ltd.

deserving of their low status, which perpetuates class stratification and discrimination through laws and policies, and educational and other institutions.

Colonization   A specific type of imperialism that includes five aspects: conquest and genocide; land theft; economic exploitation; loss of political sovereignty; and cultural colonization through imposed laws, education, language, religion, and racism.

Color-blindness   A misguided, even if at times well-meaning, attempt to pretend not to "see" group differences – especially racial ones – that results in avoidance of the topic, and leads people to conceptualize equality in terms of sameness only and to feel guilty over noticing differences. It implies that difference is bad and that it is therefore impolite to notice or dialogue about difference. It signals that people of color are expected to act white and assimilate. It encourages the erasure of power differences between groups and the denial of racism. Sometimes called the "new racism."

Community   A group of people living in the same place or having a particular characteristic in common, or coming together around similar political concerns.

Consciousness-raising   A term introduced in the United States in the 1960s, encapsulating deep conversations held amongst diverse women who explored their political, sexual, and economic lives. These conversations tended to exclude men and cover topics previously considered taboo. The women came to realize that their individual experiences were echoed in those of many other women and they critically analyzed the conditions of their lives. As a result, a number of major feminist insights emerged from these conversations. See Second-wave feminism and *testimonio*.

Curandera   A holistic, transcultural healer who largely draws from Spanish Catholic, Indigenous, and/or African and Arab spiritual and medical knowledge in what is now called the Americas. From the Spanish word *curar*, which means to heal.

Decolonial feminism   A type of intersectional feminism that emphasizes "de-" or undoing the structural, psychic, and spiritual effects of colonization and colonizing knowledge, including racist and heterosexist ideologies used to justify violence internalized by the privileged and oppressed, while also maintaining a critical, non-romanticizing feminist lens. Largely applied to indigenous cultures, seeks to restore and refashion ancestral cultures as dynamic, as well as acknowledge ongoing daily acts of resistance alongside histories of organized political struggles.

Depo-Provera   An injected form of birth control with several adverse effects, often promoted by the medical community to poor women and women of color.

Disability   May refer to a variety of physical or mental impairments experienced by many people, as well as the way in which society's lack of accommodation reinforces the disabling experience. As Susan Wendell explains, "disability is socially constructed from biological reality." Some prefer the terms "differently-abled," "challenged," or diversAbility."

Disidentification   Concept developed by José Muñoz to describe a strategy used by LGBTQ people of color. It calls for simultaneous working "on, with, and against" family structures as one negotiates the racism, classism, and sexism of dominant cultures and the sexual and gender oppression within their own homes, neighborhoods, and regional communities.

Double bind   Concept developed by Marilyn Frye. The absence of viable choices when one is confronted with irreconcilable demands. This is a characteristic of the lives of oppressed people.

Double jeopardy   Term first used by Frances M. Beal in 1970 to describe the race/gender experience of US Black women in a racist and sexist America.

Ecofeminism   An approach to the natural world that brings together feminist praxis with ecology and environmentalism. Originating in the 1970s and still evolving, it examines the traditional association of woman with nature versus man with culture, investigates the sources of pollution and depletion, and strives for a holistic, global approach to a sustainable earth for humans of diverse classes, races, and sexualities, as well as all living creatures.

Empowerment   A sense of self-worth and agency, often imparted by a supportive community through ideas, actions, and beliefs.

Erotic   As defined by Audre Lorde, "a source of power and information"; "an internal sense of satisfaction ['a depth of feeling'] to which, once we have experienced it, we know we can aspire"; "an assertion of the lifeforce of women; of that creative energy empowered." Such erotic practices nurture a sense of empowerment and interconnection that can help one resist oppressive systems and pursue social justice. See power.

Essentialism   The belief that people have a stable and unchanging, true core identity (as opposed to a relational identity that evolves through time, experience, and sociopolitical context).

Fat Studies   Academic field that politicizes fatness, challenging the medical profession and media as arbiters of women's healthy weight and physical desirability.

Femicide   Term used to describe killings of women just because they are women. *Feminicidio* in Spanish. Ciudad Juárez, Mexico, presents an egregious history of *feminicidio*.

Feminism   The radical notion that women are people. The theory of the political, economic, and social equality of the sexes. Organized activity on behalf of women's rights and interests. Feminism thus includes both scholarship and activism. As defined by Barbara Smith, "Feminism is the political theory and practice that struggles to free *all* women: women of color, working-class women, poor women, disabled women, lesbians, old women – as well as white, economically privileged, heterosexual women. Anything less than this vision of total freedom is not feminism, but merely female self-aggrandizement."

First-wave feminism   Mid-nineteenth through early twentieth-century women's campaign to gain dress, health, and vice reform; it included issues such as temperance, anti-slavery agitation, property rights, divorce rights, and education, alongside other socially oriented issues including fair wages, safe working conditions, violence against women, the health of women and their children, and suffrage.

Gender   Generally understood as the social constructions of sex. How one identifies and performs/presents oneself in society that may or may not correspond to physical sex. See sex and sex/gender system.

Gender expression   The way one self-presents externally as a gendered being by means of clothing, hair, and mannerisms, etc. (as, for example, masculine, feminine, androgynous, butch, femme, trans*, or gender-fluid). Also called gender presentation.

Gender identity   How individuals view themselves psychologically as, for example, male, female, genderqueer, two-spirit, or trans*. May or may not correspond with their sexual physical characteristics. See cisgender, trans*, transsexual.

Gender presentation   See gender expression.

Globalization   In late capitalism, a transnational interactive process between people, corporations, and national governments that is powered by economic trade and investment. Results in uneven political economic effects between developed and underdeveloped nations and an increase in migratory flows. See imperialism and transnational feminism.

Hegemonic masculinity   Concept developed by R. W. Connell and Michael Kimmel. It refers to the masculinity of those who have power in society. It defines itself in opposition to anything feminine and teaches men that the only emotions appropriate for them to display are anger and aggression. Hegemonic masculinity pushes men to look down upon women, distance themselves from men who are perceived as being gay, and attack the masculinity of men who have less power in the culture, such as men of color. See rape culture.

Hegemony   Power exercised through indirect and cultural control, as opposed to domination, which relies on coercion and force. Hegemony cleverly gets the oppressed to consent to and internalize their own oppression, making inequalities seem normal, sensible, and just.

Hermeneutics   The science of interpretation.

Heteronormativity   Concept developed by Michael Warner. The presumption that heterosexuality is ideal and normal, desirable, inherently right, and should be rewarded. It argues that same-sex or trans* desire/intimacy/sexual orientation is wrong and bad. It can lead to homo- and transphobia.

Heteropatriarchy   The societal norm of heterosexual coupling in which the man has more power than the woman. This norm is supported by a variety of institutions such as law, politics, organized religions, the educational system, and the media.

Heterosexism   Belief in the inherent superiority of one sexual orientation (heterosexual) over all others and thereby the right of heterosexuals to dominance (adapted from Audre Lorde).

Hierarchical binary oppositions   A system of thought basic to Western philosophy, in which the world is divided into two sets of categories that are seen as opposed, such as self/other, male/female, white/black, mind/body, or culture/nature; for each pair, one is viewed as superior (the norm) and the other as different, inferior, and deficient. Hierarchical binary oppositions provide an intellectual framework for members of dominant groups to deny the oppression of targeted groups by viewing oppression as the natural state of things. They also contribute to erasing the existence of people who do not fit in the binary structure, such as gender-fluid, bisexual, or multiracial people.

Hijab   Headscarf worn by some Muslim women.

Homophobia   Fear and hatred of people who love and/or are sexually attracted to people of the same sex.

Homosexuality   Medical term coined in the nineteenth century to refer to gay and lesbian acts and/or identities.

Identity   Who a person is, perceives oneself to be, or is perceived to be. It changes according to geographical, cultural, historical, economic, and life cycle contexts, is affected by power relations, and can be a source of empowerment and healing, as well as privilege and oppression. See identity politics, social location, and standpoint.

Identity politics   Ways that our politics are influenced by our social identities. Sometimes used in a somewhat essentialist way to assume that our identities determine our politics. More frequently, refers to the complex entanglements between our social identities and our beliefs. See social location and standpoint.

Imperialism   One country establishing its power and/or an economic, political, and cultural sphere of influence over most of the rest of the world.

Internalized domination   Belief of members of a dominant group that they are naturally entitled to a superior status and to the advantages derived from that status. It serves to hide the existence of dominant group privilege.

Internalized oppression   Attitude that leads people who are the target of one form of oppression to believe the negative messages against their groups and sometimes to end up acting against their own self-interests.

Intersectionality   Analytical framework that acknowledges that the experience of oppression and privilege comes from many more sources than gender. It broadens the analysis to encompass other vectors of identity and of human domination, such as race and racism, social class and classism, and sexual orientation, as well as colonialism and imperialism, disability, national origin, religion, size, and age. All these vectors are understood as being interlocking, cumulative, and interwoven.

Intersex A person born with internal or external sexual characteristics or sex chromosomes that medicine does not consider standard for either female or male. Formerly termed hermaphrodite, which is now largely considered offensive. The Intersex Society of North America is an information group whose main platform is the elimination of surgeries on intersex infants.

Intersticios Concept developed by Gloria E. Anzaldúa. Spanish word that refers to the spaces between the different worlds that women of color inhabit. Also see nepantla.

Intraracial sexual violence Sexual violence among people of the same racial or ethnic background. The most common type of sexual violence.

LGBTQ Initials used to refer to lesbians, gay men, bisexuals, trans*gender, and queer people. See queer and trans* (transgender).

Listening with raw openness Concept created by AnaLouise Keating. A way to create new pathways to dialogue through recognizing the complexity of other persons and having the willingness to be changed.

Mestiza With its origins in sixteenth-century Spain, mestiza refers to a girl or woman with racially mixed ancestry; this typically means having European white and American indigenous ancestries, and oftentimes also African, Asian, and Arab ancestries, as was the case throughout the multicultural Iberian peninsula and the Spanish and Portuguese colonies. Gloria E. Anzaldúa's theory of the "new mestiza" expands on biologically based definitions to describe people who inhabit multiple worlds because of their intersecting identities and experiences.

Motherwork Concept developed by Patricia Hill Collins. The physical and emotional labor of biological mothers or other women in the community that aims to ensure the survival of families and communities of color in the context of the social inequalities that undermine their survival.

Mythical norm Concept developed by Audre Lorde referring to a collection of dominant group identities (of race, gender, sexual orientation, class, age, ability, etc.) used to create a norm that is seen as superior and worth aspiring to achieve. Since almost no individual belongs to only dominant identity positions, this is an unattainable ideal, a myth. See hierarchical binary oppositions.

Nepantla Concept developed by Gloria E. Anzaldúa. Nahuatl word for "in-between space." Although it can be experienced as an intellectual, emotional, and spiritual moment of crisis, nepantla allows the loosening of boundaries and opens transgressive opportunities for change.

Oppression Imposition of unearned disadvantages that perpetuate social inequalities. A system that unfairly targets certain people based on their perceived group membership (e.g., race, gender, social class, or sexual orientation), not their individual characteristics. As defined by Marilyn Frye, oppression is "A system of interrelated barriers and forces, which reduce, immobilize and mold people who belong to a certain group, and effect their subordination to another group." To paraphrase Suzanne Pharr, it is based on a perceived norm that maintains its control through institutional and economic power, backed up by violence and the threat of violence. See internalized domination, internalized oppression, and privilege.

Otherize   To "other" or "otherize" is to deem someone from a specific group inferior, different, and marginal in relation to a presumed superior "self" who is deemed normal and at the center. See hierarchical binary oppositions.

PGP   Stands for preferred gender pronoun, or stated as, "What pronoun do you prefer?" For example: she, her, hers; he, him, his; they, them, theirs; ze, hir, hirs. Some now use "correct gender pronoun."

Pansexuality   Attraction to people of all genders.

Patriarchy   "Boys make the rules." Institutional systems that privilege male authority, power, physicality, ways of knowing, control, and lineage. These systems are seen by many as innate, not culturally constructed, and serve to diminish girls and women in relationship to boys and men.

Pedagogy   The art of teaching.

The personal is political   A feminist saying stemming from the 1960s claiming that an individual's story has larger political implications, and the sharing of these stories potentially heals and raises the collective political consciousness of the group, preparing and inspiring them to take action and engage in struggles for social justice. See consciousness-raising.

Postcolonial feminism   A type of feminism that focuses on intersections of gender and colonial issues. A critical approach that studies the effects of colonization and decolonization and their contemporary consequences on women in (formerly) colonized and colonizing countries.

Power   There are two main ways of conceptualizing power, one vertical and one horizontal. In the vertical understanding, there are two opposed groups, one powerful (the dominant oppressor) and one powerless (the oppressed victim). The horizontal understanding is that power inheres everywhere, circulates among subject positions, and no group ever has full power over another. Patricia Hill Collins argues that both views should be held together, in a both/and rather than an either/or formulation, in order to understand how power works in complex ways. Audre Lorde highlights the enabling power of the erotic focused on the energy of love and creativity and the embodiment of deep feeling rather than power as domination over someone or something. See erotic.

Praxis   The constant interface between theory and practice in which theory influences practice and activist experiences help refine thought.

Privilege Unearned advantages that perpetuate social inequalities and are often experienced by privileged people as natural entitlements. Privileged groups are also called "dominant" groups because they establish social norms that "subordinate" groups are expected to follow. Privilege is the flip side of oppression. See internalized domination, internalized oppression, and oppression.

Queer People who do not embrace the heterosexual/homosexual binary or who are gender-fluid. Used as a political term by people who refuse binary oppositions based on gender and/or sexual orientation.

Race A political system that organizes people by sorting them into social group-ings based on invented biological categories. Such political groupings of human beings have material consequences for people's health, wealth, social status, reputa-tion, and opportunities in life, and have emotional effects. Although there is no race gene and race is not biologically real, the social significance and effects of race emerge from actual historical and political contexts.

Racism A form of oppression defined by Audre Lorde as "belief in the inherent superiority of one race over all others and thereby the right to dominance." Like other forms of oppression, racism has institutional and interpersonal aspects.

Rape culture A culture that blames the victim of rape and normalizes violence against women. It relies on the myth of an uncontrollable male sex drive, which serves to ensure male sexual right of access to women by presenting it as a natural need, enforcing the expectation of women's sexual availability. See hegemonic masculinity.

Representation Depiction or expression of individual or group interests, depend-ing on context. In visual or textual situations this involves the ways individuals and groups are portrayed, including objectifying individuals, or the use of stereotypes, both calling for feminist resistance. In political contexts it can refer to gaining the right to vote, or having politicians who speak for their various constituent groups.

Resistance Opposing, challenging, and rebuking unjust systems that perpetuate violence, inequality, and other forms of oppression. Can take direct or more subtle forms.

Ritual A collective experience, repeated and sanctified, that people perform to remind ourselves and one another that we are not alone and that what has happened to us is not an isolated instance. A way to perform, perpetuate, and (re)create cultural and spiritual authority, as well as enact personal and collective power, healing, and transformation.

Rules of gender Concept created by Harold Garfinkel and discussed by Kate Bornstein. Societal expectations for rigid distinctions between males and females. These supposedly natural rules are in fact constructions that contribute to marginalizing transgender and gender-nonconforming people. See hierarchical binary oppositions.

Second-wave feminism 1960s–1980s revival of feminism that raised awareness of gender-based inequities in legal, familial, and governmental structures, challenged the sexual double standard, revised old canons of humanities, social sciences, and science, attacked sexism in language, media images, and children's literature, and worked for sexual and reproductive health. Lesbian feminist and women of color feminist organizing emerged simultaneously. Also characterized by mass demonstrations, consciousness-raising, underground newspapers, self-help education, and guerrilla street performances. See consciousness-raising.

Self-healing Caring for oneself; a commitment to our own body-mind-spirit wellness. It can sustain us as we do political social justice work and work hand in hand with communal healing.

Seneca Falls Convention The political and activist gathering that is generally recognized for inaugurating the women's rights movement in the United States in 1848.

Sex Generally understood as the biological sexual characteristics with which one is born. See gender and sex/gender system.

Sex/gender system Concept developed by Gayle Rubin: "The set of arrangements by which a society transforms biological sexuality into products of human activity." This definition acknowledges that sex and gender cannot be easily pulled apart along the lines of nature versus culture but that they constantly interface with one another. See sex and gender.

Sexism A form of oppression defined by Audre Lorde as "the belief in the inherent superiority of one sex over the other and thereby the right to dominance."

Sexual orientation Refers to the gender of people to whom one is most attracted sexually. Could be opposite-sex, same-sex, both (bisexual), neither or none (asexual), or fluid (pansexual).

Sexual terrorism Concept created by Carole Sheffield. A continuum of violence and threat of violence against women that includes marital rape and battering, as well as sexual harassment, and whose goal is to keep women in subordinate roles to men. It also applies to "corrective rape" of lesbians in various parts of the world.

Sexuality Sexual/erotic feelings and experiences. Sometimes also used to refer to sexual orientation.

Social location The time and place in which we live and the information to which we have access, as well as the social categories or groups to which we are perceived as belonging based on vectors such as race, class, sex, sexual orientation, gender identity, ability, and national origin. See identity, identity politics, and standpoint.

Spirit From the Latin *spiritus* for breath, an internal and/or external invisible life force. Following Laura E. Pérez, sometimes written as "s/Spirit" to note that, for some, Spirit with a capital "S" is considered an immanent divine being and spirit with a lowercase "s," akin to soul, connotes an internal or deeper aspect of being.

Standpoint   Our worldview, the ways in which we make sense of our life experiences and of the world around us based on our social location. Adrienne Rich refers to it as the "politics of location." See identity, identity politics, and social location.

Suffrage movement   Organized and international efforts for women to obtain the vote, which was one of the major achievements of First-wave feminism.

Testimonio   Spanish word for testimony; it forms an integral part of the Latin American social movements' tradition of oral autobiography that challenges official dominant stories, including those that erase, distort, or demean women's diverse voices. Considered an effective tool for consciousness-raising, social justice, creativity, and/or healing. See consciousness-raising.

Third-wave feminism   A term used to refer to the work of 1990s–2000s multiracial, often genderqueer, feminists who wrote in the personal narrative form and whose activism focused on engaging with popular culture. They criticized society's sexual double standard as well as Second-wave feminism's perceived lack of pro-sex attitudes.

Transcultural   Concept introduced by Cuban scholar Fernando Ortiz and engaged by US and Latin American scholars. In juxtaposition to the dominant assimilation model used to describe cultural encounters, this process accounts for cultural loss, the creation of new cultural forms, and the persistence of non-dominant worldviews and practices, while foregrounding the role of power.

Trans* (Transgender)   An umbrella term for individuals whose gender identity and/or gender expression differs from their sex assigned at birth. Includes transwomen (formerly referred to as MTF, male-to-female), transmen (formerly referred to as FTM, female-to-male), or genderqueer.

Transnational feminism   Analytically and through activism, attending to the ways that global economic shifts unevenly affect the lives of women, including the globalization of women's work and the ways migrating women maintain social relations across national and cultural borders. Foregrounds collective political praxis by women throughout the world in critique of free market capitalist values. See globalization.

Transphobia   Fear or hatred of trans* people. Beliefs that presume the desirability/normalcy of cisgender identities and heterosexuality, and deem trans* or gender-nonconforming desire/intimacy as wrong and bad.

Transsexual   A medical term that falls within the trans* category. People who feel that their sexed bodies/the sex they were assigned at birth do not match their gender identities. They may take surgical measures and/or hormonal therapy to effect a transition.

Triple jeopardy   Term that includes class dynamics, in addition to race and gender, when looking at the experiences of women of color.

Womanist   Concept created by Alice Walker as an African American alternative to the term feminist, in reaction against mainstream feminism's inability to fully include race issues in the 1970s and early 1980s. Definition is purposefully grounded in African American vernacular language, history, and culture and progressively broadens to include lesbian existence, female solidarity, and men, culminating in a holistic and spiritual worldview based on love.

Women of color   The terms "women of color" and "people of color" began to be used widely in the United States in the 1970s and 1980s to indicate coalitional and intersectional identities among groups facing oppressions based on race and other factors. These terms were created by people belonging to these groups and should not be confused with the earlier terms "colored women" and "colored people," which were derogatory terms used during the Jim Crow segregation era in the United States to refer to African American people. The two sets of terms are not interchangeable.

Women's Studies   An interdisciplinary field (it includes scholars trained in various fields, from English and Comparative Literary Studies to Social Science and History, and increasingly, researchers in the Natural Sciences) focusing on analyzing, critiquing, and bettering girls' and women's status in society worldwide through scholarship, and promoting activism for social justice.

Xenophobia   Fear and hatred of foreigners and immigrants.

Timeline*

Date	Event
612 BC	Sappho, Greek (Lesbos) lesbian feminist poet approximate date of birth
1650	Anne Bradstreet becomes first published poet in British-American colonies
1691	Sor Juana Inés de la Cruz, in New Spain, writes the famous letter "Respuesta a Sor Filotea [Reply to Sister Philotea]" in which she defends women's right to education
1773	Phyllis Wheatley, who was forcibly brought from Africa as a slave, becomes first published African American woman poet
1775–1783	*American Revolution*
1792	British author Mary Wollstonecraft's *A Vindication of the Rights of Woman* is published
1830s–1840s	American women's social reform activism, including abolition, temperance, dress and health reform, women's rights and utopianism
1831–1838	*Members of the Cherokee Nation forcibly relocated in the West, following the "Trail of Tears"*
1836	Lowell Mill Girls strike. They dominate textile manufacturing in Lowell, Massachusetts
1838	Flora Tristan's *Peregrinations of a Pariah* published in original French
1840–1845	*The Lowell Offering* periodical published by Lowell Mill Girls
1844	*Maine the first US State to grant married women the right to hold property*

Women in Culture: An Intersectional Anthology for Gender and Women's Studies, Second Edition.
Edited by Bonnie Kime Scott, Susan E. Cayleff, Anne Donadey, and Irene Lara.
© 2017 John Wiley & Sons, Ltd. Published 2017 by John Wiley & Sons, Ltd.

Date	Event
1848	Seneca Falls Convention. Elizabeth Cady Stanton presents "Declaration of Sentiments"
	"First-wave" feminism begun
	US defeat of Mexico. Treaty of Guadalupe Hidalgo grants United States almost half of Mexico's territory, which becomes the SW of the USA
	Chinese laborers arrive on West Coast of United States
1850	*US Fugitive Slave Law*
1851	Sojourner Truth gives "A'n't I a Woman" speech
1852	Harriet Beecher Stowe's *Uncle Tom's Cabin* published
1861–1865	*American Civil War; Emancipation Proclamation 1863*
1869	*Wyoming the first US territory to grant women the right to vote*
	National Women's Suffrage Association and American Women's Suffrage Association founded in United States
	Hungarian doctor Károly Kertbeny (Benkert) creates the term "homosexuality" to refer to same-sex acts
1870	*Married Women's Property Act in Great Britain*
1872	Victoria Woodhull (with abolitionist running mate Frederick Douglas) first woman to run for President of the United States.
1883	Cooperative Women's Guild founded in Great Britain
	Sarah Winnemucca's *Life among the Piutes* published
1884	Helen Hunt's *Ramona* published
1885	María Ruiz de Burton becomes first California/Mexican-American writing in English, *The Squatter and the Don*, critiquing denial of rights after United States annexed Mexican territory
1889	Hull House, the first settlement house in the United States, founded in Chicago by Jane Addams and Ellen Gates Starr
1890	National American Woman Suffrage Association founded, bringing together Woman's Suffrage Association (1869) and American Woman Suffrage Association (1869)
1892	Anna Julia Cooper's *A Voice from the South* published
	Charlotte Perkins Gilman's "The Yellow Wallpaper" published
1893	*New Zealand grants women (including Maori women) the vote*
1895	African American journalist and suffragist Ida B. Wells-Barnett's *The Red Record* published, reporting on lynching of Blacks in the United States
1896	National Association of Colored Women founded in Washington, DC
1898	*Spanish American War: Puerto Rico, Guam, and the Philippines become US colonies. United States annexes Hawaii*
1899	Egyptian Qasim Amin's *The Liberation of Women* published in original Arabic
1903	Women's Social and Political Union (WSPU) founded in Great Britain by Emmeline Pankhurst
1909	NAACP (National Association for the Advancement of Colored People) founded
	The Uprising of the 20,000: Led by Yiddish-speaking female immigrant workers, a coalition of working women hold 11-week strike against New York's shirtwaist industry

Date	Event
1910	Emma Goldman's *The Traffic in Women* published
1911	Ethel Smyth composes "The March of the Women" in Great Britain
	International Women's Day observed for the first time
	Luisa Capetillo, Puerto Rican suffragist, labor organizer and women's rights activist publishes *Mi opinión, sobre las libertades, derechos y deberes de la mujer, como compañera, madre y ser independiente* [My Opinion on the Liberties, Rights, and Duties of Woman, as Companion, Mother, and Independent Being]
1912	National Woman's Party founded by Alice Paul and Lucy Burns
1914	Huda Shaarawi founds the Intellectual Association of Egyptian Women
1914–1918	*World War I*
1915	Women's International League for Peace and Freedom founded with Jane Addams as its first president
1916	First birth control clinic in United States opened in Brooklyn by Margaret Sanger
1918	*Women granted the vote by Canada (excluding native women), Germany, Soviet Russia, and United Kingdom (for women over 30)*
1920	*United States grants most women the vote through the Nineteenth Amendment to the Constitution (voting rights of Black, Native American and Chinese-American women still curtailed)*
	Women's Bureau of US Department of Labor founded
1928	British author Radclyffe Hall's *The Well of Loneliness* published
1929	British author Virginia Woolf's *A Room of One's Own* published
1930	*Turkey grants women the vote*
1932	Karen Horney's *Feminine Psychology* published
1933	Frances Perkins becomes first female US Cabinet member as Secretary of Labor
1935	National Council of Negro Women founded in United States by Mary McLeod Bethune
1937	Zora Neale Hurston's *Their Eyes Were Watching God* published
	Harlem Renaissance in full swing
	Philippines grants women the vote
1939–1945	*World War II. The Holocaust.* Women, many of them Jewish, vital to underground resistance in Germany and occupied Europe
	Japanese interned in United States and Canada
	Rosie the Riveter becomes the icon of women in the wartime workplace
	France grants women the vote
1945	*Italy, and Japan grant women the vote*
	Hungary grants all women the vote (limited suffrage in 1918)
1946	*Korea grants women the vote*
1947	*Pakistan grants women the vote as it becomes a state*
	People's Republic of China grants women the vote
1948	*Israel grants women the vote as it becomes a state*
	Desegregation in race and gender of the US military
1949	Simone de Beauvoir's *The Second Sex* published in the original French

Date	Event
1950s	Women returned to home sphere, post-war. *Rise of Civil Rights Movement in the United States*
1950	*India grants women the vote three years after becoming a state*
1952	*California grants American Indians the full right to vote, including voting for local politicians*
1953	*Mexico grants women the vote*
1954	*Brown vs. Board of Education, US Supreme Court rules out racial segregation in schools*
1955	*Rosa Parks refuses to give up her seat in the front of the "colored" section of a public bus, setting off the Montgomery bus boycott that ended segregation in transportation in the United States* Founding of The Daughters of Bilitis (DOB), the first lesbian organization in the United States, by Del Martin and Phyllis Lyon
1956	*Egypt and Somalia grant women the vote*
1959	*Tunisia grants women the vote three years after becoming a state*
1960s	"Second-wave" feminism begins
1960	*First contraceptive pill approved by US Food and Drug Administration*
1961	*Presidential Committee on the Status of Women established by US President John F. Kennedy. Its recommendations made in 1963*
1962	Rachel Carson's *Silent Spring* published Dolores Huerta co-founded with César Chávez the National Farm Workers Association, which became the United Farm Workers Union Lucille Ball the first woman to run a major TV studio, Desilu Productions *Women granted the vote by Monaco and Algeria (as it becomes a state)*
1963	Betty Friedan's *The Feminine Mystique* published *Afghanistan, Iran, Kenya, and Morocco grant women the vote*
1964	*Civil Rights Act outlaws discrimination based on race, color, religion, or national origin in employment and public accommodation, ending segregation. Title VII of the act bars employment discrimination based on sex by unions and private employers*
1965	*Voting Rights Act strikes down barriers to African American vote* *US troops deployed in the "Vietnam War" which lasted until 1975* *The first dictionary of American Sign Language is published*
1966	National Organization for Women (NOW) founded Compton Cafeteria Riots in the Tenderloin District of San Francisco set off transgender movement, involving many people of color
1967	*Equal Rights Amendment to US Constitution introduced*
1969	Stonewall Inn Rebellion continues gay liberation movement National Association for the Repeal of Abortion Laws (NARAL) founded Redstockings' "Redstocking Manifesto" published Julia Kristeva's *Desire in Language* published in original French Maya Angelou's *I Know Why the Caged Bird Sings* published

Date	Event
1970	First Women's Studies program in the United States established at San Diego State University
	Kate Millett's *Sexual Politics* published
	Shulamith Firestone's *The Dialectic of Sex: The Case for Feminist Revolution* published
	Sisterhood is Powerful: An Anthology of Writings from the Women's Liberation Movement published, edited by Robin Morgan
	Toni Cade Bambara's *The Black Woman* published
	Radicalesbians' "The Woman-Identified Woman" published
	Socialist feminism through 1970s
	Lesbian Feminist Liberation Movement begins
	Street Transvestite Action Revolutionaries (STAR) later renamed Street Transgender Action Revolutionaries co-founded by Sylvia Rivera and Marsha P. Johnson
1971	Boston Women's Health Collective's *Our Bodies, Ourselves* published
	First National Chicana Conference, Houston, Texas
	The Furies Collective, a commune with newspaper in Washington, DC, voices lesbian separatism and critique of anti-gay attitudes in the feminist movement
	Switzerland grants women the vote
1972	*Title IX outlaws discrimination in federally supported education programs in the United States. It had a major effect in securing women's equal participation in sports*
	Shirley Chisholm, first woman to run for US President in the modern era
	Chicago Women's Liberation Union's *Socialist Feminism: A Strategy for the Women's Movement* published
	Ms. Magazine, edited by Gloria Steinem, launched
	Sherry Ortner's "Is Female to Male as Nature is to Culture?" published
	Elizabeth Martinez's "La Chicana" published
	"I Am Woman," hit song by Helen Reddy, released
1973	*Roe vs. Wade, US Supreme Court decision makes laws denying abortion illegal*
	National Black Feminist Organization founded in United States
	National Alliance against Racist and Political Repression founded in Chicago
	Homosexuality is no longer listed as a mental disorder by the American Psychiatric Association
	Judy Freespirit and Aldebaran's "The Fat Liberation Manifesto" published
1974	Women of All Red Nations (WARN) established by Lorelei DeCora Means, Madonna Thunderhawk, Phyllis Young, and Janet McCloud
1975	First "Take Back the Night" march in Philadelphia, PA, USA
	International Women's Year celebrated
	Gayle Rubin's "The Traffic in Women" published
	Fatima Mernissi's *Beyond the Veil* published
	Hélène Cixous's "The Laugh of Medusa" published in original French
	Yolanda López, Virgin of Guadalupe series of paintings (1975–1978)
	Susan Brownmiller's *Against our Will* concerning rape published

Date	Event
1976	Marge Piercy's *Woman on the Edge of Time* published
1977	Combahee River Collective's "A Black Feminist Statement" published
	Luce Irigaray's *This Sex Which Is Not One* published in original French
	Nawal El Saadawi's *The Hidden Face of Eve* published in original Arabic
1978	Mary Daly's *Gyn/Ecology* published
	Susan Griffin's *Woman and Nature: The Roaring inside Her* published
	Gloria Steinem's "If Men Could Menstruate" published
1979	Judy Chicago's art installation *The Dinner Party* opens in San Francisco, USA
	Sandra Gilbert and Susan Gubar's *The Madwoman in the Attic* published
1980	Adrienne Rich's "Compulsory Heterosexuality and Lesbian Existence" published
	Iraq grants women the vote
1981	Angela Davis's *Women, Race and Class* published
	This Bridge Called My Back: Writings by Radical Women of Color published, edited by Cherríe Moraga and Gloria E. Anzaldúa
	Heidi Hartmann's "The Unhappy Marriage of Marxism and Feminism" published
	Sandra Day O'Connor becomes first female member of US Supreme Court
1982	*All the Women are White, All the Blacks are Men, But Some of Us Are Brave* published, edited by Gloria T. Hull, Patricia Bell Scott, and Barbara Smith
	Carol Gilligan's *In a Different Voice* published
	Letty Cottin Pogrebin's *Anti-Semitism in the Women's Movement* published
	The Politics of Women's Spirituality published, edited by Charlene Spretnak
	Leila Ahmed's "Western Ethnocentrism and Perceptions of the Harem" published
	Greenham Common Women's Peace Camp established, Great Britain
1983	Alice Walker's *In Search of our Mothers' Gardens* published
	Sally Ride becomes first US woman in space
	Women's History Reclamation Project, later the Women's History Museum and Educational Center, now the Women's Museum of California, founded by Mary Maschal
1984	bell hooks's *Feminist Theory* published
	Audre Lorde's *Sister/Outsider* published
	Chandra Talpade Mohanty's "Under Western Eyes" published
1985	Wilma Mankiller elected Cherokee Nation's first female Principal Chief
	Donna Haraway's "A Cyborg Manifesto" published
	Gayatri Chakravorty Spivak's "Can the Subaltern Speak?" published
	Alice Jardine's *Gynesis: Configurations of Women and Modernity* published
1986	Sandra Harding's *The Science Question in Feminism* published
	Paula Gunn Allen's *The Sacred Hoop: Recovering the Feminine in American Indian Tradition* published
1987	Inauguration of Lesbian and Gay Archives of San Diego, now Lambda Archives, San Diego
	Gloria E. Anzaldúa's *Borderlands/LaFrontera: The New Mestiza* published
	Hazel Carby's *Reconstructing Womanhood* published
1988	Suzanne Pharr's *Homophobia* published

Date	Event
1989	Ynestra King's 'The Ecology of Feminism and the Feminism of Ecology" published
	Diana Fuss's *Essentially Speaking: Feminism, Nature and Difference* published
	Trinh T. Minh-ha's *Woman, Native, Other* published
	Amy Tan's *The Joy Luck Club* published
	The Tribe of Dina: American Jewish Women's Anthology published, edited by Melanie Kaye Kantrowitz and Irena Klepfisz
	Susan Wendell's "Toward a Feminist Theory of Disability" published
	Nira Yuval-Davis and Floya Anthias's *Woman-Nation-State* published
	Kimberlé W. Crenshaw's "Demarginalizing the Intersection of Race and Sex" published
1990s	"Third-wave" feminism begins
1990	Patricia Hill Collins's *Black Feminist Thought* published
	Eve Sedgwick's *Epistemology of the Closet* published
	Judith Butler's *Gender Trouble* published
	ADA (Americans with Disabilities Act) passed
1991	Riot grrrl punk rock underground movement begins in Washington, DC, and Seattle, Washington, USA
	Susan Faludi's *Backlash* published
	Jenny Morris's *Pride Against Prejudice* published
	Chela Sandoval's "U.S. Third World Feminism" published
	Deniz Kandiyoti's "Identity and its Discontents" published
1992	Mary Louise Pratt's *Imperial Eyes* published
	Rigoberta Menchú Tum awarded the Nobel Peace Prize
1993	*Janet Reno becomes first woman US Attorney General*
	Maria Mies and Vandana Shiva's *Ecofeminism* published
	Intersex Society of North America founded
1994	*Violence against Women Act in United States*
	Kate Bornstein's *Gender Outlaw* published
	Ella Shohat and Robert Stam's *Unthinking Eurocentrism* published
1995	Winona LaDuke's *Mothers of our Nations* published
	Anne McClintock's *Imperial Leather* published
	Carolyn Merchant's *Earthcare: Women and the Environment* published
	To Be Real published, edited by Rebecca Walker
1996	Eve Ensler's "The Vagina Monologues" opens in New York, USA
1997	*Madeline Albright becomes first woman US Secretary of State*
	Third Wave Agenda published, edited by Leslie Heywood and Jennifer Drake
	SisterSong Women of Color Reproductive Justice Collective organized in United States
	Greta Gaard's "Toward a Queer Ecofeminism" published
	Rosemary Garland Thompson's *Extraordinary Bodies* published
	Uma Narayan's *Dislocating Cultures* published
	Dorothy Roberts's *Killing the Black Body* published

Date	Event
1998	Judith Halberstam's *Female Masculinity* published
	Aurora Levins Morales's *Medicine Stories* published
1999	Aihwa Ong's *Flexible Citizenship* published
	Dragon Ladies: Asian American Women Breathe Fire published, edited by Sonia Shah, preface by Yuri Kochiyama, and foreword by Karin Aguilar San Juan
2000	*Vermont is the first US state to recognize "civil unions" with all state benefits for same-sex couples*
	The Netherlands grants marriage rights to same-sex couples
	Anne Fausto-Sterling's *Sexing the Body* published
	Chela Sandoval's *Methodology of the Oppressed* published
	Manifesta published, edited by Jennifer Baumgardner and Amy Richards
2002	*this bridge we call home: radical visions for transformation* published, edited by Gloria E. Anzaldúa and AnaLouise Keating
	Colonize This! Young Women of Color on Today's Feminism published, edited by Daisy Hernández and Bushra Rehman
	Ann Laura Stoler's *Carnal Knowledge and Imperial Power* published
	Val Plumwood's *Environmental Culture* published
2003	*US invasion of Iraq in a war continuing to 2011*
2004	*California law broadens the definition of sex in its discrimination prohibition to include gender identity and expression as protected categories in employment and housing*
	First gathering of the International Council of Thirteen Indigenous Grandmothers in Phoenicia, NY, October 11–17
	Massachusetts the first state to grant same-sex marriage rights
2005	*Kuwait grants women the vote*
	Inderpal Grewal's *Transnational America* published
	Andrea Smith's *Conquest* published
2006	Lisa Duggan and Nan D. Hunter's *Sex Wars: Sexual Dissent and Political Culture* published
	Incite!'s *Color of Violence* published
2007	AnaLouise Keating's *Teaching Transformation: Transcultural Classroom Dialogues* published
2008	*Barack Obama elected as first African American US President*
2009	*Still Brave: The Evolution of Black Women's Studies* published, edited by Stanlie M. James, Frances Smith Foster, and Beverly Guy-Sheftall
	The Intersectional Approach: Transforming the Academy through Race, Class, and Gender published, edited by Michele Tracy Berger and Kathleen Guidroz
	The Fat Studies Reader published, edited by Esther Rothblum and Sondra Solovay
2010	Catriona Mortimer-Sandilands and Bruce Erikson's *Queer Ecologies* published
2011	*"Don't Ask Don't Tell" (banning out lesbians and gays from service in US armed forces) effectively repealed*

Date	Event
2012	Sharon P. Holland's *The Erotic Life of Racism* published
2013	*Defense of Marriage Act, denying marriage to same-sex couples, ruled illegal in United States*
	Alison Kafer's *Feminist, Queer, Crip* published
2014	Ana Castillo's *Massacre of the Dreamers: Essays on Xicanisma, 20th anniversary updated edition* published
2015	*Saudi Arabia grants women the vote*
	Same-sex marriage is legalized throughout the United States

* Many authors represented on this timeline have numerous notable publications. We have selected what we consider the most important work related to the evolution of Women's and Gender Studies.

Acknowledgments

About.com. "African American History and Women Timeline." http://womens history.about.com/od/aframwomentimeline/a/aaw1492_time.htm (accessed December 18, 2015).

Adam, Maurianne, Lee Ann Bell, and Pat Griffin, eds. *Teaching for Diversity and Social Justice*, 2nd ed. New York: Routledge, 2007. See especially "History of Racism and Immigration Timeline."

Francis, Lee. *Native Time: A Historical Time Line of Native America*. New York: St. Martin's Press, 1998.

Inter-Parliamentary Union (IPU). "Women's Suffrage." http://www.ipu.org/wmn-e/suffrage.htm (accessed December 18, 2015).

Katz, Jonathan Ned. *Gay American History: Lesbians and Gay Men in the U.S.A.* New York, Plume Press, 1992.

The Kentucky Foundation for Women http://womenshistory.about.com/od/aframwomentimeline/a/aaw1492_time.htm http://www.kfw.org/feminist-timeline/ (accessed December 18, 2015).

Mann, Susan Archer. *Doing Feminist Theory*. Oxford and New York: Oxford University Press, 2012.

Ruiz, Vicki L., and Virginia Sánchez Korrol, eds. *Latina Legacies: Identity, Biography, Community*. New York: Oxford University Press, 2005.

Wikipedia. "Timeline of Women's Suffrage." http://en.wikipedia.org/wiki/Timeline_of_women's_suffrage#1960s (accessed December 18, 2015).

Zimmerman, Bonnie, ed. *Encyclopedia of Lesbian Histories and Cultures*. New York: Garland, 2000.

Index

Women in Culture: An Intersectional Anthology for Gender and Women's Studies, Second Edition.
Edited by Bonnie Kime Scott, Susan E. Cayleff, Anne Donadey, and Irene Lara.
© 2017 John Wiley & Sons, Ltd. Published 2017 by John Wiley & Sons, Ltd.